JUN 24 '80	DATE DUE		
NOV 9 1980			
DEC 1 1980			
AUG 1981			
NOV 1 5 1983			
JAN 4 1986			

THE
INQUISITION IN
HOLLYWOOD

THE
INQUISITION IN
HOLLYWOOD
Politics in the Film Community
1930–1960

Larry Ceplair & Steven Englund

Anchor Press/Doubleday
Garden City, New York
1980

The Anchor Press edition is the first publication of *The Inquisition in Hollywood*. Anchor Press edition: 1980

Most of Chapter 3 originally appeared in *Cinéaste* in a somewhat different form.

Library of Congress Cataloging in Publication Data

Ceplair, Larry.
   The inquisition in Hollywood.

   Bibliography: p. 477.
   Includes index.
   1. Moving-picture industry—United States.
   2. Blacklisting of entertainers—United States.
   3. Communism—United States—1917–
   I. Englund, Steven, joint author. II. Title.
   PN1993.5.U6C4   791.43′09794′94
   ISBN: 0-385-12900-9
   Library of Congress Catalog Card Number 77-25587

*To our parents, and to those
who resisted.*

Acknowledgments

Many people gave generously of their time and effort to assist us in the completion of this book. We are grateful to the men and women who submitted to our endless queries about their personal, professional, and political pasts, and indebted to those who read all or part of the manuscript and commented on our facts and conclusions. If there are errors in this book, it is not the responsibility of Sonja and Edward Biberman, Lester Cole, Philip Dunne, William Fadiman, Mimi Flood, Dorothy Healey, Paul Jarrico, Ring Lardner, Jr., Alfred Levitt, Lee Lowenfish, Albert Maltz, Ben Margolis, Abraham Polonsky, George Sklar, or Gore Vidal.

The book has also benefited from the material loaned to us or brought to our attention by Elizabeth Anspach, Gregory Bernstein, Philip Dunne, Pauline Lauber Finn, Sheridan Gibney, Dorothy Healey, Albert Maltz, Ed Medard, Deborah Rosenfelt, David Talbot, and Barbara Zheutlin.

Numerous archivists and librarians have answered our questions, provided us with material, and generally eased our research task. Our thanks to Allen Rivkin and Blanche Baker of the Writers Guild of America West, Kenneth Clark and Carolyn Stein of the Motion Picture Association of America, Gene Gressey of Wyoming University's Special Collections, Dione Miles of the Walter Reuther Library at Wayne State University, Emil Fried of the Southern California Library for Social Studies and Research, and the librarians at UCLA, University of Wisconsin Center for Theatre Research, University of Southern California, University of California's Bancroft Library, and the Hoover Institution.

We received the excellent editorial assistance of Bob Hutchins, whose skill, time, care, and attention to the quality of the prose and the validity of the ideas immeasurably improved the manuscript.

CONTENTS

Introduction

He hath disgraced me and hind'red me half a million, laughed
at my losses, mocked at my gains, scorned my nation,
thwarted my bargains, cooled my friends, heated mine enemies
—and what's his reason?

—*The Merchant of Venice*, III, i.

"Los Angeles, June 4, 1976. Three filmmakers have been ordered to
appear before a Federal grand jury here concerning a film they are
making on the Weather Underground. Subpoenas were served on
Haskell Wexler, winner of an Academy Award for his work on
'Who's Afraid of Virginia Woolf'; Emile de Antonio, well-known
leftist documentary filmmaker; and Mary Lampson, a production asso-
ciate."*

They seem to come in waves, these assaults on the moviemakers by
the suspicious and righteous functionaries of the Department of Justice and their counterparts in Congress. In 1920, while still establishing
themselves in Hollywood, the film moguls obediently listened while
cabinet member Franklin K. Lane exhorted them "to combat social un-
rest" in their films.[1] Jack Warner, Louis Mayer, Adolph Zukor, and
their colleagues spent the thirties and forties parrying government
efforts to censor or license their films and take away their theaters. By

---

* New York *Times*, June 5, 1976. The film makers refused to comply.
Represented by the Southern California chapter of the American Civil
Liberties Union, and supported by a petition signed by thirty-two Holly-
wood film notables, Wexler, de Antonio, and Lampson publicly resisted
this effort at "prior restraint of artistic expression." The Department of
Justice withdrew the subpoenas.

1947 the men in Washington, expanding the scope of their project, sought to expose the "subversive" nature of Hollywood films and film makers. Subpoenas (printed on pink paper) flowed out to screen artists of all categories. Four years later, a second, more extensive bombardment nearly demolished organized radicalism in the film industry.

The times change, the names change, the films change; above all, the tactics and strategy of repression change, as they are continually refined. Only the goal of government remains the same: control. Interest has recently flared in the era of "subversion" that was the late forties and early fifties. A spate of books focusing on the spy trials, the loyalty oaths, the Attorney General's lists, and the notorious blacklists has appeared, each attempting to depict and explain the spirit of the times.

Many of the victims of that earlier era in Hollywood, after years of struggle, have enjoyed a comeback of sorts in the late sixties and seventies—not only within the movie industry which had so unceremoniously dumped them, but also in public opinion. As this book was taking shape we witnessed an event that symbolized this mood change. A local group of radical students of the media staged a "Blacklist Evening" which included the presentation of a film produced by the Hollywood Ten followed by a panel discussion with five former blacklistees: Karen Morley, Will Geer, John Randolph, Paul Jarrico, and John Bright. The auditorium was jammed with people, all of them listening intently to these elders who spoke about the dangers they had faced and survived—dangers which most of the people in the room knew only at third or fourth hand.

Events such as this are increasingly frequent. The blacklisted are in demand as panelists and sages. One of the Ten, Albert Maltz, displayed a rack full of cassette recordings of interviews which he had granted to students of repression in the preceding five years. This partial rehabilitation of the outcast is as long overdue as it is pathetically insufficient, but the task of learning anything significant and endurable from the Ten's experience has barely begun. And there is a vast amount to be learned; for despite the renewed interest in the 1947–62 period, very little systematic research or historical analysis has appeared in the growing bibliography about the repression of radicals and radicalism in the Hollywood film industry.

Virtually all accounts overlook the pasts of the men and women who were blacklisted, as well as the larger political and professional contexts in which these people lived and thrived for the generation before the *coup de grâce* of 1947. Most writers devote a dozen or so pages to a brief review of the thirties and forties, studding them with familiar anecdotes and conventional judgments and conclusions. Their accounts usually open, in fact, in a congressional hearing room in 1947, from which proceeds yet another recounting of the dramatic confrontations between the House Committee on Un-American Activities (HUAC) and those most "unfriendly" of witnesses, the Hollywood Ten. In opening their stories where they should have concluded them, these writers deprive the reader of the real drama and, more importantly, the real point.

What is overlooked in focusing only on 1947 is that the blacklisted Hollywood artists were, in many important ways, successful radicals. The men and women who were cut down in the late forties had spent, many of them, the better part of two decades giving of themselves personally, professionally, and financially to a host of progressive and radical causes. Their selection as targets in 1947 was not, therefore, random; they were not naive and innocent victims, nor had they been playing at radicalism. The label "Communist subversive" was pinned on them only in part because they were members of the Communist Party (CPUSA). The real charge was that for ten and twenty years the film people had worked effectively for causes regarded as anathema by the new conservative or reactionary majority in Congress, as well as by most of the press and several powerful national interest groups. As the pendulum of history began its swing from Rooseveltian liberalism to McCarthyite reaction, the Hollywood activists were standing directly in its path, and, in the persons of the Hollywood Ten, were the first to be felled.

In spite of the frequency of blacklists in many professions and many parts of the country, this phenomenon came to be associated in the public mind with Hollywood. A letter to the New York *Times* rightly noted that "the blacklist probably never would have gotten noticed if, say, it were coal miners rather than movie stars involved."[2] Yet coal miners, auto workers, janitors, professors, and lawyers—anyone associated with the progressive movements of 1935–48—became enmeshed in the strands of the Cold War "internal security" dragnet: informing, investigating, prosecuting, recanting, oath taking . . . blacklisting. Hollywood was not unique on *this* score, but it was unique. The atmosphere of hysteria which HUAC utilized to sweep up the anonymous small fry from other industries and professions could not have been generated by a congressional hearing which peered into the political past of, say, a "Harlan County Ten." Hollywood was more an image than a place, a mythmaking machine feeding the fantasies of a moviegoing country. The lives of a few of Hollywood's inhabitants were regarded as national property; the words they spoke, the stands they took, the fates they met were as publicized as their movies. As a symbol of "dangerous" radicalism, Hollywood was only the tip of an iceberg, but it was a flashing neon tip that captivated the nation's attention—precisely as HUAC hoped it would do.

The relatively small parade of movie people—some fivescore marchers, nearly all of them screenwriters—wending its way through these pages, however, generated much more information than, for instance, the many thousands of government employees and school-teachers who were fired at the same time for the same sorts of reasons —that is, for long-term membership in the progressive movement. These people espoused many of the same doctrines, contributed to the same causes, read the same newspapers as their comrades in the film industry. The Hollywood contingent represents the fates of its anonymous and mute colleagues around the country.

THE
INQUISITION IN
HOLLYWOOD

1

The Screenwriter in Hollywood

> But if we were not artists or thinkers or questioners, we were
> nimble and knowing artificers. And we worked like hell. It is
> as hard to make a toilet seat as a castle window, even though
> the view is a bit different.
>
> —*Ben Hecht*

The Rise of the Screenwriter Class

The mating of Hollywood mogul and eastern magnate produced, by
the early thirties, an industrial-financial colossus: one of the most lucrative businesses in the United States, with gross assets of over two
billion dollars, an annual gross income of one billion dollars, and an
annual production rate of more than six hundred feature films. The
eight "major" (i.e., consolidated) Hollywood studios—Metro-Goldwyn-
Mayer (MGM), Paramount, Twentieth Century-Fox, Warner Brothers, Radio-Keith-Orpheum (RKO), Columbia, Universal, and United
Artists—dominated the film industry and markets not only in America,
but throughout the world for the next quarter century. Among them,
the majors controlled 80 per cent of the total capital investment in the
movie business; they produced 65 per cent of all feature films and 100
per cent of all the newsreels in the United States; they controlled 80
per cent of the nation's first-run movie theaters, and received about 95
per cent of all film rentals.[1]

The majors stood in the vanguard of American big business in the
practice of market control and stabilization. Though they scavenged
each other viciously in the scramble for theater chains and the hiring
of talented personnel, this "competition" merely camouflaged their

deep mutual understanding. The majors were one large family financed by the same banks, taking the same risks, making the same product with the same conventions, interchanging a stable corps of artists, battling common enemies, and adopting standardized policies in a whole range of areas, from foreign and domestic public relations and marketing to labor contracts and trade union policies.

The birth of the eight majors, with their near-monopoly over moviemaking in this country, had a great impact on the product itself. The venturesome dispositions and peddler mentalities of the founders came to be more and more circumscribed and transformed by the practice and viewpoint of cost accountancy and profit maximization. The procedures, policies, and perspectives of the New York financial world invaded the relatively unstructured world of the silent film and early Hollywood.

The force of financial investment tilted Hollywood in the direction of business orthodoxy, but the resistance of the moviemaking artists, and the very nature of the process and product itself, preserved some pulse of creativity. The curious universe that emerged from, and enclosed, these tensions, struggles, and contradictions was the studio system. Like an armed truce or a Calder mobile, power relations within the "classic" studio represented an uneasy balance of contending forces within moviemaking: art/profit, innovation/standardization, refinement/vulgarity, expertise/instinct, specialization/integration, creativity/predictability. The functional result was a phenomenon unique to the industrial world: a modern assembly line process in the guise of a feudal manor.

The screenwriter came to Hollywood along with "mike" booms and the Great Depression. The advent of the "talkie" not only capped an evolution in production methods and imposed the need for a producer to standardize moviemaking; it also created a permanent need for professional writers who could turn out shootable, full-length scripts with dialogue. But by the time screenwriters assumed their places in the hierarchy of moviemaking, the artistic aristocracy had lost its battle for creative authority to the financial-managerial class, whose representatives, the producers, now dominated the whole picture-making process. The great historical irony which every screenwriter had unknowingly to brave was that the very forces of production which had called him into existence and defined his crucial task denied him the artistic authority and creative satisfaction which directors and stars had once tasted and which his apparent importance would seem to demand.

Success in the form of high salaries or steady employment failed to compensate a significant minority of screenwriters for their constant subordination and artistic debasement in a business where their contribution was essential. Unaware of this contradiction, which would define not only the practice of their profession, but their personal and political lives as well, writers of every description heeded the studios' waving checkbooks and journeyed to Hollywood. (See Appendix 1.)

There is no mystery or complexity in the motivations that brought these people to Hollywood: money was the biggest, if by no means the only, lure. Some of the most serious writers in America—Robert Sherwood, Elmer Rice, William Faulkner—went to Hollywood when they needed money. Lesser-known screenwriter hopefuls came to Hollywood in many instances with families to support and debts to pay. All, famous and non-famous alike, were frequently bowled over by the amounts of money handed out in weekly salaries—up to (and occasionally over) $1,200 per week at a time when the income tax was almost nil and the dollar worth four to five times its current value. Aldous Huxley and wife were stupefied at the $15,000 which MGM offered him for only eight weeks of work on *Madame Curie*.[2] John Howard Lawson cooed over his pot of gold from RKO: "So yesterday I signed up for one job to write an adaptation and dialogue here in the East at $7,500 for six weeks' work . . . what could be sweeter!"[3]

Most movie writers could not share in Huxley's wide-eyed exclamation or Lawson's clucking satisfaction. As late as 1939, the median weekly wage for screenwriters was only $120.[4] As a group, screenwriters did not earn anything like what their counterparts in directing, producing, or lead acting made. In 1931, for example, screenwriter salaries accounted for only 1.5 per cent of the total payroll of the motion picture industry. That worked out to an amount of around $7 million to be distributed among 354 regularly employed writers (average yearly pay=$14,209.22) and 435 part-time writers (average yearly income=$6,111.12). Directors, for their part, took home 5 per cent of the total (average yearly pay=$29,744.75); and while movie stars made far more than anyone else except studio owners, the average actor received even less than the average screenwriter (i.e., around $4,100 per year).[5] In a world where large salaries were a sign of one's perceived worth to the studio and of one's prestige in the industry, it is almost astonishing that as late as 1941, only *five* screenwriters made the list compiled by the Department of the Treasury enumerating the two hundred people in Hollywood who earned more than $75,000 a year.* Finally, all Hollywood salaries, not just screenwriters', have to be seen in the light of the seasonal unemployment which affected all but the highest levels of creative personnel. For writers, the hiring year peaked in the last five months of the year and bottomed out in the spring. A writer, even a major one, had reason to experience a stab or two of anxiety when option time rolled around and he or she was caught between projects or bogged down in an unworkable, unpopular script. It was rare for writers to average more than forty weeks of work a year.†

While money was the most obvious attraction of movie writing, a profound impetus was the chance to leave one's mark on a new mode of creative writing and communicating. No matter that movie writing was downgraded by the eastern literati; the challenge of celluloid captured many writers' imaginations. Indeed, the sneers of the highbrows were a measure of the attraction of a medium which reached so many more millions of people, and moved them so much more directly, than books or plays could do. The sneering was also partly attributable to the fact that screenwriting was a special and difficult art, at which many of America's most prestigious authors did not succeed.

Among screenwriters themselves, Dudley Nichols best expressed why the movie writers stayed in Hollywood: "In spite of its complicated mechanics, the motion picture is the most flexible and exciting storytelling medium in the world. Its possibilities are enthralling."[6] Whatever their ambivalence, insecurity, frustration, or obsession to be Something More, nearly all screenwriters admitted their childlike infatuation with their trade. Each generation experienced a different sort of delight. The early thirties group (Allen Rivkin, Mary McCall, John Lee Mahin, etc.), years after their willing or unwilling departures from

---

* Jo Swerling, $97,500; James K. McGuinness, $91,875; Anita Loos, $88,375; John Lee Mahin, $79,166; Virginia Van Upp, $75,800. Two years later the number had increased to seven: Ken Englund, Morrie Ryskind, Lamar Trotti, Charles Brackett, Harry Tugend, Jo Swerling, Sheridan Gibney. *Variety*, June 25, 1945.

† In a survey of unemployment undertaken by the Pacific Coast Labor Bureau in 1938, over one hundred screenwriters replied to a questionnaire designed to reveal regularity of employment. The median employment period for 1936 and 1937 was thirty-three to thirty-seven weeks. In the thirty-week period September 1, 1936, to March 31, 1937, only 52.8 per cent of the screenwriters who responded to the survey worked full-time. *Survey of Unemployment, Employment, Earnings: Motion Picture Industry, Los Angeles Area*, April 1938, pp. 122 and 128.

the writers' buildings, still radiated the joy they felt about being in Hollywood and writing movies. They all admitted to being "Mertons of the movies." The late thirties and forties generation (Ring Lardner, Jr., Michael Wilson, Edward Huebsch), on the other hand, regarded the film form as a high art. Raised on "fine" films, they understood the potential of the medium in a way that their "greenhorn" forebears did not. Much less torn by the desire to be recognized novelists or playwrights, they devoted themselves to movie writing.

In sum, the love of movies as entertainment or art, the fun and stimulation of being with one's comrades in the writers' buildings, the studio commissaries, the famous watering holes or restaurants (Lucey's, The Formosa, Musso & Frank's), or Stanley Rose's bookstore, and especially the thrill of seeing one's story and dialogue come to life on the screen, were intense pleasures. Along with the money, they contributed to keeping the writers in Hollywood.

Work and Status in Hollywood

Every writer in Hollywood—whether he wrote his scripts at Fox's Normandy village-like writers' building, in MGM's sterile cubicles, in Paramount's seedy but comfortable rooms ("where," Ken Englund remembered, "the chair springs would poke through the worn leather and goose you just when you thought you were alone and safe"), or at Columbia's special version of the Château d'If—rapidly discovered and sooner or later learned to live with an unpleasant truth: the tie that bound the screenwriter was not between him and the moviegoer, but between him and the producer. The busy hive of the studio production system was a far cry from the private and tranquil garrets of their New York and university experiences. In Hollywood, they were uncomfortably well-known and closely scrutinized by their superiors. As former MGM (later RKO) story department chief William Fadiman related: "The story department in every studio has a cross-filed card index on writers that would make Linnaeus' *Systema Naturae* seem the jottings of an amateur."[7]

The story department, not the screenwriters, bore the responsibility of supplying production with filmable properties. The corps of writers existed for the most part to prepare and adapt the properties acquired, synopsized, classified, and presented by the bureaucracy of the studio. Writers were encouraged to submit original story ideas, but the fixed notions of producers were so rigid that it was unusual for a writer to write and sell five or six originals in the course of a career. In general, the job of the screenwriter was to adapt and transform: he took the material handed him by the story department and made it over into the schematic, concentrated, formalized geometry of a screenplay (in which a ten-paragraph description of "dawn breaking" becomes EXT. PANORAMIC SHOT—SKY—DAWN BREAKS).

A common source of frustration for the movie writer was the story conference, where the scripter's ideas, treatments, and drafts were decimated like Indians in a Western. These frequent palavers brought the writer together with his producer and, sometimes, the head of production. Here he received reactions to his most recent material, as well as directions and "suggestion" for further work. From the writer's perspective, the problem with story conferences was partly, of course, that all too frequently he heard his work harshly and unfairly criticized on the basis of standards and goals which he did not fundamentally share by people with no skill or experience at writing and slight understanding of the difficulties it entailed. Mainly, though, the agony and helplessness of the writer in a story conference stemmed from his confrontation with an omnipotent and largely alien force. "Excessive" artistic innovations or experimentations outside of time-worn genres invariably bowed before the remorseless inquisition of the producer: where's the action? who gets the girl? where are the laughs? where's the menace? (to which one exasperated writer replied, "You, you're the goddamned menace," and got up and walked out of the conference).[8] The incessant jabber, questioning, and pleading of a story conference merely highlighted the power gap. Writers finally had to do the indicated rewrites, or somebody else would. The best movie writers—Hecht, Stewart, Trumbo, etc.—all knew that ranks of sharpshooters waited to take their places at the parapets. "I made the changes," Hecht noted sourly, "because if I hadn't the scenario would have been taken out of my hands altogether and gleefully mangled by a group of studio hacks trained to read the producer's mind."[9] Stewart commented: "You couldn't make mistakes because there were other writers waiting to step in and fix your script up the way you were fixing somebody else's."[10]

So it always came back to the relationship between the writer and his producer. It seemed that no matter where the writer wandered in the studio maze, the producer appeared to thwart his progress. He had to be dealt with and satisfied. So the writer had to learn early that it was the producer's idea of a good screenplay which mattered, not his own. *The Courtier* thus figured as importantly in the writer's library as Bartlett's or Roget's. Although many of the producers possessed a literate sensibility and sound notions of what constituted a "good" screenplay, a notion is not a formula or a list of easily followed steps, nor, for that matter, an infallible thermometer of audience reception.

Writing departments possessed no accepted definition of script construction, no received body of detailed rules such as those governing classical French tragedy, Alexandrian couplets, or Shakespearean sonnets. Neophyte writers were told to "think in terms of the camera," "write for the eye, not the ear," and "maintain dramatic relationship of shots." Producers wanted shootable material; i.e., convincing, clever dialogue, crystal-clear narrative and continuity, entertaining subjects, "drama." Moreover, they needed scripts of this quality quickly and regularly. Hailing, as many of them did, from carnivals, nickelodeons, and amusement parks, studio executives compensated for any lack of aesthetic criteria by a "feel" for what would sell. They claimed to possess a kind of anatomical Richter scale on which they relied for their pronouncements about the taste and salability of movies: a sinking in the stomach, a tug of the heartstrings, or Harry Cohn's oracular stimulus—a tickle on the buttocks. For Philip Dunne or Donald Ogden Stewart, fresh out of Harvard's and Yale's English and drama departments, it was unnerving, not to say frustrating, to be so judged.

As things developed at Columbia, the writers became more wired to Cohn's New York delicatessen connection than anything else. Because fresh sturgeon was unavailable in L.A. in those days—the law forbade its public sale due to the great risk of spoilage in primitive refrigerators—Cohn, in typical mogul fashion, had quantities of the delicacy flown in daily from the East Coast. This he would dispense with great panache to his creative personnel during lunch in the executive dining room. But you only got the stuff if your day's output had . . . well, tickled the big man's buttocks. Ken Englund recounts one dreadful luncheon in the late thirties:

> Like Charles Laughton playing Bligh, Cohn would run a gimlet eye down the tense frozen smiles on both sides of his captain's table.
> "Bob"—addressing writer Riskin.
> "Yes, Mr. Cohn . . . ?"
> "I liked your first scene meeting between Jean Arthur and Gary Cooper [from *Mr. Deeds Goes to Town*] but watch they don't get too cute. Got me?"
> "Gottcha, Mr. Cohn!"

Cohn to dining room steward, "Give Mr. Riskin a piece of sturgeon."

Finally every man-Jack had been rewarded with a choice ration of Manhattan fish . . . except producer Everett Riskin and director Leo McCarey, whose plates sat empty. The rest of us more fortunates ate in silence, avoiding eye contact with the poor condemned wretches. You couldn't afford to traffic with the proscribed. Finally Ev Riskin broke the silence with a sigh:

"Harry, what don't you like about the first two sequences [of *The Awful Truth*]? Please tell us."

"I'll tell you! Neither Cary [Grant] nor Irene [Dunne] gives us a single laugh."

"But we're establishing the plot and their characters, Harry," persisted Ev. "The laughs will come later. . . ."

"And I don't agree, Harry," chimed in McCarey bravely. "There are several solidly funny moments."

Cohn silenced McCarey with a skewering look. "You don't agree with me, eh, Leo?"

"No, Mr. Cohn, I don't. . . ."

"Then fly in your own sturgeon!"

The writers who lasted in Hollywood learned how to do their best with whatever was thrown at them while at the same time removing (as much as possible) their ego investment in the script itself. That sort of effort is foreign to the creative process in general, but the writer's survival in the motion picture production process demanded this ability, and so quite a few acquired it to one degree or other. Movie writers tried to find satisfaction and pride in the relationships of trust and respect they maintained with their colleagues, and from the approval they received from their supervising producer and the front office. The mechanism was a defensive one, however, and to the degree it worked, they were, psychologically speaking, no longer artists, but rather middle-level executives in a large collective enterprise.

Adapting to the practice of screenwriting was one thing; accepting the methods of executives and producers was another thing entirely. Writers like Ben Hecht and Ken Englund, hardened by the competitive worlds of journalism and radio writing, may have managed the collaborative and emergency repair side of screenwriting better than New York litterateurs, but few screenwriters enjoyed the overpopulated, dog-eat-dog world engendered by the lure of film (and film salaries) and the producers' manipulation of the ensuing labor supply. Screenwriters competed for the available assignments and credits, but only one third of them received even a shared credit during any one year in the thirties.‡ Leonard Spigelgass wryly recalled: "There were six of us writing Shearer, six of us writing Garbo, six of us writing Ruth Chatterton, six of us writing Robert Montgomery, and six of us writing Clark Gable. Which one [of us] would they choose? It was a great lottery."[11]

With "teams of writers" being "thrown into the breach," the problem of allocating credits was an endless and sticky one. Of the forty-three musicals and musical comedies produced at MGM by Arthur Freed over the course of a quarter century, *not one* was formally accredited to a single screenwriter. And for that matter, only one team of writers—Comden and Green—managed to turn out shootable scripts for Freed without back-up teams, polishers, rewriters. In his nine years at Twentieth, Kenneth Macgowan could remember only two screenplays out of the thirty he produced and the fifty-two which aborted that could be credited to a single writer. (The films were *Young Mr. Lincoln*, by Lamar Trotti, and *The Return of Frank James*, by Sam Hellman.)[12]

A less grand but probably more irritating studio practice was the regimentation and quantification of a screenwriter's hours and output. All screenwriters were expected to abide by a strict set of studio rules governing their output and attendance. At all the majors, writers were told to report to their offices at nine or ten in the morning, take no more than an hour or hour and a half for lunch, and not depart for home until five or six in the evening. They also worked half a day on Saturdays. This constituted the minimum. Rush jobs, of course, required, and received, all the time and effort necessary to finish them by the deadline. Writers' memoirs are filled with anecdotes about the long lunches, the gossip and bull sessions in each other's offices, and the general goofing off, but the truth of the matter is that this sort of diversion was only the occasional oasis between long periods of hard slogging. Output was carefully regulated; most studios expected ten to twenty pages of material a week. That meant that up to four scripts a

---

‡ In the year ending October 1, 1935, the majors produced 301 features. Five hundred and nine writers (out of the 1,500 in Hollywood) received credits; 317 were credited with major contributions to the final shooting script, 130 were credited with minor contributions; 72 original treatments were sold. *Variety*, November 4, 1935, p. 11. These percentages had not varied much ten years later, during one of Hollywood's biggest box office years ever: the studios employed 366 screenwriters in 1945; 1,320 were enrolled in the Screen Writers Guild. *The Screen Writer*, December 1945, p. 37.

year were expected from an individual writer.[13] And writers did not get very long to "acclimatize" themselves to studio life. Nathanael West had barely stepped through the gates at Columbia when he was thrown an assignment.[14] The producers and their factotums also spent a lot of time making sure their Indians were on the reservation, though few studios went as far as Warner Brothers, which had a fence built around the writers' building and parking lot and secured it with a guard who was responsible for keeping track of the writers' whereabouts so that they wouldn't sneak off the lot during the working day.[15]

Why weren't screenwriters accorded anything like the recognition which their importance to the film industry should have engendered? For one thing, as we have seen, the writers were the last to arrive on the scene. In the early thirties' scramble for places in the talent hierarchy, they found themselves the youngest, most inexperienced creatures in the barnyard, confronting a rigidified pecking order. More to the point, the screenwriters had arrived in the wake of a terrible battle between directors and producers. In place of lost authority, some directors received the compensation of neon lights: Ernst Lubitsch's *Trouble in Paradise*, Capra's *Mr. Smith Goes to Washington*, Leo McCarey's *The Awful Truth*. This habit was combined with the producers' calculating "celebration" of the movie stars and their input—all for the purpose of heightening box office sales. It clearly did not serve management's interest to reveal the dirty little secret that writers were the ghosts in the movie machine.

Finally, there was something offputting—almost subversive—about screenwriters and the screenwriting craft. They were not only newcomers, they really *were* different from all the others, unique in their origins, talents, and contribution. Acting, producing, and directing required technique and skill, of course, but you could acquire these things on the job, or, in a pinch, "by the seat of your pants." (This was especially true in Hollywood, where an actor's personality and looks outweighed his talent in guaranteeing success, just as a director's dependability and submissiveness or a producer's toughness and profit-mindedness counted for more than artistic sensibility, independence, or integrity.) Screenwriters also had their Hollywood corruptions—docility, vulgarity, conformity. But by and large screenwriting demanded a degree of training, talent, and intelligence which excluded from its practice anyone "passing through" on the way to something higher. On-the-job practice was of course essential for writers—as it is for those in any specialization—but one could not acquire the fundamentals of literacy and imagination while standing on the set. Writing for the screen could not be faked or picked up or imbibed.

This group of men and women provided the refined material from which all films were made. Intelligent, educated, and literate in ways that most actors, directors, and producers were not,* the movie writers' importance and personal uniqueness discomfited co-workers. There could be no denying that in spite of his low status, ill-treatment, and impotence, a writer's influence was decisive. The actors', producers', and directors' names loomed larger than the writers' in the film credits, but it was clear from the start that the writer's mark was indelibly engraved on a movie.

The memoirs and biographies of other Hollywood artists show how mistrusted and unappreciated writers were within the studio system. The great Thalberg, who rarely conceded any weakness or failure of comprehension where show business was concerned, complained with exasperation one day to Anita Loos, "I can keep tabs on everyone else in the studio and see whether or not they're doing their jobs. But I can never tell what's going on in those so-called brains of yours."[16] "They went through absolute hell," Bette Davis recalled.[17] The writers were "instantly blamed if a director or a star could not cope with the matter in hand," wrote David Niven.[18] Director William Dieterle frankly admitted that in his long Hollywood experience, writers were distinguished by the ill-treatment they were accorded.[19] Nor did screenwriters' literary confreres contribute much support or confer much stature. On the contrary, many in the literary world demeaned movie writing and its product. As a result, the screenwriter frequently fell victim to a whole range of personal doubts and anxieties, all of which could be summed up by the word "ambivalence." The "scripters" were ambivalent about their profession: they both loved and hated Hollywood and their work there; they both sought and rejected it, they felt both pride and shame; they manifestly submitted to their condition and spiritually rebelled against it.

A common sign of ambivalence was the geographic bind. Some screenwriters literally could not settle down in Hollywood, even though they lived and worked there. These people remained obsessed by the need for New York's literary or dramatic distinction. The New

---

* "A survey taken in the late Thirties . . . indicated that 57% of working Hollywood producers had a university education, while the corresponding figure for directors and assistant directors was 53% and 55% respectively. For writers, the proportion was a notable 80%." John Baxter, *Hollywood in the Thirties*, New York: Paperback Library, 1970, p. 14.

Yorkers who remained behind reinforced this *idée fixe:* a sojourn to Hollywood to replenish one's coffers might be a necessity; relocating there was a sellout. A few screenwriters thus took pride in not being tied to Hollywood, in living like itinerants out of suitcases and traveling back and forth on the "screenwriters' circuit," which stretched from the Garden of Allah, the Hollywood Plaza, and the Chateau Marmont in Los Angeles to various *pieds-à-terre* on the West Side of Manhattan. They paid close heed to the reigning literary value system which attributed much more significance to a failed novel or play than to a good screenplay. Ben Hecht and Charles MacArthur, for example, stayed in Hollywood only as long as it took them to repay their debts and pool some reserves (usually less than a year). Then they would return to New York, live extravagantly, and write their next Broadway play. If the play succeeded (as did *The Front Page* and *Twentieth Century*), then they could afford to remain in New York for a few years . . . until the next time the well ran dry, and it was back to the studios for another stint with the typewriter gang.

Screenwriters also bowed low before the god Novel, who already held so many journalists, free-lancers, English teachers, and critics in spiritual bondage. Nearly every screenwriter had a novel cooking on some back burner, a novel which would rescue him from the obscurity of the writers' building and elevate him to the highest niche of the literary pantheon. To be sure, a small number of movie writers actually did turn out reasonably successful novels—Blankfort, Trumbo, Endore, Maltz, Schulberg—but not one of them ever made nearly enough money from the sale of his novels to escape screenwriting. Here, too, the sadly overlooked fact was that many great and successful novelists produced many more mediocre screenplays.

Once permanently lured to Hollywood and hooked up to the studios, the screenwriter discovered the relative anonymity of his new craft. His first brush with it came via the dissolution of authorship inherent in shared credits; the second when he saw how fleeting was the movie "byline" in any case. To the eastern literati, mesmerized by the immutability of books, a big drawback in writing for celluloid was the transience of the screen credit. A film had its day—anywhere from seven to seventy of them—and that was that. Afterward, no one could pull it off the shelf or pick it up at the nearest bookstore or library. It wasn't until 1943 that John Gassner, a theater critic, and Dudley Nichols awarded a handful of screenplays the "dignity of print" by collecting them in a published volume, *Twenty Best Film Plays*—a tiny percentage of the approximately nine thousand produced screenplays and perhaps thrice that number of unproduced ones—many of which were undoubtedly more brilliant and deserving. (Ring Lardner, Jr., for one, insists that his best work went unfilmed.) Two years later, they produced a second anthology, *Best Film Plays of 1943–1944.* This time, however, only ten screenplays were included. No subsequent volumes in this series appeared.

Nor did Gassner exactly start a publishing trend in the biannual tradition, say, of "The Best Plays"—now in its sixty-third year. Through the mid-1950s those two volumes contained the only published screenplays. This was a cruel and undeserved fate for the screenwriters, but the simple fact was, and is: published screenplays don't sell. There is more than a bit of pathos in movie writers' habit of collecting their own scripts in elegant leather-bound volumes with expensive gold lettering, standing unread on a compensatory shelf in their home libraries.

Again and again the writers complained of their anonymity; it was something to which they could never completely resign themselves. In the late forties and early fifties, when many screenwriters came to national attention during the HUAC hearings, they came blinking out from the writers' buildings, astonished that anybody outside of the studios knew who they were. When Lester Cole sued MGM for breach of contract, his lawyers asked the obvious question which nobody in court could answer: namely, how could the plaintiff have brought "disrepute" to the studio and film industry with his politics, as MGM accused, if nobody in the public domain knew who he was or which films he wrote, let alone what his politics were?[20]

From the outset writers of movies had to learn to derive satisfaction from the work itself. They succeeded to a greater or lesser degree, depending on their individual dispositions and circumstances. Cole, an especially good example of the "well-adjusted" writer, claimed that his satisfaction as a writer of movies came from endeavoring "to put forth truthfully and well" the story, situations, and characterizations of the material he was assigned. "I don't expect [the audience] to see that work and relate it to me personally," he said, adding that in this sense a screenwriter's relationship to ticket buyers is not at all like the personal tie between a published author and his readers. "As an author they don't know me."[21]

Despite their anonymity, however, virtually all screenwriters were held fast by the large salaries and by the unique, peculiar, and undefinable sense of challenge and accomplishment presented by their craft. Moreover, there were producers in the Hollywood studio system who, in the course of seeking the salable, appreciated and encouraged the estimable. The writers' frustration thus, ironically, resulted from the taste of artistic success and the wish for more, not the failure ever to taste it. The very possibility of self-expression was not always stolen by the front office, for no successful Hollywood producer lacked altogether a sense of showmanship or an appreciation, within careful limits, of talent and innovation. And even when producers did try to expunge art by fiat, the guerrilla tactics used by the screenwriters often outmaneuvered the cleverest producer. Writers, in fact, were the cleverest of all the bushfighters, devising all kinds of stratagems for evading the controls instituted by the front office regulars.

In sum, writers—and directors and actors as well—escaped from their jailers often enough to feel really frustrated about the time they had to spend behind bars; but this was a rarefied sort of frustration which came from knowing that there was perhaps one chance in twelve that one would actually be permitted to write his own kind of script and turn out an *I Am a Fugitive from a Chain Gang* or a *Grapes of Wrath*. It could, and did, happen, and not always accidentally or "illegally." *Citizen Kane* may not have represented RKO management's aspirations to create a new *Cherry Orchard* or *Rite of Spring*, but it, and its kind, frequently did reflect the artistic byproducts of the ongoing search for vehicles to please the box office and make profits.

Nevertheless, after allowance is made for studio management's tolerance, even regard, for artistic talent, the producers' tendencies lay finally in the direction of controlling, exploiting, and channeling the artistic impulse toward goals largely uncongenial to it. Not surprisingly, many of the screenwriters found ways to escape, or mitigate, the discontents arising from their work situations. But ultimately, of course, there was no *real* alternative within the movie studio system, and that was the point which the writers slowly learned. In their anger and frustration, all writers, irrespective of status or background, tended to band together. Whether at the Garden of Allah, at Musso & Frank's Grill in Hollywood, whether at Stanley Rose's bookstore or at the Writers' Club (the Guild after 1933), the movie writers drew much relief, sustenance, and joy from consorting with each other. The young John Sanford, a recently arrived screenwriter, described his colleagues' feelings about assembling nightly at Musso's in the mid-thirties: "It was our preserve; it resembled an eating club; there was no other place to eat dinner. 'Meet you for dinner,' meant Musso's. Between six and nine in the evening everyone you wanted to see was there; you would know at least eighty percent of the people dining in the back room. We liked each other. We read and respected each other's work."

The screenwriters' *esprit de corps* was stronger than, say, the directors', for their camaraderie was rooted in compassion, in the literal meaning of the term, co-suffering. Then and now, the Hollywood screenwriters were known for their black self- and Hollywood-deprecating wit and, in some notorious instances, their reliance on the bottle. Raymond Chandler claimed that "at the writers' table at Paramount, I heard some of the best wit I've heard in my life."[22] Gregariousness, bibulousness, cynicism, bitchiness, and humor may be signs of despair or escapism. And yet much of the talk, much of the consorting and creating together—at meetings, in offices, over lunches, at dinner parties—turned out fruitfully. Hollywood resounded endlessly to the echo of the writers' wit, insights, and demands, but underlying all the hot air was a growing consciousness, solidarity, and understanding—qualities which, by the early part of the thirties, would impel the screenwriters into the vanguard of trade union and political activity in Hollywood.

The transformation of professional conflicts into trade unions and political consciousness—while never automatic, direct, or simple—nonetheless occurs with such regularity as to constitute one of the few dependable characteristics of our society and historical era. No work-site is immune to it. The radical political activism in Hollywood which HUAC sought to uproot was not unique to Hollywood, nor was it simply the collective response of cosmopolitan intellectuals and artists to international events. It emerged also from the screenwriters' struggle to form a trade union to mitigate the worst frustrations of the Hollywood studio system.

2

The Founding of the Screen Writers Guild, 1933

The case of the Hollywood Ten goes back to the formation of the Screen Writers Guild in 1933.

—*John Howard Lawson*[1]

"[The producers] owned you; you were a commodity; they were paying you so much a week, and you belonged to them. And there was never any kidding about that."[2] One of Hollywood's most successful screenwriters, Donald Ogden Stewart, thus described the plight of the only group of writers in the world who were obliged to write not what they wanted to say, but what corporate executives wanted said. No other writers—from cub reporters to successful Broadway playwrights—were so highly paid, and no others were required to betray the autonomy and creativity which characterize their profession. That many of the screenwriters managed to remain highly creative artists is a credit both to their perseverance and skill and to the new medium in which they worked, film itself.

Though some individual screenwriters occasionally escaped from the constraints of the studio system, it was not until the onset of the Depression that the conditions for a collective solution came into being. Sound had brought screenwriters to Hollywood; the studio system had put them in the writers' buildings; the Depression, by reducing their assignments and wages, opened their eyes to the need for concerted action—the formation of a trade union. The drive toward unionism drew its energy from the screenwriters' struggle to improve their professional situation. Their goals included higher wages, fewer hours, regularized hiring practices, standardized contracts, and effective arbitration, but because the screenwriters were unusually articulate, intellectual, educated, and, in many instances, political, the struggle between labor and management over the Screen Writers Guild took on unmistakable ideological implications. The battle over trade union recognition and the right to bargain collectively ended by politicizing the screenwriters more fully than any other studio employees.

The Screen Writers Guild, internally divided though it would become, remained the most politically conscious and active trade union in Hollywood for fifteen years after its founding in 1933.* It served as the prototype for other talent guilds; its members were the backbone of every other political and social organization in the film community; and three times within the first decade and a half of its existence it seriously shook the studio front offices. Probably the greatest homage to the threat posed by an autonomous writers' guild was paid by the shrewdest producer of them all, Irving Thalberg, who threatened to shut down the largest moviemaking machine in the world, MGM, unless the screenwriters' organization ceased and desisted.[3]

Thalberg and his peers were used to simple economic equations in their relations with organized labor. As a result, the Producers' Association† was able to reach agreement relatively quickly with the already existing unions of skilled and semiskilled manual laborers—carpenters, painters, electrical workers, and the army of stagehands, technicians, and gaffers organized by the International Alliance of Theatrical Stage Employees (IATSE). It cost studio front offices very little to accede to the demands of these workers, for the salaries and

---

* There had been two previous attempts to form a screenwriters' union: the short-lived Photoplay Authors' League in New York (1914–16) and the Screen Writers Guild in Hollywood (1920–27). Neither had been successful in winning a contract from the studios. The writers' branch of the Academy of Motion Picture Arts and Sciences dominated labor relations between writers and producers from 1927 to 1933. A detailed account of the early attempts to form a writers' guild is to be found in Christopher Dudley Wheaton, *A History of the Screen Writers Guild (1920–1942): The Writers' Quest for a Freely Negotiated Basic Agreement*, University of Southern California: unpublished Ph.D. thesis, 1974, pp. 13–37.

† Producers' Association is a shorthand manner of referring to the Motion Picture Association of America, Inc., and the Association of Motion Picture Producers, Inc. The former, once known as the Hays Office, was headquartered in Washington, D.C., and was basically concerned with self-regulation and public relations. Included in its membership were the major studios, the Eastman Kodak Company, and the two major suppliers of sound equipment, ERPI branch of Western Electric and RCA. The AMPP was located in Hollywood, and was concerned with labor relations almost exclusively. Only the producing companies belonged, which meant that United Artists was not a member.

benefits paid out to them constituted only a small fraction of the cost of production. On the surface, film industry management appeared liberal and farsighted in granting concessions to well-established unions and technicians vital to the movie-making process. When the creative personnel who, if organized, might challenge the studio system, however, formed guilds, studio management proved intransigent, shrewd, and unscrupulous.

In any event, only the writers' organization proved troublesome to the studio executives. Directors were too few, too loyal, too highly paid, and generally too deluded about their "artistic authority" to develop a militant trade union consciousness, while the actors became the most tame and domesticated of unions once they had signed a contract with the producers in 1937. The blood-letting between studio management and the SWG, which endured for nine years, showed where the real conflict in Hollywood lay—not over money, but over the control of moviemaking. The producers willingly paid gargantuan salaries to the best actors, directors, and screenwriters, but steadfastly resisted any encroachment on creative decision-making. In fact, the high salaries were partially intended to secure the producers' autocracy, that is, to soothe the itch for artistic autonomy with the balm of wealth.

The specter of shared control was already haunting owners and production heads when the advent of sound obliged studio management to bring to Hollywood a flood of professional actors and writers from the East. These imports were not docile neophytes, but, quite often, veterans of bloody labor battles on Broadway. Actors Equity, the granddaddy of militant East Coast show business trade unions, had been sniffing around the studios since its victory in the 1919 "Battle of Broadway." That same year the Dramatists Guild had launched a strike which closed down virtually every stage production in New York and Chicago and won for its members a standard contract assuring playwrights final say over script changes and equal say (with producers) over the disposition of the film rights of their plays.

The arrival in Hollywood of hundreds of artists fresh from these eastern wars, combined with the onset of the greatest depression the world had known, ensured that fundamental questions of organization and control would be raised. Studio owners, sensing a new era of labor militancy, threw down one of management's most dog-eared trumps— a company-formed union called the Academy of Motion Picture Arts and Sciences. Conceived by Louis B. Mayer in 1927, the Academy embraced the five basic categories of film makers: producers, directors, actors, writers, and technicians. For all its limitations—most notably the lack of a binding enforcement procedure for its labor codes—this union managed to forestall serious labor organizing among the Hollywood artists for over five years. Once the changes wrought by the sound revolution and the early, worst, years of the Depression ceased to dislodge and frighten the movie artists, however, the Academy's role as an agency of studio management became obvious to all. Its acquiescence in a series of pay cuts and layoffs in the late twenties and early thirties left the talented personnel helpless before the economizing of the producers.

Ironically, President Roosevelt's bank holiday in March 1933—which launched the New Deal—persuaded studio management that the moment had arrived to resurrect the *old* deal of paternalistic labor/management relations which the Academy had been created to camouflage. Throughout Hollywood, the artistic personnel (directors, actors, writers) were herded into studio commissaries or sound stages to listen to "heartrending" homilies from studio owners and production heads, who informed their wards of a 50 per cent salary slash for everyone making over $50 a week, to remain in effect for two months. Louis B. Mayer even swore an oath to his startled artists that MGM would repay "every penny" once "this terrible emergency is over."[4]

To quell anticipated rebellion in the ranks, the employees were assured that the decision to cut salaries had been "unanimous," reached with "pain," and approved by the Academy. In fact, according to Jack Warner's later admission, the Academy had merely "arranged" a decision which the studio executives had reached unilaterally. "My brother Harry," wrote Warner, "came out from New York, and along with all other film executives in Hollywood we agreed on a fifty percent salary cut across the board for producers, stars, directors, and all others in the creative end of the business."[5]

This time the "we're all in this together" ploy didn't work. Many artists, particularly screenwriters, saw the selfishness and arrogance beneath the histrionics of the studio bosses. They remembered the 10 per cent pay cuts which had been levied in 1927 and 1931, as well as the savage staff cutbacks of 1930 and 1931. Nor did the Academy's "approval" impress, especially after it became known that the executives had convinced it to appoint a committee to reassess the standard industry practice of awarding long-term contracts to actors and writers, thereby threatening the one island of security which remained for screen artists in a sea of industrial uncertainty.

The events of March 1933 finally shattered the Academy's moral and professional stature in the eyes of Hollywood artists. Many of them were certain that the salary cuts of 1933 had been necessary not "to keep the studios running," but simply to maintain the studio profit margins and executive salaries at their high levels. The really staggering production costs at the major studios were not the salaries of the artists, but the Croesus-like bonuses handed out to executives at the end of each year. In the thirties an unbelievable 20–25 per cent of the net earnings of the majors went to remunerate a tiny handful of production chiefs, studio owners, and New York executives.[6] These bonus arrangements were not well-kept secrets in Hollywood. In fact, when the writers and actors composed a telegram to President Roosevelt in October 1933 which noted their grievances with the code which the National Recovery Administration had promulgated for the film industry, it was on the subject of executive bonuses that they concentrated their fire: "Executives of Paramount and Metro-Goldwyn-Mayer have taken millions of dollars out of their companies in bonuses. . . . The same individuals who bankrupted the major companies by their policies still control them through representation on the receiverships and in the formation of new companies. These same individuals are writing the motion picture code and directly or indirectly will be the code authority who administers it. . . . We deplore the attempt to saddle the sins of these financial buccaneers on the creative talent of the business."[7]

A series of *Variety* headlines the following year merely confirmed the suspicions of the disbelieving employees. On December 16 the headlines read: FILMS TEMPT WALL STREET; one week later, the paper reported that the studios were looking forward to a big box office year in 1935; at the end of January 1935 it was noted that "Current month is the busiest in the history of the industry since the inception of talkies."[8] Finally, a government study which was released in November 1935 proved conclusively that the motion picture industry had not only survived the Depression, but had materially enhanced its position *vis-à-vis* other amusement industries, through the policy of wage slashes: movie box office receipts as a percentage of total amusement expenditures rose from 78.86 per cent to 84.12 per cent between 1929 and 1933; the salaries of Hollywood employees declined by 16.1 per cent.[9]

A handful of screenwriters had already recognized the divergence between the studio executives' greed and their pious mouthings. Kubec Glasmon, Courtenay Terrett, Brian Marlow, Lester Cole, Samson Raphaelson, John Howard Lawson, Edwin Justus Mayer, Louis Weitzenkorn, John Bright, and Bertram Block had fortuitously met on

February 3, 1933, to discuss the revival of the Screen Writers Guild. The new salary cuts strengthened their determination to organize a Guild with teeth. The head of production at Paramount, Emanuel Cohen, without intending to do so, hastened the process by publicly admitting that talented personnel were suffering the most in the "crisis" because they were not protected by long-term collective bargaining contracts as, for example, the technicians and stagehands were. On their way out of the commissary, Brian Marlow turned to Lester Cole and whispered, "Okay, then, the obvious conclusion to this crap is our need to have a union."

But what kind of union? With what self-image? Making what kind of demands? All screenwriters agreed on the need for a standard contract which spelled out reciprocal responsibilities and obligations; the need for a fair and consistent procedure for allocating credits; the need for a means of enforcing the collective bargaining agreement; and the need for a Guild shop.

A standard contract would, according to Donald Ogden Stewart, protect "the average, ordinary craftsman from the unfair practices of a powerful monopoly, ready to take advantage of a tremendous oversupply of employees."[10] Leo Rosten (a centrist) carefully documented the nature of the exploitation which Stewart (a leftist) exposed:

> For two decades [1921–41] the movie writers in the low salary brackets (of whom there are plenty) were not given the protection of minimum wages or minimum periods of employment. They were discharged with no advance notice; their employment was sporadic and their tenure short-lived. They were laid off for short-term periods, under contract but without pay. They worked on stories on which other writers were employed, without knowing who their collaborators (or competitors) were. Their right to screen credits was mistreated by certain producers who allotted credit to their friends or relatives or—under pseudonyms—to themselves. They were frequently offered the bait of speculative writing without either guarantees or protection in the outcome.[11]

The circumstances of most screenwriters, those forced to free-lance their services to the small studios, independent producers, and "quickie" film makers, were far shakier than those Rosten documented for writers employed by the majors. In a letter to Samuel Ornitz, one of these less fortunate, John Natteford, chronicled some of the prob-

lems. Most of the minor studios, for example, did not sign contracts
with their writers.

> The writer without the protection of an agent to negotiate his
> agreement, and a written contract to define it, might expect to
> discover that his friend the producer had forgotten everything
> they had shaken hands upon unless it was to his own advantage.
> He might also expect to have the assignment prolonged, at the
> pleasure of the producer, by weeks of unnecessary waiting for
> changes and readings, and by months of efforts to collect his final
> balance.

Natteford suspected collusion between producers and executives,
from the poorest to the richest, in the matter of salaries for writers.

> While impossible to prove, it is well known that there exists an un-
> written agreement among these producers, as among the producers
> [at the majors], that no offers are to be made to an employee who
> is working, and no competitive offers made to one not working.
> Under this condition, the prices paid for services are rock bottom.

Frequently, the rock-bottom prices were not paid at all.

The very small studios—the "fly-by-nighters"—were almost Dick-
ensian in their treatment of writers.

> Here actual crookedness, larceny, plagiarism, and other evils
> enter the picture. In this field we meet the "promising" producer
> who has his picture cut and is off to New York with the negative
> under his arm before enforced collection can be made. Here we
> encounter the "if and when" deal—if the picture is sold, the writer
> gets his money. Pictures are seldom sold outright; the production
> is assigned to some concern for distribution and somehow or
> another never grosses enough to pay its bills.[12]

Neither steady employment nor dependable, cashable paychecks
protected screenwriters—from the highest- to the lowest-paid—from
being bilked, at one time or another, by the credit allotment procedure. The system of credit allocation was very arbitrary, as producers
tended to base their judgments on the same anatomical twitches and
sensations they used to rate a script's film (and financial) potential.
Later the task was thrown to the Academy of Motion Picture Arts and
Sciences, which concocted an arcane system of sifting and measuring.
The peak of absurdity in credit allocation was attained in 1934 when it

came time to draw up the list of writer-contributors to MGM's *Stamboul Quest*. The major byline went eventually to Herman J. Mankiewicz, based on an original by Leo Birinski, but the Academy's detective-like tracking down produced a veritable army of contributors:

Treatment: Donald Ogden Stewart
Construction: Wells Root, Birinski, Richard Schayer, Oliver H. P. Garrett, Stewart
Dialogue: Schayer, Root, Gottfried Reinhardt, Oscar Sheridan
Special sequences: Herbert O. Yardley, Lewis Waller, Allen Rivkin, P. J. Wolfson, C. Gardner Sullivan, Schayer.[13]

This might have made comedy material except that for a screenwriter, as for any writer, his professional life's blood was the quality and quantity of credits he received. Time and again a writer would contribute to a film and receive no credit whatever, or see himself obliged to share credits with one, two, or more colleagues whose contribution was negligible compared to his own. Every screenwriter, no matter the length of his credit list, thus hated this system. "A writer without a credit on a script he has written," Carl Foreman told us, "is professionally emasculated." According to John Howard Lawson, credits frequently went to writers who had the ear of the producer and a convincing tongue.[14] This "mess," as Nunnally Johnson termed it,[15] turned writer against writer, and further demeaned the writing department's status in the studio system, all to the benefit of studio management.

Finally, the experience with the Academy had shown the writers that no labor code, no matter how many concessions from management it contained, had any worth without a carefully spelled-out enforcement procedure. A Guild shop was necessary to maintain enrollment at a level of strength sufficient to enforce the collective bargaining agreement against the concentrated wealth of the studios.

Subsequent events would show that SWG members differed markedly on the weight they assigned to any one of these demands and their willingness to go to the barricades for them. The ten "founding fathers," however, were as one on the need to build a strong union, not simply as a counterweight to producers' power, but as a lever to transform the writers' role—by increasing their authority—in motion picture production. Contrary to the prevailing opinion among producers (and others in Hollywood opposed to a writers' union), this position was not the work of "a bunch of Communists and leftists." In fact, in

the early 1930s very few writers in Hollywood were sufficiently politicized even to consider membership in any organized radical group.
Lester Cole does not deny that there "were some leftists among us."

> Bright, Lawson, myself, we'd fall into that category. But, on the
> other hand, men like Louis Weitzenkorn and Edwin Justus Mayer
> were not leftists—they were Dramatists Guild members who had
> been part of the strike in New York. So they were, you could
> say, militant apolitical writers, or apolitical militant writers, who
> had undergone an experience with one unjust system and wanted
> to develop a means to alter the injustice they felt from this [unjust
> —studio—] system.

The first task, in the Founders' view, was to forge a lever, "a powerful organization among the writers—one sufficiently powerful to back
up its demands by shutting off the source of supply for screenplays."[16]
The second goal—alliance with other writers' organizations, like the
Dramatists Guild—made it clear that these screenwriters understood
their "derivative" and "adaptive" function in Hollywood and the con-
sequent necessity (if a writers' strike was to make itself felt) of closing
down studio access to all story material.
The third proposal was the most far-reaching. It asked for remuneration on a royalty basis which would, in turn, give the authors increased control over the content of their work by making them part
owners of the movies made from their scripts. At the very least they
could not be taxed with the old saw that "it was not their money that
was involved." To enforce this proposed reform, the Ten demanded
"full access to the [studios'] books—full right to audit them for the
purpose of determining the accuracy of the gross figures."
It became clear at the group's second meeting, at the Hollywood
Knickerbocker Hotel on February 10, 1933, that the program outlined
above was the program of a militant trade union. Howard Green, president of the impotent Writers' Club and spokesman for conservative
trade unionism, agreed that a stronger guild was indeed necessary, but
he warned that the new guild must be purely "economic" and must
not encroach upon "political or ideological" terrain. Demands for a
national writers' union and royalties were not in themselves, Green's
argument to the contrary notwithstanding, "political" or "ideological."
The writers' fight to win concessions from studio management, however, would quickly cause such labels to adhere. The conservatives
wanted nothing to do with class conflict.
The vast majority of screenwriters had not thought this extensively

about the nature of screenwriting or its relation to the studio system. They were, however, very upset by the arbitrary pay cuts and wanted, somehow, to curtail the producers' power over them. Advanced union consciousness may not have existed in Hollywood in 1933, but widespread desire to *do something* about the treatment of writers certainly did. So as soon as the news got around that a handful of writers were talking about organizing a guild, their meetings were flooded with interested participants. Once the group had assembled, however, differences emerged.

The SWG Right included many of the most successful screenwriters in Hollywood, men and women with long-standing, secure, often personal relationships with the producers. That they wanted a guild to exist at all largely reflected their wish to protect the younger people entering the profession from its worst excesses and a few unfriendly producers. The Right had no intention of siring a labor union that would antagonize the producers, change the studio system, or betray their own self-images as artists and architects. Spokesmen such as Rupert Hughes actually regarded the SWG as "a great boon to producers," which, by eliminating "sand from the gearbox" of film making and instilling in screenwriters a "spirit of team work," would inculcate a cooperative spirit among all the creative personnel whose talent coalesced to make movies.[17]

If, in retrospect, it seems clear that the Right was naive and mistaken in its professional self-image and perception of the studio system, its views were good illustrations of the consciousness which often takes root when one group of workers (a so-called labor aristocracy) in any given vocation is raised above the rest. The conservative screenwriters in the SWG were an elite, highly successful group of older men and women with privileges, perquisites, and relationships to management not available to most of their fellow writers. On the other hand, the conservatives enjoyed not one bit more of artistic authority or control over script content than the lowest of their peers, nor, for that matter, did their privileges carry over into credit allocation, contract negotiations, promotion, or tenure if their work ceased to please. Nevertheless, their higher salaries, their ostensible amity with many producers, and their freedom from certain irritating constraints frequently meant more to these labor aristocrats than the bonds of solidarity with other screenwriters, especially when the trade union bond threatened to undo the other, more important, bond with the authentic aristocracy of management. In this lay the basis of their false perceptions. The Right saw the effect of the studio system on the younger writers, but did not draw the necessary conclusions from it.

The Left consisted of screenwriters who were generally younger, more recently arrived, more attuned to conflict and struggle, and less well paid than the conservatives; they were distinguished also by a heightened appreciation of film, both as a form of art and as a medium of social commentary, and their relationship to it. They were not satisfied with grinding out "entertaining" scripts to order. For them the SWG was not a matter of *noblesse oblige*, but an opportunity for professional transformation and salvation. More than any of their colleagues, these writers were aware of Hollywood's exposed flank in its dependence on story material. Given the peculiar weakness of the screenwriter as writer—that he adapted other people's material into scripts—only a nationwide confederation of authors could cut off the flow of properties to the studios. With this weapon in its arsenal, the Guild Left believed it could, in the short run, induce recognition and good faith bargaining from the owners and managers of the studios, and, in the long run, gain increased authority over script content, anchoring that authority in a percentage ownership of the finished product.

Thus the Left defined itself by its eagerness to plant the new Guild firmly in the midst of national trade unionism and by its willingness to regard writers as "workers" who had, or should have, solidarity with other workers. Producers were seen, not as colleagues or fellow artists, but as adversaries; they were management's representatives before they were film makers. Their desire to make a profit always counted for more than their desire to turn out fine pictures, let alone their willingness to allow writers self-expression or control over creative output.

The SWG Left, locked into a caste system with a formalized chain of command, saw little to recommend in personalized solutions to the problems screenwriters encountered in Hollywood. Its interests lay in collective sensibility and militancy, much as the conservatives' interests opposed these qualities. The difference between them, from a historical perspective, was not so much a matter of sincerity as of practice and perception. The Left valued Guild unity to the extent that it consistently compromised its radical demands in the interest of unity. In general the Left perceived the situation far more realistically than the Right and proposed a strategy and tactics based on this awareness which, in the long run, promised the only reasonable solution to the underlying problems and contradictions of the screenwriting profession.

The SWG Right and Left frequently came to blows in their efforts to persuade the majority of screenwriters grouped in the SWG Center. The Center thought the Guild was a fine idea, but nearly from the start its members were placidly willing to let their more zealous colleagues from the SWG extremes thrash out policies, frequently using voting proxies provided by absent centrists. The Center undoubtedly hoped that the Guild would procure an improvement in status and an end to the many abuses, but it was, generally, less successful than many of the luminaries of the Right and Left, hence more accustomed to suffering the art/profit dichotomy and the indignities of the studio system in silence.

Yet for all its inertia and apathy, the SWG Center understood the fantasy elements in the words of rightists like Rupert Hughes—understood, that is, that producers were only amicable and cooperative and team-spirited when it suited their economic interest to be so. They understood also the need to have a Guild which could obstruct the shattering reversals (e.g., the 1933 pay cut) in which producers were wont to engage when warranted by business considerations. Thus the Center consistently voted for progressive candidates for the Guild offices and consistently supported the progressive platform: "uniform contracts, the function of the Guild as the sole representative of the writers, the right of the Guild to protect its members in all disputes and to enforce its decisions, and—last but not least—the closed shop."[18]

External Enemies

This lack of unanimity did not hinder the launching of the Screen Writers Guild in April 1933. By April 5, some two hundred writers had left the Academy for the SWG. They met to approve a constitution and bylaws and to elect officers. John Howard Lawson was elected to the presidency by acclamation. A trade union neophyte, Lawson had done his homework well. He impressed the gathering with his command of the legal and strategic opportunities available to a writers' union. More importantly, with his opening remark—"The writer is the creator of motion pictures"—Lawson galvanized the audience by reminding them all of the fundamental contradiction in their work situations and, by implication, promising them that the formation of a guild was the vital first step toward resolving that contradiction.

For all his militancy, Lawson himself was not politicized in these years (though he was rapidly to become so, mostly as a result of his involvement with the SWG). Outside of a small knot of conservatives, few writers were, and they did not advertise their beliefs. The Guild had factions, but they were divided by questions of definition and strategy, not politics and ideology. Lawson's candidacy represented the triumph of optimism and solidarity. Musing over the reasons for his election, some four decades later, Lawson said: "I was almost the only person who was totally trusted by all the groups within the Guild. They all felt that . . . I would serve only the interests of the writer and that I would be perfectly honest with everybody."

From this beginning the Guild grew fairly quickly. It had 640 members enrolled within a year and 750 by October 1934.[19] The Writers' Branch of the Academy was thus denuded of all but a handful of writers. (See Appendix 2 for a roster of SWG officers.) By means of the bank holiday, the New Deal had finally convinced the screenwriters of management's arbitrariness. The National Industrial Recovery Act (NIRA) was to provide a challenge which would get the Guild off to an auspicious start. The act established the National Recovery Administration (NRA) to oversee the writing of codes of trade and labor-management cooperation within each industry. Economic stabilization through planning, cooperation, and fairness to all parties was the official goal.‡

Studio management, like management in other industries, however, saw in the provisions of the NIRA the potential for increased industrial authority with a concomitant freedom from legal restraint. The producers wanted a regular and systematic method of dealing with their talented personnel, many of whom, executives felt, were earning more money than they were worth. The NIRA codes seemed to provide management with the opportunity to do its patriotic duty by reducing salaries across the board and getting away with it. The screenwriters and screen actors newly organized within their guilds (SWG and SAG), for their parts, welcomed the NIRA because they thought it would offer them government support in gaining recognition and collective bargaining agreements from the studios. They soon discovered, along with other newly formed unions around the country, that the NIRA was not a silver platter, but a brass bell opening

---

‡ "Title I [of the act], 'Industrial Recovery,' proclaimed the intent of Congress 'to promote the organization of industry for the purpose of cooperative action among trade groups.' Sections provided for codes of fair competition and for exemption from antitrust laws. . . ." (Arthur M. Schlesinger, Jr., *The Coming of the New Deal,* Boston: Houghton Mifflin Co., 1959, pp. 98–99.)

round one of a violent struggle over union recognition and industrial reform in America.

The hearings in Washington, in September 1933, on the subject of the motion picture code offered a glimpse of the labor-management conflict in Hollywood—and the problems which would be posed by this new government agency. Despite the lengthy testimony of the actors and writers who went to Washington to help draw up the code, the finished product openly favored management. Several of its key provisions effectively functioned as salary-limiting devices that amounted to permanent government-sanctioned pay cuts. Conspicuously lacking were provisions recognizing the authority of the newly founded guilds or improving the status of writers and actors in the film industry.

Far from battling in alliance with government against management, the guilds now found themselves facing a two-front war, with government the more formidable adversary. The final version of the code appeared in October, and the SWG and SAG moved immediately and simultaneously to eliminate the controls that the NRA administrators had provided studio management. The actors, who had launched their Guild a few months after the writers, in July (with the advice and counsel of SWG people), held a mass meeting on October 8, ostensibly to oppose the code—in fact, to swell the ranks of the SAG. The strategy worked. Enraged by the government's partiality, a stampede of actors and actresses left the Academy of Motion Picture Arts and Sciences and joined the SAG.

A week later, a mass meeting of writers and actors fired off the first of a long series of telegrams to Washington criticizing the NRA code. At the same time, reports leaked out in *Variety* and the *Hollywood Reporter* that the directors and cameramen were holding secret talks about organizing guilds of their own. Eddie Cantor, capitalizing on his reputation and his friendship with the President, carried word of the talent guilds' fury directly to Roosevelt at Warm Springs. The President, fearing that a highly publicized labor dispute over an NIRA code would adversely affect public opinion of the agency, suspended, by executive order, the controversial provisions in the motion picture code and subsequently had them permanently excluded. In their place, writer-producer and actor-producer committees—soon to be known as the "five-five" committees because each group had five representatives—were created to resolve all questions of wages and hours.

Now that it was clear that real labor-management bargaining, and not salary fixing, would have to occur, studio management opted out.

It tried to have nothing to do with the "five-fives" which implied, by their very existence, a recognition of the guilds (the representatives of the writers and actors were selected by the SWG and SAG). Moreover, it was now clear that the producers would not be able to ram their views down their employees' throats, as they had been accustomed to doing. Thus the front offices did not hasten to elect their own representatives to the "five-fives," and, when forced by the NRA to capitulate on this front, rejected every proposal made by the actors and writers.

In May 1935, as the producers' stubbornness was mounting daily, the Supreme Court announced its historic decision in the case of *Schecter Poultry Corp.* v. *United States* (295 US 495), declaring the National Industrial Recovery Act unconstitutional. The "five-fives" were formally buried. But the fight had just begun. Government simply withdrew from the field, leaving the actual partisans to an unmediated confrontation.

The studios, led by MGM, the flagship of their fleet, persisted in their opposition to the writers' collective demands. Company unions, manipulation, and intimidation figured high on the producers' list of strategies. In September, just prior to a report that the producers had resumed negotiations with the Writers' Branch of the Academy, Louis B. Mayer indicated his willingness to tear up the contracts of any SWG member not satisfied with conditions at MGM. "Mayer is reported to have said that a writer engaged by his firm works for this studio first, last, and all the time and that he, as the head of the studio, will not recognize writer allegiance to any other body."[20] Three days later Mayer offered to release Oliver H. P. Garrett from his MGM contract, saying that the studio "did not wish to embarrass him" in his position as Guild leader and MGM contract holder. Garrett declined, noting that he liked his contract—which was "materially better than is that generally signed by writers here"—and, in any case, that SWG members intended to live up to all their agreements.[21]

Irving Thalberg was the most uncompromising of them all. *Variety* reported that he was attempting to sign all the key writers and actors at MGM to personal service contracts,[22] i.e., contracts obligating the artists directly to the head of production instead of the studio. One had a choice, it was rumored, of indenturing oneself to Irving, in which case membership in any guild would be prohibited, or instantly departing from MGM. Thalberg's enmity to the Guild was uniquely vindictive and more damaging than that of other heads of production. His reputation for brilliance, his knowledge of film making, literature, and the fine arts, and his paternalistic involvement with all the talented people in his employ had long made Thalberg the most attractive boss in Hollywood (even for such "hard cases" as Hecht, Lawson, and Stewart). Now, his utter hatred for the SWG (which he felt partly because he interpreted membership in it as an act of personal disloyalty to him) severely shook many writers. No reminiscence of any MGM writer of the time would be complete without a description of Thalberg's fanaticism on the subject of the SWG. "For the first time in this confrontation with his underlings," wrote Frances Marion, "Irving was not the benign teacher but the little czar. . . . [W]e would not have blinked had L.B. [Mayer] roared out a threat to close the studio unless we gave up the guild idea, but when Irving Thalberg made this threat in chilling tones we were shocked into a dread silence which revealed his enormous power over us."[23] Similar comments were made by John Howard Lawson and James Cain.[24]

Whether by design or accident, however, the cries of personal betrayal and ingratitude clouded the issue which most producers, with their unerring feeling for the jugular, knew was decisive: control. RKO production chief B. B. Kahane (who had earlier told screenwriter Anthony Veiller, "I'll show you a blacklist that will blast every one of you fellows out of the business"[25]) testified before the National Labor Relations Board that the source of his and his colleagues' opposition to the SWG was their fear that writers would use it to extort concessions in the area of creative authority in film making by threatening to bottle up story material and thereby stop production.[26] Neither Kahane nor the most optimistic Guild activist thought that screenwriter control lurked in the near future. But Kahane wanted to abort the issue, while the Guild wanted to provide an atmosphere in which it could grow.

In November 1933 MGM became the first studio in Hollywood to institute a unit system of control[27] under which writers were assigned to specific producers on specific assignments. This effectively reduced the number of writers employed at any one time by a studio. (That is, it eliminated the need for the large staff of writers normally in any studio's employ.) "By charging producers for writers' time, it will force them to be used or dropped," *Variety* prophetically noted. Within a week, ten writers were dropped at MGM, and two weeks later *Variety* reported a significant decrease in the number of contract writers all over Hollywood, adding its prediction that thereafter the hiring of screenwriters would occur on a week-to-week, per-picture basis.[28]

By increasing the pool of unemployed writers and threatening the
extinction of long-term contracts, the studios effectively intimidated
those who remained employed and increased anxiety among middle-
and low-rank screenwriters whose accomplishments were not sufficient
to assure them steady employment under the new system.

A few screenwriters—Cole, Lawson, Sheridan Gibney, Mary
McCall—insist that personal service contracts, the unit system, and
verbal threats were not the only ways in which producers responded
to the forming of the Guild. Blacklisting by some of the more determined bosses and heads of production—Thalberg, Zanuck, Warner,
B. B. Kahane—occurred on a studio-by-studio basis against some of
the better-known activists. The effort was not concerted, however, so
the "listed" men and women—nearly always big-name screenwriters—
could find employment at other major studios. It was, nevertheless, a
taste of what was to come.

A purely local guild, for all its mobilizing and educational potential,
could not threaten any studio at that time. The pool of unemployed
or underpaid writers (now increased as a result of studio reorganiza-
tion) was simply too large for the basic trade union strike strategy
to prove effective. Producers would have no trouble finding strike-
breakers. Further, a screenwriters' strike would not affect the acquisi-
tion of story material, merely its adaptation. What was needed, therefore—and, by 1936, was seriously in the offing—was an amalgamation
of the SWG with all the major authors', playwrights', and journalists'
guilds across the country.

Internal Problems

Ironically the strategy which was destined to gain for the Guild the
power it needed to buck the producers on the vital issues of Guild recognition and creative control was also the strategy that very nearly
sank the SWG in internal disunion. The question of a national writers'
federation and the increasing talk of a strike (symbolized by the battle
for Article XII of the SWG bylaws*) aroused much discord between
Left and Right within the Guild.

This was not the first time that an attempt to weld a strong union

---

* This bylaw prohibited SWG members from signing an employment contract with any studio which extended beyond May 2, 1938. Guild policy
makers hoped, thereby, to foil the producers' tactic of co-opting key
screenwriters with long-term contracts which could legally and economically obstruct a walkout.

had mobilized the conservative element within the SWG. They were, as a result of their privileged positions in terms of salary and perquisites, the most arousable constituency in the Guild. Since they felt strong within the studios, it was of little consequence to them that their periodic assaults on Guild leadership and policies left the organization weak and divided. Though not by nature seekers of union office, the Right had been a discernible faction within the SWG since its inception. Their program of polite unionism, however, proved ineffective and they were not able to translate their negative energy into Guild policy, bylaws, or Board positions. As a result, they chose to make their presence felt through periodic disruptions instead of the ongoing persuasive techniques employed by the more popular left-of-center bloc.

The debate over the Guild constitution provided the first occasion for organized conservative action. Two provisions especially rankled them: the assessment of annual dues on the basis of a writer's salary (which offended their sense of privacy); and the granting of a fining power (up to $10,000) to the Guild counsel for use against writers who acted in ways prejudicial to the Guild (which offended the Right's sense of autonomy and threatened their independent political stance). Determined to amend this "left-wing" document, thirty conservative screenwriters organized themselves into a "Liberal Group" just prior to the 1934 SWG elections and nominated a slate of candidates "in order that the Hollywood writer can get a square deal from producers without resorting to the alleged radical and militant tactics of some of the present Guild leaders."[29] The "present Guild leaders," in order to avoid friction, became part of a "harmony ticket" sponsored by 129 writers representing the Center and Left. The politics of solidarity easily won the day, but the "Liberal Group," despite the inclusion of three of its members on the "harmonious" new Board, did not accept its defeat gracefully or renounce its position.

Within twenty-four hours of the election, Howard Emmett Rogers, a right-winger, engaged in the first recorded instance of Red-baiting in the SWG. Speaking for publication in *Variety*, Rogers tried to discredit the victory of the "harmony ticket" by attacking one of its best-known candidates, Samuel Ornitz. Not only was Ornitz a radical, said Rogers, but he had been a "principal speaker at a Communist meeting."[30] Ornitz was, in fact, a long-standing member of the Party, having joined in New York in the mid-twenties. Ornitz's "Redness" had little to do, however, with the real issue—the strength and militant posture of a screenwriters' union.

Red-baiting, a tactic as old as the headlines of November 8, 1917, announcing the success of the Bolshevik Revolution, was common in political and trade union conflicts during the thirties, especially in the period following the passage of the National Labor Relations Act, the founding of the Committee for Industrial Organization (CIO), and the establishment of a Popular Front against fascism in 1935. A vote for Roosevelt, if mentioned in the wrong company, risked earning one a Red tag; so, for that matter, did loyalty to a union. Emmet Lavery and Karl Tunberg—one a devout Catholic, the other an apolitical liberal—regularly were obliged to deny Communist affiliation (of which they were regularly accused by virtue of their leadership positions in the SWG). In Tunberg's case, the accusation was heard so frequently that his mother asked him why he had kept his Party membership a secret from her.

These accusations harmed, not individuals, but the Guild which everyone claimed to support. The fabric of solidarity was badly rent. The progressives who dominated the Board grew so frightened of schism that they modified their approach not only toward the conservative screenwriters but toward the producers as well. A tenuous unity was thus preserved in 1934 and 1935, but at the price of failing to accomplish any of the goals which the ten "founding fathers" had set back in February 1933. To make matters worse, by early 1935 a group of progressives grew so disgusted with what they saw as Guild "temporizing" that they, too, were muttering about schism.[31]

The passage of the National Labor Relations Act (Wagner Act) in July 1935 brought matters to a head, both within and without the SWG. Under the provisions of this law, the SWG could legitimately claim to be the sole agency representing screenwriters for the purposes of bargaining collectively with the studio executives. The Act was an NIRA with teeth. Lawrence Beilenson, SWG counsel, advised the membership that if the law's constitutionality were upheld—an uncertainty in 1935, given the conservative tenor of the Supreme Court—the Guild would reap immediate and far-reaching benefits.[32] Within a few days of its signature into law, the SWG informed all the major studios and independent producers by registered letters that it formally claimed for itself the right to represent all screenwriters in their relations with management.[33]

The letters had no effect whatever. The Producers' Association went blithely on bargaining with the Academy, whose Writers' Branch now represented 38 members (as against Guild membership of 770). Behind the producers' temerity lay the hope that the Supreme Court would underwrite their gamble. They simply battened down the studio hatches and waited. This aroused fury within the Guild. At a public hearing before the House Patents Committee, Jack Lawson ripped the producers, and publicized the screenwriters' plight:

> [The screen] writer has none of the protection, none of the dignity, as yet, that has been attained in other fields. One finds cases in Hollywood . . . of very well-known writers . . . who are treated practically as office boys. . . . [T]he reason why the moral standard of movies and the esthetic standards are so low today is due precisely to ignorance of [the need for creators to control the output]. Do you suppose it is the writers who want to put the absurdities, the repetitious paragraphs, the indecent allusions which one often finds in motion pictures? Of course not. It is the executive. . . . [H]e has failed to recognize the importance and value of the creative workers who are there to give him that very entertainment value [which movies often fail to have].[34]

Although it was the producer's ox which Lawson had intended to gore, it was the Guild's conservative bloc which responded. Two days after Lawson's Washington appearance, sixty-four screenwriters—led by Mahin, McGuinness, and Rogers—dispatched a letter to the SWG Board calling for the formal repudiation both of Lawson's remarks and of his status as a spokesman for the Guild. Shaken and pressured, SWG president Ernest Pascal responded with a statement claiming that Lawson was misquoted.[35] This was a lie and a stall, and the conservatives knew it. Four of them fired off to Pascal a telegram which presaged a polarization of the Guild:

> It may seem vitally important to you to save the face of a man who launched a vicious attack on the integrity of men with whom he has worked and on an industry that we have allowed all too long to be the target of continued unjustified attacks. In our minds it is more important to show loyalty to that industry. . . .[36]

Discomfited though the SWG Board may have been by the tone of Lawson's remarks, and uncomfortable though it may have been at having to stand between him and a pugnacious right-wing counterattack, the Guild officers nevertheless rallied to Lawson's defense and commended his loyalty to Guild principles.[37] The conservatives could not forgive Lawson for what they saw as his public demeaning of screenwriters ("office boys") and his gratuitous distortion of the labor-management connection in Hollywood (pitting writer-workers against producer-managers). Nor, it soon became clear, could they forgive the Guild executives for endorsing Lawson and, implicitly, his position.

Though they may not have liked Lawson's words, studio management were only too pleased with their divisive effects on the Guild. Lawson's next pronouncement, however—delivered on March 29, a few weeks after the hearings—drew blood from the tiger. The SWG, Lawson said, had voted to join with the Authors' League, the Dramatists Guild, the Newspaper Guild, and the newly formed Radio Writers Guild in a united front of writers. The negotiations had been going on behind the scenes for many weeks, and would continue even after Lawson's announcement as the various organizations strove to iron out the many difficulties raised by such a project.

The very notion of a national confederation of writers, whose purpose was to increase their creative authority over scripts, escalated the screenwriter-producer conflict to a new level. A storm of abuse issued from the front offices in the days following Lawson's announcement. The moguls assembled and affixed their signatures to a statement of intransigence on the matter of Guild recognition. The studios were not impressed by the proposed amalgamation, said the statement; they would not capitulate to a Guild shop; they would fight the screenwriters with every resource at their command. Mayer, Cohn, Zanuck, Warner, *et al.* were not deluded as to the true ends of a national writers' organization—the writers were seeking not a standardized contract with the studios, but rather "control of man power and material in the writing field."[38] As Zanuck wrote to Pascal in an exchange published in *Variety* at the end of April, "your article [in *Screen Guilds' Magazine*] definitely promises the screenwriters that eventually they will be able to control the screen destinies of the stories they work on. I can imagine nothing that would kill this business any quicker."[39]

Zanuck, for tactical reasons, chose to read more radical intent into the amalgamation than it actually represented at that time. The control provision, set out in Lester Cole's minutes of the founding of the SWG in February 1933, had long since disappeared as one of the Guild's stated goals. Recognition had become the paramount issue. If the amalgamation had been realized, undoubtedly the issue of authority and control would have been raised. In 1936, however, Pascal was not lying when he implored Zanuck to believe that the latter's allegation about SWG goals "*is not true.*"[40] It was only when the producers had made clear their intention to ignore the Wagner Act that the writers had again begun to discuss control of material and personnel through amalgamation. Articles by Ernest Pascal and E. E. Paramore/ Lawrence Beilenson in *Screen Guilds' Magazine* argued that amalgamation was a useful tactic to gain studio recognition and a collective bargaining agreement. Philip Dunne recalled that it was also intended as a device to block scabbing in case the SWG was forced to strike the studios to win or uphold a contract.

Zanuck and the other studio executives ignored Pascal's plea. They politicized the conflict with the SWG much as the conservative faction within the Guild had been doing—with Red-baiting. They were assisted by the major Los Angeles daily newspapers—the *Times* and the *Examiner*—both of which printed articles attacking the amalgamation and the SWG as, in the words of William Randolph Hearst, "a device of communist radicals."[41] The heads of production thoughtfully mailed this measured commentary, special delivery, to all their screenwriters.[42] Irving Thalberg creatively referred to SWG leaders as "a bunch of Reds."[43]

Under these circumstances it was not surprising that the producers and the Guild Right should finally discover one another. Both viewed the trade union militants and their demands with horror; both wanted corporate and creative harmony to reign in Hollywood. More immediately, both were furious with Lawson, amalgamation, and Article XII.

Conservative screenwriters could not tolerate the amalgamation: in their eyes it threatened derogation of status, from professional to laborer, and loss of autonomy to an "unrepresentative" umbrella group. A local guild of writers was one thing; it did not eliminate the possibility of cooperation with the producers. A well-organized national writers' confederation, however, would drive a permanent wedge between producers and screenwriters. For the successful conservatives who so closely identified themselves with "the industry," who prided themselves on their social and professional relations with the executives of that industry, and who spoke incessantly of harmony and integration, the prospect of amalgamation, and all that it would mean, left them profoundly distressed. The SWG Right feared that the numerical superiority of the New York writers and their different needs would combine to control the proposed confederation and orient its policy in a manner detrimental to the interests of screenwriters in Hollywood.

Amalgamation and Article XII together smacked of "collectivism" to men like Rupert Hughes, Mahin, and McGuinness. In their minds the concepts of labor and union became indelibly tagged with objectionable political and ideological labels. Thus the way was paved for conservatives to read "anti-American" radicalism into tactics and strategies which were standard fare for union building; witness Rupert Hughes' hysterical outburst over the prospect of a national writers' confederation:

> The attempt to crowd these incompatibles into one mass union, to divide it into compartments into which individuals must be cabined, cribbed, and confined, and then controlled by committee can only be ludicrous and destructive. [There is a new spirit in the Authors' League] that is destroying the Americanism of the League, and menacing the ancient freedom of the writer with regimentation, coercion, and segregation.[44]

The conservatives quickly developed a more "American" alternative to the increasingly extreme SWG. In April 1936 McGuinness and Mahin met with Thalberg, their boss at MGM (home of most of the SWG's right wing). "Irving," they said, "you are going to have to recognize the writers one day. You will be happier with the union we have in mind than you are with the SWG." Mahin's testimony as to the origins of a schism is disputed by every other screenwriter to whom we have talked; veterans of the rupture of 1936, no matter what their political hue, swear (though they cannot prove) that Thalberg conceived the idea for a new writers' guild and drew up the blueprints for it. The charge of conspiracy is, of course, impossible to document, and ultimately it is of little historical consequence. Nevertheless, several things are certain: MGM freely provided the use of its facilities—meeting rooms, offices, secretaries, messengers, lawyers, mimeograph machines, etc.—to the dissident conservatives and permitted them time off from their scripting labors to launch the Screen Playwrights, Inc. (SP).[45] Second, according to MGM vice-president Eddie Mannix (testifying with astonishing candor at an NLRB hearing a few years later), the contract which the producers would soon sign with the SP in March 1937 was virtually identical to a draft drawn up by Thalberg a few months prior to his unexpected death in September 1936.[46] Third, five of the primary founders of the SP—McGuinness, Grover Jones, and Howard Green of MGM, Howard Estabrook of Paramount, and Robert Riskin of Columbia—received writer-producer or writer-director contracts within a few months of the launching of the new guild.[47] Finally, Bess Meredyth, an MGM writer and charter member of the SP, utilized the services of one of the studios' most prominent legal advisers, Colonel Walter K. Tuller (senior partner in Los Angeles' most prestigious law firm, O'Melveny, Tuller & Myers), to draw up a lengthy legal brief challenging the validity of the proposed amalgamation.† She then had the brief published as a paid advertisement in *Variety*.[48]

Still, the founding of the SP may not have been a conspiracy, merely a set of interesting coincidences; its progenitors, however, acted conspiratorially from the outset. Throughout the early spring of 1936, while the Right was secretly discussing a schism with Thalberg, its members were publicly promising their solidarity with, and continued participation in, the SWG—if, that is, certain demands were met. An opposition group, headed by McGuinness, Mahin, Rogers, and Patterson McNutt, which claimed to speak for the conservative membership, surfaced on April 26 and asked for postponement of the annual membership meeting while these demands were negotiated. They set a modest list before the SWG Board: seven amendments to the proposed amalgamation agreement, eight amendments to the SWG constitution and bylaws, postponement of a final vote on amalgamation until the two constitutions had been amended, a retreat from the implications of Article XII, and five seats on the new Board. The next four days were filled with a series of caucuses, midnight meetings, and interminable negotiating sessions as representatives from the Right, Center, and Left met continuously to find some common ground on which to preserve the SWG.

Beginning on Wednesday, April 29, a series of "historic" compromises was announced. The Council of the Authors' League agreed to accept six of the Right's amendments outright, with approval on the seventh pending. On May 1, the SWG Board announced that the next day's vote would be not on amalgamation, but the *principle* of amalgamation, that the eight amendments to the Guild constitution had been accepted as the basis for future discussions, and that the slate of nominees for executive positions had been drastically altered. Seven people (including militants Dorothy Parker, Dudley Nichols, Sheridan Gibney, and Francis Edwards Faragoh) were dropped and five oppositionists (McGuinness, McNutt, Bert Kalmar, Robert Riskin, Samson Raphaelson), along with former Guild president Ralph Block and

---

† O'Melveny & Myers (the firm's current name) informed us that they have no records indicating that Bess Meredyth was ever a client of theirs, which leads to the supposition that MGM may have subsidized her "legal research."

leftist Lester Cole, replaced them. At the membership meeting on May 2, the Board assured the opposition that Article XII would be dropped as soon as the producers recognized the SWG.[49]

The center and left factions had deduced the schismatic intentions of the Right and had moved to block them by capitulating on every front. The opposition group formally recognized the surrender in a signed statement published in *Variety* on May 1:

> To the members of our conservative group: The committee of five representing your interests met with the executive board last night and arrived at complete agreement with the board on the adoption of the amendments to the proposed new constitution which will remove all objections of this group and will assure autonomy in the government of the affairs of motion picture writers in their own field.
>
> The executive board agreed to cooperate fully by postponing the legal vote on ratification at the annual meeting Saturday and not to reconvene for the purpose of amalgamation until the amendments have been incorporated in the constitution. (Mahin, McGuinness, McNutt, Riskin, Rogers)[50]

While the Right undermined the SWG, studio management assaulted it frontally. Jack Warner told his writers that management would not "tolerate" passage of Article XII. Said Dalton Trumbo, testifying before the NLRB, "Warner claimed we were being misled by our leaders, who were a bunch of radical _____ and soap box _____." He also said that "many of our leaders were at that minute under investigation by the Department of Justice."[51] (This latter point was a complete fabrication.) Other writers testified that Thalberg had made similar comments and threats but had sugared them with a sop to their vanity: "unions are for laborers, not dignified people like writers."[52] Producers were dangling carrots as well as wielding sticks. Between the announcement of the compromise of May 1 and the announcement of the SWG tallies on May 4, over twenty writers were reported to have signed long-term contracts with their studios.[53]

Seemingly unintimidated by the producers, the Guild members voted, 188 to 32, for Article XII and, 193 to 25, for the principle of amalgamation with other writers' guilds. The total number of ballots cast, however, was ominous. Less than half the registered Guild membership had voted. Many conservatives and moderates had either munched the carrot or felt the stick and stayed home.

Thus despite the "victories," the reigning mood within the SWG was one of apprehension—well founded, as it turned out, for the Right and studio management launched a double envelopment almost immediately. Two days after the SWG meeting, the producers (who had themselves met, secretly, on May 3) issued a statement pledging an unconditional refusal to negotiate with the Guild. Eight days later, they published an intransigent and shoddily written proclamation: studios would not purchase any plays or books which had "strings tied to them as to how and who should make the screen treatment."[54] Meanwhile the producers began to pressure individual writers as never before. Writers were "encouraged" to sign mimeographed letters of resignation from the SWG which the producers distributed among them.[55] They were treated to regular telephone calls from their superiors, notably Zanuck, inquiring about their current status with the Guild. Recalled Dalton Trumbo, "Shortly after I joined [the SWG] in 1936, the Producers' Association offered [SWG] members a simple choice: resign from the Guild and accept a company union or get off the lot."[56]

At the height of this campaign, the producers' most intensive assault against the Guild, the writers' organization was dealt a mortal blow from within. On May 5, the conservatives began quitting the SWG. Within a few days the departures reached the proportions of a hemorrhage as panicky centrists, caught between the producers' attacks and the defections in large numbers of their most successful comrades, reluctantly left the Guild, or stopped coming to meetings and paying dues, amid rumors of the launching of a new writers' union. By the eighth it was clear to everyone that the rumors were accurate. The Right called a meeting for the evening of the eleventh and invited all writers to attend. The producers announced, on the morning of the eleventh, their recognition of this new group and their willingness to bargain with it.

A New Guild

The writers did not flock to the new union, Screen Playwrights, Inc.—only seventy-five showed up on the 11th—but they did flee the old. Active membership in the SWG dwindled steadily throughout the spring and summer of 1936. The Board did what it could to stanch the flow. On May 9, following a meeting open to the entire membership (at which fewer than one hundred screenwriters appeared), the Board acted on its own initiative to rescind Article XII. With *Variety* running daily stories about producers like Zanuck offering long-term contracts to "test" writers' loyalties to the Guild, the Board hoped to take some of the pressure off moderate and apolitical writers who might not normally have wavered in their loyalty. At the same time, in a desperate effort to shore up the remaining strength and give the SWG some backbone, the Board voted to effect an immediate union with the Authors' League of America.

These measures, which were accompanied by impassioned appeals from SWG officers, hardly stemmed what by June was a complete rout. "Barely hanging on by its toes," as Allen Rivkin said, the SWG even had to discontinue its co-sponsorship of the *Screen Guilds' Magazine*. The Guild's active membership having fallen to less than fifty, it was decided to hold meetings "underground" so as to run less risk with the producers, who remained implacably hostile toward even this limping remnant. A number of screenwriters—Cole, Lawson, Englund, Gibney, Trumbo, McCall, Rivkin—remained convinced all their lives that a tacit blacklist was in effect against SWG loyalists at this time at several studios—particularly MGM and 20th. Such a charge is impossible to prove even though indications of it appear at each crisis point in Hollywood labor-management relations. What is undeniable is that Guild membership was not something one flaunted in 1936. By the autumn of 1936 it seemed that the Guild was moribund.

Only one hope remained for the handful of SWG stalwarts isolated by the ascendance of the Screen Playwrights: the possibility of regaining credibility through a petition to the National Labor Relations Board. No other strategy, certainly nothing that entailed direct confrontation with the SP or the producers, would have sufficed. The Guild faced years of tedious labor in preparing its case. "I remember the four years it required to recover from that blow," Dalton Trumbo told a younger generation of SWG members thirty-four years later; "four years of evidence-gathering, affidavits, house meetings, planning sessions, legal briefings, recruiting parties, none of which was secret, but all of which were certainly as private as they could be kept, not because their purpose was shameful, but because at that time it was not possible to organize a guild or union *without* privacy."[57]

Meanwhile the Screen Playwrights—launched officially on May 21—proceeded to construct the gentlemen's club of their dreams. They had, it seemed, found the key to peace in Hollywood: shake, do not bite, the hand that feeds you. The published announcement of the SP's inaugural meeting lavished praise upon studio management. The labor problem in Hollywood, it seemed, stemmed not from the producers—in truth, only a tiny handful of them were unreasonable—

but rather from the "radical" demands, methods, and opinions of the leadership of the SWG, that is, from "a group of writers with a lust for power." That obstacle removed, an accord could be reached on the basis of the essential interdependence of the film-making process. The nature of production in the movie business created the possibility of, and need for, cooperation, not conflict. The SP would be "an association of writers . . . with whom the producers can meet in a spirit of amicable and effective cooperation. . . ." According to the SP,

> The better producers believe that the happiness and security of the writers is an asset in their business. They have promised us complete cooperation in the solution of problems and the righting of wrongs.[58]

Indeed, in terms of concrete gains, the cordial spirit worked wonders, for the SP had more to show in less time than the SWG. The five-year contract which the SP signed with the producers in March 1937 granted recognition of the new union, a minimum wage ($125 a week), standardized contracts, notice of termination of writers on a week-to-week basis, notice, on request, of whether other writers were working on the same material, no speculative writing without payment, and participation in the credit allocation procedure.[59] The SP did live up to its code of *noblesse oblige:* these contract provisions were intended to alleviate the plight of the middle- and low-rank screenwriters.

But the public image of the Screen Playwrights as a puppet persisted throughout the four years of its existence and deprived the organization of any acclaim for the benefits it won. Rank-and-file screenwriters, who had eagerly swelled the membership of the SWG, did not join the SP, so clear was it that the new association was the creature of management and its "gains" the handouts bestowed by relieved producers.

Nor did the SP wish to become a mass or democratic union. On the contrary, its charter was that of an elitist organization, charging high dues and limiting its membership to writers under contract to major studios and recognized as successful (i.e., those who had been on a studio's staff for two years or who had three screen credits). Smaller fry could be admitted to second-class membership—"the lesser writers will be allowed membership with nominal dues and, while having no vote, will nevertheless have the higher bracket scripters bonded to handle their problems with equal fervency"[60]—if they could muster a three-fourths majority vote of the Board to support their individual applications. Not surprisingly, SP membership never numbered over 125. This exclusivity was, in the words of SP co-founder John Lee Mahin, "a deliberate attempt to protect ourselves from the elements we had left behind in the SWG."

For all the status, career protection, and increased "perks" it gained for its most celebrated members, the Screen Playwrights offered little to the rank-and-file screenwriters who would have had to pour into the new organization if it were to sustain itself over the long haul. In exchange for deserting an autonomous guild and joining a company union, a screenwriter gained very few fundamental concessions: nothing in the way of increased stature or better treatment within the studio; nothing in the way of increased job security, preferential hiring, or better assignments; and certainly nothing in the way of greater control over material or authority in moviemaking. More important still, the SP offered no protection from a new round of pay cuts or from the rumored maximum weekly salary for writers.

The SP led a short life. The organization was doomed for the simple reason that it did not, and could not, do what unions of the thirties existed to do. The Screen Playwrights was an attempt to redefine the terms and divisions, methods and goals, the very personal and collective identities which the history of industrial relations in the American film business was implacably enforcing upon changing reality: the SP asserted amicability in the face of obvious conflict, promoted the interests of a professional elite in the face of trends toward class and trade union consciousness and solidarity and maintained a paternalistic stance in the face of popular desires for participation and democracy. As such, the SP could not endure, and its founders sensed this from the outset. Even had the SWG been completely obliterated and its rival left alone in the field, as the Academy was in 1927, the SP would still have lasted only until the inexorable cycles of profit and loss of the film industry, the conflicts of the moviemaking process, and the contradictions and frustrations of screenwriting coalesced to shatter the Right's fragile dream of "amicability" and partnership.

The SWG Revived

As it was, however, the SWG was not dead—or even, after the initial shock, quiescent. The union consciousness which had launched it so enthusiastically in 1933 stayed dormant only a short time, just long enough for the wave of studio counterattacks and right-wing sabotage to abate. Within months of the Supreme Court decision of April 12,

1937, upholding the constitutionality of the Wagner Act,‡ many screenwriters were again prepared to heed their old leaders, or at least to regard them sympathetically. All were buoyed by the hope of an NLRB petition and representation election (by secret ballot).

On June 1, 1937, some four hundred writers gathered openly for an SWG-sponsored meeting and applauded the decision to file a representation petition with the NLRB. By August, NLRB investigators had arrived in Hollywood to begin an intensive month-long examination of the circumstances surrounding the formation of the Screen Playwrights. In September, dozens of writers and producers trooped to hearings in Washington to testify. Finally, on June 6, 1938, the NLRB announced that certification would be voted on in Hollywood on a studio-by-studio basis. Writers bound by a studio contract as of June 4 were eligible to cast secret ballots for the union of their choice.

The result was a foregone conclusion. The SWG, strongly supported by the actors and directors guilds, won by a tremendous margin—267–57, sweeping the election at every studio where votes were tallied.[61] Two months later, on August 10, 1938, the NLRB formally certified the Screen Writers Guild as the sole bargaining representative of motion picture writers. The producers chose not to contest the decision. On September 12, for the first time in the history of the film industry, representatives of management sat down at a bargaining table with a committee representing an autonomous union of screenwriters. Over five and a half years had elapsed since the Guild first demanded studio recognition. The victory was sweet.

Or, rather, semi-sweet. Management had no intention of granting substantive concessions. Instead, they haggled endlessly in the bargaining sessions, while quietly continuing to recognize and deal with the Screen Playwrights. Again the SWG was forced to call in the NLRB. In January 1939 that body issued an unfair labor practice citation against the producers, accusing them of having, since 1935, "interfered with, restrained and coerced employees in the exercise of their rights."[62] It further accused management of conspiring with the SP even after that union had been legally deprived of its right to represent screenwriters. Within six months the NLRB issued the producers yet another unfair labor practice charge, and this time enforced it with an action voiding the studios' contract with the Screen Playwrights,[63]

---

‡ *N.L.R.B.* v. *Jones & Laughlin Steel Corp.*, 301 U.S. 1. Within one year of this decision sixty-five labor groups in Hollywood filed petitions and grievances with the NLRB.

which expired a few months later (it had, at the time, twenty-nine members).

Still the negotiations dragged on. Ultimately, the approach of World War II motivated the producers to give in and sign a contract. They wanted to put their labor troubles behind them and face the war (and its profit potential) as a united industry. The unanimous strike vote (in May 1941) taken by the SWG may have been an inducement. Eight years and some months had elapsed since the SWG had first asked the Producers' Association for a contract.

"The 1941 contract was terrible," said former SWG executive secretary (1945–46) William Pomerance. "It tied the Guild in a knot." In addition to the provisions granted to the SP (minimum wage, an end to speculative writing, notice of termination, etc.), the Guild won an 85 per cent union shop for three years, when it would become 90 per cent (and ultimately 100 per cent), and "exclusive control" over credits. But the former was vitiated by a no-strike clause, which meant that the collective power of the Guild was available to the writers only at contract renegotiation time—which is to say, every seven years—and was never available to other guilds or unions in Hollywood, thereby delivering a mortal blow to the possibility of a permanent Popular Front in the film industry (see Chapter 6). The screenwriters' new right to arbitrate among themselves on screen credits was potentially divisive and, more important, was enforced by an arbitration and conciliation clause worded in such a way that individual writers, in the event of disputes with management, would have to seek redress without the assistance of the Guild. These problems would debilitate the SWG in the HUAC/McCarthy era and contribute to the collapse of the SWG as a political force in Hollywood.

The SWG wars did, however, bear fruit. The internal and external Guild battles produced a highly politicized left wing which was to have a significant impact on the Hollywood community and the rest of the nation in the late thirties and forties. The factors of professional contradiction and labor-management struggle helped transform the SWG Left's union consciousness into political consciousness, schooled them in partisan struggle, sowed the seeds of a heightened awareness of the links between professional, economic, social, and cultural matters, and thus prepared them for the larger national and international questions which moved to the fore in Hollywood and the United States after 1935. A well-trained bloc of Guild activists was ready to work for the various organizations which were soon to comprise the Popular Front against fascism and racism.

The Communist Party in Hollywood: Intellectual Ferment Brutalized By Politics

> [I]n times when the class struggle nears the decisive hour
> . . . a small section of the ruling class cuts itself adrift, and
> joins the revolutionary class, the class that holds the future in
> its hand. . . . [A] portion of the bourgeoisie goes over to the
> proletariat, and in particular, a portion of the bourgeois
> ideologists, who have raised themselves to the level of
> comprehending theoretically the historical movement as a
> whole.
>
> —*Karl Marx and Friedrich Engels*[1]

> "Hell," he shouted, "in those days anyone with guts and brains
> was a Communist or fellow traveler."
> —*A radical being refused a naval
> commission during World War II, quoted
> by Leslie Fiedler*[2]

The Contradictions of Hollywood Communism in the Thirties

The screenwriters who were active in the Hollywood left-wing movement combined artistic talent and a high level of intelligence with considerable moral courage and elevated social ideals. These attributes, which would have demanded expression in any era, gleamed especially brightly in the 1930s when they were successfully harnessed by a number of *ad hoc*, loosely knit organizations like the Anti-Nazi League or the Motion Picture Democratic Committee (see next chapter). By all accounts screen artist Communists played a significant role in animating the Popular Front. Men like John Howard Lawson, Sam Ornitz, Herbert Biberman, and John Bright, however, believed that their activist skill derived not from their affiliation with the Popular Front but rather from their less publicized membership in the Communist Party. The Party, with its ongoing process of political consciousness-raising, turned its sons and daughters into the singularly effective organizers and spokespeople they were.

The Hollywood branch of the Party bred social consciousness and channeled political activity as no other organization of the time did or could. In the decade 1936–45, the CPUSA made itself nearly synonymous with serious political engagement, and like any idea "on the march" it raised in many thoughtful people's minds the question, "Shall I?" Whether flowing with the Communist current or finally resisting it, the progressive, the liberal, the radical, or the socialist of the Depression had to face the question arising from his or her own commitment and activity: join the Party? Those who did paid a price—and not only the most obvious one of external repression. Communist screenwriters in the thirties faced some basic, inescapable contradictions.

"The Communist Party struggled quite openly with the relation between long-term goals and short-term actions. We wanted to reform society in a radical way, but the immediate tasks took up most of our time and energy. In effect, then, we were a reformist party; the ground for a revolutionary effort on our parts did not exist." Screenwriter Paul Jarrico was being honest as he looked back over his fifteen-year association with a party which has been variously labeled "subversive," "fifth column," and "agent of a foreign power." The basic appeal of the CPUSA in the mid-thirties—its vision; its links to the Soviet triumph of 1917; its camaraderie; and especially its proven ability to mobilize large groups of people behind progressive, civil libertarian, and labor issues and causes—must have proved enormous for people like Jarrico, because he and his comrades lived with a number of unsettling contradictions in the Party.

These contradictions extended into the most important aspects (political, professional, personal) of a writer's life. First, although Party rhetoric was replete with revolutionary phraseology, most adherents—including the vast majority of Hollywood screenwriters—did not perceive themselves as the vanguard of violent upheaval or, still less, of a dictatorship of the proletariat. Second, despite the American-centered impulses which led them to join the CPUSA, Party members uncritically supported the U.S.S.R. in the public and tended to confuse "the national interests of Russia with those of the United States" (Jarrico) in private. Third, and most crucially, American Communists, unlike their counterparts in France or Italy, lacked a place, *as Communists*, in the American polity. A French citizen could expect, as a matter of course, to join the Party, attend its meetings, read its literature, march in its demonstrations, vote for its candidates for office, and support its principles in the workplace or the neighborhood cafe without being indicted, subpoenaed, jailed, or discharged. American Communists, however, were obliged to pursue their social and political work in secrecy. This policy had its advantages, but it had costs as well. In the critical area of labor organizing, for example, American Communists customarily hid their Party allegiance when they worked with rank-and-file laborers—and as a result, while they did organize numerous workers, they failed to sink any deep Communist roots into the American labor scene.* Another anomaly was that the CPUSA contained a large percentage of middle-class and professional people (25 to 30 per cent). Though most of the American Party members had witnessed, and a number had felt personally, the effects of the Depression, they were more rooted in the bourgeois culture of upward mobility and class fluidity than in the proletariat culture of class struggle and stratification.

The Hollywood screenwriter who was also a Communist lived with a professional contradiction of which the writers themselves had virtually no awareness. They did not believe that the professional goal of writing a "good" or "shootable" and financially successful script and the political goal of changing society were incompatible. The radical

---

* According to former Party member Max Gordon, "Many Communists were confronted with the choice of keeping quiet about their revolutionary convictions, except on a 'private' basis, or of being debarred from positions of influence and leadership among fellow workers (to say nothing of loss of job). Since the latter usually meant futile isolation, they chose the former." ("The Communist Party of the Nineteen-Thirties and the New Left," *Socialist Revolution*, 27 [January–March 1976], p. 20.) Former CIO militant Len De Caux noted that "some camouflage was necessary as Communists moved into battle for progressive causes. It was expected, if not demanded, by the allies they battled alongside." (*Labor Radical*, Boston: Beacon Press, 1970, p. 246.)

Two Hollywood labor organizers with whom we talked, however, disagreed on the question of Communist identity. William Littlejohn (cartoonists) felt that any such revelation would have seriously hampered organizing activity in the Hollywood animation departments. Ted Ellsworth (costumers), on the other hand, believed that wardrobe workers were so anxious to have a union that Communists, if they were competent organizers, would have been entirely welcome.

screenwriters were like so many Penelopes: in the daytime, at the office, they unraveled the efforts of their evenings and weekends as political activists, for the movies they wrote reinforced the reigning cultural ethos and political-social order. No Communist (or, for that matter, liberal) screenwriter, of course, would have agreed to write an obviously anti-black, anti-Semitic, or anti-brotherhood script, but then Hollywood turned out very few movies which were so blatantly racist that they offended accepted social definitions and values. Racial and ethnic stereotypes abounded in every writer's scripts, however, as did the myths of democracy, justice, material success, etc., which were intricately interwoven into the film genres which dominated in Hollywood.

Paul Jarrico, John Howard Lawson, and other Communist screenwriters chose to accept the contradictions attendant to political radicalism in America because the traditional conduits to change—populism, progressivism, socialism, democratic reformism—seemed corroded or blocked. The Communist Party, by contrast, offered them a political education, identity, purpose, and effectiveness not available elsewhere in the United States in the 1930s. Even so, the forces of conservation and reaction appeared too powerful for Communists to defeat on their own. The Popular Front alliance (the closest thing to a mass progressive political movement this country has seen) created the final unsettling contradiction for Party members. Some of the very qualities which lent the Communist Party appeal to its new literary recruits—its insistence upon unquestioning assent to Party decisions and unswerving belief in the Party leadership's infallibility and the inevitability of the historical fulfillment of the movement's vision—aroused varying degrees of hostility and distrust in its liberal allies.

The policy of forming alliances, as well as the tactical shifts and the subordination of traditional Party programs necessitated by this Popular Front policy, were unique in the history of American communism. But it is essential to note that the screenwriters were attracted by, and joined, the Communist Party under these specific conditions. The "ecumenical" communism of the thirties produced a considerably "softened" Party stance and image which increased the ranks of the CP and did not impede the flow of large numbers of non-Communists to progressive causes with which Communists were associated. National and international Party leaders, however, did not cease to think of themselves as the "vanguard of the Left," infallible interpreters of history. They were alone in this perception, for when the Soviet politburo had occasion to reconsider "objective historical circumstances" and alter Party policy dramatically in the summer of 1939, after Soviet Russia signed a non-aggression pact with Nazi Germany, Communist Party allies did not see the acts of an oracle, but the machinations of a ruthless, cynical, opportunistic, untrustworthy movement in the service of a foreign—Soviet—regime. Overnight, the CPUSA lost most of its allies and a few of its own members, finding itself not only isolated, but under attack from a new—liberal—quarter as well as more vulnerable to a renewed onslaught from traditional conservative and reactionary foes.

In spite of these contradictions the Communists in Hollywood accomplished much in their heyday, from 1936 to 1946. One negative measure of the Party's achievement was the barrenness of the Hollywood political scene after the CP's destruction at the hands of HUAC, 1947–55. For a decade the progressive forces had relied on the Communists as shock troops. In their absence, and given the anxiety and fear which HUAC detonated by its attack on the Party, the entire liberal-radical movement collapsed. Without the radical Left, the Screen Writers Guild, which had fought strenuously for union rights and against reaction in the thirties and forties, renounced its involvement in politics swiftly and completely. It gradually evolved away from trade union militancy in the late fifties and early sixties to become, in the words of one of its toughest old-line (and anti-Communist) members, Allen Rivkin, "nothing more than a residual collection agency." Of the Popular Front organizations which had fought with such determination against fascism and racism, only the tiny Southern California Chapter of the Arts, Sciences, and Professions survived the destruction of the radical cadres supported by Hollywood Communists. Without a Communist presence, effective movements to ban the bomb, support the Rosenbergs, lobby for peaceful co-existence, march for civil rights, and oppose the Korean and Vietnam wars simply did not materialize in the film community.

The destruction of the motion picture Left not only transformed the political atmosphere in Hollywood, but also adversely affected the kind of product which the studios turned out. Movies of the fifties did not display any evidence of the populist spirit which infused some of the more notable thirties' and forties' films. On the contrary, studios complacently turned out hundreds of movies which not only debased women, ignored blacks and other minorities, and exalted war and imperialism, but also caricatured the "evils" of communism. In short, without its radical, largely Communist, backbone, Hollywood progressivism collapsed and died.

Historical Background

Twenties left-wingers had been largely spared the temptation to become Communists. The repressive political atmosphere of that decade, which had begun with the "Red Scare" and continued with the illegal raids launched by Attorney General A. Mitchell Palmer on the offices of the Industrial Workers of the World and the newly founded Communist groups, resulted in arrests, deportations, and harsh anti-syndicalist laws that were hardly conducive to free speech and militant trade union activity, let alone to joining the Communist Party. In addition, the CPUSA itself, like many of its fraternal branches around the world, was caught up in a series of highly unattractive purges and internecine struggles.

Coincidentally with the advent of the Great Depression and Stalin's consolidation of full power in the U.S.S.R., however, the American Communist Party emerged as a small, unified, centralized pro-Soviet party exerting a disproportionate influence on the American Left. The Party had pockets of strength among workers and minorities because it worked harder, longer, and more effectively in these groups' behalf than, for example, the waning Socialist Party or the increasingly conservative and elitist American Federation of Labor. Moreover, communism's ideology and literature won over large numbers of middle-class professionals, intellectuals, and artists in Depression America. "Marxist literature seemed to me the noblest body of literature ever penned by man," recalled Albert Maltz, echoing the thoughts of many young people of his generation.

Party membership totals climbed steadily from 1930, reaching a peak, in 1938, of 75,000 people in the Party and 25,000 in the Young Communist League.[3] These figures represent only a fraction of the total; turnovers were high, and Party veterans of the thirties now estimate that anywhere from one quarter of a million to 1 million people joined the Party or one of its fronts.[4] The Party's influence on the Left, however, remained precarious because the CPUSA, like Communist parties everywhere in the period 1928–35, firmly advocated a policy of non-collaboration with other leftist organizations. Believing the collapse of the capitalist order to be imminent, the Sixth World Congress of the Communist International in 1928 imposed upon member parties "the duty of drawing a distinction between the sincere, but mistaken, social-democratic *working men*, and the obsequious social-democratic leaders cringing at the feet of imperialism."[5] In other words, national Party leaders were instructed to preach class conflict and separatism. They were to channel the efforts of their parties toward radicalization, dual unionism,† unrelenting struggle with all other political groups, and preparation for "the eventual assumption of power."

This was hardly a program conducive to winning large numbers of educated, successful, sophisticated men and women like the screenwriters to communism. Nor did the CP show much interest in attracting Hollywood film artists through the creation of special cultural or social organizations adapted for these creative or talented people. The important cultural satellites the Party did establish—the John Reed Club and the Film and Photo League—were designed to attract the uncelebrated, the hopeful, the working- or lower-class person open to the "revolutionary" art forms of proletarian culture (proletcult), social realism, and street documentary films. Though a small group of dramatists and future screenwriters came into frequent contact with New York Communists and CPUSA viewpoints, the most the Party in America hoped for (or received) until the mid-thirties was sympathy coupled with casual interest on the part of the vast majority of liberal and radical artists and intellectuals. In the early thirties, Communist-sponsored events or activities attracted only small groups of intellectuals and artists. In June 1931 a group of film people attended a National Cultural Conference sponsored by the John Reed Club of New York; during the latter part of 1931 a group of writers traveled to Harlan County, Kentucky, to support the National Miners Union strike (Theodore Dreiser, John Dos Passos, Sherwood Anderson, Waldo Frank, Edmund Wilson, Malcolm Cowley, Mary Heaton Vorse); a Committee of Intellectuals—including Em Jo Basshe, Langston Hughes, Matthew Josephson, Sherwood Anderson, Sidney Howard, Samuel Ornitz, Lincoln Steffens, and Grace Lumpkin—formed in September 1932 to support the presidential campaign of William Z. Foster and his running mate, James W. Ford.

Much happened to change this state of affairs. Internationally, of course, the dramatic growth of fascism obliged the Soviet Union

---

† Under the auspices of the Communist-founded Trade Union Unity League, Communist labor organizers established new, or dual, unions alongside established, corrupt, or conservative old ones in an attempt to win the rank and file away from the latter.

(hence the Comintern) to seek allies against the fascist threat. On the home front the founding of the Committee for Industrial Organization (CIO) in 1935 not only represented the fruition of a long-standing Communist Party ideal—unionization of industrial workers on a mass scale—but, as importantly, furnished the Party with a greatly expanded potential for recruitment among the newly organized. This meshing of foreign and domestic needs led the Party, after 1935, to reverse its political strategy from exclusion to alignment. During the summer of that year, the chairman of the Communist International, Georgi Dimitrov, announced Soviet support for a People's Front against fascism, which had the effect of plunking the CPUSA, with its political and organizational expertise, influence, and activism, into the midst of progressive and liberal politics in Depression America. As the Party's new policy unfolded, the CPUSA briefly succeeded in generating an enthusiasm and energy in left-wing circles equal in intensity to the excitement generated by Roosevelt and his early New Deal coalition.

The CPUSA in Hollywood

In Hollywood, the Communist Party did not play an important role until 1936, although the hawk-eyed editors of *Variety* "spotted" its presence as early as 1933, and announced with the usual *Variety* hyperbole and neologisms:

> Communism is getting a toehold in the picture industry . . . [among] a crowd of pinks listed on studio payrolls as writers, authors, scenarists and adapters. And though most of the new red movie recruits are getting anywhere from $500 to $1,500 a week their program calls for a fantastic sovietizing of the lots. Meeting place of the pinks is Venice. There they gather at least once a week to plan for the millennium when studios will be writer-controlled and producers will be hired hands. Most of the leaders of the literary-communist movement are easterners who have hit Hollywood during the past two years.[6]

In reality the "movement" which frightened the trade papers (and infuriated the producers) was the newly founded talent guilds, with their militant union consciousness—events in which only the tiniest handful of Communists (acting without Party direction) played a catalyzing role. As an organized entity and collective force, the Party simply did not yet exist in the film world. Through its trade union front, the Trade Union Unity League, the Party had attempted to introduce industrial unionism into Hollywood in the early thirties. The Motion Picture Workers Industrial Union did enroll a few thousand backlot and sound stage workers in its ranks, but it could not break through the craft union orientation of the vast majority of studio workers. The Party itself was never very successful in recruiting movie lot personnel directly into its ranks. The task of organizing workers in steel, mining, textiles, etc. always appeared more pressing. By the time the Party did emerge in Hollywood, in the late thirties, most studio labor (workers and artists) had already been organized. Although Party members came to exert significant influence in the Screen Writers Guild, and some influence in several other studio labor organizations, communism's primary appeal and purpose in the screen world lay elsewhere.

Communism became, for a large and influential minority of screen artists, both the principal symbol of social idealism and the primary means of living out those ideals. In an era of causes, when the antifascist cause captured the allegiance of many screen artists, the Communist Party appealed to them because it seemed to be the best means of defending democratic values. As Hollywood became steadily more politicized in 1935 and 1936, the Party's past achievements took on a new luster. Its unstinting support for black prisoners such as Angelo Herndon and the Scottsboro boys, its success in helping to organize migrant agricultural workers and longshoremen in California, and its early (or "premature," as HUAC would later term it) anti-fascism combined with the Party's Popular Front strategy and Americanized political vocabulary to move communism into the realm of acceptable left-wing political alternatives. Overnight, Leninists became Jeffersonians as Earl Browder and the CP politburo strove to move their ideology and organization from the shade of Bolshevism into the patriotic glow of traditional American radicalism. "It was as though a new day had dawned for the American movement," wrote old-line activist George Charney. "We were not only Communists, we were Americans again. . . . [W]e were readily convinced that [Marxism and Americanism] were not only compatible but inseparable."‡

‡ *A Long Journey*, Chicago: Quadrangle Books, 1968, p. 59. Party newcomer (he joined in 1936) Richard Collins, a screenwriter, told HUAC in 1951: "the people who became Communists, at least in my time, didn't join because the Communists were going to overthrow our form of government by force and violence." United States Congress, House of Representatives, Committee on Un-American Activities, 82nd Congress, 1st session, July 6,

National Party leadership moved quickly to attract the intelligentsia. It issued a call for an American Writers' Congress to be held in New York on May Day, 1935, at which the Party hoped to enlist all sympathizer, fellow traveler, and Communist writers in the great front against fascism. (On October 1, the "call" went out for a similarly oriented American Artists' Congress.) The cause, the terms of the appeal, and the Congress itself (which illustrated, said literary critic Kenneth Burke, "the vitality and organizational ability of the Communist Party"[7]) proved enormously attractive to Hollywood writers, both present and future; Guy Endore, John Howard Lawson, Melvin Levy, Samuel Ornitz, George Sklar, Philip Stevenson, and Nathanael West signed the appeal (as did novelists Erskine Caldwell, Theodore Dreiser, James T. Farrell, and Richard Wright). These writers, and many more, united behind a proposal to found a League of American Writers as a nationwide Popular Front organization based on a platform of socio-political "againsts":

> fight *against* imperialist war and fascism; defend the Soviet Union *against* capitalist aggression; for the development and strengthening of the revolutionary labor movement; *against* white chauvinism (*against* all forms of Negro discrimination or persecution) and *against* persecution of minority groups and of the foreign-born; solidarity with colonial people in their struggles for freedom; *against* the influence of bourgeois ideas in American liberalism; *against* the imprisonment of revolutionary writers and artists, as well as other class-war prisoners throughout the world.[8] (Our italics.)

The document was characteristic of the new, ecumenical, moderated communism: it retained the revolutionary vocabulary of class struggle while studiously avoiding any mention of the revolutionary goals of international communism (e.g., overthrow of the bourgeois capital-

---

1951, *Communist Infiltration of Hollywood Motion Picture Industry*, Washington, D.C.: U. S. Government Printing Office, 1951, Vol. 1, p. 257.

Memories and recollections, always a problem for the historian, are especially troublesome in the case of ex-Communists. Although in this particular case the reminiscences agree, the more general rule is that informers, like Collins, tend to denigrate or whitewash their Party experience, while long time Party members who left in the 1950s (as a result of the Khrushchev revelations) or 1960s (as a result of the Soviet invasion of Czechoslovakia) tend to regard their years in the Party as important and beneficial, to themselves as well as the United States.

ist state). The drive to attract young, unestablished, working-class, and black writers, educable to the virtues of the proletarian novel and the use of art as a weapon, was superseded by a strategy aimed at aligning bourgeois literary and screen luminaries in the anti-fascist mobilization.

Despite the Party's new cultural stance, and the support it received from several noted screenwriters, communism in Hollywood was still in its infancy. John Dos Passos fondly recalled that when he journeyed to Hollywood, in debt, to accept a screenwriting assignment (*The Devil Is a Woman*) in 1935, the Reds of filmdom could fit around a poker table:

> My old companions of New Playwrights' Theatre days who foregathered [at the Faragohs'] in the evenings to play poker amused me by putting aside a tithe of their winnings for the Party. Communism for the high-salaried screenwriters had become a secret solemn rite.[0]

The Los Angeles branches—as distinct from the yet-to-be-born Hollywood (film community) units—had experienced a steady rise in enrollment since the bitterly fought California gubernatorial campaign of 1934, but they tended to maintain a lower profile than their New York counterparts (which accounted for half the CPUSA's total enrollment). Municipal and state authorities in California were notoriously anti-Red. The Los Angeles Police Department's "Red Squad," under the direction of William Hynes, rigidly enforced the harsh state criminal syndicalist statute.*

Hollywood was first organized into neighborhood clubs or street sections. Although the Party preferred industrial or shop branches, which enrolled workers from the same worksite, certain areas and professions did not lend themselves to this type of grouping. Since

---

* The act, passed on April 30, 1919, and aimed against the Industrial Workers of the World and the newly formed Communist Labor Party, defined criminal syndicalism "as any doctrine or precept advocating, teaching or aiding and abetting the commission of crime, sabotage . . . , or unlawful acts of force and violence or unlawful methods of terrorism as a means of accomplishing a change in industrial ownership or control, or effecting any political change." Any person who organized, helped organize, or joined an organization advocating or teaching or aiding "criminal syndicalism" was "guilty of a felony and punishable by imprisonment." Between 1919 and 1924, 531 persons were charged with violating the act. Its constitutionality was upheld in the case of *Whitney* v. *California*, 274 U.S. 357 (1927).

moviemaking was the only industry in Hollywood, and the Party's great push for film "names" had not yet begun, neighborhood clubs, which enrolled recruits from the same area but different occupations (including some motion picture personnel), became the nuclei of the Communist movement in Hollywood.

The assignment of forging a movie industry section of the CPUSA was delegated to a "cabinet-level" hierarch, V. J. Jerome, generally known as the Party's "commissar" of cultural affairs. He and Stanley Lawrence, an experienced organizer, arrived on the West Coast in 1936 to weld the growing number of Party film members into homogeneous talent branches: writers, directors, actors. These branches freed their middle-class, literary adherents from the normal demands and chores of industrial or proletarian Party membership and permitted the screen artists ample opportunity to make maximum use of their professional positions, creative skills, and social connections and influence to advance Party goals.

The Party's unusual flexibility in matters of organization, duties, dues, and discipline toward its film artist members went one step further in 1937 when it allowed its youngest screenwriter members (mostly those in their mid-twenties) to split off into a special detachment. Staff writers Richard Collins, Budd Schulberg, Ring Lardner, Jr., and others were passionately interested in exploring how to communicate their emerging radical political and social ideas in scripts. They also wanted a forum for discussing revolutionary theories of film and revolutionary film-making techniques. The men and women in this special detachment viewed Soviet and European films, read volumes of Marxist aesthetics, and spent much time discussing revolutionary cinematography, but when they went to the studios in the morning, the giant theoretical leaps of the previous evening were of necessity reduced to small steps toward the introduction of more "realism" into the standard Hollywood myths.

In matters of political doctrine, however, no flexibility was granted. No deviation from the established Party line was permitted *any* Communist. The requirement of political orthodoxy did not, in this era, extend into a Party member's creative or professional work, unless the point of view constituted flagrant opposition to Party values and goals. Literary and film creations were, of course, subject to extensive, often scathing criticism in the Party (as well as the "bourgeois") press, but the Party's leadership never tried formally to control or even to influence movies by manipulating Red writers or censoring their scripts.

What the Party did offer to Hollywood scripters was the Writers' Clinic—an informal "board" of respected screenwriters (e.g., Lawson, Lardner) who read and commented upon any screenplay submitted to them. Although their criticism could be plentiful, stinging, and (sometimes) politically dogmatic, the author was entirely free to accept or reject it as he or she pleased without incurring the slightest "consequence" or sanction. Some screenwriters, however, such as Lawson, had such strong personal and professional authority that neutral or negative responses from them discouraged a number of writers. Bess Taffel felt that the criticism she received did not help her in her screenwriting endeavors—"they told me how they would have written it; they did not deal with what I had written." Two HUAC informers, Budd Schulberg and Edward Dmytryk, complained loudly and unconvincingly of the harsh treatment accorded their creative labors by their former Party comrades.

The special place occupied by the screen artists within the CPUSA enhanced the reputation of the Hollywood talent branches within the Party. Regular Party functionaries spoke admiringly of the commitment and the activity of the movie Communists. "They identified themselves completely with the total struggle," recalled former Los Angeles County chairperson Dorothy Healey. "Some, like Dalton Trumbo, did whatever they were asked. They played a vital role in the 1938 Kern County agricultural strike, arriving in a long caravan of cars and physically interposing themselves between the vigilantes and the strikers." A key Party educator of the thirties added: "I respected the Hollywood people whom I had occasion to work with; they had a facetious humor that downtown Communists lacked—they were freer somehow."

Nevertheless, something of a distance remained in the relationship between the movie Reds and the rest of the Party. Noted Albert Maltz (a member of both a New York literary branch and a Hollywood talent branch of the Party), "There was a distinct theoretical narrowness among Party leaders and they exhibited a limited tolerance for debate and criticism from the intellectual and artistic members." And the same educator who spoke of his "respect" for the screen artist Communists also added: "screenwriters were an egoistic group of people who varied tremendously as to their quality as Party members. Thus there was always a great deal of suspicion between the Party and its creative types."

Special treatment, however, no matter how congenial or how carefully shaped to fit the needs of a "bourgeois" artist or intellectual enrolled in a disciplined "proletarian" organization, is not, of itself, a sufficient foundation on which the writer or painter can mesh his aesthetic with his political commitment. Every creative person who was drawn toward the Communist Party in the thirties (whether in the United States or elsewhere) struggled to integrate the impulse and demand to act collectively for social ends with the need and wish to create individually through artistic expression. Almost none succeeded. Those who chose one horn or the other, however, did not find either full satisfaction or coherence of purpose. Albert Maltz, for example, chose to see himself as a writer and tried (not always successfully) to avoid political activity when he wanted to write his novels. Removing himself from the scene did not, however, free him from a nagging sense of guilt "because of the need I felt to be active as a citizen." John Howard Lawson, on the other hand, surrendered the writer's mantle for the cape of Party administrator. Neither man seemed able to bridge the gap between the private act of writing and the public act of militancy.

John Howard Lawson

No single person better incarnates the values, aspirations, and durability, as well as the doubts and hesitations, of the Hollywood "career" Communist than Jack Lawson, for two decades the most respected Red in the movie industry. In an era of activists, the extent of Lawson's activities, and the pervasiveness of Marxist ideas in all his speaking and writing (except, of course, for screenplays), set Lawson apart from his comrades and made him a standard by which others were judged or judged themselves.

Lawson's communism was the product of the painful choices which, like every screen artist activist, he had to face: the challenge of interweaving art and politics, which in turn had to be balanced off against the desire to "make it" and the need to support one's family. The challenge was constant, but its manifestations varied, confronting Lawson with a series of specific choices: choosing between living in New York and pursuing playwriting or moving to Los Angeles to write scripts; balancing the social worth of literary projects or studio assignments against the needs of the Party, the podium, or the picket line. In making these choices over time, Lawson progressed from political rhetorician to political activist, from trade union advocate to Guild founder and militant, and finally from part-time Communist to full-time Party loyalist.

By the time he became a screenwriter Lawson was already partially politicized: he was a left-wing playwright aware of the need for more expressionistic forms of drama and a theater of social concern; a son whose father had been wiped out by the Depression; a compassionate middle-class liberal outraged by the treatment accorded Sacco and Vanzetti; a social reformer irritated by the utopian pretensions of Soviet Russia. Nonetheless, during the twenties Lawson had remained conscientiously a writer, not principally an activist. Like many future movie writers, he felt that he was called to be a playwright, that the drama was his "true voice." This self-image was all the more powerful because of two important successes Lawson had achieved early in his career with *Roger Bloomer* (1923) and *Processional* (1925). The first play was notable for its novel expressionistic form and technique rather than for its dramatic content; the second enjoyed a certain influence both for its use of expressionism and for the "social" dimension of its subject matter (the play was about a coal miners' strike). By 1928, however, Lawson's best plays lay behind him, and his political consciousness had already begun seriously to affect his art and his self-image as an artist. He grew restless; his dramatic projects "reflected the confusion, the romantic groping and petty handling of great themes which afflicted me in the late Twenties."[10] With his creativity inexplicably running dry and with the New Playwrights' Theatre folding, Lawson took an offer from MGM to write for the movies.

Lawson was attracted to Hollywood for the standard reasons—a vague, if "deep" interest in the potential of film, and the need to make a buck. The optimistic Lawson was one of the pioneer writers in the new world of sound movies. He seemed luckier than many, for his first assignment was to write the screenplay for Cecil B. De Mille's first talkie, *Dynamite*. The experience, however, offended Lawson's pride and professional sensibilities. Not only did he have to share screen credit with several other men (even though he had done seven eighths of the script work), but he found the emerging studio system "ruthless and irresponsible" in "prevent[ing] writers from dealing honestly and creatively with their work."[11] Like so many other "wounded" litterateurs Lawson packed his bags and returned home in 1930 at the first real opportunity, an offer from the new, left-wing dramatic ensemble, the Group Theatre. "We were determined that we would not return to Hollywood,"[12] he said as he stepped into the revolving door between Hollywood and Broadway.

The Group Theatre took two years to stage *Success Story*, Lawson's final dramatic hit. In the meantime he supported his family in

New York through a contract with RKO which permitted him to take Mammon's money while courting the divine Muses. *Success Story* helped to establish the Group Theatre as a major force in the American theater, but Lawson's rendering of the play's major theme—Jewish ghetto boy yearns to "make it" but in so doing severs his ties with his "roots" and is finally lost on that account—lacked structure and so inadequately expressed the author's own desperate dilemmas that he strained the artistic, or universal, possibility of his work. Indeed, after *Success Story*, Lawson's increasingly urgent need to express his political views, his wish to be a fine dramatic artist, and his obligation to support his family weighed on him and led him to write plays which reflected his own turmoil and conflicts but were lacking in clarity of vision or command of material. Lawson's growing restlessness, moreover, made it impossible for him to take much pleasure or interest in his dramatic work. In 1932 he wrote to his close friend, Sam Ornitz, that "the trouble with me is, I am no longer *really* interested in the [Theatre] Guild play or in the rather pale new one which I undertook. . . ."[13]

The two new plays—*The Pure in Heart* and *Gentlewoman*—opened and closed rapidly in 1934, but this career setback provided Lawson the opportunity to confront his doubts about himself and politics and to resolve them. In the April 10, 1934, edition of *New Masses*, Communist Party literary critic Michael Gold termed Lawson "A Bourgeois Hamlet of Our Time," and mercilessly exposed the ideological confusion which blighted the plays. That confusion, said Gold, stemmed from an "inner conflict" in which Lawson and his dramatic characters wandered, lost, "repeating the same monotonous question: 'Where do I belong in the warring world of the two classes?'" In a candid reply Lawson concurred with most of Gold's criticisms, but he denied the charge that he had learned "nothing" in the ten years since *Processional*. On the contrary, wrote the playwright, "my work shows an orderly development" from "bourgeois romanticism" to "genuine literary use to the revolution," that is to say, an evolution from art for art's (or the artist's professional) sake to art subordinated to politics. Gold was right to be impatient with the slow pace of his progress and the tedium of his "preoccupation with bourgeois decay," admitted Lawson, but "I . . . object to hasty judgments against intellectuals whose progress toward the left has been slow and who are aware that there is no sense in lip service without a lasting comprehension of the issues." Lawson concluded his reply with an "apology" to Gold for boring him with the monotonous question "Where do I belong in the warring world of the two classes?"; but he gave his pledge to answer it "with due consideration, and with as much clarity and vigor as I possess."[14]

It was a moment of crisis for Lawson, as it might have been for any thirties artist who took both his work and his political philosophy seriously. Lawson's uniqueness lay not so much in the answer he would shortly give to Gold's question, but in the total commitment that the answer would claim from him for the rest of his life. In joining the Communist Party soon after the exchange with Gold, Lawson chose his priority and honored it more rigidly than any other activist screenwriter. Lawson came to be known as the perennial apologist for Soviet activity and the staunchest defender of the CPUSA's line. The ranking Party spokesman, Lawson generated from his own force of mind and personality a powerful magnetism which continues to affect former Hollywood Party members to this day. But Lawson's strengths were also his weaknesses. Once in the Party, he put aside doubts and hesitations. His blindness to the faults of national and international communism presently became as renowned as his devotion to left-wing causes. Lawson's rigidity stemmed, in part, from the extended period of soul-searching which preceded his entry into Party ranks, but the ranks which he entered also played a role in forming his image as a true believer. The New York CP, which Lawson joined in 1934, had just begun to alter its strategy from exclusivist class struggle to broad alignment with middle-class sympathizers and fellow travelers. The writers' branch, to which Lawson was assigned, had recently been established to attract and accommodate intellectuals who gave priority to their artistry over their activism, but the larger Communist cosmos in which it existed had not yet diluted its hard-line Marxist-Leninism with the complaisance necessitated by a Popular Front strategy. Lawson's early New York experiences, coupled with his enduring closeness to the Communist Party's eastern hierarchy even after he had moved permanently to Los Angeles, always kept him somewhat different and apart from his Hollywood comrades.

In 1934, however, Lawson was still several years away from moving to Hollywood. During the mid-thirties he ceased to shuttle back and forth between the West and East and threw himself into activism in New York. He was named unofficial chairman of the committee of northern liberals and Communists created to call national attention to the Angelo Herndon and Scottsboro cases. Lawson and the committee visited the imprisoned blacks and wrote articles about southern justice and about the general situation of blacks below the Mason-Dixon Line.

Lawson was arrested and ordered to leave Birmingham, Alabama, twice in 1934: once for demonstrating against an attempt by the White Legion to intimidate black steelworkers who were on strike; once for criminal libel stemming from articles he had written on the violation of black civil rights in Birmingham. He later wrote of this experience: "My work in the Guild and my brief adventures in the south deepened my conviction that *commitment* is essential to the artist's creative growth."[15]

Returning to New York, in 1935, as the Party was launching its Popular Front strategy, Lawson participated actively as a member of the Executive Board of the League of American Writers and treasurer of the Medical Committee to Aid Spanish Democracy. He became a contributing editor to *New Masses*, the leading Communist cultural publication, and launched himself on "an intensive reevaluation of my work as an artist."[16] The resulting *Theory and Technique of Playwriting* (1936) was one of the seminal books on social theater written during the thirties and an influential source of education and inspiration for the second generation of left-wing writers in America.

In 1937 Lawson migrated permanently to Hollywood. He still would have preferred a career as a dramatist, but it was clear by then that he could no longer make a living speaking through his "true voice." After a brief period of energy, the various New York leftist theater groups had gone into decline, under the burden of an accumulating debt and too narrow an audience appeal. Lawson was one of many casualties which bourgeois radicals sustained in their attempt to create a politically conscious popular culture in a society enthralled by mass entertainment.

Personally, however, Lawson was the artistic victim of his own inability to resolve the age-old problem of political vs. artistic commitment. While Lawson returned to Hollywood in the hope that *Blockade* (United Artists, 1938) would be a radical statement, his "return to the fleshpots"[17] (as he put it) in fact signified the end of his quest to combine writing and activism. Lawson's attempts to write "proletarian theater" had flopped,† and the possibility that he could

---

† Harold Clurman, director of the Group Theatre, told Lawson in 1937 that he did not know enough about the working class to write good plays about it, and rejected Lawson's latest effort, *Marching Song*. (*The Fervent Years*, New York: Hill & Wang paperback, 1957, p. 175.) The play was accepted by the Theatre Union, but failed to attract an audience. The failure of Lawson's play, followed by the poor reception given a production of Bertolt Brecht's *The Mother*, delivered the killing financial blow to the Theatre Union.

write "proletarian" screenplays was nil—as any writer with any experience in Hollywood knew. Thus Lawson, like the other Reds in the Screen Writers Guild, never managed to make himself into a Communist screenwriter; he was, and remained, the screenwriter *and* the Communist *par excellence.*

In any case, Lawson's best creative efforts tended, after 1936, to be strongly influenced by Party ideology. In spite of his personal literary hopes (he continued to try to write plays), he was, in a sense, "right" to pick politics, for his gifts as radical activist far outshone his modest endowment as a creative writer. Culturally and politically, by the late thirties it made no great difference to Lawson where he lived; his basic commitment had been etched in granite. In fact, his political consciousness, coupled with his matter-of-fact acceptance of the need to support his family, insulated him and most Communist screenwriters from the debilitating self-censoriousness of many of the New York litterateurs (Ben Hecht, for example) who constantly vowed to make a sojourn in the studio brothel their last one and who, just as constantly, broke their oaths.

In 1937, when John Howard Lawson transferred to the Hollywood branch of the Communist Party, it was in its healthy adolescence. Although precise membership totals are difficult to establish, we would estimate that about 300 movie people (artists, technicians, backlot and front office workers) joined, for varying lengths of time, the talent branches of the Party during the decade of its greatest activity in Hollywood—from the outbreak of the Spanish Civil War to the first wave of HUAC subpoenas. The combination of subpoenas, contempt citations, and blacklists pried 250 names of "Communists" from the mouths of "friendly" witnesses. Another 40 to 50 Party members had died, had left Hollywood early on, or were overlooked by the FBI and the informers.

Screenwriters predominated, though there are three widely divergent estimates of the total number of them who enrolled, at one time or another, in the Party. Frank Tavenner, HUAC counsel, cited 78;[18] the Committee's "friendly" witnesses put the finger on 145; and a leading Communist screenwriter of that era now estimates that the writer membership in the Party stood at nearly 200. It would seem clear that Tavenner's figure reflected only the number of writers against whom HUAC had assembled (in its own eyes) a "watertight" case to validate Party membership (e.g., "Party cards," signed articles in Communist publications, mention by several informers, etc.). The informers' 145

may well have included the names of people who were not Party
members *per se*, although they were active in the Popular Front (in
this sense almost none of the names listed by the informers were "out
of the ball park"). On the other hand, it is quite possible that the
informers overlooked Communist writers who had died, left Hollywood, had only a fleeting connection with the Party, or played an
obscure role within it. The estimate of 200, made thirty years after
the fact, seems nonetheless quite high. (If accurate, it would surely
include every movie writer who had spent even a single evening at
a Party activity.) We would estimate that the informers' total (145)
is closest to the actual number of active Communist screenwriters in
Hollywood between 1936 and 1947.

Actors were the next largest contingent, accounting for 50 to 60
Party members. Directors and producers numbered between 15 and
20; 50 or so Communists worked in the animation departments,
composing departments, back lots, and front offices of the studios;
leaving a remnant of some 10 to 30 unaccounted-for names.

These people were organized into talent branches. There were probably between five and seven such units, the actual number varying
from time to time (there were fewer in the mid-thirties, 1939–41, and
post-1946; more in 1936–39 and 1943–46). Branches enrolled from ten
to twenty people and were generally organized along professional lines
—i.e., writers joined one of the two or three writers' branches; actors
joined the actors' branch; and the remaining members were parceled
out among the other branches. But this was simply a rule of thumb. In
practice, most members were allowed to join any branch they wanted,
in accordance with where they lived, who their friends were, what
skills they possessed, etc.

Branches were the basic organizational unit; they met at least once a
week. Contrary to popular images, however, they were not clandestine
conspiracies hatched in the basements and alleyways of Hollywood;
they were relatively open meetings held in the comfortable living
rooms of some of the most eminent film artists in America. Keeping
records was not a high-priority activity in the talent branches (unlike
Party units elsewhere in America): lists and rosters, membership cards
and minutes never flourished in bureaucratic abundance among Hollywood Communists because of the importance of protecting the public
images of men and women whose renown provided the Party—and the
Popular Front—with so many golden eggs. Similarly, regular dues
were a hit-and-miss proposition among movie Communists because
their public fund-raising efforts were so staggeringly successful. Most

Hollywood members did not contribute the standard percentage of income which Communists elsewhere in the nation paid as a matter of course (usually between 1 and 4 per cent of their salary, depending on their income level). Nevertheless, the Hollywood branches were absolutely the largest contributors to the CPUSA. What they gave—in the form of dues or contributions to Popular Front groups—dwarfed the amounts paid elsewhere in the United States.

Since most members of every Communist Party belonged to other organizations—organizations which could act openly and effectively—and since the branches were seen as the nerve centers of political activity within a given area, the branch meetings necessarily emphasized problem-solving and tactics. This stress on practice, however, did not take place in an intellectual vacuum. Each branch provided its members with an opportunity to situate their activity in a theoretical context. The Hollywood branches were particularly known for the frequency and heat of their debates over theoretical matters. The debates, notably those concerning culture and radical criticism, could be long, detailed, thoughtful, and acrimonious.

The ABCs of Marxist theoretical education—dialectical materialism, the labor theory of value, the history of the CPUSSR—had to be taught to the new members to prepare them for intelligent discussion of the topics raised at weekly branch "educationals": Marxist aesthetics, the problems of blacks and women, collective security, the finer points of popular organizing and Communist praxis. A corps of Party educators, bearing countless Party pamphlets, stood eager to tutor those unfamiliar with Marxist theory, who comprised the vast majority of the new recruits. A very few took to the basic texts with relish, like Ring Lardner, Jr., who proclaimed himself an "intellectual" convert to Marxism-Leninism,[19] while the remainder would probably have agreed with Budd Schulberg, who told HUAC, "I honestly don't think I ever mastered it."[20] A clear dichotomy exists in the memoirs and recollections of former Hollywood Communists on this matter of "interest" in Party educational efforts. Informers, like Collins and Schulberg, and bitter veterans, like Endore, claim they were bored with theory; while those who remained loyal to the Party through the years of persecution and appreciative of their Party experience—Lardner, Michael Wilson, Abraham Polonsky—were stimulated and motivated by their Marxist education.

Most newcomers in the thirties attended "study groups" as well as branch meetings. These groups—which were phased out in the forties when the Party attempted to become more traditionally American in appearance—were small (six members), but numerous and quite open. Like the various Party youth groups in operation elsewhere, they were designed as prep schools for admission to the branches. Scarcely a liberal or sympathizer in Hollywood missed getting an invitation, between 1936 and 1946, "to come talk films with us." Those who accepted found themselves, to their amusement or consternation, at a weekly get-together of a Marxist study group. As Ken Englund, Mary McCall, and John Paxton noted in interviews, new people in Hollywood, or old-line liberals, were considered fair game, and the study groups—rarely advertised as CP creations—were trying to bag as many quail as they could.

The Party, in sum, was a demanding mistress. Alongside talent branch and study group meetings, Hollywood Communists also met frequently in "fractions." Fractions met periodically to discuss the problems and opportunities posed by membership in other, non-Communist organizations (the Screen Writers Guild, the Anti-Nazi League, etc.) where it would be useful to develop and carry through a common strategy. The fractions functioned exceedingly well, and it was through them that the policies, effectiveness, and ideals (though not usually the dogma) of the Party were transmitted and magnified, well beyond actual Party strength in numbers, within a union, a Popular Front organization, or a political campaign. The very organization and discipline of the CP, which alienated many other artists and intellectuals of the thirties, allowed the activism, courage, and idealism of the screen Communists to become a palpable and influential presence in the Hollywood world.

The Impact of Communism on Screenwriters

There appeared in Hollywood, in the late thirties, a noticeable tendency to identify the left-wing screenwriter with communism. While this indiscriminate labeling was often as false, if less ill-intentioned, than that practiced by the investigators of the Tenney committee (of the California legislature) or HUAC in other eras, it was nonetheless true that many radical screenwriters were also Communist Party members. By mid-World War II, in fact, the Hollywood branches of the CPUSA included approximately 150 screenwriters, or over 15 per cent of the total Screen Writers Guild membership (and 25 to 30 per cent of those most regularly employed). The New Deal and the Popular Front offered many avenues of activism to committed liberals and socialists, but by 1936 it seemed increasingly clear to some of these left-wingers that joining the Party was the most serious and effective means of attaining their goals. (For many workers in Europe today that perception is still operable: a Spanish Communist recently told a reporter from the Los Angeles *Times*, "I had not read Marx but I saw the injustices of our employers. I came to see that the Communists were the only group confronting the government and helping the workers.")[21]

The writers were reformists, dissenters, seekers of justice, who joined the Party for the most exemplary of reasons: it was the "only political force concerned about, and willing to work to stop, fascism" (Sidney Buchman)[22]; "it was dedicated to ending serious inequalities" (Bess Taffel) and it was "an answer to unemployment" (Budd Schulberg[23]; it offered a "means of education and study" (Virginia Schulberg Viertel)[24] and it had "the appeal of the Marxist critique" (Sylvia Jarrico); it offered the comradeship of a "high quality of person" (Ring Lardner, Jr.),[25] as well as "significant fellowship" (Jean Butler) and "brotherhood" (Albert Maltz); it represented the socialist means to a socialist future.

Once in the Party, however, what kind of Communists did the screen artists turn out to be? Did they, in British Marxist critic Christopher Caudwell's terms, simply ally themselves to the "revolutionary vanguard of the proletariat class," or did they assimilate ("proletarianize") themselves and, in the process, "*really* live in the new world [of the coming proletarian revolution] and not leave [their] soul[s] behind in the past"?[26] Hollywood activists were an unusual element within the Communist Party simply because they were unusual in any surroundings. While the Party's normally strict admission procedures and membership obligations were loosened somewhat for the Hollywood branches, this is not what set the writers apart from either working-class cadres or the Party's other professional branches (doctors, lawyers, white-collar workers, etc.), for the latter also enjoyed the relaxed load of theory which the Hollywood branches carried. Rather, what finally distinguished the screenwriter in the Party were the same things which singled out Hollywood within the United States and screenwriting among the professions: the glamour of the motion picture business, and the writer's role in moviemaking. The screenwriters were the CP's "movie stars," hence uniquely valuable to the Party for their small share of the aura which has always surrounded "Hollywood" in American culture. Thus to answer one of Caudwell's questions: the Party had no incentive to "proletarianize" its screenwriter cadres; on the contrary, it needed their names and their diligence as screenwriter activists. Moreover, the screenwriters puzzled Party hierarchs, and were unclassifiable in normal Party categories, for the singularity of their professional position: they were at once workers in an industrial assembly line process and individual artists and craftsmen. They were hybrids, fitting none of the Party's (or society's) preconceptions of "workers" or "bourgeois intellectuals."

The complete agreement between the Party and its Hollywood adherents on the issue of resistance to fascism hid a knotty tangle of differences which were not resolved, and barely even faced. Every screen artist who joined the Party in those years hoped that membership would provide more workable syntheses in the areas of political action and artistic output. But the idealistic nature of the film people's goals repeatedly clashed with the practical nature of the Party.

The Communist Party's success among the left-wing, professional, middle-class intellectuals of Hollywood lay in its appeal to social idealism together with its provision of the means (and will) to live out ideals in action. The anti-fascist cause especially captured the hearts of the writers. As an organization, the Party appealed to them because it seemed to be the best means to a higher end. But the writers' "higher end" (anti-fascism) was only provisionally a top priority for the Party's national and international leadership. Their final goals always remained in the realm of working-class advancement, inter-class conflict, revolution, and the defense of the Soviet Union, while the screenwriter activists were primarily concerned with social and international goals—the triumph of the Republic in Spain, the containment of Hitler, Mussolini, and Tojo, the success of the CIO, and generalized improvement of the conditions of the lower classes and minorities. These interests were not mutually exclusive; in fact, there was considerable tactical and strategic overlap between them. Nevertheless, these divergences created a basis for confusion.

The Party leadership in this country never really understood the motivations of this mutant strain, nor were they ever particularly sensitive or sympathetic to the professional plights of middle-class Party members. V. J. Jerome acknowledged the difficulties intellectuals and professionals encountered in the CPUSA—"their academic training, their aloof habits of work and thought, their instilled, illusory ambitions, retard their alliance with the working class for common struggle"—but also noted that the Party had not "given consistent and understanding attention" to the question of transforming their values.[27] Nor, he could have added, did the Party give much thought to the frustrations and disappointments which bedeviled every Communist screenwriter: none of them—not Lawson, not Cole, not Lardner, not Stewart, not Jarrico—ever truly managed to combine his views and his vocation in a satisfying fashion. In his screenplays, no screenwriter could ever express himself even as an autonomous author, let alone as a Communist writer. Hence he was victimized both by internal division and by the waspish criticism of non-Hollywood Party members.

The frustration stemmed from the feeling of being forever doomed to remain a part-time conscious political activist—a guy who came home from a hard day at the studio confecting schlock to dull the minds of the moviegoing public only to launch himself into an equally hard night (or weekend) of telephoning, writing, speaking, meeting, or partying for causes and organizations which strained valiantly to shake the populace out of its political torpor and escapist fantasies. *This* was a more rarefied, excruciating form of frustration, unusual and laudable, perhaps, for being politically conscious—but also more painful, for that very reason.

The CP's policy of support for guilds and unions, of course, provided an extra-Party means of tackling the vocational exploitation of the Hollywood film artists. Even here, however, the focus was more on the guilds as a force in national and international issues than as a force in economic restructuring. The writer was not recruited so as to end his or her exploitation, but to be mustered in the ranks of an anti-fascist, pro-Russian army.

Finally, in the realm which most concerned artists and intellectuals —development of a new synthesis between the world of political and social action and that of artistic and literary expression, in short the creation of an entirely new literary and political vision—the Party and its creative members found little common ground. Party leaders had little understanding of the artistic or literary process and little patience with it. They wanted either a full-blown "prolet-lit" (in the pre-1935 era) or famous literary names (in the post-1935 era); outside of this, they did not push or educate their members toward creative solutions to the problems of integrating literature and politics. In fact, Party theoreticians and critics were known and disliked for the "meat cleaver" they wielded on efforts of Communist artists to attain social realism in their work. As a result, numbers of writers and artists drifted away from the Party relatively soon after joining or milling around at its fringes. The screenwriter probably lasted longer, on the average, than other writers, because he received much less individual critical attention, given the nature of the film-making process. For their part, the screenwriters did not push the Party toward a more advanced theoretical position on the cinema, nor did the Party push the screenwriters to develop one. In the extant literature (written prior to their expulsion from Hollywood) there is nothing comparable to the stance Albert Maltz took *vis-à-vis* the Party on the issue of literature and the role of writers. (See Chapter 8.) In place of theory or analysis, Communist screenwriters offered practical admonition: "not to distort, to malign, to misrepresent motives"[28]; to encourage positive attitudes[29]; to "tell straightforward stories."[30]

Even in the one major film periodical founded with radical assistance, *The Hollywood Quarterly* (1945), the emphasis lay more on evaluating "economic, social, aesthetic, educational, and technological trends,"[31] than on the development of a Marxist or radical aesthetic. Even though John Howard Lawson and Abraham Polonsky sat on the Editorial Board and Sylvia Jarrico was managing editor, left-wing screenwriters did not take advantage of this forum to break new theoretical ground. The political repression which savaged them in mid-1947 (when the *Quarterly* was well into its second volume) obviously contributed to the absence of an ongoing debate on social film theory, but there was nothing in the articles submitted by future blacklistees Ben Maddow and Lester Cole for Volume 1 which presaged the opening of such a discussion. Maddow contributed a descriptive essay on Eisenstein and the historical film while Cole simply supplied a standard screenwriter's lament, about the butchery that was performed on one of his scripts.

In the realm of film scholarship and theory the left-wing Hollywood screenwriter was thus a radical idealist rather than a Marxist aesthetician. The great movies of the thirties whose themes and treatments most impressed the Communist writers, and which they hoped to be permitted to emulate, illustrated American radical and progressive themes in the tradition of Thomas Paine, Thomas Jefferson, and Abraham Lincoln: *I Am a Fugitive from a Chain Gang, Juarez, The Story of Louis Pasteur, The Life of Emile Zola,* and *The Grapes of Wrath.* These American "models," among the best the studio system produced, were different from the advanced films made elsewhere. They failed to emulate either the radical form or content of *Mother* (Pudovkin) and *Potemkin* (Eisenstein) in Soviet Russia; *La Kermesse Héroïque* (Feyder), *La Belle Équipe* (Duvivier), and *La Grande Illusion* (Renoir) in Popular Front France; the documentary realism of Joris Ivens; the documentaries produced under government auspices by Pare Lorentz in this country (*The River* and *The Plow That Broke the Plains*) and John Grierson in Great Britain (*Drifters* and *Night Mail*); or the postwar neorealism of Roberto Rossellini (*Open City* and *Paisan*) and Vittorio De Sica (*The Bicycle Thief, Shoeshine,* and *Umberto D*) in Italy. Communist screenwriters knew and admired these films, but their Hollywood experience had sharply diminished their hopes and expectations, sometimes without their ever realizing it.

This point is clearly illustrated by the question of alternative film making. None of the Communist screenwriters ever seriously considered joining the Film and Photo League or Frontier Films (although, typically, they contributed advice and money to the latter) nor did they doubt the rationale used by everyone who wrote for the movies, whether a radical or a conservative, i.e. that someone had to live inside the infidel fortress and joust with infidel culture. Thus at the end of World War II, when Leo Hurwitz, one of the founders of Frontier Films, approached a number of left-wing screenwriters with the idea of a "radically-oriented United Artists film collective" to make progressive films on an independent basis, Lawson alone showed enthusiasm for the idea. Albert Maltz called the proposal "economic nonsense." Given the expense of making a movie and the problems of distribution (which Frontier Films had never solved), "how could we take this project seriously?" Besides, the anti-fascist cause had just triumphed, the CP was near the height of its popularity in Hollywood, and films were being viewed by record numbers of people. The left-wing writers chose to interpret these developments as reasons to remain within the Hollywood studios. To their way of thinking, studio doors and producers' minds genuinely appeared to be opening to "real" social content as evidenced by films like *Cornered, Crossfire, Pinky, Home of the Brave,* and *The Boy with Green Hair.*

In retrospect, however, the historian can only wonder on what basis the Communists built their confidence: *Cornered* had been stripped of every anti-fascist reference and turned into a cops-and-robbers picture despite the fact that it was written, directed, and produced by Communists; *The Boy with Green Hair* underwent radical surgery by the MGM hierarchy; the anxiety engendered by the effort to produce his own vision of *Crossfire* and yet not run afoul of RKO executives led Adrian Scott to ulcers and gastritis. And *Pinky, Home of the Brave,* and *Intruder in the Dust,* films which most of the Communist screenwriters saw as a triumphant step forward in Hollywood's "fight against racism," the CP hierarchy saw as, at best, sidesteps in the nation's fight against racism. V. J. Jerome delivered the "official" CPUSA judgment in mid-1950:

> It cannot be disputed that, in a formal sense, these films seem to leave behind the traditional Hollywood cliché Negro. . . . In each of [these] motion pictures, we see an attempt, or at least the outward intent, to make a serious and dignified presentation of the Negro, in a full-drawn, central role.
>
> So obviously does this represent a sharp departure from Hollywood's past patterns that, to those who are content with first impressions, these films constitute nothing short of a revolutionary change. Regardless of what must be said in criticism . . . it would be anything but realistic not to see in this new screen depiction of the Negro . . . a new tactical concession [forced] from the enemy. At the same time, it would be even more unrealistic not to see in this very concession a new mode—more dangerous because more subtle—through which the racist ruling class of our country is today re-asserting its strategic ideology of "white supremacy" on the Hollywood screen.

Jerome's bill of particular omissions and commissions included: substituting "fairness" to Negroes for realistic portrayals of their social and economic conditions, emphasizing the pivotal role of an individual, morally superior, white middle-class savior, and dramatizing "reformist, segregationist, paternalistic" solutions to the Negro problem.[32] Hollywood Communists who disagreed with Jerome's critique could not voice their criticism in Party ranks or print them in Party journals: "Disagreements . . . were flatly rejected, labelled 'anti-leadership' and 'pro-revisionist,' and ordered withdrawn."[33]

The point is, finally, that the magnetic force of Hollywood—its cultural product, its production system, its remuneration, life-style, and values—held all the screenwriters, as well as all screen artists and screen executives, firmly in place. Communists were a special, but not distinct, species within the motion picture genus. As a group, they stood for progressive ideas, for selfless charitable work, for professional, social, and political improvements, for important alterations in the content of movies. Had their cinematic ideals been realized—any of them, for any length of time—those ideals might have altered Hollywood as well as the minds and lives of the screen artists. But they were not realized. They remained ideals, and the Red screenwriters remained well-meaning screenwriters.

The satisfaction which comes from successfully blending one's work with one's philosophy is, in any era, or any country, an important aspect of a fulfilled life. Yet its attainment is rare. We have stressed the dilemma of a Donald Ogden Stewart who wrote *The Prisoner of Zenda* by day and broadcast social alarms at night. But what of the auto worker who builds Chevrolets Monday through Friday and fights against pollution and highway taxes on weekends? Or munitions factory workers who join in anti-war demonstrations? The screenwriters, thus, represented a rarefied variant of a typical American dilemma.

It is likely that no group, however "revolutionary," could have led its members to find a resolution of this dilemma for themselves, nor fomented the social revolution necessary to transform the conditions which created such contradictions. Certainly, given the religious and insular forces which have shaped American society, the CPUSA of the inter-war years was not the instrument of such change. For in a very real sense, no group, and very few individuals, could be anything but quasi-Communist in America. As an organization, praxis, and ideology, European communism never "took" in America, even among American Communists, the way it did on the continent of its origin or on the continents where European imperialism had created facsimiles of its own class-structured societies. The heritage of militancy, perduring class conflict, polemicism, centralization, and blind loyalty to the U.S.S.R. never permanently rallied large percentages of the population to its cause. Furthermore, from the outset, anti-communism flourished so in the United States that many people who might have been tempted, for one reason or another, to join the Party chose to try something else instead. Many of those who did join it had to mute their communism to remain professionally effective, but in trying to remain effective, they further watered down their communism.

In this screenwriters were not alone among American Communists, most of whom failed to assimilate or even understand Marxism-Leninism. They, and their middle-class comrades, were courageous American radicals in the Jeffersonian or abolitionist traditions who joined an organization (in this case, the CPUSA) not as a response to class exploitation, but because they regarded it as the most effective means to live out their principles in the twentieth century. It was a choice, after all, which over 200,000 other Americans made. Those who stayed Communists fought the HUAC with the same principles which had animated their anti-fascism and their wartime patriotism: justice, decency, fairness, equality, democratic rights, and (for some) socialism—democratic socialism, that is. They were formally, though not publicly, Communists, and were in many instances beholden to the

Party for the cultivation of their senses of brotherhood, solidarity, socialism, and courage, not to mention their knowledge of activist tactics and strategy. In the end, however, they chose not to stand openly as Communists and thereby left themselves open, again and again, to charges of "betrayal," "cowardice," and "duplicity." As important and "formative" as their communism might have been, therefore, it remained, historically speaking, a personal, not a social, phenomenon—and this by *their decision* not to make it an issue in their political struggles.

In sum, Hollywood screenwriters and the American Communist Party were wedded in a marriage of convenience. The union lasted because the Party did not push the writer to jeopardize his position and the writer did not push the Party into cinematic sophistication. The Party thus gained effective fighters for its Popular Front strategy, but its aesthetic theory remained unrefined; the writers gained an effective outlet for their ideals and frustrations, but remained entrapped within their bourgeois craft. Both pluses were destroyed after 1947. Each partner was driven back whence it had come: the CP went underground; Hollywood gave up its radical screen artists and then politics altogether. For a variety of reasons, the ingredients had never jelled.

Though the Communist Party did not aid the screenwriters in their attempts to revolutionize Hollywood or Hollywood films, and though it did not transform them into true Marxist-Leninists, nevertheless the Party experience was an extremely positive one for most of those who stuck with it. First, and most importantly, communism provided a channel for social-political activity. For a few this was the Party's sole function. Screenwriter Guy Endore, for example, though loyal to the CP for the duration of the New Deal and Cold War, observed years after his Party days ended:

> I wasn't really a Communist. I didn't agree with [all of the Party's doctrines]. [What] united me with it was simply the fact that they represented the most extreme protest against what I saw going on in the world. . . . I was a Communist only in the sense that I felt it would stop war and it would stop rac[ist] feelings, that it would help Jews, Negroes, and so on. I wasn't a Communist in wanting the Communist Party to run the world or in wanting the ideas of Karl Marx to govern everything.[34]

More commonly, however, the artistic branches of the Party gave their members valuable personal experiences which remained with them for the rest of their lives. Jean Butler, for example, discovered "a sense of fellowship like nothing I had ever known before," while Albert Maltz, whose membership in the Party paralleled Endore's in its duration, observed that:

> If you ask yourself, "why did Communists work so hard in the Thirties?" the answer must be the commitment and community created by the Party experience. It actuated a passion for social justice which cultivated one's own innate passion and decency. The clarity of vision of what needed to be done, and the presence of so many like-minded comrades, engendered a strong sense that the goals would be reached.

> Anyone who joined the C.P. came into a really extraordinary, formative experience when you consider the general state of American consciousness in the Thirties. I shook hands with black comrades every day, worked side by side with them as well as with female comrades, with not the slightest racist or sexist overtones. Thirty years before the "re-discovery" of women's rights, Communist men would be asked by fellow comrades, male and female, "where's your wife? why isn't she here? has she read the pamphlets? what are you, some kind of male chauvinist?" The brotherhood fostered by that experience was indelibly imprinted on all of us.

This "indelible imprint" played its most valuable role for the Hollywood Reds in the Cold War years. During the era of repression from 1947 to 1955, the Party experience of many of the victims helped them collectively to rise to the occasion, to display personal resources of solidarity, courage, honor, decency, patience, integrity, and transcendence of which any group could be proud. Moreover, their Party education had conditioned the Hollywood Reds to understand "domestic fascism" (HUAC), discern its nature and purposes, and resist it earlier, more systematically and enduringly than any other radical or progressive entity would.

The Party not only stood the Communist screen artists in strong stead in times of political and professional defeat, it also brought the members closer together professionally, raising many of them above the petty considerations which gnawed at all screen artists. Most screenwriters with whom we talked agreed that the competitiveness among Communists was much below the Hollywood norm. Henry Ephron, a non-political screenwriter and playwright of the forties and fifties, recently lauded Ring Lardner, Jr., for the latter's refusal to pick up an easy screen credit by superficially rewriting a script by Ephron and his wife.[35]

Finally, it was within the Party that a handful of radical writers learned something about the revolutionary nature of "democratic film content" (e.g., anti-racism) and "socialist film content" (e.g., emphasis on economic and social problems of capitalism), and of the struggle that would be necessary to achieve these goals in the Hollywood film industry. Though writers like Jarrico, Lardner, and Wilson never solved the mysteries of this sphinx, they wrestled with the challenge throughout their careers.

To live continuously with the contradiction between vocational activity and political belief—even if the disjunction is not always consciously recognized—saps one's sense of professional accomplishment, no matter how strong one's views, how great one's talents, how thick one's hide. If the worker can become even in a small way part of the struggle to challenge the cause of this discrepancy, however, his alienation will perhaps not be felt as keenly, even when (as in the Hollywood studio system) the reality of his work is far too powerful to be changed by the political or trade union action of a few hundred radicals. For many radical screen artists, the Communist Party symbolized their seriousness of intention in this regard, even if it could not do much, or lead them to do much, to alter reality. Mainly, though, the Party provided an opportunity for sublimation. If one could not control one's own scripts, at least one could prove his mettle by aspiring to do so and talking about it, by joining the Party, and by working hard on behalf of the many causes which the Party supported. For Lester Cole, at least, the interchange was uncomplicated: "If I could not change dialogue, I would change people's minds." An earlier writer put it even more bluntly in his *Aeneid:* "Flectere si nequeo superos, Acheronta movebo." ("If I cannot move the powers, I shall raise Hell.")

The Impact of Communism on Hollywood

The screen Communists never controlled a Hollywood Popular Front organization in the years (1936–39) of the "grand liberal-radical alliance," when mutuality of aim and enthusiasm as well as the sheer size of the coalitions ensured that the Red contingents did not seem bloclike, hence threatening, to liberal and moderate allies. The Communists, however, exercised a persuasive impact on Popular Front policies and rhetoric because of the Party's emphasis on careful preparation and hard work (and the Communists' near-perfect attendance record at all meetings and activities), as well as the clarity, ardor, and confidence with which Communists argued their views. Too, the Communists rarely allowed tedium to interfere with the accomplishment of their organizational goals: non-Communists bitterly recall the willingness of CP members and fellow travelers to stay to the end of every meeting, no matter its length or dullness.

In 1939–41, however, the situation changed significantly. The Molotov-Ribbentrop Pact, and the resulting change of international Party line, highlighted the bloc-like nature of the Communist Party. The change of the CP's official line, and the apparent unanimity with which individual Reds hailed and enforced it, drove liberal allies out of Popular Front groups, leaving the Party in "control" of the now compromised and uninfluential "rumps."

The issue, therefore, of "control" was a false one in Hollywood. The Communists played crucial roles in the victory of liberal measures and the defeat of conservative ones, but the Party "triumphed" only when its interests directly coincided with the position of the large liberal coalition—as happened during the Popular Front and World War II. Popular Front organizations, then, represented a "Communist victory" only in the sense that the Communists supported an increasingly popular cause. Beyond the Front, however—inside the guilds and unions, that is, where a Communist viewpoint might stand in opposition to a liberal position—the Party could never hope for more than a clear, forceful expression of its views. If Party members pushed too hard for an unpopular position or policy, schism could ensue, risking the destruction or the hamstringing of the organization or (in the forties) the wholesale purging of Communist members from an organization's rank and file and leadership. In contrast to the liberal hue and cry of the late forties concerning the Communist "menace" past and present, knowledgeable liberals in the late thirties generally believed that the Communist Party, for all its impressive organization and discipline, did not "control" much of anything, neither studios nor guilds nor political organizations.

Communism made no dent whatever on the functioning of the studios and their "system," nor did it even intend to. Indeed, all across the United States, and throughout the capitalist industrialized world, mid-thirties communism had little choice but to focus on the task of building unions and improving working (and working-class) conditions. The studios, like their counterparts in automobile manufacture or mining, proved to be far too massive and brutal for organized labor (let alone a small, semi-clandestine, sectarian political entity like the CP) to change or destroy. In Hollywood, the complex division of labor, the close collaboration among crafts, and, above all, the strong personal-professional bond between artists and producers in the film-making process ensured against any Communist "power plays." Moreover, the rigidity of the basic film genres—comedies, musicals, melodramas, cops-and-robbers, Westerns, etc.—simply did not lend itself to radical propaganda.

It is only when one turns to the Screen Writers Guild and the various Popular Front organizations that one discovers Communist "successes" in Hollywood. The Communists probably worked harder and longer for the Screen Writers Guild than for any other organization in Hollywood. Many of the leading labor activists who founded the Guild were, or would become, Communists (Lawson, Cole, Bright, Ornitz, and Faragoh); later in the decade younger writers joined the SWG and the Party practically simultaneously (Jarrico, Schulberg, Lardner, Collins, Butler). Communists stood in the forefront of loyal Guild militants who sustained and rebuilt the SWG during its schism and its ensuing rivalry with the conservative Screen Playwrights; they helped organize the near-strike of 1941 which brought the Guild its first contract with the studios; and they played a critical role in launching and editing the Guild magazine, *The Screen Writer*. Yet, although the SWG Communists succeeded formidably in improving the professional position of the Hollywood writer, they did not manage to create the radical union of their Marxist aspirations. Key Guild liberals, such as former presidents (and strong anti-Communists) Sheridan Gibney, Mary McCall, and Emmet Lavery, never felt that the Communists succeeded in taking control of the SWG, despite their "mastery of parliamentary procedure," their wizardry with proxy votes, and their "iron-buttocks" attendance at meetings.

At crucial points throughout the thirties and forties, the Reds were obliged to back down on issues which would certainly have transformed the role and identity of the SWG: increased writer control over the selection and shaping of story material, construction of a strong national writers' confederation, automatic support for strikes of other guilds and unions, etc. Indeed, in terms of actual power, the CP was never able to wield the force of the organized right wing within the SWG, who, with fewer numbers and no formal organization, exercised great (negative) impact on Guild policy and extracted (with the threat of schism) many more concessions from harassed liberal SWG officers than the Reds could ever do. In sum, not unlike their comrades in labor organizations around the country, SWG Communists turned out to be more loyal to trade unionism than to communism. As such, they made a decisive contribution to the founding and growth of Hollywood's most enduring guild, but they sank no political roots or traditions of their own in this union, and when the moment of the Communists' persecution arrived, the Guild turned its back on them.

Along with Guild and Party activity, the screen Communists joined every Popular Front organization of note in Hollywood: the Anti-Nazi League, the Motion Picture Artists Committee, the Motion Picture Democratic Committee, etc. They made their presence felt in all of them, but as talented activists (the most effective mobilizers, organizers, canvassers, etc.), not as avowed Communists. Communism, in other words, was a known and active force; individual Reds, however (except for a small, "notorious" handful), always remained hard to identify. Since the Party and liberal lines coincided on issues of domestic and foreign anti-fascism, Popular Front victories were celebrated as CP victories in the Communist press, but no one seemed to mind. "The Communist Party was much in evidence in all anti-fascist activity," noted Edward and Sonja Biberman, "but then so were the Republican and Democratic parties. People did not wear their party affiliations on their sleeves in those days." Ray Spencer, staff executive of the Motion Picture Artists Committee and founder of the Hollywood Theatre Alliance,‡ knew that many Communists were actively involved in both organizations. "Their presence there reflected their own need for an organized and unified response to the evils of fascism. They did not instigate or manufacture the need; nor did they control the organizations which served it."

Liberals, moderates, and even conservatives pushed and lobbied just as hard as the Communists for their particular viewpoints, for their unique manners of phrasing, for their own practical and theoretical preoccupations, and the results represented a compromise and served the functions of anti-fascism, not specifically the factions which made up the anti-fascist front. Roger Baldwin, a founder of the American

---

‡ The Hollywood Theatre Alliance grew out of the dream of Ray Spencer to create a group which would "do good theater that reflected, at the same time, the social scene." The sponsors, donors, and audiences came mostly from the motion picture industry. "Even the moguls were entranced," said Spencer; "they came frequently to our first production." That production, *Meet the People* (written by Ben Barzman, Jay Gorney, and Edward Eliscu), was a huge success, playing for one year in Los Angeles, and then moving up to San Francisco. Divisive internal quarrels and poor choice of follow-up productions sank the Alliance in 1941, two years after its founding.

Civil Liberties Union, recently summed up this aspect of the Communist question for his biographer: "I knew what I was doing; I was not the innocent liberal and I was not a fellow traveler either. I wanted what the Communists wanted and I traveled the United Front road—not the party road—to try to get it."[36]

4

The Great Popular Front, 1936–39

> We were all part of some kind of a democratic
> movement. . . . What was marvelous about Hollywood . . .
> in the Thirties was that the writers, and through the writers
> the directors and even some of the producers, did become
> politically conscious of what democracy really was.
>
> —*Donald Ogden Stewart*[1]

Early Political Consciousness in Hollywood

A newcomer to Hollywood in 1933 would certainly have been
impressed by the seriousness and acrimony of the labor/management
confrontation recounted in Chapter 2. This never-never land of the
public imagination had obviously not been able to avoid the trade
union/employer brawls which occupied most American industries
during the thirties. But he or she could have been forgiven for not ap-
preciating the extent to which this traditional conflict would explode
in the film-making business. Many of the most important American
industries (mining, railroads, construction) had, after all, experienced
bloody labor/management confrontations, which had not led to advanced political-social consciousness or broader-based political activism. Nothing indicated that the motion picture industry would be
shaken by an epoch of political "fallout" exceptional to the American
(as opposed to the European) experience. Even people familiar with
Hollywood, like Louis Nizer, did not spot any omens in the ongoing
labor struggle.[2]

An acute observer would certainly have spotted a constant reactionary political thread in the Red-baiting of the producers and, especially, in the progressive/conservative split within the SWG; but even
he or she would have been puzzled by the frequency with which polit-

ical right-wingers like Charles Brackett and Morrie Ryskind turned up
on the side of militant trade unionists like Lawson and Cole in intra-
union disputes—notably the division engineered by the Screen Playwrights. In sum, there was no contagious bacillus—certainly nothing
that need necessarily infect or politicize the entire Hollywood community—apparent in the clash between the writers and their masters.

The spores left by the Guild-studio clash, however, when exposed
to depression and local, national, and international political upheaval,
germinated into political consciousness and activism. Frustrated, angry,
and politicized in ways uncommon to other Hollywood crafts, those
writers who chose militancy played a decisive role as catalytic agents
in the political process in Hollywood. As the thirties progressed, however, the anti-fascist, reform-oriented movement grew enormously and
the politically active nucleus of screenwriters became a smaller part of
a larger whole. They remained the most active group in Hollywood,
their names adorned the letterheads of every progressive or radical organization which emerged, but their story, from 1936 until 1947
(when the first batch of HUAC subpoenas nailed a disproportionate
number of them—sixteen of the first nineteen "unfriendly" witnesses
were, or had once been, screenwriters), merges into a wider current of
national and international developments.

In the early thirties that main current was only a tiny rivulet. John
Bright, one of the few politically aware screenwriters, complained that
in those days one "had to walk all the way to downtown Los Angeles
to find even a remnant of the Industrial Workers of the World."[3] Yet
within a little over three years, Mary McCall would "complain" in a
humorous piece in the Screen Guilds' Magazine:

> We're up to our necks in politics and morality just now. Nobody
> goes to anybody's house any more to sit and talk and have fun.
> There's a master of ceremonies and a collection basket, because
> there are no gatherings now except for Good Causes. We have al-
> most no time to be actors and writers these days. We're commit-
> tee members and collectors and organizers and audiences for ora-
> tors. When the director yells, "Cut!" for the last time . . . life
> begins. Then we can listen to speeches, and sign pledges, and feel
> that warming glow which comes from being packed in close with
> a lot of people who agree with you—a mild hypnotism, an exhila-
> rating pleasurable hysteria.[4]

What caused this rapid transformation?

The Depression simply could not be ignored. Its impact on film people's lives and minds extended far beyond the salary or staff cuts among artistic personnel at the major studios. "[A] great deal of visible poverty existed all over Hollywood. . . . Barring a few indigenous fortunes . . . and a paper-thin crust of new-rich stars, producers, technicians, and land sharks . . . , the rest of us gnawed on the bare bread of poverty, unemployment, and low wages"[5]—gnawed on it directly, or lived in the constant fear of having to gnaw. Only exceptional insensitivity or insulation excused one from having to confront the spectacle of the misery of one's fellows. Not even a hard-working, successful young actress like Karen Morley could turn a blind eye. "My God, the Depression was terrible. Even for those of us with a little money it was terrible. I felt awash in a sea of unemployed. People came to my door all the time looking for odd jobs and meals. My fan mail was full of requests for assistance. And people constantly rooted around in the garbage cans behind our house."

This parade of suffering was not enough, by itself, to alter consciousness or activity. It needed agents to catalyze and channels to carry the dawning awareness, but few such existed in the Hollywood of the thirties. Indeed, such was the dearth of political interest there that the first stirring of activity had to be instigated by one of the moguls—Jack Warner—who organized a pageant for Roosevelt during the 1932 presidential election campaign. (He remembered being amazed at "how many Democrats crawled out of the woodwork."[6])

Political awareness existed, but it was largely confined to a small handful of screenwriters who had garnered the rudiments of a political education before coming to Hollywood. Men like Lawson, Cole, Trumbo, Faragoh, Ornitz, and Bright possessed sufficient political savvy to feel frustration with the absence of leftist organizations, attitudes, or structures. But what lay within them which resonated to the social forces of the decade and motivated them to transform their frustration into activism? It is, finally, impossible to say. Tracing the roots of an individual's political consciousness is about as useful as tracing the origins of a great river: at a certain point the effort becomes futile as the thing itself becomes indefinable, disappearing into a thousand nameless, changing, overlapping rivulets. Throughout the twenties Dalton Trumbo worked the night shift at a Los Angeles bakery, and in addition to making him ambitious in the usual petit bourgeois ways, the experience rendered him permanently open to the group solidarity, advanced sensitivity, and intellectual courage associated with political radicalism. Who knows why or how this happened? George Sklar's father was an assembly line worker and a socialist. His teenage son read Marx and Engels; but why this political acculturation "took," while in many other similar cases it did not, is extremely difficult to know. Lester Cole, too, came from working-class roots; he was also the son of a committed socialist. A high school dropout at fifteen, Cole claims to have been class-conscious, though not politically active, "from my earliest memories." Samuel Ornitz, on the other hand, came from secure middle-class roots. His father was a successful dry goods merchant. Yet he, unlike his two brothers, who were to become steel company vice-presidents, opted for social conscience and outspoken criticism from the time he climbed atop his first soapbox—at age twelve.

Albert Maltz's father was a successful, self-made immigrant who could afford to send his son to fine universities: Columbia and Yale. Like Lawson, Faragoh, and Herbert Biberman, Maltz passed through, and was steeled by, the social theater movement in New York. Yet Michael Blankfort and Melvin Levy, who underwent the same tempering process, bent under the hammers of HUAC. John Bright issued from the same Chicago newspaper world of scrambling, cynical crime reporters as Ben Hecht; yet while the former used the experience as a base for his communism (he was one of the very first in Hollywood), his older colleague remained apolitical. Bright's close friend and screen collaborator, Kubec Glasmon—also from the Chicago newspapers— helped found the Screen Playwrights.

What is important, finally, in the absence of "explanation," is simply the fact of the existence of strong radical faith on the part of a small handful of the early writers and the presence of radicalizing historical factors like the Depression and its issue, the New Deal, an awakening labor movement and a revitalized Communist Party. The melding of these various factors provided a foundation for the reconstruction of a left-wing movement and culture, which had been lost in this country following the repressive Red scare of 1919-21.

That earlier movement, in the pre-World War I years, had generated sufficient spiritual fervor and political activity to rally many men and women to the cause and suffuse them with optimism and energy. The Great War, the Russian Revolution, and the reaction of the immediate postwar years shattered the leftist movement in America, and Europe as well. Such was the enormity of the cultural/spiritual gap in American society filled by prewar socialism that its absence, if not the memory of it, left an indelible mark on many young artists, writers, and intellectuals of the twenties. They did not feel at home with the restructured Left, the glossy refurbishment of the American Dream (Roaring Twenties version), or the new, "Bolshevized" Communist Party. They spent the decade in search of a replacement. And just as the "movement" had become atomized and fragmented, so too the search became individualized. The searchers thought of themselves as "exiles," "orphans," or "lost." If their political opinions (they would not have said "faith") were strong and their minds critical, they were nonetheless isolated, undisciplined, unorganized, hence ineffectual.

The early career of John Howard Lawson exemplifies the left-wing rootlessness of the twenties. He graduated from Williams College on the eve of the war. Three years (and two produced plays) later, Lawson—along with Hemingway, Dos Passos, and Cummings—served as a volunteer ambulance driver in France and Italy. Dos Passos remembered Lawson, with whom he sailed to Europe on the S.S. *Chicago*, as

> an extraordinarily diverting fellow, recently out of Williams, with bright brown eyes, untidy hair and a great beak of a nose that made you think of Cyrano de Bergerac. There was a lot of the Gascon in him at that. He was a voluble and comical talker. He had drastic ideas on every subject under the sun. He was never away from you for ten minutes that he didn't come back with some tale of abracadabrating adventures that had happened in the meanwhile.
>
> He was already writing plays. . . . It wasn't long before Jack and I were telling each other how, when we got home from the wars, we would turn the New York theater inside out.[7]

Lawson was motivated partly by the sort of moral fervor which would impel the sincere and committed of a later generation to go to Spain, but his was just as importantly a search for meaning, identity, belonging. "This European experience," Lawson later wrote, "was the root and beginning of the cultural development of my generation. It initiated the passionate and troubled exploration of social reality which has led in so many directions."[8] Lawson's European search continued after the war. In the spring of 1919 he returned to Paris and playwriting. Living off a $5,000 stipend which Paramount Pictures paid him for an unproduced play (*The Spice of Life*), Lawson became immersed in a new form of theater: expressionism. His next plays, *Roger Bloomer* (1923) and *Processional* (1925), represented a melding of the European expressionist forms with American social content. Their success led Lawson, now living in New York, to join with Michael Gold, Francis Faragoh, Em Jo Basshe, and John Dos Passos in founding the left-wing New Playwrights Theatre in 1926—"a theater that would have some contact with workers and reflect realities of American life."[9]

About the time that Lawson was writing for the New Playwrights (and getting arrested for demonstrating against the imprisonment of Sacco and Vanzetti), a generation of writers who had been molded by a different set of circumstances was coming to the fore. College graduates and high school dropouts of the late twenties walked square into a Depression which severely limited their personal opportunities. At the same time they encountered new and shifting political opportunities and constellations—the New Deal, resurgent left-wing activism orchestrated by a highly disciplined Communist Party, the militant trade union movement, and a deteriorating international socio-political situation in the face of rising fascism. Moreover, the frustration and futility of the Sacco-Vanzetti protests had proved to everyone on the left the ineffectualness of one-shot moral efforts in the face of a determined and brutal policy of state repression.

Unlike most of the writers of Lawson's generation, many of the younger writers did not come from "good" families. Their social and economic background did not permit many of them time off to drive camions across the Alps or spend a year in Paris, though a few (Blankfort, Lardner, Schulberg) did have the means to go to the U.S.S.R. to see firsthand the "experiment" in socialism which was in progress there. The early family and work experience of many of them was distinctly lower or lower-middle class, rooting them strongly in an American social experience of deprivation, insecurity, discrimination, and injustice. Many of them discovered—along with a small number of the earlier generation—that simply writing about their perceptions and feelings was not enough; the younger men and women felt the need to relate their work and themselves to their times and their fellows.

This early Depression generation thus acquired the disposition and the need to work together to create a movement, whether professional (unions), cultural (the Left Theatre), political (the Popular Front), or all three. In the Sacco-Vanzetti protest, the Unemployed Councils, the John Reed Clubs, the Broadway trade union movement, the Left Theatre, and (for a very few) the American Communist Party, many of them learned the rudiments of both collective consciousness and organizing. This is not to say they came to Hollywood either as dedicated social revolutionaries or as experienced activists, or even that they came armed with a bill of particulars and intentions. But the events and circumstances they would encounter as screenwriters would elicit from them a firm, collective, adversary response, the success and lessons of which would inspire and condition a similar response to the changing national and international social, political, and economic situation. In sum, the Depression screenwriters did not have to renew the pre-World War I movement or clear the field for plowing (the Depression had done that); they had but to replant the seeds of political energy, vitality, faith, and commitment in the fertile, albeit different, soil of the thirties.

First Stirrings: the EPIC Campaign, 1934

The buoyancy of the twenties' economy and the corresponding quiescence of the labor movement (partly due to the success of the Red Scare and the partisanship of the American judiciary in issuing and upholding pro-management injunctions) led to a somewhat muted class conflict in the United States in the decade following the war and the Russian Revolution. The Depression rapidly and radically altered these circumstances. Massive unemployment inevitably helped to increase conflict between labor and management across the country, which, in turn, led to a heightened awareness of the "social crisis." This crisis was particularly intense in California. Although in retrospect it seems fairly clear that the provision of jobs and income was all that was needed to reestablish order, at the time, the proposals, means, ideas, and definitions put forward by many of the unemployed and their spokespeople appeared to threaten a good deal more than "mere" economic ends.

Such was particularly the case with the so-called EPIC gubernatorial campaign of 1934 in California, where the most well-known muckraker of the twentieth century, Upton Sinclair, ran as the Democratic candidate on a platform promising to "End Poverty in California" (EPIC). The victory of an outspoken radical like Sinclair, who had previously run as the Socialist Party candidate for governor of California, in a primary election of a major political party reflected the desperation felt by California's voters. Indeed, a socialist had never before or since come so close to such a high office. But then the economic crisis which convulsed the state was equally unique. By June 1934, 700,000 workers were unemployed in California, half of them in Los Angeles County, where one fifth of all residents barely subsisted on welfare (at the rate of $16.20 per family per month).[10] Since the fall of the preceding year the rural economy of California had been the scene of bloody clashes between migrant laborers and management, culminating in a series of strikes involving thousands of workers in every phase of agriculture. Vigilante teams, financed by employers and tolerated by civil authority, roamed the San Joaquin and Imperial Valleys, breaking up strike meetings, disrupting picket lines, ransacking union headquarters, and beating up labor organizers. Thus the election campaign of 1934 became a focal point for the passions and frustrations which the Depression had unleashed in California. The discontent which had provided the impetus for the EPIC campaign, however, also nourished a climate of fear and suspicion which could be maneuvered and manipulated by the entrenched powers in their counteroffensive against Sinclair.

Ironically, there was little in Sinclair's platform which threatened the established political and economic interests of California. The powers of a state governor are quite narrowly circumscribed, and the only measure with real bite that Sinclair could possibly have convinced the legislature to enact was increased corporate taxation. As often is the case, however, perceptions and ploys, threats and opinions, style and appearance weighed far more heavily than written programs in determining events. The "idea" of a sitting socialist governor, elected to office by millions of poor, unemployed, angry, organized voters, was far more threatening to "the interests" than any particular proposed reform in the Democratic Party platform.

Although virtually every large employer in the state, from citrus growers to oil refiners to cement manufacturers, moved immediately to counterattack the Sinclair campaign,* no sector of management reacted with greater savagery than the bosses of the communications industry —notably newspapers and motion pictures. The movie moguls, for their part, had special reason to fear and despise Sinclair since one of their number—William Fox—had indiscreetly provided Sinclair with

---

* These business leaders were old allies in the struggle to save California from communism, in whatever guise it appeared. In May 1934, for example, Pacific Gas & Electric, Safeway Stores, and a large number of banks, railroads, oil companies, realty firms, farm implement manufacturers, and food packers financed the formation and operation of an organization—the Associated Farmers—designed to ferret out the "un-American agitators" aiming to destroy California agriculture. (Dick Meister and Anne Loftis, *A Long Time Coming: The Struggle to Unionize America's Farm Workers*, New York: The Macmillan Co., 1977, p. 35.)

much of the muck he raked up about the film industry in his book *Upton Sinclair Presents William Fox.* In the early thirties Fox had approached Sinclair with an offer of $25,000 if the writer would produce an exposé of the fleecing which Fox had taken in the course of his losing struggle with his fellow moguls for control of the Fox studios. (Wrote Sinclair in his memoirs: "[E]very day Fox came with his suitcase full of documents and his little round pudgy lawyer to elucidate them."[11]) Whereas Fox merely intended to use the Sinclair manuscript as a blackmail device in his corporate struggles, the writer naturally wanted to have his creation published . . . and in this instance (one of the very few on record where a writer prevailed over a producer in matters of control of content, production, and distribution!) he succeeded.

Sinclair's book, which appeared in 1933, was not only highly critical of the top level of the Hollywood film industry, it was also bold in the measures the author proposed for reforming and controlling moviemaking, the most notable of which—nationalization or federal regulation—struck outright terror in the hearts of the moguls. Now, one year later, Sinclair's election campaign promise to raise taxes, expand relief, and put people back to work (in the case of the film industry unemployed, he even promised, somewhat unrealistically, that they would be rehired by the same studios which had let them go) brought the film executives out of their front offices in a concerted effort to "Stop Sinclair."

Anti-communism was the first weapon to be brought out. Sinclair was described as "a most dangerous Bolshevik beast" and a Communist seeking to "Russianize" California. MGM and Fox studios reinforced these accusations with newsreel footage purporting to depict random interviews with California voters. In the two weeks before the elections viewers of Metrotone News were treated to shots of solid, well-heeled citizens articulately supporting Frank Merriam, the Republican candidate, while "the Sinclair advocates were unshaven, poorly dressed and obviously uneducated."[12] One of the films went so far as to show trainloads of hoboes and criminals heading toward California to seek the easy life promised by Sinclair. Samuel Marx, then head of the MGM Story Department, confirmed that "[r]espectable people who like Sinclair landed on the cutting-room floor along with shots of tramps who spoke up for Merriam."[13] On October 13, 1934, *Variety* reported: "Trailers attacking the candidacy of Upton Sinclair for governor are being prepared at several of the studios, for screening in theatres throughout the state during the remaining two weeks preceding the November election."

The newspapers evinced the same concern for truth in their campaign against Sinclair. On October 26, the Los Angeles *Times* printed a "news photo" of a freight car loaded with tramps going to California to live off EPIC. The same day the Hearst-controlled Los Angeles *Examiner* published a photograph showing more hoboes doing the same thing. It turned out that the *Times*'s cut was not a news photograph but a still from the Warner Brothers movie *Wild Boys of the Road*, while the *Examiner*'s was a posed scene using hired actors registered with Central Casting and paid for by the studios.[14]

As would so often be the case in Hollywood, the exertions of one political extreme alarmed and mobilized the other extreme. In the instance of the Sinclair campaign, many actors and writers were deeply ashamed and outraged by the studio executives' tactics. MGM actor Fredric March, encountering Irving Thalberg at a cocktail party, publicly castigated his boss for his and his colleagues' outrageously unfair treatment of Sinclair. "Nothing is unfair in politics,"[15] replied Thalberg. (Not surprisingly, Thalberg's anti-fascism proved rather less intense than his anti-socialism. The year before his death, Thalberg was asked by writer Kyle Crichton why MGM's power and film-making potential were not used to oppose Nazism and anti-Semitism. Thalberg had no answer,[16] though he might have been thinking that Hitler and Mussolini were threatening not to raise taxes in California, but to shut down MGM offices and outlets in Germany and Italy.)

Scenes like this one probably rallied some support for Sinclair among Hollywood artists, but the really big wave which swept them into the EPIC camp broke when the producers began taking involuntary "contributions" to the Merriam campaign from studio workers' salaries. Everyone making over $90 a week was "asked" for one day's salary to save California from "Russianization."

The screenwriters—from conservatives like Morrie Ryskind to moderates like Allen Rivkin and Nunnally Johnson to left-wingers like Dorothy Parker—went livid when the producers made their "plea" for "donations." The SWG immediately adopted a resolution protesting studio management's action and pointing out that the canvass for funds was "accompanied by implied coercion and intimidation."[17] Parker, Gene Fowler, and many others joined hands with writers all around the state to form the California Authors' League for Sinclair. For many who joined this League, or others who simply went to work for Sinclair (over eight hundred EPIC clubs were in existence by election day), it was their first taste of political activism. The Democratic candidate undoubtedly benefited from this support, but the people who worked for him also grew in consciousness and insight. Carey McWilliams, the eminent lawyer, editor, and author, called the Sinclair campaign "one of the most successful experiments in mass education ever performed in this country."[18]

However successful as an experiment in politicization, the Sinclair campaign failed where it hoped to succeed. A funny thing happened to the author of *I, Governor of California* on his way to the governor's mansion: he lost the election. The presence of a candidate running on the Progressive Party ticket, whose opposition to Sinclair was greater than his opposition to Merriam, siphoned off votes which, if added to the Democratic candidate's total, would have made him governor. But the bitterness which the studio executives' tactics had created encouraged the formation of a leftist bloc in Hollywood. When Merriam ran for reelection in 1938 against Culbert Olson, a large group of film people established the Studio Committee for Democratic Political Action to work, successfully, for Merriam's defeat.

The campaign of vilification and duplicity against Sinclair had an ironic epilogue. No sooner had Merriam taken office than he announced a raise in taxes. With great loyalty and understanding, the studio heads announced that they would be leaving California—and taking their studios with them. On March 13, 1935, Fred Pelton, the MGM studio manager, was dispatched to Florida to scout new sites for the giant film company. A week later Louis B. Mayer met with the governor of North Carolina to discuss relocation there. Meanwhile, trembling at the "socialist" ramifications the tax raise might have, the studio heads moved to revive the anti-Sinclair cartel in order to lobby for a residency requirement for all citizens applying for relief or welfare funds in California. "Conditions," read the statement from the film executives, "would be unbearable if the so-called vagrants were permitted to come into the state, get a government or county dole and in short time find their way to the ballot box to have a voice in doling out funds in a reckless and unnecessary manner."[19] Their lobbying, however, was unsuccessful, as were their efforts to lower taxes or to convince anyone that they were going to relocate the studios. The Bolsheviks, it appeared, had infiltrated even the Republican Party.

The founding of the Guild, together with many screenwriters' participation in the EPIC movement—based as they were on the common experience of studio management's intransigence and imperiousness—not only made many film artists aware of the links between economic-professional and political-social issues, it also underscored the need for a collective response. The war would be a long one, however, and there would be many enemies to be faced. By 1935, in fact, an entire new theater of operations had opened up.

The Background of Hollywood's Internationalism

The political and union consciousness in Hollywood which arose out of, and concentrated on, local and statewide issues and personalities was characteristic of America during the early and middle years of the Depression. Throughout the thirties, around the nation, workers and unions battled employers while communities polarized over "social" questions in highly charged electoral campaigns at the municipal through federal levels. This was the foundation of all political consciousness in the United States in those years, but very few communities built an enduring, international activism on this base. Very few communities possessed sufficient professional solidarity and political understanding to mobilize and support movements and institutions whose origins and goals reached much beyond self-interest and local improvement.

The Hollywood film community was, along with New York City, the most important center of international consciousness and activism in the United States. These two communities led the nation in translating unionism and partisan politics into a passionate concern with the growth of fascism, the defense of the Soviet "experiment," the support of the democratically elected government of Spain, and the protection of victims of war, repression, and aggression. Such an advanced consciousness required a solid "material" base which was almost unique to New York and Hollywood. In addition to the union movement and local political struggles, internationalism drew its life from several other vitally important founts.

A strong local branch of the Communist Party was the *sine qua non* of almost all effective radical activism in the United States during this decade. The Party's most important trait was the indefatigability of its members: as a group they were without rivals in their energy and willingness to perform the daily tasks of organizing and consciousness-raising. Secondly, the Party systematically linked local events to national and international issues. In the Scottsboro Case of the early thirties, for example, the Party simultaneously aided the defense of nine black Alabama males accused of raping two white women and inaugurated a campaign to focus national attention on American racism and its roots in the capitalist system. Time and again, throughout the country, in issues touching on everything from labor abuses to imperialist aggression, the Communist Party was present and prepared with a full diagnosis and treatment. The Party was able to accomplish its task of consciousness-expanding more effectively than any other institution or group precisely because of the unity of its own organization, the sweep and power of its ideology, and the youth and apparent success of its showcase in Russia.

Even though the Party directed the major portion of its time, money, and personnel toward organizing workers, it made a decisive contribution to the growth of international consciousness in the United States by building Communist-dominated, and supporting liberal-dominated, anti-fascist organizations. Thousands of motion picture industry people responded to the appeals of these groups as well as to the thousands of Jewish refugees from Nazism who settled in the Los Angeles area between 1933 and 1945.

These political refugees were following the path blazed by the "aesthetic" refugees of the twenties, for Hollywood had gone "international" long before the rise to power of Adolf Hitler and his Brownshirts. Indeed, to European intellectuals and artists, Hollywood had exerted great attraction since the end of the First World War. John Ford went so far as to liken the postwar years to an "invasion": "There began the most remarkable hegira the world has ever witnessed. Westward and eastward the creative artistic brainpower of modern civilization has been making pilgrimages to a town on the California coast of our own United States, until today the eighth great stamping ground of the world's relentless hordes is Hollywood."[20]

With its cultural and geographical landscape dotted with ethnic enclaves, Hollywood was reminiscent of lower Manhattan in the decades before World War I. The "exiles" gathered regularly throughout the twenties at the homes of the Hungarian director Alexander Wajda and his German counterpart Ernst Lubitsch, while Paul Lukas, the Hungarian actor, and George Cukor, the second-generation Hungarian director, held international salons. Erika Mann, daughter of Thomas Mann, wrote that not even the advent of sound movies, which suddenly turned foreign accents into a deficit for some actors, could dent the internationalism of the movie world.[21] These "international" salons persisted throughout the thirties and forties in Hollywood, but they did not tend to attract the political "heavyweights." For example, there was "Sunday at Salka's." The Viertel house became the place to go for left-wing (non-Communist) artistic and literary conversation.

Regulars included Brecht, Feuchtwanger, Vladimir Pozner, Christopher Isherwood, Charles Chaplin, Hanns Eisler, George Sklar, and Bess Taffel.[22]

By the time of the Manns' arrival (in 1938), however, the artistic immigrants were coming for distinctly political reasons. Erika noted in her diary: "All of [the Germans and Austrians] are working hard, all of them are learning English furiously, and all of them have exactly two topics in which they are really interested—film and politics."[23] But the unity which had been so prominent an aspect of Hollywood's foreign communities in the twenties was absent. Bertolt Brecht wrote Karl Korsch: "Animosities flourish here like oranges, and like them have no core. The Jews charge each other with anti-Semitism, the Aryan Germans accuse each other of philo-Germanism." Feuchtwanger complained about the "utterly revolting gossip" and bemoaned the squabbling.[24]

Nevertheless, probably no other professional field or industrial locale benefited more from the Central European influx than Hollywood and motion pictures. Only the rosters of exiled physicists, theologians, and psychoanalysts compare to that of screen artists who fled the Nazis: actors Peter Lorre and Luise Rainer; composers Max Steiner, Franz Waxman, Erich Wolfgang Korngold, and Hanns Eisler; directors Billy Wilder, Otto Preminger, Fritz Lang, and Wilhelm Dieterle; not to mention the literary giants who had only a passing connection with moviemaking—Bertolt Brecht, Lion Feuchtwanger, Franz Werfel, and, of course, Thomas Mann. The artistic reputations of this international set certainly enhanced the position of Hollywood. S. N. Behrman thought the town "became a kind of Athens. It was as crowded with artists as Renaissance Florence. It was a golden era."[25]

And the political impact of the newcomers was as immediate and as profound as the artistic impact. The refugees arrived in waves, and each wave further vivified what Hollywood people had been reading in their newspapers. "Film and politics" were the immigrants' primary interests, Erika Mann had noted, while Ken Englund spoke of the "political yeast which the refugees brought with them." Years later, testifying before HUAC, the conservative film writer James K. McGuinness, hardly a man to be bowled over by "liberal" causes, told the Committee that Hollywood "offered refuge to many vocal, articulate people who escaped the lash of Hitler. . . . They were accustomed to expressing themselves, and they brought home very forcibly to Hollywood the dangers of the Fascist and Nazi regimes."[26] Whether, like Fredric March, the film artists threw parties for the refugees, or, like Karen Morley, they actually married into their ranks, the Hollywood community very quickly wedded itself to the cause of its new friends.

Suddenly, Hollywood was awash with "experts" in the nature, forms, and evils of fascism. Lillian Hellman, Edward and Herbert Biberman, Sonja Dahl, Charles Vidor, Melvyn and Helen Douglas, and others had traveled extensively or lived in Europe or the Far East, where they had witnessed the rise of Mussolini and Hitler, the crimes of their parties, the usually passive complicity of the moderate and conservative governments before those criminals, and the portentous bellicosity of the new regimes. Dahl, for example, had had the chilling experience of watching the Japanese take-over of China.

One of the most active anti-fascists in Hollywood, Sonja Dahl (soon to be Mrs. Edward Biberman)† became executive secretary of both the Hollywood Anti-Nazi League and the Joint Anti-Fascist Refugee Committee. Like many of her contemporaries, she was deeply fearful not only of the spread of fascism abroad, but by the specter of counterrevolution at home. Carey McWilliams, a regular columnist for the Anti-Nazi League organ, saw the potential for fascism in the film community itself, which he described at some length in a *Nation* piece entitled "Hollywood Plays with Fascism." McWilliams named Gary Cooper, Victor McLaglen, and George Brent as sponsors of such paramilitary groups as the Light Horse Cavalry, the Hollywood Hussars, and the California Esquadrille, all of which professed the intent to "save America" and "uphold and protect the principles and ideals of true Americanism." They drilled in their spare time, received instruction in military tactics from retired army officers and active police officials, and generally basked in the friendly sunshine radiating from the Hearst press.[27]

If there was a comic touch to this sort of only-in-Hollywood operation, the fascist tendencies of American racism, anti-Semitism, and chauvinism incarnated in the Ku Klux Klan, the American Nazi Party, and the following of Father Coughlin, Gerald L. K. Smith, and Dudley Pelley frightened the Hollywood liberals and radicals much more. The clearest threat of American fascism, however, seemed to the film community to be reflected in two movements, one populist, the other elitist. In the America of the early thirties, probably no poli-

---

† Edward Biberman, a painter, actively participated in the Popular Front organizations of the thirties and forties. His paintings, many of them depicting workers and minority peoples, have been reproduced in two volumes: *The Best Untold: A Book of Paintings*, New York: Blue Heron Press, 1953; *Time and Circumstance: Forty Years of Painting*, Los Angeles: Ward Ritchie Press, 1968.

tician besides Roosevelt enjoyed the hold on a broad stratum of Americans that Louisiana governor (later senator) Huey Long exercised in the South and rural areas elsewhere. Starting out as a rural populist, Long swiftly transformed his grass-roots movement into a vehicle of his own ambitions and hatreds. At the time he seemed to personify the lower-middle-class, demagogic aspects of an emergent American fascist party.[28]

The rich, corporate face of homegrown fascism was the American Liberty League—the aristocratic club founded by du Ponts, Aldriches, and other pillars of the American business community in 1934 to spearhead opposition to Roosevelt's New Deal. The League spent vast sums of money, published lavishly designed pamphlets depicting a country on the brink of communism and bankruptcy, and generally displayed a furious level of activity.[29] The League did not catch on—indeed, the Republican Party asked it to keep its distance in the elections of 1936—and it certainly never gathered a mass following like Huey Long's. At the time, however, there seemed to be reason for worry.[30]

The Hollywood Popular Front and International Politics (1935–39)

Introduction

In Hollywood they did more than just worry. They organized and fought back, and the product of their labors (and of the labors of similarly concerned people across the country) turned out to be the most successful, most internationally oriented left-wing mobilization ever to occur in the United States—the Popular Front. To explain its success and relative longevity, one would have to regard the Popular Front as more of a social myth—like Christian ecumenism—than a formal political organization. Certainly the uniqueness and significance of the Front resided far more in its spirit than its structure. The Popular Front could have arisen only when political conditions were such that a vast array of disjointed, fractious, highly differentiated subgroups‡ could be united in a series of overlapping organizations. But

---

‡ The Viertel family provided an apt illustration of the motley quality of the Popular Front: "Berthold had his own personal kind of socialism, Peter was a New Dealer, I was a 'premature anti-Fascist,' Thomas a Democrat and Hans a Trotskyite." (Salka Viertel, *The Kindness of Strangers*, New York: Holt, Rinehart & Winston, 1969, p. 211.)

the goal of political-social unity remains as fleeting and volatile as it is popular. In meteorology, fronts are unstable surfaces between bodies of air with different temperature and pressure. They do not mix, but a contact surface is formed which endures as long as the relative pressure stays constant. The Popular Front among American liberals and radicals would last until the Nazi-Soviet Pact suddenly and dramatically curtailed the Communist Party's anti-fascism.

The most recent example of a Popular Front for mid-thirties Americans was that formed in France in 1935. Following the storming of the French Chamber of Deputies by paramilitary gangs and leagues, the leaders of the left-wing political parties and the two major labor confederations met to discuss an alliance whose purpose would be to defend the Republic and try to keep the nation from going over to fascism as two of its neighbors had already done. On July 14, 1935, hundreds of thousands of demonstrators marched through Paris to celebrate the official announcement of *"le Front Populaire,"* and a month later, at the Seventh Congress of the Communist International in Moscow, Georgi Dimitrov, Comintern chairman, called on the democratic forces of each country to launch a people's alliance against fascism.

An international strategy, the Popular Fronts genuinely grew out of, and conformed to, the particular situations within each country. In Europe they were mainly alliances of political parties and labor confederations which contended for governmental power with opposing blocs of moderate and conservative parties. In the United States, however—given the fundamentally conservative ideological consensus between the Democratic and Republican parties, their viselike grip on political power, and the subordination of organized labor to the two-party system—the Front had to establish itself from a wide assortment of *ad hoc* groups and minor parties. This is not to say the Front was not popular and enduring, but that it became so despite the dominant political and professional institutions, not because of them.

The Front thus represented an awakening of participatory politics unseen since the Populist movement of the 1890s and not to occur again until the civil rights and anti-war movements of the 1960s. The Popular Front was not a formal organization to which one could subscribe or adhere in the way one joined the Communist Party. Rather, it was a loose term applied to a functioning coalition of organizations, all of which had in common four main objectives: to press the Roosevelt administration in the direction of a world anti-fascist alliance, to aid the defenders of democracy and the victims of fascist aggression, to counter the widely perceived threat of domestic fascism, and to defeat the efforts of conservative big business to thwart the trade union movement and block the passage of social reform measures. Very soon a whole host of specific causes (the Loyalists' struggle in the Spanish Civil War, aid to refugees, etc.) attached themselves to Popular Front organizations, but the fundamental unifying factor— fervent opposition to international and domestic fascism—was never lost from view.

No paramilitary organizations led by Gary Cooper in his cavalry uniform stormed the Hollywood chamber of commerce, but the EPIC campaign had shocked and infuriated a broad spectrum of film artists and workers. In both the EPIC and Screen Writers Guild clashes, the producers, responding to their fear and self-interest, had taught the Left enduring lessons about the arrogance and imperiousness of the ruling class. Simultaneously, the European refugees articulated the truly horrifying effects of right-wing totalitarianism in power, while the Depression had brought onto the California scene all manner of homegrown counterrevolutionary alternatives. If a political front emerges in response to enemies, plenty were on hand in the Hollywood of 1935.

Dozens of groups and organizations around the country aligned themselves with the Popular Front, but only a handful played crucial parts: the League Against War and Fascism, the American Youth Congress, the Joint Anti-Fascist Refugee Committee, the League of American Writers, Labor's Non-Partisan League, the Workers' Alliance, the Writers' and Artists' Committee for Medical Aid to Spain, the Abraham Lincoln Battalion, and the National Lawyers Guild. Three of the most important Front organizations in terms of size, activity, and money raised originated in the film community—the Hollywood Anti-Nazi League, the Motion Picture Artists' Committee, and the Motion Picture Democratic Committee.

Role of Donald Ogden Stewart

Though many people contributed to getting the League started and keeping it going, one could be singled out for his exemplary contribution—screenwriter Donald Ogden Stewart.* A brief glance at Stew-

---

* The spotlighting of Stewart as an exemplar of the leftward swing and radical activism of Hollywood screen artists in the thirties is in no way meant to elevate him above the many other screen people who worked equally as hard and as effectively. Two others, in particular, merit mention in this regard especially in light of the role they would play ten years later as members of the Hollywood Ten: Herbert Biberman and Samuel Ornitz.

art's youth demonstrates the power of the causes which were prominent in the thirties: nobody could have been less spiritually prepared for social commitment than this "patrician" product of Exeter and Yale. Playboy son of a prominent lawyer in Columbus, Ohio, Stewart was editor of the Yale *Daily News* and a member of the elite social club Skull and Bones. Following his graduation from Yale, where he majored in literature, in 1916, Stewart followed the usual upper-class post-Ivy itinerary—he became a commissioned officer in the Navy, staff writer for *Vanity Fair*, writer of light humor and light plays, sometime actor, *bon vivant*, and frequent traveler in Europe and the United States. John Dos Passos remembered him as a "most skillful wisecracker," one who displayed a "certain obsession with social status" and meeting the right people.[31] Not the slightest trace of social sensitivity or political consciousness was evident. Typically, Stewart ignored the request of the Screen Writers Guild to boycott the awards presentations of the company union, the Academy of Motion Picture Arts and Sciences. (Stewart recalled later his thought process at the time: "A week before the banquet, Irving [Thalberg] invited [my wife] Bea and me to be his guests [at the awards]. I accepted without a thought. Irving was my friend. I had not the slightest understanding of unions, and certainly none as to their connection with such a free individual as a writer.[32]

Typically for an upper-class son, the first step on the road to political consciousness was taken in rebellion against his upbringing, personified in Stewart's case by Thalberg. And typical of a rebellious upper-class son who is also a writer, his self-assertiveness was first expressed on paper, and only later in his actions; in 1934 Stewart began writing a play, *Insurance*, about a young man turning against the expectations of his wealthy family. A Communist character was *de rigueur* in such plays and stories during the thirties, but Stewart very quickly realized that he did not know a Communist from a Congregationalist, and hence had not the faintest notion of what dialogue to write for one. So one day Donald Ogden Stewart walked into a bookstore and asked for "the latest books on communism." He was given two volumes by John Strachey, a widely read popularizer of communism (whom Ring Lardner, Jr., also recalled reading during his "conversion"): *The Coming Struggle for Power* and *The Nature of the Capitalist Crisis*. These books shook Stewart to his foundations: Strachey's words cut like a laser through the genteel young screenwriter's neat set of world assumptions. "I just couldn't believe that such things were happening in the world, and I certainly couldn't understand why a man would be willing to give up so much of his life for a political belief. It seemed terribly remote from Beverly Hills."[33] Unable to discuss any of these new ideas or issues with anyone in his social set, Stewart began looking for answers in liberal journals like *The Nation* and *The New Republic*, and Communist periodicals like *New Masses*.

His reading did not bring Stewart to Bolshevism, but politicization did occur—which was in itself "mysterious" in that one cannot ultimately explain the presence of the empathy and sensitivity in Stewart's heart which fused with the new ideas to which he was exposed to create a political consciousness and commitment which stayed with Stewart the rest of his life, even to the point of leading him to sacrifice career and country. Stewart's conversion, like those of many other people, was actuated by guilt: "It suddenly came over me that I was on the wrong side. If there was this single 'class war,' as they claimed, I had somehow got into the enemy's camp."[34] Almost immediately, Stewart claimed, he recognized that he had ignored the Depression and the bread lines, and he felt overwhelming shame for the salary he was earning concocting scripts about "dreamlands" while living in a world of glamour.

Stewart's guilt, like that of many of his left-wing colleagues, colored his radicalism with a certain romantic tinge, which rendered him far more empathic and sympathetic than analytic. From Stewart's perspective, change was more a question of sharing the spoils than destroying the system: "[I didn't want] to stop dancing or enjoying the fun and play in life. I wanted to do something about the problem of seeing to it that a great many more people were allowed into the amusement park. My newfound philosophy was an affirmation of the good life, not a rejection of it."[35] Thus, not untypically, he maintained his lifestyle, joined racquet and yacht clubs as soon as they opened, and admitted to the sense of security stemming from his "well-recognized eliteness."

And yet, despite Stewart's unrealistic appraisal of the goals and meaning of socialism and class conflict, the essence and strength of thirties activism resonates even in his almost too-precious memoir: "Gradually in my mind began to form the image of a 'worker' whom I had wanted to have the same sense of freedom and brotherhood that I had had at college. Unconsciously, I suppose, I wanted to tap these 'workers' for Skull and Bones. And over in the corner of my imagination, behind the worker, there crouched the image of a little man who needed my help—the oppressed, the unemployed, the hungry, the sharecropper, the Jew under Hitler, the Negro."[36] For all the sophistication and detachment of his elegant prose, and for all his love of the "good life," the underlying strength of Stewart's devotion to his "cause" was his readiness to work for it indefatigably and, when the need arose, to suffer for it unhesitatingly. If he was not ready to spurn his money and his success (however much shame he voiced about them), he never believed again that those rewards were sufficient in life, and he never stinted in his contribution of those rewards to the causes he championed.

Returning to Hollywood from the East in early 1936, the now "motivated" Stewart, aged forty-two, was "all set to do something."[37] Not knowing any "workers," Stewart decided that the Communist Party was the best link with the proletariat and the backbone of meaningful political activism. He therefore attached himself to any "real Communists" who crossed his path, and, by 1936, there was a good-sized nucleus of them in the Screen Writers Guild, all of whom were eager to cross many paths.

Association with the Party (as a "sympathizer," then a member), however, was the least of Stewart's contributions to the Popular Front. His patrician brand of activism both fitted and helped transform the contours of the motion picture political scene. He intuitively understood how to convert Hollywood's social patterns and the studio system into functioning, energetic mechanisms of consciousness-raising. A child of glamour, elitism, and fame; an appreciator of leisure and wealth; a practitioner of high literary writing, Stewart sought to use these "drawbacks" and sources of "shame" for a new, worthier end, and in this way was instrumental in putting Hollywood on something of a "war footing." He was tireless in his efforts and frank about his motives: "[A]s far as being used went, I knew about that. I had been used by the Elite—principally as a Life of the Party—and I now chose to let the using be done by the other side."[38] He became the joiner, lender (of money, fame, leisure), and speaker *par excellence*. The mind boggles at how much activity he squeezed into a twenty-four-hour day. Ella Winter, Stewart's second wife (also the widow of muckraker Lincoln Steffens and an activist in her own right), recalled that: "His sponsorship of so many committees and delegations gave rise to a satiric story: when President Roosevelt awoke in the morning, he would ring for his orange juice, his coffee, and the first eleven telegrams from Donald Ogden Stewart."[39]

Stewart's first project was to raise funds to aid refugees from fascist aggression. He was asked by Fredric March to organize a money-raising affair around the reading of Irwin Shaw's anti-war play *Bury the*

Dead. The screenwriter no sooner agreed than he was confronted by the stern disapproval of "Father Irving." Thalberg was in no mood to tolerate changes of heart in close personal friends. He sent word to Stewart—who was under contract to MGM—that his chairing the meeting would be viewed with disfavor from above. This time, however, Stewart stuck to his guns and politely informed Thalberg's messenger that he would not be acceding to the head of production's request.[40]

The *Bury the Dead* assemblage was one of the first of many such gatherings which focused Hollywood's gaze on international events—the threat of war, the results of extreme political repression, the fear of it at home, and, above all, the obligation of the wealthy, the influential, the free, and the sensitive to take a stand, to "do their part." Sonja and Edward Biberman both recall the excitement—"the happy frenzy"—of this spectacle of emergent consciousness in a town where self-centeredness and self-satisfaction had been the rule. Hundreds of individual consciences (not to mention pocketbooks) slowly began to merge into a larger current as the film capital came alive to the possibility of collective response.

The Hollywood Anti-Nazi League (1936–39)

In terms of securing national attention and raising money, the League was the most important of Popular Front organizations in Hollywood. The brainchild of a small handful of leading film talents—writers Dorothy Parker and Donald Ogden Stewart, director Fritz Lang, actor Fredric March, and composer Oscar Hammerstein—the League always appeared to be something of a "star-studded" affair, even while its executive staff planned activities and sent around petitions which persuaded hundreds of people, in and out of show business, to join the League and thousands of others to contribute to its mission. The Anti-Nazi League served as a prototype of Popular Front groups in Hollywood: a small nucleus of activist-celebrities launched the main effort which was then run on a day-to-day basis by a salaried executive director, a small staff, and a host of anonymous volunteers. The public image of the League was framed by the Executive Board—usually a dozen or two leading lights—and the lengthy list of "sponsors" which graced its stationery and included, like the Board, many of the greatest names of the movie business. For the more perceptive readers of letterheads, what was especially impressive about Popular Front organizations was the broad spectrum of political opinion represented on the Board and the list of sponsors, from studio moguls like Carl Laemmle,

Jack Warner, and Dore Schary to radical writers such as John Howard Lawson and Sam Ornitz. It was no small feat to assemble such opponents on the membership roster of an overtly "political" organization. This was one measure of the perceived danger of international fascism.

The stimulus for the League's foundation came from the underground German opposition to Hitler—an organization of no mean proportion, connected by a makeshift network of communications, throughout Europe and in the United States, bringing together a motley collection of political viewpoints, from Catholic Centrists to Communists, from princes and bourgeois party leaders to professional revolutionaries. From the outset, the German dissidents strove to mobilize American opinion against the Nazi regime, and it did not take them long to figure out the decisive role which Hollywood could play in such an effort.

No one believed this more strongly than Prince Hubertus zu Loewenstein, the exiled leader of the German (Catholic) Center Party. He wrote in his memoir: "[I]f the motion picture industry could be induced to embrace the cause of anti-nazism this would mean an important boost for our efforts."[41] The Prince had opposed Nazism from the beginning, going so far as to organize a group of young Catholic boys into a shock troop—*Stosstrupp*—to counter Nazi tactics. He detailed his opposition to Hitler in two widely read books: *The Tragedy of a Nation: Germany 1918–1934* and *After Hitler's Fall: Germany's Coming Reich*. His words and actions did not please the Nazi leaders and Loewenstein, fearing for his life and doubting the possibility of continued effective opposition to Hitler within Germany, fled to Austria in 1933. There he founded a short-lived newspaper, *Das Recht*, and an equally short-lived anti-Nazi movement. The Nazis deprived him of his German citizenship in 1934 and forced the Austrians to expel him in 1935.

After narrow escapes from the Gestapo's clutches, Loewenstein made his way to Paris, where he conferred with Willi Münzenberg, a Swiss-German revolutionary-without-portfolio for the Comintern.†

---

† Münzenberg, who had been born in Erfurt, Germany, August 14, 1889, had moved to Zürich in 1910. During World War I Münzenberg had been identified with the Zimmerwaldian (revolutionary) Left, after the war he became the Communist International's most accomplished promoter of propaganda and front organizations. For ten years he headed the International Workers' Relief and then went on to organize the League Against Imperialism, Relief Committee for the Victims of Fascism, Committee for

Münzenberg agreed wholeheartedly with Loewenstein that Hollywood was a potentially rich source of anti-fascism. He arranged for a meeting between Loewenstein and his own personal representative in America, Rudolf Breda—or, as he was known in Hollywood, "Otto Katz."‡ Katz had, Münzenberg insisted to Loewenstein, "excellent connections in Hollywood."[42] All the anti-fascists knew him. Berthold Viertel had written of Katz and his Soviet film enterprise to Salka in October 1932;[43] Hy Kraft devoted several pages of his memoir to Katz's importance;[44] and Lillian Hellman modeled the resistance hero of her play *Watch on the Rhine* on Katz. A charismatic speaker and superb fund-raiser, Katz helped found the anti-Nazi movement in Hollywood, but appeared only sporadically thereafter.

With his help, a preliminary meeting was arranged between Prince Loewenstein and a group of film luminaries: Parker, March, Lang, Hammerstein, Stewart, etc. They agreed to hold a large banquet, not

---

the Aid of the Spanish People, and others. He also oversaw the Communist printing firm, Éditions Carrefour, which printed exposés of fascist crimes. (Becoming increasingly independent of Moscow directives, however, Münzenberg was expelled from the Communist International in 1937, and was found, in 1940, hanging from a tree in France. His death remains unexplained.)

‡ Otto Katz was Breda's real name; he was also known as André Simone. He was Czech by origin, though it seems clear he had spent much time in Germany. When Loewenstein met him, Katz was deeply involved in a vast array of anti-fascist endeavors. He had been a member of the German Communist Party since 1922, and had moved to Moscow in 1930, where he had worked in the *Meshrabpom-Russ* film collective which Münzenberg had established in 1924. Katz was summoned to Paris in 1933 by Münzenberg and sent to the United States as a fund-raiser for the anti-fascist underground. Babette Gross, Münzenberg's widow, wrote that Katz was "quick, imaginative, entertaining, witty, and loyal. . . . In Hollywood he charmed German émigré actors, directors, and writers. Katz had an extraordinary fascination for women, a quality which greatly helped him in organizing committees and campaigns." Between trips to the United States, he oversaw the publication of two exposés of Nazi terror and tactics: *The Brown Book of the Hitler Terror* (1933)—an exposure of the Reichstag fire conspiracy which was translated into twenty-three languages—and *The Nazi Conspiracy in Spain* (1937). During World War II he worked in the office of the Czechoslovakian government-in-exile, and at the war's end was appointed to a position in the press department of that country's Foreign Ministry. He was one of the victims of the Soviet purges of the early 1950s, the Slansky trials. (See Babette Gross, *Willi Münzenberg: A Political Biography*, trans. Marian Jackson, East Lansing: Michigan State University, 1974.)

merely for film celebrities and personnel, but for notables from the entire Los Angeles community, to raise money for the relief of the victims of Nazism. According to Stewart, this idea was instantly well received throughout Hollywood. To his surprise even cautious mandarins like Thalberg, Selznick, Goldwyn, and Walter Wanger pronounced themselves "sympathetic." Plans went forward for a white-tie-and-tails affair at one hundred dollars a plate to be held at the Victor Hugo Restaurant in April 1936. The banquet was a resounding success. To the dazzle of movie "names" was added the imprimatur of respectability by such figures as Los Angeles Archbishop John Cantwell, who presided, and A. H. Giannini, brother of the founder of the Bank of America and an executive vice-president of that firm, who served as treasurer for the affair.

A big "gate," however, was not the major achievement of the prince's dinner. The impetus for the founding of a Hollywood-based Popular Front organization was. Within a couple of months, the furious preparation of Stewart, Parker, et al. culminated in the formation of the Hollywood League Against Nazism (soon renamed the Hollywood Anti-Nazi League). On July 23, five hundred invited guests attended the official launching at the Wilshire Ebell Theatre, and by autumn the League was taking out full-page ads in the trade papers ("THE MENACE OF HITLERISM IN AMERICA")[45] announcing a mass meeting—this time for the little people—at the Shrine Auditorium. Again a major success was scored: some ten thousand people came to hear Eddie Cantor, Oscar Hammerstein, Dorothy Parker, Gale Sondergaard, Mayor Frank Shaw, Judge Isaac Pacht, J. W. Buzzell (AFL), John Lechner (American Legion), and other prominent members of the Los Angeles business and political scene speak out against fascism.

Propelled by these affairs, the League quickly reached the forefront of Popular Front organizations in the United States. At its peak the organization probably enrolled between four and five thousand members, including, of course, many famous film personalities, but also many more humble show business employees. Screenwriters of every political persuasion joined the League: liberals like Jo Swerling, Wells Root, Robert Benchley, Julius and Philip Epstein, Philip Dunne; radicals like Dudley Nichols; Communists like Robert Rossen, Francis Faragoh, Ring Lardner, Jr., John Bright. Even ultra-conservatives like Herman Mankiewicz and Rupert Hughes joined, albeit the latter spent a large part of his time trying to persuade the members to change the name of the group to the Hollywood Anti-Nazi and Anti-Communist League. Stewart recalled the numerous grips, gaffers, juicers, and backlot workers who joined the League; and the Bibermans spoke glowingly of the anonymous volunteers who worked day and night in their off hours to get out League propaganda, mailings, and *Hollywood Now*.

With energy, funds, volunteers, and causes to spare, the League engaged in a bewildering number of activities. Its commissions of Culture, Women, Youth, Religion, Professions, Labor, and Race mobilized and educated these varied constituencies, and an active Executive Board saw to the maintenance of unity and purpose amid the nearly uncontainable proliferation of members and causes. A newspaper (*Hollywood Now*), which systematically exposed Nazi activity within the United States and provided reports on the fortunes of fascism abroad, was published biweekly. The League also sponsored two radio shows each week on KFWB: "Dots and Dashes from Abroad" on Saturday evenings, and "The Voice of the League" on Thursdays at 9:15 P.M.

In addition the League sponsored an endless series of meetings, demonstrations, speeches, banquets, parties, and panels focusing on every conceivable fascist menace to the peace and freedom of the world. In January 1937 alone, three important events were staged: an interracial demonstration against Nazism at the Philharmonic Auditorium, with W. E. B. Du Bois as the principal speaker; an "educational" on the Spanish Civil War at the Shrine Auditorium featuring speeches by Ernst Toller, the German playwright, and André Malraux; and, on KFWB, a broadcast narrated by George Jessel, Herbert Biberman, Dudley Nichols, and Hy Kraft which satirically reviewed "Four Years of Hitler."

The League also instituted actions against the evils which their publications and spokespeople were decrying. It joined in the nationwide picketing of German consulates to protest the bombardment of Almería, Spain (which had been, on May 31, 1937, shelled by a German cruiser and four destroyers, killing nineteen persons); it boycotted Japanese goods (notably silk stockings) after Japan invaded China, and later picketed ships hauling scrap iron to Japan; it picketed the convention of the American Nazi Party held in Los Angeles; and, last but not least, it besieged Roosevelt with telegrams calling on him to express publicly America's horror with and its condemnation of German atrocities, to sever this nation's economic ties with the Reich, and to lift the arms embargo against Spain. The League took great care to snub two representatives of the fascist powers whom the studio owners had invited to Hollywood as honored guests—Leni Riefenstahl, Hitler's favorite film maker, and Vittorio Mussolini, the Duce's nephew, who was responsible for setting up the fascist film enterprise in Italy (on whose most enduring monument, Cinecittà, the Hollywood studio bosses had been consulted). In short, the League lived its commitment to the very fullest.

Nor was the League remiss in the far more difficult and dangerous task of bucking domestic and local opposition to progressivism. By the late thirties the conservative backlash to liberal New Dealism was in full swing, and the Anti-Nazi League stepped to the forefront in supporting Roosevelt's policies. Several large rallies were held to try to save the Federal Theatre Project—a WPA relief program, founded in 1935, which employed theatrical artists to write and stage plays, revues, puppet shows, etc. In the eyes of anti-New Dealers, the Project seemed to employ a disproportionate number of left-wingers and to produce a distressing number of productions focusing on social themes such as race, poverty, and the Depression. In June 1939, an alliance of Southern Democrats and Republicans succeeded in cutting off federal appropriations to the Federal Theatre Project.

This same congressional alliance also produced the most powerful and portentous embodiment of the growing conservative counter-reformation—the House of Representatives' Committee on Un-American Activities, known then as the Dies Committee after its chairman, Martin Dies (D-Tex.). Dies did not like the Anti-Nazi League. While he would have agreed that the League was indeed part of a front, he was among the first polemicists to reverse the meaning of the term "front," from "coalition" to "façade." To Dies and his brethren, the League was a front for the Communist Party, pure and simple. In a coast-to-coast radio broadcast in August 1938, Dies said that although most of the members of the League were perhaps not themselves Communists, they nevertheless were the dupes, and their organization the creature, of a small, centralized clique of loyal Communist *apparatchiks*. He announced that his committee would arrive in Hollywood in September "to hold hearings at which members of the film colony will be afforded an opportunity to reply to charges that they were participating in communistic activities."[46]

His lack of evidence notwithstanding, Dies' "candor" on the subject of Communist infiltration rallied the anti-Front forces and spurred the retreat of the fence-sitters and moderates. The producers, for their part, had rarely more than tiptoed around the edge of anti-fascism. With the exception of a few moguls (the Warner brothers), executives (Dore Schary), and independents (Walter Wanger), the studio heads fretted endlessly about the effect on their German and Italian markets of too boisterous an anti-fascist stance. (Even Wanger, the liberal theoretician of the producer caste, was trying to arrange a deal with Mussolini to make movies in Italy; and Jack Warner's "purity" as an anti-fascist became noticeable only after the Brownshirts had killed a Warner Brothers representative who happened to be Jewish.) In general, the producers could never feel very comfortable participating in an organization like the League where they were obliged to confront "social awareness" on an almost daily basis. Who knew what the consequences could be if their employees or, heaven forbid, their audiences, came to see the studio executives as "soft" on causes? More to the point, the war among producers, the Screen Writers Guild, and the Screen Playwrights was raging intensely at this time, and management certainly wanted to avoid abetting the wrong side.

Their reluctance became open hostility as the anti-League gossip and propaganda generated by the Screen Playwrights reached the producers' ears. The reactionary writers—Mahin, McGuinness, Rogers, and the others who ran the SP—protested their anti-fascism, along with the producers, but in fact they, too, were swiftly becoming anti-anti-fascist. Returning to Hollywood in 1939 from a New York sojourn, Donald Ogden Stewart found that at his home studio, MGM, the SP screenwriters had come to agree with Mahin that all Leaguers were Communists and un-Americans, hence unworthy of "even a morning snarl."[47]

In 1939, however, the strength of anti-fascism reached tidal proportions as a result of events in Spain and Czechoslovakia. The ANL could safely ignore the producers' and Screen Playwrights' growing enmity. The producers were chary of any kind of public extremism, especially mudslinging with an anti-fascist force; and the Screen Playwrights, for the moment anyway, were a moribund pride of toothless lions. Dies, however, was another matter, and the League resolutely set out to counter his baseless accusations. The Board bombarded Roosevelt and the Congress with a barrage of telegrams calling for the Committee's dissolution and then called a mass rally to denounce Dies and the Committee. Stewart prepared a special radio broadcast in which he rejected the charges made by Dies and levied some new ones of his own against congressional committees on un-Americanism. He also bared the political motive behind Dies' nationalism: "If Mr. Dies has his way there will be no one to stop him because by that time Mr. Dies will have succeeded in destroying the forces which would oppose him. . . . [H]e will have succeeded in undermining all liberal organizations—all progressive labor movements and all faith in the progres-

sive policies of President Roosevelt."[48] Dies received the message—
he canceled the Hollywood hearings, blaming "lack of funds and
time."[49]

The Red-baiting of Popular Front movements by a rattled, momentarily retreating right wing was nothing unique. No sooner had fronts
appeared in France or Spain, for example, than they were blasted as
"fronts for Communist and Soviet subversion." In Europe, the formal
political alignment of large Communist parties and Communist-controlled labor unions with larger Socialist and radical parties made the
question of influence hard to answer. It is clear, however, that in the
United States the tiny CPUSA in no sense dominated the Front or
most of its major organizations, though it did play a crucial role within
all of them. Though the charge of Communist subversion was familiar,
documentation for it was as sparse then as it is now. On the contrary, a
careful reading of the material in the archives and libraries, as well as
transcripts of interviews with dozens of participants, Party and non-
Party alike, reveals that such accusations—whether by conservatives
like Dies, Hearst, Mayer, and Mahin at that time, or by liberals like
Rosten and Rivkin later*—are not to be taken as statements about historical fact, but rather as partisan war cries intended by the conservatives to unglue a strong liberal-radical alliance, and by the liberals to
protect their flanks in troubled times.

The conservatives and their disillusioned liberal and moderate allies
introduced the terms "dupe," "stooge," and "patsy" to the lexicon of
American politics of the thirties (while the Left, for its part, was not
lacking in pejorative neologisms: "social fascists," "fascist lackeys,"
"wreckers," etc.). This war of words had gone on throughout the period of the Popular Front, but it did the movement no appreciable
harm. With the Nazi-Soviet Pact of 1939, however, and the conse-
quent shock and anger of liberals with their Communist allies, the
charges of the conservatives seemed to take on new weight and meaning. The liberal reevaluation which took place in late 1939, however,
was neither fair nor historically accurate. In fact, the usual evidence

---

* Rosten wrote that "The ruling cabal [of the Anti-Nazi League] . . . were
more determined to hold to the Communist party line than to further the
purpose—anti-Nazi—for which they were organized" (*Hollywood: The
Movie Colony, The Movie Makers*, New York: Harcourt, Brace & Company, 1941, p. 142). Rivkin and his wife, screenwriter Laura Kerr, wrote:
"The Communists stunk it up . . ." (*Hello Hollywood*, Garden City, New
York: Doubleday & Company, 1962, p. 426). Those assertions comprised
the sum total of the "evidence."

adduced to prove "Red manipulation" of the Front—post-Nazi-Soviet Pact changes in titles, programs, style, personnel, and strategy—occurred *only after* the liberals had jumped ship, leaving the Communists and fellow travelers alone at the tiller.

The liberals' leave-taking coincided with the emergence of a Communist line which differed from the anti-fascist line which had held the disparate elements of the Popular Front together since 1936. This new, "discriminating," contentious posture on the part of the Communists destroyed an effective coalition of varied peoples and groups and led many non-Communists to believe that American Communists were dominated by Moscow and hence unreliable as political allies, but it did not prove that rank-and-file Communists had been insincere in their anti-fascism or that the Communist Party dominated, manipulated, or subverted the organizations of the Popular Front.

Hollywood's Homage to Catalonia (1937-39)

The Depression, the New Deal, labor strife, the tide of European refugees, and homegrown fascism combined to form a combustible mass which, when struck by the spark of international events, blazed forth in Hollywood with anti-fascist rhetoric and action. As strong as the commitment was against Hitler, Mussolini, and Tojo, however, it increased with the fascist attack on the Spanish Republic and its Popular Front government.

On July 17, 1936, the Spanish army, led by Generalissimo Francisco Franco, rebelled against the freely elected, legally constituted Republican government. The Civil War which ensued gave rise to one of the most fervent humanitarian-political causes of the thirties. In historian Allen Guttmann's words: "Spain seemed a last chance for a representative government and a pluralistic society in a Europe that had turned with frightening speed toward dictatorship and totalitarianism."[50] The Popular Front organizations that sprang up in Hollywood and elsewhere in the United States to aid the Spanish Loyalists (i.e., those loyal to the Republican government) in their resistance to Franco did so with something of the same shame and exasperation that motivated the French underground or the Gaullist government-in-exile during the Second World War: the impulse to stand and fight in the place of one's own craven government which, in the test, was found wanting. For the Popular Front organizations devoted to the Spanish cause had to combat two opponents: France and the Roosevelt administration.

The official policy of the United States was one of neutrality toward the conflict in Spain. Roosevelt feared alienating the large Catholic voting bloc in the United States (the Catholic hierarchy, of course, staunchly supported Franco) as well as the numerous proponents of traditional American isolationism. He also hesitated at the prospect of being associated with the Soviet Union (and aligned against our traditional allies, France and Great Britain) in a political cause. Roosevelt's stubborn neutrality toward Spain drew strong support from Congress, which overwhelmingly voted an embargo on all arms shipments to either side in the Civil War, and from the American public which, despite strong sentiments one way or the other, recoiled from the risk of war. Many liberals and radicals, however, saw this *de jure* "neutrality" as *de facto* partisanship for Franco in view of the active military assistance rendered to the rebels by Hitler and Mussolini. The same impulses, therefore, that made anti-fascism the most important plank of Popular Frontism now planted the Popular Fronters squarely in the Spanish Loyalist camp.

The plight of the Spanish Republic galvanized Hollywood as no other single cause. "The thinking people in the movie community were extremely caught up in the Spanish movement," said Sonja Biberman. "They felt most strenuously that now was the time to take a stand to stop fascism. It was thrilling to see the understanding which motivated the most creative and successful people in the film industry to take time out from their busy careers." Harold Clurman, a founder of the socially committed Group Theatre in New York and a frequent visitor to Hollywood, wrote that the community life of Hollywood seemed to be centered on the circuit of parties given at the homes of writers, actors, and directors, or at the large semi-public banquets and mass rallies organized by people active in the Loyalist cause.[51]

Initially, the only channel of support for Republican Spain was the Anti-Nazi League. Following a galvanizing speech by André Malraux at the Shrine Auditorium in January 1937, the League raised large sums of money for the Loyalists. The Leaguers would have preferred to spend the contributions on arms and war matériel, but the embargo and neutrality statutes prevented such a disposition of funds, and the League instead purchased ambulances and medical supplies and promptly sponsored a domestic political campaign to "Lift the Embargo."

Enthusiasm for the Loyalist cause soon surpassed the ANL's ability to channel it. Screenwriter Dorothy Parker and playwright Lillian Hellman visited Spain in 1937 and came back to Hollywood with horrifying stories of the Civil War. Wrote Parker, in an article for *New*

Masses: "[The men who fight for Republican Spain] are fighting for more than their lives. They are fighting for the chance to live them, for a chance for their children, for the decency and peace of the future. Their fight is the biggest thing, certainly, that we shall see in our time, but it is not a good show." She went on to describe the positive efforts the Republican government was making toward the civilian population and the destructive nature of the fascist onslaught. None of her famous wit was noticeable in the section of the article where she described the effect of Hitler's aid to Franco:

> In Valencia, last Sunday morning, a pretty, bright Sunday morning, five German planes came over and bombed the quarter down by the port. It is a poor quarter, the place where the men who work on the docks live, and it is like all poor quarters, congested. After the planes had dropped their bombs, there wasn't much left of the places where so many families had been living. There was an old man who went up to everyone he saw and asked, please, had they seen his wife, please would they tell him where his wife was. There were two little girls who saw their father killed in front of them, and were trying to get past the guards, back to the still crumbling, crashing house to find their mother. There was a great pile of rubble, and on the top of it a broken doll and a dead kitten. It was a good job to get those. They were ruthless enemies to fascism.[52]

Parker and Hellman, along with like-minded film colleagues—writers like Dashiell Hammett, Donald Ogden Stewart, Dudley Nichols, Lester Cole, Julius and Philip Epstein; directors John Ford and Lewis Milestone; actors Melvyn Douglas, Luise Rainer, Paul Muni, Fredric March, Gale Sondergaard, and John Garfield—founded the Motion Picture Artists Committee to aid Republican Spain (and the equally beleaguered Republic of China) in the battle against fascism. These same people were also instrumental in launching another organization, the Hollywood section of the nationwide Joint Anti-Fascist Refugee Committee. The JAFRC was formed by veterans of the Spanish Civil War, led by Dr. Edward Barsky, directly following the withdrawal of the International Brigade from Spain. The organization supplied aid to Spanish refugees interned in French relocation camps and those who emigrated to South America. (Barsky had been head of the American hospital units in Spain; he had supervised the building and staffing of six hospitals and the operation of the moblie surgical units.)

Both committees worked hard and grew rapidly. The Refugee Committee had a nationwide membership, but even the MPAC could boast an enrollment of fifteen thousand at its peak. The MPAC generally handled public relations for the Loyalist cause—raising money, organizing cocktail parties and dinners, planning large rallies, staging benefits, shows, and lunches (at the Hollywood Plaza Hotel's "It" Cafe) which featured famous film personalities. The Refugee Committee, on the other hand, left more tangible monuments, such as the Lewis Vivas School in Mexico for the refugee children from Spain.

The MPAC proved every bit as active in Hollywood as the Anti-Nazi League. To raise money for Spain, it staged an enormously successful political cabaret revue entitled "Sticks and Stones." The revue attacked the domestic gnats which buzzed fiercely around Popular Front organizations and the foreign soldier ants swarming over the world's democracies. Its skits, contributed by some of Hollywood's best screenwriters, showcased progressive causes and satirized reactionaries like Dies and appeasers like Neville Chamberlain. An offshoot of the MPAC, the Freedom of the Screen Committee—an umbrella organization for sixty smaller Front groups and labor organizations—sponsored a showing of John Howard Lawson's film on the Spanish Civil War, *Blockade* (United Artists, 1938). That single fund-raising event sent eighteen ambulances to Spain. A year later the same Committee achieved a similar success with a money-raising exhibition of Picasso's "Guernica."

The organizations intended to keep the Spanish Civil War before the public's attention proliferated in 1937–39. Each project seemed to require a separate committee, despite the large overlap of sponsors and members. The group which made the documentary film *The Spanish Earth* illustrates both the specialized nature of many Popular Front groups and the vast range of activity of some dedicated Popular Fronters. The project had taken shape in New York among a group of screenwriters and theater and literary people: Lillian Hellman, Dorothy Parker, Herman Shumlin, Archibald MacLeish, and Ernest Hemingway combined to form Contemporary Historians. Hellman, Hemingway, and MacLeish wrote a script which was shot by the well-known cameraman Joris Ivens. In the summer of 1937, Hemingway and Ivens brought *The Spanish Earth* to Hollywood for its second important showing (the first had been at the White House). The screenings—at Fredric March's home, at Salka Viertel's house, at the Ambassador Hotel, and in the Philharmonic Auditorium—brought in more than $35,000 for the cause.

Typically, though, in a Hollywood courageous and unified in its foreign sympathies but timid and divided on internal matters, none of the leading producers, directors, and moguls who attended the showings and contributed large sums of money cared to use their power or influence to aid Ivens and Hemingway in arranging a general release for their film. None of the distributors would touch it, and ultimately the film lived a circumscribed life underground, on college campuses, and in cinematic archives. Despite all the talk and plans for having the studios make films about Popular Front concerns, only one—*Blockade* —was ever realized.

Hollywood's politicized film artists made some effort to break out of the political limitations imposed on them by studio employment. Lillian Hellman and Clifford Odets helped out on *The Spanish Earth*, the Motion Picture Democratic Committee produced *California Speaks* for the Olson gubernatorial campaign in California in 1938, and a large group of radicals organized a progressive film group, the Motion Picture Guild, Inc., in April 1939. Screenwriters Nathanael West, Tess Slesinger, John Wexley, Sidney Buchman, Ring Lardner, Jr., John Howard Lawson, Arthur Kober, Samuel Ornitz, Dudley Nichols, Lillian Hellman, Budd Schulberg; directors Herbert Biberman and Frank Tuttle; actor John Garfield; cameraman Floyd Crosby; and various others planned to make a series of socially relevant motion pictures: documentaries on migratory workers, southern sharecroppers, the New Deal, and the evils of fascism. The grand plans and the organization itself were victims of the turmoil unleashed by the Nazi-Soviet Pact, the demise of the Popular Front, and the political quarrels of the Phony War period.

It is difficult to measure precisely Hollywood's contribution to the Loyalist cause in Spain. If bodies on the line were what was needed— and men like George Orwell, John Cornford, and Julian Bell thought so—then the American film community's sacrifice was obviously inadequate. No Hollywood screen artist went from the back lots and sound stages to the mountains and valleys of Spain; only one, as far as we know—Alvah Bessie—came from Spain (via *New Masses*) to the motion picture industry. From this perspective, the three thousand American men who made up the Abraham Lincoln Battalion of the XVth International Brigade were the only people in this country truly willing to "take the stand" which everyone was talking about.

On the other hand, it is neither just nor useful for historical purposes to measure every contribution against one extraordinary standard. There are degrees of contribution and sacrifice which are lost sight of if one simply brushes off every donor except those who picked up a gun. At best, a slight majority of the people in this country voiced sympathy for the Spanish Republicans, but their feelings did not go deep enough to induce them to give up America's traditional isolationism on the Republic's behalf. A very small minority of these sympathizers gave money to the cause; and an even tinier fraction gave liberally of their time and energy. As a cohesive, identifiable community, no group gave more nor—with the possible exception of New York City—even as much as the Hollywood film community gave, in work, money,† endurance, and risk to Spain. Ambulances, publicity, funds, petitions and telegrams to President Roosevelt, aid to refugees, consciousness-raising, moral and international pressure, however, in the end counted for very little against panzer tanks, Messerschmitts, and Italian soldiers.

The Hollywood Popular Front in State and National Politics: The Motion Picture Democratic Committee (1938–39)

The fervor generated by the Spanish Loyalist cause widened the perspective and deepened the political involvement of most Popular Front activists in Hollywood. The fight against international fascism heightened the awareness of progressives of all hues to the developing signs of a right-wing reaction in America. As we have seen, the Anti-Nazi League, along with the other Hollywood Popular Front organizations principally oriented toward international issues, had to fight continually with its domestic opponents, whether the homegrown fascists of the American Nazi Party and the Ku Klux Klan, or the conservative and reactionary enemies such as the Dies Committee, the Hearst press, the Screen Playwrights, etc. The League and its Popular Front allies—especially the Communist Party—never hesitated to draw links between the progress of fascism abroad and the potential for reaction in the guise of counterliberalism and anti-New Dealism at home. Nevertheless, the international fascist threat attracted more attention

---

† Frank Tavenner, HUAC counsel, estimated (after an examination of bank records) that eight Hollywood Popular Front organizations collected close to $1 million during the late thirties. (United States Congress, House of Representatives, Committee on Un-American Activities, 82nd Congress, 1st session, July 6, 1951, *Communist Infiltration of the Hollywood Motion Picture Industry*, Washington, D.C.: U. S. Government Printing Office, 1951, vol. 2, p. 1881.)

and concern because it preceded the conservative counterrevolution in this country and seemed much more dangerous and far-reaching, and because it provided a broader emotional and unifying appeal than the more partisan issues of local and national politics. Because the Four Horsemen of the Fascist Apocalypse—Hitler, Mussolini, Tojo, and Franco—thundered far more destructively across the historical stage than the seven asses of the Dies Committee, the Anti-Nazi League, the Motion Picture Artists Committee, and the Joint Anti-Fascist Refugee Committee largely occupied themselves with the international scene.

Nevertheless, the Popular Front spawned a series of significant organizations whose primary *raison d'être* was the advancement of the causes of liberalism, anti-fascism, and anti-racism at the local, state, and national levels. Their work involved lobbying for civil rights and civil liberties legislation and campaigning for progressive and liberal candidates for electoral office. Among the most important of the organizations which emerged in the Popular Front era were the national (CIO-organized) Labor's Non-Partisan League, the New York-based American Labor Party (1936), the California People's Legislative Conference (successor to EPIC), and the Hollywood-based Motion Picture Democratic Committee (the MPDC).

Like so many of the liberal/leftist organizations in Hollywood, the MPDC emerged as something of a backlash against the predatory politics of studio management and conservative politicians—in this instance, the Sinclair-Merriam gubernatorial campaign of 1934. The collusion, duplicity, and selfish expedience exhibited by the studio executives and other California magnates, right-wing publishers, and the Republican Party, were, in the eyes of many screenwriters and actors, simply a larger reflection of the unfairness and intransigence which the producers had shown in the battles with the guilds a year earlier. The Merriam campaign bred pockets of consciousness among screenwriters and actors which endured months and years after the EPIC clubs and the California Authors' League for Sinclair had died out. Specifically, it was now apparent to everyone that local and state politics had a direct impact upon everyone's immediate self-interest, and that there existed strong connections between the progress of labor unions in Hollywood and elsewhere and the progress of liberal, New Deal politics.

This awareness was once again directed toward political activity when a progressive Democrat, Culbert Olson, ran for governor of California against Frank Merriam in 1938. Olson's unorthodox New Deal for California, reminiscent as it was of Sinclair's "socialism"—public ownership of private utilities, reorientation of the tax structure, repeal of infringements upon civil liberties, production-for-use,‡ increased social welfare activities, and improvement of the conditions of migratory laborers—reanimated the pro-Sinclair forces. The radical nature of Olson's proposals—an indication of the desperation and festering class conflict of Depression America—was only one of the extraordinary aspects of his campaign.

The MPDC sprang into existence in June 1938 to work for Olson's election. Screenwriters dominated this organization: Dashiell Hammett was the chairman; Philip Dunne, the vice-chairman; Dudley Nichols, the financial director; John Bright, the publicity director. The Board included, at one time or another, Donald Ogden Stewart, Ralph Block, Milt Gross, John Grey, Jo Swerling, Allen Rivkin, Harold Buchman, Martin Berkeley, Robert Tasker, Nat Perrin, Gordon Rigby, and Shepard Traube.

Actors, publicists, electricians, and others from the studios joined these writers in supporting the progressive cause in California. Film artists toured the state—the actors delivering speeches written for them by the screenwriters, this time without squabbles over bad lines and bad delivery. Funds were raised through the usual cocktail party circuit and appeals at mass meetings. Backlot workers and young writers tirelessly canvassed the local precincts. The Committee produced a film, *California Speaks*, which was viewed by more than a half-million voters in the week prior to the election. The MPDC also sponsored four statewide and two nationwide radio broadcasts on behalf of Olson and the New Deal.

Incredibly (due in large part to the strong support Olson received from the Hollywood film community) Olson was elected in the face of a growing nationwide conservative reaction against the New Deal and liberalism. His triumph was a small red bobber on a building wave of white water, however, for the Republicans picked up eighty-one House seats, eight Senate seats, and thirteen governorships and increased their percentage of the national vote from 39.6 (in 1936) to 47 in the national elections of 1938. An alliance of southern Democrats and traditional Republicans, united by their opposition to Roosevelt's "court-packing" scheme, their anger at his refusal to employ force against the newly formed CIO's sit-down strikers, and the issue of the "Roosevelt recession" of 1937, was responsible for the con-

---

‡ Production-for-use factories do not manufacture for the market but for the immediate consumption needs of the workers employed in them.

servative gains.[53] It was quite apparent that the new Republican-
southern Democratic alliance would dismantle the New Deal piece by
piece if it got the opportunity. However frustrated and irritated the
Hollywood Popular Fronters were with the President over foreign issues such as the Neutrality Act, their loyalty in the domestic arena
never flagged, and they rallied immediately to his cause.

Elated over Olson's victory, and lulled by the apparent reform sentiment which had swept the new governor and his New Deal for California into office, the MPDC, according to one of its founders, John
Bright, became moribund. By early 1939, however, the conservative
Republicans in the state legislature, their ranks swollen by the defection of many Democrats, launched an all-out attack on Olson's budget
and its social welfare provisions. The MPDC sprang back to life in
February. Observed Bright at the time: "The hundreds who had sat
back now realized that they must function as a pressure threat as well
—not periodically, but incessantly."[54]

With the appearance of its "Declaration of Policy" on February 12,
1939, the MPDC more or less institutionalized itself.[55] The Declaration
was an interesting mixture of mainline American radicalism, replete
with the obligatory references to the Founding Fathers and Abe Lincoln, and thirties leftist analysis and rhetoric. The warning/pledge
scenario below was a fairly common one-two (setup/knockdown)
punch of the political left wing of this era. The warning:

> Today, only the most heedless can ignore the solemn portent of
> current world events. In every corner of the globe, democracy is
> on the defensive. . . . Reaction has taken to demagogy, and the
> result is that new feudalism which we call Fascism.
>
> Only the most ignorant, of [sic] the most disarmingly treach-
> erous, of our citizens deny that the same forces are at work in
> America today. The current propaganda campaign against Presi-
> dent Roosevelt and the New Deal, backed and endowed by reac-
> tionary political and manufacturing organizations, organized and
> financed on a hitherto undreamed-of scale, shows a full under-
> standing of the techniques and slogans employed by the various
> fascist government cartels in Europe.

The pledge:

> 1. We hereby reaffirm our complete faith in the democratic proc-
>   ess.
>
> 2. We hereby pledge ourselves to strive as Americans for the de-

fense, the deepening and the strengthening of democracy, and all that it implies.

3. We hereby pledge ourselves to fight for the preservation of those individual liberties guaranteed to all Americans under the Bill of Rights.

4. We hereby reaffirm our categorical opposition to any and all forms of minority dictatorship, whatever the economic philosophy behind them.

The pledge was authored by Philip Dunne, who had "one hell of a time getting point number four past the MPDC board." Already concerned that the Committee was losing its political clout as a result of the Moscow Purge Trials and the rumors of Communist domination of the MPDC, Dunne wanted to identify the group as non-totalitarian—"to put us on record specifically as a democratic organization." The Communists and fellow travelers forced Dunne to qualify the term "dictatorship" with the word "minority" before they would accept the pledge. The Reds had no difficulty accepting Dunne's affirmations of faith in "the democratic process" and "the deepening and strengthening of democracy." The Communist Party was a stalwart upholder of Americanism during the late thirties. The Communists were always quoting Jefferson and Paine, using, Dunne recalled, the short form of their first names—Tom—only.

The pledge is a valuable artifact for what it tells us about the enduring power of the American national ideology, because the innermost thought structures of virtually *all* leftists in the thirties were determined by that ideology. They shared their conservative opponents' ideological underpinnings: loyalty to, and faith in, the American democratic tradition and its possibilities; the importance of American nationality in defining a person; the commitment to "liberty" as represented by the various founding documents of the American Republic.

The two sides, however, diverged on political, social, and economic grounds. The Right developed an exclusivist and highly class-conscious definition of nationality through its doctrine of Americanism, while the Left stressed the "revolutionary" and "original democratic" impulses of the Founding Fathers and documents. The very virulence of the Left-Right political clash indicated the degree to which they fought over the same relics and sacred texts, appealed to the same saints and gods, and looked to the same sorts of golden futures (while advocating quite different methods to get there).

When the confrontations occurred—whether in the thirties, late forties, or early fifties—both sides trumpeted the purity of their "American ideals" and their "American behavior" and accused the other side of betrayal. On four occasions in the two decades after 1935, the American government tried, unsuccessfully, to deport radical (hence un-American) labor leader Harry Bridges back to Australia; the Left loudly defended him with, among other documents, a pamphlet written by Dalton Trumbo stating that Bridges' efforts to improve the conditions of exploited American workers were the essence of patriotism and squarely within the "American pattern."[56] Similarly, when Albert Maltz, Trumbo's fellow blacklistee, stood on the threshold of going to prison for contempt before the Un-American Activities Committee, he proclaimed: "We are all of us proud of our American citizenship, or ought to be. It has concrete meaning. As it has been for generations before us, it is the mold of our total way of life. In the simplest and most profound and most pervasive manner, the daily existence of all of us has been conditioned by the fact that this, not any other, is our land; and that we are citizens of it."[57]

Despite the conservatives' heightened decibel levels, fullblown reaction was not in the offing in prewar America. The men and women of the MPDC evinced great confidence and optimism as they went about implementing their pledge. In good thirties fashion, they formed a radio committee, a motion picture committee, a publications committee, a speakers' committee, all of which urged the public to support Olson and Roosevelt, to expand public housing programs, and to promote civil rights legislation. The minutes of the meetings of the Executive Board for 1939 read like exegeses of the important social (and "anti-social") bills pending in the California state legislature and the United States Congress.

With the passing of time, the Congress took up a larger and larger share of the MPDC's lobbying efforts. In particular, its activities fixed on two diametrically opposed committees which symbolized the differences engendered by the New Deal era: the La Follette Committee to Investigate Violations of Free Speech and Rights of Labor, in the Senate, and the Dies Committee on Un-American Activities, in the House.

The La Follette Committee had won great respect and popularity among the Hollywood Left for its exhaustive hearings into the labor- and union-busting practices that were so prevalent in the thirties.[58] When La Follette launched his equally painstaking probe into the exploitation of migrant workers practiced by California agribusiness, the film community, and the MPDC in particular, actually activated its creative, speaking, and publicity-gaining skills to expand and extend Senator La Follette's efforts. The plight of the Okies and the Chicanos in California had long been an issue of concern for the Hollywood Left. Even within the relatively apolitical confines of the Screen Writers Guild, the militants were always trying to pass resolutions supporting the strikes of the Salinas lettuce-packers or the Imperial Valley fruit-pickers. The farm workers' misery and suffering were so evident and their treatment at the hands of management and hired thugs and strikebreakers was so brutal that a number of film artists—Herbert Biberman, among others—increased their commitment to activism as a result. "The spectacle moved me to anger and action," Biberman later wrote.[59] Biberman and many others in the MPDC worked hard to raise funds for the John Steinbeck Committee to Aid Agricultural Organizations which was founded in October 1938 and chaired, successively, by Carey McWilliams and Helen Gahagan Douglas. The Steinbeck Committee did more than raise money. It raised the morale of the workers by holding a Christmas party for the children of the striking Delano pickers in December 1938, and helped raise the consciousness of the citizens of California by means of the pamphlets its members wrote and distributed exposing the nature of California agribusiness. Finally, the publication of *The Grapes of Wrath* in 1939 had an enormous impact on all parts of the Hollywood community, especially the Left. It aroused a concern which the MPDC hoped to channel into a mass meeting to protest the strikebreaking tactics which the Madera County growers were employing against cotton workers, who were then on strike for higher wages. This demonstration was eventually held on March 21, 1940, at the Philharmonic Auditorium in Los Angeles. Ten thousand people came.

No sooner had the La Follette Committee finished its investigation of industry and begun to contemplate a probe into the oppression of migratory labor than the Dies Committee opened fire on La Follette and Hollywood. If Senator La Follette and his colleagues felt they could safely ignore the conservatives in the House, the MPDC and the other Hollywood Popular Front groups enjoyed no such security. On the contrary, their particular strength—the celebrity which guaranteed them and their causes a sympathetic public hearing—proved a weakness before a body like the Dies Committee. The conservatives had quickly taken note of the "unique contribution toward the realization of [the New Deal]" which could be made by politically conscious artists able "to utilize the great public mediums concentrated in Hollywood to arouse public interest in the problems of this democracy and in the constructive efforts toward their solution." (The quoted words are the MPDC's about itself.[60]) The Dies Committee saw an enemy in Hollywood which it was determined to root out and destroy. It wasted no time in pitching battle with the Olson forces, the Anti-Nazi League, and the MPDC. Investigations began in mid-1938, and in spite of periods of retreat, did not cease until the Committee won its victory in 1947–55.

Conclusion: the Decline of the Popular Front (1939–40)

Early in this chapter we quoted Mary McCall's mocking of the words, earnestness, committees, and fund-raising parties which characterized political consciousness in the Hollywood of the late thirties. There were plenty of speeches, organizations, and petitions, of course, but finally one must ask "How extensive was the political mobilization of the film community?" and "How important, nationally or internationally, was it?"

In the issue of *Screen Guilds' Magazine* immediately following the one in which Mary McCall's piece appeared, Donald Ogden Stewart ironically assured McCall that she had far less to worry about than she realized: Hollywood was hardly the beehive of political activity which she had portrayed. On the contrary:

> During the past year I have attended practically all of the "radical" meetings, symposia, and benefits . . . and I can assure Miss McCall and her possibly alarmed readers that 99.44 percent of Hollywood is still sleeping peacefully in its options. . . . I must deny emphatically her insinuation that a large minority of Hollywood writers, actors and directors are [engaged in political activity] or are, for that matter, in the least interested in anything political that does not concern their own studio or the abolition of the State and Federal Income Tax.[61]

Both observers were correct to some extent, given their differing perspectives, political philosophies, and hopes: McCall, the moderate, was fearful that writers would be distracted from their roles as observers and recorders; Stewart, the radical, was fervently convinced that writers were workers threatened, like all other workers, by fascism, and that all art—even all communication—served a social cause.

It is very difficult to furnish precise statistics about the political mobilization of Hollywood. The organizations of the Popular Front kept

almost no records (as far as we know) on matters of this sort. Therefore we can deal only in rough approximations. The total population
of the film community (excluding extras, of whom only the tiniest
fraction made enough of a living from acting to be construed as
members of the motion picture business) fluctuated between fifty
thousand and sixty thousand people during the thirties. The Motion
Picture Artists Committee claimed a membership of fifteen thousand.
The Anti-Nazi League—which included non-motion picture people in
its ranks—claimed four to five thousand members. The Motion Picture
Democratic Committee, with its focus on partisan political activity, reported a membership of only three to four hundred. So far as we
know, membership rosters are not available; therefore it has not been
possible to cross-check names and note overlaps—of which, undoubtedly, there were many. The MPAC was the sort of organization which
appealed to a wide spectrum of political opinion, and was thus an organization to which even producers and studio executives could belong. Accompanying these more conservative joiners were the activists
who were also members of the ANL or the MPDC. Thus a conservative estimate places the number of group-joining "activists" in
Hollywood in the late thirties at fifteen thousand people out of sixty
thousand, or 25 per cent.

One would need to know a good bit more than we do about the degree of commitment and the political beliefs of these fifteen thousand
to be able to say much of significance about the nature and extent of
consciousness in the film world. On the face of it, 25 per cent is quite
impressive and virtually unmatched among other professional-
geographical communities in the United States in the thirties, or after.
The records show that, time and again, the attendance at Popular
Front events, the enthusiasm produced, the information dispensed, and
the money raised occurred on a scale that both pleasantly and unpleas-
antly astonished contemporaries.

If all the details of the Popular Front in Hollywood cannot be
charted with great accuracy, we are better informed (as was HUAC)
about the number and identity of the leading activists who constituted
its heart. A core group of about two hundred progressives worked
closely with, and followed the lead of, fifty to seventy-five committed
radical activists (who were about equally divided between non-Communists on one hand, and Communists and fellow travelers on the
other). (See Appendix 3.) HUAC and the FBI did their homework
very well: the first subpoenas that went out in 1947 struck at the
nucleus—slightly enlarged then by the addition of forties newcomers to

Hollywood like Albert Maltz and Alvah Bessie; while the second wave, in 1951, went to most of the remaining "heavies." Committee Chief Investigator Louis Russell and counsels Robert Stripling and Frank Tavenner performed brilliant repressive surgery; their scalpels cut out nearly every spot of "malignancy" in the Hollywood body politic without destroying much surrounding "healthy" tissue. The men and women ordered to testify before HUAC *all* had active political pasts, the great majority of which had originated with the Popular Front organizations of the thirties; and virtually no one with an active left-wing "political" past (who hadn't reversed himself after 1939, as a few did) escaped the summons. (By contrast, the industry's blacklist and "graylist" in subsequent years, motivated by management's need to pander to conservative public opinion, looked like wholesale butchery.)

No matter which activists we discuss—the subpoenaed, the black-listed—the screenwriters constituted the absolute majority. Fifty-eight per cent of the film people subpoenaed by HUAC were screenwriters; 57 per cent of those blacklisted were screenwriters; 58 per cent of those who cooperated with HUAC were also screenwriters. The next largest industry group, the actors, comprised between 20 and 25 per cent of each category. Screenwriters were the elite corps of political con-sciousness in Hollywood in the two decades after 1933, and their lead-ers were the brains of all the organizations which sprang up in expres-sion of this consciousness. Their time, energy, and money fueled progressive politics in Hollywood, and their words advertised progres-sive ideals to the general public. Without their unique contribution, Hollywood political activism might have existed, of course, but only at the level of the cocktail party chic and movie star glamour which were a part of its veneer. The writers used this glitter and saved it from fatuity by giving it depth and substance. This contribution was as clear to the participants in the Hollywood Popular Fronts of the thirties and forties as it was to the congressional investigators of the fifties.

Political activity in Hollywood was as serious and broad-based as political activity anywhere in America in the thirties. Its look, how-ever, was unique:

The peculiar Hollywood mixture of dinner-table politics never ceased to astonish me [wrote Ella Winter], as when Miriam Hopkins wore cotton stockings to boycott Japanese silk. Or when a dinner party in evening dress drove to San Diego in Cadillacs to join CIO longshoremen in picketing a boat bound for Japan with scrap iron. Or when [during World War II] Norma Shearer raised her glass at a very exclusive banquet of top movie "brass," with the women elegantly clad in sequined evening gowns, to toast "the glorious banners of the victorious Red army."[62]

Winter did not intend her description as a put-down in the manner that latter-day anti-Communist critics of the Hollywood Popular Front decry and belittle the "cocktail party activism" of the movie world. On the contrary, she intended it as merely a thumbnail portrait of the apparent and "contradictory" surface of a deeper, far more significant reality which underlay the glamour, and to which she, along with hundreds of other men and women, contributed much of her life. The glamour may indeed have been the marquee of Hollywood's political theater, but it was not the only, or even the primary, component of the structure. But it was important and needs to be examined for what it really was and was not.

Surely an important measure of people's commitment to a cause is the degree to which they are willing to invest their free time on its behalf. Each social class or community expresses its political consciousness not only through its vocational and professional activities but through its habits of leisure and dress as well. Would film stars have increased their political effectiveness in Hollywood, or accomplished more for the anti-fascist cause, if they had worn overalls and work shoes during the San Diego picket? In Hollywood, as in any community, if one wished to raise consciousness, support, and money, one had no choice but to address people from within the cultural and vocational institutions and modalities to which they were accustomed. Simply to be heard, let alone to be effective, one has to have access to people and to people's confidence. The Hollywood community was wealthy, ostentatious, glamorous, and somewhat artificial by comparison to nearly any other segment of American society, but this did not necessarily reflect its capacity for meaningful politicization, activism, consciousness, or national effectiveness. Indeed some of these very chic traits lent Hollywood's political actions a weight and influence they would not otherwise have had.

The irony which is overlooked in restating the criticisms of "fashionable" activism in Hollywood is that a number of the very customs and institutions whose oppressiveness, inbreeding, and insularity frustrated many of the film artists in their pre-political days and held their community up for a certain amount of ridicule proved, in the hands of

activists like Donald Ogden Stewart, to be capable of transformation
into springboards of genuine political expression and education. Indeed
it was the magic of Hollywood's politicization in this period that the
cocktail party was turned into a locus of genuine exchange and expansion, and the phony glamour into an engine ensuring national attention
to important issues; the oppressive writers' buildings became fertile
meeting grounds for planning and persuasion and enlistment; the
schlocky, despised movies (occasionally) became vehicles for social
commentary; and the Screen Writers Guild, for all its impotence and
internal division, became an important platform for Popular Front
propaganda.

Anti-fascism succeeded for a long time in welding together a political-social movement called the Popular Front. Its contradictions and
fissures were many, and we shall discuss them and the Front's decline
at length in the upcoming chapters, but there is, finally, no denying
the power and uniqueness of the Front in Hollywood during the three
years that it flourished. The Fronters may not have stopped Hitler or
Mussolini, but they provided vital aid for the victims of fascism and
laid the groundwork for the moral fervor which saw this country
through five long, costly years of war. They may not have halted the
historical course of domestic reaction, but by fighting it tooth and nail
the Popular Fronters helped stave off its victory and lessen its ultimate
impact. "We fought on every front," wrote Lionel Stander, an actor
who would one day be blacklisted for his political past, "because we
realized that the forces of reaction and Fascism fight democracy on
every front. We, too, have been forced, therefore, to organize in order
to combat them on every front: politically through such organizations
as the Motion Picture Democratic Committee; economically through
our guilds and unions; socially and culturally through such organizations as the Hollywood Anti-Nazi League."[63]

1. The Biberman brothers, Herbert (left) and Edward, pose before a statue of Frederick the Great during their travels in Europe in the late twenties.

2. Two decades after witnessing the rise of repression on one continent, they experienced it on another. On the eve of Herbert's prison sentence in 1950, Edward painted this portrait of him.

3. The pre-political Donald Ogden Stewart (far right), playing what was then for him the lifelike part of an effete socialite in the MGM film *Dulcy* (1930), which also starred Marion Davies and Elliott Nugent. Stewart went on to become one of the foremost spokespeople in the Hollywood anti-fascist movement. (Courtesy, *Photoplay*.)

4. The first Hollywood Popular Front. The granddaughter of mogul Carl Laemmle joins the daughters of conservative screenwriter Morrie Ryskind and liberal lyricist Oscar Hammerstein II in a party at the Hammersteins' to collect presents and money for the children of Loyalist Spain on December 4, 1937. (Courtesy, Black Star.)

5. The only Hollywood activist to serve in Spain. Here Company Adjutant Alvah Bessie (right) poses with Company Commander Aaron Lopoff, 2nd Company, Abraham Lincoln Battalion, XV International Brigade. Taken in June 1938, near Marsa, Catalonia, where the Americans were training for the Ebro offensive.

6. Part of the contribution of the League of American Writers to the Spanish Republican cause. (Courtesy, Bancroft Library.)

7. A token of gratitude from the Spanish Republic to the Hollywood film community. The document was signed by the Spanish Foreign Minister, Alvarez del Vayo, and the legendary Spanish Communist Party leader, Dolores Ibarruri ("La Pasionaria"). 1938.

8. Philip and Amanda Duff Dunne on their wedding night in the summer of 1939, a few months before the liberal-Communist divorce.

9. To avoid the anti-Communist witch-hunters, even liberals with spotlessly anti-Communist reputations like Melvyn Douglas had to submit to a kind of clearance procedure, in this case an "interview" by *Photoplay* magazine. (Courtesy, *Photoplay.*)

IS MELVYN DOUGLAS A *Communist?*

10. Bess Taffel in the early 1940s, when she was an aspiring screenwriter.

11. John Howard Lawson, the doyen of Hollywood Communists, at the height of his professional and political activity in the film community, the World War II years.

12. Dalton Trumbo in the mid-1940s, when he was among the highest-paid screenwriters in Hollywood.

13. The second (wartime) Popular Front. A banquet for the Women's Ambulance and Defense Corps of America: Colonel Sonja Dahl Biberman flanked by Paul Robeson, English actor Philip Merivale, and Los Angeles mayor Fletcher Bowron, on her right; and actors Paul Lukas and Gregory Ratoff, on her left.

14. An average day on the picket line at Warner Brothers Studios during the 1945 CSU strike— before, that is, the intervention of left-wing screen artists. Fire hoses, tear gas, hired thugs, and "sympathetic" policemen and sheriffs all did their part to break Hollywood's only democratic union movement. (Courtesy, Special Collections, UCLA.)

5

The Disintegration of the Popular Front

[Melvyn] Douglas, and thousands of liberals like him, travelled the same road as the Communists then, not from choice, but because the Communists were hitchhiking on the liberal band-wagon. The Communists were the fellow-travellers, not the liberals.

—*Philip Dunne*[1]

The People's Front program is not socialism. It has the merit of making no pretensions to that effect. It is openly and frankly a joint platform of non-socialists.

—*Earl Browder, general secretary of the CPUSA*[2]

The Nazi-Soviet Pact and the "Great Awakening"

On August 24, 1939, newspapers around the world carried headlines informing their readers that Joachim von Ribbentrop and Vyacheslav Molotov, the foreign ministers of Nazi Germany and Soviet Russia, had signed an agreement of non-aggression between their two countries "in the event of war." War came right on schedule, one week later, as the Luftwaffe blitzed Poland and the Russian high command, in coordination with Hitler, sent the Red Army pouring across the eastern border of her Slavic neighbor. Three months later, the army created by Leon Trotsky to protect the world's first socialist revolution launched an unprovoked attack upon Finland.

The impact of these events on the world's—and particularly on leftists'—sensibilities cannot be overstated. Even though the Nazi-Soviet Pact was not an alliance; even though it was apparently one in a long series of non-aggression pacts* signed between the European powers since the early twenties (including the Rapallo Pact of 1922, the Kellogg-Briand Pact of 1928, the Anglo-German Naval Agreement of 1935, the Hoare-Laval Agreement of 1935, and the Munich Agreement of 1938); even though such hardened diplomats and statesmen as former U.S. ambassador to Russia Joseph Davies and Winston Churchill understood its necessity ("not unexpected," "in their self-interest"[3]) ("realistic in a high degree"[4])—all this notwithstanding, liberals and radicals everywhere were stunned by the *rapprochement* between the unyielding adversaries of the Spanish Civil War.

Virtually every memoir, letter, and recollection of the era testify to the disillusionment of liberals and Communists alike. For the liberal founder of the American Civil Liberties Union, Roger Baldwin, "it was the biggest shock of my life. I was never so shaken up by anything as I was by that pact. . . ."[5] For members of the Communist Party, however, who had exhausted themselves for four years in anti-fascist labor, the news had surrealistic overtones. Picture the blind John Milton, in the midst of his labors over *Paradise Lost*, being brought word that the armies of Lucifer and the Archangel Michael have agreed to cease fighting each other and instead deliver a coordinated attack upon the unprotected souls of mankind. His response probably would have been similar to Party newcomer Sylvia Jarrico's: "It couldn't be true, I thought. History just doesn't happen that way."

The astonishment of Communists was all the greater since Stalin had issued no direct warning (through the Comintern "nuncios" attached to each national party) of his impending reversal, nor had developments on the European diplomatic front (for all the twists, turns, and ambiguities of that period) augured such a startling realignment or redefinition of the forces of "light" and the forces of "darkness" in the world. All through the months of July and August 1939, however, the *People's World* and *Daily Worker* columnists had been criticizing British and French support of the dictators, their reluctance to form a mutual security or collective assistance pact with the Soviet Union, and what the Communist analysts perceived as the Western democra-

---

* In fact, it was not simply a non-aggression pact, but an agreement to divide Eastern Europe into mutually delimiting spheres of interest. The Secret Additional Protocol (which was not published until after the war) demarcated German and Soviet spheres in the Baltic region and recognized areas of Soviet "interest" and German "disinterestedness." The treaties and protocols can be found in Victor S. Mamatey, *Soviet Russian Imperialism*, Princeton: D. Van Nostrand Co., 1964, pp. 131-34.

cies' encouragement of a new German "drive to the East." Nevertheless, with the announcement of the Pact, the switchboards at both Communist newspapers in the United States lit up like Christmas trees and stayed that way, while the CPUSA's politburo went into permanent session.

They had much to discuss. Non-believers of any era do "the faithful" a disservice in underestimating the degree of doubt and conflict which beset the latter before they submit to the demands of their vows of self-discipline and obedience. Communist memoirists of every hue recorded the pain, tensions, and bewilderment felt at every level of the Party and within the hearts of nearly every individual Party member. "The treaty came as a megaton shock," Al Richmond wrote, while George Charney felt "limp and confused," and Benjamin Gitlow recalled that American Party leaders "floundered in the dark for two days and did not know what to do. The ninth floor of Thirteenth Street was in bedlam."[6] Peggy Dennis, on the other hand, accepted the Pact readily enough, but was sickened and angered by the "reversal of analysis of fascism and rejection of the years-long commitment to fight fascism" which followed in mid-September. Her husband, Eugene, a Party hierarch, "was in conflict [over the new line]. It was inconceivable to him that there could be a dichotomy between any Communist party and the Soviet Union."[7]

Party members, while still active, however, do not talk openly about their inner reservations (except perhaps to each other). Thus the entire scenario of shock-doubt-reconsideration-reversal-rationale became a secret psychological itinerary obscured by the glare of two spotlighted Party "lines": the anti-fascism of the Popular Front, now well into its fourth successful year of aggressive life; and the new neutrality calculated to blur the carefully etched distinctions between fascism and democracy. In the opinion of most non-Party leftists, the new "line" was only a narrowly conceived prop for Soviet national interests.

Disingenuously, the Comintern claimed it had no wish to sunder the Popular Front or to abandon its Popular Front strategy, but "merely" to transform the goals. No directive arrived from Moscow calling for a return, however imperceptible, to the proletarian class exclusivity of the twenties and early thirties. Nevertheless, most Communists must have known that while they themselves would (in the main) prove capable of reversing the thrust of several years of hard work and rationalizing that reversal, their liberal allies and leftist sympathizers would not. In this expectation they were not disappointed. Every Popular Front group in the United States was affected. Some split into two (the American Labor Party into an anti-Pact group led by David Dubinsky and a pro-Pact group led by Vito Marcantonio), some voted known left-wingers from office and attempted to institute antitotalitarian oaths (CIO), while most lost a large percentage of their membership (National Lawyers Guild).

The destruction, like the inception, of the first Popular Front, 1936–39, in America and Hollywood was in large measure the consequence of international events. The Nazi-Soviet Pact and the invasion of Finland immediately changed the attitudes of liberals toward the Soviet Union and, soon after, their attitude toward their immediate ally, the CPUSA, when it became clear that American Communists were not only going to accept the new line but to try to justify and act upon it as well.

The events of August to November 1939 radically altered the balance of liberal response toward the U.S.S.R. and the CPUSA, especially in Hollywood. What was once a small group of liberals (Allen Rivkin, Mary McCall, Ken Englund, etc.) openly skeptical about the prospects of the 1917 revolution and increasingly hostile to the "socialist experiment" swelled overnight. A group which had been much larger, including Philip Dunne, Nathanael West, and Dudley Nichols, and which had maintained its "critical perspective" on Russia but stayed receptive to functioning in a working alliance with Communists when circumstances permitted, dwindled. Only a small group of fellow travelers (Dalton Trumbo, Lillian Hellman, Howard Koch), who were Communists in everything but name, remained somewhat stable.

These distinctions cannot be drawn precisely. The non-Communist Left easily slid back and forth across a fairly wide spectrum of attitudes toward the Party, both in its national and international forms. In the main, liberal screenwriters lacked a firm, coherent ideology. Their stances toward communism were, therefore, finally reactive. The explanations and rationalizations which all liberals splashed over the pages of their journals—*Modern Monthly*, *The New Republic*, *The Nation*, *Common Sense*—were nearly always *ex post facto* embodiments of gut-level responses to the latest news about the Soviet Union or the latest encounter with Browder and his Party.

Recent conversations with a number of Communist screenwriters make it clear that the great majority of them were profoundly startled by the news of the Pact and the invasions of Poland and Finland. Yet nearly all came sooner or later to accept the diplomatic reasoning, even necessity, of the Pact—i.e., the Soviet Union needed to protect itself from the vulnerable isolation to which the Western democracies had consigned it in their own series of agreements, both formal and *de facto*, with the fascist powers since 1935: in their non-intervention in, and arms embargo against, Spain; in their acceptance of the Italian conquest of Ethiopia; in the Munich Conference and the failure to contest Nazi take-overs of Austria and Czechoslovakia. Such signs as these (opposed actively by all Popular Fronters at the time of their occurrence) indicated fairly conclusively to the Soviet leaders, and their international supporters, that the West had given up the ghost of collective security and even hoped to channel German aggression in the direction of Russia.

The Hollywood Communists, for the most part, understood this explanation for the Pact, but many of them did not see the need for a drastically reformulated political line which described the fascist-democratic antagonism as "imperialist war" of no concern to socialists. After all, they had been fervent anti-fascists for four or five years, contributing unstintingly of their time, talent, and treasure to the Popular Front. Now, when the Party hierarchy shifted gears, the Hollywood members did not speak out, even though they had not participated in the decision and felt decidedly uncomfortable with it. Today, some of them believe they should have protested openly. Given the nature of the Party, the relative youth and inexperience of the Hollywood members, and the style of commitment of the thirties, however, protest appeared unthinkable to Hollywood Communists. The CPUSA did not countenance criticism from the ranks. Younger members like Jean Butler "never had the nerve to criticize the new line openly. I was young and unsure and I didn't want to stick my neck out." A more important determinant of silence was the sense of commitment which fueled the political activism of the thirties' Party joiners. At the same time they decided to become part of a disciplined and dedicated collective, they also decided to make certain personal considerations secondary—and to stick to this reordered set of values. Within this altered scheme, the privilege of disagreement took a back seat to the demands of unity and obedience, which were, in the eyes of the new recruits, the ingredients of effectiveness.

Whatever the degree of moral outrage Hollywood Communists felt, they were loath to desert the Party at the first severe testing. They had joined the CP imbued with the belief that long-term, effective political action depended upon organization, obedience, discipline—goals which could be maintained only if individuals stifled their personal doubts

and swallowed their fears. Moreover, once educated by the Party, a recruit rapidly gained an appreciation of "the complexity" of most issues
and the paucity of dependable information available to make final de-
terminations on one's own (Communists were chary of the "facts" and
opinions presented in the "bourgeois" press). They came instead to
trust the national and international Party leadership.

In retrospect, it is clear that this position would have been a lot
more valid if the CPUSA of the late thirties had practiced the
democratic centralism which it preached—i.e., if its leaders had
supported and encouraged extensive debate from below before reaching major decisions. In the thirties, though, rank-and-file Communists,
as Dorothy Healey was to admit many years later, were not even
privy to the debates raging in the politburo and Central Committee
of the Party. In this atmosphere of *de facto* centralism, frequent,
vociferous dissent branded one a factionalist, or "Trotskyist," and
led to expulsion. Few Hollywood people cared to risk that fate. As
screenwriter Guy Endore wrote in his memoir, "I often wanted to
run out of the Communist Party, but there was just no place
to run. . . ."[8]

The question for most Hollywood Communists—probably for most
intellectual Communists anywhere—was then, and is now, "How long
do I put up with it?" At what point—the forced collectivizations, the
purge trials, the repression of the anarchists in Spain, the Pact, the
Khrushchev revelations, the Hungarian invasion—does one finally
jump ship? The Pact came so early in the lives as Communists of most
movie people that they could swallow it without choking, while the
sources of news about the collectivization, the purge trials, and Spain
were too suspect to be trustworthy to Communists.

Liberals vs. Communists

Thus the international events which rocked and then wrecked the
Popular Front did so by clarifying the motives and ultimate loyalties
of liberals and Communists alike. Anti-fascism, anti-racism, pro-labor
sentiment, and electoral politics constituted only part of the impulse
which drove the American CP to ally with other elements of the Left
in a Popular Front in 1935. Popular Front membership embodied, in
the last analysis, a tactical mode of implementing a broader strategy
aimed at preserving and strengthening democratic institutions as the
most favorable atmosphere for revolutionary work at home, and
democratic states as the most likely enemies of fascist aggression

abroad. Most liberals were not revolutionaries or even, necessarily, supporters of socialism. They were active in the Front because they were anti-fascist and pro-New Deal; they had no other motives, no "further" ideology which their role in the Front served as a tactic. As long as history did not press the alliance or complicate matters the partnership between liberals and Communists in the Popular Front held rather well.

The sudden evaporation of the Popular Front in the aftermath of the Hitler-Stalin Pact reflected a deeper, and previously latent, disjunction between the way Communists and non-Communist liberals viewed politics and political action. However high the pitch of emotional or intellectual dedication of liberals to the work of the Front's various organizations, their work here meant, paradoxically, both more and less to them than it did to the Communists. Front work meant more to liberals in the sense that they invested the temporary and vulnerable Front associations with more meaning, hope, and expectation than the Communists did—indeed, to some extent they invested the same devotion in the transitory Front that the Communists invested in the Party. They were thus liable to disappointment when their Communist partners clearly demonstrated a different attitude toward the Front and to bitterness when "their" Front collapsed like a sand castle in the flood tides of European *Realpolitik*.

Though more emotionally bound to the Front than the Communists, the liberals as a group remained less politicized than their allies. For most liberals, political action did not result from formal commitment to a systematic, enunciated ideology, practice, and organization; rather it tended to remain *ad hoc*, albeit passionate. For most Communists, however, political action tended to become the standard expression of who they were as people. This dissonance meant, most obviously, that the Communists *as a group* plugged harder, longer, and with greater singleness of purpose as the going got rougher, while most liberals became overwhelmed, confused, and finally frightened by constant encounters with a superior adverse force.

At a different level, the thirties liberals' lack of formal ideology and organization meant that their political action quite easily became distracted, diffused, and diverted by events. Communists within the guilds and Popular Front organizations acted according to a definite program which permitted them to select ways and means, weigh propositions and possibilities, allocate funds and efforts—i.e., to organize and channel activity for maximum effectiveness in achieving interlinked sets of goals—while the liberals showed a tendency to react, to attempt too much, to fail to see conjunctions or predict outcomes.

Finally, this dissonance in political perception engendered a mutual distrust which limited the period of joint activity. For the Communists, of course, it was an article of faith, almost of self-definition, that all but a handful of non-Communist leftists were fundamentally "different" and ultimately unreliable. Neither the Party leadership nor membership relied, in their strategic equations, on the dependability of liberals; hence, within Party ranks, there existed small possibility of disillusionment or the blind fury which stems from it. Many liberals, however, especially those new to political activity, knew nothing about communism, its history and practice, nor would they come to know with any assuredness who among their fellow Fronters was a Communist. The CPUSA was not *formally* participating in these various groups and causes. Thus no one had reason to suspect or expect that the next man's or woman's loyalty and allegiance to the cause in general or the immediate task at hand were any different or any less than his or her own. When the "great awakening" of the Pact came, this brand of liberal grew angry, and finally altogether disillusioned with the utility, even possibility, of collective political action. They drifted out of Popular Front organizations. (When the movement regrouped after Pearl Harbor, some of them once again rallied and invested themselves wholly in the new organizations and groups, once again heedless of the nature of their allies. Then 1947 and the HUAC hearings opened their eyes and sent them scurrying for the second time within a decade.)

While the liberal rank and file in Hollywood displayed an almost willful innocence about the realities of partisan political action, their leaders and spokesmen—people like Melvyn Douglas and Philip Dunne —possessed far more in the way of infighting acumen and skills. The latter knew perfectly well the necessity and nature of working with Communists, having fought beside and against them through the years of struggle in the guilds, and therefore they knew in advance to expect contingent loyalty. In addition, they themselves entered the political alliance with a firm political ideology, different from that of the Communists. While the Communists looked toward a socialist future and pledged their allegiance to the Party and the Soviet Union, the ranking liberals placed their faith in Roosevelt, New Deal reformism, the Democratic Party, and benevolent capitalism.

In fact, in the jungle of sectarian political activity, liberals like Douglas and Dunne behaved no differently from the most hardened

Communists. Both groups were loyal to a party and a leader, both engaged in harsh polemics with their adversaries and rivals, both lived with certain compromises of conscience. There is never anything "neat" about commitment to political action; purity of motive or perfection in choice are luxuries available only to historians in the safety of the archives. Dunne and Douglas openly criticized the reactionary designs of some southern Democratic senators and congressmen, the lack of presidential support for an anti-lynching bill, the embargo on Spain, and the administration's failure to aid refugees from Nazi Germany, but they believed that Roosevelt was anti-Nazi and interventionist—as they were—and that he was moving in their direction as rapidly as domestic circumstances permitted. For them, as for Endore, there was no other haven.

The alliance that Douglas, Dunne, *et al.* made with the Communists was no more in "bad faith" than vice versa, but other liberals were, from the outset, burdened by a strong, pervading, almost subliminal, mistrust for their partners, mistrust of a type which left them vulnerable to diversion by anti-communism. The Nazi-Soviet Pact was by no means the first instance in which well-known liberals lost faith in their Communist allies. The Red-baiting of Martin Dies in 1938 had shaken the liberal element in the Anti-Nazi League to the point where they turned their attention from the fight against fascism to fruitless and obsessive scrutinies of League membership, strategy, tactics, etc. to "make certain" that they didn't constitute a version of the Communist Party line.[9] This fretting about which tail was wagging which dog in the left-wing alliance all too often caused some weaker liberals to lose faith in their own numbers, strength, and principles, and led them to play unwittingly into the hands of the Popular Front's conservative adversaries.

The latent mistrust and divided loyalties might have been less damaging if the Popular Front could have mobilized the forces of organized labor in the United States and Hollywood. The Front did not lack for supporters from the ranks of labor—indeed most of the people who joined the Anti-Nazi League, the Abraham Lincoln Battalion, and the Motion Picture Democratic Committee had been bloodied in labor/management struggles throughout the decade. But the trade unions themselves, the real source of power for the working class, were so rent by jurisdictional and political strife that they couldn't even form themselves into a single national federation, let alone subscribe *en bloc* to a political alliance against fascism. The CIO was badly split: the leaders of Jewish unions, such as David Dubinsky of the ILGWU, were solidly pro-Loyalist, while leaders of largely Catholic unions, such as John L. Lewis of the Mine Workers and Philip Murray of the Steelworkers, refused to come out in support of the Republic.[10] The feuds within the Hollywood guilds and unions over contending political programs, parties, and philosophies (not to mention the divisive effects of management meddling) destroyed any chance of enrolling organized labor in the battle against fascism.

In Hollywood, Red-baiting did its work on the labor scene as well as in the political arena. An unsavory alliance between studio front office executives and the entrenched, corrupt, gangster-dominated leadership of the largest labor group (the International Alliance of Theatrical Stage Employees—the IATSE) destroyed any chance of building a democratic, politically active union for backlot workers in Hollywood. The IATSE bosses were, among other things, dedicated anti-Communists who steered the union away from association with any progressive causes despite (or because of) the obvious enthusiasm of many rank-and-file technicians and grips for anti-fascism, New Deal politics, or socialism.

Thus it happened. For one immediate and a few long-term reasons, the Popular Front, after three years of energetic life, went the way of most broad-based political alliances. The Pact was no mere "triggering device," but a historic event of great magnitude. Before Molotov and Ribbentrop signed the agreement, the Popular Front in Hollywood had flourished. By the late fall of 1939 it resembled a great bombed-out cathedral, a haunting, appalling, sad vestige of happier times. The faithful had scattered. Rent by schism and mistrust, their determination that faith and action could accomplish any goals broken by doubt, they gave little resistance to the depredations of the reactionary when he appeared among them. Saddest of all, an influential minority of old believers became unwitting recruits in the new anti-Communist crusade.

The remainder of this chapter will chronicle the fate of one of the Popular Front's most successful and influential organizations as it passed through the fire of late 1939. The Motion Picture Democratic Committee, founded in 1938 as an electoral wing of the anti-fascist movement, appeared late on the Popular Front scene but quickly became a highly influential and successful independent citizens' pressure group. Its disappearance from the political scene dealt a grievous blow to Culbert Olson and New Deal progressivism at a time when both the California governor and the American President were being relentlessly attacked by the right wing. More to the point, the MPDC is the only Hollywood Popular Front organization which was survived by documented evidence of the course of its disintegration. If the historian had to pick among available subjects, however, this would still be the choice because the decline of the MPDC dramatically foreshadowed the Truman-Wallace (liberal-radical) split of the post-World War II era. Moreover, the Anti-Nazi League, the Motion Picture Artists Committee, and the other Front organizations, from all that we know, each came to an end in a fashion similar to the MPDC.

Douglas, Dunne, and the Decline of the Motion Picture Democratic Committee

Few people gave of themselves more generously—in time, energy, and material resources—to the Hollywood Popular Front than actor Melvyn Douglas and screenwriter Philip Dunne. Though accused regularly of being "Reds" by the undiscriminating Dies Committee and Hearst press, it was known to every Red in Hollywood that Douglas and Dunne were the unofficial leaders of the liberal, non-Communist constituency which was, for a long while, the majority in the MPDC.

Douglas, whose face was well known to millions of moviegoers for his roles in *Theodora Goes Wild* (Columbia, 1936), *Ninotchka* (MGM, 1939), and thirty-four other films between 1931 and 1939, was a leading man in the light comedy genre. "When I first came to Hollywood," said Douglas, "I had only a dinner table interest in politics. My political involvement rose specifically out of the appearance of Nazism. Helen and I went to Germany in 1936 where we were terrified, traumatized, and profoundly shocked by what we saw and heard. On our return we looked around for a group who knew what was going on—and found the Anti-Nazi League."

He and his wife, former movie star Helen Gahagan, became active supporters of virtually every progressive cause. Indeed, by the latter part of the decade it was clear that both Douglases were destined for high places in American electoral politics. (He conferred regularly with national Democratic leaders, and served as a delegate to the Democratic National Convention in 1940; she was a Democratic National Committeewoman in 1940, vice-chairperson of the Democratic State Committee from 1941 to 1944, and a congresswoman from 1944-50. In 1950 her electoral career was destroyed permanently when Richard Nixon opposed her with a campaign strategy characterized primarily by savage and unjustified Red-baiting.)

Philip Dunne was on his way to becoming one of the most successful screenwriters in Hollywood. The son of one of America's best-known political satirists, Finley Peter Dunne (the creator of Mr. Dooley), Philip graduated from Harvard in 1929 and journeyed to Hollywood the following year to take a job as reader at the Fox studio. Four years later he was the lead screenwriter on *The Count of Monte Cristo* (UA, 1934), and his career steadily advanced thereafter —he received Academy Award nominations for *How Green Was My Valley* in 1941 and *David and Bathsheba* in 1951, as well as the Laurel Award in 1962, and in the fifties he produced and directed. At Harvard, Dunne had signed his name to a Sacco-Vanzetti protest committee roster, but like most film people he really "got politics" in the thirties—first in the 1932 presidential campaign, then in the guild wars, then in the Popular Front. "I was," said Dunne, "born and bred to liberal politics. My father was a fundamental liberal democrat, who loathed bigotry, prejudice, and exclusion. He brought me up to have very strong feelings toward Britain and France as democracies. My father was very close with Theodore Roosevelt, our family knew Franklin Roosevelt, and I was in Jimmy Roosevelt's club at Harvard."

Like every other thirties activist Dunne faced the question of joining the Communist Party. He dealt with it rather more summarily than most: "Not for a moment did I consider joining. Dictatorships were repugnant to me and it was clearly an undemocratic organization. In fact, I tried to de-recruit the recruiters." He did not quarrel with the economic analysis or socialist vision of the Party; his "problem" with it was "political." The Party tried to hook Dunne with the bait of effectiveness: "You're spread too thin; you're all over the place. We'll channel your energies." Dunne successfully resisted because he had already chosen his political channel: the Democratic Party, of which he became state vice-chairman in 1938. He also held high office in the Screen Writers Guild, the MPDC, and the Anti-Nazi League, and helped found the Americans for Democratic Action (1947) and the Committee for the First Amendment (1947).

Douglas, too, felt the hot breath of Communist recruitment: "One night, Lionel Stander kept me up till dawn trying to sell me the Russian brand of Marxism and to recruit me for the Communist Party. I resisted. I had always been condemnatory of totalitarianism and I made continual, critical references to the U.S.S.R. in my speeches. Members of the Anti-Nazi League would urge me to delete these references and several conflicts ensued."

Notwithstanding their deep-seated anti-communism, neither the Douglases nor Dunne had any difficulty working alongside Party members and fellow travelers prior to the fall of 1939. For the most part, one didn't know, with any degree of accuracy, who was Red and who was pink; nor did the question of party affiliation loom especially large at a time when everybody was united on basic foreign policy issues: against the embargo on Spain and for an anti-fascist collective security front composed of the Western democracies and the Soviet Union. "The Communists were behaving and working as part of the coalition," Dunne said; "indeed, they were gilt-edged and pure on Popular Front issues."

The prevailing belief among non-Communist progressives was that the Party had agreed to take a ride on the liberal bandwagon of patriotism and anti-fascism, so why not welcome them aboard, especially when they could be easily controlled? "We never thought they were dangerous," said Dunne, "only misguided; and we believed we could always freeze out what we thought to be a CP minority. I never believed for one moment that when the crunch came they could change the purpose of the Popular Front." Dunne's conclusion characterizes perfectly the liberal perception: "They, not we, were fellow travelers."

The Nazi-Soviet Pact and the invasion of Poland hit the MPDC like a delayed time bomb. At first there was a certain fraternity and equality in the universal shock and emotion that everyone registered upon hearing the news from abroad. Until it became clear that the various factions comprising the Executive Board of the MPDC stood at loggerheads on the issue, the illusion of unity could be maintained. In September it was still possible for the Board to agree (unanimously, Dunne said) on continued strong opposition to international fascism.

Yet divisions of opinion were already becoming apparent: the bone of contention was what attitude should be taken toward the Soviet Union and Hitler in light of the Pact. Most pre-Pact anti-fascists had shared two fundamental beliefs: that one could not be seriously opposed to Hitler and be a pacifist; and that the Soviet Union was an integral component of the collective anti-fascist deterrent to German aggression in Europe. The Pact disturbed Dunne, therefore, not because he saw it as an example of Russian perfidy—"I was not opposed to the Nazi-Soviet Pact for Russia," he said; "I saw it as the ploy of one nation-state seeking security"—but because it removed the Soviet Union from the ranks of the anti-Hitler forces and allowed the German dictator to turn his attention, and armed forces, against France and Great Britain, the first lines of American defense.

Concerned with the disintegration of the anti-Nazi front in Europe,

Dunne and Douglas became alarmed when evidence of a similar disruption began to appear in the ranks of the MPDC. Both liberals remember Herbert Biberman as their barometer of Communist drift away from the interventionist spirit which had previously animated Popular Front groups and activities in Hollywood. Melvyn Douglas remembered that the film director had chaired an anti-fascist gathering which met, ironically, the night before the announcement of the Nazi-Soviet Pact. Someone asked Biberman to comment on the rumors that such an agreement was in the offing. Douglas recalled that Biberman pounded on the table and called the rumors "fascist propaganda." Douglas continued: "After the Pact was announced we did not see much of Biberman and his political friends. They reappeared, a few weeks later, with 'Yanks Are Not Coming' placards." "Before the Pact," recalled Dunne, "every other word out of Biberman's mouth spoke of collective security. All of a sudden he added the modifying phrase, 'collective security for peace, not war.'"

The dilemma of the Hollywood Communists is obvious in Biberman's new formulations. What, in the fall of 1939, could "collective security for peace" possibly mean? With the Wehrmacht and Luftwaffe finishing off Poland, Mussolini annexing Albania, and Japan moving in on British possessions in the Far East, peace no longer existed. Yet, after three years of strenuous activity in the cause of all-out war against fascism, the Communist parties of the world were ordered to seek peace.† In their need to square the circle—to serve their anti-fascist past, to remain faithful to the lessons they had learned from World War I, and to protect the Soviet Union while adhering to Party discipline—people like Herbert Biberman fell prey to statements and positions of Orwellian self-contradiction.

It is easy to understand that liberals had little patience for this sort

---

† The British Communist Party did not change its line until the week following the Russian invasion of Poland, on September 17. According to former CPGB Central Committee member Douglas Hyde: "The Party's central committee had met one day at the King Street headquarters to draw up a stirring manifesto to the British people calling upon them to sacrifice all in the great anti-Fascist struggle. After hours of discussion the text was made final. Then, unexpectedly, in walked the British representative to the Communist International who everyone thought was still in Moscow.

"He took one look at the manifesto and told the leaders they would have to scrap it. It was, he said, an imperialist war. The Comintern had said so and that meant opposing it in the classical Marxist way. [He showed them written evidence on a postcard signed by Georgi Dimitrov.]" (*I Believed*, New York: G. P. Putnam's Sons, 1950, p. 73.)

of Newspeak, particularly when it was presented with shocking suddenness and as a non-negotiable *fait accompli*. On October 13, the Political Committee of the CPUSA released to the public the results of their seven-week debate over the stance to assume *vis-à-vis* the altered international situation. Direct pressure from Moscow, and their own belief in the infallibility of directives from that source, led American Party leaders to declare that the war in Europe had become "an imperialist war for which the bourgeoisie of all belligerent powers are equally guilty." In and of itself that interpretation would have engendered heated debate within Popular Front organizations; it was, however, the "explanation" which followed that actually destroyed the foundations of the liberal/Communist alliance.

> The present war between two imperialist groups . . . has at one blow wiped out the former division of the world between the camps of democracy and fascism. . . . Therefore the slogans of anti-fascism can no longer give the main direction to the struggle of the working class and its allies, as they formerly did in the period of the struggle for the anti-fascist peace front and people's front . . . not only the old division between Republican and Democratic parties, but also that between the New Deal and anti-New Deal camps, is losing its former significance.[11]

One week later a formal pro-neutrality resolution was introduced at a meeting of the MPDC Board, and passed before the liberals could rally their troops. The close vote (10–7) did not cushion the shock. Not only had the organization reversed its position on international affairs, but it had adopted the Communist line. The sudden capacity of the Communist/fellow traveler bloc to determine MPDC policy in late 1939 is not surprising if one recalls that 1939 was not an election year in the United States, and, as a result, many liberals seemed to be in hibernation. They were generally not as interested in the massive strikes of the Madera County cotton pickers as they were in electoral campaigns. Left pretty much to their own devices—Douglas was making movies and traveling to Washington; Dunne had recently married and his meeting attendance had slackened considerably—the radicals organized demonstrations in support of agricultural workers. They could not have agreed with Dunne, who was then vice-president, that mid- and late 1939 "was a relatively quiescent time for the MPDC as an electoral organization." In those days, no organization was seasonal, no period quiescent if one was a member of the CPUSA.

Electoral quiescence wasn't the only cause of liberal drift away

from the MPDC in late 1939. The heightened activity of the Dies
Committee had also taken its toll among the less committed progressives who feared the effect on their reputations and their earning
power of continued association with radicals. The announcement of the
Pact gave them the final justification they needed to cease attending
meetings. The more "professionally" political of the liberals remained
behind, however, determined to contest the CP "control" of *their* organization. "I was uneasy," Dunne recalls, "but I thought we could
save the organization."

Nonetheless, the time for diplomacy and negotiation had passed.
Dunne knew that in view of the October vote of the MPDC Board, "I
would have to force the issue": either the organization would return
to its old line or it would face schism. Douglas was handed that issue in
Washington, D.C., in early December. He lunched there at the Cos-
mos Club, the guest of honor of a group of twenty important New
Dealers, including Frank Murphy, Jerome Frank, Leon Henderson,
Tom Corcoran, and Harold Ickes.

> Douglas told us [Ickes wrote in his diary] that the group to which
> he belongs in Hollywood [MPDC] was willing to do what it
> could for the New Deal and I agreed with his statement that this
> group could be very influential. There are two or three Commu-
> nists, rather prominent in the organization, who will have to be
> sidetracked since they continue to be apologists for Stalin since
> Stalin's tieup with Hitler.[12]

Immediately following his return to Hollywood, Douglas wrote a
"Report to the Executive Board of the Motion Picture Democratic
Committee,"[13] intended to present the "problem" and force the organization to align itself closely with the administration in the coming
election year. The Hitler-Stalin Pact, the division of Poland, and the
invasion of Finland (and Roosevelt's sharp condemnation of the latter), wrote Douglas, had "caused a very sharp difference of opinion in
many liberal organizations." Douglas, however, chose to do battle in
his report on none of those issues; instead he took up the cudgels
against "caustic" radical criticism of Roosevelt's diplomacy.

> The fountainhead of these attacks has been the Communist Party.
> The idea is current and not without foundation that the Commu-
> nist Party and such other liberal organizations as suddenly turned
> against an administration foreign policy which they had so re-
> cently supported, had been pro-New Deal in the past not because
> of any real conviction but for opportunistic reasons.

It should be noted that the CP's new line—while caustically critical of Roosevelt and his diplomacy—was in no sense a condemnation of the entire New Deal, or of democratic society, American patriotism, alliances with liberals, or anti-fascism in themselves, or of the several causes—Spain, Culbert Olson, opposition to the Dies Committee— which anti-fascism entailed internationally and nationally. All the evidence of the 1936–39 era—from Party publications to newspaper reports to memoirs, correspondence, minutes of meetings—strongly indicates that Communist participation in the anti-fascist cause was "sincere" insofar as any political action undertaken by a collective can be sincere. There was, and is, no indication that the Party was consciously acting in bad faith, that it was saying one thing and doing another, or manipulating people and events to ends which betrayed the *manifest* causes and issues for which the Popular Front fought. More to the point, in Hollywood, the screen Communists from Stewart to Lardner—nearly all of whom joined the Party as a consequence of their anti-fascist fervor—were the incarnations of sincere "conviction," though perhaps not of independent and critical thinking.

Such considerations would have seemed a quibble to Melvyn Douglas. Whatever the level of Communist "sincerity" or "conviction" before August 1939, the "treachery" of that month permanently tainted their credibility in Douglas' eyes. "The result [of Communist bad faith]," Douglas wrote in his "Report," "has been the complete discrediting of such organizations or individuals not only in the eyes of a large portion of the public but in the eyes of those New Dealers in the administration whom we support and who have clearly expressed themselves on this subject." It was imperative, he concluded, that the MPDC give full support to the President and voice "wholehearted disapproval" of his critics.

Douglas' "Report" and the resolution which he sponsored did not fare well at the MPDC Board meeting of December 19, 1939. A number of eloquent Communists and fellow travelers—John Bright, Harold Buchman, Robert Tasker—spoke out powerfully against aligning the organization so rigidly and uncritically with the Democratic Party as well as against the excessively strong anti-Communist vocabulary which they claimed the Dunne-Douglas forces were adopting and which was playing them, wittingly or unwittingly, into the hands of the far Right. To this the liberals adroitly replied that the CPUSA was already "objectively aligned" with the Right in its isolationism. Unimpressed by this riposte, the fellow travelers on the Board joined with the Communists (as they would again in 1945–47) to reject the plea of "administration liberals" to support a Democratic President's foreign policy. The vote was unanimous. According to the minutes, neither Dunne nor Douglas was present.

The resolution, its opponents felt, would not only compromise the MPDC, but would threaten to stigmatize it for disagreeing with Roosevelt. "This resolution suggests," one Board member stated, "that disagreement with the President's foreign policy constitutes a preference for the purposes of another government, Russia. This is a false contention."[14] In effect the opponents of the Douglas resolution accurately foresaw the propaganda ploy (criticism of America=disloyalty to America) and the political tactic (the isolation of "disloyal" Americans) which would, in less than a decade, poison not just the atmosphere of the Hollywood Popular Front, but the political and social life of the entire United States.

Undaunted, Dunne and Douglas rewrote the resolution and presented it to an emergency meeting of the Board which convened three days later at Dunne's home. The tone was moderated, but the essence of the resolution was unchanged: no alliance with those who refused to adhere to the Roosevelt line. In pleading his case, Dunne begged the listeners to remember that "Washington opinion regards the MPDC as too close to the Communist Party." The time for moral posturing had passed; Roosevelt and the Democratic Party demanded assurance of the MPDC's unswerving loyalty. When queried as to the schismatic potential of his resolution, Dunne cast the die: the time for schism had arrived. "[My] resolution," he said, "is frankly intended to define our split of purpose and opinion with the Communist Party—since we can get no place until we do state this split. . . . [S]tripped to its essentials, this resolution is a repudiation of the Communist Party."[15] Dunne thus gave voice to the hitherto unspeakable: the MPDC, and the Front of which it was a part, could no longer contain and channel its divergent tendencies and had perhaps played out its historical role.

The Board, reiterating the dangers they saw in the Dunne-Douglas proposal, again voted down the resolution, but consented to Dunne's motion to submit it to a vote of the full membership. This was an unusual and somewhat dramatic step. Like most Hollywood Popular Front organizations, the MPDC was essentially a general staff which mobilized soldiers as it needed them—i.e., it planned and promoted large gatherings which featured prominent people speaking on behalf of specific causes and for specific goals. In this sense it was not like the guilds and did not normally hold large membership meetings to settle

internal disputes. But in this instance the Board was anxious to avoid
any charges of railroading or dictatorship.

Some three hundred people appeared at the Hollywood Women's
Club for the showdown meeting on January 30, 1940.[16] Melvyn
Douglas did not appear. He had resigned from the MPDC (and from
the Anti-Nazi League when his motion denouncing "Nazi aggression"
and "Soviet perfidy" was soundly defeated and he was personally
maligned). Dunne had authored a new resolution, carefully written to
avoid any accusation of Red-baiting: "We point out sharply that this
concerted campaign to lay the basis for outright suppression of the
Communist Party is reminiscent of the post [World War I] hysteria
which culminated in the now universally condemned Palmer Raids."
The MPDC Board presented a policy statement consisting of the three
basic themes common to every truncated Popular Front or ongoing
Communist front group of the period known as the Phony War
(1939–40): keep America out of the war, defend the Bill of Rights, increase economic security for Americans. Neutrality was the linchpin
of this new set of principles, for behind the call for "preparedness,"
the radical Left believed it detected the regrouping of the same unsavory alliance of business interests, conservative newspaper barons,
and jingoists which had precipitated American entry into World War
I waving the rhetorical flag of "keeping the world safe for democracy." Until the alignments and purposes of the approaching war became clearer to the Communists—that is, until the Soviet Union joined
an alliance with the West against the Axis—American entry appeared
unjustified and dangerous to them, a covert assault on civil liberties
and the gains of the New Deal by munitions manufacturers and hawk-
ish politicians.

The clouds of war—both foreign and domestic—shrouded the
debate and lent it an ominousness and anxious pessimism unfamiliar to
the Hollywood Popular Front. Both sides struggled to find haven from
the upcoming storms: the Communists in the "absolute and fundamental objective" of defending "the first socialist state"; the Dunne-
Douglas liberals in upholding what remained of an anti-fascist collective security front. The profound mistrust which divided liberal from
Communist was the product of everyone's shaken security: the Left
feared that the United States might join the wrong side in the war,
while the liberals felt that Communists were traitors and repressors.
Both sides recognized the growing conservative drive against civil
liberties, labor unions, the Left, and New Deal reforms; both viewed

with alarm the growing self-confidence and shrillness of the Dies
Committee. But for the first time in the history of the Front, the sides
could not be allies in opposing these enemies. Dunne admitted as
much: "Although the Communists fight for civil liberties, progressive
legislation, and peace, they do so for selfish, dictatorship-seeking
reasons." The MPDC membership overwhelmingly defeated Dunne's
redrawn resolution.

The Emergence of Liberal Anti-Communism

The liberals resigned *en masse* from the organization. They did not
go quietly or happily; their recriminations bore eloquent testimony to
the passion, closeness, and interdependence of the Hollywood Popular
Front. These men and women had fused tight bonds in the years of
the late thirties, personal relationships based on mutual respect, collaborative effort, and shared dangers to their careers which crossed party
lines and transcended partisan politics. After the hothouse warmth and
insulation that the Front in Hollywood provided, it was natural that
great emotion would arise when "politics" intervened to throw the activists out into the cold conflict of factionalism.

In a letter to Melvyn Douglas, writer Humphrey Cobb noted that
the liberal exodus from the Popular Front left him "keenly resenting
the fact that the communists have usurped and then discredited the
words 'liberal,' 'progressive,' 'democratic,' etc."[17] Every liberal who
departed a Popular Front organization called back over his or her
shoulder: "I have not changed." Philip Dunne wrote *Time* magazine in
a similar vein: "Melvyn Douglas has not changed. The liberals have
not changed. The Communists have."[18]

But the circumstances of the late thirties had changed the Roosevelt
liberals more than they knew or could admit. The new post-Popular
Front groupings created by the schismatic liberals (e.g., the California
Citizens Council, William Allen White's Committee to Defend
America by Aiding the Allies, the Union for Democratic Action,
Fight for Freedom) did not function in the same fashion as the old
Front organizations. Migrant labor and studio backlot workers, or
anything not directly connected with the political establishment, received little more than lip service from the new liberal organizations.
Demonstrations and mass meetings, petitions and grass roots organizing
on behalf of rural workers, oppressed minorities, or the poor went by
the boards as the liberals, lacking the ability or desire to mobilize ordinary citizens, turned to lobbying, letter writing, punditry, and other

forms of elite influencing. Also, the causes for which they fought became more "national" in scope, more one-tracked in purpose: pro-war, pro-administration. In other words, "differentiated" or non-collaborative liberals jettisoned the broad, adventurous, independent, and (upon occasion) radical politics of the Popular Front, and embraced instead the familiar figure of "practical politics" and power-oriented issues.

For many liberals, "practical politics" included an anti-Communist plank. In Hollywood, Melvyn Douglas introduced one variant of liberal anti-communism—the need for liberals to fight to keep Communists "out of liberal organizations." "It was a problem of trustworthiness," the actor stated, "not of their being Communists *per se*. Their long-term goals were not mine, and they were using my goals as expedients to achieve goals in which I did not believe. They were obstructionists." In a speech of February 4, 1940, before the California Citizens Council—a group of liberals whose names had been culled from Douglas' own contacts and suggestions offered by his New Deal connections[19]—Douglas condemned, without naming, "those groups whose thinking seems to be dominated by foreign agencies and who, not having been able to make much headway with political parties of their own, seek to infiltrate themselves into one of the major parties, there to exert their influence. The results are bitter recriminations, public name calling, [etc.]." One month later, Douglas, now chairman of the group, proposed that it sponsor a symposium devoted to the issue of communism: how it functions, what are its errors, how to combat it.

At the same time that Douglas was launching his attack on the Communists, he (and other film community liberals) had to guard their own flanks from the right-wing offensive. The liberal-Communist split beckoned alluringly to the conservatives, who leaped to exploit the breach. To protect his vocation as an actor, Douglas was forced to distance himself even further from the Communists than he might otherwise have done; he underwent the humiliation of an "interview" in *Photoplay* magazine entitled "Is Melvyn Douglas a Communist?" In that article, Douglas assumed the calculated disingenuousness that would become *de rigueur* for all liberals desirous of distancing themselves from "pink" movements and people in order to save their careers. He wrote: "I do not consider that I was allied with Communists then or at any time. . . . Even a casual investigation would have clearly established that I have as little regard for Communists as I have for the Nazis and that I have been quick to condemn their influence wherever I have found it in operation."[20] Douglas' troubles with the

right wing stemmed from his identification with the Roosevelt administration. When he was appointed by Eleanor Roosevelt as head of the
Arts Council of the Office of Civilian Defense's Voluntary Participation Branch, the conservatives launched a vicious attack against the
"frills" of this position (Douglas was being paid the munificent sum of
$8,000) and the "Communistic tendencies" and ethnic background
(wasn't his original name Hesselburg?) of the actor. Douglas resigned
the office and joined the army. The fact that one year earlier Douglas
had been cleared of "Communistic tendencies" by Martin Dies apparently carried little weight with anti-New Deal right-wingers. In
August 1939, while Dunne, Cagney, Bogart, and March felt it necessary to appear before the HUAC chairman, then in San Francisco, to
refute charges of their communism, Douglas was spared the journey
by the receipt of a telegram from Dies informing the actor that no evidence existed which linked him to the Communist Party.[21]

Liberals to the right of Douglas ventured into the sea of "Red
fascism"[22]—communism=fascism=totalitarianism, all alike inimical to
democracy, all to be fought with equal fervor.[23] The "Red fascist" po-
lemic freed its wielders from the burden of careful distinctions and the
discomfort of living with ambiguities and uncertainties. If Stalin's
crimes rivaled Hitler's for magnitude, cynicism, and horror, and if
Browder defended Stalin, then the entire American Communist Party
could be condemned as the moral and political equivalent of Nazism,
regardless of the progressive efforts to which this local Party might
have contributed in the past or might contribute in the future.‡

The first demonstration of the procedural "correctness"—and sub-

---

‡ Red fascism of the forties was similar, in political effect, to "social fascism" of the early thirties. Attaching the fascist label to political foes had
considerable currency in the twenties and thirties (as it does today).
Since Communist theory accounted for the rise of fascism, and explained
its "nature," in terms of the crisis of democratic or parliamentary capitalist
states, the Party, in the years 1928 to 1935, labeled as fascist any group
(even Socialists) who continued to play the conventional political game.
The usefulness and advisability of the policy of "social fascist" polemics
were demonstrated clearly in Weimar Germany, where Communist refusal
to collaborate with other parties of the Left greatly eased the Nazi climb
to power. Both epithets contained far more error and invective than truth;
both proved disastrous to left-wing unity and effectiveness. And the
strategies which they symbolized betrayed causes and purposes to which
Communists and liberals alike were dedicated: social fascism virtually
sold out the German working class to Hitler; Red fascism led to uncon-
scionable sabotage of democratic and constitutional procedure during the
HUAC/McCarthy era.

stantive nullity—of liberal anti-communism occurred in the spring of 1940. On May 7 the American Civil Liberties Union—a group dedicated to the unconditional defense of free speech in America—held a remarkable "trial" of a member of its Board of Directors. Elizabeth Gurley Flynn, an admitted member of the CPUSA, was removed from her position on the ACLU Board on the grounds that no Communist, *ipso facto*, could support civil liberties sincerely. It was an astonishing charge to bring against a woman who had, for a quarter of a century, distinguished herself for work in human rights, labor organizing, political progressivism, and civil liberties. The Nazi-Soviet Pact had magically invalidated this woman's (and other Party members') work and rendered it deceitful and cynical. "[A] Communist was no longer just a Communist after the Pact," stated Roger Baldwin. "A Communist was an agent of the Soviet Union."*

Baldwin was judging from appearances, but then he had little else to go by. The CPUSA's change of line (from anti-fascism to pro-peace and neutrality), signifying as it did a new set of political priorities for American Communists, not only angered liberals and justified their departure from the Popular Front, but harmed the cause of communism itself. The enmity of liberal leadership and the retirement from activism of the liberal rank and file left the Communists and fellow travelers isolated and vulnerable. It was psychologically very hard on Communists, especially in Hollywood, where the closeness and ardor of Fronters had been so complete, to watch the undoing of the alliances which had sustained everybody so satisfyingly for the past three years. Few activists in Hollywood had had any experience with the political cold; suffering for one's politics had only been an abstraction up to then. "The only way we [Communists] survived this period [1939–40] with our integrity and sensibilities intact," remembers Abraham Polonsky, "was to remind ourselves constantly that the Pact and its policy reformulations were simply tactics and temporary. The

---

* Quoted in Peggy Lamson, *Roger Baldwin: Founder of the American Civil Liberties Union*, Boston: Houghton Mifflin Co., 1976, p. 228. Beginning in 1942, certain ACLU staffers turned with increasing frequency to the FBI for information on the political affiliations of ACLU Board members, both national and local. In return for "clearances," two top ACLU executives—general counsel Morris Ernst and executive director Patrick Murphy Malin—provided J. Edgar Hoover with confidential ACLU correspondence, minutes, and drafts of position papers. ("A Statement by Corliss Lamont on the ACLU and the FBI," *In These Times*, November 16–22, 1977, p. 22.)

sigh of relief that went up among American Communists when Hitler finally invaded the Soviet Union [in June 1941] was audible everywhere."

The tragedy of the demise of the Popular Front of the thirties, aside from the obvious fillip it gave to the emerging right-wing reaction in the United States, was the truncation of the political education it entailed for thousands of people. Had the Popular Front remained a relatively harmonious organization for a full decade, its recruits would undoubtedly have widened and deepened the political dimensions of their lives and integrated political action more closely with their vocational and personal identity. It is dangerous to treat historical hypotheses too loosely, but it seems reasonable to suggest that ten years of healthy life for the Popular Front would have furnished many more battle-hardened troops for the fight against reaction in the postwar era. During its short existence, the force of the anti-fascist campaign had held the Dies Committee (and like-minded right-wingers) in check. Yet the inexorable conjuncture of historical events and political and personal contingencies denied the united Left movement the time it needed to harden. Even so, the Front had its collective fingers in every kind of pie: cultural, social, trade union, conventional party politics. No type of activity was closed off to it: demonstrations, cocktail parties, pressure groups, *ad hoc* organizations. Acting on every issue, bringing attention to international questions and problems, pointing out links between national and international developments, showing the connections between politics, culture, and economics, the American Popular Front of the thirties succeeded, for a short time, in forging new bonds of alliance between diverse leftist groups and making that presence felt in this country. The formal rebirth of a Popular Front in 1941 after the German invasion of Russia and Pearl Harbor could not hide the loss of a certain spirit of unity and optimism among progressive forces in this country which has not been seen again.

What terminated in 1939 was the existence of a powerful, activist progressive alliance which could provide effective opposition to the periodic eruptions of reaction which sweep across the American landscape, reminding everyone of who's really in charge here. The liberals of the forties and fifties had, on their own, neither the backbone nor the political consciousness to obstruct effectively militant American conservatism, as evidenced by their "resistance" to such triumphs of reactionary legislation as the Alien Registration Act (1940), the Taft-Hartley Act (1947), the McCarran Internal Security Act (1950), and the Communist Control Act (1954). On the other hand the isolated radical Left had not the numbers, the access, the style, or the will to work effectively within the American social-political system. In America the spectrum of risk for political activists invariably runs from sectarianism to opportunism. The Popular Front of 1936–39 offered, perhaps, the most promising way out of this dilemma.

The Phony War and the
Resurrected Popular Front, 1940–44

If they say to us, "We must fight this war to preserve
democracy," let us say to them, "There is no such thing as
democracy in time of war. It is a lie, a deliberate deception to
lead us to our own destruction. We will not die in order that
our children may inherit a permanent military dictatorship."

—*Dalton Trumbo, 1940*[1]

By the time Pearl Harbor was attacked—all the conditions
which had seemed to me to make for an honest and effective
and successful war against the Axis had been fulfilled. . . . [It
was] a war for the liberation of people, a war to make the
slogans into realities.

—*Dalton Trumbo, 1944*[2]

"The early forties," wrote Harold Clurman in his memoirs, "particularly that period which preceded our entry into the war, represented a
kind of stasis, pregnant with possibilities for both good and evil."[3]
Enveloped within the clouds of an impending war and threatened by a
renewed assault from the American Right, the divided American Left
reformed itself. Its new groupings struggled, independently from each
other, both to promulgate and justify their individual positions on bel-
ligerency and to defend the progressive gains of the thirties. Divided
though they were by fierce disagreement on the question of rendering
assistance to the Allied powers, left-wing groups continued to resist
conservative advances. The Communists, mainly through the League
of American Writers, responded to the increasing internal reaction
more firmly than their liberal former allies. The moderates of the
Dunne-Douglas persuasion focused far more attention on foreign pol-

icy as they mirrored Roosevelt's transformation from "Dr. New Deal" to "Dr. Win-the-War." The ACLU, however, strongly supported embattled civil liberties. To the right of Dunne-Douglas, a group of "conservative" liberals—most notably those grouped around the *New Leader*—pursued the new anti-Communist line with a growing vengeance. This, of course, not only left them unavailable for any kind of operational alliance with radicals; it made them, *de facto*, fellow travelers of the Right. Len De Caux, who was working in the office of the CIO in the prewar years, remembered that "Washington in the first half of 1941 offered a foretaste of Cold War McCarthyism. Liberals and laborites might have taken warning of the fabrications and excesses of anti-communism, had not many of them been among its chief inciters."[4]

The Conservative Reaction (1938–43)

Although numerous vigilantes from private organizations did their part, the main assault on the progressive movement was mounted by the state and federal legislatures. Around the country newly elected conservatives allied themselves with the anti-Roosevelt Old Guard to block relief for the poor, dismantle New Deal agencies, expose "subversives," and attempt to outlaw the Communist Party. Their first target was the Federal Theatre Project of the Works Progress Administration.[5] This relief agency had suffered from savage Red-baiting since its inception in 1935, but had survived to employ a large number of artists and produce an impressive number of well-received theatrical presentations. The plays produced by the Theatre Project were usually attacked, however, for their progressive content. This, along with the Project's employment of blacks, its congeniality to radical trade union activity, and its general tendency to harbor "intellectuals" and "propagandizers," made it an inviting target for the right wing, which had been rejuvenated by its victories in the 1938 congressional elections.

The Dies Committee (HUAC) spearheaded the attack on the Theatre Project, utilizing the sort of demagogic tactics which its successors would wield even more destructively ten years later. The complaisance of the American press in sensationalizing "leaks" by Dies Commitee members and staff led to a trial-and-verdict-by-newspaper-headline even before the "inquiry" commenced. The hullabaloo and subsequent "investigation" worked like a charm, and, in June 1939, the

House effectively abolishing the FTP by cutting off its funds. (A loyalty oath was instituted for all new WPA employees at the same time.)

Members of the Hollywood Left, in alliance with New York artists and intellectuals, responded rapidly to the attack on the Federal Theatre Project. The most illustrious members of the Anti-Nazi League and the Motion Picture Artists Committee fired off telegrams; the three major talent guilds (at the instigation of the Screen Writers) sponsored a national radio broadcast and mass demonstration, on June 26, 1939. Stung by this latest salvo from Hollywood, and undaunted by the hiding he and his Committee had taken from the film Left in 1938, when they had labeled the Anti-Nazi League a "Communist front organization," Dies waded into battle once again. Armed, this time, with the unsubstantiated testimony of American Legionnaires, disgruntled ex-Communists, right-wing fanatics, and publicity-seeking informers, Dies told the press that the motion picture industry was a "hotbed of communism." Liberals, radicals, and Communists, 2,500 strong, forgot their political differences over the Nazi-Soviet Pact and gathered at the Philharmonic Auditorium on February 27, 1940, to protest Dies' latest outburst.

The Committee arrived better armed this time. It had compiled a long list of "subversive" film people (including Melvyn Douglas), and Dies was sending investigators to Hollywood to get more. Concentrating the attack more carefully this time, the investigators approached the Screen Writers Guild through its president, Sheridan Gibney. According to Gibney's later testimony, he was given a list of alleged screenwriter subversives. "I was told that if I would call these writers and have them report to a certain room at a certain time at the Hollywood Roosevelt Hotel, they could clear themselves."[6] (That is, they could disclaim, or apologize for, their political past and name some of their equally "duped" associates.) Gibney promptly called the people on the list and advised them not to comply. Two or three went anyway, one of whom, Rena Vale, an ex-Communist, provided some of the names which would be typed onto HUAC subpoenas in 1947 and 1951. Gibney and the SWG Executive Board found no assistance forthcoming from their employers. The producers' neutrality, said Gibney, "in effect left the creative talent groups without the support of the producing companies and . . . in a position of being scapegoats."[7]

While his investigators were ferreting out names and future witnesses in Hollywood, Dies, at his mansion in Beaumont, Texas, was sitting as a one-man committee. There, in executive session, he heard testimony from a number of alleged and actual former Communist functionaries, most notably John L. Leech, the first of what would be a long line of people who would serve the government as professional witnesses during the coming decades. Leech had joined the Party in 1931, served as a paid Party organizer for two years, 1934–36, and been expelled in 1937. Former Communists with whom we have talked are convinced that Leech was a paid police agent during his entire Party tenure. Leech's credibility and veracity had been scathingly criticized six months earlier by Dean James M. Landis of Harvard Law School, who had presided over the United States Government's first attempt to deport West Coast labor leader Harry Bridges. Less finicky than Dean Landis, Dies attentively copied down the forty-two movie names which Leech, a former executive secretary of the Party's Los Angeles County section, spewed forth.[8]

A few weeks later Leech repeated his list for a Los Angeles County grand jury. (That same grand jury subpoenaed Herbert Biberman, Gale Sondergaard, Sam and Sadie Ornitz, Lionel Stander, and Clifford Odets to answer questions "concerning operations of Communists in the film colony."[9]) Someone leaked Leech's testimony, and newspaper headlines all over the country emblazoned their front pages with the news that Humphrey Bogart, James Cagney, Fredric March, Franchot Tone, Lionel Stander, and over a dozen other stars had been named as Communists. Dies, alone in "executive session," promised clearance to all those who would "cooperate." Within two weeks of the "leak" all but one of the named, actress Jean Muir, had appeared and all, except Stander, had been "cleared" by the HUAC chairman.[10] Republic Studios fired Stander as a consequence, while executives from the major studios responded to the news of the Leech accusations and the Dies clearance procedure with uncharacteristic openness, announcing, through a *Variety* headline: "INVESTIGATE US—WE'RE CLEAN!"[11]

The producers were much less cordial one year later, when the California counterpart to Martin Dies—Jack Tenney, chairman of the Joint Fact-Finding Committee on Un-American Activities of the California legislature[12]—announced that he intended to launch an investigation of "Reds in movies."[13] His inspiration came from Walt Disney, who one month earlier had been the victim of a well-organized strike of his cartoonists and animators. In the course of a losing battle, Disney had taken out an ad in *Variety* in which he stated: "I am positively convinced that Communistic agitation, leadership, and activities have brought about this strike. . . ."[14] In actuality, the strike had resulted from Disney's overbearing paternalism, high-handedness, and insensitivity.[15]

Not coincidentally, the lead-off witness in the Tenney Committee investigation was Herb Sorrell, who had organized and led the strikers. He was to be followed by John Howard Lawson, Herbert Biberman, and Lionel Stander. The movie executives had been asked to "contribute" funds to the Committee, but had declined. The first "official" probe into the left-wing politics of Hollywood laid a very large egg. The headlines in *Variety* provide some indication of the farcical nature of the undertaking:

July 30: COMMY PURGE BACKFIRES: WITNESSES LINKED TO TENNEY

July 31: TAKING ON ALL THE FANFARE OF A COMIC OPERA

August 1: SORRELL ATTACKS TENNEY COMMITTEE DURING HIS TESTIMONY

August 2: TENNEY COMMITTEE CLOSES HEARINGS

Some six months later, when Tenney made a second foray into Hollywood, he had learned both the magical quality of camouflage words and the importance of linking investigations to reigning national moods. Entitling this effort "an investigation of enemy aliens in the film industry," he quickly secured the cooperation of the producers.[16] Tenney came up empty-handed, but he persisted in his efforts to expose subversion in Hollywood. In autumn 1943 he urged Robert Sproul, president of the University of California, to cancel a writers' congress which the university was co-sponsoring with the Hollywood Writers' Mobilization. Tenney believed that this congress, intended as a forum for discussing the role of writers in the war, was "Communist-inspired" and would trick "a great many innocent people . . . into acting as 'window-dressing' and furthering Communist objectives."[17] His admonitions ignored, Tenney proceeded to hold two days of hearings on the congress and the Writers' Mobilization. Once again the results harmed no careers, but Tenney's increasing preoccupation with the literary world (he also accused the UCLA *Daily Bruin* of "Red" leanings) portended a destructive future. Soon after the war ended Tenney held a fourth investigation of communism in Hollywood, this time focusing on the Screen Writers Guild, which he found to be a "Communist-dominated organization."

Though HUAC disappeared for four years from Hollywood, and the Tenney Committee made few obvious inroads into the left-wing movement—largely because a receptive climate of opinion still did not exist—the seeds of doubt were planted. With management standing apart from its employees, writers and actors feared the effects of HUAC and Tenney publicity on their professional careers. Both the forthrightness of the producers' invitations and the readiness of the named actors to appear before these committees to "clear" themselves indicated the dilemma in which non-radicals were placed by lawfully constituted governmental bodies, even when these bodies acted in a clearly unjust, arbitrary, and vicious manner. Many non-Communists believed that "truth" and "reality" were the strongest weapons to use against HUAC's accusations. The accusations, however, were headlined in the New York *Daily News* (with a circulation in the millions) while the "truth" was headlined in *PM* (with a circulation in the thousands). The liberals also found that the decline of the Popular Front and the fierceness of their divorce from the Communists and fellow travelers had left non-Communists equally exposed to the forces of repression. The cushion of collective, political support, which often serves to mitigate individual fear, had disappeared.

The producers, for their part, warbled in an entirely different key when congressional investigation and pressure focused on the content of their films. Studio executives were at one with most Americans in expressing sympathy for the Allied cause, but somewhat in advance of their audience in hawkishness. While public opinion polls in July 1940, after the fall of France, still registered strongly non-interventionist sentiments in the American public, producers and studio executives Darryl Zanuck, Jack and Harry Warner, Sam Goldwyn, Spyros Skouras, and Walter Wanger were contributing heavily to the interventionist-oriented William Allen White Committee. Not surprisingly, Hollywood output began to include films sympathetic to the British, opposed to the Germans, and supportive of war readiness. The film executives also formed a Motion Picture Committee Cooperating for National Defense, in mid-1940, "to co-ordinate the industry with outside groups in the national emergency." Prior to December 1941 this committee distributed government-made information films throughout the studio-owned theaters. After Pearl Harbor it was renamed the War Activities Committee and cooperated fully and completely with the government.

The isolationist America First Committee, through two of its most prominent members—Senators Burton Wheeler (D-Mont.) and Gerald Nye (D-N.D.)—expressed outrage and opposition to the few features and newsreels which, in Hollywood's tepid fashion, seemed to be promoting American entry into the war. Wheeler accused the movie industry of conspiring with the Roosevelt administration to carry on "a violent propaganda campaign intending to incite the American people to the point where they will become involved in this war."[18] In mid-1941 Wheeler was joined in his anti-Hollywood crusade by Nye and Bennett Clark (D-Mo.), who introduced a resolution, approved by the Senate, calling for an investigation into "prowar" propaganda in motion pictures and radio broadcasts.

The Senate Subcommittee on War Propaganda, chaired by D. Worth Clark (D-Idaho), "investigated" forty-eight films (twenty-five American features, thirteen foreign features, mostly British, and ten RKO *March of Time* newsreels). Seven of the twenty-five, including the anti-fascist *Confessions of a Nazi Spy* (1939) and *Underground* (1941) and the pro-war *Sergeant York* (1941) and *Dive Bomber* (1941), came from the most pro-Roosevelt of the studios, Warner Brothers. But MGM (*Escape* and *Flight Command*), 20th (*Four Sons* and *The Man I Married*), Paramount (*I Wanted Wings* and *One Night in Lisbon*), and Columbia (*Escape to Glory* and *Phantom Submarine*) were well represented. Ironically, only four of the twenty-five were written by future blacklistees: *Confessions of a Nazi Spy* (John Wexley), *Escape* (Marguerite Roberts), *Four Sons* (John Howard Lawson), and *Sergeant York* (Howard Koch); a fifth, *Mystery Sea Raider*, was directed by Edward Dmytryk.[19]

Where the Dies Committee had simply met stubborn resistance from the Left and the SWG, Wheeler and Nye met an overwhelming counteroffensive fron studio management. Banking heavily on pro-Allied public sympathy and cashing in on the anti-Jewish nature of many of the remarks and positions of America First and its senatorial allies, Will Hays, president of the Producers' Association, and the studio executives blasted the Senate Subcommittee and denied the charges. The Producers' Association retained no less an eminence than Wendell Willkie to represent them before the Subcommittee.

The Screen Writers Guild, uninvited, lent its support to the producers' efforts. It chose to fight, however, on a somewhat different terrain. Hays and the producers, by channeling their energy into refuting the Subcommittee's specific charges, implicitly admitted (or at least did not contest) the right of government to investigate free expression; the Guild Board, on the other hand, sent off a telegram to the investigators questioning the constitutionality of the entire proceedings: "[T]he wish to convey a point of view on any aspect of life is implicit in the art of expression; . . . a dangerous contradiction exists between any attempt by legislative action to censor expression . . . and our fundamental Constitutional guarantees."[20] In *PM* John T. McManus posed an even more telling question: why didn't a congressional committee investigate why only 50 of 1,100 films made in the last two years deal with fascism when its assault so clearly threatened everything democratic and American?[21]

The Senate hearings, conducted during September 1941, received very unfavorable coverage from the newspapers. Arthur Krock and Dorothy Thompson, among others, ridiculed the intent and efforts of the senators. Willkie organized and led a very able defense, and finally the Subcommittee's case collapsed of its own emptiness.

The industry's clear victory in Washington demonstrated indisputably that unified, organized, and aroused film producers and executives constituted a formidable force—far stronger than the guilds. This strength was used narrowly and rather selfishly, though, in the defense of the product itself and their control over it; it was not used in defense of constitutional principles. When, six years later, the Thomas Committee came to town combining the strategies of both Nye-Clark and Dies—attacking films in general and film artists in particular—the producers once again defended the former, while they prepared to sacrifice the latter.

The Nye-Clark hearings, ending just before Pearl Harbor and the restoration of liberal-radical unity in a wartime Popular Front, culminated a three-year wave of conservative efforts to dismantle progressive gains of the thirties. Indeed, in retrospect, it seems clear that the war itself, and wartime left-wing unity, constituted but a lengthy interruption in the right wing's reacquisition of power. But for Hitler's invasion of Russia and Japan's attack on the United States, it is likely that the machine of anti-communism and anti-New Dealism would have ground on, despite the setbacks of Dies and Nye-Clark.

The conservatives, however, did not go into hibernation, nor did they forget about Hollywood, during the war. Representative Marion T. Bennett (R-Mo.) said, in a speech before the House: "Hollywood, in its usual extreme style, has apparently lost its head and gone completely overboard in its attempt to make Communism look good. Our temporary military alliance with Russia must not cause us to forget that, except insofar as treatment of Jews is concerned, there is no difference between Communism and nazi-ism as it affects the common man. . . . [Just because the Comintern is dissolved] there is no evidence that the American Communist Party will be dissolved or will not continue to follow the party line originating in Moscow and often reflected on the silver screen." *Mission to Moscow* attracted the wrath of the Republican National Committee, which called it "New Deal propaganda," while *North Star* incurred the enmity of William Randolph Hearst, who ordered all his editors to qualify all mention of that film with the phrase "Bolshevist propaganda."[22]

These verbal attacks were pinpricks compared to the outrages against civil liberties which occurred in the atmosphere of anxiety engendered by the speed and power of the Nazi *Blitzkrieg*. Red-baiting cropped up with increasing regularity in management's dealings with labor (notably during the Vultee Aircraft strike in Los Angeles, the Allis Chalmers strike in Milwaukee, the North American Aviation strike in Inglewood, California, and the Disney strike) and in the government's dealings with the radical opposition. In June 1940, Congress passed the Alien Registration Act, "the first federal peace-time restrictions on speaking and writing by American citizens since the ill-fated Sedition Act of 1798."[23] Mining the nativism which characterized the entire course of American history, and exploiting the wide gap which had now opened between liberals and Communists, conservative elements in Congress and the press lobbied for the Alien Registration Act by labeling the CPUSA "subversive" and its members as "fifth columnists." (This despite the fact that the Communist Party stood firmly on a platform of non-intervention and employed means of propaganda which differed not at all from other prominent anti-war organizations, e.g., the conservative America First Committee or the socialist Keep America out of War Congress. The only difference was that the latter two favored the Nye-Clark resolution.) The bill became law largely due to public confusion and ignorance; there was no widespread enthusiasm for the law.

According to the great First Amendment scholar Zechariah Chafee, not one of the thirty-nine anti-Communist bills introduced into Congress in this era, not even the pernicious Section Two of the Alien Registration Act (commonly known as the Smith Act)—which effectively gave government the right to prosecute a person for his opinions —received much notice from the citizenry.[24] The same indifference manifested itself in public non-reaction to the efforts of state legislatures (in Arkansas, California, Delaware, Indiana, Tennessee, and elsewhere) to remove the Communist Party from the electoral ballot.

The League of American Writers, the National Lawyers Guild, and the American Civil Liberties Union offered the only organized opposition. The League had been founded in New York in 1935 to enlist the support of well-known writers in the anti-fascist struggle. Its leadership was dominated by Communist writers. It is a moot point whether national Party leaders actually controlled the League, because the Communists who staffed the executive positions did not diverge from the Party line. Nevertheless, during the period (1936–39) when the Party line and liberal positions coincided, the LAW succeeded in attracting a broad, non-Communist base of support. Presided over by Waldo Frank, the omnipresent Donald Ogden Stewart, and Dashiell Hammett, the League, at its peak, enlisted nearly eight hundred writers, over one hundred of whom wrote for the film studios.* Both active and aspiring screenwriters—Lawson, Hammett, Maltz, Bessie, Gibney, Bright, Tess Slesinger, and Viola Brothers Shore—played important roles both in the Hollywood chapter and on the National Board. During its heyday in the mid-thirties, the League played a very active part in calling attention to the Loyalist cause in Spain and raising funds for it. Over four hundred writer-members responded to Stewart's appeal, "To the Writers of America." Stewart asked them to express their opinions on fascism: "We wish the whole country to know what is felt by the most sensitive instruments of national life, you American writers. Your verdict has world importance." The answers were printed in *Writers Take Sides: Letters About the War in Spain from 418 American Authors* (New York: League of American Writers, 1938). Only seven writers failed to deliver strong negative statements.

The League also became a dependable conduit of funds to such pro-Loyalist groups as the Medical Bureau of the American Friends of Spanish Democracy, the North American Committee to Aid Spanish Democracy, and the Spanish Societies Confederated to Aid Spain. The Medical Bureau organized the American Ambulance and Hospital Corps for Spain, sending a team of sixteen doctors, nurses, and drivers, and twelve tons of supplies, to the Loyalists. One historian estimates that the various pro-Loyalist committees in the United States raised

---

* The presidents were, for the most part, figureheads; the League was run by its Executive Board. In any case, Stewart's presidency of the League of American Writers represented his last radical political stand. He could not "go along with the American Peace Mobilization campaign of the Communist Party" and thus found himself "reviled by the Right and suspected by the Left." He felt like an "outcast" at the Fourth (and last) League Congress (1941) because of his outspoken partisanship for national preparedness and aid to the democracies. (Stewart, *By a Stroke of Luck*, New York: Paddington Press, 1975, pp. 252–56.) In 1941 Stewart left Hollywood to return to New York and playwriting. Although he came back to Hollywood a few times (in 1945 and again in 1947) to write scripts for MGM, he did not rejoin the ranks of radical political activism.

nearly $2 million for the Republican cause.[25] After Franco's victory in early 1939, the organization focused its attention on neutrality, domestic reaction, and refugee aid.

With the Popular Front dissolving around it, the Communist Party nonetheless sought unity among left-wingers on the basis of their opposition to repressive legislation. The League, in alliance with the ACLU, gave full support to the National Conference for Civil Liberties, which convened in New York in October 1939. (Earl Browder was a featured speaker.) In the aftermath of that conference, the League formed a Civil Liberties Committee to direct a petition campaign aimed at defeating the Alien Registration Act. The petition read:

> WE, THE UNDERSIGNED, being citizens and voters of the United States, respectfully urge the defeat of the Smith Omnibus Anti-Alien Bill, H.R. 5138, which under the pretense of regulating alien activities violates our Bill of Rights, limits freedom of publishing and would lead to unemployment in [the publishing] industry.[26]

These efforts notwithstanding, the Smith Act became law and the fears of its opponents were duly realized. Almost immediately the Justice Department attempted, through the new law, to deport (to Australia) the most effective West Coast labor organizer of the decade, Harry Bridges. As Pacific Coast director of the CIO, Bridges had lent vital support to the Hollywood guilds and democratic labor unions throughout the thirties. Dalton Trumbo now repaid the favor, penning an eloquent defense of Bridges' patriotism and service to American laborers and a harsh indictment of the Smith Act and the motives of the people now enforcing it.[27] Trumbo and other left screenwriters gave generously to the Harry Bridges Defense Committee's efforts, which eventually proved successful.

Isolated successes in cases like Harry Bridges' or the Dies Committee's probes managed, to some extent, to restrain the conservative resurgence, but they could not turn the tide. The recession of 1938, the "excesses" of the New Deal, Roosevelt's serious blunders (Supreme Court-packing and electoral opposition to key southern Democrats), and the xenophobia and isolationism aroused by the threat of a world war all contributed to the strong conservative beachhead in the 76th Congress, which convened in 1939. From their positions in the private sector, there was little progressives and radicals could do except wait for the next attack and try to deal with it as it came. The initiative was no longer in their hands, as it had been in the mid-thirties. The Communist Party, for its part, by adhering intransigently to its revised policy on the European war, not only contributed to its own isolation, weakness, and exposure, but raised serious questions in the minds of even the most sympathetic onlookers about the general capacity of Communists to act critically, morally, and independently.

Keep America out of the War

Three distinct anti-war organizations—each motivated by its own political impulse and background—appeared on the scene during the Phony War (the period of inactivity between the German attack on Poland in September 1939 and the German attack on Norway in April 1940), aiming at deterring American entry into the European armed conflict. America First represented the traditional isolationism of the right wing. The Socialist Party-inspired Keep America out of War Congress fed off the pacifist beliefs of its prime motivator, Norman Thomas. Finally, the Communist Party launched at least four anti-war movements—the American League for Peace and Democracy, the Hollywood Peace Forum, the American Peace Mobilization, and the Keep America out of War Committee (the latter organized by the League of American Writers)—none of which was isolationist or pacifist. The Communist-inspired movements, in fact, strongly supported certain local wars, e.g., Chinese resistance to the Japanese invasion; and they redoubled their efforts to aid the victims of, and refugees from, fascism.

Communist support for American neutrality, obviously, originated in the changed Comintern line which followed the Nazi-Soviet Pact, and was justified by a critique of the foreign policies of the Western democracies. Albert Maltz summed up the feelings and viewpoints of the far Left in early 1940: "Those of us who had been anti-fascist since the rise of Hitler had gone through a period of enormous bitterness because we now saw Hitler beginning the dismemberment of Europe with the assistance of the English and French governments. England had not been interested whatsoever in stopping fascism. This had been demonstrated month after month for seven years."

In fact, according to the research of David T. Catell, Maltz's analysis of British motivations was close to the mark, at least concerning

Spain. Catell has written: "If the nonintervention scheme [of the Western democracies] had to be abandoned, the evidence indicates the British were contemplating a policy of supporting not the Loyalists but rather the rebels. Some evidence of this direction had already come to the attention of the German government [in 1936]. The German chargé d'affaires in Spain reported that *sub rosa* the British were aiding the rebels. . . . Foreign Minister Delbos of France reported to United States Ambassador Bullitt on August 1, 1937, 'Eden had told him frankly that he would prefer to see Franco win. . . .' "28

Communists looked to the Soviet Union as their weather vane, and the Russian arrow pointed in the direction of neutrality because, quite simply, Stalin felt himself isolated from the West and did not care to take on Hitler alone. The official line of the Soviet Union (hence the Comintern and the CPUSA), therefore, attempted to distinguish between a "truly" anti-fascist struggle—which the Communists claimed to advocate—and the current armed conflict among "imperialist" powers—which, they said, was only a repeat of World War I. In the eyes of Comintern leaders, not only had the British and French failed to live up to their collective security promises and treaties; they had also hoped to encourage Hitler to seek his *Lebensraum* at the expense of the Soviet Union. In sum, Maltz, Trumbo, Guy Endore, and other left-wing screenwriters who spoke out or penned anti-war material during this period believed they had legitimate reasons for stating that the events of 1933–40 had none of the earmarks of a budding alliance against fascism. As Trumbo noted in early 1940:

> I bow to no one in my admiration of and my sympathy with the Finnish people. But I am, in the interest of American neutrality, obliged to ask, "why only Finland?" Did the help of the world go out to China, Spain, Ethiopia, Austria, Albania, Czechoslovakia? On the contrary! People who wished to assist these nations in the defense of their democracy were harassed, held up to public ridicule, and finally smeared with the libel of being subversive to democracy! As a result, seven nations fell before brute force and dictatorship.29

A vocal minority of Hollywood screenwriters voiced strong skepticism about the "democratic" nature of any war which the United States might enter on the heels of its refusal to aid the Spanish Republic and its passivity in the face of previous Axis aggressions and

Allied appeasements. The writers who spoke from the forums and symposia organized by the League of American Writers and the various Communist peace mobilizations reiterated that the United States had helped to undermine collective security against fascism. They said, also, that they feared a Rooseveltian "crusade" like Wilson's in World War I, since its outcome could well entail some sort of accommodation with the fascist dictators, a campaign against the Soviet Union and European communism, and the repression of civil liberties at home. After all, argued Trumbo (in his popular novel *Johnny Got His Gun*, 1939) and Endore (in his pamphlet *Let's Skip the Next War*, 1940), the results of the previous war "to make the world safe for democracy" had been death, dismemberment, armed intervention against the Bolshevik Revolution, and the Palmer Raids on radical opposition in the United States. The only way that Roosevelt could have guaranteed to their satisfaction that he would not act likewise would have been by concluding a treaty of alliance with Soviet Russia. Stalin had proved his good faith as an anti-fascist in the Spanish Civil War, Trumbo and his colleagues said, but Roosevelt had yet to do so. Any war the United States declared without a close understanding with the Russians, therefore, smacked of imperialist conflict and would not be "a war for the liberation of people." When Hitler invaded France and the Low Countries, the literary far Left hardened its heart on the issue of aid to the Allies. "To go and support England now, in the face of her whole record during the thirties, is something that we do not think is merited," said Maltz.

While the non-Communist Left split several ways on the question of war and intervention, the Communists in the League of American Writers and the peace mobilizations appeared to launch themselves wholeheartedly into the non-interventionist cause. In retrospect, it is clear that many individuals in the Party harbored doubts; they did not, however, reveal them at the time. Keep America out of War committees were formed in all branches of the League of American Writers; an *Anti-War Bibliography* (sixteen pages of anti-war music, drama, poetry, fiction, memoirs, films, art, periodicals, and pamphlets) was published in 1940; liaisons were established between all similarly motivated left-wing groups (Hollywood Peace Forum, Hollywood Peace Council, etc.); rallies were held—one of which, "America Declares Peace," reportedly drew eight thousand people to the Olympic Auditorium in Los Angeles (on April 6, 1940) to see a "Living Newspaper on Peace," written by Michael Blankfort, Gordon Kahn, and other

leftist screenwriters; speeches, manifestos, and "calls" (circulars) proliferated.

Albert Maltz

One of the most consistent spokespeople for the anti-interventionist
position was a soon-to-be Hollywood screenwriter. By the time Albert
Maltz took over an office in the writers' building at Paramount in 1941,
he had already established a reputation as an ardent left-wing opponent
of United States involvement in the European war. "There were certainly people of my generation [Maltz was born in 1908] who, like
myself, felt the weight of World War One very much. I know that
when I was in college, before I had any political leanings at all, I had a
horror of war and of the uselessness of war as objectified by World
War One. As I grew into young manhood, I read the exposés of war
diplomacy and the deals of the munitions makers, and the enormous
profits. I read the memoirs and novels of Henri Barbusse, John Dos
Passos, e. e. cummings, and ever so many others. The First World War
was definitely part of my consciousness."

It was part of the consciousness of many others of Maltz's and suc-
ceeding generations. Anti-war demonstrations were regular occur-
rences during the thirties. On April 12, 1935, for example, the Los Angeles *Evening Herald and Express* carried a story from the United
Press newswire reporting that a number of student and youth groups
(Student League for Industrial Democracy, American Youth
Congress, National Students League, etc.) were sponsoring a "nationwide student 'strike' against war [which] drew a record number of
youths from college and high school classes today, with indications the
total would approach the student leaders' goal of 150,000 participants."
The report mentioned large demonstrations at Harvard, the University
of Chicago, the University of Kansas, Texas Christian University, and
UCLA.

Maltz's stance on neutrality in 1939–41 grew out of many years of
political activity and thought. The son of a successful, self-made
Lithuanian immigrant, he attended Columbia University, where he
majored in philosophy. Though not expressly "political," Maltz's father, a building contractor, impressed his son with his strong sense of
"humanity." It was the Depression, really, which framed the younger
Maltz's political consciousness and left him open to radical philosophy
and poised for political activity. "The Depression was always with
you," he recalled, "no matter what your status was. I remember the

shanty-towns in Riverside Park [on the Upper West Side of Manhattan], the number of my classmates forced to drop out of school to go to work, and the rapid radicalization of the intellectuals whom I read and admired."

A *New Republic* account of the frame-up of a Cleveland bellboy for a gangland murder precipitated Maltz's first overt "political" activity. He was then a graduate student in the Yale Drama Department, where he had formed a close association with fellow student George Sklar. The two met for dinner one night (in autumn 1931) and discussed the possibility of collaborating on a play based on the Cleveland incident. Prior to that evening, Maltz had written only on personal themes. The resulting effort—*Merry-Go-Round*—was good enough to be staged off Broadway, at the Provincetown Playhouse (in the late spring 1932). It received good reviews, and the next day thirteen uptown theaters made offers for it. The play's exposure of the corrupt politics of a large city dovetailed with the New York State legislature's hearings into the questionable practices of New York Mayor Jimmy Walker's administration, and brought *Merry-Go-Round* a good deal of attention. Too much, in fact, because the city administration attempted to use the city's fire regulations to close down the theater where the play was to open. Newspaper pressure forced the reopening of the theater and *Merry-Go-Round* opened on Broadway after one week's delay. It played for six weeks, but it was not a financial success.

Nevertheless, the subject of the play and the playwrights' tough-minded approach to it attracted the attention of a small group of theatrically inclined left-wingers, led by Charles Remford Walker, who wanted to write and produce plays "oriented to working-class themes" —that is, plays with social meaning. The Theatre Union, which they formed in the fall of 1932, became the first true Popular Front organization in America. Its members came both from working-class (Sklar himself, Paul Peters) and middle-class backgrounds (Maltz and Michael Blankfort). "We at the Theatre Union felt very strongly," Sklar said, "that it was necessary to bring social theater to people for whom it would have meaning, at prices they could afford. We wanted to be professional, but we also wanted to reach a broad working-class audience." The Union was governed by a Board which represented every point on the left-wing political spectrum of the thirties: liberal, socialist, Communist. Some members, however, like Maltz, Sklar, and Blankfort, had no strong ties to a particular organization, but instead shared a devotion to the theater and to their conception of it. Probably for that reason the Theatre Union lasted for six years, finally succumbing, not to political squabbles (although it had some, notably between Communists and Trotskyists), but to lack of funds.

As the Theatre Union thrived, Maltz's own politics began to crystallize. Prior to 1932, the only overtly political issues which aroused him were war profiteering and race discrimination, particularly against blacks. "Things like lynchings, widely publicized with photographs, drove me wild." Groping for a means to give coherence to his feelings and sympathies, Maltz began to read Marxist pamphlets—Marx, Lenin, Plekhanov, and Engels (especially Engels' *Socialism: Utopian and Scientific*). At the same time he traveled around the United States, visiting labor trouble spots and observing the worst scenes of Depression America. The plays and short stories he wrote reflected the desperate situation of coal miners in Ohio, Pennsylvania, and West Virginia, the depredations of vigilante groups in the midwestern farm country, and the success of sit-down strikes in the automobile plants in Detroit. Maltz's writings of the thirties, including his novels, provide a sensitive tour through the experiences of the lower classes during the Depression decade. At his best in the short story genre, Maltz crafted compassionate, naturalistic depictions of the denizens of Bowery flophouses and slum tenements, and powerful evocations of the personal and social costs of racism, exploitation, strikebreaking, etc. Two of his best pieces, "The Happiest Man in the World" and "An Afternoon in the Jungle," capture in fiction what the young Karl Marx had discovered in the 1840s: people need to work to maintain their human dignity, and, when deprived of work, they are reduced to the degrading subhuman status which characterizes the déclassés and *Lumpenproletariat*.

In 1935 Maltz, his political-social consciousness broadened by the rapacity of Tojo, Mussolini, and Hitler, became a member of the Communist Party. These international predators "were encountering real opposition only from the Communist Party and the Soviet Union," Maltz says now. For the rest of the decade, Maltz threw himself into Party political work: attending and organizing meetings, writing pamphlets, making speeches. He managed to produce three more plays and his first novel (*The Underground Stream*) in these years, but they, too, were stamped with their author's political preoccupations. Maltz also devoted much of his time to turning out copy for the League of American Writers and an anti-bigotry magazine he helped found, *Equality*, whose editorial board included Franz Boas, Bennett Cerf, Dashiell Hammett, Moss Hart, Lillian Hellman, Prince

Loewenstein, Dudley Nichols, Dorothy Parker, Donald Ogden Stewart, and Ernst Toller. He also wrote the introduction to the LAW's pamphlet on anti-Semitism, "*We Hold These Truths* . . . ,"[30] and wrote and edited (and subsidized) articles in *Equality* to expose and counteract the impact of Father Coughlin and the Dies Committee. Like the World War I nationalists whom Maltz had read about in his youth, he saw in the chauvinists of the late thirties deliberate nurturers of political reaction camouflaged behind patriotic and religious rhetoric.

Obviously, Maltz's skepticism concerning the impulses of certain sectors of American government and business was, for him, nothing new. In the play *Peace on Earth*, produced by the Theatre Union in 1933, Maltz and Sklar had one of their protester-characters enunciate many of the same themes which they themselves would espouse in 1940 as members of the League's Keep America out of War Committee: "The bosses in Wall Street and Washington build up war fever—in the newspapers, in the movies, over the radio—build up hate, build up hysteria. . . . When we go out to fight it's not gonna be for the bosses. It's gonna be for a new world—for a world where there won't be any wars."[31]

Left-Wing Anti-Interventionism

The LAW's anti-war campaign failed to galvanize the Left the way other issues had a few years earlier. Its analysis of the motivation and effects of English, French, and American foreign policy in the thirties was, to a large extent, correct. The Left, however, drew faulty conclusions from, and based wrong-headed activity on, its premises. And despite their public self-assurance, many left-wingers knew this. It was one thing to argue that England and France, and even the United States, acted like craven appeasers of Axis aggression. It was quite another, however, to conclude that therefore the Western democracies were the moral and political equivalents of fascism and should be unaided or opposed in their struggle against the Third Reich; to say, as the CPUSA did in mid-October 1939: "The distinction between fascist and non-fascist governments has lost its former significance as a determining factor in international relations."[32]

The weakness of the Left's position in this matter was clearly exposed at a forum held in July 1940 at the Hollywood chamber of commerce. Howard Emmett Rogers, one of the most conservative screenwriters in Hollywood, after listening to the radicals' remarks presented his own views (beginning with the statement, "I, as most of you know, am a reactionary"). He noted that in the speeches of Carey McWilliams, Dalton Trumbo, and Theodore Dreiser there had been numerous denunciations of the perfidy of Great Britain, France, and Poland, but scarcely one mention of the perfidy of Adolf Hitler. "You may," Rogers said, "go into lengthy discussions as to the background of England and you may say that England should be punished. But is there any nation in the world today so low in the estimation of any man or woman in this hall tonight that he or she would want to see that nation conquered and destroyed by Hitler and Nazism?"[33]

For all their proclamations of "unremitting opposition to fascism," many League members were privately troubled by Rogers' question. The Nazi-Soviet Pact, with its secret territorial arrangements, did, after all, make the Soviet Union, if not an appeaser, then certainly an accommodator (some said ally) of the Axis. Moreover, the strategic about-face which Russian foreign policy entailed for all the world's Communist parties left the Reds and their allies highly vulnerable to the charge of inconsistency and uncritical subservience. The League and its allied organizations consequently worked in an atmosphere of increasing isolation, antagonism, and self-doubt. After the autumn of 1939, American public opinion grew decidedly hostile to the Soviet Union, particularly during the Russian invasion of Finland. No careful rationalizations by Party members could justify this act of Soviet aggression. Unfortunately the radical Left, including most Communist and fellow-traveler screenwriters, attempted, falteringly, to do so. They thus left themselves so morally lame that the arguments they did make, some of which ought to have been more convincing than they were, went unheeded. The shrill anti-communism of the conservative victors of 1938 and the torrent of abuse from anti-Soviet liberals in 1939 would likely have drowned out reason anyway, but still, the Communists needlessly detracted from their own cause and unintentionally aided that of their enemies.

Outspoken anti-interventionism by the Communists after the Pact fueled a particularly vicious brand of liberal anti-communism which had its genesis in the editorial offices of the New Leader. Two days after the Pact, its editors professed not to be surprised, claiming that "it was only a question of time [until] the ruthless killers of Moscow and Berlin would embrace each other."[34] A newly formed group—the League for Cultural Freedom and Socialism—attracted the participation of former Marxists like James Burnham, Dwight MacDonald, William Phillips, Philip Rahv, and Bertram Wolfe, and liberals like

V. F. Calverton, Melvin J. Lasky, and Harold Rosenberg. The League consigned the Soviet Union squarely to the camp of international reaction and affirmed that "among advanced intellectual circles in the United States the most active forces of reaction today are the so-called cultural organizations under control of the Communist Party."[85] Nor did one have to be an intellectual anti-Communist to oppose the Soviet Union in these days. Popular opinion, as measured by a Gallup Poll in December 1939, showed 99 per cent of the respondents to be pro-Finland, while an analysis of newspaper commentary revealed a strong trend of support for a German-Allied alliance against the Soviet Union.[36]

Hostility from without and self-doubt and hesitation from within hampered the left wing's anti-interventionist efforts. Problems appeared almost immediately after the New Year. Screenwriter (later novelist) Irving Stone resigned from the Board of the Hollywood chapter of the League of American Writers in January 1940, because the Board voted down two of his resolutions. Stone had opposed the recognition of the newly formed Los Angeles Council to Keep America at Peace after that body had characterized the European war as "imperialistic." On the contrary, Stone argued, "the war is one of Democracy versus Nazism and we should cooperate with the Allies to the utmost to crush Nazism." John Howard Lawson challenged Stone's interpretation and the latter's motion lost, 8–1. Stone then proposed that any matter pertaining to the international situation be referred to the membership before the Board took any action on or made any statement about it. This, too, was defeated, and Stone resigned, saying that he "considered his work on the Board personally to consist of [having been] a one-man guard against Communist influence."[37]

Three months later, on April 30, at a plenary session of the League's National Board, Eleanor Flexner reported on the difficulties the Keep America out of War Committee was encountering. "We found," she said, "that we were working as a small isolated group lacking effectiveness. . . . We have tried different types of projects but always we have encountered difficulties in carrying through a consistent line."[38] By June, interventionism had surfaced within the Board itself. Oliver La Farge, a novelist, proposed a resolution containing a strongly worded anti-fascist statement and urging "aid to those who are battling against the Fascist powers." The National Board lost all pretense of unanimity in the debate over La Farge's motion. It barely voted down (10–7) a proposal to submit the motion to a membership referendum. Lawson, Maltz, and Philip Stevenson voted with the majority, but Donald Ogden Stewart and Ella Winter voted with the minority.[39] Nine months later, in March 1941, the Hollywood chapter of the League held a meeting of its Peace Subcommittee to inquire into its ineffectiveness. Answers and improvements were not forthcoming.[40]

The difficult situation in which the diplomacy of the Soviet Union had placed American Communists was magically erased by the diplomacy of Nazi Germany. On June 21, 1941, a Communist front organization, the American Peace Mobilization, called for the observance of a "National Peace Week." The next day, June 22, the Wehrmacht invaded Russia. Literally overnight the APM rescinded its call and lifted its "perpetual peace vigil" in front of the White House. A few weeks later it was announced that the American Peace Mobilization would now be known as the American People's Mobilization, espousing a program of aid to Russia and the Allies.[41] With the Soviet Union enlisted in the struggle, the war—in Communists' eyes—was no longer "imperialistic," but a crusade against fascism. Naturally, the League of American Writers executed the same reversal as its kindred Communist front organizations. In July a "call" went out urging all writers to take "all immediate and necessary steps in support of Great Britain and the Soviet Union to insure the military defeat of the fascist aggressors."[42] Six months later, following Pearl Harbor, the League called "on all American writers to put their training, talent, and devotion to the service of our country."[43]

Panzers in the Ukraine must have seemed a godsend to Communists, especially those in Hollywood. Certainly the policy shift which the invasion entailed occurred much more swiftly, explicably, and comfortably to them than the shocking 1939 turnabout had, but it did not reassure fellow left-wingers and liberals, who continued to worry about Communist independence and trustworthiness. Fight for Freedom members, though they decided that they would support Roosevelt's efforts to aid the Soviet Union, issued a press release on June 23, 1941, which stated: "We repudiate here and now support which comes from members of the Communist Party or their sympathizers."[44] David Dubinsky commented in his recently published memoirs: "The ease with which they could turn round and round simply confirmed the feelings I had always had about their untrustworthiness as allies."[45]

Popular opinion, however, was now strongly pro-Soviet and patriotic, and the need for a united war effort pushed these questions, as well as anti-communism, temporarily into the background. A Gallup

Poll in July revealed that 72 per cent of the public favored a Russian victory while only 4 per cent favored Germany. Nearly all major periodicals either joined in the pro-Russian chorus or maintained a discreet silence during the summer and fall of 1941.[46] The resurrected National Council of American-Soviet Friendship could now attract to its congresses government luminaries like Henry Wallace, Harold Ickes, Donald M. Nelson (president of Sears and head of the War Production Board), and Fiorello La Guardia. Messages of good will flowed in from Henry Morgenthau, Edward Stettinius, Sam Rayburn, Dwight Eisenhower, and many others. Between September 1941 and December 1946 Russian War Relief collected almost $85 million in cash and kind for shipment to the Soviet Union.[47]

Widespread sympathy for Russia, however, could not solve the CPUSA's basic dilemma, dramatized in these twenty-four months by the vicissitudes of international events: a permanent discrepancy between the stated and real determinants of its actions and the effect of this gap on its position in American politics. However much the ideas and ideals of socialism and progressive action meant to individual Communists, the fact remained that the political organization to which they adhered took its instructions from the Executive Committee of the Communist International, which was entirely controlled by the Soviet government and subservient to Russian national interest. For all the justifications which could be, and were, put forth to explain and rationalize the switches in the line of the American party, and for all the words expended to try to demonstrate the close links between Soviet national interest and the cause of socialism and progress at home and abroad, the discrepancies remained.

It was hard to understand, for example, how a person who had vociferously fought fascism throughout the mid- and late thirties could suddenly find little to choose between fascism and the democracies, however flawed, of Great Britain and France, unless his outlook were determined by the current needs and rationale of Stalin's foreign office. In the same vein, it was hard to understand how a person who again and again would put himself physically on the line to defend Sacco and Vanzetti or the Scottsboro boys or to advance trade unionism among California migrant workers would yet rationalize the forced collectivization of millions of peasants and the purging of many thousands of fellow Communists as "necessary" unless his outlook were determined by the current needs and rationales of Stalin's departments of agriculture and justice.

American Party members, including the film people, did not have to experience firsthand the KGB, the Gulag, the terror, the thousands and millions of executions and forced migrations. They lived, on the contrary, with an abiding sense of strength and optimism for being members of an international political organization which had made a successful revolution and formed the backbone of radical and progressive action in the United States, France, and other countries. Since public acknowledgment or intra-Party criticism of the flaws of the international Communist movement would lead to exclusion from "the only group seriously fighting fascism," and since Stalin's worst crimes were discussed only by obviously hostile or reactionary sources, and since the abrupt diplomatic shifts were uncomfortable but, in the Communists' eyes, defensible, one could, in 1939, justify to oneself continued Party membership.

Albert Maltz does not deny that adverse information about the Soviet Union existed during the thirties. He said, however, "it seemed to be part of a decade-long fabric of lying and intervention on the part of world capitalism against the single socialist state." Maltz knew nothing about the toll of collectivization, the depredations of the KGB, or the Gulag; he did know about the purge trials and the claims made against their validity. "But if you were convinced of what the trials were," he now says, "it was easy to ignore the counter-information. My shining eyes blinded me—I could not see past the tremendous social advances the Soviet state had made."†

Still, the dilemma remained, and it could not be avoided through candor. Public acknowledgment that the Party was formally indentured to the Kremlin's policy line would have been unacceptable in the United States, where Party ranks were filled with devotees of socialism and progressive reform and where alliances with other left-wing parties and organizations were frequently necessary. Outside of the Soviet Union itself, very, very few Communists joined the Party to work for the advancement of Soviet national interest. Frenchmen, Italians, and Spaniards adhered to their national CPs for the same reasons of

---

† A latter-day believer in another cause—anti-communism—also suffered from tunnel vision of a similar sort. Using the same illogic, Irving Kristol defended the blinkered vision which kept him unaware of the CIA involvement in the organizations and periodicals for which he worked during the fifties: "Rumors there were, but they were not particularly credible. Most of these rumors issued from sources—Left-wing, anti-American, or both— that would have been happy to circulate them, true or not, and one discounted them in advance." ("Memoirs of a 'Cold Warrior,'" New York Times Magazine, February 11, 1968, p. 25.)

domestic progress and patriotism which motivated American radicals. Once in the Party, however, defense of the world's first socialist state became a fundamental concern and duty. As a result, Party members frequently had to subordinate their other international and national aims to the task of supporting Stalin's foreign policy.

Party members may not have felt they were betraying themselves in the circumstances of 1939–41 (and 1945–present), but the Party itself seriously compromised its position in the American political arena. The lack of a revolutionary tradition or situation in the United States meant that the Communist Party depended on liberal good will for realization of many of its goals (anti-racist legislation, trade union protection, etc.) and liberal support against right-wing witch-hunts. The Popular Front demonstrated these needs. The post-Pact actions of the American Communists led to the dissolution of the alliance with liberals and non-aligned left-wingers. This event, in turn, led to a perceptible strengthening of the position of traditional right-wing anti-communism—the more so as moderate liberals themselves increasingly gave vent to their own brand of anti-communism. The liberal-Communist split was only superficially papered over during the war; the followers of Dunne and Douglas wanted nothing more to do with Communists. The real significance of the split would not emerge until later on in the new decade when, the war over and Roosevelt dead, the right-wing resurgence was again in full stride. Then the loss of the liberal alliance would prove terribly damaging to the CPUSA.

Hollywood at War

The Hollywood film industry was among the most enthusiastic and cooperative of recruits to the United States war effort. Virtually everyone, mogul and grip alike, committed himself to all varieties of war support activity, from making propaganda films to buying bonds. The motives of different individuals were not necessarily equally altruistic, however. The patriotism of the movie executives was encouraged by a loving concern for profits and industrial benefits. One immediate boon which their loudly trumpeted Americanism won for studio management was escape from wartime government control of film making. In return for autonomy, the studios willingly adopted strict self-censorship and their own extraordinary wartime regulations and measures. The newly created Research Council of the Motion Picture Academy of Arts and Sciences, which included all the majors, the important independents (Goldwyn, Wanger, Disney, Hal Roach, Republic), and representatives of the three main talent guilds, distributed the assignments and oversaw the production of training, historical, and public relations films made by the Army Pictorial Division. There were, nevertheless, definite limits to the self-sacrifice of the movie executives. The revelations of the Truman Senate investigating committee, the criticisms made by the head of the Office of War Information's Motion Picture Bureau, Lowell Mellett, and the complaints lodged by the generals directing the United States occupation forces in postwar Europe all attest to the strong vein of self-interest and economic motivation within the film executives' well-publicized "Win-the-War" campaign.

The Truman committee hearings revealed that the training films which the Hollywood studios made under contract with the Army Pictorial Division were allocated to studios and cost-budgeted in such a way as to serve as sponges to soak up the large overhead which reduced commercial film making no longer absorbed. Lowell Mellett carried on a running battle with studio executives over whose point of view, Hollywood's or the government's, would appear in industry-produced films about the war. Less than a year into the war his office scored the industry for "laying excessive emphasis on the blood-and-thunder aspects of the war," ignoring the "sacrifice which will be made on [sic] every American family in the next year," and failing to portray the "virtues of American life in such a way as to give our Allies a genuine understanding of the American people." And as early as 1944, the Army made it clear that they preferred dealing with the Overseas Branch of the Office of War Information in the matter of distribution of commercial films in liberated portions of Europe—they found the government agency "easier to handle than private enterprise."[48]

At a lower rung, the war opened up important opportunities for the more politically conscious artists to express some of their viewpoints in Hollywood films. A good example was Donald Ogden Stewart's strongly anti-fascist screenplay for MGM, *Keeper of the Flame* (1943). Louis B. Mayer gave his very best talent to the film—actors Spencer Tracy and Katharine Hepburn, director George Cukor. Stewart, who had previously been as famous for his light-comedy screenplays about East Coast socialites as for his "extracurricular" political activities, was given this unusual (for him) assignment because anti-fascism was no longer "premature" and it made good sense to use a screenwriter who knew something about the subject. The Communist screenwriter was delighted. "Here was my compensation,"

Stewart wrote in his memoirs, "for the sabotage of my radical attempt to do my bit; here were my 'war aims' which coincided, I believed, with those of Roosevelt and all good Americans. . . ."[49] Sylvia Jarrico, a fellow Party member, expressed similar feelings about the renewed coincidence of Communist and democratic American goals: "We were heart and soul in the war effort. We felt ideologically well equipped for it. And we were glad to have so many others with us now. We now had a government-sponsored answer to those who said Nazism and communism were the same thing."

Keeper of the Flame was the film which Stewart, in two decades of highly successful movie writing, was "most proud to have been connected with." A surprising statement, because the film is tedious, wooden, and heavy-handed and demonstrates forcefully the difference between an internalized Marxist aesthetic and the simple mouthing of the conventional left-wing point of view. It was this latter aspect that made the movie so precious in Stewart's eyes; at last he had the opportunity to put in Hepburn's mouth a précis of the Left's position on domestic fascism: "They didn't call it fascism; they dressed it up in red, white, and blue and called it Americanism." The widowed heiress whom Hepburn portrays then goes on to enumerate the specific components of her late husband's "Americanism"—anti-Semitism, opposition to organized labor, racism, etc.

Nevertheless, the war films, deficient as they were in terms of sophisticated aesthetic or political consciousness, illustrate well the unique opportunity which the war occasionally conferred upon some of the left-wing screenwriters—the opportunity, finally, to meld their politics and their vocation. The Hollywood Left benefited in other ways from the war as well. While radical cadres in other areas and other industries were dispersed by the war, their left-wing activities blunted or diverted by the drive for victory, Hollywood screenwriters avoided, to a large extent, this diaspora of militants. In fact, the left wing within the Screen Writers Guild actually strengthened its toehold in the organization. Most of the important and well-known screenwriters, radicals and conservatives alike, were too old for the draft and devoted their efforts to propaganda work at home. A number, of course, went overseas. Michael Wilson and Michael Blankfort joined the Marines; Edward Huebsch and Ben Maddow fought with the Army in Europe; Budd Schulberg enlisted in the Navy; Arthur Strawn and Stanley Rubin, in the Air Force. A lucky few were able to continue to use their film skills: Waldo Salt, Philip Dunne, Robert Riskin, Leonardo Bercovici, Ken Englund, and Bernard

Schoenfeld worked for the film division of the Office of War Information; while Carl Foreman and Leopold Atlas worked with Frank Capra's unit in the Signal Corps. One writer, Robert Meltzer, died while serving with the Army Rangers in Europe.

Some writers, however, like Ring Lardner, Jr., Dorothy Parker, and John Sanford, discovered that even in the arm-linking fraternalism of the war, their past hemmed them in. Much as all three wanted to contribute their services to the war effort, the "excesses" of their "premature anti-fascism" were well enough known to keep the armed forces from employing them. Lardner wrote, "it turned out I was wanted wherever I applied, and then again, on second thought, I wasn't."[50] Sanford, who had legal training, as well as writing skills, could not join any branch of the service even in a civilian advisory capacity. He believes that directors Frank Capra and William Wyler, both of whom were commissioned officers, had been warned by the FBI to "stay away from Sanford." Dorothy Parker could neither enlist in the WACs nor obtain a passport as a war correspondent.[51] Sanford and Parker and Lardner remained somewhat isolated examples—anomalies at the time, auguries only in retrospect.

One could say that the period 1941 to 1945 was the best the radical screenwriters would know. They not only came in out of the political cold, but also, within the confines of the entertainment/propaganda industry which employed them, they were able to convert from heterodoxy to orthodoxy without losing their integrity. The studios called on the radicals' political knowledge and experience more than ever before or again; more so than in any other period, the radicals were assigned material congenial to their political and social consciousness. This "freedom" can be easily overstated, of course. Studio guidelines, producers' blue pencils, and the weight of the Hollywood aesthetic (genre requirements, studio pictorial style, etc.) functioned as usual during the war years, as did the customary strictures of the radicals' self-censorship, to produce scripts which even the Hollywood right wing could not fault.

Leftist screenwriters, from newcomers to Hollywood like Maltz to prominent veterans like Stewart, admitted to feeling "grateful" for war picture assignments. In view of the especially low level of the comedies, musicals, and melodramas which the studios churned out during the war, films like *Destination Tokyo* (Maltz), *Action in the North Atlantic* (Lawson), *Blood on the Sun* (Cole), and *The Cross of Lorraine* (Lardner) represented the closest thing available to "social content" or "topical" movies. In contrast to all other types of films—

which declined even by Hollywood's low standards of realism—
war pictures were permitted a potential for authenticity and ma-
ture treatment which the front office granted nothing else. The
radical writers sensed this and strove to make the most of the artistic
and political freedom opened up for them. Writing in *New Masses*,
screenwriters Paul Trivers and Robert Rossen asserted that the experience of the war was producing "far-reaching effects in the motion picture" and on the makers of motion pictures, producers included. Even
audience tastes had been upgraded—the war had matured viewers' attitudes to the point where they were much more receptive to "responsible" films.[52] The radical screenwriters were determined to cultivate
this new public taste and not to offend or destroy it with typical
Hollywood excess and exploitation, or heavy-handed propaganda.

Even the most friendly right-wing witness, writer-producer James
K. McGuinness, testified to HUAC that he could find no fault with
the performance of the radicals during World War II, especially with
the content of their scripts. McGuinness said that Hollywood
"profited from reverse lend-lease because during the [war] the Communist and Communist-inclined writers in the motion-picture industry
were given leave of absence to become patriotic. During that time [for
example] under my general supervision Dalton Trumbo wrote two
magnificent patriotic scripts, 'A Guy Named Joe,' and 'Thirty Seconds Over Tokyo. . . .' "[53]

McGuinness' conclusions were substantiated in a more systematic
fashion by sociologist Dorothy Jones, who analyzed the content of the
war movies written by the screenwriter members of the Hollywood
Ten. Jones found no evidence of subversion in the screenplays; she
discovered, rather, that "the Ten were credited with an impressive
number of top-quality war films which made a positive contribution
to the government's war information program."[54]

Jones failed to point out, however, that the Ten's war films also
avoided the wearisome formulae which weakened the output of other
screenwriters of the period. While there was nothing particularly
Marxist or Stalinist about the radicals' screenplays—that is, they did
not promote the cause of revolution, or even mention the problem of
the Second Front‡—they nevertheless did manage to avoid overem-

---

‡ Communists and fellow travelers were deeply disturbed by the delay on
the part of Roosevelt and Churchill in opening up a Second Front in Western Europe, failing thereby to relieve the Soviet Union of the massed
weight of the German Wehrmacht: "From early 1941 until the Normandy
landings of June 1944, the entire strength of the British Empire and Com-

phasizing or overdramatizing the role of the extraordinary individual (the war hero) and instead focused on the teamwork and suffering of the average soldiers. Scripts like those for *Sahara* (Lawson), *Thirty Seconds Over Tokyo* (Trumbo), *Objective Burma* (Bessie and Cole), or *Pride of the Marines* (Maltz) stressed the collective effort of the front-line troops, and they presented as authentic a picture of the reality of war as it was possible to do in Hollywood. Finally, the Ten's scripts avoided, for the most part, the more overt forms of jingoism and racism which marred many other Hollywood war films—e.g., references to "Japs," "yellow dogs," "Krauts," etc.

Thus the Hollywood Left was patriotic, but in its own fashion, coincident with mainstream war enthusiasm, but not entirely congruent. Though Communists and fellow travelers now worked for victory as assiduously as their erstwhile foes (liberals and conservatives alike), it was toward a particular idea of victory—an Allied victory *with*, not at the expense of, the Soviet Union. To that end, the Hollywood radicals lobbied for the opening of an immediate Second Front in Europe to end the war more quickly, take the pressure off the sorely pressed Red Army, and prevent the war from becoming (as many of them still feared it might) a disguised effort to destroy the Soviet regime. In the same vein—as the domestic counterpart to protecting the Communist partner among the Allied powers—the Hollywood Left, as we shall see below, worked to protect the New Deal and the rights of certain minorities at home.

At the same time, however, radicals succumbed to a certain blindness in their patriotic commitment. Noted Paul Jarrico, "during the war, the CPUSA was more patriotic than anyone, so fucking patriotic in fact that we didn't protest the internment of the Japanese or the prosecution of the Trotskyites under the Smith Act. Yes, we were right in the mainstream." Jarrico's bill of particulars could be amended to include the failure to protest the bombing of civilians in Germany and Japan or the restrictions placed on the right of labor unions to strike by the Smith-Connally Act of 1943. Indeed, the Communist Party remained adamantly anti-strike until mid-1945. Moreover, radicals of all stripes accepted the Atlantic Charter as a worthy state-

---

monwealth engaged between two and eight divisions of the principal Axis power, Germany. During all but the first six months of the same period, the Soviet Union withstood, contained, and eventually repulsed, an average of about 180 German divisions." (John Bagguley, "The World War and the Cold War," in David Horowitz, ed., *Containment and Revolution*, Boston: Beacon Press, 1969, p. 95.)

ment of war aims even though it had been written without the collaboration or concurrence of the Soviet Union, and was as filled with vague promises and as empty of concrete programs for implementation as the Fourteen Points of Woodrow Wilson had been. In short, the Communists and fellow travelers, in the name of national unity, chose to temper certain of their traditional stands and curtail some of their usual activity.

The Communist Party

A new generation enrolled in the CPUSA during the years of the Grand Alliance against the Axis. Its motivations and concerns differed as sharply from the generation of the late thirties as the latter, according to one of its members, Sylvia Jarrico, differed from that of the early thirties: "The older writers, especially those from New York, were accustomed to struggle and hardship." Men like Lawson, Ornitz, Faragoh, and Cole carried their years of service to the Party as badges of trustworthiness and signs of doctrinal superiority. The newcomers of the late Popular Front era—the Jarricos, the Butlers, Ring Lardner, Jr., Budd Schulberg, etc.—made the Old Guard somewhat uneasy. "We were," Sylvia remembers, "more obviously middle class [than they] and less inclined to talk in revolutionary terms and to come to grips with the hard questions [e.g., revolution, proletarianization, etc.]. They were critical of us for being so easygoing."

Such distinctions became even more decisive in the war years when the numbers passing through the Hollywood branches markedly increased. To become a Communist in the very early thirties, before the Hollywood talent branches were launched, was a considered act of political judgment. Len De Caux, already a veteran labor organizer, wrote of his cautious approach to the CP in the early thirties: "I certainly couldn't see socialism just around the corner. What I saw ahead was a chopping block to which I preferred not to volunteer my head. I wanted to be red but not dead."[55] Most mid- and late-decade joiners enrolled in the rush of great emotion aroused by the wave of fascist aggression and the outbreak of the Spanish Civil War. A number of Popular Front Communists, like Donald Ogden Stewart, were not ideologues but idealists, propelled far more by their liberal temperament and an emotional commitment to dramatic causes than by any meditated engagement to communism, social revolution, or the Soviet Union. The dozens of men and women who entered the Hollywood branches after 1941, however, were more overtly motivated by their

"Americanism" and impelled forward by a leftist brand of patriotism and the wartime alliance of communism and liberal democracy. Members of the CP war generation, like blacklisted screenwriter Bess Taffel, can still recall their feelings:

> My awareness of country and my patriotism began when I was meeting Communists. Up until that time, the word "patriotism" was hardly in my consciousness. I did not feel patriotic. When I came to Hollywood, I met politically-conscious people, often people whom I had long admired and whose books I had read. I saw them now as citizens who loved their country and were very concerned about it. They loved it enough to want to correct the evils and inequities they saw. I suddenly felt deeply imbued with a sense of country, with a feeling that I belonged to a country. Up to that point I had had no consciousness of it. *I now felt I belonged to the United States.* We were at war and the people who were the most active in the war effort, the most organized, were the Communists. I could disagree with none of their stands. I wanted to belong; I was impatient to belong. [Her emphasis.]

Even more than the "generation" of the late thirties, the Hollywood Communists of the war years were primarily committed to contingent Party stands and positions rather than to Party ideology, structure, or identity. Once again membership in the CPUSA appealed to large numbers of liberals and radicals as the best, most efficient, and most dramatic form available to fight for a specific goal. And once again the Party hierarchy lowered its admission standards and enrolled anyone who seemed willing to walk a mile or two with it. Party leadership strove to downplay the sectarian, conspiratorial, revolutionary, and hierarchical sides of communism, and to emphasize its role in the United Front at home and in the Grand Alliance abroad. Toward that goal, on May 15, 1943, the Soviet Union announced the dissolution of the Communist International.

If the Party relaxed its vigilance as to the "quality" of recruits, the recruits also heeded less the dangers of enrollment in the Red ranks. Thirties Communists, both the "older" and "younger" generations, entered the Party with some knowledge of, if not personal experience with, the Red scare and the repression of the twenties. Particularly in the very early part of the decade, being a Communist was fraught with clear and present risk. Later, all Party members of the thirties suffered through the 1938–41 "chill" as the conservative resurgence and the Nazi-Soviet Pact isolated the CP from its allies and divorced it from the mainstream of American politics. Even the dullest of thirties Communists saw in such repressive legislation as the Alien Registration Act of 1940 the specter of full-scale reaction.

The arrival of the "American War" and the new Popular Front came as a deliverance to thirties Communists. The signs that pointed to the Party's reintegration into the mainstream seemed to contemporaries far stronger than the signs that the new Front was purely a contingent and superficial façade, papering over the profound fissures and tensions which remained from the thirties experience. Since the rebuilt Front seemed to its Communist constituency more solidly based than the old one, they did not place a very high priority on instructing prospective new members about the possibilities of reaction and retribution. As a result of all these war-induced factors, the forties' entering class was far removed from the psychological as well as the actual reality of repression. Winning the war dominated every Party member's concern.

Despite the fact that veteran Communists delighted in the rehabilitation of the Soviet Union in American public opinion, the newer Party members proved to be considerably less animated than their forebears by a utopian vision of the Soviet Union or of a Communist or socialist future in America. Theory was not stressed as much as it had been a few years earlier, while Russia stood more as an ally in the effort to defend democracy than as the determinant of strategy and policy. Instead of criticizing Western democracy, forties Communists were intent on defending it; no longer the victims of the economic crisis of capitalism, they depended upon its rapidly recovered strength to supply the material of victory. Forties Communists, finally, did not see themselves as defending the Soviet Union, but the "free world," of which Russia was considered to be a part. United States and Soviet war propaganda, of course, did all it could to encourage such perceptions by linking closely the American and Soviet "democracies." The tone was established in films like those director Frank Capra made for the War Department, whose well-distributed "Why We Fight" series lauded the Soviet defense of "basic freedoms," leaning on quotations from, among others, Generals George Marshall and Douglas MacArthur. Stalin, for his part, spoke of "independence" and "democratic liberties" as often as he drew public breath in these years. And the statements which issued from the Allied leaders who had conferred at Moscow, Teheran, Yalta, or even Potsdam were as studded with the terms "democracy" and "democratic" as speeches at a Fourth of July picnic.

In sum, Axis aggression, by creating a new international alliance and restoring an old domestic alliance, allowed the CPUSA to reverse itself and proclaim a patriotism and an anti-fascism acceptable to a broad current of Americans. Once again, and to an even greater extent than in the thirties, being a Communist did not automatically insulate one from the center ring of American political activity.

Popular Front Redivivus (1941–44)

In spite of the new activity and optimism which writing scripts for war films injected into their professional lives, the radical screenwriters of the war years still derived their greatest satisfaction from and expended their greatest efforts in "extracurricular" work. War and refugee relief organizations sprouted up all over Hollywood. Fund-raisings, bond sales, blood drives, and war charities of all types proliferated. Older organizations like the Communist Party and the Motion Picture Democratic Committee (now renamed the Hollywood Democratic Committee to appeal to a broader base) underwent a renaissance after the stagnant days of the Phony War period. Concurrently, a new organization, the Hollywood Writers' Mobilization, managed to unify a wide range of politically different writers. For all its structural flaws—far more apparent to posterity than contemporaries—the new Popular Front emerged with a broader and apparently stronger base than anything that had gone before it.

So great was the mutual liberal-Communist enthusiasm for victory that the new Front succeeded in mobilizing behind it a greater variety of national and Hollywood labor organizations—the CIO, regional trade union councils, many individual unions, the talent guilds—than its ancestor of the late thirties. In Hollywood, the Screen Writers Guild stood, as usual, in the vanguard. On December 9, 1941, its membership dispatched a telegram to Roosevelt pledging the SWG's full support for the war effort. Locally, the Guild established its own defense committee to work closely with the Los Angeles Civilian Defense Committee. Screenwriter "captains" were appointed at each of the majors and charged with the responsibility of marshaling writers to work on civil defense projects. By mid-January 1942, the Guild had forged direct links with such federal information (read: propaganda) agencies as the Office of Government Reports, the Office of the Coordinator of Information, and the Office of Facts and Figures.[56] Also the Guild played a prominent official role in the work of the Motion Picture Committee for Hollywood (which sold war bonds), the Unity for Victory Committee (composed of the labor unions of Los Angeles County and dedicated to harmonious labor-management relations), and, in close collaboration with the Screen Actors Guild, the California Federation of Labor (which staged a weekly radio show, "This Is Our America").

The most impressive and best-known wartime achievement of the movie writers acting through their Guild, however, was the creation of an independent war propaganda and information organization, the Hollywood Writers' Mobilization. The West Coast equivalent of the Washington-New York-based Writers' War Board,* the HWM succeeded in enlisting an imposing spectrum of authors—3,500 of them, including novelists, screen and radio writers, publicists, journalists, cartoonists, composers, and lyricists—as the various amalgamation projects of the thirties had never managed to do. Launched the day after Pearl Harbor, the Mobilization intended to let the whole country know, and to remind it as often as necessary, what the war was about. The federal government was delighted with the spontaneous appearance of agencies dedicated to refining and shaping war propaganda. The Office of Civilian Defense lost no time in calling upon the HWM to produce "consistent hard-hitting [radio programs] that can be used in every town in America."[57] Indeed, within a short time, the Mobilization functioned as a kind of literary armory for the government, providing the bureaucracy with all manner of evocative propaganda material: scripts for war bond drives, documentary scenarios for the departments of the Treasury, Army, and Navy, speeches for government officials, pamphlets, biographical material, instructional brochures, in fact anything that involved the stringing together of words. As it turned out, the writers of the HWM wrote more to order as hacks for the government than they ever did for their studio producers—and were rewarded with even less recognition—but they luxuriated in their selflessness and dedication.

If similar to the old Anti-Nazi League in its numbers and its enthusiasm, the Writers' Mobilization yet differed from its predecessor in one

---

* The brainchild of mystery writer Rex Stout, the Writers' War Board came into existence on December 9, 1941, to help the Treasury Department enlist writers to sell war bonds. By the time the war ended, over two thousand writers had contributed their services to this quasi-official extension of the Office of War Information. (Lewis Gannett, "Books," in Jack Goodman, ed., *While You Were Gone: A Report on Wartime Life in the United States*, New York: Simon & Schuster, 1946, pp. 459–60; John McAleer, *Rex Stout: A Biography*, Boston: Little, Brown & Co., 1977, pp. 297–346 *passim*.)

crucial respect: its single, pragmatic *raison d'être* permitted no tran-
scendent moral cause or principle to frame, or to override, its single-
minded devotion to "winning the war." The majority of writers who
served the HWM did not share the national administration's victory-
for-the-sake-of-victory attitude. Nevertheless, the goals for a postwar
world which the Mobilization expressed, notably in the Free World
Theatre, rang with the vagueness and banality of most of the propaganda efforts of official government agencies. The nineteen plays
which comprised the Free World series' broadcasts over the ABC Blue
Network in 1943 dramatized the aims of a "century of the common
man," "no business as usual," "all people are the same," "a world of
peace and security," etc. While the writers did not trivialize any of
these important themes, neither did they make them very meaningful.[58]

The politics of the Phony War era narrowed the purposes and issues
around which leftists and progressives could unify—to campaigns to
Win the War and reelect Franklin Roosevelt. As a result, these Front
groups of the forties, especially the HWM, lacked a potential for enduring; nor could they be termed "political" in the admiring way the
Left had described the Anti-Nazi League or Motion Picture Democratic Committee as being "political"—i.e., the newer groups were not
independent, critical, and committed to a wide-ranging vision of what
society should be. Where the Anti-Nazi League had fought the Dies
Committee as part of its war against fascism, or the MPDC had taken
on the defense of the California migrant workers as an integral part of
its commitment to New Deal politics, the Hollywood Writers' Mobilization functioned as a quasi-governmental agency. It uncritically sub-
scribed even to the government's definition of the role of films during
the war: "The wartime function of the movies . . . is to build morale,
and morale is . . . education . . . inspiration . . . confidence. . . ."[59]
Missing from this document was a commitment to film as a form of artistic expression or a pledge to tell the American people the truth
about the war. By agreeing to beat their plowshares into swords at the
behest of the bureaucrats and their own desire to be "useful," the film
writers, ironically, were doing what the Communists had preached in
the thirties—and most of the writers had resisted—wielding art as a
weapon in the political struggle.

The weapons were further refined with the Mobilization's most impressive accomplishment, a Writers' Congress, co-sponsored by the
University of California, which was held at UCLA in October 1943.

The purpose of the Congress, as outlined by university president Robert Gordon Sproul in his opening address, was:

> To analyze propaganda techniques as weapons of victory; to sharpen the creative skill of writers by pooling their creative experience and knowledge; to investigate the most effective use of new media of expression; to strengthen firm and continuous cultural understanding among the United Nations; to mobilize the entire writing profession in a program of action for the free world of tomorrow.[60]

The Congress consisted of a series of seminars (motion pictures, radio, other media, and writers in exile) and panels (Propaganda Analysis, the Nature of the Enemy, Problems of the Peace, Minority Groups, the American Scene, Pan-American Affairs). Aside from Trumbo's commentary on the continued use of racial stereotypes in commercial films, the general tenor of the conferees' remarks was away from controversy or criticism. For example, screenwriter Talbot Jennings stated: "I do not believe that this is the time for pictures to raise any issues whatsoever here at home as between any race or creed or class."[61] This program, which could have been written aboard the *Prince of Wales* by Roosevelt and Churchill, stands in sharp contrast to the topics slated for consideration at another writers' "Win-the-War" congress:

> We urge [read the "call" of the League of American Writers] the immediate opening of a Second Front in Europe. Our Congress will seek ways and means of crushing our internal enemies. . . . We shall demand the democratic integration in this people's war of the total energies of the Negro people, by fighting with them against discrimination in any form, whether in civil life or in the armed forces.[62]

There could be no question of competition between the congresses. The powerful Writers' War Board (in the East) was hostile to the League's Congress, and the Mobilization, in terms of numbers, patronage, and subsidies, towered over the struggling League, which had had to borrow the $3,500 needed even to prepare the groundwork. The League did not put up a fight in any case. The Communist Party, whose members controlled the League, had no desire to pick a fight with the Mobilization or foster divisiveness in the Popular Front. The

League canceled its plans, wrote off the $3,500 plus the year of intensive planning, and expired soon thereafter.

National unity steamrollered out of existence an independent, critical leftist group. The "cause" of victory also narrowed the social and political perspective of its participants. The tunnel vision which ensued from the subordination of all else to the goal of victory became most apparent when issues arose in which most screenwriters, particularly liberals and Communists, would normally have evinced great interest. The lack of critical autonomy in the HWM was quite apparent in the letter Carey McWilliams received from Ralph Block, who had formerly been SWG president and was then serving as coordinator of HWM activities, in response to McWilliams' request for information on the internment of Japanese-American citizens in California. McWilliams, who was researching a report for the Institute of Pacific Relations, had queried Block about the attitude of the federal government toward "citizens and non-citizens of alien derivation." Block blandly described the policy, concluding his letter to McWilliams with the kind of comment one would expect from a high-level government functionary: "[I hope] that you may, through the media to which you have access, give publicity to this point of view. Your cooperation in this matter is of the utmost importance and will be of great value to your government."[63]

Within the confines of the Mobilization's drive for victory, however, the Left was not completely submerged, nor did it entirely lose its voice. HWM radicals tended to initiate non-war-oriented activities (e.g., a large demonstration against American Nazi Gerald L. K. Smith, picket line observers at the Conference of Studio Unions strike of 1945), which the government had not proposed and which a number of other writers did not especially approve. Pauline Finn, the executive secretary of the HWM, recalled that the activities of the Left did not cause many problems within the organization. Since it was not a membership group, but a clearinghouse agency for assignments, there was no official day-to-day contact which could lead to confrontations between the various political factions. "Since there were no Board or membership meetings, the cleavages were just not that obvious." Nor was the organization itself purely an American-oriented enterprise. One of the most spectacular of its productions centered on a tribute to the Soviet Union—the Western premiere of Dmitri Shostakovich's Seventh (War) Symphony—and included a tribute to the United Nations. The symphony, conducted by Leopold Stokowski, was performed before a sell-out audience at the Shrine Auditorium on October 9, 1942. The proceeds went to Russian War Relief.

In an unusual turnabout, however, it was as writers that the Communists and fellow travelers made their most significant political contribution to the goal of victory. Philip and Janet Stevenson, Leo and Pauline Townsend, Harold Buchman and Louis Solomon, and a brilliant new immigrant, Abraham Polonsky, wrote one third of the scripts for the radio show "Reunion, U.S.A.," in which they expressed many of their long-standing beliefs and some of their growing concerns with the postwar world.

Polonsky was one of the few writers who came to Hollywood with previous experience in the CP and a deep knowledge of Marxist theory. He was the only screenwriter to have had any involvement with non-literary trade union organizing. For two years, 1939–41, Polonsky had served as educational director for the Westchester County, New York, CIO and as editor of its newspaper, *The Home Front*. He worked closely with the United Automobile Workers' radical faction in its largely successful effort to maintain its position within a labor movement which had begun to look nervously over its shoulder at the baying hounds of anti-communism. Polonsky had himself been educated at City College of New York and by a decade-long connection with the Communist Party. He graduated from college in 1932 and went on to Columbia Law School, supporting himself with stipends from his job as a teacher in night school English classes at CCNY. On the side, Polonsky engaged in political activities and wrote—first short stories, then radio scripts, and finally a magazine serial which eventually became his well-received first novel, *The Enemy Sea*. Until the war, Polonsky had had no interest in movie writing. "I had had some nibbles from the studios," he said, "but Hollywood did not appeal to me as a place to live and work." In 1942 Polonsky joined the Office of Strategic Services (OSS—the precursor of the present Central Intelligence Agency). Wanting security for himself and his family when the war was over, Polonsky signed a contract for postwar employment with Paramount Pictures.

A tour of duty in London and Occupied France (1943–45) producing "black radio" programs† for the OSS and the Free French forces

---

† The "black radio" personnel produced programs broadcast from England, but purporting to originate in undercover stations within German-occupied countries and the Reich itself. The "broadcasters" masqueraded as patriotic Germans, loyal to the fatherland, but disturbed by the depredations and

opened Polonsky's eyes to the strong anti-Communist elements lurking just below the surface of the Roosevelt administration's fraternal tie to its Soviet ally. In ways that only a few Communist home-fronters suspected, the American government was laying the groundwork as best it could for a restoration of nationalistic, anti-Communist governments in Axis-occupied countries. Recalled Polonsky:

> As the War came to a close [the OSS] wouldn't let us bring any arms in for those partisan groups who were Communists. [The OSS] did not want them to be armed after the War was over. During the last year of the War there was already in motion, within Army Intelligence, anti-Communist programs for the post-War future. Before I [returned home] O.S.S. tried to recruit me to go to China in order to prevent the coming of socialism there.[64]

By the time Polonsky arrived in Hollywood in 1945, the political situation both there and in Europe had worsened for the radical Popular Fronters who hoped to keep intact both their own domestic alliance and the worldwide Grand Alliance or United Nations. Polonsky found that a number of Hollywood Communists had come to share his disquiet. The summer and fall of 1944, with their political conventions and campaign activities, gave liberals and radicals sufficient reason for alarm. The dumping of the liberal, internationalist Henry Wallace from the Democratic ticket in favor of Harry Truman, a machine politician, augured ill, especially in view of the loud and sudden reawakening of anti-communism statements and activities from the conservative ranks. The Republicans, from Dewey on down, charged that the Roosevelt administration was soft on communism, citing the President's release of Earl Browder from prison. Sidney Hillman, a founder of the CIO and the mainstay of organized labor's support for Roosevelt, also came under heavy fire from the Republicans and HUAC, which announced an investigation into his political activities. In Hollywood, too, conservatives were once again on the warpath. As early as

---

deficiencies of the Nazi leadership. Polonsky and sociology professor Howard Becker were responsible for "what must have been one of the most fantastic broadcasts of the war"—a speech by Colonel-General Ludwig Beck (presumed dead by his own hand following the failure of the German army officers' July 1944 attempt on Hitler's life) urging the Wehrmacht to rise against the Führer in order to spare Germany from total destruction and remove some of the country's burden of guilt for its complicity in the crimes of the Nazis. (Sefton Delmer, *Black Boomerang*, New York: The Viking Press, 1962, pp. 253–55.)

February 1944, the remnants of the Screen Playwrights had joined with a number of notable reactionaries (Walt Disney, director Sam Wood, actor Adolphe Menjou, etc.) to launch a militantly anti-Communist organization, the Motion Picture Alliance for the Preservation of American Ideals.

Though the official Communist Party line continued to be based on the "spirit of Teheran" and the maintenance of the national and international fronts, screenwriters like Polonsky and Stevenson shared a growing apprehension. They found an outlet in "Reunion, U.S.A.," which ran for nineteen weeks on the ABC Blue Network (Mondays, 7:30–8:00 P.M.) between May and November, 1945. The show originated in a series of seminars sponsored by the Hollywood Writers' Mobilization in 1944 on the general problems of postwar readjustment of soldiers and civilians. The first four scripts cleaved very close to the sociological-psychological theme adumbrated in the seminars, concentrating on the personal and emotional adjustments individuals and families had to undergo after the homecoming joys had subsided. Beginning with the fifth show (*One and One Makes Nothing* by Jerome Epstein), however, and continuing through to the summer recess in late August, a broader social and political perspective is evident in the scripts written by liberals as well as Communists. The focus shifted from individual to social problems: the need for meaningful jobs for war veterans and for national and international cooperation and postwar planning, along with the evils of intolerance and the benefits of political involvement.

Before "Reunion, U.S.A." returned to the air, on October 1, for its last six broadcasts, the writers had become increasingly concerned about the nature of the peace and the contours of the postwar world. The CP members within the Hollywood Writers' Mobilization had met and decided to try to convert the radio show from a simple dramatization of the social and psychological problems of returning servicemen to an exercise in political education. The Mobilization, of course, was in no wise a Communist-run entity. If the Communists were to have their way, they would need the cooperation, indeed the active participation, of their liberal co-writers, the predominantly liberal crew of directors and technicians, and the production and network staff. Milton Merlin, a non-Communist who wrote and directed several of the more political shows, remembers that the Communists were, in this situation, the most organized and active of a group of convinced, enlightened artists and craftspeople. "It was no different than the thirties," said Merlin. "They did not take over; nor could they have accomplished their goals if the climate had not been right." As it happened, enough signs of a less than glorious new world were in evidence in the autumn of 1945 to seal the bond between Communists and liberals, and "Reunion, U.S.A." switched themes yet again. The final six scripts (four by liberals, two by Communists) not only proved highly entertaining, but they also dramatized political problems in subtle and realistic ways. The critical acclaim for the show attested to the artistic quality of the radical "lesson plan." *Weekly Variety*'s staffers were enthusiastic about the three plays they reviewed (Polonsky's *Man from the Moon*, Milton Merlin's *Home Again Blues*, and Milton Geiger's *Beachhead on the Campus*), terming the show "important," "worthwhile," and a necessary addition "to the list of radio's must shows." Not even the increasing politicization of the series stilled the accolades: "The war is over, and now 'Reunion' has broadened its significance. The program brings the war vet face to face with the fact that while the war is over, the fascistic acts thought killed along with the defeated have come into greater prominence. . . . 'Reunion,' as a peacetime crusader, has found its purpose. . . . The occasion of 'Reunion' stirred hopes for a better world."[65]

The closing show of the series—*The Case of David Smith*, written by Polonsky—purported to depict the postwar medical investigation of a GI (David Smith) who suffered a complete mental breakdown as a result of his peacetime, not his wartime, experience. Fighting in the Pacific, Smith was assigned to organize guerrilla bands against the Japanese invaders of an unspecified Pacific island. Smith recruited his jungle partisans with evocative words taken right from the American War of Independence: "You must fight for your freedom." Smith told the hesitant, "I'm an American. And [you have my word] you'll be free." The natives fight; the war ends; and the former colonial power returns to take possession of its island—"all with due order and a little shooting." The severely disillusioned Smith can, of course, do nothing to make good on his "promise." Shortly before lapsing into psychosis, he writes to his fellow organizer, Sergeant Tana: "I believed in the promise I made them, the promise of freedom. Who is going to keep it, and when?" (The haunting question posed by a Communist Party activist was answered, thirty years later, by the research of a liberal historian: "The battle for freedom, as the Allies fought it, did not promise freedom for dark peoples."[66])

The other five scripts were just as hard-hitting and prescient. *Beachhead on the Campus* by Milton Geiger depicted the postwar stirrings of anti-Semitism on a college campus, confronting a returning veteran with the question: "What was I fighting for for three years?" *Peace Has Been Declared* (Milton Merlin), *Just Between Us* (Harold Buchman and Louis Solomon), and *Peter and the Werewolf* (David Hertz) dramatized, in various ways, the threat of subversion from the Right. Each depicted the guises in which the forces of disunity would endeavor to undermine the motives which had sent men and women overseas and the hopes which victory had raised. The writers counseled against isolationism, racism, xenophobia, chauvinism, and hatred.[67]

The far Left in Hollywood did not entirely cease to agitate and to express itself separately from the new Popular Front. No sooner had the war broken out, in fact, than a small group of them turned their attention, not to North Africa and the Philippines, but toward the same sorts of domestic causes which had captured them in the thirties. In particular, the scurrilous campaign waged by the press and police and municipal administration against the Mexican-American community in Los Angeles aroused the indignation and support of radicals in the film industry. The press campaign, begun in early 1942, against "pachucos" (Mexican-American youths who wore "zoot suits" and joined gangs) and "pachuco crime" climaxed in a celebrated case of injustice—the Sleepy Lagoon Case (August 1942)—and one of the most vicious race riots in recent American history—the Zoot Suit Riots (June 1943).

In the former, over one hundred Mexican-American youths (averaging eighteen years of age) were arrested for the murder of José Díaz. Twenty-four indictments were returned in August, and after a thirteen-week trial, accompanied by lurid newspaper stories, twelve were convicted of murder, five of assault. The Communist Party and a number of Front groups in which it participated—Civil Rights Congress, International Labor Defense, National Lawyers Guild—helped organize the defense and establish a support group, the Citizens' Committee for the Defense of Mexican-American Youth, which later became the Sleepy Lagoon Defense Committee. Sponsored by labor groups, professional guilds, ethnic organizations, educators, and film people—John Bright, Guy Endore, Dalton Trumbo, John Howard Lawson, Ring Lardner, Jr., Orson Welles, Rita Hayworth, Dorothy Comingore, Canada Lee, and Joseph Cotten—the Committee undertook a large-scale program to educate the Los Angeles population to the racism which existed in their midst and to gather support for a reversal of the convictions. Radio broadcasts, rallies, demonstrations, a jazz concert at the Philharmonic Auditorium—in short, all the tried and true thirties fund- and consciousness-raising methods—were removed from the cold storage of the Phony War period.[68]

Though the convictions were overturned on appeal in October 1944, the racial atmosphere in Los Angeles had become charged with conflict. Shortly after the convictions, scuffles between Mexican-Americans and white sailors broke out in Venice and Ocean Park. Some of the Mexican-Americans were arrested, and the usual inflammatory newspaper headlines about "Mexican crime" followed. On June 3, 1943, eleven sailors returned to their naval base at Chavez Ravine, claiming they had been attacked by a gang of zoot-suiters. The next evening some one hundred sailors, armed with clubs, piled into a caravan of twenty taxicabs and drove to East Los Angeles, where they severely beat several Mexican-American youths. Their appetites merely whetted by this first "invasion," the sailors returned in greater force the next two nights, joined by Army and Marine personnel. On June 7 an army of several thousand Anglos, including a number of civilians, raided the barrio and beat up every Mexican-American youth they could find while the police either looked the other way or arrested some pachucos. Hundreds of Mexican-Americans were injured; no whites were arrested.

While the authorities fiddled (the Los Angeles city council outlawed the wearing of zoot suits and the miltiary declared downtown Los Angeles off limits to military personnel), liberals and radicals burned. The stirrings among the leftists, which had begun with the formation of the Sleepy Lagoon Defense Committee, crested in July 1943. Over one hundred groups were formed within labor organizations, civic groups, churches, public schools, fraternal organizations, etc.[69] The Hollywood Left, already conscious of the use of stereotypes in the movies, press, and popular parlance and conversant with the injustice, inequality, and poverty burdening the lives of racial minorities in the United States, joined actively in the series of educational projects which stemmed from the Sleepy Lagoon Case and the Zoot Suit Riots. One of the most notable results of this flurry of attention was the film *Brotherhood of Man*, written by Lardner and Maurice Rapf, animated by John Hubley, and subsidized by the Educational Division of the United Automobile Workers.[70] The group which made the film, United Film Productions, had been formed by Karen Morley and other radicals at the insistence of the UAW. That group had also made a campaign film for Roosevelt, *Hell Bent for Election*. As the Cold War and domestic Red-baiting progressed, however, the UAW, under pressure from Victor Reuther and Philip

Murray, ceased to subsidize this group. The union formed a less "crimson" organization, consisting of the American Jewish Committee, the Anti-Defamation League, and the International Ladies' Garment Workers' Union, to continue the production of civil rights films. The new committee sponsored the making of a documentary based on the *Report of the President's Committee on Civil Rights.*[71]

In the Left's "discovery" of racism in California, however, one large area remained unexplored. Apparently no amount of awakening consciousness could penetrate the patriotic indifference of everyone, radicals and Communists included, to the plight of Japanese-Americans in the concentration camps. A few religious groups, notably the American Friends Service Committee, raised their voices against the loud chorus of silence, but in Hollywood, as elsewhere in the country, the decision to sequester the Japanese was popular. No notable left-wing organization or individual (excepting Lou Goldblatt of the CIO and A. L. Wirin of the ACLU) sprang up to protest this incarceration, whose "legality" was upheld by the United States Supreme Court. No outraged pamphlets were written, not even by wary sentinels of racism like Carey McWilliams. McWilliams wrote, in 1942: "In the long run the Japanese will probably profit by this painful and distressing experience. They had not made a satisfactory adjustment to American life prior to December 7th; and through the unforeseen exigencies of the war it is possible that they can win for themselves a far more satisfactory position in American life than they have enjoyed in the past."[72] Thorough research into the evacuation and the conditions of the camps radically altered McWilliams' thinking, and in 1944 he authored a series of articles, pamphlets, and books which exposed the racism and intolerance involved in the relocation.

The Communist Party could have made the issue a national one, as it had done with the Scottsboro boys in 1933 or the victims of international fascism in the mid- and late thirties. Instead it formally supported the internment. An editorial in the Party's West Coast newspaper, *People's World*, noted that:

> anyone sincerely interested in prosecuting the war against the Axis powers knows that is absolutely necessary to remove all Aliens of German, Italian or Japanese nationality from strategic areas, and that even American citizens of whatever national origin, may have to submit to a system whereby they can be removed from certain areas, or given permits to live or work there, as may be deemed necessary by federal and military authorities. But for

the great majority [of Japanese-Americans], plans must speedily be worked out to settle them [in camps] under federal government supervision.[73]

The Party's total commitment to wartime patriotism led its leaders to retreat from two other previously fundamental positions as well— opposition to the Smith Act and support for better working conditions for American laborers. Twenty-nine members of the Trotskyist Socialist Workers Party of Minneapolis-St. Paul were arrested and charged with "seditious conspiracy"—a Smith Act violation. The Communist Party refused to join the defense committee which sprang up in the summer of 1941 to rally support for the indictees. An editorial in the *Daily Worker* explained why: "The Communist Party has always exposed, fought against and today joins in the fight to exterminate the Trotskyite Fifth Column from the life of our nation."[74] And, in the face of obvious and growing working-class dissatisfaction with an increasing work pace and a declining real wage, the Communist Party steadfastly defended the federal government's demand, institutionalized in the War Labor Board, for industrial harmony and labor quiescence.

Toward Renewed Polarization

In an important sense, the Second World War served only as an interlude in the ongoing contests of the late thirties: between the Left and the Right, on one hand; within the left wing itself, between liberals and radicals, on the other. The two-year "moratorium" of 1942–44 had seemed to strengthen the Left by resurrecting its unity from the wreckage of the Nazi-Soviet Pact. Moreover, the international alliance of American and Soviet forces had lifted what had come to be nearly a quarantine on the CPUSA within the arena of American politics. In actuality, however, the war years saw no real restoration of liberal-radical unity or left-wing originality or vitality; at most they witnessed a temporary (if blinding) effulgence of enthusiasm and activity toward the narrow goals of military and electoral victory. The revived alliance was less a Popular Front in the impressive fashion of its predecessor than a cheering squad which included within its ranks a small contingent who worried about what would happen when the cheering stopped.

There was genuine reason for apprehension. In the same twenty-four months that registered the left-wing revival there also occurred far more solid gains for its adversaries. Big business took advantage of the booming war industries to regain the profits, influence, and confidence of which the Depression and the high tide of the New Deal had temporarily deprived them. Those same years also saw the steady strengthening of the conservative blocs in the United States Congress and in state legislatures, as well as the intransigent unwillingness of a critical group of centrist liberals to do more, even at the height of the war effort, than provisionally temper the anti-communism which had, by now, become an integral aspect of their political identity.

The war years hardly hampered the conservative resurgence, except to take an occasional gust or two out of the sails of anti-communism (and this thanks to the Russian alliance and public sympathy for the Russians). Fed by their own springs, the right-wing forces did not particularly need the splits and tensions within the Popular Front in order to drive themselves forward. The postwar schism between moderate liberals and radicals did, however, permit the Right to concentrate its attack on a more vulnerable, isolated target than liberalism itself. With most key sectors of liberalism weakening and falling silent or benevolently neutral in the face of anti-communism, the disintegration of the great center-left coalition which had characterized the thirties was completed with astonishing speed.

7

Prelude to Repression, 1944–47

The trend is obviously toward greater realism, toward a more
frequent selection of factual American themes, toward the
theory that motion pictures should not only entertain and
make money, but should also give expression to the American
and democratic ideals. . . .

—*Philip Dunne* (*1946*)[1]

[Communist writers] do not want actors jumping up and
shouting "Hooray for Stalin!" on the screen. It is the constant
portrayal of comic politicians, bankers who are scrooges and
dishonest judges that becomes dangerous.

—*James K. McGuinness* (*1947*)[2]

Long before the foreign war was over, the political wars at home had
recommenced in all their intensity. The presidential election of 1944
was seen by both parties as a crucial watershed in American history.
The winner could dictate the treaties that would end the war and
could also set the tone for postwar American domestic policy. Despite
the fact that Roosevelt had long since backed away from a program of
New Deal legislation, the New Dealers remained in office, and the Republicans were only too eager to supply a new set of faces in Washington. The strident, partisan tone of official conservatism, institutionalized in the Grand Old Party, set the stage for a new campaign of
vituperation and hate. The Republican Party leadership's indifference
or disdain toward militant reactionaries in the thirties had been slowly
transformed during the years out of power into a willingness to tolerate, and even to participate in, anti-Communist witch-hunting.

The Republican Party's new tone was enunciated clearly by its presidential nominee, Thomas E. Dewey, in his 1944 campaign. Other established Party figures—Knowland, Taft, Jenner, etc.—also sounded the Republican theme: the Roosevelt administration was "soft on communism"; indeed, it had provided domestic Communists with a congenial nest. The relief organizations created by the New Deal, the impetus given to labor organizing by the Wagner Act, and the appointments to high governmental positions of liberal intellectuals constituted an unofficial sponsorship of Red activity in the United States.

The Democrats, or so they believed, could not afford either to ignore or simply to deny the Republican accusations—if, that is, the incumbents wished to retain their hold on the mass of moderate voters. Even though the CPUSA was not illegal, and the Soviet alliance was still publicly cherished by officialdom, the charge of un-Americanism which could be leveled against local Communists, as "supporters of a foreign government," was too potent a weapon for nervous public servants to resist, particularly in the mid-forties atmosphere of anxiety over international affairs and insecurity about domestic trends. With the death of Roosevelt and the accession of the less liberal, less politically apt Harry S. Truman, the Democratic Party shifted its forces to protect its right flank: Republican charges were ridiculed, but Henry Wallace and other left wing New Dealers were sacrificed. Many of the words and some of the actions of the Truman administration promised a continuation of the New Deal, but the climate of political accommodation to which Roosevelt's first campaign had given birth— and in which Popular Front politics had thrived—chilled noticeably.

This intense rivalry between the political parties, which provided a climate favorable to reaction, formed the political backdrop for the triumph of anti-communism in the post-World War II period. Intensive class conflict, following a decade of gains for labor unions and four years of enforced wartime labor-management "harmony," formed the economic backdrop. The rallying of an impressive number of labor organizations to the left-center coalition during the war had deeply antagonized powerful economic interests in America: an anxious cartel of bankers, industrialists, and media barons represented by the United States Chamber of Commerce and the National Association of Manufacturers. The war, by massively increasing sales, productivity, profits, and the government's need for managerial expertise in the newly created war bureaucracies, had reintroduced corporate influence into Washington to an extent greater than at any time since the inauguration of Franklin D. Roosevelt in March 1933. To the business and financial elite, anti-communism had far less to do with putting the GOP back into power than it did with combating recurrent worker restiveness and weakening organized labor. Thus anti-communism functioned in this period in the same fashion as nationalism had in other periods: naked class, economic, and political objectives were dressed in more appealing, demagogic garb. In the guise of a loyal opposition and protectors of the public interest, the elites launched their attack on liberals and labor—the un-Americans.

It was not especially easy to link communism with un-Americanism and thus make it *the* issue in this country. The CPUSA had never been large enough or influential enough that its opponents could convince a large segment of the populace that it represented a menace to American security, freedom, or property. Most Americans were indifferent to it. While a majority of citizens proved favorably disposed to the Soviet Union as a heroic and reliable wartime ally, this approval did not reflect on the national Party. In fact, both the Roosevelt administration and the Party hierarchs carefully avoided mixing ideology with victory. Both assiduously ignored the problems inherent in a Grand Alliance triumph wrapped around a Red Army victory. When the shooting was over, and the Soviet Union was clearly visible as the single remaining challenger to United States hegemony in the postwar world, the Grand Alliance shattered and the ideological debate became deafening. Under these conditions, the American Communist Party could be seen as a direct extension of the "forces of darkness," of the power, duplicity, cynicism, rapacity, and terrorism of Joseph Stalin.

The alliance of extremists, conservatives, politicians, and social-economic elites was thus able to wrest a full-blown domestic Red scare out of international tensions. This was accomplished by encouraging the development of an altered and ultra-charged set of connotations for the words "Communist," "Red," "liberal," "labor," and "union." The first step in the process, linking communism in general with international evil, was not difficult to accomplish in the polarized world of the postwar era. Nor was the second step—associating American Communists with the crimes and designs of Joseph Stalin—especially troublesome in light of the CPUSA's steadfast defense of all Soviet actions, most notably the Nazi-Soviet Pact. These two steps, however, could, at best, lead to the containment of communism abroad and the effective prohibition of communism at home. The conservatives' real enemies—New Deal liberals, "premature anti-fascists," socialists, social critics, reformers, labor union militants, etc.—remained free of the dragnet.

The keystone to the reformation of opinion was thus an intricate third step: the linking of all expressions of liberalism and radicalism to communism. Here the right wing relied upon Americans' characteristic nationalism. Communism was "un-American" because it was atheistic, collectivistic, and international. This linking of Americanism to a highly specific set of values—organized religion, private property, and nationalism—made it un-American, hence Communistic, to be critical of, or to wish to change or challenge, those values and the institutions and policies which reflected them. Right-wing spokespeople hammered away at the theme that reformist activists and critics weakened America; they therefore had to be Communistic in identity or sympathy, and, in the national interest, had to be exposed and quarantined.

The jump from step two to step three required a massive and unremitting campaign, conducted on several fronts by numerous groups and individuals, from both the public and private sectors. Anti-communism became a full-time business. If conspiracy by the forces of postwar anti-communism cannot be proven, it is nevertheless not difficult to exhibit the overlaps, interconnections, parallelisms, mutual support, and common ideology which characterized all elements of the coalition.

The general structure of the American anti-Communist crusade is familiar to the student of political reaction: there is always a general staff of interlocking ecclesiastical, economic, political, and social elites which never meets but which is highly aware of its membership and which consciously confers social prestige and significance on the witch-hunt; a propaganda division composed of "deeply concerned" intellectuals and academics with access to the most influential publications; an intelligence-gathering unit composed largely of ex-military personnel, ex-FBI agents, ex-federal bureaucrats, and disgruntled former Communists; the engine of war itself—usually a congressional committee staffed with conservative politicians, preponderantly from the southern states, who have not distinguished themselves in any realm of government but who are seeking to remedy that through the anti-Communist crusade; various independent armies of local collaborators, primarily loyal to the particular industry or area in which they work or live, who assist the crusade and see to it that the anti-Communist purge is thoroughgoing within their bailiwick.

Working alongside the crusade, and deriving new notoriety and influence from it, were numerous established social organizations of the Right—the American Legion, Veterans of Foreign Wars, Daughters of the American Revolution, Knights of Columbus, etc. These groups mobilized and influenced large sectors of the public and extended the anti-Communist work of the governmental investigatory committees, thereby obliging private industry, or the public bureaucracy, to enact sanctions against uncooperative witnesses, suspected Reds, and admitted Communists and sympathizers. Finally, there were the independent "sanctioning" agencies, the executors of the judgments of the inquisition: the executive boards and employer associations in private industry; departmental heads and politically appointed administrators in the public sector; public prosecutors from the Department of Justice; the judiciary; and the commentators, editors, and publishers of key metropolitan newspapers and national magazines. To them fell the task of ensuring that the damned lost their jobs, their social standing, (in some instances) their freedom, their capacity to be heard, and their opportunity to find other employment within their professions. Much of the executioners' power to influence consumer and voter attitudes against "named" Communists derived from a studied indifference to the subtleties and complexities of ideology and the rights of the accused; that is, from their willingness to accept the images of a Red monolith and of the Republic in danger.

The relationships among the various forces described above were characterized by acknowledged, conscious, often coordinated interaction as well as agreement on the larger goals and methods of the enterprise. There remains, however, a crucial auxiliary group of moderate and liberal institutions and individuals which effectively widened the appeal and advanced the work of the crusade by praising it with faint damns. While appearing to disapprove of right-wing anti-Communists' methods and politics (though not their anti-Communist, capitalist, or democratic ideology), these influential liberals expressed far more strongly their understanding—and even justifications—of the excesses of the crusade. As events unfolded, they intensified their polemics against the Communists and pulled their punches against the Right. Their criticisms of the Right were procedural, patronizing, and narrowly political/tactical (in the nature of "bad show" and "tut-tut"), while their indictment of the Stalinists and fellow travelers was sweeping, alarmist, and ruthless. Though these liberal intellectuals were themselves reviled (and one day even pursued) by the anti-Communist inquisitors and hatchet men, this by no means brought to an end the provisional cooperation between the crusade and the "Vital Center."

These liberals acted as a crucial swing group in the political balance of forces. Most of them could boast long careers of left-wing (e.g., Popular Front) opposition to the policies and methods of traditional American conservatism, but their own anti-communism had expanded to such a point that they were not only not allies of the besieged left wing, but its *de facto* adversaries. Anti-Communist liberals, believing that communism was a "greater menace" than fascism, placed moderate politics and politicians in the service of the Right, thereby precluding any possibility of an effective liberal counterweight. They provided instead a course of political expediency which was followed by large numbers of hesitant, frightened liberals or progressives who might otherwise have rallied to the defense of the Left.

Anti-Communist liberals not only blocked the formation of a liberal-radical alliance against a reactionary wave; they also, as the historians of this era, gave final legitimacy to the anti-Communist crusade. Their protected positions in, and access to, the worlds of academe and of book and periodical publishing have permitted them a partial monopoly over both the accounts of the witch-hunt and the critical reception given to these "analyses."

The anti-Communist crusade and its adjunct organizations constituted a very complex and heterogeneous social phenomenon. The individuals involved in the war against communism differed greatly in their social origins and status, their economic roles, their income, their political opinions, and, significantly, in the various styles, strategies, and goals of their anti-communism. Whittaker Chambers, J. B. Matthews, John Rankin, and Parnell Thomas had little in common with Francis Spellman, Robert Taft, and Eric Johnston,* while the latter, in turn, had no direct links with William F. Buckley, James

---

* Eric Johnston, a significant figure in postwar Hollywood, was, during the war, president of the United States Chamber of Commerce. A successful businessman from Seattle, where he owned four electric companies, Johnston had, during his long tenure as vice-president and president of the Chamber of Commerce, developed strong links with Washington administrators and American businessmen. He was a member of the Economic Policy Subcommittee of the State Department's Advisory Committee on Postwar Foreign Policy and an outspoken foe of Soviet power. In early 1944, during a trip to the Soviet Union, it was reported that he and Stalin had strongly disagreed on the matter of American and Russian relations. In September 1945 he was hired as president of the Motion Picture Association of America.

Burnham, and Ralph de Toledano. Lionel and Diana Trilling and
Arthur Schlesinger, Jr., for their parts, inhabited an entirely different
political society from that of the conservative or ultra-Right. Yet in
the convergence of events, all of them—red-neck, southern politicians;
professional government witnesses; patrician *philosophes;* the emi-
nences of church, state, and economy; and the liberal professoriate—
played indispensable roles in the national crusade against communism.

The unprecedented power of the post-World War II anti-Communist crusade stemmed from the imprimatur given to the marauders
by established elites, as symbolized by the Republican national ticket in
1952. Only in an epoch where anti-communism had become an acceptable and desirable vocation could someone like Richard Nixon have
built, out of slander and malice, a political career which would lead
him from lower-middle-class obscurity to close political association
with the leading national hero of the time—a former General of the
Army and president of Columbia University.

The power and uncompromising aggressiveness of the postwar
Soviet Union and international communism (renewed as the Cominform in 1947) and the CPUSA's obvious links with Stalin provided the occasion and the justification for the anti-Communist crusade, but each element of the Right had its own particular (usually
domestic) agenda. Two of the varieties of anti-communism—southern
populist and northern patrician—were further bonded together by
anti-working-class and anti-reform sentiments. Anti-atheism and ideological conservatism motivated the Buckleys and Spellmans; xenopho-
bic nativism and political opportunism, the Rankins and Thomases;
anti-totalitarianism and anti-Stalinism, the liberals like Schlesinger or
Trilling; personal fortune-hunting and status-seeking, a Herbert Mathews or Vincent Hartnett; Americanism and anti-internationalism, the
American Legion. The linchpins of the apparatus—the corporate and
political elites—were fueled by their fear of trade union power and
their hatred of socialism.

The decisive factor in the domestic anti-Communist cartel was the
alliance of big businessmen and nationally known Republican politicians. Militant trade union activity, mainly in the form of larger,
more frequent strikes and broader-based popular agitation and political
participation, sent shivers of apprehension through major American
companies. At the same time, years of languishing out of power, help-
lessly watching the river of legislation enacted by the most important
reform administration in American history, had reduced the Republican Party to fury and desperation.

Unions and strikes came to represent the legacy of the New Deal, and Communist infiltration, in the eyes of men like Eric Johnston and Robert Taft. The links binding organized labor, New Deal reforms, and the CPUSA were, in fact, far less powerful than these men thought. The power displayed by the American labor movement in 1945 was the result of ten years of economic depression and the vision and hard work of union leaders like Harry Bridges, John L. Lewis, and Sidney Hillman, not to mention the courage and determination of rank-and-file workers in the steel, automotive, rubber, and electrical industries. The New Deal, through the Wagner Act and the National Labor Relations Board, provided government recognition of labor's emergence as a major force in American society. The New Deal could, however, be both pro- and anti-labor. In its pro-labor phase it passed the Wagner Act; in its anti-labor phase, Roosevelt and his aides leveled harsh and unfair charges of subversion and anti-patriotism at strikers during the years 1939–41.

Communists played both great and slight roles in the growth of labor power in the thirties and forties—great in the sense that Communist Party members—Lee Pressman, National CIO; Julius Emspack, UEW; Ben Gold, Furriers; Phil Connelly, California State CIO; Charles Smolikoff, Florida State CIO; etc.—contributed significantly to labor organizing in this period, but slight in that they did so as dedicated trade unionists rather than as Communists.

Workers, whether organized by Communists or non-Communists, did not readily accept either union discipline or the growing gap between wages and rising prices. Even during the war they did not hesitate to "hit the bricks"—between 1941 and 1945, 6.7 million strikers participated in 14,471 strikes in this country, far more than in the CIO organizational surge of the late thirties; indeed, far more than in any comparable period of United States history.[3] Few of these strikes originated in the front offices of unions; the great majority were unauthorized expressions of discontent by rank-and-file members. Though these work stoppages had no grave impact on the war effort, they did contribute to altering the balance of domestic political forces in this country by bringing into existence a dedicated anti-labor coalition of Republicans and conservative southern Democrats in Congress. This alliance passed into law, over Roosevelt's veto, the War Labor Disputes Act (Smith-Connally Act), providing for, among other anti-labor devices, criminal penalties for the advocates of "illegal" work stoppages and the prohibition of union contributions to political campaigns. Passed in June 1943, the Act required a "cooling off" period before a strike vote could be put into effect, secret ballots for strike votes in defense plants, and permission for the President to seize and operate any struck plant vital to national defense.[4]

The CIO leadership, determined to help reelect Franklin Roosevelt in 1944, circumnavigated the Smith-Connally restrictions by forming the CIO Political Action Committee in July 1943, under the leadership of Sidney Hillman, to channel funds from individual labor unions to progressive Democrats and independents. Six months later, on January 26, 1944, it was announced that the House Un-American Activities Committee had opened an investigation into the "Communist penetration of the CIO Political Action Committee." It was the first time that HUAC, or any similar congressional unit, had investigated in depth a large, mainstream, national labor organization. Dies, J. Parnell Thomas (R-N.J.), Joe Starnes (D-Ala.), and other Committee members, for all their anti-labor demagogy, were not foolhardy or quixotic men. On their own they would likely not have confronted the second largest labor confederation in the country (over 5 million strong) unless they felt that by so doing they could rally the support of other, more powerful people and institutions behind them.

Dies had accused the CIO of harboring Communists as far back as January 1939, and again in March 1941, but the HUAC chairman had not, in either instance, gone further than issuing inflammatory statements and submitting material to the Congressional Record. This time around, however, he planned a full-scale inquiry, but Sidney Hillman refused to comply with the subpoenas. Dies undertook a flank attack, ordering his Committee staff to cull all the information, verified and hearsay, in its voluminous files. The "report" which ensued charged that Communists had "penetrated" the CIO-PAC, that they worked through it to carry on their "subversive activities," and that the major objective of both was to "discredit the Congress of the United States." The bulk of the "report" was given over to case histories of the alleged Communist connections of thirty-five CIO leaders.[5]

The CIO was not HUAC's only concern in early 1944, even though it was, for the moment at least, generating the most publicity. In April 1944, several scouts had been sent back to the familiar territory of the motion picture business. This time, however, the reports they sent in to Washington spoke of a considerably changed atmosphere and alignment of forces in Hollywood. Anger and apprehension over smoldering labor militancy had aroused powerful and influential individuals and institutions within the film industry. One newly founded organization in particular stood ready to do battle alongside HUAC.

Anti-Communism Within the Film Community: The Motion Picture Alliance

The Motion Picture Alliance for the Preservation of American Ideals was the brainchild of a prominent group of Hollywood anti-Rooseveltians—foremost among them Sam Wood, the MPA's first president. "He was such a charming man—gentle, generous, dear . . . until 'It' came up. 'It' invariably transformed Dad into a snarling, unreasoning brute; we used to leave the dinner table with our guts tangled and churning from the experience." So spoke Jeane Wood, recounting her father's obsession with communism ("It"). Combating "It" became Sam Wood's reason for living in the last decade of his life.

And his reason for dying. The morning of his fatal heart attack (September 22, 1949) found him engaged in a stormy quarrel with Margaret Sullavan at MGM. Wood wanted a screenwriter removed from a scheduled film project, accusing him of being a member of the Communist Party. (In the early forties Wood had made no such fuss over working with other dedicated left-wingers: Dalton Trumbo on *Kitty Foyle* and Dudley Nichols on *For Whom the Bell Tolls*.) Sullavan said she would walk off the picture if the director had his way. Churning over that argument, Wood went to a meeting of the Motion Picture Alliance where he became further enraged at the news that Emmet Lavery was suing the group for slander. Shortly after the meeting ended, Wood collapsed and died of heart failure.

Even in death, however, he continued his fight against communism. His will specified that no prospective heir, with the exception of his widow, could inherit unless that person filed, with the clerk of the probate court, an affidavit swearing that they "are not now, nor have they ever been, Communists."

A reasonably successful second-line director at MGM during the thirties, Wood specialized in saving and finishing difficult films—notably *Gone With the Wind*. Politically unaligned, Wood had always been a fervent admirer of the views of William Randolph Hearst. The men knew each other personally and carried on a cordial relationship during and after the two films Wood made with Marion Davies. As Hearst's enthusiasm for Roosevelt curdled as a result of "excessive" federal welfare and the "dictatorial" nature of the National Recovery

Administration, Wood followed him into the Republican, anti-New Deal camp. Wood's opposition to Roosevelt did not turn into hatred, however, until the early forties. Gradually, during the war, Jeane Wood recalls, her father was transformed and possessed by his anti-Roosevelt beliefs. "Iron entered his soul," she said; he literally began to equate the New Deal with communism. He carried around a "little black book" in which he scrupulously noted the names of "Communists" who should be "purged" from the film industry, passionate supporters of FDR leading the list. By the presidential election of 1944, Jeane Wood believes, her father's vision had become completely occluded. Communists occupied his entire attention; around the house he could be heard "muttering" about their infiltration into the film industry.

Jeane Wood believes that her father was sincerely convinced that Communists were a threat and a menace to American ideals. He was also, as we have seen, influenced by William Randolph Hearst. The obsessive ingredient, however—the factor that transformed Wood from an anti-Communist to a possessed witch-hunter—was, Jeane Wood says, professional frustration and disappointment. She traces his mono-mindedness on the subject of communism to his failure to win the Best Director Academy Award for *Goodbye, Mr. Chips*. It had been his first "prestige" film and the defeat galled and disappointed him beyond measure.

Films such as *Mission to Moscow* and activities such as the Writers' Congress of October 1943 moved Wood and a number of his MGM cronies—directors Clarence Brown, Norman Taurog, Victor Fleming, King Vidor; costume designer Cedric Gibbons; and screenwriter Howard E. Rogers—along with Walt Disney, Gary Cooper, and other Hollywood conservatives to start organizing against the Reds. In February 1944, after weeks of secret meetings and planning sessions, the formation of the Motion Picture Alliance was officially announced. Not so coincidentally, this announcement was made the day before a glittering assemblage of Hollywood liberals were to gather at a dinner sponsored by the Hollywood Free World Association, an anti-isolationist, anti-nationalist organization. Vice-President Henry Wallace was the featured speaker, screenwriter Dudley Nichols was the chairman, and Governor Earl Warren, Will Hays, Walter Wanger, Olivia De Havilland, and Walter Huston were among the honored guests.

Sam Wood was the Alliance's first president; Walt Disney, Cedric Gibbons, and Norman Taurog its vice-presidents; Clarence Brown its treasurer. Among the members of the Executive Committee were screenwriters James K. McGuinness, Borden Chase, Bert Kalmar, Rupert Hughes, Fred Niblo, Jr., Casey Robinson, Howard Emmett Rogers, and Morrie Ryskind.

Future officers of the Alliance would include Robert Taylor, Adolphe Menjou, Gary Cooper, Hedda Hopper, John Wayne, Ward Bond, Charles Coburn, and Roy Brewer.

The Alliance members were not at all shy about declaring the group's *raison d'être*: "In our special field of motion pictures, we resent the growing impression that this industry is made up of, and dominated by, Communists, radicals and crack-pots. . . . We pledge to fight, with every means at our organized command, any effort of any group or individual, to divert the loyalty of the screen from the free America that gave it birth."[6] In the more colorful words of MPA member John Lee Mahin, the Alliance aimed to "turn off the faucets which dripped red water into film scripts" as well as to counter Hollywood's adverse image in the press. Sam Wood's inaugural address to the MPA set the tone and defined the strategy of the new Red-baiting era in Hollywood: "The American motion picture industry is, and will continue to be, held by Americans for the American people, in the interests of America, and dedicated to the preservation and continuance of the American scene and the American way of life." If "you are Americans," he told his listeners, then you are qualified to join the Alliance and assist it in its ventures.[7]

Thus from the outset it was all too clear that the Motion Picture Alliance was to be neither an exclusive grouping of conservative studio executives on the order of the Motion Picture Producers' Association nor a coalition of industry groups banded together in the "interests of the industry," as the Motion Picture Industry Council was to be in 1948. On the contrary, as almost every political person in the film industry, liberal and conservative alike, perceived, the MPA exemplified a new genus—one which was out for blood and which exhibited an anti-Communist zeal and tenacity greatly overshadowing its members' loyalty to the film industry. Its open invitation to HUAC to return to Hollywood to conduct a full-scale, fully aided investigation estranged the MPA from the producers. Walter Wanger probably voiced the sentiments of most of his fellow movie executives when he told *Weekly Variety:*

The MPA has made unsupported charges of Communism in the motion picture industry. It has linked throughout the country the words Hollywood and Red, without proof. . . . They could have

taken those charges to responsible groups. They could have gone
to the Producers Association. Instead they went to the press. I am
for unity. But there can be no unity as long as a group exists that
thinks more of its selfish interests and publicity than of protecting
the welfare of an industry that serves the nation best by remaining
free.[8]

Correctly sensing that a narrow, intra-studio campaign or a low industrial profile would not serve its purposes, that it would, in fact, result either in a leftist counterattack that would smother it, as the
Screen Playwrights had been smothered, or in producer indifference,
the Alliance immediately threw out lines to HUAC, the Tenney Committee, the Knights of Columbus, the American Legion, and the Republican Party. An unconfirmable rumor held that the MPA even
offered Martin Dies a $50,000 annual salary to leave Congress to head
the organization.[9] What is certain is that Alliance members "un-
officially" wrote an inflammatory letter to arch-conservative Senator
Robert R. Reynolds, which the North Carolina Democrat duly read
into the Congressional Record on March 7, 1944. Signed by "A
Group of Your Friends in Hollywood," the letter was a thinly disguised invitation to launch a congressional investigation into communism in Hollywood.

Although the letter particularly scored the "flagrant manner in
which the motion picture industrialists of Hollywood have been
coddling Communists" and " 'totalitarian-minded groups' working in
the industry for 'the dissemination of un-American ideas and beliefs,' "[10] the Alliance did not neglect, in other messages, the anti-labor
motif which characterized the anti-Communist crusade. Many years
later, former HUAC investigator William Wheeler told an interviewer: "We were invited by Hollywood people—especially those
concerned about Communist Party infiltration of craft unions."[11] Roy
Brewer, international representative in Hollywood of the International
Alliance of Theatrical Stage Employees (IATSE), was more concerned than anyone. The non-Communist, but militant, democratic,
and decentralized Conference of Studio Unions (CSU) had, in the
four years since its formation in 1941, organized and tantalized the
thousands of Hollywood studio workers who either chafed under the
IA's sweetheart unionism or were left unorganized as a result of it.
IATSE leadership had been consistently more sensitive to the needs of
the studio executives than to those of its rank-and-file membership.
The only gains that IA members won during these years were in the

form of payoffs for anti-labor actions, such as voting against the rival United Studio Technicians Guild in an NLRB election in 1939, or those required to keep pace with gains won by democratic groups such as the CSU. IA people were regularly available as scabs, strike-breakers, and thugs. By lashing his union tightly to the Motion Picture Alliance, Brewer hoped to profit from the anti-Communist crusade by destroying the "Communist-dominated" CSU and purging his own union of dissidents.

Brewer was not alone in his opposition to democratic or militant trade unionism within the MPA. The founders of the old Screen Playwrights joined the Alliance because they believed that the Screen Writers Guild was now "lousy with Reds." Walt Disney hated unions and was a veteran Red-baiter. In fact, nearly all the MPA members were renowned within their own talent guilds for their anti-strike, pro-management, pro-industrial harmony positions. Ayn Rand's pamphlet *Screen Guide for Americans* perfectly captured the anti-labor, pro-business impulse behind the launching of the Motion Picture Alliance when it advised moviemakers: "Don't Smear the Free Enterprise System," "Don't Deify the 'Common Man,'" "Don't Glorify the Collective," "Don't Smear Success," "Don't Smear Industrialists."[12]

Hollywood union activists not in the thrall of Brewer's sweetheart unionism and anti-communism were instantly alerted to the threat posed to them, their organizations, and their industry by the MPA's stated and unstated means and ends. Opposition immediately appeared. A fairly broad coalition of liberal and radical adversaries was assembled by the Screen Writers Guild, who recognized among the Alliance's members many of its erstwhile enemies of the Screen Playwrights, Inc. On April 18, 1944, two days before HUAC investigators arrived, the SWG Board sent out telegrams to more than forty labor groups in the film industry asking them to send representatives to a convocation whose job would consist of combating the "harmful and irresponsible" statements of the Motion Picture Alliance.[13] Emissaries from seventeen guilds and unions appeared at the May 2 meeting and named themselves the Council of Hollywood Guilds and Unions. Plans were made to hold a mass meeting on June 28. Approximately 1,000 delegates, representing 22,000 studio artists and workers (more than two thirds of the total) converged at the Women's Club of Hollywood to register their indignation with the words and actions of Sam Wood and the Motion Picture Alliance. More was at stake here, however, than politics. By inviting HUAC to Hollywood and by publicly announcing that communism infected the film industry, the Alliance was aiming to purge the studios of everyone with a strong left-wing viewpoint and history of activism on behalf of that viewpoint. The Left's battle with the forces of reaction had taken on another, more personally threatening, aspect: the job a progressive held was now, for the first time, at stake.

The speeches and resolutions of the May meeting were transcribed and published in a pamphlet entitled *The Truth About Hollywood*. The Foreword underscored both the ominous nature of the challenge and the unprecedented nature of the reply. "For the first time in the history of Hollywood, the workers in the motion picture industry have united to set up a program of public relations and to take action to protect the industry and its workers from anti-democratic, anti-labor attacks." The Foreword also noted, prophetically, that the Motion Picture Alliance was "only one symptom of the type of attack that may always be expected by a free screen" just as the picture business was only the first community embroiled "in the type of 'witch-hunting' described in this paper." The history, meaning, and intent of the reactionary trend in Hollywood were then explored and examined by a broad political spectrum of speakers—moderate liberals like James Hilton and Emmet Lavery, centrist liberals like Mary McCall, left-wing liberals like Oliver H. P. Garrett, and Communists like Sidney Buchman. The labor-management gap was spanned by the presence on the speaker's rostrum of liberal producer Walter Wanger and union leaders Herb Aller (Photographers), Al Speede (Electricians), and Herb Sorrell (Painters and Conference of Studio Unions). All their remarks revealed their outrage at the MPA for presuming to speak for the film industry ("So far as I know the Alliance has never held a meeting open to the industry," said Mary McCall), and for summoning outside forces of reaction to judge the people and products of Hollywood ("It has provided ammunition to the industry's chronic enemies," charged Wanger†). The speakers were practically unanimous in their denunciation of the MPA membership as spokespeople for anti-labor, anti-free expression, pro-fascist positions. The assembled delegates agreed that the time had arrived for them—the vast majority of film employees—to inform the world that they, not the Alliance, represented the true voice of Hollywood. All guilds and unions were pressed to join the Council of Hollywood Guilds and Unions, and a two-year program of action was proposed to combat anti-labor and

---

† Five years later Wanger changed tunes (and partners), saying: "I recognize that time and history have proven the correctness of the judgement of the MPA and its foresight. . . ." (New York *Times*, September 17, 1950.)

racist practices within the industry and to protect film making from attacks by "subversive and dangerous" organizations like the Alliance. Finally, in the single overtly partisan action of the day, the meeting pledged its allegiance (in a fervent resolution) to the nation's commander in chief.

The words of the united forces of Hollywood labor did not derail the anti-Communist crusade. Traditional jurisdictional rivalries and political differences would soon undermine the Council and render it useless in the approaching collision. Its very appearance and existence, however, further fed the fires of the crusade's anti-labor demonology. The working-class devil was not simply some concocted wraith haunting the minds of right-wing Cassandras; it had deep roots in the events going on nationally and locally at the time the MPA was formed. The wartime strikes, frequent as they were, were dwarfed in number by the postwar swell, as workers in war-related industries such as steel, coal, shipping, and railroads battled to achieve the wage/price parity which had been denied them by the Wage Labor Stabilization Act, which had frozen salary levels, while the cost of living had risen nearly 50 per cent since American entry into the war. The Wage Labor Board devised the so-called "Little Steel" formula—a 15 per cent wage raise—as compensation for the unions' no-strike pledge. Demanding wage increases of as much as 35 per cent, American labor set off, in 1946, an unprecedented explosion of work stoppages. Between August 1945 and August 1946 there occurred 4,600 strikes, involving 5 million workers, and resulting in the loss of 120 million man-days of production. The figures for the calendar year 1946 were even higher —over 8 million workers struck.[14]

The strikes shattered the "labor peace" of the war years and the postwar illusions of management and labor leaders that harmony could be imposed from the top down. On April 1, 1945, Eric Johnston (president of the United States Chamber of Commerce), William Green (president of the American Federation of Labor), and Philip Murray (president of the Congress of Industrial Organizations) had signed a "Charter for Industrial Peace," which looked toward a postwar future devoid of conflict and overflowing with prosperity—a strike-less world of industrial harmony in which labor-management differences were amicably resolved.[15] The vision and plans of this entente did not, however, accord with the needs of organized labor's rank and file. Indeed, in his new position as head of the Motion Picture Association, Johnston soon found himself a central figure in management's strategy of obstructing labor's demands.

Prominent corporate executives gathered in New York in the autumn of 1945, under the auspices of the National Association of Manufacturers, to formulate and coordinate their counteroffensive.[16] Shortly thereafter, at a Labor-Management Conference called by President Truman in November, the gauntlet was publicly flung: Charles E. Wilson of General Motors, David Sarnoff of RCA, Johnston, and others made clear their intent to take a hard line on wages and to lobby intensively for the repeal of the Wagner Act.[17] In the ensuing months and years, evidence accumulated to indicate that management's campaign would not be limited to the narrowly economic grounds of labor union contentiousness. A series of pamphlets issued by the United States Chamber of Commerce contained a series of "recommendations" which, in retrospect, seemed designed not only to undo the labor gains of the New Deal, but to link unions, free expression, and social reform legislation with political radicalism and to deal the latter a final, shattering blow. The 1946 Chamber publication suggested the institution of a strict federal loyalty program and an investigation of Communist influence in the cultural media, notably the motion picture industry. The 1947 report called for the Department of Justice to publish, biannually, "a certified list of Communist-controlled front organizations and labor unions." It also demanded an "anti-Communist" modification of the Wagner Act. By 1948 the Chamber was demanding federal legislation barring Communists from positions in teaching, social work, book reviewing, and libraries. The 1952 "master plan" virtually disregarded the Constitution altogether in its cry for an untrammeled investigation and prosecution of Communists, the complete exclusion of Reds and fellow travelers from all agencies and professions affecting public opinion, from all educational or literary positions, from jobs of high visibility, prestige, and salary, particularly those in the entertainment field, and from any plant or factory large enough to have a trade union local.[18]

The Hollywood version of the nationwide postwar labor-management collision was particularly dramatic. The Conference of Studio Unions represented the only hope for a democratic labor union movement in Hollywood. The organization had been founded by Herbert Sorrell, business agent of the Motion Picture Painters Local 644, in the wake of a successful strike which he had helped organize and lead against the Walt Disney Studios—a strike which had established the relatively progressive Cartoonists' Guild. At its inception, the Conference included five unions (the Screen Cartoonists' Guild, the Screen Office Employees Guild, Film Technicians Local 683, Machinists

Local 1185, and Motion Picture Painters Local 644), all rank-and-file-oriented. The founders of the CSU hoped to unite all non-IATSE locals in Hollywood and to establish locals for the unorganized trades and vocations in the picture business. Left-wing in its orientation throughout the war, the CSU broke ranks with other labor federations in the United States to support or participate in the activities of a large number of Popular and Communist front organizations, which in turn lent support to the CSU in its contests with management and the IATSE. By 1945 the Conference had enrolled nearly ten thousand members (as compared with sixteen thousand for Brewer's organization), and, as such, constituted a serious threat to the producers, who did not regard Sorrell as a "reasonable" labor leader, as they did Roy Brewer. Fearing a postwar CSU-led strike for higher wages and improved working conditions, studio executives tried to paralyze the Conference by exploiting one of the many jurisdictional disputes which were common among rival Hollywood labor federations. The California branch of the Producers' Association, responsible for formulating a common labor policy for its constituent studio members, refused to recognize a change of affiliation of the Society of Motion Picture Interior Decorators from the IATSE to the CSU. Sorrell promptly appealed to the War Labor Board, which upheld his claim. The Association of Motion Picture Producers refused to budge. The CSU leadership, fully understanding the portent which the AMPP's tactics held for their plans for postwar expansion of the CSU, launched a strike in March 1945, which lasted for eight months. The National Labor Relations Board investigated, found the AMPP to be at fault, and eventually paved the way for a strike settlement satisfactory to the CSU.

Round one had not proved peaceful, however. The strike, especially at Warner Brothers, had witnessed picket line scenes reminiscent of the worst labor-management confrontations of the thirties in Detroit, Chicago, or Oakland. Warners (and their IATSE allies) employed scabs, thugs, tear gas, fire hoses, and the studio's private police and fire departments to disrupt picket lines and break the strike. The CSU strike polarized a Hollywood film community seemingly united by the war effort. Various Popular Front organizations rushed to the aid of the strikers and sent off the usual torrent of letters and telegrams, with the usual prominent names, to the usual people and organizations: the NLRB, the California congressional bloc, President Truman, Secretary of Labor Lewis B. Schwellenbach, the Democratic National Committee.

The objections, however, fell on deaf ears. The Truman administration, for its part, proved as hostile to the Hollywood strike (or to *any* strike) as the Roosevelt administration had been in the immediate prewar years. Despite the warnings from Hollywood liberals that the Democrats stood in peril of losing their hold on film labor's loyalty, the Washington politicians did nothing. Finally George Pepper, executive secretary of the Hollywood Independent Citizens Committee of the Arts, Sciences, and Professions (HICCASP), the leading Popular Front alliance of liberals and radicals in postwar Hollywood, warned Truman that his organization would find it very difficult to "mobilize [public opinion] behind critical legislative issues [sponsored by the Democratic administration]" if more support for a fair settlement was not forthcoming from Washington. In this attempt to goad or shame the President, Pepper put him on notice that "our local situation appears but part of a nationwide pattern created by a reactionary drive against unionism, full employment, unemployment compensation, and a permanent FEPC [Fair Employment Practices Committee]."[19]

The Washington chieftains were not alone in their unwillingness or inability to see in the CSU strike an augury of coming events. The Communist Party, still blinkered by its wartime patriotic line, initially proclaimed its hostility to the strike order. Within two days of the outbreak of the strike the Party's main West Coast organ, *People's World*, placed equal blame on the producers and the CSU and appealed to the War Labor Board and Congress to arrange and enforce a settlement. Ten days later, on April 19, the paper ran a story, under the headline FOR NATIONAL UNITY—END THE FILM STRIKE, accusing the CSU leaders of "wasting forces needed for making that new world for which the President [Roosevelt] gave his life." On May 18 the *People's World* labeled the ongoing strike "a disgraceful situation." In late September, however, the CPUSA abruptly changed its attitude toward the strike. During the summer months American diplomats and military chiefs of staff—most notably Truman at Potsdam—had displayed increasing truculence *vis-à-vis* Russian demands in Eastern Europe. Word may well have come down from CP headquarters in New York (or Moscow) that the Party had better begin to assume a position "independent" from that of the Truman administration in foreign and domestic matters. On September 21 a *People's World* writer commended the CSU strikers for their fight for basic union rights, and criticized the War Labor Board and the NLRB for their impotence. Suddenly the strike had become not a disgrace but an omen: "It is no accident that Hollywood has been chosen as a testing ground in this anti-union campaign by those who see in this critical post-war period their best chance to smash democratic trade-unions . . . and, in short, to set Los Angeles—and America—on the road to reaction. . . ."[20] Thus the CP hierarchy caught up with its Hollywood rank-and-file and joined HICCASP in the ranks of CSU supporters.

The strikers needed every friendly word and body they could get. They faced formidable opposition, the strongest of which was, not surprisingly, the person who had the most to lose from a CSU victory —Roy Brewer. He had threatening letters mailed out to all the prominent film personalities connected with HICCASP. The three-page document proclaimed at length the sturdy Americanism of the IATSE in contrast to the alien nature and beliefs of its opponents. The letter ended with a question (printed in upper-case letters) which every reader was expected to publicly answer:

> [Do] you, you as an individual, support the campaign of slander, vilification, lies and scurrility now being carried on against our officers and those loyal American workers who believe in and support the I.A.T.S.E., and who, by doing so, have incurred the enmity and hatred of the entire Communist "apparat"?[21]

The letter strongly intimated that if the recipient did not declare himself for Brewer and his organization and against Sorrell and his, then that person was *ipso facto* an agent of un-Americanism, an enemy of the IATSE, and a likely candidate for boycott by the union's film projectionist members. For film artists concerned with their careers, a threat not to project their movies in the nation's theaters was dire indeed. As it turned out, Brewer had little to worry about from the vast majority of screen actors and actresses. In March 1945 the Screen Actors Guild voted, 3,029 to 88, to cross the CSU picket lines.[22] The small group of progressives within SAG, led by Karen Morley and Lionel Stander, found themselves entirely outnumbered and outmaneuvered by Ronald Reagan, George Murphy, Robert Montgomery, etc.

Even the Screen Writers Guild refused the CSU's request to respect the picket lines, albeit by a much more narrow margin. The Board cited the no-strike clause‡ in the SWG's bargaining agreement with

---

‡ The no-strike clause (Article 15 of the Basic Minimum Agreement of 1937) read: "The Guild agrees that during the term hereof it will not call or engage in a strike affecting motion picture production against any producer signatory hereto, and will order its members to perform their contracts with the producers signatory hereto even though other persons or groups of persons are on strike."

the studios as its answer to Sorrell's plea for solidarity.[23] The Board did, however, send a series of telegrams to Washington and to Eric Johnston urging governmental intervention as the most immediate manner in which to settle the strike.[24] Although the SWG included within its ranks a large minority of radicals who supported the CSU outspokenly and a much larger contingent of liberals and moderates sympathetic to the concept of democratic unionism, the Board feared taking a partisan stand which would polarize the Guild and run afoul of the studios. Leftist screenwriters, then and later, critized the Board's shortsightedness and its failure to affiliate the SWG with other Hollywood unions or to support strikes by other motion picture workers. This policy "far removed" the SWG "from the Hollywood labor scene," wrote radical Arthur Strawn; "it was as if we had no Guild," lamented liberal Philip Dunne.[25] Thirty years later, former Communist Abraham Polonsky recalled that the CSU was the only natural ally for what he termed a "terribly isolated and vulnerable SWG. A thriving CSU would have bolstered us immeasurably."

Without allies, and with the strike dragging on, Sorrell decided to single out one studio—Warner Brothers—and, by putting maximum pressure on it, to break a link in the studios' chain of resistance. On October 5 a mass picket was thrown up around the studio. Three days later the studio's police and fire departments, equipped with fire hoses and tear gas, and a vigilante squad of one thousand IATSE thugs, led by IA officials and equipped with chains, rubber hoses, blackjacks, and metal cables, attacked the CSU picket lines. In the melee that followed, many injuries were sustained, but the strikers held their lines.

At this point the Hollywood leftists—led, as always, by the screenwriters—finally made their presence felt. The baldness of the IATSE/studio/police alliance evoked protest from liberals and radicals alike. Lester Cole appeared before the SWG Board and urged it to call a membership meeting to vote on the following resolution, which he had authored:

> The Guild takes the position that the spirit of the Minimum Basic Agreement [between the Hollywood unions and guilds and the Hollywood studios] has been broken by Warner Brothers in its violation of the civil liberties of the strikers and that writers will not work at Warner Brothers until a specific settlement between the striking groups and the studio has been reached.

Conservatives and liberals on the Board voiced strong opposition to this measure, saying that "anything which the Guild could do in the situation was not of sufficient importance to warrant the possibility of breaking up the SWG, which they believed might result if such a proposal were presented to the membership at this time." Cole's motion was narrowly defeated by an alliance of conservative and liberal Board members. A second motion—to provide legal aid to any writer arrested while picketing at Warners—also went down to defeat. The most that the radicals could extract from the SWG Board was an official protest against the actions of the studio police and an official delegation to a newly created organization, the Citizens Committee to Clarify the Strike Situation.[26]

The Board's refusal to involve the Guild deeply in the strike did not deter the radical screenwriters from further action on behalf of the CSU. They joined with a group of prominent Los Angeles citizens (UCLA professor Franklin Fearing, Assemblyman Augustus Hawkins, Carey McWilliams, Thomas L. Griffith of the NAACP, et al.) to form a committee of observers. The group sent a telegram to Warner Brothers informing studio management that the signatories would be on hand Tuesday, October 9, as "witnesses to the picketing at your studio."[27] Perhaps as a result of such outside interest, there was no further violence on Tuesday, or in the days thereafter as the observation continued. Meanwhile, at a mass demonstration in support of the CSU, Dalton Trumbo delivered a blistering attack on studio producers for their willingness to back corrupt, undemocratic unionism even to the point of violence and illegality. In an ironic peroration, Trumbo "thanked" the producers for "alert[ing] American labor to the true nature of the dangers confronting it."[28] Then, on October 15, the SWG Board relented to the demands of its left-wing members and issued a statement in support of the CSU's demand for reinstatement of all strikers in the studio positions they had held prior to the work stoppage.[29]

Gradually the tide turned in favor of the CSU. The NLRB ruled against the producers and the aroused Hollywood Left agitated, demonstrated, and observed in support of the CSU. The pickets, protected by such witnesses as Lawson and Cole, continued, and finally the studios gave in: the new affiliation of the interior decorators was recognized. The Hollywood Left had won what would turn out to be its last important battle. The increasing unwillingness of the majority of SWG membership to face the powerful historical tides sweeping the United States and Hollywood in the late forties weakened the Left considerably. Part of the problem was that the SWG packed even less weight in the postwar world than it had during the thirties. The membership could not even oblige studio executives to rehire writers returning from service in the armed forces, and it did not even bother to try to force Columbia and MGM to take back Lawson and Bright, two members who had been fired for their involvement in the CSU strike.

In any event, the Left had small opportunity to savor its victory. Another, worse, CSU strike broke out less than a year later, in September 1946. (Actually there had been a second strike, in early July 1946, which had lasted three days and resulted in the CSU'S winning a 25 per cent wage raise from the studios.) This third strike would drag on for three years, resulting in the disappearance of the CSU, the purge of left-wing labor leaders, including Sorrell, from all Hollywood unions, and the end of the democratic labor movement in the picture business. The issue which launched the strike was manufactured by Brewer and the Producers' Labor Committee, all of whom were spoiling for another go-round with the CSU. Once again it was a question of jurisdiction, this time over set and prop building. Sets had always been erected by Carpenters (AFL) from material brought to them by grips (IATSE). Now, the IA claimed that "set erecting" was different from "set building," and claimed jurisdiction over the former for a scab carpenters' local it had established during the 1945 CSU strike. The Painters (CSU) refused to paint "hot sets" (i.e., those "erected" by IA people). The executives immediately locked all CSU personnel out of the studios.

As the minutes of the Producers' Labor Committee revealed, when they were read to a congressional subcommittee eighteen months later, the set erection dispute had been a co-production of Brewer and the studio executives. The minutes had been turned over to Sorrell's attorney, George Bodle, by Pat Casey, an MGM executive appalled by the conspiracy. Bodle testified:

> The minutes show that the producers' labor representatives were in constant conference from September 11, 1946, through September 24, 1946, consulting each other and agreeing upon a policy of uniform action. . . . The minutes further reveal that Roy Brewer . . . was called in and present at most of these meetings, and that arrangements were made to have the carpenters ordered to work on "hot sets" and upon their refusal to "terminate their employment"; that the IATSE was to provide replacements for the studios; that the policy was decided after advice from the New York executives to attempt to keep open [the studios, and to] call on IA to do the struck work.[30]

Even without knowledge of the behind-the-scenes maneuvers, few members of the Hollywood Left doubted that Brewer and the studio executives were trying to ensnare Sorrell in another, protracted strike. Sorrell proved deaf to counsels of restraint; he lunged for the bait. The strike erupted. The 1945 scenario of telegrams, violence, protest, and counterprotest was repeated. Again, Lester Cole's motion for a special SWG membership meeting was voted down by a worried Board;[31] again the studios' police departments, augmented by recruits from municipal forces,* entered the fray with gas canisters and fire hoses; again IATSE goons disrupted picket lines while police and sheriff's deputies stood by. In other words, the opponents were the same. This time, however, support for the CSU had noticeably lessened. The anti-Communist crusade had begun to take its toll on the Left. Brewer's merciless Red-baiting voice had joined the larger national chorus. In a letter to *The Screen Writer*, Brewer called the Guild a "fellow traveler organization" in cahoots with Communists within the CSU.[32] Pat Casey, who had been, up to the 1946 strike, the chairman of the Producers' Labor Committee, did not agree with Brewer. He told the House Sub-Committee that he did not think the strike was "communistic-inspired." He continued: "My God. I have heard Communist, Communist. It gets down to where if you do not agree with somebody you are a Communist. . . . There is no question but so far as our trouble out there is concerned the fellows in those studios are anxious to work and to get that dough Saturday night. I don't think they have anything to do with communistic affiliations."[33] The Red-baiting had the effect Brewer sought: no Hollywood union dared to offer even verbal support to the CSU.

In the midst of the new strike, and of Brewer's stepped-up campaign of Americanism and anti-communism, national elections were held. The Republicans, running on an overtly anti-labor, anti-Communist platform, enjoyed major congressional gains, picking up eleven seats in the Senate and fifty-four in the House, while garnering enough new governorships to emerge with a majority of the state houses. Organized labor was a bigger loser than the Democratic Party; its staunchest supporters were swept out in the Republican wave.[34] Once in office, the triumphant conservatives launched an immediate offensive against

---

* "Hundreds of film strikers were arrested daily in late 1946 and early 1947 by Los Angeles police who were often on studio payrolls (MGM bought up the entire Culver City police force)." (Daniel J. Biederman, "The Making of a Zealot," *The Nation*, June 22, 1974, p. 781.)

unions. Dozens of proposals to curb the power of organized labor
were introduced in the federal and state legislatures. The most
significant result of hundreds of hours of hearings and debates on this
subject was, of course, the Taft-Hartley Act of 1947, but it was accompanied by many similar state laws.

The election results, coupled with the Brewer campaign, undercut
the CSU's left-wing support. Among organizations, only the Communist Party and HICCASP openly supported the strikers, and CP assistance, under the circumstances, was of little help. These material and
psychological factors overwhelmed the CSU in 1947 and the strike
came to an unsuccessful end. Brewer fought the CSU at the studio
level with means more effective, in the long run, than assaults on
picket lines. Working closely with studio management after the lockout of CSU members who refused to work on "hot sets," the IATSE
established new locals of scabs to fill the holes left by the strikers and
lockouts. Where such outrageous instances of collusion and strike- and
union-breaking might have previously been met with a concerted response from Hollywood labor unions and guilds, in 1946–47 they succeeded. Gradually the CSU picket lines dwindled, members reluctantly deserting Sorrell for Brewer and the assurance of work. What
left-wing support the CSU had initially rallied was by now itself under
such overwhelming pressure that it had to look to its own survival. In
1949 the CSU had ceased to exist and Sorrell had been purged from his
own local. By then, however, other events had transpired which
dwarfed the entire issue of the CSU's cause.

Though the CSU drew its final breath in relative obscurity, its destruction (and the identity of its saboteurs) had many ramifications
for the Left in Hollywood. Within the unions it spelled the end of de-
centralization and democracy. The ranks of the IATSE were swept
clean of left-wing spokespeople. The disappearance of the CSU took
away from the other progressive unions and guilds throughout the film
industry a dependable source of labor solidarity. A former Communist
who is still active in the Hollywood labor movement summed up the
consequences of the defeat of the CSU strike of 1946: "It was a devastating loss. It was a complete disaster for everything progressive, autonomous, or liberal in the Hollywood labor movement. Hundreds were
blacklisted; their homes and lives were shattered; some committed
suicide."

The shock waves from the dissolution of the CSU radiated well beyond the labor unions. HICCASP—a much broader and more influential organization than the Motion Picture Democratic Committee of

the 1930s—was split down the middle by the CSU strike and the question of which candidates to support in the 1946 elections. By the end of 1946 it was reduced to a radical caucus, the numerous and influential liberals having jumped ship. HICCASP's diminishment, coupled with the CSU's defeat, left a broken movement and an isolated assortment of radicals and Communists, with no organization to stand between them and those groups now ready to "clean up" the film industry, and only the Communist Party to stand behind them when the witch-hunters arrived.

HICCASP and the Third Popular Front

The story of the decline of HICCASP illustrates how virulent the liberal/radical split of 1939–41 remained. Not even war-time unity and Communist patriotism could heal it. Nevertheless, while it endured, HICCASP "was much more impressive than the MPDC," said Ellenore Bogigian, the Committee's chief of staff, "because it benefited from the increased political organizing and consciousness which had gone on in Hollywood since 1939." HICCASP incarnated the tremendous progressive revival of the war years, gathering together the numerous individuals and organizations which flourished in that period. Like the Popular Front groups of the thirties, however, the new organization's excitement, optimism, and activity concealed from its members the legacy of past partisan conflicts and the latent internal divisions. Few activists recognized or reflected upon such considerations. Even men and women who had been badly burned in the 1939–41 dissolution of the Front now flocked to HICCASP as to a "promised land, a dream world." In fact, this political garden bloomed with extraordinary rapidity on the cratered battlefields of the Phony War period.

HICCASP began life as the Hollywood Democratic Committee, which was formed by radical veterans of the Motion Picture Democratic Committee, Communists, and some newcomers to the Hollywood political scene. The Nazi-Soviet Pact had delivered a death blow to the credibility of the MPDC as a political force, at least as far as the 1940 campaign was concerned. By 1942, however, with the passing of the excitement of America's entry into the war, activists like Lawson, Trumbo, Bright, and studio composer Johnny Green began to perceive the disturbing signs of militant conservatism which accompanied the bellicose patriotism of the day. Worried by what they saw, they organized to assist the reelection campaign of Governor Culbert Olson and the congressional campaign of Will Rogers, Jr. In both the state and national campaigns the issues and stands polarized political opponents. Racial tensions were exploited by Republican candidates, who also augured their party's 1944 position of hostility to welfare and labor. The progressives, under the circumstances, had to be satisfied with a split decision: victory for Rogers, defeat for Olson.

Undistracted by events in North Africa, Europe, and the Far East, domestic political factions immediately turned their attention to the 1944 elections: the conservatives were eager to extend their gains; liberals and radicals were grimly determined to stop the Republican advance and retake the offensive. The first organized expression of this nationwide progressive impetus was the Hollywood Democratic Committee. Over two hundred screen artist left-wingers gathered at the Hollywood-Roosevelt Hotel on January 14, 1943, to reconstruct a permanent organization, on the order of the Motion Picture Democratic Committee, that would nominate and elect "honest and responsible" public officials. By the following summer the HDC had been joined by the CIO Political Action Committee, the National Citizens Political Action Committee (a liberal/labor alliance of people who were pro-Roosevelt but not necessarily pro-Democratic Party), and the Independent Voters Committee of Artists, Writers, and Scientists for the Re-Election of President Roosevelt (the New York-based counterpart of the HDC).† All these groups had in common a concern about the quality of victory, both at home and abroad; a stance independent of both political parties; a devotion to the person, and symbol, of Franklin Roosevelt. In each, Communists stood in the forefront of the organizing efforts, though they were greatly outnumbered by liberals on the lists of sponsors and boards.

The new organizations shared one other characteristic: conspicuously absent from these gatherings of liberals and radicals were the

---

† The National Citizens Political Action Committee's officers included former senator George Norris, Sidney Hillman, James G. Patton (National Farmers Union), Freda Kirchwey (*The Nation*), Bishop R. R. Wright, Jr., and R. J. Thomas (United Automobile Workers).

Initiating sponsors of the Independent Voters Committee of Artists, Writers, and Scientists included Helen Keller, Ethel Barrymore, Van Wyck Brooks, Thomas Hart Benton, Michael Todd, Serge Koussevitzky, and Norman Corwin.

In the spring of 1945 the Independent Voters changed its name to the Independent Citizens Committee of the Arts, Sciences, and Professions, and opened a legislative office in Washington which they shared with the Hollywood Democratic Committee. On June 6, 1945, the HDC changed its name to HICCASP; on March 14, 1946 HICCASP affiliated with ICCASP.

moderate and conservative liberals who had turned to strident anti-communism in late 1939, and who now stood intransigently aloof from this third Popular Front, forming instead their own organizations. The first ones were founded prior to the United States entry into World War II: Committee for Cultural Freedom (by Sidney Hook and John Dewey) and Union for Democratic Action (by James Loeb, Jr.). During the war, in the summer of 1944, the American Labor Party in New York split over the issue of including left-wing trade union representatives within its governing body. Alex Rose and David Dubinsky opposed Sidney Hillman on this issue, lost, and formed the Liberal Party as, in Dubinsky's words, "a rallying center for those labor and liberal forces that wanted a genuinely independent outlet for political action free of the two major parties and of the Communists as well."[35] In January 1947 the centerpiece of the anti-Communist liberal movement was established—Americans for Democratic Action. James Loeb, Jr., was joined by Eleanor Roosevelt, Paul Porter, Reinhold Niebuhr, Arthur Schlesinger, Jr., Joseph Rauh, Melvyn Douglas, Philip Dunne, and other liberals desirous of protecting what they called "the Vital Center" from the competing totalitarian ideologies of fascism and communism. Their position was clearly stated in the ADA's inaugural manifesto: "We reject any association with Communists or sympathizers with communism in the United States as completely as we reject any association with fascists or their sympathizers."[36]

Each Popular Front group had at its head one person whose enthusiasm, organizational capacity, and patience with detail helped guide it over the factional stresses to victory in the 1944 elections: Sidney Hillman of the CIOPAC, Beanie Baldwin of the NCPAC, and Jo Davidson of the Independent Voters. The head of the Hollywood Democratic Committee possessed all the leadership talents of his eastern counterparts, but differed in that he was a member of the Communist Party. A violinist, George Pepper developed arthritis in his fingers and was obliged to quit his profession. He threw himself into political work, organizing musicians for the war effort and Hollywood people for the 1942 elections. Under his very able direction, the HDC grew rapidly, and by mid-1943 it had become the major outpost of progressivism west of the Hudson River. All who knew and worked beside Pepper attest to his intelligence, discipline, and uncanny knack for bringing together people of diverse partisan viewpoints. In Bogigian's words: "He put together the HDC like a watch and polished it like a jewel." Such care paid off. Membership skyrocketed. Within a year 1,000 people had joined; there were 2,700 members by 1945, the year that the

HDC changed its name to HICCASP; and 3,200 in 1946, the year it became officially affiliated with the national Independent Citizens Committee of the Arts, Sciences, and Professions.

Pepper, as executive secretary, provided the organizational genius and guiding spirit, but policy was thrashed out by a very active group of officers and Board members. The Communists were a decided minority on the Executive Board, and liberals monopolized the roster of officers: the playwright Marc Connelly was chairman; Gene Kelly, John Cromwell, a director, and E. Y. Harburg, a composer, were vice-chairmen. The Communists and fellow travelers were represented on the Executive Board by Henry Blankfort, Sidney Buchman, Edward Dmytryk, John Howard Lawson, William Pomerance, Robert Rossen, and Frank Tuttle; the liberals included Olivia De Havilland, John Garfield, Ira Gershwin, Sheridan Gibney, Johnny Green, Miriam Hopkins, Emmet Lavery, Lewis Milestone, Edward G. Robinson, and Orson Welles. The organization issued a bimonthly publication, *Target for Today*, which endorsed candidates, recommended positions on pending legislation in Sacramento and Washington, particularly those dealing with civil rights questions, and publicized racial injustices. It initiated the Council for Civic Unity, which wedded together over fifty organizations dedicated to promoting civil rights for minorities, and sponsored a United We Stand (against racism) rally at the Shrine Auditorium in March 1944.

By the middle of 1944, the Hollywood Democratic Committee and related organizations across the country were alive and active and could look forward to about one good year of successful political activity before succumbing to external and internal pressures. That it would decline precipitously after 1946 does not gainsay the militancy, strength, and optimism which bore along this third, peacetime Popular Front, much as those qualities had borne its wartime "father" front and its anti-fascist "grandfather" front.

In 1944 the entire American Left was in full agreement on the necessity of reelecting the President. Roosevelt's power as a rallying point against all the domestic forces of darkness cannot be overestimated. Centrist liberals and Communists alike shared the feeling that Franklin Roosevelt alone could stem the tide of domestic reaction and preserve the Grand Alliance in Europe. His symbolic importance grew in direct proportion to the widening gaps within the third Popular Front.

Throughout the summer and autumn of 1944 the Dewey-for-President forces, backed full force by the Motion Picture Alliance,

staged an enormous political show that bore as many of the markings
of an anti-Communist, anti-labor expedition as it did of an electoral
campaign. The Hollywood Democratic Committee, agreeing with
Lawson's estimate of a future "so freighted with possibility of danger" and with Trumbo's sense that the "situation is desperate,"[37]
mobilized all its resources. In a campaign reminiscent of that the
MPDC helped wage for Culbert Olson in 1938, the HDC organized,
demonstrated, and canvassed indefatigably. Specialized committees
were set up, celebrity-packed banquets held, and rallies, broadcasts,
and advertisements sponsored. Secretary of the Interior Harold Ickes
spoke to a glittering assemblage at the Ambassador Hotel, and vice-
presidential candidate Harry Truman appeared before a noisy throng
at the Shrine Auditorium. The Hollywood branch of the Communist
Party, following national Party policy, threw itself into this election
with determination.

In the wake of Roosevelt's victory, the Hollywood Democratic
Committee merged with the national organization, ICCASP, and the
refounded progressive alliance reached its pinnacle. From one coast to
the other, Helen Keller, Serge Koussevitzky, Bennett Cerf, Albert Einstein, and Thomas Mann linked arms with James Cagney, Edward G. Robinson, Eddie Cantor, Orson Welles, and Lillian Hellman.
By June 1945 the HDC had become HICCASP, "the first step in
creating a national, nonpartisan, political organization of cultural
workers that will markedly influence the peace."[38] HICCASP was
taking in staggering contributions—its monthly receipts during 1945
and 1946 averaged $13,000—and it was taking on every cause and
issue which arose, from full support for the United Nations and
international cooperation in the peaceful use of atomic energy to
opposition to the stationing of American troops in China and Indo-
china; from vigorous labor and civil rights activism to opposition to
HUAC and the MPA. It actually seemed that "happy days were
there again" as everyone from John Howard Lawson to Ronald
Reagan to James Roosevelt joined forces. Optimism never ran so high
as on this, the eve of FDR's fourth victory, of the end of the war, of
the founding of the United Nations . . . and, as it happened, of the
end of the left-wing political movement in Hollywood.

Even without the shattering impact of outside forces, the internal
unity of the revived Front would have been difficult to maintain. The
differences between moderates and radicals had only been papered
over, not eradicated. They reappeared almost immediately in the
debate within the Screen Writers Guild over whether or not to main-

tain the existence of the Hollywood Writers' Mobilization, an organization which had performed outstanding service during the war and which seemed to many an excellent vehicle for united action by screenwriters on a variety of postwar fronts. Red-baiting by the Tenney Committee had damaged the Mobilization, however, and the Guild Executive Board, which was subsidizing the HWM to the tune of $2,500 a year, was, by mid-1945, wary and concerned with its own reputation. Lawson and the SWG radicals vocally defended the Mobilization, arguing that the organized body of screenwriters needed a political and cultural arm, and that the Mobilization served the purpose admirably. Therefore, they argued, the disappearance of the Mobilization would simply create an operational vacuum which would have to be filled by a similar institution. The opposition, led by Emmet Lavery and Allen Rivkin, believed just as strongly that the Mobilization's *raison d'être* ended with the war and, moreover, that the organization was becoming a serious liability to the SWG. Richard Collins told HUAC that the Communists wanted to maintain the HWM because "it had become an excellent vehicle for the presentation of material, political material, cultural material, and I think they felt it could probably be used for the same purposes in the post-war period. The difference was, of course, that during the war everyone was in complete agreement, and after the war the fissures began to develop internationally and also, therefore, in the Mobilization, in the guild. So, they couldn't—there was not the unanimity as to what the Mobilization should do. . . ."‡

As always, the Guild liberals' main concern was the health and unity of the writers' union *as* a writers' union, while the radicals argued that organized writers could not avoid political stands. It was clear to Guild moderates that the politics of peace would prove far less unifying for their membership than wartime patriotism had been. Given the postwar atmosphere—the Cold War brewing, Roosevelt dead, Tenney

---

‡ United States Congress, House of Representatives, 82nd Congress, 1st session, Committee on Un-American Activities, July 6, 1951, *Communist Infiltration of the Hollywood Motion Picture Industry*, Washington, D.C.: U. S. Government Printing Office, 1951, Vol. 1, pp. 230–31. Similar problems beset the Writers' War Board in the East. Edward Klauber, assistant to the director of the Office of War Information, was instrumental in cutting off OWI's subsidy to the Writers' War Board, calling it a "political liability." Klauber felt that there were too many "private" projects (i.e., campaigns against the use of racial and minority stereotypes in the media) mixed up with the Board's "government aid activities." (*Weekly Variety*, June 13, 1945, p. 31; June 27, 1945, p. 31.)

on the horizon, FBI and HUAC investigators combing the studios, warnings from high-level studio executives (notably Spyros Skouras of 20th Century-Fox) about the "high costs" of political activism, the intra-industry Red-baiting of the MPA—it was no longer tolerable to allow the SWG Reds a subsidized forum. The radical minority was powerless to prevent the Board from voting to terminate the SWG's subsidy of the Hollywood Writers' Mobilization. The radicals retained the name and managed to keep a semblance of the organization afloat for two more years, using it as one forum, among many, in their campaign to warn the public about censorship and cultural repression. The "new" Mobilization sponsored a series of forums—"Counter Attack: Against the Plot to Control America's Thinking"—every other Monday at the El Patio Theater, and arranged cultural exchanges with the Soviet Union. On April 30, 1946, in cooperation with the American Society for Russian Relief, the HWM screened Soviet director Victor Eisimont's *Once There Was a Girl* at a benefit to raise money to reequip the First Medical Institute of Leningrad. Under the chairmanship of Dalton Trumbo, the Mobilization also organized a discussion about the Soviet film industry at which Soviet director Konstantin Simonov was the featured speaker.

During the twelve months between the Guild's abandonment of the HWM and the liberal-radical schism within HICCASP, events on the international scene prefigured dramatically the ending of the domestic alliance between liberal Democrats and Communists and gave the domestic anti-Communist crusade the opening it needed to mobilize, finally, the American public behind its cause. Following Truman's unexpectedly uncompromising stance *vis-à-vis* Stalin at Potsdam in July, the sudden cutting off of Lend-Lease to the Allies in August, and the foot-dragging on a Soviet request for a large loan to aid its domestic reconstruction program, the word went out to the Communist parties —particularly the CPUSA—to engage in "independent political action." This policy did not prefigure a return to the "imminent revolution/class against class" position of 1927-35; it did mean, however, that all future issues which concerned Communists and liberals would be debated and scrutinized "on their merits." In practice, the new policy required the American Party members to assume tougher, more critical stances within the Popular Front organizations to which they belonged. Where, for example, Communists gave automatic support to the decisions made at Dumbarton Oaks in 1944, they heatedly attacked the Council of Foreign Ministers Meeting in London in September 1945, Churchill's "Iron Curtain" speech at Fulton, Missouri, in July

1946, and the Marshall Plan in early 1947; where, between 1942 and summer 1945, the Party adhered faithfully to its no-strike pledge, in the months and years after V-J Day it fully backed militant labor union activity. In particular, three events signaled the new strategy of the CPUSA: the purge of Party General Secretary Earl Browder, the "trial" of screenwriter Albert Maltz for the "crime" of revisionism, and the Party's withdrawal of electoral support for select Democratic Party candidates favored by its liberal allies.

Earl Browder's tenure in office coincided with the Communist Party's highly successful Popular Front policy. The tremendous growth of the Party in those years, the decrease of Red-baiting during the war, and the military alliance between the Soviet Union and the United States all led Browder to an extreme of ecumenism, which did not sit well with European Communist leaders once the international alignment had changed. Browder came to believe that the CPUSA, as then constituted, was, in the context of the American liberal political tradition, an impediment to left-wing unity, hence to achieving social, economic, and political change at home and peace abroad. In his desire to bring his organization into the national political mainstream where it could play a greater role in postwar policy formulation, Browder took the unprecedented step of dissolving the Communist Party of the United States and replacing it with the Communist Political Association in May 1944. Since a transformation of this magnitude could not have occurred without Moscow's express approval, Browder's blank check, coming shortly after the dissolution of the Comintern in May 1943, showed the extraordinary concessions which the Soviet Union was prepared to make to extend the Grand Alliance into the postwar world.

In mid-1945 word came down from the Kremlin, via French Communist leader Jacques Duclos, that "Browderism" was an error, and that Browder was "the protagonist of a false concept of the ways of social evolution in general, and in the first place, the social evolution of the United States."[39] The Duclos article, personally approved by Stalin, appeared in *Cahiers du Communisme* in April 1945 and in the *Daily Worker* on May 24. Within two months the Communist Party was re-formed in the United States and Earl Browder was ousted from its leadership. (In February 1946 he was excluded from the Party altogether.) The new leader, William Z. Foster, was an apostle of class struggle who had no objections to carrying out the new policy of independent political action. He established, as preconditions for alliances, liberals' endorsement of a third—the Progressive—Party, denunciation of the Truman and Marshall Plan doctrines, and support for the foreign policies of the Soviet Union. "Communists in the trade unions and people's organizations were under instruction to make these the main issues in their activity; coalition relations were severed when they failed."[40]

Hollywood Party members justifiably believed that these events were occurring at a far remove from their influence. Returning war veterans like Michael Wilson, however, openly scorned Browder's strategy and threw their weight behind the Duclos article. "I came back from the war tough and angry," Wilson said. "I was intolerant of the Browder period; I believed the Cold War was waiting in the wings." Ring Lardner, Jr., for his part, recalls that the film Communists were "flattered" when Foster felt it necessary to come to Los Angeles to explain to them what had happened.[41] But no Hollywood Red, from the unquestioning defenders of the new format like Jack Lawson to the most skeptical critics of one more revision of Party tactics like Jean Butler, knew for certain what effect, if any, such distant changes would have on their political lives. The "case" of Albert Maltz quickly showed them. In the week following Browder's expulsion from the Party, an article on literary criticism authored by Maltz appeared in *New Masses* (February 12, 1946). The article was written in response to an "invitation" issued by *New Masses* editor Isidor Schneider in the form of an article he wrote, "Probing Writers' Problems," for the October 23, 1945, edition of the magazine. "I hope," wrote Schneider, "that articles representing all viewpoints, and in greater detail than is possible in [mine], will emerge from the discussion." Maltz's piece, entitled "What Shall We Ask of Writers?" attacked the Party position of the thirties which envisioned art as a weapon in the class struggle. Terming such an outlook the "vulgarization of the theory of art" and a "straitjacket for the writer," Maltz openly admitted that "in order to write at all, it has long since become necessary for me to repudiate [this view] and abandon it." Simply in terms of content, Maltz's article—which had developed out of discussions between him and his friends from the Theatre Union days, George Sklar and Michael Blankfort—was not, by any means, an aberration from the unstated assumption of Communist writers of all categories that the goals of proletarian literature and the means of Party literary criticism were inappropriate to the American cultural scene. CPUSA hierarchs, at least since the dawn of the People's Front movement, had seemed to concur. In a speech before the first American Writers' Congress in 1935, Browder himself had publicly promised freedom of creative expression to writers who joined the Party. In his speech Browder stated:

> We believe that the overwhelming bulk of fine writing also has political significance. We would like to see all writers conscious of this, therefore able to control and direct the political results of their work.
>
> By no means do we think this can be achieved by imposing any preconceived patterns upon the writer. On the contrary, we believe that fine literature must arise directly out of life, expressing not only its problems, but, at the same time, all the richness and complexity of detail of life itself.[42]

In the very issue of *New Masses* in which Maltz's piece appeared, Party culture critic Isidor Schneider wrote approvingly of the screenwriter's views.[43]

Times had changed, however, and an example had to be made to show that tighter control would henceforth be exerted on all Party members, screenwriters included. On February 12, the New York flagship fired its first salvo at Maltz. Mike Gold, the doyen of CPUSA literary critics, was called upon to administer the reproof. Gold's four pieces, which appeared in the *Daily Worker*,[44] utterly savaged Maltz's stance, reviling him as a revisionist heedless of the class struggle, the needs of a Marxist party, and "the greatest crisis in American history," and as a screenwriter who "let the luxury and phony atmosphere of Hollywood at last poison him." Maltz should know, veteran Communist that he is, Gold wrote, how the "breadth" of Browderism almost wrecked the Party and "misled" young writers:

> Now that [Browderism] is over, we are painfully trying to get back on the Marxist rails of history. The young writers Maltz worries about will never be misled by this return to Marxism. But they would be derailed and damaged if they learned to tolerate Trotskyites and to be as non-political as Albert Maltz tells them they can be.
>
> That way lies the ivory tower, the floundering in the marsh, the negative and passive literature of the cafes and esthetic cliques. Albert is preaching a terrible confusion.

Other Party regulars, seeing which way the intra-Party cultural winds were blowing, joined in the attack. Samuel Sillen, editor of *New Masses*, and Howard Fast, darling of the New York hierarchy, joined in the verbal and written onslaughts on Maltz.

Maltz himself, and many of the screenwriters, were utterly taken aback by the severity of the Party's rebuke. At first something of a defensive reaction took shape in the form of *ad hoc* meetings and outraged exclamations. "The Maltz article caused an enormous furor in the Party's ranks," recalled Dorothy Healey. "The cultural side of the Party program always attracted a good deal of attention from the membership, but this time the debate attracted the big brass from New York." Maltz was not completely without support within the Party. He received a number of letters urging him to resist—even to lead a breakaway movement. Bess Taffel, for one, was infuriated. "I think it was the first time that I ever spoke out at a Party meeting," she recalled, "and I spoke with great anger." While many screenwriters within the Party agreed with Maltz intellectually, though, they disagreed with him politically. With few exceptions, the members of the Hollywood talent branches decided that Party unity was more important than theoretical correctness in the matter of Marxist literary criticism.

Very soon Maltz stood isolated as it became clear that the "big brass" were indeed serious. Nobody was willing to risk expulsion by speaking up too loudly on his behalf, and, in truth, Maltz himself had no stomach for martyrdom. He felt nothing but repugnance at the prospect of becoming the focus of a schismatic movement. Over three decades later he said to us:

> Underlying everything intellectual, however, was a powerful emotional factor: such a furor had been raised over my piece that I had to retreat or be expelled. The times did not allow for a debate in the pages of *New Masses*, and expulsion over *this* matter was completely unacceptable to me. I felt the Party was the best hope of mankind; that it would be the force which moved the world toward brotherhood. I was truly in a state of shock over the accusations that I had taken an anti-Party and anti-Marxist stance.

In a frenzy of self-doubt and personal anguish (this was, he said, "the most unsettling experience of my life, infinitely worse than going to prison; nothing compared to it"), Maltz began to feel that perhaps Gold's and Sillen's criticisms were well-taken, that perhaps he had made a theoretically impossible separation between literature and politics and had not fully considered the balance of forces in the world in 1946. Perhaps, too, he realized, his anger over various other Party matters had shown through in his article.

Presently, therefore, after a brief show of resistance, Albert Maltz collapsed entirely. His recantation appeared in *New Masses* on April 9.[45] In it he acknowledged that his first article "was a specific example of revisionist thinking" and of "distorted marxism." With that the matter rested. A chastised Maltz remained within the fold, nothing lost but face. Maltz fared much better than those writers in the Soviet Union who were found to have gone against the newly tightened Party controls over intellectual and literary output. Shattered reputations, arrests, even executions, were the lot of the Soviet writer or artist or thinker caught in the path of Zhdanovism, a ruthless campaign launched, in 1946, by Andrei Zhdanov—member of the Politburo, secretary of the Central Committee, commissar of ideological affairs, and a leading force in the formation of the Cominform—to mobilize Soviet culture for the Cold War. It represented a return to the most vulgar forms of "art as a weapon." In a speech he delivered in Leningrad, Zhdanov stated:

> Our literature is not a private enterprise calculated to please the varied tastes of a literary market. We are in no way obliged to provide a place in our literature for tastes and tempers that have nothing in common with the ethics and qualities of the Soviet people. . . . We demand that our comrades, both those who give leadership in the literary field and those who write, be guided by that without which the Soviet order cannot live, i.e., by politics. . . . [T]he writer must educate the people and arm them ideologically.[46]

Many years later, at the time of Khrushchev's 1956 speech revealing Stalin's crimes, Maltz severed all relations with the Party. His action occurred, ironically, at the same time that the Party, as part of its post-Stalin "thaw," published an article "forgiving" Maltz and praising his "plea for the highest quality in art," his condemnation of "the tendency to praise the political program of a work of art no matter how poor a work it was," and his argument for "conditions of freedom which would enable writers to explore, investigate, experiment, test." The Party definitely suffered from its attack on Maltz, concluded the writer in the *Party Voice:*

> But with the rejection and condemnation of Maltz's position, the climate in our movement became increasingly restricted and confined. More and more, we applied a political means test to all cultural work. Standards of beauty, taste, distinction and style became sloughed over or ignored.[47]

Indeed, as a result of the Maltz affair, the CPUSA's already blemished image did take another beating in the eyes of liberals and fellow travelers who closely watched this display of discipline which had arisen out of a call for a free debate. The seeming willingness of Communist intellectuals to be corseted by an organization in which they had previously been cosseted drained away a significant portion of the good will still remaining among non-Party left-wingers.

The "new" Communist Party leadership did not seem to care much about the opinions of their erstwhile liberal allies in this or any other matter. By mid-1946, with United States and Soviet Union foreign policies on a clear collision course, the CPUSA broke completely away from the unofficial alignment with the Democratic Party which had characterized Roosevelt's later years in office. Most liberals and liberal organizations that did not comply with the new independent CP line were simply written off as unredeemable losses or good riddances. The new head of the Party in Southern California, Nemmy Sparks, ruthlessly began to restore "discipline" in the Hollywood branches of the CP. Ellenore Bogigian, who had been very close to Sparks's congenial, accommodating predecessor, Paul Cline, said of Sparks: "He displayed nearly criminal policies toward other, non-Party organizations. It was the first time I ever saw such direct interference in the affairs of previously allied organizations, so many broken promises, so much rechanneling of funds. His insensitive muscle-flexing gave the Communist Party a bad name in a broader circle than ever before." Dorothy Healey, who worked very closely with Sparks for over twenty years, does not dispute the particulars cited by Bogigian. Healey adds, however, that Sparks's seeming ruthlessness was a cover for an insecure man sincerely intent upon putting into effect a hard-line policy directive from his New York superiors.

The most serious casualty of the new Communist militancy was HICCASP, an organization already sorely beset by the death of Roosevelt, the anti-labor policies of Harry Truman, and the heating up of the Cold War. HICCASP members did their best to hold the organization together, even as the Communist Party line of independent action made unity more difficult. The Executive Board began meeting twice a week in order to resolve the issues which were undermining its unity and wasting the considerable assets—moral as well as financial—which had accrued since November 1944. By mid-1946, however, even the liberals had begun to hold "fraction" meetings. In desperation the Board named a special "unity" committee, composed of two representatives from each "side," to hammer out a compromise manifesto on which HICCASP could take a united stand. The committee—consisting of Ronald Reagan and Don Hartman from the moderates, Linus Pauling and James Roosevelt from the centrists, Dalton Trumbo and John Howard Lawson from the radical Left, and chaired by the "impartial" radio writer True Boardman—met for three days and nights at James Roosevelt's home.

The resulting statement of policy turned out to be mainly the work of the Center and the Left. For some reason, Reagan and Hartman hardly contributed to the proceedings. A non-participating observer remarked that "they seemed bored with it all." The five-page document which the committee presented to the Board on July 10 was a vague farrago of platitudes which satisfied almost no one. But it was all HICCASP had, and the Board optimistically published it as a pamphlet carrying the unfetching, ambiguous title "Your Future Is in Your Hands Now!" The preamble sought to rally the Old Guard of the New Deal—"To protect, extend, and implement the ideals of Franklin D. Roosevelt," while circumnavigating the renewed factionalism of the political tendencies by calling on people to unite not as Republicans, Democrats, or Communists, but as members of HICCASP. The program of action reiterated the traditional goals of internationalism, anti-racism, and anti-reaction.

This effort to restore unity was, however, overwhelmed by the dissonant uproar which greeted HICCASP's next encounter with a substantive political issue: the question of whom to endorse in the 1946 California race for a seat in the United States Senate—the anti-Communist liberal Will Rogers, Jr., or the opportunist liberal Ellis Patterson, who had previously enjoyed CP electoral support. The Los Angeles Party hierarchy understandably opposed Rogers, but the grim, intolerant manner in which it mobilized its cadres for Patterson decimated the organization. Sparks made it clear that he would bring "charges" against HICCASP Party members who sought to act with moderation or compromise within the Executive Board. Party members were instructed to force a vote on the Rogers-Patterson issue despite warnings from all concerned that such a policy would precipitate a schism within the Popular Front organization. Dore Schary and other liberals pleaded with HICCASP Communists to join them in ducking the whole issue by endorsing neither of the candidates, but Sparks would not relent in his determination to force a showdown. In a tense and emotional meeting, the HICCASP Board members met to decide the issue of the senatorial endorsement. "The Communists won the vote," said Bogigian, "but lost the organization. It created a bitterness within HICCASP theretofore unknown."

The HICCASP which formally endorsed Ellis Patterson was already an organization whose liberal membership was noticeably diminished since the heyday of wartime fraternity. The decision for Patterson, and the accompanying atmosphere of polarization, reduced liberal membership in the Popular Front organization still more sharply. The Communists who remained behind thus acceded to a position of more control than they had ever enjoyed before. Under their direction HICCASP soon cut its Democratic moorings entirely and joined the far more radical cause of launching a third party for the 1948 elections. On December 30, 1946, representatives from the National Citizens Political Action Committee and the Independent Citizens Committee of the Arts, Sciences, and Professions met in New York to form the Progressive Citizens of America, which would, in turn, be transformed into the Independent Progressive Party in July 1948.

The Reality of Appearances

It is fair—and important—to inquire if the Hollywood Reds appeared to be the foreign agents and social subversives—the Stalinists—that everyone, including liberals, said they were. "Stalinist" was a term of opprobrium used in the thirties and forties to designate those who renounced public critiques of the Soviet Union and its "socialist experiment," who implacably defended Stalin's actions in the face of evidence which indicated these actions were indefensible, and who followed blindly the tactical, strategical, and doctrinal line handed down by Moscow.

Were the Hollywood Communists "Stalinist"? The initial answer must be "yes." Communist screenwriters defended the Stalinist regime, accepted the Comintern's policies and about-faces, and criticized enemies and allies alike with an infuriating self-righteousness, superiority, and selective memory which eventually alienated all but the staunchest fellow travelers.

As defenders of the Soviet regime the screen artist Reds became apologists for crimes of monstrous dimensions, though they claimed to have known nothing about such crimes, and indeed shouted down, or ignored, those who did. "There was very little available knowledge of the U.S.S.R.," said Albert Maltz, "and those who claimed to 'know' were not sympathizers, hence were suspected of being part of the two-decade-long capitalist crusade against the lone socialist state." Even given the Western societies' patent anti-Communist sentiments and policies, this argument about "suspect evidence" and "impeachable witnesses" does not excuse the purblindness. After 1929 bits and pieces of evidence came increasingly to light to indicate that the Soviet regime was undertaking actions and policies of dubious morality, perhaps even criminal or genocidal in nature. With the arrival of the Spanish Civil War and the purge trials in the U.S.S.R., highly damaging reports of Communist and Soviet ruthlessness and homicide began to pile up. In 1935, Edmund Wilson wrote to disillusioned fellow traveler John Dos Passos and echoed the feelings of Hollywood Reds and anti-fascists of the time:

> In regard to Russia, it seems to me a mistake to form any too definite opinion because we really know nothing about it. I don't see any reason to disbelieve that they had a counter-revolutionary conspiracy backed by Germany on their hands, as they say they had [in justifying one of the early purge trials]. . . . Stalin, however much he may want to maintain his power, is certainly a good deal different from Napoleon. Stalin is a convinced Marxist and old Bolshevik; Napoleon cared nothing about the principles of the French Revolution and betrayed it. Also, he had megalomanic imperialist ambitions which one can hardly imagine Stalin entertaining. Stalin, whatever his limitations, is still working for socialism in Russia.[48]

However, twenty-seven months later, in April 1937, Wilson had significantly changed his line. He wrote to fellow traveler (and still "Stalinist") Malcolm Cowley:

> I believe you are mistaken about the trials. . . . [Y]ou sound as if you had read nothing but the official report. You ought to read the Trotskyist and socialist stuff, too—and some of the most illuminating material has appeared in that little sheet called THE INTERNATIONAL REVIEW. Also, [W. H.] Chamberlin, who, in spite of his fundamental stupidities, is really about the best reporter on Russia. I guess that all the trials have been fakes since the time of the Ramzin sabotage trial. They have always been intended to provide scapegoats and divert attention from more fundamental troubles. In the case of these recent trials, I imagine that not a word of these confessions was true. The victims had, I suppose, been guilty of some kind of opposition to the regime; and the technique evidently is to tell them that they can only vindicate themselves by putting on acts which will be helpful to the U.S.S.R.[49]

Wilson's reconsideration proved that, by the late thirties, it was possible for intelligent, informed men and women of socialist convictions as well as unimpeachable personal and political integrity to begin to voice suspicions and even condemnations of Stalin's actions.

The men and women who remained in (or joined) the Party, however, did not attempt to give public voice to their reservations or their criticisms, if any, of Soviet communism. The liberal perception of the Reds as duplicitous, opportunistic, cynical, untrustworthy, and irresponsible obstructionists was therefore not hopelessly wide of the mark. In all too many crucial situations the Reds appeared to their allies to be automatic and puppet-like in the words, actions, and unanimity with which they defended a policy or doctrine clearly not of their own making. Communists did not publicly divulge their individual or collective hesitations, reservations, or second thoughts about the Party line. Nor did they attempt to explain to the public, their allies, or adversaries the personal and political faith, prior commitments, and organizational discipline which led them to accept the sudden changes of line and reversals from abroad and to defend and justify actions of a foreign government about which they, like everyone else, knew little.

Viewing the Hollywood Communists from the historian's perspective, it is necessary to conclude that on occasion these men and women undermined their credibility, mis-served their cause, and misled their contemporaries with their behavior, their attitude, and their words. The American Communists in general, and the film Reds in particular, never displayed in this era any independence of mind or organization *vis-à-vis* the Comintern and the Soviet Union; hence, much as their activities and accomplishments in many realms—notably anti-fascism, domestic and international—redound to their credit, in the last analysis the CPUSA, and its Hollywood talent branches, could not escape some association with the actions, errors, and crimes of international communism. However perfunctorily and mechanically they may have defended the U.S.S.R., however "oblique" to their *major* preoccupying domestic and international goals the defense of Stalinism probably was for most of them, and however uninvolved in (and ignorant of) the actions of the Soviet regime they personally were, the screen artist Reds nevertheless defended that regime unflinchingly, uncritically, inflexibly—and therefore left themselves open to the justifiable suspicion that they not only approved of everything they were defending, but would themselves act in the same way if they were in the same position.

As it turned out, the Communists in Hollywood were not *simply* "automatons" in their personal responses and reactions to Moscow. Though they did not publicly divulge hesitations and doubts, it is clear from extensive interviews with many Hollywood Reds of the era that most of them harbored, from the beginning to the end of their involvement with the Party, a strong sense of conscience and an occasional sense of reserve, even shock and disapproval, where certain Party decisions, methods, and leaders were concerned. Indeed, all but two or three screen artists eventually broke with the Communist Party of the United States over precisely the sorts of reversals or revelations which lost the Party its allies and sympathizers in the late thirties. Nearly all would have agreed with Albert Maltz's rueful "if only": "No one I knew in the CP would have stayed in the Party had they known then what they found out later." At the time, however, it was literally inconceivable to Reds that Russian Bolsheviks could be acting in the ways indicated by the "bourgeois" press or the "renegade Left."

Most dedicated Communists of the thirties were incapable of making the conceptual leap from their own socialist idealism and belief in Bolshevik morality to the image of torture and repression signified by the anti-Soviet information. Santiago Carrillo, one of the most intelligent and eloquent of Eurocommunists, summed up recently his own reaction to the news of the purge trials of the thirties:

> One cannot deny the impact of the Moscow trials, and of the astonishing confessions made at them, . . . [we] could not conceive of the infernal machine by means of which those confessions were obtained. It is true that history and the Twentieth Congress of the Communist Party of the Soviet Union have confirmed many of the atrocities denounced by the Trotskyists at the time, but to choose where the truth lay, between what they said and what Stalin and his companions said, was, as it were, a question of faith, and we chose to believe the Soviet leaders.[50]

The fact that the Hollywood Communists actually harbored doubts, which, when augmented over the years by other matters of conscience, would eventually lead to a break with the Party, is irrelevant from any perspective except that of historical truth. At the time it would not, and should not, have mattered to the Communists' contemporaries that the Reds had their doubts. The point was, they acted as if they had none; and their latter-day post-Party efforts to "explain" themselves and their strategy remain unconvincing.

While this extended discussion of the nature and the appearance of Hollywood communism may be useful for understanding the liberal-radical split and the isolation of the Reds in the political community, the considerations raised here do not clarify the question of responsibility for the fate which Communists (and eventually many liberals) in the film world met at the hands of the conservatives and reactionaries of HUAC, the Catholic Church, the American Legion, and compliant studio management. Undependable as allies in the progressive cause, guilty of being apologists for the crimes of a foreign power, American Communists in general, and Hollywood Reds in particular, were still in no wise the subversives which the congressional investigators and professional witch-hunters construed them to be. There is no evidence to indicate that the Hollywood Reds ever, in any way, conspired, or tried to conspire, against the United States Government, spied for the Soviet Union, or even undermined any social institution in this country. They of course vociferously attacked a host of adversaries—from California growers and studio management to conservative politicians, certain congressional committees, and a host of other socio-religious-political organizations—but these attacks were public and publicized, and the battles they fought differed not at all from those waged by the far more numerous liberals and progressives, who were sometimes their allies. Nor did they ever try formally to propagandize Hollywood movies in the literal sense of "subversion," i.e., "to undermine the principles of, or corrupt."

From the perspective of the men and women who trampled over the political movement in Hollywood after 1947, it would have made no difference if the CPUSA and its film branches had, in fact, developed and adhered to a critical "American path" to socialism. Whatever path they had chosen, it would have been antithetical to the vision, the interests, the whole set of arrangements, values, and relations which made up the right-wing vision of American society. That vision, by early 1947, had already launched a veritable holy war against "international communism," far removed in scope and power from the anti-Soviet diatribes of 1939-41. A reflective, critical American Marxist would by the late forties be in a far more difficult position *vis-à-vis* the Right than the apologetic party-liner of the Hitler-Stalin Pact era, when the domestic Right was isolationist, for he would have found much to criticize and disapprove of in U.S. actions toward the Soviet Union and the countries of Western Europe after 1945. While individual Communists might have deplored many of the more ruthless methods Stalin employed in the Russian take-over of Eastern Europe, none could have

denied that American foreign policy was following an equally determined path toward carving out spheres of influence with different,
but equally implacable methods (infiltrators, financial threats, A-bomb
rattling, etc.). Secondly, the two previous witch-hunts in American
history—the Alien and Sedition period and the post-World War I era—
thrived on similar ascriptions of foreign agentry with far less in the
way of proof—or reality (although the Jeffersonian Democrats and
the Industrial Workers of the World and left-wing Socialists did
travel paths parallel to foreign events: the French Revolution in the
former case, the Russian Revolution in the latter).

In summary, it would seem that the liberal charges against the
Hollywood Communists were largely substantiated by history, while
the right wing's view—that Red film artists were subversives aiming to
undermine first movies, then the state and society—was profoundly erroneous and predetermined by the Right's own distorted political vision and agenda. By appearing as "agents of Moscow," American
Communists only helped clear the path for the conservative-reac-
tionary crusade; they did not set it into motion or determine its course.

Hollywood on the Eve of the Subpoenas

While liberals and Communists fought one another over whether to
endorse Patterson or Rogers, and HICCASP, the last hope of a revived
Popular Front in Hollywood, dismembered itself as a result of Communist intransigence, events on the national and international scene
were transpiring which would dwarf these squabbles and devastate the
resulting splinter groups of liberals and Communists. Left-wingers of
the mid-forties displayed an incredible shortsightedness in allowing issues such as electoral endorsements to divide them at a time when the
Motion Picture Alliance, HUAC, and Jack Tenney thirsted for
liberal-radical blood, Churchill quarantined Eastern from Western
Europe, Henry Wallace was fired from the Cabinet for supporting accommodation with the Russians, and Truman broke faith with the
progressive traditions and hopes of the New Deal era and instituted a
loyalty investigation of federal employees. Unity on the Left could
not have halted the anti-Communist crusade, but it might have
lessened the number of victims and the extent of the victimization.

Some did see the writing on the wall. Communist screenwriter
Philip Stevenson, for one, foresaw the domestic implications of the
Truman Doctrine, the President's program to provide American mili-
tary aid to the conservative governments of Turkey and Greece, both

engaged in civil wars with indigenous left-wing and nationalist forces. Stevenson wrote a letter to the liberal Democratic senator from California, Sheridan Downey, warning against an impending Alien and Sedition Act.*

> It seems all too possible. The movement on foot to outlaw a legal political party [CPUSA], the numerous bills in Congress to shackle labor, strongly suggest that the real purpose of the undeclared war on Russia may rather be suppression of popular rights. . . .
> The Truman administration is moving in the direction of suppressing popular liberties at home under cover of patriotic emotions roused by an undeclared war abroad. The first steps are already preparing.[51]

Other screenwriters noticed that movie producers, for their part, were also beginning to hedge on promises made during the war and in the immediate postwar period. The majors had, it is true, produced one important anti-racist short subject—*The House I Live In* (RKO, 1945)—and were planning a series of anti-anti-Semitic movies—*Crossfire* (RKO, 1947), *Gentleman's Agreement* (20th Century-Fox, 1947)—and "realistic" black movies—*Pinky* (20th, 1949), *Home of the Brave* (United Artists, 1949), and *Intruder in the Dust* (MGM, 1949). By early 1947, however, producers began to retreat. RKO reneged on its promise to Scott and Dmytryk to allow them to make a picture examining the life and problems of blacks,[52] and Dalton Trumbo could point to a long list of commercial films—including *Song of the South*, *Abie's Irish Rose*, and *Duel in the Sun*—in which

---

* Radical screenwriters with a historical bent, such as Stevenson and Albert Maltz, referred regularly to the Alien-Sedition period as a warning to others and a lesson to themselves. One of the most frequently read and heavily underlined books in Maltz's extensive library is Claude G. Bowers, *Jefferson and Hamilton* (Boston: Houghton Mifflin Co., 1925). Maltz identified closely with the Republican newspaper editors who firmly resisted and challenged the Adams administration's attack on free speech.

Philip Dunne, too, perceived the striking similarity between the two periods, writing in an article circulated to SWG members: "Attempts to force conformity of opinion are nothing new in the United States. The Alien and Sedition Acts of the first Adams administration, directed against the Jeffersonians who were thought to be too sympathetic to the French revolutionaries, afford what is almost a direct parallel to the anti-Communist proposals of today." ("On 'Loyalty' *Affidavits*," November 1947.)

racial stereotypes persisted.[53] In the summer of 1947, radical director
Irving Pichel wrote:

> The screen remains a medium, but is not a voice. It does not speak
> for itself, but as though it were merely an accomplished actor
> memorizing and repeating words that have been applauded in
> other media and have been precensored, sifted, filtered against de-
> viation from the most commonly accepted and widely held social
> generalizations.[54]

Most left-wingers would have agreed with Pichel that Hollywood
movies had indeed become a "caponized medium," incapable of con-
ceiving socially meaningful film projects.

In fact, economic circumstances conspired with political developments to forbid anything like an innovative climate in postwar Hollywood. Falling box office receipts followed hard upon the movie boom
of 1945–46, as economic recession, changing taste, and court-ordered
divestiture of theaters from major production companies combined to
cut profits drastically. As a result of decreasing attendance, higher foreign tariffs and tighter currency restrictions, strikes, and litigation
costs, studio net profits sank sharply in 1947 (from $121 to $87 million) and again in 1948 (to $48 million).[55] Management acted swiftly
and mercilessly: twelve thousand workers were cut from the studios'
payrolls, while the number of actors, writers, directors, and staff
producers under contract was halved.[56] Louis B. Mayer reduced both
his bloated retinue and his inflated salary by 25 per cent.[57]

Under normal circumstances—as during a similar slump in the thirties—producers would have cast about for new themes and ideas to
make their movies more appealing. The early thirties, after all, had
been the breeding ground for such Hollywood staples as gangster
movies, musicals, and screwball comedies. These genres, however, like
all new genres, made their impact as "entertaining" modes of social
criticism. Whether the genre creator uses sarcasm, exposure, irony,
realism, caricature, or comedy of manners, he is essentially creating a
new—and critical—framework for viewing his surroundings. Criticism
of American values at this time, however, was a risky venture. Help-
lessly dependent on the American government for its support and intervention in the foreign market, where it could force reduction of
import quotas and relaxation of currency restrictions, producers were
forced to weigh carefully the decision to launch new genres.

While the movie producers had their bill of particular and pressing
needs ready to tack on Washington's door, the government, for its

part, stood ready with an equally lengthy set of demands. This film industry-government courtship had been going on for at least a decade. As much as the government thought it was doing for the industry, film spokesmen, notably A. H. Giannini in 1938 and Walter Wanger in 1939, complained that it was not enough. These men were also disturbed by what they saw as Washington's attempt to "suggest" changes in film content, a trend which became increasingly evident as Hollywood's need for government assistance escalated.[58]

The government did its utmost to promote overseas markets for American films. In the late thirties the State Department invited the majors to cooperate in a million-dollar propaganda program it was initiating in South America. This project gave the studios a subsized shove into a virgin market, the proceeds from which would go far toward making up the losses from the rapidly closing European markets.[59] In 1943 *Variety* reported that the "motion picture industry is the only commercial setup that has been permitted to operate in the North African and European war zones." Forty carefully selected Hollywood films, pre-dubbed, followed the victorious Allied armies into North Africa, Italy, France, etc.[60]

Government officials appreciated both the film industry's need for federal support and the tremendous ideological and economic impact American films could have on foreign audiences and the national balance of trade. On the other hand, the State Department was not interested in assisting an industry whose product might contain "elements which create erroneous impressions about the United States among people who lack a background of understanding what is normal in the United States."[61] As early as January 1944 representatives of the State Department and the Hays Office met to discuss the establishment of a film bureau in Washington to permit the movie industry "active participation in post-war plan[ning]."[62] Shortly afterward, when it became evident that foreign government film monopolies and national subsidies were replacing the old "free" world film trade, the studios ousted Will Hays as the industry spokesman and replaced him with the more urbane, politically and socially connected Eric Johnston. Unlike Hays, who was originally employed to exercise his authority within and upon the film industry itself, Johnston was, from the outset, designated as chief Washington lobbyist for the movie studios. Spending nearly all his time in the capital, Johnston worked closely with the Departments of State, Justice, and Commerce, the Coordinator of Inter-American Affairs, the Director of Reconversion, members of Congress, and, often enough, with the White House and

President Truman—in short, with anyone who could promote the sale of American films abroad.

While Johnston, and Hays before him, were currying favor with Washington's most powerful officials, the Department of State was sending off an inquiry to all of its field offices asking certain questions about "American Motion Pictures in the Post-War World." The query contained the following statement:

> Especially in the post-war period, the Department desires to coop-erate fully in the protection of American motion pictures abroad. It expects in return that the industry will cooperate whole-heartedly with the government with a view to insuring that the pictures distributed abroad will reflect credit on the good name and reputation of this country and its institutions.[63]

The replies to the query were critical of Hollywood's use of gang-sters, frivolity, and glamour; one, from the Dominican Republic, cited the deleterious effects of *The Grapes of Wrath* and *Tobacco Road* on this country's image. The Department's *Memorandum* on the subject of postwar international information dropped some not too gentle hints on the subject of the responsibility of motion picture producers. On page 2, fully italicized, appeared the admonition that *"The United States Government and specifically the State Department cannot be indifferent to the ways in which our society is portrayed in other countries."* Further on the memo encouraged studio executives to or-ganize themselves to assist "not any particular public policy but rather the generalized concern of the Nation about the way it appears through the world and impinges on the awareness of other peoples."[64]

Eric Johnston received this and other messages and transmitted them loud and clear to his employers in Hollywood. He went from studio to studio and from guild to guild carrying the banner of the Truman administration's foreign policy and insisting that the film industry live up to its role in the fulfillment of that policy. Speaking to RKO em-ployees in March 1947, Johnston noted that the Truman Doctrine marked a "new era" in United States diplomacy. Divulging to his lis-teners the contents of "talks" he had had with Secretary of State George Marshall and Chairman of the Senate Foreign Relations Com-mittee Arthur Vandenberg, Johnston announced the official United States policy of "worldwide countering of Soviet expansion" and em-phasized the support which the American film industry must render to this "cause." Pointing out how "new diplomatic developments directly affected" the interests of the motion picture industry, Johnston again emphasized that the studios and their personnel would be expected "to play a part in implementing the State Department policy." He told the workers at Paramount Studios that when he is in Washington, he is "in and out of the State Department every day."[65] In other words, the message Johnston brought to Hollywood was that the rifle the film industry had shouldered in World War II could not be put down; it had to keep marching to the drums of another martial conflict—the Cold War with international and domestic communism.

With the pressures and prejudices brought by Johnston permeating the front offices, screen artist left-wingers now stood exposed to potential desertion by the same studio management which had traditionally displayed benign indifference to radical political activity (albeit sharp watchfulness for radical scriptwriting). With many liberals divided and cowed, and an important contingent of them defecting to the enemy; with the principal democratic labor movement in Hollywood on the verge of complete collapse and the national labor organizations under violent attack; with the Motion Picture Alliance frightening movie industry employees away from politics; with HUAC and associated governmental agencies, notably the FBI,[66] actively pursuing their investigatory work with the close cooperation of the MPA; and with studio management now indentured to the Cold War mentality of State Department bureaucrats, the remaining radical political activists in Hollywood had only the Screen Writers Guild to turn to. But it, too, broke and ran under the full force of the attack.

Political dissension and economic adversity had visited the SWG in the immediate postwar years with the same effects that they had inflicted on every other organization in Hollywood. By the summer of 1947 there were nearly 1,500 experienced or aspiring screenwriters in the movie capital. Of these, 262 were employed by the majors, 178 by independent film makers. That total, 440, represented a 25 per cent decline from the peak figure of 588 employed writers in March 1946.[67] Such statistics, irrespective of the political climate, would have made concerted Guild action in pursuit of writers' interests very difficult. With the added political factor, however, it became clear by the end of 1947 that the SWG faced not only a crisis of bargaining leverage as a labor organization, but a larger internal crisis of unity— soon to be followed by a public collapse of integrity as a union of writers and intellectuals.

Very early after the war's end, the anti-Communist crusade began to make life hellish for the movie writers and their Guild. No matter how divided Guild membership was over the question of postwar policies and actions, every move the screenwriters made as a collective group was met by Red-baiting of unprecedented savagery and effectiveness. Writing in the spring of 1947, screenwriter Garrett Graham noted that "for nearly a year now . . . Hollywood, and particularly the screen writers, have been the targets of an unparalleled campaign of cumulative calumny."[68] Ken Englund, then just beginning his career of activity in the SWG, believed that the mounting attacks on the organization seriously weakened the Guild to the point where it was rendered incapable of taking a strong stand in the storm which was breaking. The Guild would do well merely to survive, many members, including Englund, felt; it could not afford to do much else.

The strength and responsiveness the Guild did display toward the furies of the anti-Communist crusade came from its organ, *The Screen Writer*. Unlike the SWG Board, which waffled and retreated under the direction of its moderate and liberal majority, *The Screen Writer*, when edited by Communists Dalton Trumbo and Gordon Kahn between 1945 and 1947, stood firm and, for a time, even rallied some of the liberals as well. Right up to the morrow of the HUAC hearings in October 1947, when panicked Guild moderates systematically removed every radical from positions of responsibility within the SWG, left-wing editors and contributors to *The Screen Writer* defiantly returned the fire of the anti-Communists. Articles regularly appeared which roasted the MPA, the Tenney Committee, HUAC, the Taft-Hartley Act, and every other counterprogressive force which showed its face. Month in and month out the magazine, in farsighted polemical analyses, warned its readers of the meaning, nature, and dimension of the anti-Communist crusade. Beyond trading blows with the besiegers, the radicals of *The Screen Writer* also kept up pressure within the Guild for militancy on union matters relating to writer demands, support for the CSU strike, and alliances with other guilds and unions. The latter priority struck the radicals as especially imperative. The SWG Board had succumbed before the need to show solidarity with the CSU strikers for fear of exposing the SWG to further attack from the Right; *The Screen Writer* editorial staff, which warmly supported Herb Sorrell and his federation, believed the Guild was increasingly vulnerable because of its lack of support for other progressive labor groups. If the CSU were to win its third strike, as it had won its first two, SWG radicals reasoned, the tie between the two labor organizations would pump badly needed blood into the "splendid but lonely" Screen Writers Guild.

It was a hard time for radicals to press any claims, however, even on purely union matters. The right-wing crusaders had already succeeded in polarizing the atmosphere to such an extent that all matters connected with working-class solidarity or union militancy, especially those involving writers and intellectuals, smacked of creeping communism. Thus when the moderate screenwriter James Cain proposed that the Guild join with other authors' groups around the country to create an American Authors Authority, conservative forces in Hollywood and in the national journalistic establishment engaged in Red-baiting to the point of wrecking any possibility for the appearance of what was essentially nothing more than an effective copyright organization for writers of all political stripes. A Special Supplement of *The Screen Writer* (March 1947) was devoted to detailing and explaining the functions and mechanics of the Authority. Basically, it was similar to ASCAP, the music business organization, which banned all outright sales of any material. Instead the rights were assigned to the Authority, which would, in turn, copyright the material. If an entrepreneur or producer or editor wanted to use the material, he or she would have to pay a leasing fee to the Authority. Each subsequent use would require an additional leasing fee. It was, in short, an ongoing royalty arrangement. The apolitical nature of the AAA proposal was attested to by the impressive fact that the badly divided screenwriters managed a 343 to 7 consensus in favor of Cain's idea.[69] Moderate and conservative writers who stood in resolute opposition to buttressing the CSU rallied enthusiastically to the creation of an office which would, in Guild president Emmet Lavery's words, "work for the small writer as well as the big writer." For all its fervor, the mode of Lavery's defense of the AAA provided telling evidence of the political atmosphere in which it was written:

> The whole battle for licensing and for the AAA is a highly capitalistic maneuver designed to take a little more capital from one group of capitalists—producers, publishers, radio chains, television —and put it in the pockets of another group of capitalists, the writers. It is not something that squares with the Communist Party line. . . . The Kremlin would not understand it nor care for it.[70]

The anti-Communist crusaders did not heed Lavery's words. The October, November, and December editions of *The Screen Writer* reprinted eighteen pages of viciously hostile newspaper commentary from around the country, commentary which characterized the proposed Authority as "totalitarian," "a little Kremlin," and (contradictorily) "a literary tsardom." "We were," recalls former SWG executive secretary William Pomerance, "attacked from all points of the compass." The Red-baiting worked. The SWG backed away from the Cain proposal, as did Cain himself. The radicals alone continued to push it, including it in their platform for the 1947 Guild elections.

Thus on the eve of the worst disaster ever to overtake its members, the Screen Writers Guild—once *the* labor organization in Hollywood whose very existence troubled the sleep of studio front office inhabitants—felt itself, in the words of Pomerance, "powerless." Fearful of further internal divisiveness, fearful of a new siege of Red-baiting, fearful of the "recklessness" of its own left wing, and the wrecking qualities of its right wing, the SWG Board retreated before what it construed as the superior forces of management, public opinion, and the anti-Communist crusade. The Guild had been weak in the past, but the price of its weakness was never so high nor exacted so completely from its own membership as it would be in the years 1947–53.

The SWG lost every battle it mounted against the studios in the postwar years. William Pomerance, then executive secretary, remembered how Eddie Mannix "killed me on the issue of rehiring screenwriter war veterans; before a packed room of writers he effortlessly demonstrated the Guild's lack of power on this question."

At the same time, the SWG, at the behest of its French counterparts, unanimously voted to petition the American State Department to renegotiate the loan agreement with France, because it contained a protocol freeing American films from the import quota. The French film makers feared that a wholesale importation of Hollywood films would make it even more difficult for the French film industry to reestablish itself. Eric Johnston informed the writers that "the moving purpose behind the agreement was a desire to promote the ideal of world unity," and to prevent future wars by removing "excess nationalism" and allowing a "freer exchange of goods." Nor could the Producers' Association president resist a Red-baiting *coup de grâce:* "You may be interested in knowing that when the loan agreement was up for approval in the French Assembly, the only spoken opposition to the film provisions came from a few Communist deputies." The loan was not renegotiated.[71]

Probably at no other time in this century, not even at the depths of the Depression or the height of the New Deal, did this nation witness two years as fraught with potential for cataclysm, as filled with unyielding factionalism, as charged with confidence and uncertainty, optimism and fear, potency and despair, as the two years between the summer of 1945 and the summer of 1947. Counterrevolutionaries of all stripes, who had been on the defensive in the thirties, allied with representatives of corporate America, returned to respectability and power by the war matériel policies of the Roosevelt administration, to surge forward on every front. The united Left of the old Popular Fronts, a shadow of its former self, fought back staunchly, but its ranks were decimated by CP reversals, the defection of the anti-Communist liberals, and the depredations of the anti-Communist crusade. The conservative backlash which the latter symbolized may well have been irreversible and irresistible—certainly it embraced the most powerful elements of American society, politics, and economics—but disunity within the progressive coalition rendered it, especially the radical contingent, more isolated, impotent, and vulnerable than it would otherwise have been. The autumn of 1947 marked the beginning of the end.

The Congressional Hearings
of October 1947

"I won't do it. I stop here! Right now, I stop! Somebody has
to say no to them. It's needed to say . . . to say no. . . . To be
against them."

"To be against the government? . . ."

He nodded. "Yes. To be against the rottenness."

—*Albert Maltz, The Cross and the Arrow*[1]

The Investigation Commences: Congressional Pressure and
Producer Resistance, March–September 1947

Like a beacon in the darkening political night of postwar America,
Hollywood attracted the moths of reaction again and again. Ostensibly
the attackers cried out against "Communist subversion" in film making, but in truth their main target was the populist and liberal themes
which, in HUAC's eyes, appeared all too frequently in the films made
by the artists, intellectuals, and Jewish businessmen who dominated
an industry which in turn dominated the public imagination. Obviously, Hollywood movies changed no person's political consciousness;
at best, or worst, they reinforced mainstream social values. But to
right-wingers of the 1940s, even mainstream social values—if they had
a liberal tinge—were anathema. "Subversion" simply served as a pretext
for silencing a cultural and humanitarian liberalism—a liberalism of the
heart—which, in the eyes of America's right wing, regularly "infected"
the atmosphere in which Hollywood movies were made. To its
way of thinking the movie industry had to be brought round and
made to express proper American values.

The previous forays of legislative committees into Hollywood had been repulsed for a number of reasons, ranging from public antipathy to the fact that no body of investigators had yet proved capable of pitting Hollywood against itself by exploiting preexistent hierarchical, professional, and political divisions within the film industry. Studio bosses and their eastern exhibitor counterparts had proved too autonomous and too resilient for Dies, Wheeler and Nye, and Tenney. Legislative accusations had moved the film executives to resistance rather than to the expected collapse. Now, however, in a national atmosphere of Russophobia, Parnell Thomas and his colleagues could persevere in their exposure and denunciation, knowing that economic sanctions would bring recalcitrant studio management to heel. Though his predecessors had not been able to frighten producers into selling out their own left-wing employees, Thomas—supported by the economic power of the American Legion, the Catholic Church, and like-minded groups—would do so. The threat of mobilized public opinion —of a mass box office boycott, that is—would shortly arise to terrify studio management in a way no amount of reactionary bluster from the politicians could do.

Once the producers were enlisted, willingly or otherwise, in the anti-Communist cause, the crusaders could rely on a new form of economic sanction—discharge from studio employment—to give unprecedented gravity to their denunciations and exposures of individuals; to create a kind of reign of terror among screen employees. As soon as Eric Johnston volunteered the "full cooperation" of the Producers' Association, a HUAC subpoena was transformed from an annoyance or summons to do political battle to the kiss of professional death (or an invitation to become a stool pigeon). Such considerations greatly raised the stakes of the battle between congressional reaction and Hollywood radicalism, though they did not in any sense change the political essence of the struggle. What was changing rapidly was the identity of victor and loser, and the enormous price—blacklisting and a prison sentence—which the loser would have to pay.

If the tactic of issuing subpoenas was itself unfamiliar, the names of the "unfriendly" witnesses* to whom the pink slips were dispatched

---

* During the closed hearings which HUAC held in Los Angeles in May 1947, Parnell Thomas referred to a group of witnesses from the Motion Picture Alliance (Robert Taylor, Richard Arlen, Lela Rogers) as "friendly witnesses, cooperating with the Committee." The New Jersey congressman further defined them as "volunteers of information," whose "Americanism is not questioned." He did not use the term "unfriendly," however, when he referred to the uncooperative Hanns Eisler. That label was pinned by

were utterly predictable: they were those same men who for nearly a decade and a half had openly worked for causes ranging from the Roosevelt reelection campaigns to international anti-fascism to organizing and supporting union activity. By 1947 the question of exactly who was an active member of the CPUSA—given the Party's policies and vicissitudes in Hollywood in 1939–45—was rather harder to answer than at the height of the Popular Front, though the names of the leading, and even second-string, radicals were thoroughly familiar to everyone in the film community, from producers to grips. What Hollywood only suspected, HUAC knew. Long before nineteen Hollywood leftists were called to account in 1947, congressional investigators, working with FBI files, had compiled long lists of alleged Communists in the movie business. The job of verifying the allegations had been painstakingly carried out, although Communist Party affiliation was not terribly hard for diligent infiltrators to ascertain. Beginning with John Leech and Rena Vale in 1940, continuing through the informers of 1951–53 (Larry Parks, Edward Dmytryk, Martin Berkeley, Elia Kazan, etc.), and ending with William Ward Kimple in 1955, HUAC never seemed to lack long lists of names to investigate or expose. Leech and Kimple were the most notorious of a large group of police undercover agents who infiltrated the Los Angeles branches of the Communist Party. Kimple, an acknowledged member of the Los Angeles Police Department Intelligence Squad—the Hynes Red Squad—worked within the Party from 1928 to 1939, eventually becoming the membership chairman of the Southern Section. He told the Committee in 1955 that he was "in the position . . . to positively identify the Communist Party membership of close to a thousand people."[2]

After the war, infiltrators swarmed about Hollywood in such numbers as to have justified an FBI boast that "when five or six of you [radicals] are gathered together, I am with you." Right-wingers were equally diligent in ferreting out names for HUAC. During the hearings he held in Los Angeles in May 1947, Parnell Thomas told the press that "hundreds of very prominent film capital people have been

---

the *Hollywood Reporter* on nineteen screenwriters, subpoenaed to appear in Washington in October, whose hostility to HUAC had been made clear through speeches and paid advertisements. Eleven actually testified; ten were cited for contempt of Congress, convicted, and sentenced to jail. They became known as the Hollywood Ten. The eleventh, Bertolt Brecht, answered the Committee's questions, denied he was a Communist, and immediately left the United States for the German Democratic Republic.

named as Communists to us." The providers were the Motion Picture Alliance for the Preservation of American Ideals.[3] When its show trial commenced in October 1947, the Committee knew who was, and who was not, vulnerable to its Red-baiting, and knew it with far greater certainty than the Dies or Tenney committees had known.

The conservative Committee members not only knew the identities of the Hollywood Communists, they were angered and indignant that studio producers and front office executives, who should have known and cared, acted as if they did not. Indeed, the hearings that began early in 1947 were, perhaps, designed as much to spread anti-Communist anxiety among film industry management as to censure individual Reds. This was no easy task; the major producers were tough and independent entrepreneurs, not easily stampeded by the latest in an endless series of Washington-provoked spookings. The producers knew perfectly well how insulated their movies were from contact with anything resembling Communist political propaganda. They understood even better than their radical underlings that the Washington probe sought, not a handful of left-wing writers, but control of film making. On this matter the producers were prepared to do battle, even to the extent of appearing to take a stand with left-wing screen artists. Only when the Committee convinced the producers that their profits and control were imperiled by seeming solidarity with the "unfriendly" witnesses would studio management abandon that tack for one of grudging compliance with HUAC.

The producers' opening move, made by their spokesman and nominal leader, Eric Johnston, was a deft one. To protect his employers' autonomy from the encroachments of government and pressure groups and from the charges of Communist subversion of Hollywood film making, he appeared before HUAC, in March 1947, as an "expert on the containment of communism," along with fellow "experts" Jack Tenney, J. Edgar Hoover, and right-wing hate-group coordinator Walter S. Steele.† He used the opportunity to deride the charge of

---

† Walter S. Steele symbolized HUAC's original, and continuing, close link with America's "hate underground." Steele, chairman of the American Coalition Committee on National Security, a confederation of 114 patriotic organizations, first appeared before the Committee on August 16, 1938, naming 640 organizations as "Communistic." Included in this list were the ACLU, the CIO, the Boy Scouts of America, and the Camp Fire Girls. Frank Donner notes that Steele's "testimony was significant because it marked the emergence of the vigilante network that became so important to the functioning of the Committee." (*The Un-Americans*, New York:

"Communist infiltration" of Hollywood, claiming they "have suffered
. . . overwhelming defeat" every time they tried to influence scripts or
production, and to deflect Congressman Rankin's "suggestion" that the
studios summarily fire everyone suspected of Communist sympathies.[4]
In fact, Johnston was no less a cold warrior than HUAC. In his book
We're All in It, he extolled America's role as a "world power." America, he wrote, is "the powerhouse which stands in the way of the sole
remaining aggressive force loose on the globe—Communist Russia—the
only force likely to start another war. Around our huge powerhouse
of the West, the free world must rally—or go down."[5] Johnston knew,
contrary to the Committee's contention, that Hollywood producers
had already enlisted in the Cold War—on the side of the "free world
powerhouse." And he thought that HUAC's efforts to "restrict" or
"influence" motion picture content could only adulterate the themes
of democracy and freedom which Hollywood films already contained. HUAC members were not persuaded by Johnston's argument
or swayed by his eloquence; the Committee and its allies continued to
put pressure on the studios. In April, an obviously worried Jack
Warner broke ranks with the producers' anti-HUAC front and called
for "An All Out Fight on Commies."[6] When Johnston realized that his
March testimony had not dissuaded Thomas from opening a "massive
investigation" of the film industry, he met with the HUAC chairman
to pledge the "full cooperation" of the Producers' Association. He told
the press that the producers "are just as anxious as any member of the
Committee to expose any threat to the screen and to the American
design of living," but that the investigation must be "fair, dignified and
objective."[7]

On May 9, 1947, Parnell Thomas and John McDowell (R-Pa.) arrived in Los Angeles, established themselves at the Biltmore Hotel, and
proceeded to interview fourteen "friendly" witnesses. The Motion
Picture Alliance, whose ranks produced nearly all the "friendlies,"
proved so garrulous in its bill of particulars that the HUAC representatives were obliged to extend their stay in order to hear Robert

---

Ballantine Books, 1961, p. 13.) In fact, two of HUAC's chief investigators,
J. B. Matthews, a peddler of the Protocols of the Elders of Zion, and Robert
Stripling, a "white-supremacy Southerner," had been vociferous anti-
Semites before becoming involved with HUAC. (See David Wesley, *Hate
Groups and the Un-American Activities Committee,* 2nd ed. (revised),
New York: Emergency Civil Liberties Committee, 1962, pp. 8–10.)

Taylor, Richard Arlen, Adolphe Menjou, Leo McCarey, Howard Emmett Rogers, James Kevin McGuinness, Rupert Hughes, and others detail the extent and nature of "Communist subversion" in Hollywood. The hearings were held in executive (secret) session, but deliberate leaks to the newspapers and the trade papers spoke of the large numbers of screenwriters being named by the witnesses. Rupert Hughes, for example, was quoted as telling Thomas and McDowell that the Screen Writers Guild was "lousy with Communists today."[8]

With HUAC actually in town and the Alliance screen artists wildly pointing their fingers, the united front of studio executives began to fray. While most producers were simply angered by the audacity of the inquisitors and their gumshoes, a few were genuinely frightened. Jack Warner, for one, behaved before the Committee like a cornered villain from one of his studio's gangster movies, blurting out the names of every left-winger or liberal he could think of (all of whom he labeled "Communist")—which meant most of the SWG activists who had been or currently were under contract to Warner Brothers. Some of the men fingered by Warner—Julius and Philip Epstein, Sheridan Gibney, Emmet Lavery—had not only never been Communists, but were known for their criticism of communism.

More typical of the movie moguls' reaction to HUAC at this early date was Louis B. Mayer's public disdain ("Nobody can tell me how to run my studio") and private caution. Shortly after the Thomas probe began, Mayer called screenwriter Lester Cole to his office. He told me, Cole later testified, "that a number of stories had come to him in regard to my activities, my political beliefs. . . . He wanted to find some way to put an end to this. . . . [He] really had plans for me at the studio . . . and he didn't care what I believed, but since these were his plans, would I not in some way attempt to modify my activities[?]"[9]

Mayer's hold-the-line strategy clashed strongly with the surrender proposals Eric Johnston offered at a June 2 meeting of the Producers' Association. There he outlined a three-point program "to meet the issue of Communism in Hollywood." First, said Johnston, the producers must publicly "insist" upon an open investigation by the Committee; second, they must not employ "proven Communists" in jobs which might provide them with any influence on film content; and third, the producers should hire James Byrnes, former Secretary of State, to represent them before HUAC and the public.[10]

Willing to concede points one and three, the producers still balked at two. If putting out press releases calling for an "objective and fair investigation" of everything from studio story departments to commissaries would help Johnston in his duel with Congress, then he was free to do so. And if hiring a high-priced Washington notable was part of the cost of improving Hollywood's defenses, then the producers would foot the bill. But when it came to the delicate question of hiring and firing within their own studios, the producers would not yet agree to be dictated to—not by the Committee and certainly not by Johnston. The studio heads and managers, accustomed to having their own way, had no intention of tossing overboard such valuable writers as Dalton Trumbo, Metro's highest-paid screenwriter, or Lester Cole, who was about to be elevated to the rank of producer, simply because another committee of red-necked, Red-obsessed congressmen didn't like these writers' politics. It was by no means yet clear that a witch-hunt was in the producers' best interests. For the moment, at least, the idea of a blacklist was distasteful, and the expense of permanently ostracizing many of their finest screen artists was prohibitive. This steadfast defense of industrial sovereignty was clothed in a robe of moral principle. MGM's Eddie Mannix nobly announced to the assembled producers that he was "not about to join in any 'witch-hunt'" to "hurt Communists as long as I [am] able to protect the material on the screen [from subversion]."[11]

But the pressure was mounting. The departure of the Committee from Hollywood did not bring peace to the troubled souls of the major-studio producers. Thomas had left behind many all-too-obvious signs of his determination not to be sweet-talked, bargained, or stonewalled into going away: HUAC agents haunted the executive office buildings of the studios, dropping dire warnings about impending "unpleasant consequences" should management not agree to cooperate. One of them, H. A. Smith, announced to the press, "I plan to hold a number of meetings with industry heads, and the full resources of the House Committee and our investigative staff are at the disposal of those [studio executives] who want to put their house in order before Congress does it for them."[12] Shortly thereafter Smith informed Eddie Mannix that he would be subpoenaed to appear before the full Committee in Washington if he did not discharge Lester Cole immediately. When Mannix balked, Smith reminded him that more was at stake than the inconvenience and embarrassment of a subpoena and an appearance; that an "open" investigation by HUAC could "bring them [Mayer and Mannix] a good deal of trouble."[13] Mannix, with Mayer behind him, held the line, though not without increasing the pressure on Cole.

The Strategy of the "Unfriendly" Witnesses

On September 21, 1947, the House Un-American Activities Committee issued subpoenas to forty-three members of the Hollywood film industry requiring that they appear as witnesses before the Committee during its October hearings in Washington. (See Appendix 4 for a list of the subpoenaed people.) The timing probably caught many of the recipients off guard, while many others, the "friendly" witnesses, were not at all surprised—they had, after all, assisted in the preparation of the invitation list. The nineteen left-wingers who were summoned had watched the storm clouds gathering over Hollywood since the end of the war. The logic of events—HUAC's continued presence in the film capital since 1944, the periodic release of lists of names by Jack Tenney, the Red-baiting of the Motion Picture Alliance, the Hearst papers, and the *Hollywood Reporter*—presaged a show trial, but the Left did not know when or how the storm would break. If and when it did, they thought they could rely on the forms of resistance which had traditionally sprung up to thwart such invasions. It would have required prophetic vision to foresee that the revived Popular Front of the postwar era would prove narrow and frightened, that the producers' usual anti-Washington sound and fury would signify nothing, that the Truman administration would support the House Committee's probe, and that the Cold War had weakened the fervor of the many public-spirited citizens normally sympathetic to liberal or radical causes.

The "unfriendly" Nineteen were sensitive to the winds of political change, and the stands taken by their fellow witnesses sobered them all. The large number (coincidentally, also nineteen), if not the fervor, of the "friendly" witnesses was a surprise. Sam Wood, Ayn Rand, Adolphe Menjou, Roy Brewer, and the rest were old foes. More troubling were the stances of the "neutral" witnesses, notably Eric Johnston and SWG president Emmet Lavery. Within a week of the arrival of the subpoenas Johnston announced to the press that the producers had no desire to "shield or defend" members of the Communist Party.[14] Emmet Lavery, for his part, made it clear that in his testimony he intended to defend only "the reputation" of the Guild.

The "unfriendly" Nineteen, as it soon became clear, harbored more far-reaching and radical intentions. As a group, they had much in common besides their current predicament and their hostility to HUAC. Indeed, a casual observer might have thought them interchangeable. The number itself had no mystical significance. Between fifty and sixty high-profile activists composed the core of the Hollywood radical movement of the thirties and forties. Without question these nineteen men qualified to a man for membership in this group on the basis of their long-term dedication either to the guilds, the Communist Party, or the myriad organizations and causes of the Popular Fronts. If these were the only criteria, four dozen other radicals who worked in the film industry—e.g., Donald Ogden Stewart, Abraham Polonsky, John Bright, Paul Jarrico, Michael Wilson—should also have been subpoenaed. Although the method used by HUAC to select these nineteen men remains shrouded in mystery, it is clear that they shared four characteristics of particular relevance to the Committee's ends: all lived in Hollywood and were closely associated with motion pictures; sixteen were or had been writers; all were actively engaged in pro-Soviet activities; only one was a veteran of World War II. Perhaps of less political import, all of the Nineteen were men and ten were Jewish. Most significantly, the great majority were, or had been, members of the Communist Party of the United States. Out of this commonality of profession, experience, and politics emerged the Nineteen's desire to defeat the House Committee.

To realize this aim, however, the Nineteen had to overcome some potentially troublesome differences arising from conflicts of personality, disagreement over legal strategy, and professional inequalities. As events would indicate, some of the victims of this first roundup of screen left-wingers had made themselves inviting targets for Thomas through the sheer openness and magnitude of their activity—alleged Party membership cards, by-lines in Communist periodicals, names on "Communist front" letterheads, etc. But others who had not been Communists—Pichel, Milestone, Koch—would be far more difficult to brand.

Personally, they were an individualistic, strong-minded, opinionated, articulate, often contentious group of intellectuals. Though a few of them had been close friends, they in no sense constituted a social clique. As in any group of strong and diverse personalities, strain and discord existed, but during the numerous strategy sessions, harmony more or less prevailed. Professionally they covered a wide spectrum of success and financial security. Trumbo, Scott, Lardner, Parks, Koch, and Dmytryk enjoyed high salaries and long-term contracts at major studios, while Cole was on the verge of being made a producer. Maltz and Rossen, equally gifted and successful, chose to free-lance.

Still relatively young, these men were at the summits of their careers and had every reason to expect to remain on top. By contrast, Sam Ornitz, Herbert Biberman, Alvah Bessie, and John Howard Lawson were no longer in demand. Ornitz, the doyen of the group, had worked steadily in the twenties and thirties but had, like so many other writers, slowly slipped out of fashion. Bessie and Biberman had both failed to impress the studio bosses with their abilities. Lawson had been in great demand during the war, but his extensive activity during the CSU strike seriously damaged his career.

The potential disagreements resulting from the personal, professional, and political differences never threatened to divide the Nineteen. (Actually, the eighteen, because Brecht, an alien, wanted to be left free to work out a position that would not risk the loss of his recently issued exit visa—to Switzerland—as soon as the hearings had ended. He feared that close association with the Americans would be used as an excuse to delay his departure. The other eighteen understood.) Agreement on a series of fundamental points was immediate: the eighteen artists wanted to retain their jobs in the film industry, stay out of jail, avoid any possibility of informing, and "get" the Committee. Only the last question posed any difficulties—how, and at what sacrifice?

Nor was there disagreement over choice of counsel. Ben Margolis and Charles Katz, charter members of the National Lawyers Guild (NLG) who had been in the forefront of civil liberties cases in California since the thirties, were the first to be retained. In an effort to build as "broad an image or front as possible," the Nineteen also secured the assistance of Robert Kenny, a former judge and state attorney general, and Bartley Crum, a corporate lawyer (and a Republican) from San Francisco who had moved from representing William Randolph Hearst in the thirties to supporting Harry Bridges and fair employment for blacks in the forties.‡ Finally, Margolis and Katz recom-

---

‡ In the fifties, according to FBI files secured by the National Lawyers Guild, Crum became an informer, furnishing the FBI with information about the San Francisco chapter, pronouncing himself "very happy to cooperate with the FBI" in its investigation of the NLG, promising to search his files for further information, and offering to be "a willing witness at any hearing concerning the NLG." (Letters from Special Agent-in-Charge, New York to Director, FBI, October 1, 1953 and October 26, 1953, FBI National Lawyers Guild file, pp. 4,961 and 5,179, quoted in Percival Roberts Bailey, *Progressive Lawyers: A History of the National Lawyers Guild, 1936–1958*, Rutgers University: Unpublished Ph.D. thesis, 1979, pp. 505–6.)

mended that Samuel Rosenwein, a New York member of the NLG, and Martin Popper, a Washington-based attorney for the Civil Rights Congress, be brought in to handle developments or litigation in the East. Only the original counselors attended all the meetings, while Kenny attended a large number and Crum came to one or two at the end.

All the lawyers agreed that the only chamber in which the case could be won was the United States Supreme Court. Defeat in the congressional hearing room, on the floor of the House of Representatives, at the trial level, and in the lower appellate court was anticipated, but the high court was still, in late 1947, a solid preserve of Rooseveltian liberals. It was certain in the minds of the Nineteen and their lawyers that justices Hugo Black, William O. Douglas, Frank Murphy, Wiley Rutledge, Robert Jackson, and Harlan F. Stone would uphold the "unfriendly" witnesses before HUAC.

But the triumphal climax in the Supreme Court Building lay far in the future; for the moment it was a question of finding the means of providing the liberal justices with the best constitutional arguments. The problem was a brain-twister. As Ring Lardner, Jr., noted, "the first thing to recognize, we felt, was that the Committee had [us] in a rather tight bind, with strictly limited choices, none of them pleasant to contemplate, especially if you were indeed a Communist."[15] Five possible paths through the labyrinth suggested themselves, three of which were rather quickly dismissed; the remaining two engendered prolonged discussion.

First, the Nineteen could denounce the Committee outright, deny its right to exist by attacking its constitutionality, and refuse to answer its questions. So unrestrained an attack would certainly lead to instant contempt citations and professional doom, and would foreclose any possibility of using the widely publicized hearings to make a further statement. It would also damage the case the Nineteen wanted to present to the public: that no committee of Congress had the right to inquire into the political opinion or group memberships of American citizens. Moreover, there existed no possibility that any court would uphold such a challenge, for the legal precedents buttressing Congress' right to form investigative committees were clear and long-standing.

As a second alternative, the Communists among the Nineteen might simply deny their Party membership, thereby shutting down the circus before the main show commenced. This strategy appealed to no one. Not only was it obvious that the FBI and HUAC investigators had been diligent in their evidence-gathering; it was equally well known that the left wing was riddled with informers—indeed one might even turn up among the Nineteen—and the legal, and professional, penalties for perjury were much greater than those for contempt.

More to the liking of at least one purist among the Nineteen, Alvah Bessie, was the third possibility: open admission and proud defense of one's communism and political past. Such a strategy had to recommend it both a certain moral immaculacy and the promise of raising the "real" political issues underlying the hearings. If the hearing had been a formal political trial before a judge and jury, this approach might have been the best. The rules which governed a congressional hearing, however, left many traps for such high-minded and unwary defiance. For one thing, this approach overlooked the certainty that a witness would be gaveled into silence by the Committee chairman. For another, it implicitly granted the Committee's right to ask questions in the first place—something the Nineteen were determined not to do. Equally problematic, once having answered the "Are you now or have you ever been?" query with a burning "Yes! And here's why . . . ," the witness would then legally have obligated himself to reply to the interrogators' next question, "Who were the other members of your cell?" If he refused to name names—and none of the Nineteen had the slightest intention of doing so—he would be charged with contempt and left without constitutional grounds for contesting the citation. Finally, the candid approach would certainly have lost the Nineteen both public sympathy and their jobs.

A word should be said about this question of candor, for there is a strong tendency among latter-day anti-Communists, and even sympathetic left-wingers, to belabor the "unfriendly" witnesses for their "lack of forthrightness" before the Committtee. It is a fact that confirmed ideologues like Lawson and Biberman did not push for using the congressional hearing room as a political soapbox in the same way, for example, Trotsky had once used a tsarist courtroom to espouse his political beliefs. The House Committee did not permit anything like the unrestrained soliloquies which the Russian courts of the early twentieth century tolerated. The words "pounding gavel" stud the transcripts of the hearings and indicate the frequency and relish with which a contumacious witness' words were drowned out.

A far more compelling justification for the Nineteen's lack of "candor" was the particular perception of the Committee which *all* of the "unfriendly" witnesses shared. The left-wing screen artists saw HUAC differently from the civil libertarians, liberals, and the unaligned public. The Nineteen did not consider Thomas, Rankin, Nixon, *et al.* representatives of the national government. Rather, they saw them as political adversaries, camouflaged in congressional robes, in the ongoing war between reaction and radicalism. In Ben Margolis' words, "HUAC was an instrument of political repression; it was merely putting into action the conservative politics of the era." Albert Maltz said that the "unfriendly" witnesses had not intended "to conduct a sideshow or a legal maneuver," but rather to combat in HUAC the entire postwar right-wing movement which sought to silence critics and regiment the words and thoughts of everyone from artists to government employees.[16] "One is destroyed," he stated on another occasion, "in order that a thousand will be rendered silent and impotent by fear."[17] Maltz believed that this was the method of fascism, and that in HUAC the Nineteen "were fighting another form of fascism." In short, the "conservative politics of an era" had perhaps succeeded in conquering a part of the national legislature as well as gaining the tacit support of the executive branch, but this did not, in the Nineteen's eyes, endow the Committee with any greater authority or right than the Ku Klux Klan or the American Nazi Party possessed. It did not, in other words, alter the fundamental political nature of the struggle; it simply meant that the traditional enemy was disguised, better fortified, and far more dangerous. With such a perception, the Nineteen *had* to challenge all of HUAC's claims from the start, and that meant contesting its right to interrogate American citizens.

This political vision only partly dictated the legal strategy, however. For accompanying the Nineteen's wish to defy and defeat HUAC was the necessity—reflex, really—of protecting their jobs and careers as well as their families' financial security. Given the public statements of Eric Johnston and the private admonitions of sympathetic producers like Mannix, the Nineteen and their lawyers knew that a point-blank refusal to cooperate with the Committee would ineluctably lead to professional disaster. And not one of the "unfriendly" witnesses, for all his implacable rejection of HUAC, could contemplate with equanimity the end of his professional career. They were courageous activists, not career revolutionaries or ideological martyrs. Suffering, when it came, was thrust upon them unwillingly, though it was borne with good grace by most. Thus the legal strategy they devised had the triple aim of 1) opposing HUAC, while 2) not discrediting themselves in studio executives' eyes with "indecorous" outbursts of intransigence, and 3) providing the constitutional basis for a favorable Supreme Court opinion. Specifically, the Nineteen and their lawyers sought to devise a strategy which would permit each of them sufficient time at the microphone before the gavel and contempt citation of Chairman Thomas silenced them. The Nineteen thus had to accept conditionally the Committee's existence and, provisionally at least, play its game. The tightest and safest constitutional route would have been to refuse to answer by reason of the entire Bill of Rights. Such a stance might have obscured the issues which the Nineteen wanted to spotlight. Two other realms of constitutional refuge remained, the First and Fifth amendments. Each presented its own problems, however, and the lawyers and their clients spent many hours sifting through the precedents and the possibilities.

Though a later generation of "unfriendly" witnesses would turn to the Fifth Amendment as the only available device to avoid being either sent to jail or forced to inform, the Nineteen found it not to their liking. From a strictly legal point of view, it was not a sure haven. Through the years lower courts and Congress had indicated that the Fifth could be used in legislative investigations, but the Supreme Court had never expressly ruled on the issue.[18] The nine justices would thus have to be depended upon to extend old principles to a new situation. In any case, witnesses who used the Fifth would have been cited for contempt. Secondly, the Fifth was morally abhorrent to most of the American public. Whatever the intentions of the framers of the Fifth,[19] and whatever legal capaciousness its wording technically permits a "refugee" (". . . nor shall [any person] be compelled in any criminal case to be a witness against himself . . ."), the fact remained that public opinion regarded "taking the Fifth" as a sure sign that the taker had something to hide (rather than that he had simply chosen to refuse to aid the state in its prosecutorial task). Since the Nineteen saw the confrontation with HUAC as a political battle, they required a strategy which would appeal to, or at least not offend, the very public whom they wished to enlighten or persuade. Just as important, the Nineteen were not willing to cultivate public sympathy and understanding at the expense of their pride in their political pasts; that is, they did not want the public to believe that membership in the Communist Party constituted a criminal act or a shameful memory. Similarly, as front-line troops in the domestic Cold War, the "unfriendly" witnesses could not abandon or implicitly deny what they considered the achievements of Communists in recent world history: the Popular Front, the successes of the Red Army, the resistance movements in Axis-occupied countries, etc. As Charles Katz noted, "For the group to intimate [as they would by taking the Fifth] that their political beliefs could conceivably be criminal under our country's institutions and principles would in fact be tacitly to concede in the public eye what Dies and Rankin had long been trying to prove."

That left the First Amendment: "Congress shall make no law . . . abridging the freedom of speech . . . or the right of the people peaceably to assemble." This concept has a long and noble history in the United States, from John Peter Zenger's defense of freedom of the press to Eugene V. Debs' refusal to be silenced by a court injunction, to the efforts to silence Communists and labor organizers during the twenties. Standing on such hallowed ground gave the Nineteen the moral, historical, and legal basis they needed to challenge the Committee's jurisdiction without appearing to be captious, self-seeking wreckers of congressional procedures. More fundamentally, the tradition of the First struck a resonant chord in the "unfriendly" witnesses themselves. Both in their public and private statements, they constantly reiterated their regard for their responsibilities as American citizens, defenders of the Constitution, and bearers of the radical tradition of Zenger, Paine, Altgeld, Debs, etc. The decision for the First did not stem from patriotic posturing on the Nineteen's part. Rather, these men, and the movement of which they were a part in Hollywood and New York, were passionately imbued with a unique mix of democratic radicalism and patriotic idealism. This faith of the Nineteen's went deeper than their critical posture toward American democracy as it actually functioned, and is, finally, what explains their surprise and bitterness when the public, their employers, and the courts ultimately turned against them.

American radicals have a deep-seated faith in the political tradition from which this government and society stem. The Nineteen saw HUAC as an illegal aberration—a betrayal of "Americanism." The antidote which the Hollywood radicals prescribed, therefore, was a restorative, not a toxin: they called for the responsible action of American citizens to reclaim the traditional political rights and civil liberties to which they had an inalienable guarantee.

Ideological and emotional considerations blended, moreover, with tactical and career-minded common sense, for the First would definitely win for the Nineteen greater sympathy and support within the film community, particularly from liberals for whom civil liberties were sacred and censorship abhorrent. Finally, the First Amendment defense recommended itself legally: the Supreme Court had not (yet) explicitly limited its use by witnesses testifying before the Congress. Nevertheless, for all its sentimental, political, professional, and legal advantages, the First also carried with it the sure promise of citations for contempt of Congress and a protracted and expensive court battle to avoid imprisonment and fines. In short, if not exactly the martyr's stake, the First was certainly no springboard to redemption; it provided, in the end, a field of honor on which the adversaries could meet.

The attorneys relied heavily on two Supreme Court opinions as the legal basis for their advice to the Nineteen on the probable success of a First Amendment strategy: *Kilbourn* v. *Thompson*, 103 U.S. 168 (1880) and *West Virginia State Board of Education* v. *Barnette*, 319 U.S. 624 (1943). Katz and Margolis read the former as having set down the rule that "it is simply not the business of government to compel the unwilling private citizen to disclose, at peril of his liberty, his politics or his political associations." *Barnette*, which did not actually involve the power of a congressional investigating committee, as *Kilbourn* had, nevertheless spoke directly to the issue of the power of the state to compel a private citizen to avow his loyalty or be punished for remaining silent. In a 6–3 decision, the Court expressly overruled a decision it had made three years earlier upholding a compulsory flag salute requirement. In the course of his majority opinion, Justice Jackson enunciated a theory of the First Amendment which caught and held the legal gaze of Charles Katz. Twenty-five years after the strategy sessions, in a letter to Albert Maltz, Katz could still recapture his delight in the precedent:

> In retrospect, some of us (and probably I more than my brethren) were clearly wrong in our assessment of the added strength given to Kilbourn by Jackson's opinion in the West Virginia case. Yet that opinion had . . . seemingly destroyed the whole super-patriotic cabal, specifically including (almost by name) the proponents of the views of the House Un-American Activities Committee.
>
> We were young men in 1942—and in 1947. Jackson's judgement was olympian—electrifying. And during the months between the date of the first service of the subpoena early in 1947 and October 27, 1947, when Jack Lawson first appeared, I clung feverishly to the words of Jackson, certain that what he had taught would not be forgotten in less than 5 years.[20]

The pros far outweighed the cons, in the Nineteen's eyes, and they rallied around the First Amendment. The strategy question resolved, they discussed the mode of its presentation to HUAC. Although each witness was left to formulate his own particular manner of approach (and there was lively argument over the degree of politeness to accord the inquisition), the group decided that each would read a critical statement before answering any of the Committee's questions and then, in the guise of answering questions, of giving testimony, would side-step the questions about their political or union affiliations. The statements presented no problems. Though emphasizing different aspects of the conservative reaction—Ornitz and Scott stressed the persecution of minorities; Biberman, Trumbo, and Bessie drew parallels with European fascism; Lawson, Lardner, Cole, and Maltz focused on the Bill of Rights; and Dmytryk exposed the blacklist—each statement represented a clear, forthright, radical political stance.

So much for the straightforward statements. The second, allied tactic was the admittedly obscure one of refusing to answer HUAC's questions without expressly saying, "I refuse." The ploy was urged on the group by Robert Kenny, a lawyer whom Lardner described as "a negotiator, a politician, an attorney much more cautious than Margolis or Katz." Kenny somehow convinced everybody that a witness' "trying to answer in his own way," while being gaveled down by the Committee chairman, would stand a defendant in better moral and legal stead before the courts of public opinion and justice than concise refusal to reply. More particularly, such a tactic would give a future jury of twelve sympathetic people an "arguable issue"—i.e., did the Nineteen's "answers" really constitute answers?—not a clear violation of law on which a judge's instructions would leave a jury very little room to acquit. Moreover, by agreeing to "talk" to HUAC, the "unfriendly" witnesses would not appear contumacious in the eyes of that crucial body—studio executives—and would not be liable for blacklisting.

If the First Amendment strategy was sound, the testimony tactic was dubious. By adopting the answering-by-not-answering approach before the Committee, the Nineteen were relegating their First Amendment defense to a fallback position, usable only in the courts. They thereby disarmed themselves of their clarion call to the American public in general and the Hollywood film community in particular.

Final agreement on this complicated plan of attack was not reached without some unspoken reservations. Alvah Bessie claims that three of the Nineteen signed statements swearing they were not Communists and deposited them, secretly, with their producers in the hope that such a hedge would protect them from any adverse legal and professional consequences which might ensue from unforeseen weaknesses in the collective plan of attack.[21] Walter Goodman writes (without attribution to source) that Scott and Dmytryk wanted to be more candid with HUAC and were "beaten back by the hard-nosed faction led by Lawson who wanted a united front and a rousing issue."[22] Margolis and Maltz, however, remember differently. Dmytryk, they say, hardly spoke at any of the sessions and Scott voiced no disagreement with the final strategy. Moreover, any call for candor was ludicrous even for ex-Communists (which Scott and Dmytryk were not) to advocate because they would still have to name names or face a contempt citation.

A consensus achieved, and afterthoughts notwithstanding, the Nineteen gave unanimous and unstinting support to the plan which they adopted. For the next three years they would display to the public and their adversaries a solid front.

The Political Battle Against HUAC

The second, and in some respects more important, front of the war between the Nineteen and the Committee—that of public opinion— opened immediately after the issuance of the subpoenas. Both sides understood the decisive role of non-combatants, but where the Committee needed only passivity, indifference, or fear from the public, the Nineteen needed active popular support in the form of organized, collective mobilizations like those of the Popular Front era. As their attorneys busied themselves with the legal aspects of the case—a Motion to Quash the Subpoenas on the grounds that the object of the Committee's investigation lay "wholly within the domain of thought and speech and opinion" safeguarded by the First Amendment[23]—the "unfriendly" witnesses moved to rally liberals of all shades. Employing tested thirties tactics, they made speeches, raised money, established committees, and took out ads in the newspapers and trade papers. And, at the outset anyway, their cries did not fall on deaf ears; the Nineteen were not seen as Cassandras, but as Paul Reveres. Many people, perhaps a majority, in the Hollywood film community agreed that HUAC posed a serious threat to the movie industry. Even the liberal anti-Communists recently congregated in the Americans for Democratic Action deplored, in an ad, signed by Melvyn Douglas, which appeared in the *Hollywood Reporter*, the harm done to "cultural freedom" by HUAC's "careless and callous investigating methods."[24] Nor, for that matter, did most studio producers and executives find anything to disagree with in the Nineteen's two-page manifesto that appeared in the trade papers on October 16:

The issue is not the "radicalism" of nineteen writers, directors, actors who are to be singled out, if possible, as fall guys. They don't count. No *one* of them has ever been in control of the films produced in Hollywood. The goal is control of the industry through intimidation of the executive heads of the industry . . . and through further legislation.[25]

This outpouring of anti-HUAC feeling proved quite short-lived, however, hence a source of bitterness and disappointment for the "unfriendly" witnesses—who had assumed the HUAC-phobia represented personal solidarity with their cause, which it did not.

Appeals for procedural punctiliousness from liberal anti-Communists and tacit support from front office businessmen constituted but slight assistance to the Nineteen's purpose. If HUAC were to be destroyed, efforts and sacrifices beyond anyone's previous experience would have to be made. Initially three groups seemed to have the requisite qualities of number, organization, anger, and determination to "go the distance": the Progressive Citizens of America, the Committee for the First Amendment, and the Screen Writers Guild. Though indistinguishable from one another in their earliest outcries of rage, the three groups soon came to diverge widely in the extent of the direct aid they offered the "unfriendly" witnesses.

The most active and enduring support for the Nineteen came from a group which dared not to speak its name. Besides, it had never been the policy of the Communist Party, even at the height of the first Popular Front, to give formal public support to any cause or organization for fear of driving out non-Communists and eliciting gratuitous opposition. Although the Party's leaders verbally supported the Nineteen and the principles for which they battled, the national Party itself was besieged on too many other fronts to offer anything in the way of material assistance. Within a year Communists would be purged from the CIO and fired from government and teaching positions and would see their leadership decimated by a series of Smith Act indictments and convictions.* The national leadership instructed

---

* Even before the Nineteen appeared in Washington, the ranks of Party members and allies had been thinned out by HUAC and the judicial system. Seventeen members of the Joint Anti-Fascist Refugee Committee's governing body were convicted of contempt of Congress in June; Eugene Dennis, the Party's general secretary, was sentenced to one year in jail in July for refusal to testify before HUAC; and Leon Josephson received a similar sentence on a similar charge in October.

the Hollywood branch to manage as best it could on its own. With a strong pocket in the Screen Writers Guild and a dominating influence in the Progressive Citizens of America, the Hollywood Reds provided the most tangible and reliable assistance.

The Progressive Citizens of America

The PCA was formed in late 1946 by the Communist and fellow-traveler remnants of the various independent citizens' groups discussed in Chapter 7—the Independent Citizens Committee of the Arts, Sciences and Professions and the National Citizens Political Action Committee—and by mid-1947 had moved to the outermost edge of the Democratic Party. Many of the activists in the national organization were Communists, and the Hollywood branch was Red-dominated. The organization itself, however, was not officially Communist, nor even a Communist front group, as the American League for Peace and Democracy had been. Rather, control of the PCA had devolved to the far Left only when moderates and liberals left, or refused to join, the organization. If the PCA enjoyed an intense, though brief, spurt of life, it was largely due to the fact that Communists had fewer and fewer baskets into which they could put their eggs. Only the Civil Rights Congress and the National Lawyers Guild, among visible and effective nationwide organizations devoted to aiding citizens accused of political crimes, now remained open to Communist influence. The PCA, for its part, was the CP's only effective lobby and political pressure channel.

Although the PCA provided continuing support for the Nineteen, it functioned less well as a political action group. As a merger of two highly active left-wing groups—NCPAC, which was oriented toward grass-roots campaign mobilization, and ICCASP, which was oriented toward fund-raising and speaking—the new organization might have been expected to undertake integrated and "complete" political activity along a wide range of left-wing issues and causes. Instead, something of an internal split between its old constituent parts persisted, with the result that two separate staffs were maintained and an ongoing series of duplications of effort and disagreements over tactics occurred.

In July 1947, two months before the subpoenas arrived, the Board of the PCA called a Conference on the Subject of Thought Control in the United States as a means to warn the public of, in Howard Koch's words, the "alarming trend to control the cultural life of the American people in accordance with reactionary conceptions of our national interest."[26] In contrast to Koch's "radical" vision of the purpose of the Conference, Gene Kelly's "liberal" view offered a preview of the differing perceptions which were soon to widen into tactical and strategic cleavages: "the meeting was a protest against the Committee's published statements in the press categorizing certain writers, directors, actors, etc., as 'unfriendly'† and thereby smearing them publicly before they had a hearing of any kind."[27]

Held in the posh Beverly Hills Hotel, the Conference recaptured, for one last time, the atmosphere of the thirties: it covered a wide range of political, social, and cultural issues, showcased an impressive array of famous and passionately involved speakers, attracted wide press coverage and national attention, and produced a long list of radically worded resolutions. The entire left-wing community of California participated either as speakers or discussants. No areas of culture and thought control techniques were left untouched: the press, radio, literature, film, music, art, architecture, drama, and even medicine, science, and education. Vigorous and critical debate culminated in many strong resolutions calling for freedom and the mobilization of public opinion. The Conference voted unanimously to urge the abolition of HUAC as well as all the "little HUAC's" at the state level. Every speaker warned of the new restrictions and intimidation creeping into his or her profession; many drew parallels between America in the late forties and Germany during the Third Reich.

When the subpoenas arrived in September, the Progressive Citizens of America immediately closed ranks behind the Nineteen. Starting in October the PCA launched a daily broadsheet—"The Other Side of the Story"—intended to dispense an "antidote to the poison many of you are reading in your newspapers or hearing over the radio these days."[28] On the eve of John Howard Lawson's lead-off testimony for the Nineteen the PCA sponsored a very successful conference on Cultural Freedom and Civil Liberties which brought together, at New York's Hotel Commodore, noted liberals and radicals such as Robert Kenny, Senator Claude Pepper (D-Fla.), Harvard professor Harlow Shapley, and two of the Nineteen, Lardner and Parks. A letter from Henry Wallace criticizing HUAC was read.[29]

In short, the Hollywood radical Left proved prescient in perceiving the reaction and its methods and energetic in responding. But they

---

† Kelly had telescoped events in his letter. At the time of the conference no Hollywood people had been labeled "unfriendly." That nomenclature arrived with the subpoenas in September.

seriously miscalculated both the force of the repression and the dismaying alacrity with which former allies would submit to it. Perhaps blinded by their own fervor, unity, and strength of purpose, Hollywood leftists did not realize how isolated in the national community they had become as a result of their knee-jerk apologism for the Soviet Union, which left them open to the charge of treason. What did not register properly with the radical Left in late 1947 was that while liberals had loyally stepped forward, it was not to support suspected Communists, whom many regarded as "agents of a foreign power," but to defend civil liberties and oppose political reaction.

The Committee for the First Amendment

Lucey's restaurant, on Melrose Avenue, directly across from Paramount and RKO studios, had long been a favorite watering hole for film artists, union organizers, and studio workers. In September 1947 writer Philip Dunne met there for lunch with directors William Wyler and John Huston and actor Alexander Knox. "We were principally concerned," said Dunne, "with the assault on civil liberties, what to us looked like persecution of the so-called 'unfriendly' witnesses, and the reputations of hundreds of others whose names were being slandered." They also feared the beating the film industry was taking at the hands of Parnell Thomas and the conservative press. Out of their multi-faceted concerns arose a group called the Committee for the First Amendment (CFA). Dunne, Wyler, and Huston were the Committee for the First Amendment. They wrote all its publicity and press releases, conducted its liaison work with the Nineteen, the producers, liberal congressmen, etc. They were assisted, on occasion, by an informal steering committee composed of director Anatole Litvak, writer Julius Epstein, actor Shepperd Strudwick, producer Joseph Sistrom, and press agent David Hopkins.

The founding meeting of the Committee was held a short time later at the home of songwriter Ira Gershwin. Writer Abraham Polonsky, representing the radical Left at what was mainly a liberal gathering, noted that the Gershwin home was "jammed. You could not get into the place. The excitement was intense. The town was full of enthusiasm because they all felt they were going to win. Every star was there. We Communists had not created the organization, but we believed in its usefulness and helped to organize its activities." Not surprisingly, given the CFA's resources of funds and personnel, these activities were widespread and highly visible: two national radio broadcasts, a series of one- and two-page ads in the trade papers, and a highly publicized, star-studded trip to Washington, D.C., on a chartered airplane. Determined to advertise their intention to defend civil liberties and their industry, the CFA pitted the glitter and celebrity of names like Humphrey Bogart, Danny Kaye, Myrna Loy, Katharine Hepburn, Fredric March, Richard Rodgers, and Moss Hart against the concentrated power and effectiveness of the little-known members of HUAC. Studio power, in the form of vocal support for the CFA from the producers, would have stood the Nineteen's cause in greater stead than the roster of over 300 household names which graced the anti-HUAC ads Dunne and Wyler and Huston composed. As it was, only a few of the most powerful producers and executives—Pandro S. Berman, Walter Wanger, Sam Zimbalist, Jerry Wald, Arthur Hornblow, Jr., and William Goetz among them—contributed meager sums to the cause. Considering the inflated salaries earned by high-ranking studio executives and producers, the amounts they contributed were as token as the number of names of producers which appeared in the CFA ads: Samuel Briskin ($200), Pandro S. Berman ($50), William Goetz ($1,000), Arthur Hornblow, Jr. ($500), Fred Kohlmar ($250), Joseph Pasternak ($50).[30] Nevertheless, recalled attorney Ben Margolis, "it was a major support effort for the Nineteen's cause. It had a broad basis within the industry and the tacit backing of the industry executives." Despite Margolis' evaluation, the Committee for the First Amendment did not arise primarily to help the "unfriendly" witnesses. Noted Dunne: "Ben was wrong. The CFA was in the business of supporting *rights*, not causes."

In order to attract the broadest possible base of support, the CFA leaders did not publicize their Committee as a direct support group for the Nineteen. Dunne, Wyler, and Huston did not particularly care whether or not any of the "unfriendly" witnesses were now, or had ever been, Communists. They privately suspected as much, but they were confident that the CFA's cause could not be compromised by revelations about the Nineteen's political affiliations. According to Wyler, "what mattered to us was that the Nineteen challenge HUAC in a dignified manner on the basis of the First Amendment."

From the start it was clear that the CFA would not include Communists in its membership. Partly this policy was the decision of scarred liberal veterans of the last Communist "surprise," the Nazi-Soviet Pact, but it was largely the tactical ploy of men who knew "we were going to be called Communists or Comsymps anyway and weren't anxious to give the opposition real grounds for saying so" (Dunne). To this end, they constantly warned CFA members, petition signers, and, even more emphatically, the participants on the radio broadcasts and the chartered airplane trip of the harmful effect "dangerous political affiliations" could have on the CFA's goals. That is, the CFA founders pointedly asked all Communists and fellow travelers to keep their distance. An examination of the rosters of names involved with the various CFA activities indicates that the far Left, for the most part, heeded Dunne's admonition—sixteen radicals signed the ads; only one, Larry Adler, traveled to Washington. Dunne and Wyler carefully policed their Committee, and Wyler felt so sure of its liberal purity that he could write to *Hollywood Reporter* publisher William Wilkerson: "no member of our group is a Communist or sympathetic to the totalitarian form of government practiced or advocated by Communist parties in different parts of the world."[31]

The Screen Writers Guild

The Committee for the First Amendment, an *ad hoc* White Knight arriving to smite HUAC, retired from the fray only after its opponent turned out to be many fearsome monsters, not one lone dragon. The Screen Writers Guild, a long-standing organization nominally devoted to the protection and welfare of its members—hence, it could be supposed, profoundly concerned with attacks on freedom of speech—never even donned its armor or mounted its horse. Emmet Lavery, then president of the SWG, said in retrospect, "Many of our members did not want to confront the Committee"—they feared imperiling not only their careers, but the existence of the Guild itself.

In fact, since the end of World War II, the writers' union had come to resemble a battlefield on which radicals, liberals, and conservatives regularly fought. The far Left never really threatened to dominate, but its superior organization and devotion to unions often won for its chief spokespeople a disproportionate number of high Guild offices. From these positions the Left kept up a steady flow of pressure, rarely winning its aims, but constantly challenging the skills and organization of the majority and wearing down its patience. By 1946 this majority had already reached something like its threshold of toleration for the far Left. The events of 1947 added fear to the Guild moderates' impatience with screenwriter Communists, and the stage was thus set for intra-Guild bloodletting even before the subpoenas arrived in September.

As for HUAC, the Guild was, of course, strongly opposed to, and offended by, that Committee's pretensions and allegations. But with more to lose than their colleagues in the CFA, the SWG liberal leadership more anxiously protected the reputation of its organization and more openly divorced itself from the fates of its members among the Nineteen. When his subpoena arrived, Lavery told the SWG Executive Board that the hearings were "really a good opportunity to project what the Guild was really like and to explode HUAC's accusations with truth." At no time did Lavery suggest that his testimony might also present an opportunity to stand behind the eleven screenwriters among the Nineteen.

Acting with the Board's approval, Lavery proceeded to place himself and the SWG "at the command of the FBI for any investigations they might care to make."[32] Lavery had made a similar offer when he testified before the Tenney Committee in 1946. He was not, it seems, opposed to an investigation of Hollywood; rather he opposed probes by "improper" agencies. Just prior to his departure for Washington, Lavery issued a position paper which the Board circulated to Guild members. He promised to "defend the principle of freedom of the screen at every point"—except where it came to the treatment of members of his union hauled before a congressional committee for reasons precisely concerned with the exercise of artistic and political freedom of expression. There, Lavery and the Board washed their hands:

> in the matter of individual activities of Guild members, either within or outside the industry, the individual defense or individual presentation is a matter for each individual witness. As the chief executive officer of the Guild, it is not my purpose at Washington to act either as "prosecutor" or as "defending counsel" for individual witnesses before the Committee.[33]

The governing body of the Guild thus assumed a highly questionable position *vis-à-vis* the Nineteen. As a trade union, the SWG's only *raison d'être* was the protection and welfare of its screenwriter members, whatever their political views and associations. The Nineteen had not been subpoenaed merely as radical activists, but as screen artists charged with subverting movies with their left-wing beliefs. They thus stood indicted *as screenwriters* (or directors or producers or actors), and were unarguably entitled to the protection of their guild. Under these circumstances, for the Guild to separate itself from its eleven members was to separate itself from the principle on which both the Guild and the Nineteen professed to stand.

Nevertheless, on the eve of the hearings the list of HUAC's opponents gave the Nineteen reason for optimism. Aside from solid and wide-ranging liberal and press hostility toward the Committee, the "unfriendly" witnesses enjoyed unfaltering aid from the Progressive Citizens of America—and from individual Communists. The Committee for the First Amendment had arisen to march, if not exactly in step with the Nineteen, at least comfortably close to its exposed right flank, while even the SWG's qualified position did not yet augur ill, for the screenwriters among the Nineteen still believed they might be able to bring their union around.

Washington, D.C., October 20–30, 1947

Albert Maltz was not especially eager to go East. He was hard at work on a novel, *The Journey of Simon McKeever*, and, like many writers, he hated to be interrupted. HUAC, however, "was a cancer on the body politic which had to be excised." Lester Cole felt "nervous, apprehensive, uneasy," but "determined." Ring Lardner, Jr., who would recite the most quoted line of the October hearings ("I could answer it [your question on Communist Party membership], but if I did, I would hate myself in the morning"), "had no confidence in my ability to outduel the Committee verbally." As a group the Nineteen felt confident that they could walk successfully over the abyss on the thin constitutional wire they had strung during their pre-hearing strategy sessions. HUAC, however, had held some pre-hearing strategy sessions of its own. As the Committee's hearings unfolded, they came to resemble a drama staged in four acts. The impresarios of the Committee deliberately calculated the witnesses' appearances to suit the purposes of the spectacle they were producing. What proved to be most disruptive to the plans of the "neutral" and "unfriendly" witnesses was that no one knew until each day dawned who would be summoned to the bar and in what order.

Act One, Scene One saw Jack Warner walk to center stage and repeat before a packed house (and a listening national radio audience) the craven performance he had delivered *in camera* the previous May. After a short, wan disclaimer wherein he "assured" HUAC that no "subversive propaganda" ever found its way into any of Warner Brothers' films—not even *Mission to Moscow*—Warner launched into a windy, stuttering, obsequious protestation of his "Americanism" and his loathing of communism. Without being asked, he volunteered the names of twelve "Communists" whom he had "spotted" and "fired" from his studio: Bessie, Kahn, Koch, Lardner, Lavery, Lawson, Maltz, Rossen, Trumbo, Wexley, Odets, and Irwin Shaw.[34] Warner's complaisance in throwing fellow screen artists to the wolves came as a horrifying shock to the watching Nineteen, the listening CFA, and even Warner's colleagues, most of whom were furious that one of their highest-ranking members would thus break ranks and wave a white flag over the Producers' Association's intended stone wall. (Eric Johnston went out of his way to inform the Nineteen that he and his confreres "are embarrassed by the fact that Jack Warner . . . made a stupid ass of himself" both in the October hearings and those of the spring. Paul McNutt, former governor of Indiana, ambassador to the Philippines, and chairman of the War Manpower Commission, who had been hired as a special counsel for the Producers' Association in mid-September, had told the Nineteen: "I have spent all day reviewing his testimony in an effort to have Warner appear in a less idiotic light."[35])

Aspersions on Warner and reassurances to the Nineteen could not, however, dispel the foreboding which Warner's testimony brought to the hearing at its outset. Had Louis B. Mayer and Dore Schary, two other ranking studio executives, been permitted to testify on the heels of Warner, Mayer's phlegmatic immovability and Schary's elegant derision might have helped to redress the balance. But Parnell Thomas understood too well how to stage an effective show trial. Mayer's and Schary's testimonies were buried amid the further accusatory performances of the "friendly" witnesses and the physical removals of the "unfriendly" witnesses.

Act Two introduced a long stream of "friendly" witnesses—Sam Wood, John Charles Moffitt, Rupert Hughes, James K. McGuinness, Morrie Ryskind, Fred Niblo, Jr., Richard Macaulay—who matter-of-factly named three dozen "Communists" whom they knew to be working in Hollywood. At one point, while McGuinness was struggling to remember the names of more "subversives," Thomas interrupted to tell him not to worry, the Committee had a list of seventy-nine names.[36] As Warner had done, though without the frenzy of a cornered rat, the "friendly" witnesses defended Hollywood against the charge that its films were subversive. Their performances differed from Warner's in style (they were completely self-possessed), predictability (the former Screen Playwrights among them had been denouncing Communists for fifteen years), and accuracy (no howlers like calling Lavery a Communist to cast doubt on their recitals).

Screenwriter Richard Macaulay closed out this act with the recital of twenty-nine obviously memorized names.‡

If Act Two seemed to promise an impending tragedy, Act Three was strictly comic opera. A squad of Hollywood leading men had cast themselves in the role of "concerned patriotic citizens" defending a shrinking studio beachhead against an invading Bolshevik menace. Thomas and his colleagues sat impassively as Robert Taylor, Robert Montgomery, Ronald Reagan, Gary Cooper, and George Murphy related how they had vigilantly scrutinized prospective scripts for their "Communistic" content, tried to warn their colleagues and superiors of "subversive" activity, and generally tried to set a high standard of patriotic Americanism. Unlike the previous slate of "friendly" witnesses, this group did not defend Hollywood against the "Red" charge; indeed, they came closer than anyone, even Sam Wood, to substantiating the accusation. Their function was not to provide the Committee with information, but with luster. They did not name names but lent (their) names. These actors, like Adolphe Menjou earlier, provided HUAC with the means of neutralizing the impact on public opinion of the hostile and equally celebrated Committee for the First Amendment, due to arrive in Washington for the start of the final act on Monday, October 27.

In the weekend between the testimony of the last "friendly" witnesses, including Walt Disney, and the first "unfriendly" witness, John Howard Lawson, the Committee for the First Amendment opened its campaign to win over public opinion. Thus far that opinion was hardly solid in its support for HUAC and its project. Indeed many important newspaper reviews had been running against the Committee's work. The New York *Times*, the Washington *Post*, the Louisville *Courier-Journal*, and other leading dailies had been printing editorials blasting HUAC for the fashion in which it had chosen to conduct the investigation "now under way in Washington." Wrote the *Times*: "We do not believe the Committee is conducting a fair investigation. We think the course on which it is embarked threatens to lead to greater dangers than those with which it is presently concerned."[37] Intent on expanding this beachhead among the enlightened public, the CFA dispatched its planeload of stars—Bogart, Bacall, Kaye, et al.—to Washington on Sunday, October 26, and sponsored,

---

‡ 1947 HUAC hearings, p. 198. When the left-wing informers began their name game in 1951, they proved Macaulay quite accurate. Only three of his names (Marian Spitzer, John Collier, and Ranald MacDougall) were not reiterated.

that very night, a national radio broadcast ("Hollywood Fights Back"). One after another the stars stepped up to the ABC microphone to denounce HUAC, uphold the First Amendment, and defend Hollywood, but left unmentioned the nineteen "unfriendly" witnesses. The CFA had timed its demonstrations to support not Lawson, but Eric Johnston, who was also scheduled to appear on Monday. By contrast, the Progressive Citizens of America's Sunday convocation in New York was specifically intended to hearten the Nineteen.

On the morning of Act Four the Grand Alliance for the Defense of Hollywood appeared formidable. Never again would the Nineteen's cause appear as tightly linked with that of the CFA and the producers. The demonstrations of the former and the spoken and printed words of the latter's representative, Eric Johnston, seemed to promise a united front. Indeed, for several days now, the head of the Producers' Association had been wearing his liberal cap—taking out full-page ads in the New York *Times*[38] and the Washington *Post* which reprinted letters he had written criticizing HUAC to the leaders of Congress; and meeting privately with the Nineteen and their attorneys to say that "we share your feelings, gentlemen, and we support your position,"[39] and to spike all rumors of a blacklist.

Although HUAC never made public the process by which it scheduled the appearances of the "unfriendly" witnesses, it appears that the order was determined by the weight of the "evidence" the Committee's investigators had amassed on each: John Howard Lawson, Dalton Trumbo, Albert Maltz, Alvah Bessie, Samuel Ornitz, Herbert Biberman, Edward Dmytryk, Adrian Scott, Ring Lardner, Jr., Lester Cole, and Bertolt Brecht. Had the hearings continued, Waldo Salt would have been the next witness.

From the start, the whole of the raucous fourth act seemed to be taken from another play altogether, from guerrilla theater rather than classical tragedy. No sooner was John Howard Lawson sworn in than he asked permission to read a statement—a privilege which the Committee had granted to many "friendly" witnesses. Thomas insisted on reading the statement before granting permission. Outraged by the force of Lawson's written critique of HUAC, Thomas denied the screenwriter's request, and ordered Stripling to begin the interrogation. HUAC's strategy thus immediately pre-empted the Nineteen's. The Committee had no intention of providing a soapbox for the radicals' attempt to discredit it. They took the battle directly into the court of the "unfriendly" witnesses. Every time Lawson started to say something beyond a direct response to Stripling's very narrow questions, he was gaveled into silence. For half an hour Lawson fenced with the Committee, growing angrier and angrier as Thomas' gavel cut him off. The few protests he registered had to be shouted over the din: "This Committee is on trial here before the American public. . . . The question of Communism is in no way related to this inquiry, which is an attempt to get control of the screen and to invade the basic rights of American citizens in all fields."[40] At length, as Lawson steadfastly continued to refuse to give a straight reply to Stripling's oft-repeated "Are you now or have you ever been?", Thomas terminated the testimony altogether, cited Lawson for contempt of Congress, and ordered him off the witness stand. A sergeant at arms forcibly, and indecorously, "escorted" the screenwriter from the committee room.

Lawson's shouting disturbed a lot of observers who might otherwise have sympathized with one whose treatment at the hands of HUAC differed so radically from that accorded all previous witnesses. Sympathy for Lawson's act of lèse-majesté before a duly constituted congressional committee quickly dimmed, however, in the wake of the testimony of the next witness, HUAC investigator Louis J. Russell. Waiting in the wings to play his role in the set piece, Russell stepped forward as Lawson was led away and calmly read from a prepared document detailing thirty-five instances of "Communist affiliation" on Lawson's part. The memorandum cited dates of articles written for the Daily Worker and New Masses and listed nearly two dozen "Communist front organizations" in which Lawson held membership. (Russell even introduced into evidence what he claimed to be a "Communist Party membership card" made out in the screenwriter's name.*) The evidence appeared conclusive.

The mood in the liberal camp during the lunch recess was glum. The CFA had flown to Washington to stand behind the firm, dignified testimony of Eric Johnston. Instead, as a result of Thomas' sly scheduling, the stars were now inextricably linked in the eyes of the public with an offensive flouter of congressional decorum and a Red. Also, the tenor and force of Lawson's written and spoken arguments carried him, and the Nineteen, farther into the war than most liberals wished to go. In his statement Lawson termed the hearings "illegal and indecent"; and Thomas "a petty politician, serving more powerful

---

* There is reason to believe that this card and the nine which were introduced later were fabrications. The Communists with whom we talked claimed they were not issued cards, precisely to avoid this sort of exposé.

forces" which "are trying to introduce fascism in this country." The
Committee itself, wrote Lawson, was trying "to subvert orderly government and establish an autocratic dictatorship." Lawson reserved his
choicest epithets for the "friendly" witnesses and their "evidence,"
calling them "a parade of stool-pigeons, neurotics, publicity-seeking
clowns, Gestapo agents, paid informers, and a few ignorant and frightened Hollywood artists." The peroration of the statement irretrievably
shifted the confrontation from legal, procedural, and even constitutional grounds to the realm of politics and ideology:

> I am plastered with mud because I happen to be an American who
> expresses opinions that the House Un-American Activities Com-
> mittee does not like. . . . The Committee's logic is obviously:
> Lawson's opinions are properly subject to censorship; he writes
> for the motion picture industry, so the industry makes pictures
> for the American people, so the minds of the people must be cen-
> sored and controlled.
> Why? [Because] J. Parnell Thomas and the Un-American in-
> terests he serves . . . [are] conspiring against the American way
> of life. They want to cut living standards, introduce an economy
> of poverty, wipe out labor's rights, attack Negroes, Jews, and
> other minorities, drive us into a disastrous and unnecessary war.
> The struggle between thought-control and freedom of expres-
> sion is the struggle between the people and a greedy unpatriotic
> minority which hates and fears the people.†

Although Lawson was not permitted to read any of this statement,
the force with which he opposed HUAC had an invigorating effect on
at least one of the Nineteen. That night Ornitz wrote to his wife,
Sadie, "I thought Jack was splendid on the stand. He took the first
blow for all of us. We have the benefit now of knowing how to ride
this low punch."[41] Lardner believed that "Jack finally brought the real
political conflict out into the open," even though "his words and delivery probably were not very good public relations." Thirty years
later one of the "unfriendly" witnesses, Edward Dmytryk, claimed he
was not "delighted" with Lawson's testimony. In the film *Hollywood
on Trial*, he told an interviewer: "my disillusionment began with Lawson's testimony."
    Nor was the Committee for the First Amendment pleased with Law-

---

† All the statements of the Ten are reprinted in Robert Vaughn, *Only
Victims: A Study of Show Business Blacklisting*, New York: G. P. Putnam's Sons, 1972, pp. 316–34.

son's performance. It spent the lunch-recess ruing the consequences of what Dunne saw as "Jack's major tactical blunder." Eric Johnston, for his part, was now confirmed in his suspicions that Lawson was a Red, and, as such, the screenwriter, and the other "unfriendly" witnesses who stood with him, constituted a clear and present danger to the studios; the producers could in no wise appear to support Communists. Johnston went before HUAC that afternoon and delivered a carefully worded testimony wherein he chastised the Committee for its unproven attacks on the film industry and cautioned the congressmen about some of their methods. The motion picture producers, he warned, intended to use every means within their power to keep the screen "free," both from subversion and from governmental coercion. Communists in Hollywood, however, were a different matter. They should be exposed, because "an exposed Communist is an unarmed Communist. Expose them," he invited the Committee, "but expose them in the traditional American manner." Lest there be any doubt about the cordiality of Johnston's invitation, he repeated it in his closing words: "I have never objected to your investigating Hollywood. I told you we welcomed it, and we sincerely do."[42]

Johnston's words delivered much the same blow of shock and chagrin to the Nineteen as to the liberals. Both camps realized, for the first time, that the studios might "chicken out." Johnston's testimony distinctly blunted the edge of the Nineteen's delight with Lawson. The Producers' Association president's warm invitation to HUAC to pillory the Communists in the movie industry fell as an entirely unexpected blow. Trailing back to the Shoreham Hotel late in the afternoon to try to evaluate the implication of Johnston's reversal, the "unfriendly" witnesses drew small solace from Bertolt Brecht's sympathetic hypothesis that if there had been people like Lawson in Germany in the early thirties, Hitler would never have come to power.

Ornitz, the oldest and most experienced radical among the Nineteen, scolded himself and his comrades for their error in trusting the other camp. As Ornitz wrote Sadie, describing Johnston's "[turning] tail under fire": "The mistake we made was to expect anything else. First he made all the beautiful liberal speeches and then delivered the good old coup de grace." Ornitz now saw how cleverly HUAC had manipulated both its stature as a governmental body and American patriotic sentiment. "We underestimated the strength of the enemy, his advantageous strategic position, namely, the last refuge of scoundrels. It was this that sucked Eric Johnston into their polecat refuge." The Committee's outrageous but effective treatment of Lawson clearly demonstrated there would be little pretense of fairness or equity in the Thomas Committee's dealings with the rest of the "unfriendly" witnesses. For the most part, they would be denied the rights accorded to every other testifier. What Ornitz described as the "glamour tactics" and "glory tactics" of the Popular Front-style alliance of liberals, producers, and radicals—"this great box office production"—proved entirely useless in light of HUAC's ruthlessness and determination.

Thus, unexpectedly, it was HUAC, not the Nineteen, which precipitated the confrontation. In view of the Committee's *modus operandi* with the "unfriendly" witnesses, as well as the evidence it unquestionably had and intended to present about each of them, the Nineteen had no means left to them of preserving their "dignity," their alliances, and their skins while still fulfilling what they believed to be their primary responsibility to inform the American people of what really was taking place in Washington. Lawson's gut response to his treatment by Thomas and Stripling and the words he had chosen to hurl at them reflected the traditions of radical dissent for which he and his colleagues had been subpoenaed in the first place. On the morning of the twenty-seventh Lawson unknowingly performed a prophetic function by reminding the Nineteen of who they were and what their real mission was after a weekend during which many of them had perhaps permitted themselves the illusion of thinking that victory would come easily and quickly to yet another Popular Front *redivivus*. On Monday morning and Monday afternoon the "unfriendly" witnesses encountered the real issue: a malevolent superior force which obliged them to stand alone and defiant.

The rest of Act Four played itself out, both sides remorselessly determined. Gone was the anticipated bearding of HUAC, its place taken by the censorial raps of the pounding gavel, the hectoring drawls of Thomas and Stripling, the sarcasm and unrestrained fury of the "unfriendly" witnesses, the constant hovering of the sergeants at arms, and the drone of Louis J. Russell and his revelations. The nine American citizens who followed Lawson to the witness chair tried, each in his own fashion, to express their view of what was actually occurring. Most of them, however, had little chance to register any form of a protest before being geveled (and hauled) off the stand. Only Maltz was allowed to read his full statement, while Bessie was permitted to read four paragraphs (or about half) of his. Maltz believes that he and Bessie (the third and fourth of the "unfriendly" witnesses to be called) were allowed to read their statements so as to mute the criticism which had begun to flow over the stark difference in treatment accorded the first two "unfriendly" witnesses—Lawson and Trumbo, and the last group of "friendly" witnesses—including Lela Rogers and Walt Disney.

In general, the testimony alternated between statements of constitutional principle and the rights of American citizens on the one hand, and criticism of HUAC's "fascistic" intentions on the other. Ornitz stated in measured tones: "I say you do raise a serious question for me when you ask me to act in concert with you to override the Constitution."[43] Speaking from the deepest roots of his consciousness, Maltz told his inquisitors, "Whatever I am, America has made me. And I, in turn, possess no loyalty as great as the one I have to this land."[44] Lardner and Trumbo decried HUAC's attack on labor unions and its efforts to link the witnesses to communism and communism to the Screen Writers Guild, while Bessie stressed what he saw as the true political nature and historical purpose of HUAC:

> The understanding that led me to fight in Spain for that Republic, and my experience in that war, teach me that this Committee is engaged in precisely the identical activities engaged in by un-Spanish committees, un-German committees, and un-Italian committees which preceded it in every country which eventually succumbed to fascism.[45]

The demeanor of the other "unfriendly" witnesses who appeared on the stand ranged from the relative civility and self-possession of Scott and Ornitz to the anger and evident frustration of Biberman, Bessie, and Cole. Whatever his attitude, delivery, or substance, however, each witness was cited for contempt of Congress and in each instance his testimony was followed by Russell's bill of particulars. (Although these memoranda were entirely confected of hearsay, fabricated, and circumstantial evidence, it was a fact that only one of the eleven "unfriendly" witnesses who testified—Bertolt Brecht—had not, at one time or another, been a Communist.) In 1947 the protestations of loyalty and constitutional principle rang hollow in the face of those ten lists of alleged "subversive" behavior and Communist affiliation.

The Aftermath, November 1947

On the train ride back to Hollywood, Lester Cole and Louis B. Mayer discussed the hearings. The mogul brooded mournfully over the "bad press" and the notoriety which the whole incident had given to Hollywood. "Mayer," Cole later testified, "was obviously wrought up, and I

would say, anything but calm during the entire conversation." Nevertheless, the MGM boss remained personally friendly and sympathetic
to Cole. Mayer expressed his doubt that the matter would soon "blow
over" and his fears that his plans for making Cole a producer would
now "be much more difficult." No mention was made of termination
or of a blacklist.[46]

"Bad press" would also describe the problems besetting the Thomas
Committee. HUAC's harsh treatment at the hands of the New York
Times, the New York *Herald Tribune*, the Washington *Post*, and
other major publications had led to a temporary suspension of the motion picture hearings (which was to last almost four years). Hailing
this decision as one to be greeted with "a sense of relief," the *Times*
also printed a "Report from the Nation," a survey by its corre-
spondents of the public response to the hearings. Dallas, Chicago,
Omaha, Denver, Los Angeles, and San Francisco reported outright disapproval of HUAC's methods, while Boston and New Orleans were
unfazed by the Committee's revelations. On the front page of that
same edition, however, a different response to the Ten's behavior captured the headline: STENCH BOMBS, FIST FIGHTS DISRUPT PCA FILM PRO-
TEST. Twelve "unfriendly" witnesses and Margolis had journeyed to
Philadelphia to speak before a PCA-sponsored rally on behalf of the
Nineteen. The *Times'* reporter called it "one of the most tumultuous
meetings ever witnessed at historic Independence Hall Square."
Members of the audience of twelve hundred shouted out: "Shut up,
you Communists" and "Go back to Russia, you bums."[47]

The curtailment of the hearings gave the Nineteen, eight of whom
were now spared the ordeal of testimony, an illusory sense of victory.
Weekly Variety came to the asinine conclusion that HUAC's "feelings were hurt" and it was taking "very hard" the opposition of the
Producers' Association and the picture company presidents.[48] Far more
encouraging was the large reception hosted in New York by the Civil
Rights Congress, at which over four hundred people cheered the announcement that the Nineteen would fight the contempt citations and
continue to work for the abolition of HUAC.[49] Two days later some
of the returning "unfriendly" witnesses were given a noisy reception
by five hundred cheering partisans at the Los Angeles airport. Lardner
addressed the faithful, telling them that even though HUAC had
suffered a setback, the fight was far from over.[50] The Progressive Citizens of America planned a large rally for Gilmore Stadium on November 16, and the Committee for the First Amendment promised it
would organize ten more radio broadcasts and set up a permanent

speakers' bureau. Behind the scenes Dunne, Wyler, and Huston conferred with studio bosses in what Dunne termed "a desperate effort to head off a blacklist."

The air of victory and the feeling of optimism were illusions, and evaporated like dew. The radio broadcasts never happened; the speakers' bureau never formed. Within a fortnight the Hollywood Ten, as they were now called, would be fighting for their professional existence as, one by one, their pillars of support crumbled under overwhelming, unexpected internal and external stresses.

Once the producers decided to blacklist the "unfriendly" witnesses, the CFA lost its rallying cry and the vast majority of its troops. An anti-blacklist organization proved impossible to form in an industry town where the bosses were doing the blacklisting and the unions and guilds were ducking for political and economic cover. Two sources of external pressure combined to render the CFA an empty shell. The stars began to hear that prominent individuals were using Red-baiting and nativist slurs against them. Ed Sullivan confided to Humphrey Bogart, "the public is beginning to think you're a Red!"[51] and John Rankin told the House of Representatives, while commenting on a petition from the CFA:

> I want to read you some of these names. One of the names is June Havoc. We found . . . that her real name is June Hovick. Another one was Danny Kaye, and we found out his real name David Daniel Kamirsky. . . . Another one is Eddie Cantor, whose real name is Edward Iskowitz. There is one who calls himself Edward Robinson. His real name is Emmanuel Goldenberg. There is another here who calls himself Melvyn Douglas, whose real name is Melvyn Hesselberg.[52]

In connection with the dissolution of the CFA, it should be noted that the Committee's founding triumvirate of Dunne, Huston, and Wyler by no means collapsed under pressure, but continued the struggle "in the only ways now available to us. We lobbied, pressured, pleaded, argued, fought within our guilds and signed the *amicus curiae* brief." Dunne even acted as a character witness for Trumbo. But these were the ineffectual, if valiant, actions of a few generals without troops. In any organized, collective sense, the liberals disappeared from the fray within two weeks of the end of the hearings. Perhaps in different circumstances the CFA adherents could have laughed off, or violently protested, Rankin's blatant anti-Semitism and xenophobia, but in late 1947 insecurity and nativist anxiety flourished, and liberals felt less and less inclined to offer their names and reputations on behalf of Communists. Their hesitancy was reinforced, soon after the CFA delegation returned to Hollywood, by direct warning from the studio executives. Some, like Gene Kelly, had been approached even before the trip to Washington. L. K. Sidney, Mayer's assistant, came to Kelly's home and "begged him not to go."[53] Even before the chartered airplane took off, rumors were afloat that agents were being summoned to the offices of high-level executives and told to control their clients. The pressure mounted when the hearings were over. Throughout Hollywood the word went out that the era of political demonstrations was over. The studios could no longer afford, and would no longer tolerate, activism.

Dunne and Wyler, for their part, vowed to continue the liberal fight without the stars. The Committee of One Thousand,‡ which tried to rise from the ashes of the CFA, turned out to be more sparrow- than phoenix-like. It proved to be merely a letterhead organization of national liberals whose chirp was drowned in the raucous din of the next several years. By 1948 it, too, was moribund. All that remained in Hollywood to fight political reaction and the blacklist were the organizations—the very small organizations—formed by the far Left and the blacklistees themselves. The era of alliances had ended. As liberals and Communists reflect on that era, they reach varying conclusions about the quality of resistance offered by the CFA. Karen Morley, speaking at a blacklist retrospective, concluded: "The liberals were not cowards; they simply did not know what to do when their prestige had no ostensible effect on events. They were very naive." Wrote Dalton Trumbo of their vulnerability before events: "Whatever position each of them held in the world had been achieved lonesomely, without institutional support or grants-in-aid, and their futures held no hopes of tenure."[54] And Abraham Polonsky commented:

There was nothing in their character or background to give them the fibre to stick with it when it got tough. I am glad they did what they did. They were sympathetic to us then, and they welcomed us back to Hollywood [when the blacklist began to

‡ Among its initiating sponsors were: Van Wyck Brooks, Albert Einstein, John Fairbank, Dorothy Canfield Fisher, Christian Gauss, Melville Herskovits, Helen Keller, Archibald MacLeish, Rexford Tugwell, Rabbi Stephen S. Wise, and Lillian Hellman. The Hollywood contingent included Deanna Durbin, Florence Eldredge, and Fredric March.

weaken]. They were, you must remember, part of the industry, not members of the Communist Party; the industry was abandoning Communists and liberals had to protect their jobs.

Philip Dunne's perspective, not surprisingly, differs strongly from those of Morley and Polonsky:

As for "lack of fibre," I might point out that the Communists were drafted by subpoena into the war against HUAC. The liberals volunteered. We couldn't defend their peculiar politics, we could and did defend their rights—at considerable risk to our own reputations and careers. We failed not because we "lacked fibre" but because the motion picture producers did.

Leaving the question of internal fortitude aside, the historical evidence is clear on one point: with very few exceptions, Hollywood liberals retired from the political arena. The famous article ("I'm No Communist") which Humphrey Bogart wrote for *Photoplay* magazine in March 1948—wherein the actor admitted he was a "dope" (albeit an "American dope")—demonstrated both the inordinate pressure brought to bear on the stars who went to Washington and the degree to which many of them capitulated to this pressure. The article was a palpable attempt to separate Bogart from the Ten and save his career. Most of the other troopers of the CFA recanted in the privacy of their souls or studio executive offices. Their contrition was contagious and enduring. No *ad hoc* committees arose to fight the blacklist, ban the bomb, fight for civil rights, publicize abuses of minorities, oppose McCarthy, or carry on *any* of the traditional struggles for which the Hollywood liberal community had been world-famous in the preceding era. The Hollywood Communist Party, the Progressive Citizens of America and its successor, the Southern California Chapter of the Arts, Sciences, and Professions, carried on these multifarious fights as best they could under the threat of professional ruin and almost total social quarantine.

In the great fear that led the mass of liberals to abandon the anti-HUAC fight, the rationale for their retreat was a specious distinction between victim and principle. "I still defend free speech," says the frightened moderate, "but I detest Communists and won't support the Nineteen." Though it is theoretically possible to be committed more to a principle than to the cause or individual which stands behind it, defense of the principle from an attack has little meaning outside of individual cases. Victims of the breach of a principle, no matter what one may think of their politics, incarnate that principle. The liberals of the late forties and early fifties who opposed the blacklist and supported the First Amendment yet ignored the Ten, and then the dozens, and finally the thousands of blacklistees because they disapproved of communism simply provided themselves with a ready excuse for their fear before HUAC. The liberals ended up halting far short of the actions which a real commitment to liberalism would have entailed: unflinching defense of the constitutional rights of flesh-and-blood Communists. Closer to home, liberal aloofness made their own persecution easier for HUAC, McCarthy, the movie studios, and the Motion Picture Alliance for the Preservation of American Ideals. For once these "crusaders" had hunted down the Communists and fellow travelers, they turned on the liberals. The Americans for Democratic Action, the liberal flagship, which counted Dunne and Douglas among its officers, nearly disappeared in the ferocity of the Red-baiting of the early fifties. Many individual liberal screen artists eventually took a turn on the black- and graylists. Those who remained active in the movie business did not escape the backlash. The liberals should have listened more closely to the warning issued by the lawyers' forum at the July 1947 Conference on Thought Control:

> If the prosecutions of any of those who have taken the lead in challenging the authority of [HUAC] succeed—and it is immaterial whether we agree with the views or politics of those being prosecuted—no progressive citizen is safe. Their defense is our own first line of defense.[55]

The Collapse of the SWG

No sooner had the Committee for the First Amendment faded into the wings than the Screen Writers Guild marched center stage and purged radicals from positions of leadership, cut the blacklisted screenwriters adrift, and publicly washed its hands of its left-wing political tradition. Throughout the summer of 1947 the Executive Board of the SWG had been the scene of divisive debate over the whole question of the Guild's future existence and identity. This preoccupation with its own internal politics stemmed from the Board elections of winter 1946, when a slate of candidates which included several leading left-wingers (Cole, Lardner, Harold Buchman, Hugo Butler, Leo Townsend) had squeaked into office. Within nine months the very presence on the Board of such men as these became intolerable to a group of moderates

led by Allen Rivkin and Emmet Lavery. The combination of the subpoenas and section 9H of the new Taft-Hartley Act* precipitated the
final clash between left and center in the SWG. The moderates were
convinced that anything short of a purge of the leftists would destroy
not only Guild unity but also the vestige of political nonpartisanship
which the union still retained in the eyes of the industry. As the national political climate worsened, liberal Guild leaders became almost
frantic in their desire to cleanse their union of the strong taint of communism. The moderate forces moved immediately to prepare for the
crucial election of late November. Acting as liberal whip and campaign manager, Rivkin organized an "All Guild Slate" (i.e., one devoid
of left-wingers) to unite the "entire union" and "keep the Guild out
of politics." Behind this facade of "Guild interest," of course, lurked
the politics of a Right-leaning liberal faction.

In the midst of this anti-Left politicking, SWG president Emmet
Lavery traveled to Washington to testify before HUAC and continue
his electioneering. Following six "unfriendly" witnesses, Lavery perfunctorily contested the Committee's right to question people about
their political beliefs, and then proceeded to rehearse at length his own
brand of liberalism and vehement anti-communism. The only reference Lavery made to the five screenwriter members of his guild who
had just been cited for contempt was to advise HUAC not to turn
them into "political martyrs":

> My only concern with respect to this whole proceeding, Mr.
> Chairman, is merely that people might go back home and think
> that they have been political martyrs. An election in November
> which is coming up in our Screen Writers' Guild might be
> seriously affected, and not for the better, if people thought the
> Government had interfered more than was necessary in the nor-
> mal operations of the Guild.[56]

---

* It required every officer of every American labor union to file an
affidavit attesting to his or her lack of Communist affiliation. No union
whose entire staff of executives did not sign could petition the National
Labor Relations Board for certification elections or rulings on unfair labor
practices. The unions, fearing a wave of company-formed rival unions and
management intimidation of labor organizers, could not, they believed,
afford to lose the services of the NLRB. Within one year of the law's appearance, over 81,000 union officers had filed the required 9H affidavits
with the NLRB.

The hearings concluded, Lavery pursued his attack on the radicals, particularly the eight screenwriters among the Hollywood Ten. Though his second term as Guild president was ending and he would not be returning directly to California (his play *The Gentlemen from Athens*—"a tribute to the democratic process"—was soon to open in New York), Lavery sought to influence the coming SWG election as best he could. He wrote a full report on the hearings and prepared a series of recommendations, both of which were read by Mary McCall at a membership meeting on November 6. Lavery's implicit message was that the Ten had knowingly harmed Guild interests by linking the writers' union with communism in the public mind; that is, they had deliberately associated their refusal to answer the question about Guild membership with their refusal to answer the question about Communist Party membership. Therefore, Lavery insisted, the Guild must dissociate itself from the Ten, yet take "militant decisive action" to express its disapproval of HUAC by standing "squarely behind" studio management in the latter's request for "sweeping reform" of congressional investigating procedures. In short, the "defense of the good name of the industry" mattered; defense of the Ten could only detract from that cause.[57]

Lavery's comments were printed and distributed to SWG members. Along with them went a critical commentary or rejoinder written by four of the Nineteen (Cole, Collins, Kahn, Lardner) which sharply disagreed with the recommendations of the outgoing president and criticized his testimony before HUAC. Lavery had, they felt, cooperated with HUAC by fully answering Stripling's questions; he had failed to present clearly to the congressional Committee the midsummer Guild resolution condemning HUAC's methods and purpose; and he had championed a faction while pretending to be concerned with "the defense of the Guild" as a whole. They also countered Lavery's claim that the Guild was "bigger than any of the individuals involved in it" and his contention that "the Guild does not have to choose sides between Parnell Thomas and individual screen writers in an issue not of the Guild's choosing" with an explanation of their own "logic" before HUAC:

> We figured out that as long as the Thomas-Rankin Committee existed, there was a clear and present danger to ourselves personally, to this Guild and to what freedom there is in picture-making. We reasoned that the only way to lick this danger was not to toss pellets of mixed cooperation and chastisement at the Committee,

but to challenge it at the very foundation of its existence: its right
to enforce answers in violation of the First Amendment.[58]

Lavery's "farewell address," though condemnatory of the Ten, was
a reasonably impersonal and dispassionate statement. The All Guild
Committee functioned, however, as a fiercely partisan and censorious
electoral machine. One of its supporters, James Cain, wrote a leaflet in
which he noted that although Jack Tenney, Parnell Thomas, and Rupert Hughes were reprehensible men,

> these gentlemen say we are loaded with Communists, and whether
> we like it or not, this charge is true. As we are now constituted,
> the party line is more important to certain members commanding
> a majority of the Executive Board than the interests of the mem-
> bership and leftist propaganda more important to the *Screen
> Writer* than material of interest to writers.

This "Pravdushka"—these travelers of the "Moscow road," as Cain
termed the leftist nucleus within the Guild—abused their positions and
cost the Guild money, prestige, and the confidence of the membership.
Vote the All Guild Slate, Cain promised, and you will thereby banish
"all politics" from Guild activity."[59]

Cain's leaflet summarized well the feelings of the All Guild partisans.
Its style may have occasionally descended into Red-baiting reminiscent
of the Right, and its assertions were sometimes overstated or false
(e.g., the Left by no means commanded a majority of the Board, nor
did *The Screen Writer* focus only on political issues; in fact, an entire
issue of *The Screen Writer*, and large parts of many others, were
devoted to Cain's pet project, the American Authors Authority—a
purely union issue). Yet, on the whole, the mimeographed circular was
not simply a travesty of truth in the style of Motion Picture Alliance
propaganda. The leaflet reflected accurately the briar patch into which
the times had flung both political and union issues. Traditionally it had
been possible, if difficult, to distinguish issues and domains; the mid-
thirties struggle between the Guild and the Screen Playwrights raged
largely over union matters, though political divergences characterized
(and perhaps motivated) the contending sides. By 1947, however, the
major issues which divided movie writers—section 9H of Taft-
Hartley, support of the Ten, the Guild's image and reputation—were
irreducible alloys of professional *and* political elements. The All Guild
view of the Ten, for example, was that the "unfriendly" witnesses'

problems with HUAC were their own personal political affair. The Ten replied that it affected screenwriters professionally when a breach was opened in the First Amendment by a duly constituted body of Congress investigating the relationship between an artist's political views and his professional work. The eight screenwriters among the Ten believed that whatever their political views or whatever anyone felt about how they had conducted themselves before the Committee, they were entitled to the support of their union because HUAC threatened not merely Communists but screenwriters as screenwriters.

The All Guild Slate easily triumphed in the election of November 20. The new Board immediately adopted a resolution supporting Lavery's views, applauding his conduct before HUAC,[60] and effectively abandoning the Ten (though they disguised the actions in ringing statements of anti-HUAC and anti-blacklist rhetoric). The Board then commenced to purge almost all left-wingers and suspected left-wingers from the SWG executive and administrative structure. The sweep of the moderates' broom was reflected in the composition of the Guild committees for 1948. Prior to November 1947, leftist liberals, radicals, and Communists constituted fully a third of the membership of every committee; afterward, it was a rare committee which included even two left-wingers out of twelve or more members, and most committees had none at all. Many of the most distinguished screenwriters and loyal SWG activists—Lawson, Cole, Bright, Lardner, Kahn, Stewart, Ornitz—disappeared from prominence, influence, or power within the organization they had helped to found and build. Indeed, it is fair to say that the Left ceased to exist in any organized, meaningful sense in the Screen Writers Guild.

Their absence was unmistakably apparent not only in political matters pertaining to HUAC and the blacklist, but in purely professional conflicts with studio management (e.g., allocation of screen credits, eligibility for Academy Awards). Throughout the late forties and early fifties the SWG's strong statements of defiance to government and management were inevitably followed by retreats when either foe stood firm. The Guild instituted, then dropped, an anti-blacklist suit; refused to press for the reinstatement of Cole, Lardner, and Trumbo; and waged, then retreated from, later battles to preserve the screen credits of all blacklisted writers.

The sweep of a "historical force" is strongest in retrospect. The autumn of 1947 was unquestionably a critical watershed in the history of progress and reaction in Hollywood. It is easy to note how, after 1948, the national conservative tide, augmented by right-wing film industry undercurrents, swept across the movie industry, encountering no significant opposition. It might have been different. The progress of reaction might have been arrested (as it was enhanced) by the actions of a few. The decisive collapse was the producers' unexpected recourse to the blacklist. Until then, the history of HUAC in Hollywood was not essentially different from the history of the Dies and Tenney committees. The film business was, of course, considerably more shaken and mobilized by Parnell Thomas than it had ever been before; but ostensibly the studio line held. Lardner, Scott, Trumbo, Cole, and Dmytryk returned to their jobs; the rest of the Ten returned to the familiar task of finding jobs. On the surface HUAC had appeared to suffer a defeat. The hearings had been unexpectedly canceled; no new ones were scheduled. Yet within a month the producers handed HUAC the victory which it might not have been able to win for itself.

Studio executives and movie financiers gave in to what they saw as the vastly superior force of hostile public opinion. The times, if not exactly HUAC, managed to do what Tenney, Dies, or previous times had never accomplished: convince management that its material interest would be more damaged in ignoring HUAC and the hearings than in surrendering their much-vaunted images as unchallenged rulers of their industrial domain. This negative logic of the producers appeared to be more unanimous than it actually was at the time; evidence exists to indicate that an important minority of powerful studio bosses—Mayer, Goldwyn, Schary, Cohn—were looking for a way to arrive at a different conclusion. If strong intra-industry support for the Ten had been forthcoming from some of the highly influential moderate and liberal screen artists who enjoyed social and professional access to high-level studio management, a number of key moguls might have hesitated. If, in addition, the blacklisting of the Ten had been greeted by united Guild outcries and action, even strikes, these same chief executives might have refused Eric Johnston's second plea for blacklisting as they had refused (in June) his first.

Instead of stiffening the producers' spines, however, most Hollywood liberals, both in the guilds and the CFA, provided everyone with what appeared to be the best face-saving device: the separation of people and principle. In effect, the liberal formula ran along this line: "we support the right of people to freedom of expression, but we do not stand behind the Ten who are denied that right." As transposed into the managerial key, the tune ran: "we are opposed to a blacklist, but we are not going to hire Communists."

This logic-chopping destroyed the functional solidarity that might have arisen out of Hollywood's well-publicized loathing of HUAC—a loathing which Eric Johnston and John Howard Lawson held in common. The atmosphere of the times might have been overcome if a few prominent, powerful individuals in Hollywood had stopped to reflect on the meaning and strength of their own commitment to liberal values and the identities of the men who were to be persecuted (respected colleagues, fine screen artists, hard-working and self-sacrificing activists in progressive causes). These things might have occurred and might have proven decisive for a turning of the tide. They did not. After the Waldorf conference, the tragedy unfolded in gradually increasing, eventually awesome amplitude. The logic of *de facto* capitulation and *de jure* outcry created its own momentum and cosmos. Events continued to push the liberals and producers backward from this line of retreat, thereby increasing the distance between them and the blacklistees and further decreasing the likelihood of reconsideration.

The Influence of Hollywood Communists on American Films and American Politics, 1930–47

> [T]he humanist writer did not meekly deliver what the philistine ordered, but struggled tenaciously to preserve human values in all his work; . . . Hollywood writers in particular, dealing like all their kind in the radioactive commodity of ideas, were accountable to the peoples of the world for the effects of their ideas.
>
> —*Michael Wilson*[1]

The Debate over "Influencing Content"

Despite the badgering of the members of the House Committee on Un-American Activities, Mayer, Warner, Johnston, and Schary had remained adamant on the question of Communist content of Hollywood motion pictures. Warner, who wriggled and crawled before every other accusation, stood firm on the issue of "subversion":

> With all the vision at my command, I scrutinize the planning and production of our motion pictures. It is my firm belief that there is not a Warner Brothers picture that can fairly be judged to be hostile to our country, or Communistic in tone or purpose.[2]

The protest of hawk-eyed vigilance contained, of course, an implicit truth—the producers had ample reason to police story material for the screen. Not because any screenwriter attempted or intended to "subvert" the minds of the viewing audience, but because every writer, no matter his politics, had a point of view which he tried to transmit in his scripts. The producers' and executives' concern was to see that only their own point of view reached the screen. Occasionally this point of view reflected the political atmosphere and paralleled the concerns of

the radical screenwriters (e.g., during World War II); far more frequently, however, the paths of the writers and the executives diverged
(on labor, minorities, the Spanish Civil War, the Cold War). Whatever the historical era, however, the Hollywood screenwriter *never*
had final say over what appeared on the screen. That was *always* the
province of the front office.

Radical screen artists knew this; nevertheless, they did not renounce
the challenge of writing better scripts. For many this goal involved a
struggle for believable characters, realistic motivation, natural dialogue, and plausible climaxes—that is, better form—as well as political
or social substance. The screenwriters wished to see themselves not
only as prestigious spokespeople in the fight against fascism, but as radical artists striving to improve their craft and their medium, struggling
to express their views, and, through their professional work, helping to
change the way people thought. The debate over film content, therefore, moved from the studio story conferences (where, in any case,
the writer always lost) to the Party meetings, and meetings of the
Hollywood branch of the League of American Writers, where old
guard writers and novices argued strenuously over the possibility of
influencing film content, educating the public, and "using" the film as
a potent weapon in the campaign to reform society.

The issue boiled down to this question: despite all the built-in safe-
guards by which any studio ensured the formulaic and ideological
homogeneity of virtually its entire film output, and despite the orthodox Marxist view which held that any kind of cultural expression, such
as film, was merely the predetermined, inalterable reflection of underlying economic and social realities, was it nonetheless possible for the
individual radical writer, sitting in his office at MGM, to create a
screenplay which would, in some small but important way, change or
enlighten public thinking on some crucial social, political, or economic
issue? In other words, could he or she write movies that would actually
live up to what HUAC would one day be saying about Hollywood
films—i.e., that they were undermining the prevailing social consciousness and cohesion of the United States?

The "younger" Communists in Hollywood (those who joined the
Party in 1939 or after) tended to believe, or hope, that this sort of
radical self-expression was desirable—and possible. Noteworthy among
them was screenwriter Paul Jarrico. The son of a zealous socialist-
Zionist Russian immigrant, Jarrico, along with future screenwriter
Michael Wilson, stood in the forefront of radical student politics at
UCLA and Berkeley in the early thirties. "There were," remembers

Sylvia Jarrico, "many links between the Berkeley students and the International Longshoremen's and Warehousemen's Union. The former felt a strong urge to be part of the working class; we only seemed to be in the know—the workers understood things better. Many students went right from the campus to the docks when the strike broke out." Like many of the younger screenwriters, Jarrico started early in the business—upon graduating from college—but unlike most, including many future "leftists," Jarrico's radical political consciousness (he was a Young Communist in 1934–35) predated, and to some extent determined, his vocation. "I started out as a political person and then became a cultural worker [i.e., writer, then screenwriter], and I would be a political person even if I were not engaged in cultural activities. I simply grew up thinking that fathers go to political meetings every night." By 1937, Jarrico, then under contract to Columbia Studios, and his wife Sylvia, the brilliant daughter of Russian Jewish immigrants and herself a "veteran" left-winger, began to center their political activity around a group of young, left-wing screenwriters—Ring Lardner, Jr., Richard Collins, Budd Schulberg, Arnaud d'Usseau—and, by 1939, they had both formally joined the Hollywood CP.

Jarrico and his group, partly because they were the first generation of screenwriters to "grow up" on movies, partly because of their youth and idealism, firmly believed it was possible to influence, in a politically progressive way, the scripts they turned out. Forty years later Paul recalled the fight he and his circle put up within the Party to convince the comrades of their view:

> I had a lot of illusions at first. At the time I think most of us who worked in the industry had the impression we could influence film content. There were big fights in the Party on this issue between the people [like Lawson] who said, "you guys are kidding yourselves; you can't influence film; film is part of the superstructure; its function is to defend the base; the producers are not going to let you get away with anything that is really radical," and their opponents, like myself, who believed that film was potentially an educational medium which reached millions and millions of people. If you could change their attitude toward women, workers, Blacks, and minorities in general—*and you could*—then that was an important contribution. Sure they wouldn't let us make a really revolutionary picture, but if we were good writers and skillful at our craft we could subtly affect the content [toward progressive ends]. It was a battle we did not resolve at the time. . . . At a certain point [late forties], however, the Cultural Commission [of the CP] came down hard on those of us whom it considered to be

"right-wing opportunists" (because we believed that film content ought to be a major focus of Party work). There were knock-down/drag-out fights on the subject in New York. I would have to say that essentially we lost [and the "left sectarians" won].

Jarrico's own early hope to "influence content" reposed in the screenplay he wrote for the film *Tom, Dick and Harry* (RKO, 1941). From his retrospective summary and judgments about the script, it is possible to see precisely how Jarrico and his group "essentially lost" the battle to make film content the "major focus of Party work" within or without the studios:

> I had a lot of illusions about what *Tom, Dick and Harry* had to say. It is one of those cases where I thought at the time I was making a social and political contribution, but later decided that I had not. When I wrote the script, I believed I was attacking the American success myth and the Cinderella myth in a consciously political way. The screenplay tells the story of a girl who dreams of marrying wealth, but who then proceeds to fall in love with a guy who doesn't believe in success. It was a romantic comedy, even good entertainment, but certainly no manifesto. The girl winds up with the guy she loves because they "ring bells to-gether"—all of which is a fine romantic concept, but it has noth-ing to do with defeating or weakening the success or Cinderella myths. In fact, my story is just another form of it. You don't marry wealth or Prince Charming; you marry the "bell-ringer." It's pure romanticism, but at the time I thought it was politics. I would have to say now that if it had any political importance or relevance, they were very small. Yet I'm not ashamed of the pic-ture, only of thinking that it was more than it was. It would be an illusion to think that there was anything profound in its observa-tion of society or that it transmitted any real social insight into the mass audience which viewed the film and thought it to be a good romantic comedy.

Historically speaking, of course, the question of *Tom, Dick and Harry*'s "radical" content cannot resolve the issue of whether or not left-wing screenwriters could express their political and social view-points in their scripts. As a matter of fact, Jarrico's judgment on his script for this film is well taken. What *Tom, Dick and Harry* proved was only the ludicrousness of trying to interlard radical themes in the standard Hollywood fare assigned, or allowed, to screenwriters. In these instances, the radical actor or writer was reduced either to "Red" inserts (e.g., Lionel Stander whistling "The Internationale" while waiting for an elevator in *No Time to Marry* or Jarrico himself having the family in *Tom, Dick and Harry* listening to a radio news broadcast revealing the merits of anti-trust litigation) or to moralistic banalities ("money isn't everything," "nice guys finish first," "honesty is the best policy"). Certainly as regards such films as *Tom, Dick and Harry* the Lawson faction was correct in its assessment that little could be done to "radicalize" them, and that it was perhaps counterproductive even to try because of the risk of antagonizing the front office (and courting discharge) over the jejune issue of political inserts.

There was, however, another category of films made in Hollywood about which no writer—no matter how pessimistic or "orthodox" his feelings about the larger question of influencing content—ever proved blasé: the so-called "topicals," or movies dealing with current social, economic, political, and cultural issues and subjects. Hardened radicals and screenwriter veterans like Lester Cole and Edward Huebsch can still recall the pain they felt when movies like *Blood on the Sun* (UA, 1945) and assignments like *Viva Zapata* and *Mother Night* were gutted, truncated, or rejected: "It was worse than going to jail; the evisceration of a politically meaningful script cut right into my soul" (Cole); "Both my heart attacks occurred after producers rejected politically oriented scripts I had written" (Huebsch).

Films about current events were nothing new in Hollywood; for many years one of the handiest, least expensive sources of story material to feed the ravenous studios was the daily newspaper, whose headlines, by attracting the public's gaze, seemed to promise pre-sold and profitable film ideas to hungry producers. But if producers were hungry, they were also wary, and current problems and issues often proved highly "charged" items. It went without saying that no studio policy maker ever knowingly countenanced a radical or revolutionary film or even the honest depiction in a film of radical or revolutionary material. On the other hand, events like the Bolshevik Revolution, the Spanish Civil War, anti-Semitism, and the Depression arrived uninvited, but not necessarily unwelcomed, at the front offices' doorsteps. The only standard by which studio executives judged such socio-political foundlings was whether movies about them seemed likely to turn a profit without arousing an excessively negative reaction.

The challenge from the studio's point of view would then be to homogenize the subject in question by shaping it along the lines of a standard Hollywood genre while steering clear of both the Hays and

Breen offices* and the radical writer who may have been assigned to
the project. If Lenin's *What Is to Be Done?* had proven to be an international best seller, Darryl F. Zanuck would undoubtedly have made a
bid to purchase it and, once in hand, might have employed Ring
Lardner, Jr., to turn this classic blueprint of Communist Party organization into a behind-the-scenes story of a struggling small-town newspaper, with Tyrone Power as Lenin, the editor, and Donna Reed as
Krupskaya, his adoring but neglected assistant.

Such worked-over renderings as these proved very dicey, however,
and despite the apparent "ready-made" profitability of "topicals," very
few ever got made because the producers could not figure out ways to
bypass their own hired watchdogs of film "morals." In the economic
balancing act which the producers were obliged to perform, the fear
of mass boycotts mobilized by the guardians of public morality and
patriotism counted for more than the potential profits to be reaped by
exploiting an event's currency and interest. As a result, half a dozen
scripts on the Spanish Civil War were finally shelved, the script of
Black Fury (Warner Brothers, 1936) was gutted to make coal company management seem less rapacious than it actually was, and no films
were made depicting the rise of Hitler and Mussolini for fear of cutting off the Italian and German markets. The sensitivity of MGM executives in this matter extended even to their allowing Hays and Breen
to convince them to scrub Sinclair Lewis' best-selling novel *It Can't
Happen Here*, after a pre-production outlay of $200,000, because it
was "too dangerous." Louis B. Mayer claimed it was canceled "because
it would cost too much." Lewis and Sidney Howard, who adapted the
novel, claimed that pressure from the Hays Office, who feared "mob
uprisings," an offended Republican Party, and an international boycott
caused the film to be shelved. Hays merely noted that it was MGM
which made the decision.[3] MGM did produce, thoroughly sanitized,

---

* Both Will H. Hays and Joseph I. Breen had been appointed, the former
in 1922, the latter in 1934, to head off censorship campaigns directed against
the Hollywood studios. Hays, postmaster general in President Warren
Harding's Cabinet, was appointed president of the Motion Picture Producers and Distributors of America, Inc. and given near-autocratic powers
to aid him in his efforts to preserve the "freedom of the screen" from the
efforts of over thirty state legislatures to enact strict censorship statutes.

Breen, a well-known Catholic intellectual, was appointed to head the
newly created Production Code Administration (PCA) as a means of heading off the boycott campaign against Hollywood films launched by the
Legion of Decency the previous year. The film executives agreed not to
distribute, release, or exhibit a film without the PCA's stamp of approval.

successes from other mediums (*Three Comrades*, from a novel by Erich Maria Remarque, and *Idiot's Delight*, from a play by Robert Sherwood) whose stories were situated in Germany and Italy, respectively. In the first film all party labels were scrupulously removed; in the second, a new country was invented. Even so, the Italian government was furious.

Films about the Depression in America always carried upbeat endings, usually focusing on some Roosevelt-like savior promising to clean the Augean stables of corrupt bankers and industrialists. Current, burning social themes such as anti-Semitism, racism, the plight of minorities in America, poverty, labor conflict, and the role of women were hardly touched at all. When they were, in the late forties, the studios' obvious reserve and desire to placate "all" sides of an issue usually had the effect of denaturing the script, the movie, and the issue. In sum, "topicals"—despite the sensations created by *Scarface, Little Caesar, Public Enemy, The Grapes of Wrath, The Informer,* or *Mr. Deeds Goes to Town*—represented only the tiniest dose of realism in the steady diet of Westerns, musicals, comedies, and melodramas which rolled off the Hollywood assembly line.

A good example of the calibrations of self-interest which went on in the studio front offices as they contemplated topicals was the Spanish Civil War. The dilemma here was how to write entertainingly about the ongoing drama in Iberia without offending a host of vested interests from the Roman Catholic Church to the fascist regimes in Europe to the neutral American, British, and French governments. Nonetheless, Spain was considered such "hot stuff" in the late thirties that a number of studios and independent producers—Universal, MGM, Walter Wanger, etc.—were determined to cash in on the ready-made drama attending events like the bombing of Almería and Guernica, the siege of Toledo, the battle of Jarama, and the retreat across the Ebro River—though they were also "working overtime to see to it that there is no taint of partisanship in the scripts."[4] It amounted to solving the great puzzle of how to keep the action and the drama while dropping the history, to write about the Civil War without mentioning Spain or the contending sides and issues, that is, to tell *a* story without telling *the* story.

Enter the studio specialists in puzzle-solving: the screenwriters. In the Hollywood production process, where screenplay creation was often like sidling among bric-a-brac, or skating smoothly over numerous thin egos, the left-wingers proved as a group to be more consistently deft at crafting "playable" scripts on time than other screenwriters. Nevertheless, left-wing screenwriters were not necessarily or frequently selected to write "topical" scripts in the thirties except the early gangster genre, invented, in part, by Communists Faragoh and Bright. When they were, the selection had nothing whatever to do with permitting the writer his "say," but rather with profiting from the man's superior knowledge of the Spanish Civil War or fascist regimes to create a playable script—in which his "say" was even less likely to get said. Nevertheless, the great hope—or illusion, as Jarrico said later—of any left-wing writer was that he could somehow outsmart the producers and "censors" in subtle ways that would permit an important minimum to "get said."

The moguls and executives, for their part, were never very frightened by the possibility of being "outsmarted" by the Reds. Executives like Eddie Mannix of MGM were, as a matter of policy, totally *au courant* in terms of the Hollywood political scene. The dossiers compiled by the studio security offices, and the rumors collected in the story and writing departments, on the political activities of all employees bulged with data—although until the forties (and HUAC) the question of an individual's specific party affiliation might be unimportant. But in general, except under certain special, highly politicized conditions—e.g., the Guild wars or the EPIC campaign—the front office did not care about an employee's "ideology." Robert Lees, who was to be blacklisted in the fifties for his refusal to cooperate with HUAC, told the Committee:

> there has been no question of political affiliations in terms of my employment that I have discussed or have been asked to discuss by any of the people I have worked for. Even up to the very last time I was hired [by Paramount in 1951], the general concept seemed to be that a man was hired on his ability as a writer and not on any kind of political affiliations he might have. . . .[5]

Of course, Lees was no problem—the Abbott-Costello, Martin-Lewis films which were his specialty did not exactly lend themselves to sophisticated political commentary. Those subjects which did, such as Spain, were not problems either; there was little likelihood of a writer's politics affecting a shooting script. F. Scott Fitzgerald's fictional Pat Hobby was called in to do a rewrite on a film about Spain. The head of production told him: "Clean up the stuff about Spain. . . . The guy who wrote it was a Red and he's got all the Spanish officers with ants in their pants. Fix up that."[6]

Anti-communism and the raising of the red specter were pure public relations, to be indulged in when the front offices felt pressured by national conservative interests into "cleaning house." PIX REDS MUST FLEE H'WOOD, MAYER WARNS screamed a *Variety* headline in 1936;[7] but in fact neither Mayer nor his factotums did any serious political pruning until years later, because they needed good writers, and the left-wingers figured among the best. Indeed, by the late thirties anti-fascists were being assigned to write the increasing number of topicals dealing with fascism.

It was therefore not surprising that the liberal Walter Wanger assigned the radical Clifford Odets to write a script on Spain in 1937—*The River Is Blue*. Odets had been lured away from the Group Theatre by money, and wrote three scripts in the mid-thirties. One was produced (*The General Died at Dawn*, Paramount, 1936), and the two others were shelved. Wanger knew that Odets was a Red, and Odets knew that he knew. Odets' screenplay was deemed unshootable, for technical, not political reasons, and Wanger, in the usual time pinch and desperate for material to fulfill his ambitious production contract with United Artists, offered another Red, John Howard Lawson, the opportunity to rewrite the script. Unlike the young Paul Jarrico, Lawson had few illusions about the propaganda possibilities of any single Hollywood film; he knew too well the economics of film production and distribution to believe that he would be allowed to make a film exalting the Loyalist cause. Lawson undertook the assignment knowing from the outset there would be carefully prescribed limits:

> We could not call the Loyalists by name, we could not use the actual Loyalists' uniform. This I accepted because it was the only way in which the picture could be undertaken. And there was complete understanding between Wanger and myself; there was no attempt on my part to introduce material without discussing it because I would consider that dishonest and would never attempt to do that with a film that I was making.[8]

Lawson also knew that he would have to overlay the historical and current Spanish material with a fictional spy/intrigue caper, thereby further distorting the Loyalist cause by reducing it to a background for another wheezy Hollywood melodrama. (Lawson at this time was devoting virtually all his non-studio time to Popular Front anti-fascist, pro-Loyalist propagandizing.)

With the limitations imposed by "circumstances," it made little difference whether the screenwriter, Lawson, was the head of the Hollywood CP or a deacon in the First Presbyterian Church. In a field so mined with "givens," Lawson could hope at best to offer only "a simple message." Thus, *Blockade* would show the "horror visited on women and children by the bombing of cities and the starvation of civilian populations."[9] He also hoped to warn the American people that Spain was but a dress rehearsal for a second world war. Any decent, sensitive Hollywood screenwriter, even a conservative like Morrie Ryskind or a moderate like Allen Rivkin, could have hoped and attempted as much. Wanger, however, needed Lawson's expertise on Spain—and he got it, virtually shorn of the politics for which John Howard Lawson lived.

The film itself was not well received—by the Left, the Right, or posterity. It was too obviously undertaken with one eye on the Hays Office and the other on the Roosevelt administration. The events in the film clearly take place in Spain, the site of some ongoing political struggle; but the two warring sides are not identified and, according to a review in the progressive journal *Coast*, the film skirted "everything that might be called a moral or ethical issue."[10] Looking back on the thirties, a former Communist, Granville Hicks, recalled how excited he and other comrades were about the reports that Lawson was going to script a film about the Spanish Civil War, "which, we were told, was going to strike a great blow for the Loyalist cause in Spain. But when the picture appeared, it did not even indicate on which side the hero was fighting."[11]

Like many ex-Communists, especially those confessing in the early fifties, Hicks was being somewhat coy about his "premature consciousness." No politically active person—nor any regular reader of newspapers—could mistake the side on which Marco (Henry Fonda) fought. On the other hand, unless the viewer was already in the Loyalist camp, the film's dramatic ending probably provoked little more than a reinforcement of any anti-war feelings which already existed:

> (Close-up on Marco, who has just been told he can go on leave)
> "Leave? (He shakes his head bitterly)
> "You go on leave to find peace—away from the front—but where would you find it? The front is everywhere— They've turned our country into a battlefield—there's no safety for old people and children—women can't keep their families safe in

their houses—they can't be safe in their own fields—the churches
and schools and hospitals are targets!
(His voice almost breaking—torn by his own emotion)
"It's not war—war is between soldiers—this is murder. . . .
We've got to stop it! Stop the murder of innocent people! The
world can stop it! Where's the conscience of the world?"
(Fade-out)

If Granville Hicks didn't recognize the side on which *Blockade* was
fighting, the American Catholic Right did. Diluted as the issue of fascism vs. democracy was in the film's spy story and romance, *Blockade*
nevertheless set off a minor political bombshell when it opened at the
Radio City Music Hall. Commotion in the Church hierarchy was so
great that Wanger was forced, by pressure from the banks, to halt
production on his newest film-in-progress, based on Vincent Sheean's
memoirs as adapted for the screen by John Howard Lawson, about the
underground resistance to the Nazis. Meanwhile, Catholics trained
their guns on *Blockade*. Pickets were thrown up around Radio City,
displaying what *The Nation* termed "fantastic accusations of [the
film's] 'war propaganda' ";[12] the Knights of Columbus and similar
groups noisily protested to the Hays Office; and many parish priests
ordered their congregations to stay away from the film. The Boston
city council attempted to ban the film; Fox West Coast Theatres refused to show it as a regular first-run feature; and, at its national convention, the largest Hollywood trade union, IATSE, declared it propaganda and passed a resolution informing the producers that union
projectionists "will not be responsible for the handling of propaganda
films by its members."[13]

Lawson went to his grave in 1977 proud of the fact that he had
scripted the only commercial film of the thirties which attempted in
some way to explain the Loyalist cause.† He did not think *Blockade*
was aesthetically a fine film, however.

I wouldn't say it was a bad picture because it's touched by the
greatness of the subject, but there are moments in "Blockade"
when you can see a definite conflict going on right before your
eyes on the flickering screen between the documentary aspect . . .
and the second-hand spy story which is the central theme and
central story of "Blockade." You just cannot fit them together.

---

† One other commercial film about Spain, Paramount's *Last Train from
Madrid*, was unabashedly apolitical—an Iberianized *Grand Hotel*.

This is my fault; no one else's fault but mine. I just didn't know how to find a key to [their integration]. And the key has not been found yet; . . . perhaps there is no key.[14]

After the release of the film, and the resultant outcry from the conservatives, Lawson wrote that the film had made a point unintended by him or Wanger: "The importance of Blockade [is that it offers] clear evidence that the screen is not at present free, and that even the simplest humanitarian statement is regarded as 'alarming' and 'dangerous' to those who want to keep the motion picture in swaddling clothes."[15] Thus did the older, detached Lawson place his finger squarely on the reason for the near-total absence of serious political-social content in films turned out by the old Hollywood studio system: the implacable, "non-negotiable" demand of producers that all films, "topicals" included, be entertaining before they were truthful or informative, and bland rather than provocative. Nonetheless, in the fervor of the Popular Front, radical screenwriters tenaciously searched for Jack Lawson's elusive "key" which could successfully make the didactic diverting. Finding it, however, was only the first step; the writer had next to open the producers' lock, an unpredictable, perpetually changing mechanism of taste and fear which barred the corridor to the production of most "topical" film scripts.

John Wexley, a radical writer who succeeded, waxed ecstatic over the results. He termed his work on Confessions of a Nazi Spy (Warner Brothers, 1939), "the most exciting and exhilarating work I had ever done in Hollywood" and predicted that it "will prove a turning point in the motion picture industry. . . . Aside from any question of its merit, I believe . . . exhibitors will spring upon the prints of 'Confessions of a Nazi Spy' as manna from heaven because by the very nature of its subject it lends itself to every form of publicity exploitation and sensational advertising."[16]

Wexley's pride and emotions clouded his rational judgment, however. Although Warner Brothers, satisfied with early returns on Confessions, indeed dusted off three properties of a similar, anti-fascist nature (The Bishop Who Walked with God, Underground, and Boycott[17]), within two months all were again shelved. Bending to pressure from the Roosevelt administration, the Hays Office, and a few isolationist congressmen, Jack Warner announced that there would be "no [more] propaganda pictures from Warner Brothers." Instead, Warner said, his studio would increase its production of light comedies to counteract the effects of war.[18]

The impact of the Nazi *Blitzkrieg* across Europe in the spring and summer of 1940 kept the Warner's projects—and dozens like them in other studios—in story department files and off the sound stages. *Variety* reported: "Belief is strong in some [studio] circles that Uncle Sam will crack down on American distribution of any films objectionable to Adolph Hitler should he happen to come out on top in the European conflict."[19] Nor were war movies big box office. The American people were not belligerent in the summer of 1940. They were scared by the prospect of a massive European war and stayed away in droves from reminders of the impending carnage. As a result, the studios were forced to change the titles of war movies already in production: Republic changed *The Refugee* to *Three Faces West;* 20th changed *I Married a Nazi* to *The Woman I Married;* Columbia changed *It Happened in Paris* to *The Lady in Question.*[20]

While World War II increased the producers' appetite for "topical" films (because it whetted the public's), the anti-fascist and patriotic enthusiasm of many screen artists did not confuse the taste buds of the studio executives. Scripts about the war, about the ever popular British ally and the increasingly popular Soviet ally, still had to avoid controversy. Writers still had to detour around accurate representation of the social and political conditions of America's allies. The three films which Hollywood produced about Russia in 1942, *Mission to Moscow* (Warner Brothers), *Song of Russia* (MGM), *North Star* (Samuel Goldwyn), were Sovietized versions of *Mrs. Miniver.* Though written by radicals (Howard Koch, Paul Jarrico and Richard Collins, Lillian Hellman) and released at a time when Lend-Lease was popular, the Russians were valiantly holding off the Nazi armies at Stalingrad and Leningrad, and the Signal Corps was producing a paean to Russian courage (*The Battle of Russia*),‡ all three films managed to avoid an intelligent or in-depth treatment of any of the problems involved in the building of a socialist society and the contradictions of an alliance between a capitalist and a Communist country. These omissions were deliberate. As Mayer told HUAC: "The final script of *Song of Russia* was little more than a pleasant musical romance. . . . We did not attempt to depict Russia."[21] Jack B. Warner, when asked whether he thought the statements about Russia contained in *Mission to Moscow*

---

‡ In Frank Capra's film, General MacArthur was quoted on the exemplary courage and heroism of the Russians; the film's narrator mentions the Russians' "love of their soil" and their exhibition of the "determined will of a free and united people." *The Battle of Russia* was one in a series of "Why We Fight" films produced for the Army Signal Corps.

were "right or wrong," replied to HUAC: "I have never been in Russia. I don't know what Russia was like in 1937 or 1944 or 1947, so how can I tell you if it was right or wrong?"[22]

None of the screenwriters who worked on the Soviet scripts retained pleasant memories of the experience. Richard Collins told HUAC that the "big brass" at MGM (Mayer, Sam Katz, Joe Pasternak) paid very careful attention to the script of *Song of Russia*. MGM, said Collins, "wanted to make a picture about Russia because Russia was in the news," but Louis B. Mayer did not want to make a film about Communists. An earlier script had been turned down by David Selznick because he had deemed it too favorable to Russia and because it contained the term "collectivized farm." Collins and Jarrico were given specific instructions on how to sanitize the script for MGM's purposes. "So we decided," Collins continued, "not to mention what kind of farms these were. And then we took out words like 'community' and did a general job of cleaning it up on this level."[23] Lillian Hellman was so incensed at the changes director Lewis Milestone and producer Samuel Goldwyn made in her script *North Star* that she bought back her contract from Goldwyn for $30,000.[24] Howard Koch recently wrote that his screenplay for *Mission to Moscow* "was not original but a re-creation of events that took place in that period as recorded in [Joseph] Davies' book (*Mission to Moscow*), in his personal reminiscences and in the minutes of the League of Nations and those of the Moscow trials." Warner had taken a very deep interest in the project—at the request of President Roosevelt—and oversaw the production.[25]

The war thus did not alter the consciences or consciousness of movie producers—they continued to search for safe and profitable film formulas or to break new ground in old ways. Darryl Zanuck, for example, stood in the forefront of moviemakers who felt an urge to "forge ahead, to move into new ground." "We must," he stated a bit sententiously, "begin to deal realistically in film with the causes of wars and panics, with social upheavals and depression, with starvation and want and injustice and barbarism under whatever guise." Lest the priorities of corporate realism be lost in this torrent of noble ideals, however, Zanuck added (he was speaking to a large group of writers at UCLA in October 1943), you must "dress [this new realism] in the glittering robes of entertainment."[26] He tried to show the writers what he meant in his next film—a pet project—*Wilson* (written by Lamar Trotti, directed by Henry King, released in August 1944). This film biography of the twenty-eighth President, with its irrelevant musical interludes (the Wilson family gathering around the piano at moments of national or diplomatic crisis), only succeeded in proving how self-contradictory was the wish to coat realism with glitter, and how often the impulse for "realism" was itself ideologically conceived. (Zanuck's Wilson was an obvious apotheosis of Franklin D. Roosevelt, who was seeking a fourth term of office. Early in the film there is a series of short takes depicting Wilson signing a host of important reform acts: the Federal Reserve Act, the Clayton Antitrust Act, the Adamson Act, etc.; in his peace endeavors, he is described as the "spokesman against selfish nationalism.")

The film itself was "small"—a dramatization in black and white of a personalized ideal of political integrity and world peace. The promotion and advertising, however, were big, and, ironically, it was the cost, the marketing, and the trailers—not the content—which most offended radical screenwriters at the time. It took an ideologue, Ring Lardner, Jr., to remind the businessman, Zanuck, that the size and shape of the market for the "new" realism was too small and unrepresentative to make a blockbuster of a film like *Wilson*. "[I]t would have been sounder policy to make a picture about Wilson for perhaps half the cost of Zanuck's production and sell it honestly and on its merits to the ever-widening audience for such screen fare," wrote the Communist screenwriter in *New Masses*.[27] Excessive and misguided advertising, necessitated by front offices fearful of not recouping their ill-advised huge outlays, would attract, and dissatisfy, a wider audience than would care for any film which treated political content in even a cursorily sophisticated way, and would offend the smaller audience of moviegoers who reacted favorably to films like *Sahara* or *Thirty Seconds Over Tokyo*. Most serious, in the conventional syllogistic illogic of studio moneymen (*Wilson* lost money. *Wilson* was a political film. Political films lose money), experiences like Zanuck's with his latest movie would kill all likelihood of other, smaller, better political films being made in Hollywood.

Lardner's critique indicated the war-sharpened desire of all leftist screenwriters—liberal as well as Communist—to make serious and realistic movies. Philip Dunne was anxious to put into effect the documentary techniques he had learned in the Motion Picture Bureau of the Office of War Information; Carl Foreman felt that he had learned "how to make films" during his tour of duty with Capra's Signal Corps unit. Lester Cole told us that the assignment to write a script on Emiliano Zapata represented, for him, the culmination of his screenwriting career. But John Wexley's experience with two anti-Nazi films, *Hangmen Also Die* (United Artists, 1943) and *Cornered* (RKO, 1945), and Lardner's experience with Samuel Goldwyn proved yet again that in Hollywood it was the politics of the distributor and exhibitor which dominated.

In May 1942, American newspapers reported the assassination of Reichsprotektor Reinhard Heydrich by what was assumed to be a group of Czechoslovakian patriots. German *émigrés* Fritz Lang and Bertolt Brecht conceived of a movie based on the revenge the Nazis might have taken on the population of Prague. Lang telephoned Wexley, who lived in Bucks County, Pennsylvania, and asked him to write the script; he wanted to draw on Wexley's skill as a screenwriter (*Angels with Dirty Faces, The Amazing Dr. Clitterhouse, Confessions of a Nazi Spy,* etc.) as well as his political beliefs. Wexley believed that Lang eliminated or reduced to microscopic proportions any mention or shot of Jews and that his aesthetic execution stereotyped the characters and reduced the dramatic thrust of the story. "Enough of the original point of view—that the people of Czechoslovakia hated the Nazi oppressors and those who reacted the strongest were the workers and the Left—remained," said Wexley, "that I was satisfied with the film. But I had expected more from Lang."

Two years later, Wexley was approached by Adrian Scott to write a script based on a one-page story idea of Ben Hecht's. It was a manhunt premise and Wexley, who had recently read a State Department White Paper detailing the police state Juan Perón had established in Argentina and the dictator's sympathies for the Nazis, suggested: "Let's have the main character chase his prey to Argentina and show that it is harboring Nazis." It was clear from the beginning, both to Scott and executive producer William Dozier, that Wexley's script would be critical of the Argentinian government. They were not disappointed. Wexley's script dramatized his belief that fascism was still alive in South America and that a parallel existed between the Argentinian secret police, against which the movie's hero collided, and those of the recently defeated European fascist governments.

Edward Dmytryk, a director whose career was in the ascendance at RKO, was assigned to the film. Although he was a member of the Communist Party, and presumably imbued with the anti-fascist feelings which had motivated most Hollywood people to enroll in the CPUSA in the forties, Dmytryk was also strongly career-oriented. He wanted the films he directed to be commercial successes. After reading the script, he told Wexley that it was "too much of an attack against fascism." (Years later, while pursuing his career as an informer, he told

HUAC, the readers of *The Saturday Evening Post,* and the readers of his memoirs that he objected to Wexley's script because it was "wordy" and "uncinematic," and that it contained "long speeches loaded with Communist propaganda thinly disguised as antifascist rhetoric. . . .")[28] Wexley's fear that Dmytryk intended to "whitewash" the Perón government was enhanced when he learned that the director had flown to Buenos Aires to confer with Argentinian officials about the validity of Wexley's criticisms.

On his return, Dmytryk convinced Scott and Dozier that the film would not only lose money if Wexley's script was not altered, but that RKO might face a full boycott of its entire program by Argentina and countries friendly to it. John Paxton, who had written *Murder, My Sweet* for RKO (which Dmytryk directed in 1944), and who was a close friend of Scott's, was assigned the rewrite. He was told to make it more of a manhunt picture. The finished product carried no political labels, and the villains (Wexley's secret police) had no apparent superiors. The government of Argentina was not criticized, and the motivations and purposes of the characters became murky and amorphous. Paxton called it "a very poor film. I had no feeling for the script. It was a hack job on my part." Wexley said that enough had been left in to make it an effective movie: "It was superior to most 'B' melodramas and an alert viewing audience could fill in the gaps."

At the time, however, Wexley tried to shame Dmytryk and Scott into restoring the cuts they and Paxton had made in his script—especially the criticism of the Perón government. Wexley asked John Howard Lawson and Albert Maltz, whom he termed "distinguished, politically wise writers," to try to influence Scott and Dmytryk. Wexley denies that he approached Lawson and Maltz as Communists; Dmytryk claims that it was an example of "Party procedure."[29] Two meetings were held on the subject. Lawson and Maltz did not think that the two scripts were as dissimilar as Wexley claimed. There the matter ended. The film made money for RKO and improved the status of Dmytryk and Scott at the studio. It did, however, have two important consequences: one, it provided Dmytryk with an incident he could use to certify his "break" with communism; two, it proved that screenwriter, director, and producer Communists were far more vulnerable to the dictates of the studio system than to the demands of their ideology or the influence of fellow Party members.

As *Cornered* neared completion, the vicissitudes attendant to the creation of a new film genre, the anti-anti-Semitic film, demonstrated conclusively the unpredictable and frustrating nature of social and political film making in Hollywood. As the war began to wind down, the predominantly Jewish moguls and studio executives, who had generally refrained from calling attention to their religion either by ostentatious support of Jewish causes or by sympathetic portrayal of Jewish people or their plight, noticed the climate of opinion had significantly altered and at almost every studio an anti-bigotry project took shape. Ring Lardner, Jr. (Goldwyn), and Adrian Scott (RKO) were involved in two of them. Even though the former's script proved unacceptable and the latter's became a profitable, award-winning film, both emerged from the experience with unhappy thoughts about film making in Hollywood. Scott's "success" with *Crossfire* drove him to ulcers; Lardner's failure with *Earth and High Heaven*, followed by a similar disappointment with a film he did for the Cagneys on Custer and the Little Big Horn, made the screenwriter "despondent about the chances of getting anywhere with significant content. . . . I began the postwar period with a less optimistic attitude about 'political' films, accepted more commercial assignments (like *Forever Amber*), and started brooding about getting out of Hollywood."

Toward the end of 1944, Goldwyn hired Lardner for what the producer described as "the delicate and important job of adapting Gwethalyn Graham's *Earth and High Heaven*, about anti-Semitism in Montreal." Lardner did a short treatment, which Goldwyn liked, and was authorized to write the screenplay while Goldwyn traveled to Europe. He read Lardner's first draft on his return.

> He said [recalled Lardner] I had "defrauded and betrayed" him. Defrauded because I hadn't followed the agreed-upon treatment. I maintained the changes were minor and normal, and asked what he meant by betrayal. He said one of the reasons he had hired me—just one of the reasons—was that I was a gentile. "You have betrayed me by writing like a Jew." (When I told this to Gordon Kahn, he asked: "How did you do it? From the right- to the left-hand side of the page?")

Lardner returned to his office to pack up his gear only to be stopped by Goldwyn's wife, Frances. She had persuaded Sam to continue with the project and told Lardner to ignore what her husband had told him, that "he was just nervous because of the subject material."

> She conned me (probably with his knowledge) into working two or three more weeks on it without pay. But he said I still treated the subject in too direct a fashion. Over the next two or three

years at least six other writers did versions, none of them pleasing to Goldwyn.

By 1946, when Scott began his approach to the RKO chiefs with the *Crossfire* project, the atmosphere for pro-Jewish films had noticeably improved. The successful completion of a popular war against Nazi Germany combined with the shocking revelations of the holocaust primed the sensibilities of the moviegoing public. In addition, the issue of an independent Jewish state in Palestine had caught on in Hollywood. Even Ben Hecht shucked his cynicism and plunged into fund-raising for the Irgun, and non-Jewish luminaries such as Gene Kelly and Philip Dunne became active in the cause of a Jewish homeland. Over seventy-five film writers, directors, and producers, members of the Hollywood Branch of the American Arts Committee for Palestine (Philip Dunne, William Wyler, and Jerry Wald among them), gathered at Lucey's on October 2, 1947, to hear Senator Claude Pepper (D-Fla.) speak on the subject of a Jewish homeland.[30] Finally, collective ethnic consciousness among Jews, emerging over the course of a decade, crystallized in a recognizable, cohesive Jewish voting bloc.

The main force behind *Crossfire* (RKO, 1947) was Scott, who had long wanted to make a film about anti-Semitism. His impulse sprang not from his philosophical Marxism, but from his personal beliefs and his desire to make serious, dramatic films. Scott, like Wexley, believed that the forces of fascism and racism had only been temporarily defeated in World War II, and he wanted to dramatize the evils of prejudice and bigotry.

For almost a year Scott and Paxton, old friends from their days as critics on *Stage* magazine in New York and three prior screen assignments in Hollywood, discussed their approach to the subject: they needed a theme which they could sell to the RKO executives; a theme, that is, which did not reduce the film to an agitprop tract. "I finally decided," Paxton recalled, "that a cops-and-robbers format might work best. The tension and menace thus created would provide the most interesting and acceptable mode of treatment for the theme." Scott approved of Paxton's treatment, to which he attached a memo (see Appendix 5) whose wording indicated the difficulty he anticipated in getting the project approved. In fact, Scott wrote later, "we *worried* more about [the script] than we *thought* about it. We wondered if they really would let us make it."[31] (Severe stomach pains plagued Scott during the preliminary stages of the film.)

Much to Scott's surprise, executive producer William Dozier agreed that anti-Semitism was on the rise and that he, too, was "concerned" about it. Studio head Peter Rathvon thought anti-Semitism was a good theme for a film—that "the sterility of general motion picture production was something which bothered him [and] here was a good useful way to introduce a new subject matter" (Rathvon's eagerness was also undoubtedly prompted by the news that 20th Century-Fox had scheduled an anti-anti-Semitic film: *Gentleman's Agreement*). Dore Schary, head of production at RKO, approved Scott and Paxton's treatment. And movie censor Joseph Breen applauded it[32]—if, that is, Paxton would minimize the drinking, not condone prostitution, and insert a speech by an army major in which it was made clear that Monty (the anti-Semite) was not typical of army personnel. Even with all these green lights—with all the ifs coming up positive—Scott did not shed his fears or his stomach pains; nor could he free himself of the self-censoring mechanism which the studio system had bred within him. In what could stand as an epitaph for all politically conscious screen artists working in a commercial medium, Scott bitterly summed up his experience with *Crossfire:* "We are magnificently adjusted to bans, and ripe for more bans. . . ."[33]

"What Am I Doing Here?": The Studio System and the Alternatives

Why then did Scott, and the two hundred plus Communist and fellow-traveler film artists like him, remain in Hollywood? A very small group of radicals—Leo Seltzer, Leo Hurwitz, Sam Brody, Paul Strand, etc.—preferred the Communist-backed Film and Photo League or the independent Nykino and Frontier Films to employment with the majors. (However, no one in the United States seemed able to retain his or her vocational purity. Both Hurwitz and Brody, when times were tough, in the late thirties and forties, accepted jobs in Hollywood studios.) According to Seltzer, the choice—to steer clear of Hollywood—though monetarily unrewarding, was professionally gratifying to a degree unavailable to the Hollywood film employee: "Ours was a total involvement in what was happening in the world on a very practical and realistic level. We filmed the everyday social scene, the economic struggles, and we put it together to represent a realistic, not dramatized point of view. . . ."[34] Suffering *from* their art, not *for* it, studio-employed writers rarely experienced anything approaching a close connection between their vocation and their politics. We asked a number of the writers we interviewed why they had not attempted to script alternative film projects—why they had not broken away from the Hollywood industry whose possibilities were so limited. None of them had an answer. It had never been a real or rational possibility to them. Lawson later claimed that he had been arguing for years, within the confines of Communist branch meetings, that "The struggle against the corrupting influence of the commercial film must be combined with the struggle for an independent motion picture art, genuinely free from Wall Street control."[35] Still, there was no escaping the contradictions: while Lawson was writing his book, he was also writing scripts on the black market, asserting even less control than when he worked openly for the majors.

Though it was an endeavor rich in film possibilities, alternative film making was poor in remuneration. Most of the left-wing screenwriters were married, with two or more children, and were unwilling to begin scrambling for the money necessary to keep food on the table. Second, the independents had to scrounge for funds to buy equipment, film, etc. Sam Brody recalled that the huge efforts in time and energy expended in this direction "drained the group [Nykino] of most of the creative drive and energy needed to create such long range projects [as features]."[36] Third, the independents had no assured distribution network. Their films played in union halls, living rooms, and auditoriums on a hit-or-miss basis.

These obstacles would have stymied all but the most dedicated of film artists, but there were two other factors which clinched the argument: a dispute over the nature of cinema and the role of dialogue, and the Hollywood writers' perception of the importance of Hollywood films in the formation of the consciousness of the American people. In the early days of the alternative film projects writing and directing skills were not important; expert camerawork was the basic skill required for filming hunger marches, rent strikes, picket lines, etc. And even when Hurwitz *et al.* broke away from the "heat of the action" documentary style of the Film and Photo League to form a group (Nykino) to make dramatic-documentary films, their bias remained cinematic rather than literary and, according to Hurwitz, the Hollywood people could not adapt.

> Hollywood films depended on words. They were safer and more bankable than images. And if your career is concentrated on nothing but writing dialogue, you will stop thinking in terms of images and create only in terms of conventions. The film story is thus told in terms of talking about the events at hand, rather than

developing an image of the events. George Sklar and Vera Caspary did a script for us on the subject of child labor. They had no feeling for images; no sense of how to build an event in filmic terms. It was, like most Hollywood films, a filmed dialogue. We rewrote it into a shooting script. Sklar and Caspary thought our script was awful.

George Sklar drew a different lesson from the episode. Hurwitz, he said, offered a "dubious generalization" and "example" to prove his point. "I was not a screenwriter; I had never written a screenplay (only a treatment with Maltz in the early thirties). And Vera had refused to work on scripts, she only wrote original story ideas." They had attended a preview of Frontier Films' *The Wave* (a documentary about Mexican fishermen), at which the invited film people were asked to contribute ideas, scripts, etc. Sklar remembered that the audience was impressed by the film, and that Vera offered to write a story. She asked Sklar to adapt her idea. "It was a very intensive job. We spent three exhausting weeks on it. It was full of imagery, a very fluid script. But I did not write in individual camera shots, just master scenes." Hurwitz and Strand did not read *Payday* for a few weeks. Finally, they showed Sklar and Caspary the changes they had made. "Not only had they broken it down into a shooting script," said Sklar, "and ruined some of our imagery, but they had rewritten the dialogue, a subject about which they knew nothing." Sklar and Caspary were incensed. "They treated us worse than a Hollywood producer would have. A Hollywood producer would at leave have employed a professional to do the rewrite." In short, nothing in the experience of alternative film making during the thirties offered a compelling attraction to professional screenwriters.

Finally—and most obvious to the Hollywood writer who had to face the question "What am I, a committed radical (or Communist), doing in an industry which produces such a steady stream of bourgeois claptrap?"—Hollywood films were too important to be left to the Hollywood producers. Though not a screenwriter herself, Sylvia Jarrico had sat in on enough debates about the question of the radical screenwriter in Hollywood to understand the rationale of those who stayed:

The writers may not have thought that they could get Hollywood to deal with more realistic material but they had an obligation to try because they understood the power of film—they thought it the most potent educational invention in history. They did not look to alternative film making. They believed that socially responsible writers belonged in the film industry because feature films were the most significant way in which the people of the world were being educated. The medium reached so far, that any victory was important.

Though the Hollywood writers did not join the crews or staffs of the alternative film groups which regularly appeared in the thirties and forties, radical screen artists did contribute time, money, and advice to most of them. In December 1936, Donald Ogden Stewart chaired a fund-raising program presented by the New Film Group of Los Angeles, which wanted to produce a series of pro-labor films. Dudley Nichols, Marc Connelly, Sherwood Anderson, Fritz Lang, Fredric March, and Walter Wanger sponsored, in 1938, Films for Democracy, a group formed "to safeguard and extend American democracy." In addition, radicals provided material to the film committees formed by the various Popular Front groups such as the Motion Picture Democratic Committee and the Hollywood Democratic Committee. For the latter, Richard Collins and Abraham Polonsky undertook to write a police training film on the treatment of minorities, and Robert Lees, Fred Rinaldo, and Robert Rossen prepared a project on slum clearance in Los Angeles.

Leo Hurwitz, though he deplored the effect that Hollywood had on screenwriters—"they were skilled and professional, but narrow and slotted"—agreed that they did win some important victories within the Hollywood film industry. "They changed movies by means of having a slight civilizing influence on the Hollywood product and by opening the doors on aspects of life normally closed for Hollywood." Party critics of the thirties, however, were far less tolerant of the efforts of radical Hollywood screenwriters. For instance, at the Western Writers' Conference of the League of American Writers on November 13, 1936, Donald Ogden Stewart, Sam Ornitz, Guy Endore, Budd Schulberg, and others were criticized because they "lacked courage to sacrifice their jobs in the struggle against fascism." They were also accused of insincerity and of attempting to blame poor screen stories on producers and the public.[37] Party polemicist Mike Gold, in an address to the Fourth, and last, Congress of the League of American Writers in 1941, reflected on the preceding decade, and attributed "good" Hollywood movies to the radical atmosphere, not the efforts of radical screenwriters:

In America, our people's movement of the Thirties was felt in many directions. The proletarian seed sown in a few first novels about strikes and unemployment grew by a hundred branches until it brought new dignity even to Hollywood. Pictures like The Informer, Emile Zola, Mr. Deeds Goes to Town were not being made in Hollywood before 1930.[38]

Gold missed the point. Communist screenwriters could not themselves, directly, improve or change content through political inserts—whistling of "The Internationale," speeches about democracy—or by writing Communist films stressing the importance of the collectivity over the individual and graphically depicting the plight of the dispossessed, the nature of their struggle, and their inevitable class triumph, or by imitating Russian Marxist aesthetics. Lawson, for one, was very forthright about the lack of success in those directions:

As a matter of undeviating practice in the motion picture industry it is impossible for any screen writer to put anything into a motion picture to which the executive producers object. The content of motion pictures is controlled exclusively by producers; [all aspects of a film] are carefully studied, checked, edited and filtered by executive producers and persons acting directly under their supervision. . . .[39]

Informers Richard Collins, a screenwriter, and Meta Rosenberg, a story editor, confirmed Lawson's statement in their 1951 testimony before HUAC. Collins made it clear that anything smacking even remotely of "Communist material," including words such as "community," "communal," etc., was blue-penciled or "cleaned out" of all scripts, especially those dealing with Russia. Rosenberg, also an admitted member of the Communist Party, stated that the executives above her at Paramount were very aware of propaganda and political issues and "were very concerned about what writers were hired and what stories were bought."[40] Four years earlier, in 1947, Louis Mayer and Jack Warner had emphasized their control over screen content, while "friendly" right-wing witnesses—Sam Wood and Adolphe Menjou—averred that the producers were remarkably vigilant about keeping "Communist propaganda" and "Communist influence" off the screen.

The debate over "Communist propaganda" and "content," though interesting, nevertheless obfuscates the real impact of the radical screenwriters on Hollywood. They were not part of an aesthetic movement—that is, they were not promoters of proletcult or social realism manifestos, nor were they recruits in a cultural crusade to liberate the Hollywood film castles from the hands of the infidels. They were, instead, artists with, in Abraham Polonsky's words, "a generalized political awareness . . . who were trying to make films that reflected this awareness in one way or another when they had an opportunity to do so."[41]

And it was as political people that they made their presence felt. Wherever creative or political folk gathered in Hollywood between 1933 and 1950—at the writers' buildings, the studio commissaries, the Screen Writers, Screen Actors, or Screen Directors Guilds, the Hollywood League of American Writers, the Anti-Nazi League, the Motion Picture Democratic Committee, or the Hollywood Theatre Alliance—a nucleus of Communists was present. Their viewpoint (or line) could not be ignored or sidestepped. The insistence and articulateness of the film Communists altered the atmosphere of Hollywood—and influenced film content and political behavior—in the same haphazard, unpredictable way that cloud seeding alters the weather.

But the Hollywood "clouds" required unheard-of amounts of "seeding" and a lengthy period of "seeding" time—both of which the reactionaries were determined to cut off. The witch-hunters created an atmosphere on their own, in the late forties and fifties, which made progressive social content in films difficult if not impossible.

Without an examination of the original scripts the radicals turned in to their producers, we cannot evaluate completely the quality of their cinematic radicalism. The finished film alone cannot provide evidence of how much the producers changed, or how much they did not have to change as a result of the success of the studio conditioning process on left-wing screenwriters. Nevertheless, as we look back over the fifteen years (1933–47) during which politics dominated the lives of screenwriters and thoroughly infiltrated the Hollywood milieu, three judgments concerning the impact of politicized screen artists on commercial films seem obvious. One, forces far stronger than the consciousness of screenwriters determined what was deemed suitable for filming, whether those forces were intangible ones like personal preferences or studio policy, historical ones like the Depression or World War II, or tangible ones like box office receipts and pressure from government agencies and congressional committees. Two, if the atmosphere for progressive films or "topicals" existed, the radical screenwriter could have a "say" only if the studio line happened to coincide exactly with

the Party line, which really occurred only once, during World War
II. Three, if Hurwitz was correct in his estimation that politicized
screenwriters did somewhat alter trends in the Hollywood film world,
they did it in the same manner that they affected policies in the SWG
or in the Popular Front organizations—that is, in their guise as liberals.
In short, Communist screenwriters did not revolutionize, Stalinize,
communize, Sovietize, or subvert the output of the film industry. They
did try to approach their subject matter more objectively and straight-
forwardly than was the norm; they endeavored to add realism and
delete racial distortions and ethnic stereotypes; they aimed to accentu-
ate any real elements or story material they found within their assignments. If the majority of the films made from their scripts seem politically indistinguishable from the films made from the scripts of
non-radical screenwriters, it is not necessarily because they lacked skill
or determination, but because the studio executives were more skilled
and determined—and by far more powerful.

10

The Hollywood Ten: From the Blacklist to Prison
November 1947–June 1950

The Committee will be deprived of its basic weapon and in
effect be abolished only if the motion picture industry stands
firm.

—*Ring Lardner, Jr.*
November 7, 1947[1]

"Soon after we returned to Hollywood," attorney Charles Katz
remembers, "we received word that Eric Johnston was reverting to his
pre-October position and that he was carrying Spyros Skouras [20th
Century-Fox] and Nicholas Schenck [Loew's, Inc.] with him." In
light of Johnston's long-standing anti-communism and his testimony
before HUAC, this rumor could have surprised nobody. His apparent
support of the "unfriendly" witnesses was simply an alternative gambit
that he had essayed, more or less in good faith, when the executives
had rejected his original counsel. In the wake of the testimonies of the
Ten, however, Johnston felt no further obligation to continue hard-
lining the Thomas Committee. In fact, he thought the hearings would
lead to box office disaster if studio management did not move deci-
sively to counter the publicity which followed Russell's revelations.

A handful of liberal editorials supporting the First Amendment
meant little to Johnston when weighed against the mobilizing potential
of aroused religious (Legion of Decency, Knights of Columbus), patriotic (Daughters of the American Revolution, American Legion),
and educational (Parents Teachers Association) groups. When it came
to questions of politics, no press was good press in Johnston's eyes.
Veterans of Foreign Wars' post commanders could, he believed, repel
far more box office dollars than favorable editorials in New York
newspapers could attract. Unless the studios separated themselves

cleanly from the "exposed Reds," profits would fall under the weight of the Ten's comportment, Russell's dossiers, and the contempt citations.

The New York-based executives reached similar conclusions. Their concern with profit and loss gave them a different view of the hearings and public opinion from that of the Los Angeles-based moguls and heads of production. These corporate financial overseers could, when they chose, exercise irresistible pressure on the studio barons. Thus, although men like Zanuck, Mayer, and Dore Schary seemed "determined," even as late as November, to protect their "unfriendly" employees, Skouras, Schenck, and Peter Rathvon (RKO) decided that the time had come for the industry to cut its losses. In the face of all the other difficulties undermining the profitability of Hollywood movies—television, foreign trade restrictions, antitrust prosecutions—the accountants and financiers felt that the industry could not afford a show of solidarity with the Ten. Thus Johnston's hand was considerably strengthened when he returned to Hollywood after the hearings and began to reformulate the studios' "Communist policy."

He immediately, and publicly, voiced his "disappointment and disapproval." The performance of the "unfriendly" witnesses was a "tremendous disservice" to the film industry, the Producers' Association president told the *Hollywood Reporter*. "Their refusal to stand up and be counted for whatever they are could only result in a confusion of the issues. . . ." He called upon the government to "adopt a national policy with respect to the employment of Communists in private industry," and urged the motion picture industry to "take positive steps to meet this problem [of internal communism] and do it promptly."[2]

In a last-ditch effort to circumvent eastern pressure to institute a blacklist, several of the Hollywood studio bosses (Zanuck, Mayer, and Schary) requested a collective letter of "explanation" from the eighteen "unfriendly" witnesses who had returned to Hollywood (Brecht had gone back to Germany). This letter, and the individual ones which each of the five artists under contract were also asked to write, would constitute part of the studios' attempt to silence the baying patriotic wolves. Howard Strickling, an MGM publicist, told Lester Cole to write "something that might be used in some way to help make [Cole's] position clear, and something which perhaps the studio could use."[3] Four years later Dore Schary testified:

> I tried to get Scott to sign a statement that he was not a Communist to show the Board of Directors in my efforts to keep him em-

ployed. He said he would sign an affidavit that he did not sympa-
thize with any party which sought to overthrow the government
by violence, but he would not say that he had never been a
Communist.[4]

Lardner did not write a letter nor, to the best of his knowledge, did
Trumbo or Dmytryk.

The group's letter, addressed to Nicholas Schenck, and Cole's letter,
entitled "STATEMENT," represented another means of implementing the Nineteen's HUAC strategy. Even with contempt citations and
the threat of unemployment hanging over them, the "unfriendly"
witnesses refused to budge from their position that no congressional
committee (and, by extension, no employer) could institute a political
opinion test for employment. While continuing to insist that freedom
of association remained a sacrosanct right of political minorities in this
country, regardless of historical conditions, the Nineteen acknowledged that the political atmosphere of the era required forthright admission of their feelings about the United States. Without renouncing
the right to criticize undemocratic government agencies, both letters
contained strong statements of loyalty. The letter from the eighteen
proclaimed the group's loyalty to the United States and to the "motion
picture industry and to its continued leadership of the screens of the
world, based upon its fullest expression of the democratic faith and
heritage which is America's." "We are," the letter concluded,

> either voters in the Republican, the Democratic, the Independent,
> the Communist, or any other column, which we believe is irrele-
> vant and totally immaterial, so long as our citizenship occurs
> under unquestioned allegiance and devotion to the American peo-
> ple and the government they peacefully, soberly, and patriotically
> elect to represent them.[5]

Cole, who recited in writing the pledge of allegiance, and swore that
he "did not believe in violence and force to overthrow our government, and . . . was not an agent of a foreign power," also took a shot
at HUAC: "I further solemnly swear that I will continue to resist,
with all my strength, under all pressure, economic and social, the current drive to subvert [the pledge of allegiance], in spirit if not in letter, to read: 'I pledge allegiance to the Thomas-Rankin Committee,
and to the anti-democratic forces for which it fronts; one nation
divided, with fear and insecurity for all.' "[6]

Just as the Nineteen and their lawyers had misjudged the effect that HUAC's hostility toward them would have on the impact of their prepared statements, so too they miscalculated the issue before the motion picture executives in November—it was no longer a question of loyalty, but a question of the behavior of the Ten before a congressional committee. Nothing short of effacing the recent past would have saved the Ten's position in the film industry, and further efforts at "explanation" were probably doomed from the start. On the other hand, regardless of their own deep respect for their American citizenship, the "unfriendly" witnesses found that the symbolism and vocabulary of patriotism had been completely preempted by their political enemies. Thus the display of loyal Americanism seemed cynical or disingenuous; in either case, it was too little too late. The letters were not even released to the press—indicating that the die had already been cast in New York.

The executives and producers gathered at the Waldorf-Astoria Hotel in New York on November 24–25 to decide the fate of the Ten. The meeting was called by the three most powerful employer groups in the industry: the Association of Motion Picture Producers, the Motion Picture Association of America, and the Society of Independent Motion Picture Producers. As it turned out, the boards of directors of two studios—RKO and Fox—had already decided to fire their "defiant" employees. Though the decision was not communicated to the screen artists for another week, the careers of Dmytryk, Scott, and Lardner had effectively ended in late November. Peter Rathvon, president of RKO, declared later that Dmytryk and Scott were fired because they "brought themselves into disrepute" by their defiance of HUAC and by their post-hearing political activity (meetings, speeches, interviews, paid advertisements, radio broadcasts), "all adding up into defiance of the institutions of the United States Government." Their conduct had "crystallized" against the movie industry the "fluid public opinion" aroused by the announcement of the HUAC inquiry. "This country," concluded Rathvon, "is full . . . of organizations that like to pass resolutions and take sides on issues. . . ." He named the American Legion and the Hearst papers as organizations "beginning to take hold of this thing"—i.e., the issue of "Communism in Hollywood."[7]

Eric Johnston once again confronted the assembled moguls, executives, and producers with a set of choices; this time, however, he cracked the whip. They had, he informed his colleagues, to take a formal position on the hearings, "to fish or cut bait!"[8] Only two courses remained open to the industry: studio management could retain the Ten and make a public statement promising to keep subversive material off the screen; or they could fire, or refuse to employ, the Ten. Johnston rattled off a half-dozen reasons in favor of the second alternative:

1. The tenor of newspaper editorials had begun to turn against Hollywood;

2. The American Legion was threatening a boycott;

3. An audience in Chapel Hill, North Carolina, had stoned the screen of a movie theater showing a Katharine Hepburn film (she had been prominently featured as a supporter of the Committee for the First Amendment);

4. Boycotts were being instituted in Glendale, California, and Independence, Kansas, against films associated with the Ten;

5. Spain, Chile, and Argentina had threatened to refuse to accept films produced by studios which employed the Ten;

6. RKO and 20th Century-Fox had already decided to fire Dmytryk and Scott, and Lardner, respectively.

Only Sam Goldwyn protested that these matters were not weighty enough to justify a blacklist of ten screen artists. No other producer spoke out against Johnston or for the first alternative. James Byrnes, chief counsel for the Producers' Association, did point out that any action the studios took could not be collective—they would have to act individually against their left-wing employees.[9]

The next order of business concerned Mayer's question: how do we undo the effect of HUAC's attacks on Hollywood and prevent further encroachments on our autonomy? Even though they had agreed on the necessity of sacrificing the Ten, the producers determined that they would abase themselves no further, that they would draw the line of retreat on the graves of Trumbo, Cole, Maltz, et al. Mayer noted that the Committee had a lot more names, and that "this could just be the beginning" unless the producers were to launch a convincing counterattack.[10] The assembly responded by appointing Mayer, Joseph Schenck (20th Century-Fox), Walter Wanger, Dore Schary (RKO), and attorney Mendel Silberburg to a committee to draft a declaration announcing the abandonment of the Ten and the adoption of a policy of self-regulation.

The producers' real feelings and motives remain hidden. When speaking for the public record (confined, for the most part, to the depositions and testimony they delivered in the breach of contract and conspiracy suits brought by their former employees), they had to stand firmly on the contractual pretexts which "legalized" the Waldorf decisions. Mayer, for example, could not tell the world he was discharging Lester Cole because the latter was a Communist or even simply because he had been cited for contempt of Congress; the studio contracts contained neither a "politics" nor a "criminal" clause. Thus, whatever the producers said among themselves, or whatever the "real" reasons, the formal justifications for the institution of a blacklist had to be framed in "moral" terms.

In the broadest sense, of course, the decision not to hire certain artists—that is, to capitulate to political reaction at the highest level of government—was highly political. Reduced to its essence, however, the decision to blacklist was economic—fear of adverse box office required their dismissal.* Dore Schary's claim, seventeen years later, that no one at the Waldorf meeting argued "for the establishment of a blacklist in any form whatsoever"[11] cannot be taken seriously, although it was true that the producers believed that a limited blacklist marked the last, not the first, episode in their collective confrontation with HUAC. The Committee would henceforth either leave Hollywood alone or face an industry stonewall; Hollywood would go back to business as usual. "I urged us," said Schary, "to word the declaration in a manner that would not induce panic or create an atmosphere of fear—that we were not going to institute a [political] clearing house."[12]

The "clarity" of Schary's memory, seventeen years after the fact, contrasts sharply with the confused and garbled words of Peter Rathvon four months after the Waldorf meeting. At that time, Rathvon stumbled all over himself as he tried to explain the rationale which had guided the executives in November 1947. He claimed that the Ten, by their behavior before HUAC, had destroyed a distinction which the industry had drawn and had been prepared to stand behind: "a distinc-

---

* These fears were not borne out by the evidence that the Producers' Association's lawyers presented at the various breach of contract trials which members of the Ten instigated, nor by the reception of films on which blacklisted artists had worked. There is no proof that any film produced, directed, written by, or starring an "unfriendly" witness could not attract crowds to the theaters, win prizes, or be sold to television for large sums of money. In fact, there is overwhelming evidence to the contrary.

tion between a man whose political beliefs led him to an attitude of mind where he was prepared to destroy the institutions of the United States, [and] a man who had no such beliefs, but adheres to membership in the Communist Party."[13] He neglected to mention how this distinction would, in fact, have been made. No matter the standard, however, the result would be blacklist for those who did not meet it.

On December 3 the Waldorf Statement was communicated to the world. (See Appendix 6.) One week earlier RKO management informed Adrian Scott and Edward Dmytryk of their immediate termination as employees of the studio:

> By your conduct [before HUAC] and by your actions, attitude, associations, public statements and general conduct before, at, and since that time, you have brought yourself into disrepute with a large section of the public, have offended the community, have prejudiced this corporation as your employer and the motion picture industry in general, have lessened your capacity fully to comply with your employment agreement, and have otherwise violated the provisions of Article 16 [the morals clause]† of your employment agreement with us.[14]

MGM, for its part, indefinitely suspended Cole and Trumbo. Zanuck of 20th could not bring himself personally to dismiss Lardner; his assistant passed the discharge word down.

By the first of December 1947, for the first time in the history of the American film industry, ten perfectly capable, experienced screen artists found themselves at the end of their professional careers as a consequence of their political beliefs.

The Value of the Ten

In terms of productivity, talent, and proceeds, what had the studio executives agreed to relinquish when they made their pact with the Washington devils at the Waldorf conference? It has long been fash-

---

† Article 16 read: "At all times commencing on the date hereof and continuing throughout the production and distribution of the Pictures, the [artist] will conduct himself with due regard to the public conventions and morals and will not do anything which will tend to degrade him in society or bring him into public disrepute, contempt, scorn, or ridicule, or that will tend to shock, insult, or offend the community or public morals or decency or prejudice the corporation or the motion picture industry in general. . . ."

ionable among those who write about this period of Hollywood history to disparage the artistic capabilities of the Ten—without supplying a persuasive analysis of their scripts, or systematically noting the critical response, financial returns, or awards garnered by their films. Murray Kempton slashed hardest and most elegantly: "Their story is a failure of promise. . . . The promise at the beginnings of most of them appears now to have been largely smoke and thunder. . . . [T]hey got rich fabricating empty banalities to fit Hollywood's idea of life in America. . . ."[15] Walter Goodman repeated Kempton's words and added some pejorative (and inaccurate) asides of his own: "[They] were craftsmen, more or less adept at setting down on paper the ideas in a producer's head. It was not arduous work. . . . [Their] careers parodied the writer's craft. . . ."[16] Stefan Kanfer diminished their work with superciliousness: "True, they were responsible for pap, but they were also concerned for the Little Man. . . ."[17] Hilton Kramer simply repeated the old bromides: "[They were] loyal, pampered, high-priced hacks."[18] These assessments follow from the critics' ill-concealed efforts to diminish the Ten politically. The producers, for their part, weighed the "unfriendly" witnesses on a profit and loss scale.

Though the scale finally tipped against the Ten—and the hostile witnesses who came after them in 1951–53—the weighing process was not as easy or clear-cut as it may have seemed to contemporaries. Indeed, left-wing screenwriters as a whole were highly regarded by their employers. Although they comprised only one ninth of the screenwriter population of Hollywood, they authored or co-authored one fifth of the scripts filmed between 1938 and 1974—attesting to their ability to turn in intelligent, shootable scripts on schedule.‡ In terms of financial gross and awards, however, the radical screenwriters, as a group, did not approach this proportion. Between 1938 and 1947, the decade of the most intense left-wing political activism, this group

---

‡ The total of radical screenwriters (140) was derived from adding the number of blacklisted writers to the number of writers who informed to HUAC. (Howard Suber, *The Anti-Communist Blacklist in the Hollywood Motion Picture Industry*, unpublished Ph.D. thesis, UCLA, 1969, pp. 174–276.) The screenwriter population (1,320) was given in *The Screen Writer*, December 1945, p. 37, and May 1946, p. 41.

According to the totals tabulated in *Film Daily Year Book*, the eight majors produced 3,145 films between 1938 and 1947. Left-wingers scripted 600 of those films. (*Who Wrote the Movie and What Else Did He Write?*, Los Angeles: Academy of Motion Picture Arts and Sciences and Writers Guild of America West, 1970.)

of 140 men and women received 19 out of a total of 142 Academy Award nominations for best achievement in screenwriting and won 4 of the 29 Oscars handed out (the winners were Donald Ogden Stewart, Sidney Buchman, Ring Lardner, Jr., and Howard Koch). Six screenplays by radicals were included in John Gassner's highly respected collections of the thirty "Best Screenplays" of the 1930–45 era: *Mr. Smith Goes to Washington* and *Here Comes Mr. Jordan*, both by Sidney Buchman; *Little Caesar* by Francis Faragoh; *Watch on the Rhine* by Dashiell Hammett and Lillian Hellman; *Dragon Seed* by Marguerite Roberts; and *Casablanca*, co-written by Howard Koch. Finally, of the three dozen writers whose work Richard Corliss analyzed in his *Talking Pictures*, only five left-wingers (Koch, Trumbo, Lardner, Buchman, and Polonsky) received attention. In sum, blacklisted screenwriters, counting awards, nominations, and listings, accumulated 14 per cent of the available accolades of their profession while contributing 20 per cent of the material on which recognition was based.

The financial value of the radical screenwriters to the studios is less clear, since executives and producers did not usually "blame" writers for films which lost money. In terms of profitability, we have no record of the radicals' contributions to studio coffers. We do know, however, that the left-wingers did not write (perhaps because they were not selected to write) a large proportion of Hollywood's biggest box office hits. Collectively they scripted ten of the ninety-one top-grossing films made before 1952.

The artistic quality of the films scripted by left-wingers cannot be measured by statistics; it is a matter, finally, of taste and opinion. Focusing only on the Ten, however, the corpus of intelligent film criticism recognizes only one of them among the most gifted film-making talents in Hollywood annals: Richard Corliss, a long-time student of the art of scriptwriting, singled out Lardner as "a major screenwriting talent."[19] Corliss was much harsher toward Trumbo: "Trumbo's reputation as a top screenwriter is all but inexplicable. Those of his films that cannot be dismissed as sophisticated but uninspired hack work are inevitably cursed with either preachy self-importance or cheery (but still preachy) patriotism."[20]

Whether because of their extended "vacation" from the studios, or because of their politics, or because they simply lacked great talent, radical screenwriters and directors receive short shrift from critical or aesthetic surveys of Hollywood if they are mentioned at all. If we focus only on the Ten, we find, outside of Corliss' book, no other retrospective, critical or otherwise, which discusses a member of the Ten. Nor have articles been devoted to analyses of their careers. A search through the periodical card catalogue of the library of the Academy of Motion Picture Arts and Sciences reveals only one quasi-critical article—on the one turncoat, Edward Dmytryk. In it, Romano Tozzi arrives at some rather questionable judgments: "Dmytryk's career is a very interesting one . . . his greatest achievements are still to come. . . . [H]e has the requisite integrity and idealism."[21] On the other hand, neither Andrew Sarris nor Stanley Hochman includes Dmytryk in their surveys of important Hollywood directors: *The American Cinema: Directors and Direction, 1929–1968* (a survey of two hundred directors);[22] *American Film Directors* (a survey of sixty-five directors).[23] But, while present-day critical and artistic judgments are of interest to film historians and buffs, they did not, of course, figure in the Waldorf delegates' debate over the weighted value of the Ten.

The evidence indicates that, in terms of capital worth, the producers did not sacrifice much to HUAC. Five of the men were under contract at the time of the October hearings: Cole, Lardner, Scott, Dmytryk, and Trumbo. Of the remaining five, Bessie, Biberman, Lawson, Ornitz, and Maltz, only Maltz was in demand by the studios. He eschewed long-term contracts in favor of one-picture deals, however, hoping thereby to earn sufficient money and gain the necessary time to pursue a career as a novelist. His subpoena happened to arrive as he was finishing *The Journey of Simon McKeever*, but he could easily have been under contract. His last two films—*Cloak and Dagger* (Warner Brothers) and *The Naked City* (Universal)—did excellent box office, both ranking among the top fifty grossers for the years in which they were released. Henry Ephron, a non-political screenwriter of this era, wrote in his memoirs that Maltz ranked among the top two or three writers at Warner Brothers in the mid-forties.[24]

Ornitz, the oldest of the Ten, had enjoyed a successful, though not renowned, professional career in the thirties, but he had not received a screen credit since 1944. Biberman, who had been in Hollywood since the mid-thirties, never really found himself in great demand as a director. After 1944 he had only one directing credit, though he had worked on two other films, as writer-producer and producer. Bessie, who came to Hollywood in 1943 after several years as a regular contributor to *New Masses*, had failed to live up to his early promise at Warner Brothers. Following four screen credits, and an Academy Award nomination, between 1943 and 1945, he had only a shared credit for a small independent (*Smart Woman*, Allied Artists) to show for his postwar efforts in Hollywood.

John Howard Lawson's craft and reputation as a writer had not declined since their high-water mark in the late thirties and the war years, but his notoriety as a radical had finally rendered him unpalatable to studio bosses. Despite the critical and financial success of his war films (*Sahara*, *Action in the North Atlantic*, and *Counter-Attack*), Lawson had had only one screen credit (*Smash-Up*, Universal, 1947) since Harry Cohn had fired him during the CSU strike of 1945. In short, in the only professional currency which mattered in Hollywood —"what did you do recently?"—four of the Ten held very little.

By contrast, the five contractees were rich, and highly valued by their studios. Dalton Trumbo, just short of his forty-second birthday, had recently signed (with MGM) one of the most lucrative screenwriting contracts in Hollywood annals, giving him a $3,000-a-week salary. His wartime track record at MGM—three money-makers in a row (*A Guy Named Joe*, *Thirty Seconds Over Tokyo*, and *Our Vines Have Tender Grapes*)—had earned him both the contract and the free time to attend the United Nations Founding Conference in San Francisco in 1945 as a speech writer for Secretary of State Edward Stettinius and to spend six weeks in the Pacific as a war correspondent. Those activities, along with his work as editor of *The Screen Writer*, did not interfere with his productivity as a screenwriter—Trumbo completed four scripts in three years, even though he received only one screen credit (for the original idea for a film produced by Republic Studios, *Jealousy*, 1945).

Edward Dmytryk, age thirty-nine, and Adrian Scott, age thirty-six, were two of RKO's most dependable artists. Dmytryk had directed eleven films since 1942; Scott had produced six. Their most recent collaboration, *Crossfire*, would be a box office success and would receive a large number of brotherhood and humanitarian awards. Studio head Peter Rathvon was undoubtedly sincere when he said he "sure hated to lose those boys. Brilliant craftsmen, both of them. It's just that their usefulness to the studio is at an end."[25]

Lester Cole, though only a few years older than Dmytryk or Trumbo (he was forty-three), had screen credits dating back to 1932. At one time or another in his long career he had worked for every major studio except RKO, finally signing a long-term contract with MGM in 1946. Just before the HUAC subpoena intervened, Cole stood on the threshold of a successful career with the largest studio in Hollywood: his option, calling for a salary of $1,350 a week, had just been picked up in the autumn; he was assigned to write one of MGM's biggest productions, *Zapata;* he was about to be promoted to the rank of writer-producer. All this despite the fact that his three films for Metro, *Fiesta, The Romance of Rosy Ridge,* and *High Wall,* had not recouped their collective production costs at the time of his blacklisting.[26]

Ring Lardner, Jr., the youngest of the Ten (thirty-two), was also the "hottest" property among them. His 1946 screenplay *Cloak and Dagger* (written with Maltz) ranked fiftieth in grosses; his 1947 screenplay *Forever Amber* (also co-authored) ranked fourth. Before the Waldorf conference convened Lardner had signed a new contract giving him $2,000 a week, and he was hard at work on two important films for 20th, *Britannia Mews* and *The House by the River.* After a decade in Hollywood, with an Oscar already to his credit, of distinguished lineage, Lardner had one foot in the screenwriters' pantheon before Thomas and Johnston combined to slam the door shut on his career.

Yet none of this mattered. No ten men, whatever the level of their skill, are indispensable to a huge industry overflowing with talent, both tested and untested. Conversely, the Ten's shattered careers, disrupted lives, and prolonged legal battle to stay out of jail purchased almost four years of respite from HUAC for the studio executives—not a bad bargain, actually, if screen artists are viewed merely as capital goods. The cost-benefit analysis which underlay the Waldorf decision totaled blacklist.

By the winter of 1947–48, the several strands of the Hollywood political story—having been temporarily interwoven in Washington—once again unraveled. The liberals, as an organized force, had effectively disappeared from the scene; the Ten and the radical Left were engaged in a two-front legal battle, against the studios and the contempt citations; and the producers, with the reluctant support of the guilds, were trying to unite a frightened and fragmented industry to do battle against the intra-industry Left and the national Right.

The Industry vs. HUAC, 1947–50

With the banning of the Ten "unfriendly" witnesses from studio employ, the executives fulfilled the first, and to their minds, lesser promise of the Waldorf Statement: to "eliminate subversives." Professing unconcern with the outcome of the Ten's civil litigation against the studios, the producers moved quickly to enforce their second pledge—"to safeguard a free screen"—by promulgating a strategy to counter any further incursions into Hollywood by their "real" enemy, the congressional Right. The success of this or any other anti-HUAC strategy required unity in the film industry.

None existed. Though the Motion Picture Alliance for the Preservation of American Ideals had been in regular and frantic session since the October hearings, fretting over Thomas' handling of the "unfriendly" witnesses, Alliance members continued to support HUAC fully.[27] Anti-Communist liberals, for their part, would neither join with the Communists in an anti-HUAC alliance nor publicly support the producers' Waldorf Statement. In a letter to Chat Patterson, national chairman of the American Veterans Committee, Melvyn Douglas wrote: "My only suggestion would be that liberals do not allow themselves to be confused or cajoled into joining hands with the Communists. . . . I consider this a serious mistake from the standpoint of both ideology and practical politics. I see no reason for fighting fire with fire when water is available."[28] Three weeks later, James Loeb, Jr., the national executive secretary of Americans for Democratic Action, wrote Douglas to criticize the Waldorf Statement, calling it a "disastrous decision."[29] These private outcries were rarely translated into forthright public stances. No liberal group called for the outright abolition of HUAC, although most called for its reform. The liberal guilds and unions, such as the SWG, held back in fear, while the more conservative ones, Actors and Directors, did not seem to disagree with the Committee's means or ends.

Ironically, if the studio bosses had pursued a unity strategy in the summer or fall, they might not have had to undercut their own credibility by banishing the Ten in November. Now, with a half-score lambs delivered over to the wolves, it proved difficult to establish harmony and tranquility in the barnyard.

To carry out the decisions of the Waldorf meeting, the executives set up two committees, one for each coast. The eastern committee, consisting of Barney Balaban, James Mulvey, Spyros Skouras, and Albert Warner, served mainly in an advisory capacity. The Western committee—Louis B. Mayer, Joseph Schenck, Henry Ginsberg, Dore Schary, and Walter Wanger—implemented the Waldorf Statement. Directly upon its return from New York, the West Coast group deputized Mayer, Rathvon, Wanger, and Edward Cheyfitz (representing Eric Johnston and the Producers' Association) to meet with representatives of the three major talent guilds for the purpose of "explaining" the employers' position and enlisting the employees' aid "to protect the industry and all those engaged in it" from the Thomas Committee and "to disavow any intention of a witch-hunt."[30]

They met on November 27. Ronald Reagan represented the actors, William Wyler the directors, and Sheridan Gibney, George Seaton, and Harry Tugend the writers. The implications of the Waldorf Statement greatly disturbed the guild representatives. The screen artists, too, wanted to "protect the industry," but not at the cost of a blacklist, especially an extended blacklist. None of the guild representatives challenged the blacklisting of the Ten "exposed Communists." In short, though contemporaries did not put it so baldly, the pressing question for the guilds' membership was not the existence of the Waldorf blacklist, but fear of its open-endedness. Rathvon, who had inaugurated the dismissals, now tried to reassure those whose political pasts had not yet caught up with them. He told them, "we were not going to set up nothing [sic]" by way of a formal blacklist. "We weren't going to fire people. We weren't going to fail to hire people because they were under suspicion."[31] "Communists," i.e., exposed HUAC witnesses, were, of course, excepted from Rathvon's blanket promise, but the producers hoped, with the cooperation of the guilds, to implement a publicity program which would prevent further exposures and suffering and protect "innocent people."

Late in the afternoon of the following day the Executive Board of the Screen Writers Guild convened a special meeting to hear a report from Gibney, Wyler, and Reagan. Gibney told his Board that the producers wanted the assistance of the guilds to keep "innocent people from being victimized."[32] The phrase "innocent people" needed explanation, however; it had not yet caught on as the industry-wide euphemism for "everybody but the Ten." The producers told "us," said Gibney, that unless the guilds united with management behind the Waldorf Statement there could be no assurance that the Thomas Committee would not reopen the hearings and "hurt many innocent people."[33] "Our reply," continued Gibney, was that we "could not cooperate in order to save the producers in the position already taken [at the Waldorf]" and that, furthermore, Rathvon's reassurances notwithstanding, the guilds continued to fear that they would be used as political "screening agencies."

The guilds' seeming recalcitrance on the matter of the Waldorf Statement should in no wise be construed as belated support for the Ten or for a recrudescence of left-wing politics in general. Only the day before the guild representatives were to meet a second time with the Mayer committee, the Screen Directors Guild clearly displayed its feelings about the blacklisting of one of its members. At a membership meeting on December 2 Robert Rossen rose to urge a Guild protest against the firing of Edward Dmytryk and was roundly booed. The members then passed a motion stating that no one who refused to sign the Taft-Hartley "non-Communist" affidavit could hold a Guild office.[34]

At the December 3 meeting between the representatives of the guilds and the producers, the latter accused the former of dragging their feet on the matter of intra-industry "unity." Reagan, Gibney, and Wyler repeated their profound concern with the methods management would employ to determine future hiring and firing policies. The guild representatives were determined to draw the line at "honest liberals." Again the producers spoke reassuringly: there would be no dragnet. In fact, conceded the Mayer group, management understood "that the Guilds would have to take a stand in opposition to the [Waldorf] statement"; the producers simply "hoped it would be couched in such terms as not to bring down upon the battered brow of the industry another storm of adverse public opinion."[35]

In any event, the Mayer committee failed to extract a formal statement of acquiescence from the guilds. On the contrary, the directors passed a resolution opposing the principle of blacklisting incarnated in the Waldorf Statement, calling it "fundamentally insincere" and criticizing the policy of the producers as one which promoted the very "atmosphere of fear which the statement professes to deplore."[36] The writers could not agree among themselves on the wording of any kind of statement, so they issued none, but they did vote to fight future firings and to sponsor *amicus curiae* briefs in the civil litigation suits.[37] The actors also issued no formal reply to the Mayer committee, but in mid-January the Screen Actors Guild passed a resolution requiring all its officers to sign anti-Communist affidavits.[38] The guilds' stubbornness in this relatively minor matter of support for the Waldorf principles became meaningless and hypocritical as a result of their *de facto* acquiescence in management's blacklisting of the Ten. No guild representative, and no guild, at any time demanded or urged the rehiring of the Ten, and in the eyes of the producers *this* posture and this posture alone was crucial.

Thus by the end of the year, as far as the entire industry was concerned, the Ten were non-persons. In early January SWG members handily defeated—333–224—a resolution presented by left-winger

Hugo Butler calling on the Guild to fight for the reinstatement of the three fired writers and to provide them with legal counsel in their breach of contract suits against the studios.[39] The attitude which predominated in Hollywood was aptly expressed by liberal producer Dore Schary: "I was faced with the alternative of supporting the stand taken by my company or of quitting my job. . . . I like making pictures. I want to stay in the industry. I like it."[40]

Limiting industry losses to the Ten, however, proved much harder than anyone suspected. Despite all the fulminations against HUAC, the atmosphere of censorship and intimidation engendered by the Thomas Committee engulfed the film-making capital. "A studio executive in charge of reading scripts" told Lillian Ross that a new kind of self-censorship was emerging in Hollywood:

> It's automatic, like shifting gears. . . . I now read scripts through the eyes of the D.A.R., whereas formerly I read them through the eyes of my boss. . . . I'm all loused up. I'm scared to death, and nobody can tell me it isn't because I'm afraid of being investigated.[41]

A month later *Variety* reported that anti-Communist films, once avoided as box office death, have "become the hottest [theme] to hit the screen this year."[42] The studios had responded to the broad hints of Representative Richard Nixon (R-Calif.) to make films which warned the American people about the dangers of communism.[43] Incredibly, in the face of poor box office and a survey indicating that the public had no interest in anti-Russian or anti-Communist films, the studios turned out over fifty such movies.

What should have proven even more disturbing to industry liberals who were silent about the Committee's activities was that the promising postwar trend of movies with social content came to a jarring halt. In August 1948 *Variety* wrote that "studios are continuing to drop plans for 'message' pictures like hot coals." For example, 20th Century-Fox shelved the script for a film called *Quality*, in which a black nurse fell in love with a white doctor;* while Columbia fastidiously scrubbed *Portrait of an American Communist* because the script called for sympathetic treatment of the lead character before his conversion to "Stalinism."[44]

---

* 20th did not cancel *Quality;* the film's name was changed—to *Pinky*—and Dudley Nichols' script was rewritten by Philip Dunne.

In sum there existed substantial grounds for the Ten to sing a chorus of "I Told You So," had they but the breath and the heart.

The Ten's Fight to Stay Out of Jail, 1947–50

"Auld Lang Syne" no doubt held a special poignancy for the Ten as it ushered out 1947. The blacklisted screen artists discovered how soon old acquaintances could "be forgot and never brought to mind." Having been participants in, indeed at the center of, some of the mightiest Hollywood political battles of the preceding fifteen years, they now stood suddenly deserted and exposed, lepers rather than colleagues. Lardner remembers how "numbed" he felt at the overnight disappearance of nearly all supporters and co-combatants. The Ten were reduced to depending on themselves, their lawyers, their fellow Communists, and a small group of non-Party sympathizers.

The Nineteen reduced itself to the Ten in late November. Brecht left for Switzerland, and the other eight, who had not been cited for contempt of Congress, tried to return to the business of making motion pictures. Gordon Kahn and Waldo Salt, especially Kahn, remained active in the campaign to "Save the Hollywood Ten," while the others offered money and moral support. Howard Koch alone broke ranks with the strategy which had been agreed upon in early October—he announced, by means of an ad in the *Hollywood Reporter*, that he "had never been a member of the Communist Party." Koch softened the blow of his defection somewhat by reserving the right to refuse to repeat this statement before HUAC, and by admonishing the industry to "stand firm" and "defend ourselves by defending each other."[45]

The careers of Salt and Kahn alone suffered serious disruption between October 1947 and April 1951; five of the others worked regularly in those years, while the sixth, Richard Collins, enjoyed as many screen credits (zero) as he had between 1943 and 1947. Dore Schary fired Salt in November, but not for "political reasons."[46] Kahn's last contract with a major studio, Warner Brothers, had expired in February 1947, and he received few calls thereafter.

Foremost among the non-Communist liberals who strongly supported the Ten's efforts to stay out of jail and to warn the American people about the dangers of HUAC were Thomas Emerson of the Yale Law School, Walter Gellhorn of the Columbia Law School, Carey McWilliams, I. F. Stone, Henry Steele Commager of Amherst College, and Alexander Meiklejohn, a former law professor and university president, who had just finished delivering a series of lectures on free speech at the University of Chicago, Yale, Dartmouth, and other universities.

Without jobs and powerful allies, the Ten's fight became a defensive one, no longer to beard the HUAC lion, but to keep from being mauled by it. The terrain of battle now centered on extensive anti-HUAC speaking tours to inform the public and raise money for legal expenses and on legal contests to fight the contempt citations and sue the studios for breach of contract. For the first time the judicial front became as important as the political and propaganda fronts of the "radical-reactionary war"—as did the professional, as the Ten scrambled to eke out what work they could on an anonymous or exile basis.

In those years between the hearings and jail the focus of activity shifted from the homes of potential supporters and donors to the offices of lawyers and agents and to the courtrooms and congressional chambers of the United States Government. On November 24, the same day the producers began their Waldorf conclave, the United States House of Representatives met to consider the contempt citations which its Committee on Un-American Activities had just voted against ten screen artists. The Ten's efforts to combat the citations had already been set in motion, while Congress had been in recess. The attorneys had "requested" Speaker of the House Joseph Martin (R-Mass.) not to certify the contempt citations alone—as House rules entitled him—but to wait until the House had reconvened. Since the conservatives had no more desire to hide the proceedings from the public than did the Ten, the latter won a minor victory—their only one.

The conservatives, notably the members of the Thomas Committee, used the occasion and the forum to defend their handiwork of October by means of a scurrilous excoriation of the "unfriendly" witnesses. Two of the Ten—Maltz and Trumbo—were singled out for debate and recorded vote, while the remaining eight were dispatched seriatim by voice vote. The crux of the case against the "unfriendly" witnesses was political: they had, in Thomas' words, "over a period of years" engaged in "Communist activities" and no amount of "fog about constitutional rights [and] the First Amendment" should obscure this political conspiracy against the United States. The Ten's recalcitrance before HUAC exemplified their politics, said Thomas. "The reason these ten individuals refused to answer the question was because [sic] they were Communists. They knew we had the evidence that they were Communists. . . ."[47] Maltz was singled out by Representative McDowell of HUAC as "a colonel in the conspiratorial, political army of Soviet Russia. . . ." Maltz deserved, said McDowell, "the medals that are given to a comrade" whose long-term activities and efforts have amounted to dedicated political criticism of the policies of the United States Government, particularly the Congress.

> [T]his man was the most arrogant, the most contemptible, the most bitter of all these people who do not believe in their own country. Here is a typical Communist intellectual, burning with a bitter hatred of the country he was born in, its Government, its officials, and its people.[48]

It is unclear why McDowell singled out Maltz, whose testimony was less angry and strident than some of the others'. Furthermore, there was an interesting contrast between the dignified, albeit critical, tone of Maltz's written statement (which began "I am an American and I believe there is no more proud word in the vocabulary of man") and the scurrilous, demeaning tenor of the Pennsylvania congressman's attack.

Only a handful of (mostly Democratic) liberal congressmen spoke out against the pillorying of the Hollywood film artists. Some, like Chet Holifield (D-Calif.), reiterated that constitutionality cannot be flouted because of a political war or an anti-Communist atmosphere: "The issue is whether we believe in the basic principles of a Government by law, or whether we turn, in the cowering fear of the moment, under the pressure of hysteria, to the variable judgment of scared men.[49] Others, like Herman P. Eberharter (D-Pa.), agreed about the constitutional issue—"we can support the recommendations of [HUAC] or we can support free speech. We cannot have both."— but went on to expose the real motive of Thomas et al.: "I cannot escape the conclusion that there is some justification for the charge . . . that the purpose of this committee was not to destroy an existent subversive threat in Hollywood, but to intimidate and control the movie industry."[50] Jacob Javits (R-N.Y.) and Emanuel Celler (D-N.Y.), while not contesting Congress' right to conduct a political investigation, did criticize the means and tactics of HUAC.[51] This liberal opposition was engulfed by the tide of votes affirming the Committee's contempt citations: 347–17 (in Maltz's case); 240–16 (in Trumbo's).[52]

The vote occasioned no surprise among the Ten or their lawyers. Nor, given the political circumstances, did the unprecedented alacrity with which Attorney General Tom Clark requested and received indictments from a federal grand jury (on December 5). (This in contrast to the Roosevelt Justice Department, which had been noted for its foot-dragging in HUAC-related cases.) Shortly afterward the federal district court to which the case was assigned denied the Ten's request for a collective trial. The screen artists would now be obliged to undertake, on an individual basis, the expense of a full trial defense. Lawson once again led off, with Trumbo to follow. After both these men had been convicted, however, the prosecution and defense agreed to a formula: the other eight screen artists would not be tried in the lower court, but would accept for themselves the final verdict (following the exhaustion of the appeal process) rendered on Lawson and Trumbo.

The groups which now materialized to aid the Ten in their legal and political fight were administered by the Ten themselves, their families, and the hundred or so left-wing families living in Hollywood, in all a very tiny percentage of the thirty thousand people who worked in the film industry. Within this much reduced left-wing contingent (the Freedom from Fear Committee and the Committee to Free the Hollywood Ten) life and activity persisted, along with dedication to the tasks at hand and faith in a felicitous outcome. Sylvia Jarrico recalled the passion and stubbornness of some of those who supported the Ten: "We thought the Ten would win at every stage of their trial and appeals. Our community held together really well during this struggle. The issues were so clear-cut that I felt I made a point every time I opened my mouth."

The battlements were fortified, for the most part, with Communists. The Hollywood branch of the Party had been momentarily strengthened by the hearings. Screenwriter Alfred Levitt, a relative newcomer to the Hollywood Left, noted that "the 1947 hearings shook up the radical community pretty badly, but at first there was a show of solidarity. Many more people might have left the Party then if it had not been under attack." The Party, however, and the leading front organization with which it was involved—the Progressive Citizens of America—had bigger worries than the plight of the Ten. The Smith Act indictments threatened a wholesale incarceration of the CPUSA's national and state leadership, while the PCA was preoccupied with the project of founding a third party to elect Henry Wallace to the presidency of the United States.

Herbert Biberman tried to compensate for the lack of support and resources with sheer drive, determination, and energy. "He was," remembered Maltz, "the super dynamo behind all our activities." Biberman worked closely with Pauline Finn, a former employee of the Screen Writers Guild and director of the Hollywood Writers' Mobilization, to establish the PCA-sponsored Freedom from Fear Committee. Operating from a small house on Yucca Street in Hollywood, a small staff of volunteers raised funds, arranged national speaking tours for the Ten, gathered signatures for the *amicus curiae* brief written by Alexander Meiklejohn and Carey McWilliams, and organized a national Stop Censorship campaign. Much of the money that the Committee raised came in the form of cash from people opposed to HUAC, but fearful of being identified with the Ten. Edward Biberman remembered that "the state of fear and terror in those months was such that anyone who even offered anonymous cash gifts seemed courageous."

Though upward of $150,000 was raised, neither the fund-raisers ("New Year's Eve with the Hollywood Ten" at Lucey's restaurant, "Election Night with the Ten" at the Butler home, or "A Thanksgiving Meeting with the Ten" at the El Patio Theatre) nor the countless speeches, nor the pamphlets, nor Gordon Kahn's "objective study," *Hollywood on Trial*, nor the movie *The Hollywood Ten*, generated anything like the broad-based support necessary to force the Thomas Committee to cease and desist, the courts to find for the Ten, or the studios to scrub the blacklist. The theme of "we're first, but you're next" was repeated *ad infinitum*, but though many heard, few responded.

In the heat of the warnings and appeals, the trials opened. The legal strategy of the Ten had long been agreed upon. Unlike their confrontation with HUAC, the judicial resistance would be constitutional and procedural, not political. The main argument, stated in each defendant's trial brief, was that the "particular questions put to the defendant . . . violated the rights reserved to the defendant under the first, fourth, fifth, ninth, and tenth amendments to the Constitution to be protected from official inquisition that can compel disclosure of his private beliefs and associations."[53] The Ten's lawyers had gathered evidence to establish that the Committee considered the Communist Party to be a criminal conspiracy, that the purpose of the hearings was to inflict penalties upon those it believed to be Communists, and that the proceedings were specifically directed against the "unfriendly" witnesses. In sum, the lawyers for Lawson and Trumbo argued that the purpose of the hearings was not to investigate "un-American activities" but to punish men whom Thomas and his colleagues believed to be political criminals.

However well grounded in legal principle and substantive evidence, the Ten's fate rested on a hope and a prayer—that the federal judiciary had not been seriously infected by the political conservatism and anti-communism which floated in the late forties air. They hoped in vain. One month before Lawson's trial opened in mid-April 1948 attorney Kenny received a letter from former congressman Maury Maverick (D-Tex.), informing him that:

> [T]he tide is going against you. . . . No one even dares to support the Ten. . . . [L]egislative and judicial personal opinions and mass psychology, backed by the people, is [sic] aggressively against. Not a single judge, Congressman, or Senator (other than Marcantonio,† who will hurt) will rise to say a word in defense. . . . In other words the Ten are regarded as war criminals, more so than ever.[54]

Maverick's sense of doom was borne out a few days later. On March 18 the Ten's main line of legal defense—the First Amendment—was sundered. Dr. Edward Barsky and sixteen members of the governing board of the Joint Anti-Fascist Refugee Committee had been cited for contempt of Congress on December 30, 1946, for refusing to produce the records of their organization or to answer HUAC's questions. In the case of *Barsky et al.* v. *United States*, Circuit Court of Appeals judge E. Barrett Prettyman ruled that "Congress has power to make an inquiry of an individual which may elicit the answers that the witness is a believer in Communism or a member of the Communist Party."[55] In sum, the prior intentions and conclusions of congressmen are not at issue when Congress duly establishes an investigatory committee. Samuel Rosenwein, one of the Ten's eastern attorneys, did not appear too downcast. He wrote Martin Popper on June 17: "Upon us has now fallen the signal honor of carrying on the struggle to scale the Olympian heights. The Supreme Court will not be able to keep us out because we have history on our side."[56]

With the *Barsky* precedent in hand, the federal judge at Lawson's trial had little difficulty in confining the issue to the defendant's contemptuous recalcitrance before HUAC rather than the broader political questions of the Thomas Committee's constitutionality or its hidden agenda. The right of HUAC to ask the questions it did was ruled non-justiciable (i.e., outside the provenance of the judge's powers).

---

† Vito Marcantonio was first elected to Congress in 1934, after serving as a longtime assistant to Fiorello La Guardia. During his tenure of office (until 1950, with a two-year "vacation" from 1936–38), he was the most consistently pro-labor, civil libertarian Representative.

Lawson was found guilty of contempt of Congress on April 19, one week after his trial began. Trumbo's verdict came down on May 5.

In June the Supreme Court of the United States refused to review the *Barsky* case. Shortly thereafter the same Circuit Court of Appeals with which Lawson and Trumbo had filed their appeals upheld the conviction of Gerhard Eisler (alleged Comintern delegate to the CPUSA) for contempt of HUAC. While the appeal was pending the Ten demonstrated their solidarity with the Barsky group by publishing an ad in the trades and participating in a protest at the Embassy Auditorium in Los Angeles. In the autumn of 1948 the Ten themselves received some welcome support from Albert Einstein, Thomas Mann, E. B. White, and others. These luminaries, acting under the auspices of the National Council of Arts, Sciences, and Professions, signed a statement written by Maltz urging organizations to submit *amicus curiae* briefs on the Ten's behalf. The soon-to-be-convicted writer made one last impassioned plea for assistance: "[The Hollywood Ten] are the last barrier in the Courts to these modern witch hunters. If the Hollywood Ten win, the Bill of Rights will be affirmed and the inquisitions will cease. If they lose—then it will be a dark, dark time for free thought, free speech and free culture in America."[57] Nineteen organizations, mainly left-wing CIO labor unions and Communist-dominated rump groups left over from the Popular Front era, and four hundred individuals responded either with briefs of their own or with signatures on the one prepared by Alexander Meiklejohn.‡

On June 13, 1949, Circuit Court of Appeals chief justice Bennett C. Clark ruled in the cases of *Lawson* v. *United States* and *Trumbo* v. *United States*:

So that there may be no mistakes or misunderstanding and because the point here involved has proven to be one of constant recurrence, we expressly hold herein that the House Committee on Un-

---

‡ Among the non-Communist writers who signed the brief were Philip Dunne, Julius Epstein, Melvin Frank, Albert Hackett, Edwin Justus Mayer, Peter Viertel, Norman Panama, Arthur Miller, and Marc Connelly. The organizations included the American Civil Liberties Union, National Lawyers Guild, American Jewish Congress, Methodist Federation for Social Action, and eight CIO unions: American Communications Association; Food, Tobacco, Agricultural & Allied Workers; International Fur & Leather Workers; International Union of Mine, Mill & Smelter Workers; United Electrical Workers; United Furniture Workers; United Office & Professional Workers; United Public Workers. (Most of these were expelled from the CIO in the next few years.)

American Activities, or a properly appointed subcommittee thereof, has the *power* to inquire whether a witness subpoenaed by it is or is not a member of the Communist Party or a believer in communism and that this power carries with it necessarily the power to effect criminal punishment for failure or refusal to answer that question. . . . This is equally true of the inquiry whether appellants were members of the Screen Writers Guild.[58]

In the accompanying reasoning Justice Clark resituated the issue of the Ten v. HUAC in its political and ideological context. Indeed, the judge's language clearly subsumed the legal and constitutional questions into his own definition of nationalism—a nationalism defined and reinforced by the prevailing Cold War climate:

> No one can doubt in these chaotic times that the destiny of all nations hangs in the balance in the current ideological struggle between communistic-thinking and democratic-thinking peoples of the world. Neither Congress nor any court is required to disregard the impact of world events, however impartially or dispassionately they view them. It is equally beyond dispute that the motion picture industry plays a critically important role in the molding of public opinion and that motion pictures are, or are capable of being, a potent medium of propaganda dissemination which may influence the minds of millions of American people. This being so, it is absurd to argue, as these appellants do, that questions asked men who, by their authorship of the scripts, vitally influence the ultimate production of motion pictures seen by millions, which questions require disclosure of whether or not they are or ever have been Communists, are not pertinent questions. Indeed, it is hard to envisage how there could be any more pertinent question. . . .[59]

After reading this opinion, Ben Margolis began to formulate the opinion he would state many years later: "It simply didn't matter how strong a case you could argue with facts or constitutionality in this period; if your case involved the Communist Party you could not win it."

At the time, however, the Ten and their lawyers believed that a friendly majority on the Supreme Court would undo the expected defeats at the trial and intermediate appellate levels. It was virtually gospel in the ranks of the "unfriendly" witnesses that Black, Douglas, Jackson, Murphy, and Rutledge would vanquish HUAC with the First Amendment. Even without the unexpected deaths of Murphy (on

July 19, 1949) and Rutledge (on September 10, 1949), however, it is possible that the "Roosevelt Court" would not have lived up to its "liberal" image, given the highly charged political atmosphere in Washington in 1950. The replacements, though, did not help matters: the conservative Attorney General Tom Clark, who had directed Japanese relocation in World War II and had authored the Attorney General's list of subversive organizations in December 1947, and Sherman Minton, whose subsequent record on civil liberties belied his previous loyalty to the New Deal as a senator from Indiana and then a presidential assistant.

With only Black and Douglas dissenting, the Supreme Court, in April 1950, denied *certiorari* to (i.e., refused to hear) the Lawson and Trumbo cases. On June 11 the two writers entered the federal penal facility at Ashland, Kentucky, to begin their one-year terms. In the course of that same month their eight comrades, according to the earlier agreement, underwent brief trials (lasting less than an hour) and were convicted and sentenced. Adrian Scott was not sentenced until September 27; he was suffering from stomach and intestinal problems and was too ill to travel to Washington. No appeals followed; it had been agreed that Lawson and Trumbo alone would chart those waters. The legal battle was over, lost. At his sentencing Ring Lardner, Jr., told the court:

> Everything I know about the history of inquisitions and test oaths confirms my conviction that there is only a minor difference between forcing a man to say what his opinions are and dictating what his opinions should be. Whenever men have been compelled to open their minds to government authority, men's minds have ceased to be free.[60]

By June 1950, Lardner and eight of his nine colleagues had lost their physical freedom as well.

Just before they entered their several places of incarceration, the Ten completed a hurriedly produced film about their case which they intended to serve as a means for carrying on the fight and raising funds to pay their astronomical legal costs. That film, *The Hollywood Ten*, a twenty-minute political tract narrated by Academy Award-winning actress Gale Sondergaard, wife of Herbert Biberman (and herself one of the first witnesses to be called in the second round of HUAC hearings which began in 1951), was noteworthy for its utter lack of self-pity. The Ten clearly had no desire to appear as martyrs but as (once again) political activists doing the job they had been doing since the thirties. The didactic body of the film showed the Ten sitting at a table, commenting on political repression in America during the late forties. Biberman spoke of "thought control," Maltz and Cole of the "Cold War" and its domestic effects; Bessie described a "developing nightmare of fear," and Dmytryk spoke of "government by stool pigeon." Periodically a member of the group would punctuate the narrative with a pointed question directed at the viewer: "HUAC is now free to operate," said Ornitz. "How will *you* answer their questions?" The film ended on a direct challenge by Biberman: "There need be no more [like us]—it depends on you."

The film, like its makers, was blacklisted. The only distribution network which agreed to handle *The Hollywood Ten* was composed of the wives and friends of the jailed men. Sadie Ornitz, Sylvia Jarrico, Gale Sondergaard, and others carted the film from meeting hall to auditorium to living room. Even this circumscribed distribution discomposed business and government circles. Although the powers did not fear that domestic commercial exhibitors would risk boycott and Redbaiting by allowing *The Hollywood Ten* to be shown on their premises, foreign distribution was another question. *Variety* reported that "the Motion Picture Association of America, the United States State Department, and other groups concerned with U.S. public relations abroad, reportedly are agitated over [efforts] to give the film wide distribution overseas."[61] Official and unofficial pressures emanating from the United States Government and American corporations hindered foreign, as well as domestic, play of the film.

The Ten's Fight Against the Blacklist, 1947–55

The Ten were as successful in civil litigation as they had been in their criminal proceedings. Individually and collectively they filed eight civil suits charging breach of contract and conspiracy to blacklist against the studios.* They lost every one—albeit they settled some out of court. Even when they won at the trial level—as Cole, Lardner, and Scott managed to do—the jury verdicts were either overturned by an

---

* The individual suits: *Cole* v. *Loew's, Inc.*, won at the trial level, reversed on appeal, dropped in January 1952; *Dmytryk* v. *RKO*, dropped; *Scott* v. *RKO*, won at the trial level, new trial ordered, appeal opposing new trial order denied; *Trumbo* v. *Loew's, Inc.*, dropped; *Lardner* v. *Twentieth Century-Fox*, won at trial level, reversed on appeal, settled out of court. The collective suits: *Cole et al.* v. *Loew's, Inc. et al.*, settled for $107,500; *Maltz et al.* v. *Loew's, Inc. et al.*, dropped; *Young et al.* v. *Motion Picture Association of America, Inc. et al.*, settled for $100,000 (see Chapter 12).

appellate court or new trials were granted by the trial judge. With the
exception of Federal District Court judge Leon R. Yankwich, who
presided over *Cole* v. *Loew's, Inc.*, no magistrate in the country
proved sympathetic to the Ten's claims that their testimony before
HUAC had not harmed their employers. Yankwich alone found the
producers' reasons baseless. In his statement accepting the jury's verdict
in Cole's favor, on December 20, 1948, the judge noted that at no time
in his conversations with Cole did Louis Mayer broach the subject of
the "morals clause." For Mayer, then, continued Yankwich, neither
morality nor communism was ever at issue.

> [T]he policy that was adopted was not the policy that MGM
> wanted to adopt. It was the policy that Mr. Eric Johnston sought
> to have adopted at the [producers'] meeting in July [1947] and in
> which he was not successful. . . . Mr. Johnston indicated [in his
> testimony in this trial] that it was his insistence, his high-pressure
> methods that resulted in the adoption of this policy.[62]

Yankwich's temerity did not go unnoticed by the witch-hunters. The
Tenney Committee concluded that this case, the judge's opposition to
the state's criminal syndicalism statute twenty years earlier, and his
regular participation in ACLU forums rendered Yankwich "not
qualified, because of his obvious bias and sympathy for pro-Communist, pro-Soviet causes, to sit on the federal bench."[63]

Loew's, Incorporated, MGM's parent company, appealed on the
basis of "misrulings" and "prejudicial error" on Yankwich's part. The
appellate justice, Walter Pope, who heard the case agreed with the appellant's contention that communism was indeed an issue in this case
and, further, that Mayer's failure to warn Cole about the "morals
clause" prior to the hearings did not prejudice the studio's case in
discharging the writer after the hearings. Finding that "the net effect
of the [HUAC] hearing was to make Cole a distinct liability to his
employer," Pope reversed the judgment and remanded the case.[64] Similarly, when 20th Century-Fox appealed an adverse finding in the
Lardner case, the appellate judge found that "the conduct and the ultimate conviction of Lardner in the circumstances of the case could not
help but hurt Fox and everybody else in the motion picture business."[65] Scott had been awarded $84,300 by a jury in April 1952. Federal judge Ben Harrison overturned the verdict and ordered a new
trial, because the jury "failed to appreciate the whole picture of the
situation." He added that Scott and Lardner, whose suit was tried si-

multaneously with Scott's, were not "men of courage. If they had been, they would have stood up and been counted."[66]

Again and again, the Ten found that juries proved much less "politicized" than judges. The former remained unswayed by the evidence which the studio lawyers had gathered to demonstrate that the politics or behavior of the "unfriendly" witnesses and their convictions for contempt of Congress had had any appreciable impact on studio reputations or receipts. Despite the most strenuous efforts of a small army of lawyers and investigators, the only hard bits of evidence which management could produce to prove box office damage were the picketing of a Chaplin picture in New Jersey and the stoning of a Hepburn film in North Carolina. Since neither of these stars had anything to do with the Ten, the Nineteen, or HUAC (except that the actress had signed, along with hundreds of others, a Committee for the First Amendment petition), the relevance of this evidence was immediately placed in question. Studio executives like Louis B. Mayer could not, when pressed, cite "direct evidence" that Cole's or Trumbo's films were being attacked by audiences.[67] Eddie Mannix rattled off some unfavorable press and radio statements about the Ten, but could offer no figures or percentages to prove that such negative commentary had affected the studio's grosses. Nevertheless, Mannix insisted that "any criticism" is "harmful," adding that he had "information, whether true or untrue, that organizations in America were about to put on a campaign against the picture business, particularly against the members who had defied Congress."[68]

The Ten's attorneys mustered a formidable case for their clients simply by shooting more holes in the already tattered evidence offered by studio management. It proved relatively easy to show, for example, that the success or failure of a movie associated with one of the Ten had nothing to do with political or "moral" questions. Peter Rathvon had to admit that *Crossfire*—directed by Dmytryk and produced by Scott—continued, even after the hearings, to prosper financially and reap awards.[69] George Hickey, western sales manager for Loew's, tried to show, by reading from his collection of booking cards, that Lester Cole's movies were being canceled as a result of the unfavorable publicity connected with his appearance before HUAC. It turned out, however, that of the nine cancellations, two occurred at theaters which had closed down altogether and the remaining seven at theaters which had canceled a number of films. In fact, some of Cole's films had been retained by these seven. To underscore the point that these cancellations reflected the entertainment value of the film, and not the politics of its writer, and to impeach further Hickey's extrapolations, the plaintiff's attorney could point to the fact that a film—*Cynthia*—having nothing to do with the Ten had been canceled at more theaters than any Cole picture.[70]

The plaintiff's refutations did not stop there. An Audience Research Poll, conducted by George Gallup for the producers themselves, indicated that only 13 per cent of the respondents believed that the Hollywood film industry shielded Communists, while over 85 per cent could not name one or more of the "unfriendly" witnesses. Gallup concluded:

> The evidence points to the fact that the public has little awareness of possible Communistic influences, if any, in pictures being produced today. Also, few could name any particular player whom they thought of as a Communist or Communist sympathizer. . . . Findings from these studies indicate that the congressional investigation—at least that part of it which is now being completed—will have little immediate effect on the boxoffice.[71]

While Gallup canvassed the citizenry, the studios' attorneys, Loeb and Loeb, had scoured the country for organizations and witnesses who could claim both to know about, and to hate, the Ten. They finally managed to assemble thirteen such groups, including the Knights of Columbus of Lafayette, Indiana; the Sheridan Women's Club of Sheridan, Wyoming; the Catholic War Veterans of Santa Fe, New Mexico; five Veterans of Foreign War posts; and two American Legion posts. On further examination, however, it turned out that only three of these worthy assemblies had actually adopted resolutions condemning Hollywood Communists, while none had barred their members from attending films connected with the Ten, or with any other radical or liberal film artists.[72]

In every case which came to trial, then, juries found for the screen artist plaintiffs. Counting retrials, five panels did not accept the defendants' assertion that the issues of communism or contempt of Congress provided justifiable grounds for a studio to invoke the morals clause and breach its contract with an employee. Each time the sanctity of the formal commercial compact outweighed, in the jurors' minds, the testimony and evidence presented by Loeb and Loeb. And each time a judge intervened to overturn the conclusions of the juries. Jurors were not necessarily less infected by the prevailing anti-Communist mood than judges; rather, the jurors were more moved by the obvious contrast between plaintiffs and defendants—the Ten made a far more sincere, sympathetic impression than Johnston, Mayer, Mannix, or Rathvon—as well as by the specifically legal and moral dimensions of the case. In America, however, judges have the final say; the Ten, and the blacklisted screen artists who followed, never succeeded in winning judicial recognition of the existence of a conspiracy to blacklist.

The Lives of the Ten

Three days before Christmas, 1947, Albert Maltz wrote to Robert Kenny appraising the situation of the Ten to date. "I think we have *done magnificently*. And the basic reason for this, as I see it, is because [sic] we have *fundamentally* challenged the Thomas Committee and the entire reactionary movement of which it is the spearhead." Maltz acknowledged the difficulty of the fight, but termed it "a good fight, a very good one, a proud one."[73] Ten months later, in a private letter to his co-defendants, Maltz's tone had changed radically. "We are," he wrote then, "financially and physically depleted." They were no longer "the functioning unit" they had once been. The various fund-raising drives they had organized that summer were "almost disastrous failures." The group had only $2,000 in its coffers, when almost $50,000 was needed to continue the appeals process. If they failed to appeal, not only would they go to jail, concluded Maltz, but the Thomas Committee would continue as "a roving Star Chamber" and little Thomas Committees would appear "everywhere."[74]

The Ten's physical cohesion, so important to the group's morale, had been attenuated by the individual scramble for money to live on. Dmytryk had gone to England to find work; Scott to Paris and Lardner to Switzerland to do likewise. Cole, Lawson, and Lardner had their homes up for sale, while Ornitz and Bessie were living off loans and "charity" from friends. Trumbo could not even secure a loan. He wrote his agent, "In the last week I have discovered that no bank will lend on my cars, although they are both late models and in excellent condition." Even Trumbo's home, a ranch in Ventura County, which he owned outright, would not fetch "a penny" in mortgage loans.[75] Dmytryk's savings were being siphoned off by alimony payments to his former wife. Only Maltz and Biberman appeared solvent, but the legal expenses and the lack of regular income strained their resources as well. Dmytryk secured two directing jobs in London and Maltz, Cole, and Trumbo were offered black market writing jobs, albeit at greatly reduced rates. The various criminal and civil cases, as well as the day-to-day expense of maintaining their families, quickly drained these irregular sources of income.

Between 1948 and 1950, although only seven of the Ten—the writers—could function anonymously in the United States, the professional atmosphere was still considerably looser than it was to become following the opening of the second round of HUAC hearings in 1951. In the months after the 1947 hearings no one in Hollywood realized the path on which America was heading, and independent producers had not yet caught on to the exploitable situation of blacklisted writers. Thus Maltz received a fair sum—$33,750—for a script which was submitted under the name of a friend. Maltz soon tasted, however, the gall of his new status. Two weeks after purchasing his newly published novel, *The Journey of Simon McKeever*, 20th Century-Fox shelved the screenplay. An outcry from the Motion Picture Alliance for the Preservation of American Ideals had been heard in New York, and the studio's Board of Directors pulled the project out of the production schedule. In a letter to the Screen Writers Guild, Maltz spoke of the "absolutely unprecedented" nature of Fox's action and of the "spreading net" of fear which caused it.[76] Five years later, Maltz and Lardner learned that commercial publishers in this country did not care, in the case of the Hollywood Ten, to buck the Cold War climate either (see Chapter 12). As on the scriptwriting black market, the Ten were not completely shut out from the world of publishing until after 1951. Before entering prison, Lawson saw the publication of his cultural history of the United States: *The Hidden Heritage: A Rediscovery of the Ideas and Forces That Link the Thought of Our Time with the Culture of the Past*, New York: Citadel Press, 1950. While he was in prison, Samuel Ornitz oversaw the final proofs of his novel: *Bride of the Sabbath*, New York: Rinehart, 1951.

Jail and the Surrender of Edward Dmytryk

Obviously none of the Ten wished to go to jail, but by the time the moment of incarceration arrived, they had resigned themselves to their fate. None of them, with the possible exception of Dmytryk, considered the possibility of recanting and, whatever his inner thoughts, he remained outwardly solid and steadfast. Something of the attitude which steeled these men for the upcoming tribulation was demonstrated by Biberman when he was asked by his parole adviser if, given similar circumstances, he would again behave in an "unfriendly" manner toward HUAC. Biberman replied:

> If I were brought before a Committee which in my opinion was threatening the foundation of our liberties by its action—how could a man who conceived of citizenship and duty as I do not challenge what he was deeply convinced his duty impelled him to challenge as evil and destructive?[77]

Lawson, Trumbo, and Scott served their time at Ashland, Kentucky; Cole and Lardner at Danbury, Connecticut; Maltz and Dmytryk at Mill Point, West Virginia; Sam Ornitz at Springfield, Missouri; Bessie and Biberman at Texarkana, Texas. Cole and Lardner were pleasantly surprised one day to find that a new inmate at Danbury was none other than their old acquaintance Parnell Thomas. The New Jersey congressman had been sentenced for padding his office payroll. Lester Cole happened to pass the former HUAC chairman, now busily at work in the prison's chicken coop. Cole said something of a political nature, to which Thomas replied, "I see that you are still spouting radical nonsense." Said Cole: "And I see that you are still shoveling chicken shit."

According to their letters and memories the Ten did not suffer physically in prison so much as they simmered inwardly. They were model prisoners and got on quite well with their inmates, most of whom knew nothing and cared less about the screen artists' "turpitude." Maltz wrote to Kenny that the other prisoners were surprised to learn there even was such a crime as contempt of Congress, while "Communism [to them] was only a word."[78] Behind the exterior of well-behaved jailbirds, however, impatience and anger and bitterness seethed. Wanting to return to society as soon as possible, they spent part of their leisure time filling out parole applications—none of which succeeded. Biberman wrote to his attorneys that his anger at being locked up intensified rather than cooled as the days went by. He could find no "positive values in this 'experience,'" but implied that negative emotions like bitterness, self-pity, or the desire for revenge constantly threatened to occupy his thoughts and constantly had to be fought. He wondered "how long it will take to have [these feelings] wear off—when one is free again?"[79] Bessie was much less contained in his letters to Kenny, exploding in one: "I curse the day that Warner Brothers called me in New York in January 1943 and asked me if I would like to write motion-pictures."[80] Just after his release Maltz wrote Kenny that his time in prison "was the hardest year I've ever put in. To be locked up is a very, very deep violation of one's living spirit."[81]

Preying on all their minds was the stark specter of professional and financial destitution once they were released. The jobs and salaries offered to the imprisoned Ten in sponsorship of their parole applications could not have allayed their anxiety. Lester Cole, instead of the writer-producer position which was to be his at MGM, now had the prospect of a position as an assistant copy writer in the advertising department of the Sealy Mattress Company at a salary of $400 a month. Herbert Biberman could look forward to a new life as an assistant buyer for the Pacific Coast Textile Company at $100 a week. The others collected a series of vague promises and offers from various publishers, agents, and producers.[82] Though the jobs themselves may not have eased the minds of the Ten, the very existence of *any* job offer at all, given the temper of the times, represented courage and generosity on the part of the offerer. As grateful as they were to their sponsors, the Ten felt infinitely more thankful for their attoneys— Margolis, Katz, Kenny, Rosenwein, and Popper—who rendered, frequently without remuneration, constant legal services.

The intensity of the professional anxiety weighing upon the Ten in prison was poignantly illustrated by the collapse of one of them, who appeared before HUAC to recant his political past and announce his new politics less than a year after the jail door had slammed shut behind him and he was struck by the realization: "I am actually locked up." Although one of the youngest members of the Ten, Dmytryk had been in the film industry the longest. In 1923, at the age of fifteen, he had taken a job as messenger boy at Paramount Studios. He slowly worked his way up—with one year off to attend the California Institute of Technology—from part-time projectionist, to full-time projectionist, to cutter, to film editor, and finally, in 1939, to director. After five years of "B" films, he directed his first important feature, *Tender Comrade*, written by Dalton Trumbo, in 1944 at RKO. The pursuit of a career had not allowed Dmytryk much time for politics, and he had not been a part of the Popular Front of the thirties. He was first attracted to the Left in 1942, he claims, when he was asked to lecture on film cutting at the Hollywood League of American Writers' School. There he discovered a place "where professionals could really get together and talk over their trade."[83] One professional thing apparently led to another—political—thing, for Dmytryk joined the Communist Party in 1944, "in the love feast days" when being a Communist "didn't stop you from being an American."[84]

To this point in the story, none of Dmytryk's former comrades offer any disagreement. From here on, however, motives and interpretations diverge widely. Dmytryk claims he left the Party in 1945, following the meetings with Lawson, Maltz, and Wexley about *Cornered*.[85] Not one of the Ten or their attorneys with whom we talked confirm this fact. They all remember that he was present at every Party meeting which involved the Ten between 1947 and 1950. Dmytryk claims that his disillusionment with the Ten began after the hearings; that he could no longer, even by implication, be linked to a political group which put means over ends every time, whose political line superseded everything and everyone.[86] He told HUAC, in his second appearance, "before I went to jail, I had already made up my mind, as soon as my jail sentence was over, I would issue an affidavit and disclose whether I had been a member of the Party."[87] Albert Maltz, his fellow prisoner at Mill Point, believes that the "chemistry" of transformation only began "after the jail doors closed shut." Prior to this, as Maltz made clear in a letter to *The Saturday Evening Post*, Dmytryk had behaved and spoken exactly like all of them. (The *Post* did not print the letter and Maltz paid to have it appear as an ad in the *Hollywood Reporter*, May 29, 1951.) Once in jail, Dmytryk believed that he could resurrect his professional situation by separating himself clearly from the notorious Ten. On his release, however, he realized that unless he did a great deal more reposturing, not only would he never work in Hollywood again, but he might never get a passport to work in England either.

There is no dispute about the sequence of events which followed Dmytryk's about-face. In September 1950 Bartley Crum visited Mill Point to assist Dmytryk in writing a statement attesting to Dmytryk's loyalty to the United States. Crum released it to the press the next day. In it Dmytryk reversed the stance he had taken before the Committee in October 1947, stating:

> that I am not now, nor was I at the time of the hearing, a member of the Communist Party, that I am not a Communist sympathizer, and that I recognize the United States of America as the only country to which I owe allegiance and loyalty.[88]

The affidavit was sent to the Attorney General of the United States, other members of the Department of Justice, and to the press. Neither forewarned nor forearmed, a shaken and angry Maltz approached Dmytryk to discover his intentions. Dmytryk replied that it was simply a tactic to secure his reemployment in Hollywood, that he was still opposed to the Committee, still opposed to the Motion Picture Alliance, still, in short, "the same man I always was."[89]

Dmytryk emerged from jail in November and within two months had begun to meet regularly with a "rehabilitation" committee consisting of Ronald Reagan, Roy Brewer, and four others appointed by the newly formed Motion Picture Industry Council.[90] The Council had been formed by Brewer in March 1949. He invited all the Hollywood unions, guilds, and producer groups to appoint representatives. The Council's purpose was to bring the "Communist problem" in Hollywood to the attention of the studio executives, publicize the efforts of the film industry to purge itself of "subversives," "clear" repentant Communists, and heap vituperations on any HUAC witnesses who took the Fifth Amendment. Between 1949 and 1951 its presidents included Brewer, Dore Schary, Cecil B. De Mille, Ronald Reagan, and Allen Rivkin.

The MPIC was a charter member of the Council of Motion Picture Organizations, formed in August 1949 by the producers, exhibitors, and distributors. Its purpose was to create "a national policy-making authority to plan, organize, and supervise a comprehensive, continuous public relations program. . . ."[91] Ned Depinet (RKO) was president; Roy Brewer and Ronald Reagan were among the vice-presidents.

On April 25, 1951, Dmytryk went before HUAC a second time. In this, the second step of his "clearance" procedure, he answered all the Committee's questions and named two dozen of his former comrades. The experience proved to be cleansing for him: "For the first time in three and a half years," he wrote in his autobiography, "I felt free of guilt."[92] Two weeks later his "recantation" article appeared in *The Saturday Evening Post* and he was offered a contract, in his own name, by the King Brothers to direct a film entitled *Mutiny*. Early in 1952 he signed a four-picture contract with the Stanley Kramer unit at Columbia. Dmytryk worked steadily in Hollywood thereafter.

By May of 1951 the remaining nine "loyalists" were out of jail, and facing a well-enforced blacklist which rendered them virtually unemployable in commercial writing professions. "Freedom" was a relative concept in the Hollywood to which they returned: though out of prison, they were not free to pursue their careers, to continue their political activity, or to be anything other than scorned "agents of a foreign government." A new wave of repression had begun to sweep over the film industry in the spring of 1951. It left in its wake many, many more victims and uncovered a new species of political animal, which Lawson termed "the artist stoolpigeon."[93]

11

The Devastation: HUAC Returns to Hollywood, 1951–53

> During the past year the Committee is pleased to report that the spirit of helpful cooperation evidenced by motion-picture industry figures has been excellent. Further, it can be stated on considerable authority that perhaps no major industry in the world today employs fewer members of the Communist Party than does the motion-picture industry.
> —*Annual Report of the Committee on Un-American Activities for the Year 1953*[1]

The Cold War Prelude

As severe as it was, the fate of the Hollywood Ten turned out to be only a small foretaste of the political, professional, and human destruction that was to occur in Hollywood shortly thereafter. The last of the Ten went to prison in September 1950, leaving the echoes of their forebodings to send a chill through the film community. The jailing of successful screen artists shattered the pervasive illusion that Americans could not be punished for their political beliefs and activities. The high stakes of the HUAC-Hollywood contest would occasion much soul-searching, retrenchment, and even capitulation on the part of liberals and radicals as the film industry braced itself for the battering it now feared would come.

The storm broke in the spring of 1951 with devastating fury. The Committee (now chaired by John S. Wood, D-Ga.) resumed its project of political inquisition and repression with renewed vigor. Its hold on public opinion had been considerably strengthened by a series of national and international events whose significance far outweighed the defiant resistance provided by the Hollywood Ten: the conviction of Alger Hiss, the fall of China to the Communists, the first successful atomic explosion by the Soviet Union, the arrest of atomic spy Klaus Fuchs in England, the dawning of Joseph McCarthy's special brand of anti-communism, the passage of the McCarran Internal Security Act (requiring the registration of all Communists and Communist organizations, establishing a registration agency, the Subversive Activities Control Board, and providing for "internal security emergencies" and the detention of suspected "subversives"), the outbreak of the Korean War, the Supreme Court's approval of the Smith Act (in *Dennis* v. *United States*), and the arrest of Julius and Ethel Rosenberg. These events, and many others like them, "haunted the fifties" (to paraphrase I. F. Stone) and ushered in a period of political repression such as this country had not seen since the years following World War I when, in California alone, between 1919 and 1924, 531 individuals had been charged with violations of the state's Criminal Syndicalism Act; 264 had been tried, 128 had been imprisoned.[2]

This time around, however, the methods of repression were more refined. Subpoenas from congressional committees and requests to appear before administrative boards replaced the forced entries, unconstitutional searches, and illegal arrests authorized by the Department of Justice between 1919 and 1921; but the effects were the same. An "invitation" to appear in itself unsettled most of the recipients, many of whom had not been consciously political. One person summoned to appear before an administrative tribunal, Edmund O. Clubb, a China expert in the Department of State, recalled his state of mind when he opened the letter which informed him that he was under suspicion as a security risk: "My brain understood the significance of the words contained in the letter, but I could not perceive in my heart how an officer with my record could be summoned by an administrative tribunal to such picayune questions as those contained in the interrogatory just handed to me—vague inquiries into my political attitudes as a young man, and one lone concrete item that meant absolutely nothing to me."[3]

Thousands of Californians faced similar chilling and incomprehensible experiences. In 1948 the Los Angeles city council and the Los Angeles County Board of Supervisors approved a loyalty oath for municipal and county employees; a year later the Regents of the University of California agreed to a similar oath, enforced by a "sign or resign" stipulation, which applied to members of both the faculty and the staff. In 1950 the California legislature passed the Levering Act, which withheld the salaries of public employees who refused to swear that they were not at that time, nor had they recently been, members of a subversive organization (i.e., an organization on the Attorney General's list). Three years later the Dilworth and Luckel bills, providing for the dismissal of schoolteachers as well as public employees who refused to answer questions about their political views or activities before a school board, or a committee of the state legislature, or a congressional committee, were enacted. "These were the years," wrote Eason Monroe, head of the Southern California chapter of the American Civil Liberties Union,

> of the slow steady purge—out of employment, out of community organizations, out of public posts of one sort or another, [and] out of political candidacies—of anyone who either had in his own personal record membership in the Communist Party or associated groups, or was a member of any family in which these relationships were characteristic, or who had friends [who espoused such views], or who had ever attended a meeting, or who read the wrong literature, or for any reason at all.[4]

Meanwhile the FBI, or the specter of the FBI, haunted everybody even remotely suspected of harboring left-wing political views or participating in left-wing activities or associations. The Reverend Stephen Fritchman, who arrived in Los Angeles in January 1948 to assume the rectorship of the First Unitarian Church, found that his new (very liberal) congregation contained many members, including film community people, "who had repeatedly been visited by the F.B.I. to know whether they were ready to talk about their past associations . . . ; were they ready to talk and name their friends? I was told again and again of these merciless house calls by the pair of crew-cut, well-dressed, dead-pan visitors."[5]

In Hollywood, even before the new subpoenas arrived, the FBI prowled and movie industry activism subsided before the threat of further prosecution. When MGM executives called in Donald Ogden Stewart "to answer some questions," the Popular Front war-horse saw that his days as a Hollywood film writer had ended, and, to avoid the fate of the Ten, he migrated to England. " '49, it was '49," the screenwriter recently recalled. "And I was asked to come into the office [in New York]. And it was suggested that I clear myself . . . and give names and so forth. And that was the end of that beautiful contract. . . . And [my lawyer] just went over to them and settled on the contract."[6]

Gordon Kahn also left the country, but the circumstances of his departure reflected more clearly than Stewart's the pending nightmare of surveillance, rumor, harassment, and fear. Kahn's widow, Barbara, remembered:

> In the summer of 1950 rumors of a second, more thorough round of HUAC hearings increased. I was in the East at the time, recovering from hip surgery. On August 16 I received a letter from Gordon, postmarked Chihuahua, Mexico. In the letter he told me that friends had advised him to leave the country; they were certain that his name was at the top of the HUAC list. He feared that a subpoena meant inevitable imprisonment, so he had packed his bags and, in the middle of the night, driven toward the Mexican border. A cloudburst and a flash flood had almost cost him his life along the way, and once at the border, he had to bribe his way past suspicious Mexican officials.
>
> Still on crutches, I returned to Los Angeles. Life became a nightmare of suspicion and anxiety. Letters to Gordon had to be enclosed in envelopes addressed to a Mexican family in order to avoid FBI interference. I had to negotiate the sale of our home and most of our possessions while being hounded by FBI agents.

The rumors and apprehensions affected other radicals in a different manner. For example, Communist screenwriters Leo Townsend and Richard Collins and Communist actor Sterling Hayden, "out of the dictates of conscience," called the FBI in 1950 to confess their "subversive pasts" and provide long lists of names of former political associates. (Those named had no idea that the left-wing flank had been so badly exposed by their former comrades.) Prominent liberal Edward G. Robinson testified at his own request before HUAC, bringing with him stacks of documents and records to wipe away the red clouds of suspicion which hovered over his career. "The most terrifying thing about the atmosphere," remarked radical director Joseph Losey, "was seeing people succumb, and seeing all protest disappear. Because if you did protest, you'd had it."[7] Screenwriter Al Levitt, who, along with Losey, would soon be on the blacklist, recalled the large number of broken lunch and dinner dates, the phone messages which went unanswered, the unending chain of embarrassed excuses from good friends whom one had known, and been seeing socially, for years. Dashiell Hammett lost more than friends and social engagements. In April 1951, he was sentenced to six months in prison for refusing to name contributors to the Bail Fund of the Civil Rights Congress, on whose board Hammett served. While he was in prison, the Internal Revenue Service mailed him a back-tax bill for more than $100,000.[8] Soon after the second wave of HUAC subpoenas, "the left-wing community in Hollywood virtually disappeared," said Levitt, "its organizations becoming either defunct or totally transformed in activity and purpose"; its cadres frightened, broken, confused.

The ground for HUAC's return had been partially prepared by Edward G. Robinson's eagerness to be "cleared." Representative Francis E. Walter (D-Pa.), future chairman of HUAC, remarked on December 21, 1950:

> This Robinson hearing was a good thing. The time has arrived when we should find out what influences have been at work in Hollywood, who was responsible for the charges of Communism, and who is and who is not a Red.
>
> I think we should offer everybody who has ever been accused an opportunity to come before us and clear his reputation of these charges. I favor a full and complete investigation of the charges and rumors.[9]

Although Robinson had been cleared, Pandora's box had been irrevocably opened. Republicans in Congress attacked HUAC's "bill of health" for Robinson, because the Committee had not called any witnesses to testify to the actor's "Red connections." These critics demanded a new set of hearings, to hear both anti-Robinson witnesses and, finally, the remainder of the original Hollywood Nineteen.[10]

The Committee's appetite was further whetted by the emergence of a thriving new media industry in Hollywood—television, which, the Committee noted, could have

> a tremendous emotional impact upon the [viewing] audience. . . . Because of the vast new potentialities of television it seems logical that Hollywood motion pictures will some time in the future be presented on a large scale to television audiences.
>
> The Committee hopes that its investigation of Hollywood will have a far-reaching effect and prevent a large-scale future Communist infiltration of the television industry.[11]

But though television offered HUAC a whole new world to conquer, the Committee did not confine its investigations to the emerging networks and studios during its second visit to Hollywood. This time around no branch of the industry was to escape the dragnet; radio, theater, and music, as well as film and television, received "coverage" during the fifties investigations.

If the second HUAC assault on the entertainment world was thus considerably broader in scope than the 1947 hearings, it was more carefully focused. Indeed, the two probes differed markedly in that the second expressly circumvented the executives in the several branches of the industry. The Waldorf meeting had taught the Committee that it was far more expeditious to put individuals on trial than a whole industry. Industrial bosses were obviously willing to sacrifice even their most accomplished employees (not to mention significant portions of their own executive autonomy); but they drew the line at "cooperating" with HUAC programs which seriously questioned the products' "image," "reputation," or ideological soundness—at frontal assaults which threatened box office receipts or profits, that is.

The first hearings and their aftermath had demonstrated to HUAC that while studio bosses and New York executives were prepared to admit that left-wing activism flourished in Hollywood, they would not, under any circumstances, allow that Hollywood films had been "tainted" by left-wingers. The hearings which followed (and which dragged on intermittently for five years) aimed at the more feasible goal of eradicating liberalism and radicalism in Hollywood. HUAC's project was therefore more of a mop-up than a vengeful assault. Only the unwilling, the unrepentant, or the dissembling would feel the Committee's steel; the cooperative had nothing to fear from HUAC or the studios. Shortly before Leo Townsend sat down at the HUAC witness table to confess his past and name names, he sat down with the executives at Warner Brothers, where he was under contract, and apprised them of his plans. The producers there offered understanding and the assurance "that my testimony would in no way affect my employment at their studio."[12] Indeed, nearly all studio executives looked on benignly as artist after artist trooped forward to avail himself of the pardon awaiting those willing to talk. *Variety*, probably for the first time in its long history, actually published an understatement about the future of informers in the motion picture industry: "There is some belief that if a man purges himself and answers frankly, he will probably escape suspension or discharge from his studio."[13]

Nothing withstood the unrelenting, eerily reconciliatory pressure of HUAC and its growing number of camp followers, certainly not the remnants of the radical Left fully engaged in the campaign to win paroles for the eight "unfriendly" witnesses who were still in prison. In the midst of Arts, Sciences, and Professions-sponsored activities involving such personages as Thomas Mann, Linus Pauling, and Robert

Morss Lovett, the Left was suddenly hit by the new flood of subpoenas. Sylvia Jarrico remembered their impact: "We were planning a large welcome home demonstration for the eight. We thought our fight to rehabilitate their reputations was going pretty well and that they would come out of jail as heroes. Then the subpoenas hit. HUAC's timing couldn't have been more perfect."

Hollywood Collapses Completely

In early March 1951 eight radical screen artists—actors Larry Parks, Gale Sondergaard, Howard da Silva, and Sterling Hayden, and writers Richard Collins, Waldo Salt, Paul Jarrico, and Robert Lees—received subpoenas. (Parks, Salt, and Collins had been among the Nineteen; this was their second go-round with HUAC.) This time there was no outcry, no gathering of the liberal-radical tribes, no formation of a Committee for the Fifth Amendment. Indeed, the hush surrounding the new subpoenas was so deafening that Sondergaard, da Silva, and Salt spent precious funds to place an ad in *Variety* commenting critically on the silence.[14] The guilds refrained from even token support. In fact, the Screen Actors Guild had volunteered to be a fellow traveler of the Committee: in October 1950 SAG executives, with the unofficial assistance of the Motion Picture Alliance for the Preservation of American Ideals, had drafted a loyalty oath similar to the one already employed by the armed forces and defense industries. Though the oath proved unacceptable to the rest of the industry,[15] SAG's accommodating stance sobered everyone. A proposal for an industry-wide loyalty board surfaced in June 1951. Nine of the organizations represented in the Motion Picture Industry Council favored it, two were neutral; only the opposition of the Screen Writers Guild (which voted it down 176–143) kept it from being implemented.[16]

When Sondergaard formally petitioned her Guild to lend support to its subpoenaed members at the forthcoming hearings, the response of the SAG Board, dated March 20, 1951, was swift and direct:

> Your letter (1) attacks as an inquisition the pending hearings by the House Committee on Un-American Activities into alleged Communist Party activities by a few individuals and (2) asks that the Guild protect you against any consequences of your own personal decisions and actions.
>
> The Communist Party press also has attacked the hearings as a "warmongering, labor and freedom-busting . . . witch-hunt . . . by Congressional inquisitors." The Guild Board totally rejects this

quoted typical Communist party line. We recognize its obvious purposes of attempting to smear the hearings in advance and to create disrespect for the American form of government.

. . . Like the overwhelming majority of the American people, we believe that a "clear and present danger" to our nation exists. The Guild Board believes that all participants in the international Communist Party conspiracy against our nation should be exposed for what they are—enemies of our country and of our form of government.[17]

The letter made it unmistakably clear that "unfriendly" witnesses were on their own before HUAC and studio management:

if any actor by his own actions outside of union activities has so offended American public opinion that he has made himself unsaleable at the box office, the Guild cannot and would not want to force any employer to hire him. That is the individual actor's personal responsibility and it cannot be shifted to his union.*

Although ultimately arriving at the same destination, the Screen Directors Guild nearly broke apart on the issue of the proper extent of collaboration with the anti-Communist crusade. In the fall of 1950 the SDG Board passed a bylaw requiring a loyalty oath of all members—with the implicit threat of blacklisting for those who refused to sign it.[18] The campaign had been spearheaded by Cecil B. De Mille, who also, according to director Robert Parrish, "seriously proposed that every director be required, at the close of every film he directed, to file with the Guild a report on *whatever he had been able to find out* about the political convictions of everyone connected with the film, particularly writers and actors. This information would then be on file at the Guild so that directors could check on the 'loyalty' of those who wanted jobs."[19] The Board presented the bylaw to the membership for a vote—a vote conducted openly, with signed ballots. Under those procedural circumstances, needless to say, the measure passed overwhelmingly. Many directors were angered by the manner in which the oath was railroaded through the Guild. Guild president Joseph Mankiewicz, who had been out of town during the balloting, determined to hold an inquiry into the whole matter of loyalty oaths and Guild voting procedures.

No sooner had Mankiewicz announced a full membership meeting,

---

* In July 1953, SAG members overwhelmingly voted to ban known Communists from the organization.

however, than De Mille moved to block it and to initiate a drive to re-call the president from office. De Mille and his followers literally locked the Mankiewicz supporters out of the SDG building on Sunset Boulevard in order to prevent them from gaining access to the mailing lists. Such was the temper of the times, however, that even the twenty-five directors who supported Mankiewicz felt obliged to sign a loyalty oath in order to validate their good faith and prove the "disinterested" nature of their opposition to loyalty oaths.

Eventually (on October 22), a general meeting of the SDG membership was held to resolve the conflicts. The De Mille faction displayed such xenophobia and nativism that Rouben Mamoulian finally arose to say that for the first time since he had arrived in America from Russia he was afraid to be speaking with a foreign accent. William Wyler, accused of treason by De Mille, offered to punch the eminent director of biblical epics in the nose. With tempers seething, and schism impending, John Ford, "a politically unpredictable animal," arose and quietly demolished De Mille's case. The members then voted to repudiate the De Mille faction and obliged the entire Board to resign.[20]

Four days later Mankiewicz sent out a letter to all members of the Screen Directors Guild of America urging them to sign the loyalty oath.[21]

The Screen Writers Guild, to forestall another attack on its vulnerable position, itself began to collaborate with the Committee. Rather than trifling with loyalty oaths, the SWG Board authorized its president, Karl Tunberg, to turn over to HUAC investigators all of the union records—an act far more deadly than SAG's loyalty oaths, which required only *pro forma* activity. For nearly two decades SWG radicals had spoken freely at Board and membership meetings, never dreaming that their words would come under the malevolent scrutiny of a congressional committee investigating left-wing "influences." Tunberg was also assigned the task of explaining to the Committee "how we had foiled a Communist attempt to take over the Guild; that we had, therefore, cleaned our own house and should be left alone." Before going to Washington to testify at the 1951 hearings, Tunberg met with Maurice Benjamin, a lawyer for the Producers' Association, who assured him that "studio executives were desirous of keeping the red stamp off Hollywood" and would thus be happy to coordinate their strategy with the SWG's and assist Tunberg in any way—a radical departure from the usual treatment accorded SWG officials by studio management. HUAC counsel Frank Tavenner also proved cordial to Tunberg. The two conferred prior to Tunberg's appearance before the Committee and Tavenner approved of the general tenor of the remarks the SWG president intended to make.

In short, the guilds foreswore even token opposition to the hearings and instead offered, in varying degrees, their cooperation to the Committee and its crusade. The screen artist guilds, along with the other unions, guilds, and producer associations of the film industry, also offered their collective endorsements to HUAC by forming a Hollywood Cold War organization, the Motion Picture Industry Council (MPIC), a public relations outfit aimed at protecting the "good name" of the motion picture business. As the months went by, however, that task came to require tacit cooperation with, rather than public fulminations against, HUAC. With the arrival of the new subpoenas in March 1951, the MPIC took its stand directly alongside HUAC, announcing its support for "any legally constituted body that had as its objective exposure and destruction of the international Communist conspiracy."[22] Animated by its founder-president Roy Brewer, the MPIC was already famous for the merciless Red-baiting in which it had engaged during Henry Wallace's presidential campaign in 1948. The MPIC could also turn prickly with HUAC when the Committee attempted to return to its old technique of muddying the film industry's reputation. In early 1952, following the publication of HUAC's less than congratulatory annual report on the state of "cleanliness" of Hollywood, the MPIC launched "a big newspaper play as a means of building public good will." According to *Weekly Variety*, "the organized industry came off strongly on the press relations aspect of the [HUAC] report. Editorial writers across the country generally took Hollywood's side in the controversy."[23]

In the spring of 1951 the dozens of subpoenaed witnesses who chose to oppose HUAC could look to only two groups for support, the local branches of the Communist Party or the Hollywood chapter of the Arts, Sciences, and Professions. Since the membership of these two groups was, by now, virtually identical and all were the recipients of subpoenas, the "unfriendly" witnesses could really look only to themselves.† Writing to Biberman, Maltz commented on the parlous position of the second generation of hostile witnesses:

---

† In addition to the thousands of subpoenas, Communists had been, by the end of 1956, hit with 145 Smith Act indictments; there had been 108 convictions. Membership in the Party had decreased to 10,000 (from 43,000 in 1950). (David Caute, *The Great Fear: The Anti-Communist Purge Under Truman and Eisenhower*, New York: Simon & Schuster, 1978, pp. 185 and 208.)

we had the hope of winning. But [they] have a smaller torch to carry, yet the same consequences; have less support, and more certainty that they are walking the plank. In a way we reached bed-rock only when the [Supreme] court turned us down; they begin walking bed-rock from the first moment.[24]

The Cloning of the "Artist-Stoolpigeon"

A bare majority of the 110 men and women who were subpoenaed‡ in the second set of hearings found "bed-rock" too hard; 58 of them decided, after varying degrees of self-examination, to avow their Communist pasts, acknowledge that they had seen the light, and (as proof of regeneracy) provide the Committee with the names of others who had strayed. Every witness was approached by a HUAC investigator and urged to follow this path. Those who elected to do so—i.e., those unwilling to face the prospect of appearing on the industry's blacklist —were coached on how to testify. "Sincerity" was important because many of the hearings were televised and the Committee was concerned about improving its image as a constructive force. A witness demonstrated his or her "sincerity" by affecting a cooperative attitude during the questioning and congratulating HUAC for its good work, in short by appearing to agree that the Committee was necessary and beneficent after all.

No amount of celebratory lather, however, freed the informer-witness from the indispensable condition of self-exculpation—the name game. The question "Who were the other persons who were members of the cell?" marked the decisive moment of every "friendly" witness' testimony. No would-be informer could appear taciturn in his response to this question. A certain minimum number of names was necessary; those who, before they appeared publicly before the Committee, could convince HUAC counsel that they did not know the names of enough former comrades to give a persuasive performance, perhaps because their involvement in the CP was too slight or too distant, were provided with names. The key to a successful appearance—i.e., one that guaranteed continued employment—was the prompt recital of the names of a few dozen Hollywood Reds.

Of the 58 informers, 31 were "important" Hollywood artists*—19

---

‡ Some of those who were named avoided subpoenas by leaving the country: Barzman, Bright, Butler, Kahn, and Stewart. Other prominent radicals, for reasons never explained, never received a "pink slip": Arnaud d'Usseau, Guy Endore, Ian McLellan Hunter, Dorothy Parker, and John Wexley.

* By "'important' Hollywood artists" we mean those who had at least four screen credits prior to being subpoenaed. Two of the people listed in Ap-

writers, 4 directors, 5 actors, 1 producer, and 2 composers. As a group, these 31 men and women recited an average of 29 names apiece (a mean of 21, a total of 902), which, when duplications are taken into account, amounted to over 200 Hollywood Communists. Individually the 31 varied widely in the number of names they gave to HUAC, ranging from Martin Berkeley's 155, Pauline Townsend's 83, and David Lang's 75 to 6 for Clifford Odets (who claimed to have been a Party member for only a short time—six months—in the thirties), 7 for Sterling Hayden (who claimed that he had only been in the Party for a short time, that he had been assigned to a non-talent branch, and that he "never knew the last names" of some of the members), and 1 for Gertrude Purcell (who was not asked for any names—and did not receive another screen credit). The informers with more "tender" consciences exposed the most obvious Reds—Lawson (named 27 times), Biberman (16), Cole (15), Jarrico (14), and Lardner (14)— hoping thereby to spare as yet unnamed radicals. The effort was futile. Virtually no Communists or former Communists escaped exposure, the lives and careers of the frequently named artists were even more lastingly blighted.

These unseemly rituals served no legislative or investigation function for the Committe—no amendments or additions to federal law resulted. HUAC needed no further fodder for its grinder; its research had been thorough. The "name game" substantiated the witness' "conversion" by demonstrating his or her willingness to betray former comrades. There was no alternative to this deed, virtually no way out for even the "friendliest" and seemingly most "sincere" penitent. The witnesses had been made aware that their professional future hung in the balance; a witness stepped before the Committee "guilty" and unemployable simply as a result of having been subpoenaed. For many artists it was the most important appearance of their lives, the one recognized forum for purifying one's name in the minds of studio executives and political clearance agencies.

If anyone showed how *not* to inform before HUAC, it was the first witness of the reopened hearings, actor Larry Parks, who had originally been subpoenaed in 1947 as part of the Nineteen. Parks had been coached by HUAC, but once in public he chose to extemporize and

---

pendix 7, however, had none, but their closeness to a large group of radical screenwriters confers the label of "important" upon them: Pauline Townsend, who worked with her husband, Leo, on many of his scripts, and Betty Anderson (who testified under her married name, Elizabeth Wilson), who was secretary of the Anti-Nazi League and the Motion Picture Democratic Committee and belonged to a writers' branch of the Hollywood CP.

temporize—to admit to his own Communist past but refuse to name his comrades in the Party. In effect he tried to escape with a striptease instead of the expected full exposure. The Committee remained implacable in its demand for names. Parks reduced himself nearly to groveling and pleading, protesting:

> I don't think this is a choice at all. I don't think this is really sportsmanlike. I don't think this is American. I don't think this is American justice.
> I think it is not befitting for this committee to force me to make this kind of a choice. I don't think it is befitting to the purpose of this committee to do this.[25]

Parks opened the gates through which so many who succeeded him would follow. His momentary hesitation finished him in Hollywood despite his ultimate, wrenched compliance. The Los Angeles *Examiner* announced in a banner headline on March 23, 1951, his capitulation: LARRY PARKS LISTS NAMES OF 10 HOLLYWOOD REDS. The next day the column head for the paper's page-one story about Parks bespoke the price to a witness of public writhing and soul-searching: LARRY PARKS LOSES $75,000 SCREEN ROLE. An actor new to stardom, Parks appeared in only three other films, in supporting roles, before his death in 1975.

Had Parks's testimony not provided sufficient contrast to the demeanor of the Ten in 1947, screenwriter Martin Berkeley indelibly engraved the second hearings with perfidy. Richard Collins, another turncoat member of the Nineteen, had barely provided Berkeley's name to HUAC on April 12 than Berkeley sent a telegram to the Committee accusing Collins of perjury and stating "it is well documented that I have fought Communism consistently inside my guild and out."[26] Berkeley went on to muster the support of several leading liberal screenwriters to intercede on his behalf with the studios. Then Berkeley dropped out of sight. He surfaced in Washington on September 19, where, to everyone's astonishment, he admitted to seven years of Communist Party membership. He then proceeded to name names, 155 of them. His was a comportment without peer in the annals of the film hearings.

A few other witnesses, expecially among the actors and actresses (Sterling Hayden excepted), matched the indignity of HUAC's questions with undignified displays of their own. Lucille Ball donned her most famous persona—the scatterbrained "Lucy Ricardo"—in order to wriggle out of damaging allegations about her political sympathies. Ball was spared a recital of names by her obvious apoliticism and obsequiousness—she swore that she was never a member of the Party but had registered as a Communist voter in 1936 to please her Socialist grandfather. She also swore that she had not cast a vote for a Communist candidate.[27] Edward G. Robinson and José Ferrer just wiggled, while Lloyd Bridges arranged for his testimony to remain secret, and writer Abe Burrows put on a cretinous performance. By and large, however, Parks, Berkeley, Ball, and Burrows were exceptions to the rule. The informers as a group tended to be direct and serious—an altogether credible lot. The testimony of screenwriter Leo Townsend is representative of that of most of the "friendly" witnesses during the second hearings, revealing as it does the submissiveness which HUAC (and, by extension, the producers and right-wing pressure groups) required of repenters:

> Before I name these names I would like to preface this with a very brief remark. I feel that the purpose of this Committee is an investigative one so that the Congress of the United States may intelligently legislate in the field of national security. As a loyal American interested in that security, I feel I must place in the hands of this Committee whatever information I have.
>
> Also I feel that since the American Communist Party in the last four years hasn't openly and honestly stated its aims and goals and has evaded the issue of its allegiance to the Soviet Union, I think that the American people have a right to know which people have not made up their minds [to recant].

Townsend also pointed out that perhaps only "five or six of the people I knew in the Party would commit acts of violence. But I don't know which five or six this might be." If he remained silent, he said, he would share responsibility for any of their future actions.†

Townsend's testimony, like that of the great majority of informers,

---

† 1951 HUAC hearings, Vol. 2, p. 1,524. Leo Townsend challenged our analysis of the motives and staging, at least in his case, of the informing process. "My testimony was not manufactured. My informing was a matter of conscience for me; I had discovered that I had made a terrible mistake in joining the Communist Party, that Stalin had been responsible for as many deaths as Hitler. Nor did it save my career. Two weeks after my testimony I was dropped by Warner Brothers. I knew I would be, but it was the price I had to pay for having joined the Communist Party."

However one looks at Townsend's testimony—either the past or current one—the fact remains that the cost of penance was not very high. He was working regularly within a year, authoring or co-authoring eleven screenplays between 1953 and 1957 for 20th, United Artists, Columbia, and Universal.

dramatized the Committee's theatrical genius. Avoiding obvious obsequiousness, which would certainly not have been believable, the witnesses, their attorneys, and HUAC counsel arranged soliloquies which spotlighted a seemingly complete and authentic reversal of the fundamental ideological position and organizational loyalties which had animated a significant portion of the speaker's life. Standing before a congressional committee whose forebears and present members he, like all the other informers, had ardently opposed since 1938, Townsend not only criticized and disowned the same Communist Party in which he had spent six very active years of his life, but reversed his long-term opposition to what he had always called "domestic fascism" and virtually congratulated the Committee on its exploratory function. He (and the others) went a step further: they proffered help to Wood, Doyle, Jackson, Walter, *et al.* in realizing HUAC's project, which was to extirpate, by exposing, the roots of the progressive movement and to silence, by frightening, all possible sources of liberal criticism. And finally, Townsend, like the other "reborn Americans," consented to sink into political obscurity and quiescence once this final political episode was over, thus effectively terminating (on a reactionary note) a long career as a left-wing activist and ideologue. In sum, HUAC's second-round "victory" over Hollywood again resulted from the behavior of a group of witnesses—this time, however, consisting not of a display of recalcitrance but of the spectacle of approximately one sixth of the Communist community within the Hollywood entertainment industry breaking under pressure and renouncing its commitment.

For all their compromises, the informers did manage to hold the line on one issue: they did not, for the most part, renounce their own political pasts. Parks, Townsend, Collins, and Dmytryk generally refused to admit that their motives in joining, or their activities while working in, the Communist Party were malevolent. Whatever the American Party had since become in their eyes, or whatever crimes and errors they now believed the Soviet Union had committed in the name of communism, these former Reds asserted over and again that *their* personal reasons for remaining Communists were idealistic, not revolutionary or subversive—i.e., as Communists they wished to fight injustice and social evil and help to bring about a better world.

By painting the Communist Party in Hollywood as a passionate, busy group of social meliorists, often bored with dogma and theory, the informers were, to be sure, partly telling the truth as they had witnessed it. But they were also creating a picture which tended to buttress the credibility of their present reversals. As they had joined the CPUSA for idealistic and "American" reasons, so now they could oppose it *on the same grounds*. The informers thus made themselves appear, not as revolutionaries engaged in a cunning ploy, but as loyal citizens who had seen a new light.

From prison eight of the Hollywood Ten listened by radio to these penitent displays of candor by which so many of their former comrades elected to save their careers by condemning anew the "victims" alongside of whom and for whom they had once fought so hard. It was an altogether disheartening spectacle. Maltz wrote Biberman (both were by then out of prison):

> The new Hollywood business is very grim, very savage. I watch it with an inner sickness. . . . Oh the moral horror of this parade of stoolpigeons, what a sickness it spreads over the whole land. That which we predicted is here—the complete triumph of the Motion Picture Alliance for American Ideals. My God.[28]

But it did have its lighter moments. After Lester Cole had been fingered by three different witnesses (including the Ten's Judas, Edward Dmytryk) in less than a fortnight, a fellow inmate of Cole's at Danbury Prison turned to the writer and said: "Lester, if you *are* a Communist, you had better get the hell out. Any group with that many finks in it is no damn good!"

Why did the informers inform? There was a strong tendency at the time for cooperative witnesses to tie their candor before HUAC to their current disillusionment with communism. At the hearings nearly all the informers spoke of some degree of blighted faith in the God That Failed (or His earthly minions), disappointment which, they said, had culminated in their departure from the Party at some point between 1942 and 1948. Time has not altered this perception. In a documentary film, *Hollywood on Trial,* made in 1976, Edward Dmytryk told an interviewer that he had informed because "I didn't want to be a martyr for a cause I didn't believe in." Roy Huggins, former Red screenwriter and current television producer, remarked in 1971, "if I'm going to go [to jail, I told myself in 1951], I want to go for something that I'm actually guilty of" and "I had long since decided that one of the great errors of my life had been that of believing that the Soviet Union represented the glorious future."[29] Huggins is now, however, appalled at his cooperative spirit, ascribing it to being "caught unprepared" and having "a failure of nerve." Dmytryk and Kazan have evidenced no regret of any kind.

The informers' attempt to link their "political disillusionment" to their decision to inform in a cause-and-effect relationship was a bold, and successful, but largely duplicitous gambit. It conveniently ignored the fact that some of them did not leave the CP when they claimed they did. Indeed, at the time of the Duclos Letter in 1946 (cited as "the final straw" by a number of informers), there had been nothing like a mass exodus from the Hollywood branches of the Party. It seems clear that Dmytryk and Berkeley, for example, whose memories were so clear and sharp on the subject of identifying former comrades, suffered lapses when it came to recalling the exact date of their own departure from the Red ranks.

A motive which several of the informers admitted to, and which surely loomed in the minds of all fifty-eight, was the fear of going to jail. And yet even that consideration, initially so overwhelming, could be dispelled by rational consideration: the Fifth Amendment obviated any necessity of spending time behind bars.

In short, it finally came down, not mainly to disillusionment, nor to prison even—neither of which necessitated informing—but to the blacklist. *This* was the material, obvious, and basic "American" truth which no one cared to mention at the time, and very, very few have admitted years later. The reality which informed informing was this: four dozen witnesses so feared losing their careers and their income that they cooperated. Sterling Hayden and Elia Kazan eventually stepped out from behind the shrubbery that every other informer was beating around and forthrightly conceded that they had exposed their comrades in order to save their own careers. But even Kazan and Hayden did not say as much at the time—nor would they have been encouraged, perhaps even permitted, to do so by the Committee or the studios. The aura of pious sincerity, not to say sanctity, which had to suffuse the proceedings was essential to all concerned. How would it have looked, after all, if fifty-eight men and women had stood in the dock and prefaced their candor with the simple admission, "Mr. Wood, I'm doing this because I don't want to cease earning $50,000 a year"? Kazan, however, did tell Lillian Hellman, "I earned over $400,000 last year from theater. But Skouras says I'll never make another movie [if I don't cooperate]."[30] Hayden, in his autobiography, was equally forthright: "I think of Larry Parks [who] consigned himself to oblivion. Well, I hadn't made that mistake. Not by a goddamned sight. I was a real daddy longlegs of a worm when it came to crawling. . . . I [then] swung like a goon from role to role. . . . They were all made back to back in an effort to cash in fast on my new status as a sanitary culture hero."[81]

Most informers escaped the objectionable fates they had feared. While Isobel Lennart went on to write numerous important films for MGM, Lester Cole worked in a warehouse; while Richard Collins turned out a screenplay a year after his testimony (and this after not having enjoyed a single screen credit between 1945 and 1951), Alvah Bessie worked the lights at the Hungry "i" nightclub in San Francisco; while Martin Berkeley wrote a succession of mediocre screenplays for Universal and United Artists, Sidney Buchman ran a car park; while Roy Huggins and Meta Reis Rosenberg went on to fine producing careers, Robert Lees, Fred Rinaldo, Alfred Levitt, and Edward Huebsch struggled to make themselves over into maître d's, newsprint salesmen, photographers, and TV repairmen.

Not every informer's career improved or continued as a result of his or her cooperative testimony, but the majority thrived. Leopold Atlas, George Beck, Melvin Levy, Larry Parks, Gertrude Purcell, and Sol Shor each had between zero and three credits in the fifties and sixties. On the other hand, Lucille Ball, Mac Benoff, Martin Berkeley, Lloyd Bridges, Lee J. Cobb, Richard Collins, Edward Dmytryk, Sterling Hayden, Harold Hecht, Roy Huggins, Elia Kazan, Roland Kibbee, David Lang, Isobel Lennart, Clifford Odets, Stanley Rubin, Bernard Schoenfeld, Budd Schulberg, Leo Townsend, and Frank Tuttle were very gainfully employed in the post-hearing era.

Contrary to the victims' angry feelings, the informers did not *cause* the destruction which overtook their uncompromising colleagues. By April 1951 it was eminently clear to even the most blithe Hollywood radical that HUAC did not need the exposés provided by the informers; that the Committee had sufficient nails, wood, and bloodthirsty onlookers for all the crucifixions. Even if no one had "confessed," it is clear that Wood and his cohorts would have coldly, briskly, and efficiently marched the entire list of "Hollywood Communists" through the witness box, one at a time, listened to their recitals of the Fifth, and waited for the studios to blacklist them. In the atmosphere of 1951, courage seemed to have lost all social validity; it no longer seemed to serve any positive function—except, perhaps, to posterity. Courage was reduced to a purely personal matter. And yet, if

58 chose to cooperate with HUAC and the clearance agencies, over two hundred chose differently.

Portrait of an Intransigent: Bess Taffel

"The subpoena hit me just as my career in Hollywood had taken a sharp upward swing. I'd written the original screenplay for a Darryl Zanuck production [*Elopement*] which was then shooting; I'd sold a script and done a screenplay at Columbia; and now was back at Fox developing a new project. Unassailable proof that I was on my way up appeared in the form of my first invitation to a 'Class A' Hollywood party. I was never to go." Leo Townsend's testimony brought Taffel's private political views and activities to public notice, forcing her to face decisions she had never thought she would have to make.

After coming to Hollywood in her early twenties, Taffel got to know a number of men—Lawson, Maltz, Ornitz, and others—whose novels, plays, and theoretical writings had played an important role in her artistic development. In no wise did the left-wingers fit her preconceived image of "Communists." "They were not wild-eyed fanatics; they were reasonable, intelligent people who were not content to sit back and savor the lush rewards of success, but instead gave up much of their lives and resources to make the world a better place. I respected and admired them, and I wanted to be like them." Joining the Communist Party in 1943 at the height of its patriotic epoch, Taffel nevertheless refrained from great activity. For her communism was more an idealistic than a political stance. And when the Party's idealism began to wear thin, as it did for her during the controversy over Maltz's articles in *New Masses* (1946), she drifted away from Party functions and meetings. Townsend told HUAC as much: "she attended [meetings] quite infrequently, and then disappeared completely."

She did, however, draw close in a personal way to a small group of non-Party left-wingers—Charles and Oona Chaplin, Hanns and Louisa Eisler, Lion Feuchtwanger, Clifford Odets, Salka Viertel. Taffel was in New York in 1947 when she read in the newspapers that Hanns Eisler, a film composer, was the brother of Gerhart Eisler and Ruth Fischer, two of the Comintern's most important American representatives.

The [Hanns] Eislers and I had become quite close, but guilt by association was very real at that time and I was scared. Many of his friends were refugees from Hitler, still tired from their struggle with the Reich, and with no heart to fight the U.S. government. Attendance at the weekly salons at the Eisler home dwindled to a small group—the Chaplins, the Feuchtwangers, Salka, and myself. I did what I could; at the very end [when they were deported] I was the "unidentified companion" who drove them to the airport. I did not think seriously then about the possible danger this relationship might hold for me.

When the subpoena arrived, however, Taffel thought about it a lot.

Hanns's house had been under constant surveillance and I was sure my frequent comings and goings had been noted. I suspected my phone had been tapped. I had helped Hanns translate his statement to the Committee. At the Eislers' request, I'd written numerous letters to consulates in an effort to get them a visa to any country but Germany. (Mrs. Eisler was emotionally unprepared to return there.) I'd maintained a correspondence with friends in Paris who might know of a job for Hanns and facilitate a French visa for him. I have reason to believe that at least one of those letters was opened and read before it was returned to me. I remembered a cable from Paris in which a typographical error of a single letter gave an innocent message the sound of some dark, international intrigue. I remembered the extraordinary way it was delivered to me. There was the sudden visit from a member of the Immigration Department who questioned me about the Eislers after they'd gone.‡

Since she had not been active in the Party for years, Taffel half expected she would "somehow escape" a subpoena. "Until it was in my hands, I felt deep inside that it would never happen. The new [1951] hearings brought with them agonizing suspense—the daily listening to radios, the constant poring over newspapers. People were being named all around me. Each day's end brought momentary relief followed quickly with fear of tomorrow." She was totally unprepared for the appearance at her door one summer evening in 1951 of HUAC's Hollywood investigator, William Wheeler.

---

‡ Eisler had appeared before HUAC in September 1947. The Committee accused him of perjury and asked Immigration authorities to deport him. A hearing was held and a deportation warrant issued in February 1948. Eisler and his wife were granted permission to leave voluntarily if they signed a declaration promising never to return to the United States. The couple left the country, for Czechoslovakia, on March 26, 1948.

Mr. Wheeler himself: Not your ordinary marshal. Everything became unreal. It was twilight and I didn't think to turn on a light. We sat in the half-dark and he told me ever so gently that I'd been named [in executive session by Leo Townsend] and the Committee would like to ask me some questions.

I took the subpoena from him. I told him, "This is death, you know." He knew. He was sympathetic, sincere, sorry. He'd do his best to help me, except, of course, in the matter of work. He could do nothing about that. He gave me his card and said, "We haven't informed your employers about this, and there's no need for you to do so either."

I sat very still, afraid to utter a word, afraid to let him know I was not going to cooperate, afraid he might misinterpret a word, a gesture to mean that I was. When he left, I sat in the dark, numb, wanting comfort, human warmth, but afraid to call anyone, afraid they might be watching to see whom I'd turn to, afraid to involve anyone else.

In the morning I went to see a man who, I'd heard, had already received a subpoena. We talked. I remember he laughed a lot and I thought, "How strong he is, how unafraid." Later he capitulated to the Committee.

When I had first considered the possibility of being called I knew exactly what I'd do. Oh, I'd talk all right. I'd welcome the chance to put the record straight. I had nothing to hide and a lot to be proud of. I'd *like* to tell them about quitting my lucrative job at Paramount to work for the Army, writing rehabilitation scripts for returning GIs on "subversive" themes like "How to Look for a Job," or about receiving a military Citation of Merit for my work, or about the wartime radio scripts I wrote for the Red Cross.

But I'd name no names. Let them send me to jail. The truth is, I really didn't believe they would because I was going to be polite, reasonable. That was all *before* the subpoena. Now, as I sat there in the gathering darkness, I wasn't so sure. I was afraid to risk it. Besides, I knew by now that I'd never be given the chance to carry it off. The moment my answers did not suit their purposes, they'd switch to the naming part of their ritual and then dismiss me. I finally abandoned my naive fantasy completely when I heard that Anne Revere [a subpoenaed actress], who'd also planned to speak out, went to Washington to observe some hearings and then returned and decided to take the Fifth. Otherwise, she said, she'd just go to jail without anyone's noticing or knowing why, a painful and useless gesture.

By 1951, defying the Committee, or challenging it on First Amendment grounds, had disappeared as an alternative. The Ten's fates—particularly the Supreme Court's denial of *certiorari* to Lawson and Trumbo—demonstrated the hopelessness of this tack. Nor, for that matter, did the Communist Party encourage anyone any longer to be a "hero." Heroic postures were altogether too expensive in legal and human fees, took too much time (when Party members were in prison) away from the struggle. Those who now determined to oppose HUAC were therefore counseled to take the Fifth.

The great majority of those who decided to fight HUAC did take the Fifth Amendment. But other forms of resistance were also essayed. Nine artists "ducked" their subpoenas in order to establish a tradition for those who simply could not face the prospect of appearing before HUAC. Writers Michael Uris, Fred Rinaldo, Louis Solomon, Leonardo Bercovici, Edward Huebsch, Hugo Butler, actresses Karen Morley and Georgia Backus Alexander, and director John Berry went "underground" for several weeks to show others one way of, in Karen Morley's words, "keeping out of jail, avoiding legal expenses, and, in the case of some writers, continuing careers." The Committee announced that it was ordering the arrests of the avoiders, but ended up dropping the notion. A few weeks later, with subpoena-ducking established as a non-crime, the nine resurfaced. "It was no way to live," said Morley. (Nationwide, a number of other radicals, fellow travelers, and Communists went underground for varying lengths of time to avoid prosecution and jail.)

Communist screenwriter-producer Sidney Buchman developed his own, unique form of "resistance." He appeared before the Committee, which was meeting in Los Angeles, on September 21, 1951. For almost three hours he dueled the congressmen, admitting to his own membership in the Communist Party but refusing to name any names and refusing to use the Fifth Amendment. Just before his flat and final non-compliance, Representative Donald Jackson (R-Calif.) left the hearing room—for reasons which were never explained—and left the Committee without a quorum. Thus Buchman could not be cited for contempt.

In January 1952 Buchman was issued a second HUAC subpoena. He tried, twice, to convince a United States District Court to quash it on the grounds that the summons represented an abuse of congressional power—that it was "arbitrary, harsh, discriminatory, unnecessary." Twice denied, Buchman then refused to honor the subpoena. By a vote of 314–0, the House found Buchman in contempt of Congress. Buchman told the press that his failure to heed the second subpoena "was a calculated risk accepted with a preference for facing a judge and jury rather than a congressional body." On March 12, 1953, Buchman was found guilty of contempt, fined $150, and given a one-year jail sentence, which was then suspended.[32]

The "unfriendly" witnesses who used the Fifth Amendment developed three variations on the theme. The "full Fifth" was the complete stonewall—say nothing to HUAC except one's name and address. Paul Jarrico and Michael Wilson (among others) who struck this chord came the closest to imitating the Ten in their anger and intransigence. Then there was the "slightly diminished Fifth" for those, like Carl Foreman or Robert Rossen (in his first appearance), who were willing to tell HUAC that they were not now members of the Communist Party but unwilling to answer the question of whether they had ever been members, or any other questions about the Party. Some tried to employ a "fully diminished Fifth"—to speak at length about oneself, but refuse to talk about anyone else. Bess Taffel and Anne Revere considered and dropped this tactic; Lillian Hellman urged the Committee (both by letter and in person) to allow her to use it. As it turned out, for Hellman as well as the other hostile witnesses, the Committee permitted only the first two alternatives. Tavenner told the "unfriendly" witnesses, and their lawyers, that they would be cited for contempt of Congress if they tried to pick and choose among questions. Taffel was thus in a quandary:

I didn't want to take the Fifth. In spite of its honorable history and all the efforts to keep it in proper perspective, it had been so subverted in the public mind that most Americans remained ignorant about its use and regarded it as "something to hide behind." It creates such an atmosphere of guilt around you that you actually *feel* guilty. I had to keep reminding myself that I'd done nothing wrong. But the Fifth doesn't allow you to say *anything*, not even to correct the most outrageous question. Your only possible response is the droning repetition of the language of the Fifth, an exercise that makes it difficult to sustain any composure or sense of dignity.

So I considered the alternatives. Cooperation was out of the question. It was not even a matter of protecting anyone; they obviously knew all the names. It was simply that I was viscerally incapable of allying myself with these men whom I considered evil, who were cynically, knowingly destroying innocent people. I think I would have vomited. I could not join them in their human sacrifice even though they *did* know the names.

And I was unwilling to perjure myself as, I was convinced, the cooperative witnesses were doing. The pattern of their testimony bore out my feeling that they were repeating scenarios given to them, providing expected responses involving self-denigration, the admission of having been duped, the spewing out of anti-Communist sentiments, and, of course, the lists to be named.

There were modified forms of the Fifth, but I eventually rejected those. They were, I had observed, a signal of weakness to the Committee, who promptly bore down on the witness in an effort to break him down or trap him in contempt. Such witnesses were kept on the stand for hours, sometimes recalled the following day. I wanted none of that.

I *had* no alternatives—there was only the Fifth—and I was most uncomfortable with it. Terrified, in fact. It immediately designated me as a "hostile witness," which meant that the Committee would be visibly, sneeringly hostile to *me*. In that withering atmosphere, I'd have to keep my wits about me to use the Fifth correctly—and the Fifth is very tricky. You have to be ahead of the interrogator. You have to recognize the question that "opens the door"—no matter how innocent it may appear—and avoid it or forfeit the privilege. The specter of a contempt citation is always present in the hearing room.

My lawyer, A. L. Wirin, also warned me about perjury. I was advised to respond to the most factual questions with such qualifying phrases as "I believe," "to the best of my recollection," etc. Wirin insisted that I practice using these phrases. A hostile, frustrated Committee, intent upon punishment as this one was, could, if it chose, find cause for a perjury citation in an honest error, an unintentional misstatement under oath.

A particularly exasperating aspect of the Fifth is that you can implicate others without naming names simply, ironically, by the very act of using the Fifth. For instance, what if they ask you about someone like Charles Chaplin? I knew that Charlie had never been a Communist, nor a member of any organization. It was against his basic philosophy. But the Committee won't let you say that; you have to answer, as always, "I refuse to answer on the grounds that it might tend to incriminate me," and thereby make it seem as if Chaplin were a Red.* I lived in dread that I might, thus, be forced to add to the troubles of a dear friend and a good human being. My major preoccupation now became thinking of questions that might be put to me. Every day I recalled something else they might ask. I was in a state of chronic terror.

Meanwhile it appeared that Mr. Wheeler had been true to his word not to tell the studio about me. Every morning I went to work, dragged myself through the day, smiling, greeting people, wondering how they'd act if they knew. I couldn't sleep. I began taking sleeping pills at night and wake-up pills during the day.

Somehow the word got out. One day Fred Kohlmar, my producer at 20th, called me into his office. "I hear you got a pink paper," he said. He was a very kind man and, I believe, genuinely concerned about me. He urged me to engage Martin Gang as my attorney. I told him why I couldn't, that Gang was the lawyer to whom the cooperative witnesses went as part of their effort to be cleared by HUAC [see below]. I think Fred understood. "You'll be back here again," he reassured me, meaning that for now, at least, I was no longer in the studio's employ.

The Committee heard from Bess Taffel on September 18, 1951, three months and two postponements after Wheeler first visited her. The drama for which she had perhaps overprepared herself was completed in two minutes. Wirin had told Tavenner that Taffel intended to take the full Fifth, and HUAC, sated with informers (Townsend testified that same day, Berkeley the next) and triumph, deigned not to waste time embarrassing a small fry like her. "My relief was enormous," she remembers; "It was over!"

So, of course, was her career as a Hollywood screenwriter. In subsequent years she managed to author some black market television scripts using a pseudonym, and she ghost-wrote a theatrical story which did not sell. She was approached twice by movie producers willing to let

---

* Chaplin was subpoenaed by the Committee in September 1947. After three postponements of his appearance, he sent HUAC a telegram: "I am not a Communist, neither have I ever joined any political party or organization in my life." The Committee members must have believed him because they wrote back that his appearance was no longer necessary—that they considered the matter closed. (Charles Chaplin, *My Autobiography*, New York: Simon & Schuster, 1964, pp. 447 and 449.)

her write scripts (under a pseudonym), but the terms were "utterly demeaning and humiliating" and she turned them down.

Amplifying the Reactionary Crusade: the Clearance Procedure and the Graylist

As much as it dominated attention, HUAC was not the only aspect of the anti-Communist crusade and the reactionary resurgence in the Hollywood of the early fifties. The Committee delivered an attack which shattered the Popular Front of radicals and liberals, but its means were ultimately limited both by its enabling legislation, which sanctioned only the persecution of Communists and egregious fellow travelers, not liberals, and by the minimal procedural formalities and decorum required by HUAC's status as a committee of the U. S. Congress. Moreover, the Committee's time in Hollywood, destructive though it was, could not but be limited by the sheer scope of HUAC's Americanizing project in many other parts of the United States.

Thus to magnify HUAC's pulverizing blow to the film industry came the foot soldiers of reaction: the fanatical and vengeful, the opportunists, the scavengers, the small and craven emboldened by the behavior of national politicians, studio bosses, key labor union leaders, and the heads of major national pressure groups. The people and organizations which assembled in HUAC's shadow threw their nets far wider than the Committee and obeyed far fewer rules. The important "smear and clear" organizations were:

1. American Business Consultants, formed by three ex-FBI agents in 1947. They published *Counterattack* on a regular basis and in June 1950 printed the "bible" of the graylist, *Red Channels*, a list of 151 people in show business and statements of Communist front activities of each.
2. Wage Earners Committee, formed in October 1951. Published the *National Wage Earner*, which listed 92 "subversive" films, picketed selected movies, and issued defamatory circulars on many others.
3. Aware, Inc., established in December 1953 by a group of New York actors and Vincent Hartnett, who formerly worked for ABC. They published *Confidential Notebook* regularly, and supplements similar to *Red Channels* periodically.

These groups followed the lead of the Motion Picture Alliance for the Preservation of American Ideals in designing an insidious two-step of censure and redemption—they cast subversive aspersions on the names of any political activists of the thirties and forties who had not clearly voiced an anti-Communist or anti-Soviet position in the intervening years; they then offered their services to cleanse the tainted of the odor of treason. By 1951 no one who had not undergone a clearance procedure could work in the entertainment industry. Thus the minuet of cooperation with HUAC became only one of the prescribed steps in the choreography of clearance. Other steps were added which entailed continued degradation and humiliation at the hands (and feet) of individuals and organizations eager to profit from the circumstances and climate, impatient to pursue both their enemies and their self-interests. Such, finally, was the extent of the required self-abasement that most politically committed radicals ultimately "preferred" the blacklist and black market to supplication before their persecutors.

The blacklist, however, was rather exclusive. One's name could not be inscribed on its rolls unless one had refused to cooperate with HUAC, either by taking the Fifth or by refusing to appear after being named by an informer. Film industry executives swore, of course, that no list of names circulated among the studios. They claimed they did not have to compile such a document; that the United States Government Printing Office did it for them, listing, in the various publications of HUAC, the names of all the men and women who had appeared before a congressional investigating committee and refused to cooperate. In all, 212 screen artists, producers, and studio workers were so "listed" by the Committee, and hence blacklisted by the film studios. As lengthy as the list of subversives in Hollywood was, it contained but a small portion of the names (over 60,000) compiled by HUAC. HUAC was lavish, both in its compilation of dossiers (over 1 million) and in its distribution of the information they contained to employers—some 60,000 individuals became "known" to their bosses via this channel.[33]

While the blacklist emerged as the studios' response to official anti-communism, something known as the "graylist" emerged in its shadows as a means of attacking liberals and fellow travelers. Many of the constituent elements of the crusade against communism looked to haul in a bigger catch than the "Stalinists" for whom they so ostentatiously baited their hooks. The graylists never enjoyed the publicity or effectiveness of the blacklists, but they touched many more people. Taking up where HUAC left off, the American Legion and a private firm called American Business Consultants culled HUAC and Tenney Committee reports, appendices, and hearing transcripts, back issues of the *Daily Worker*, letterheads of defunct Popular Front organizations, etc. to compile a list of people who could not be accused of "communism" but who had, at one time or another, dallied with liberal politics or causes. The Legion published two magazines, *Firing Line* and *American Legion Magazine,* and ABC put out a periodical entitled *Counterattack* and an index called *Red Channels;* all these publications carried attacks on individuals, organizations, and industries, as well as long lists of names of "subversives." No studio was without a full set of these blacklists and graylists; no studio failed to "honor" these judgments from without; no studio was without its "executive vice president in charge of clearance."

The blacklist was a kind of professional cancer, but at least the afflicted person knew what he had done—and what he must do to "cure" the disease. The great frustration of the graylist was that it seemed to many sufferers to be an ailment which had no origin, diagnosis, or treatment. One simply stopped hearing the telephone ring. No one was secure from reckless accusation or mistaken identity. Actress Martha Scott was confused with singer Hazel Scott, who had been a HUAC witness in 1950, and found her name on Aware, Inc.'s list of subversives. For her and others, it was like fighting an unseen enemy. Screenwriter Louis Pollock, a man without any known political views or associations, suddenly had his career yanked out from under him because the American Legion confused him with Louis Pollack, a California clothier, who had refused to cooperate with HUAC. The screenwriter described, in an affidavit, the "graylist effect":

> Sometime in 1954 I stopped selling. . . . All I could do was keep writing, try not to believe that in some mysterious way my work had slumped, and hope desperately to start selling again. . . . [I experienced] a fear of lack of talent which now gnawed at me constantly. . . . Trying to write with waning confidence in myself was the worst ordeal I went through those days. . . . Sometime around this period I turned to sleeping pills as a steady nightcap, was put on medication by my doctor to reduce my blood pressure, and took to filching my wife's tranquilizers. . . . After a few years of not selling and not getting work, I broke down to the point where I became panicky and was plagued day and night by the fear of complete destitution. I was not for some months able to sit down and write another speculative word on the typewriter. . . . I did some hysterical things.[34]

Had Pollock been more knowledgeable, he could have sought the aid of the various clearance agencies which had sprouted in Hollywood and New York: Roy Brewer's Motion Picture Industry Council,

Martin Gang's private office, the American Legion's national office, and, on occasion, the Anti-Defamation League of the B'nai B'rith. Arnold Forster, general counsel of the Anti-Defamation League, told HUAC that his organization helped any Jewish person from the entertainment industry who was willing to "follow our suggestion to voluntarily communicate with the F.B.I. or HUAC and offer to answer all questions." We helped no one, continued Forster, "who at any time pleaded the fifth amendment." The League attempted to get its clients a hearing before HUAC and, that accomplished, their jobs back. To expedite the latter task, Forster made use of the services of Hearst columnists Victor Riesel and George Sokolsky and Frederick Woltman (New York *Telegram*).[35] Sokolsky was a friend of J. B. Matthews, an ex-Communist front personage who became the first important congressional informer in 1938. From there he went on to become the research director of HUAC and, in 1953, executive director of Joseph McCarthy's Senate investigating committee. Matthews' article—"Did the Movies Really Clean House?"—which the *American Legion Magazine* ran in December 1951, precipitated the Producers' Association/ American Legion conference in Washington the following spring.

Alternatively, had Pollock been employed at RKO, he could have been cleared by the unusual procedure instituted by Howard Hughes shortly after he took control of the studio in 1948. The test which Hughes devised for the artists on his payroll was quite simple. Liberal director Joseph Losey, who failed it, explained how it worked:

> I was offered a film called "I Married a Communist," which I turned down categorically. I later learned that it was a touchstone for establishing who was [or was not] a "red": you offered "I Married a Communist" to anybody you thought was a Communist, and if they turned it down, they were. It was turned down by thirteen directors before it was made [by Robert Stevenson]. . . .†

The first real clearance agency in Hollywood, however, was established by the fanatical anti-Communist labor (IATSE) leader Roy Brewer in the late forties. He believed that a recognized and certified "sanitation" organization would encourage Communists to confess, thereby protecting the motion picture industry from further external

---

† *Losey on Losey*, ed. Tom Milne, Garden City, N.Y.: Doubleday & Company, 1968, p. 73. The film died at the box office, but was sold to television some time later under the title *The Woman on Pier Thirteen*.

assaults and assuring a further besmirching of the Communist Party, the Popular Front, and progressive political action in general. Brewer was quoted as saying that "the people who had broken with the Party had to be helped, both because it was the right thing to do and because it hurt the Communist Party"; his chief investigator, ex-Communist (and ex-FBI agent) Howard Costigan, noted, "since these people had used their position to aid the Communist Party, they were under special obligation now to help publicly destroy it."[36] Richard Collins and Edward Dmytryk, among the first of Brewer's successfully rehabilitated clients, referred other ex-Communists to the MPIC. Once Brewer and Costigan satisfied themselves that the recanter was sincere, they would advise him or her of the established procedure: 1) to seek an interview with an agent of the FBI and give him all the information one had about radical politics; 2) to petition HUAC to hear a full and public recantation, including denunciation of former comrades; and 3) (if the person were famous enough—e.g., Dmytryk, Kazan, Edward G. Robinson) to write a magazine or newspaper article renouncing past activism.

Upon the satisfactory completion of these tasks, the individual was assured by Brewer of the support of the Motion Picture Alliance, whose intervention with the studios sufficed to win back the jobs of the "cleansed." As self-appointed, but widely acknowledged, arbiter of the fates of a large number of men and women, Roy Brewer quickly attained an importance and legitimacy in Hollywood which he had not enjoyed as a reactionary labor boss. Similarly the Motion Picture Alliance, once outcast among liberals and regarded as a pariah by producers and executives, achieved an elevated status in Hollywood in recognition of the crucial function it was performing for studio executives not anxious to dirty their own hands cleaning others'.

Where Howard Hughes was simply a feudal lord obsessed with purging his domain of Reds, and where Roy Brewer was a right-wing eminence willing to serve his country and his industry by stamping "non-objectionable" on ex-Communist penitents, Martin Gang was a certified liberal attorney. Gang became the "man to see" in Hollywood for those ex-Communists who could not stomach the thought of kowtowing to Brewer and the Motion Picture Alliance or for those fellow travelers or premature anti-fascists who feared that they would be named, either before HUAC or in the pages of the various witch-hunt indexes. Until 1951, at least, Gang enjoyed a good reputation with the liberal community. As a member of ICCASP, he had been active in the defense of the Nineteen and had contributed $100 to the

Committee for the First Amendment. In 1950 he had written the imprisoned Dalton Trumbo, asking to try the screenwriter's suit for breach of contract against Loew's, Inc. Gang believed Trumbo had by far the strongest case.[87]

By 1951, however, Gang, like many of his liberal co-religionists, registered the permanent change in direction of the political winds, and tacked accordingly. Far from perceiving this new brand of politics as ignoble, Gang saw himself rather as a "frustrated crusader" trying "to keep a lot of innocent people from being hurt unnecessarily."[88] The first such "innocent" was Sterling Hayden, who had retained Gang as a show business attorney long before the actor had visited the FBI in the autumn of 1950. With his career on the line, Hayden engaged Gang to expand his legal services beyond the usual contract negotiation to consultation with the studios and HUAC. The word of Gang's successful efforts on behalf of Hayden—who barely missed a day from the shooting schedule of his film which was then in progress—spread, and some two dozen other Hollywood black- and graylistees made their way to Gang's office door. Gang claims he cleared every one of them.

The studios, of course, badly needed the services of people like Brewer and Gang. High-priced and valuable talent needed advice and clearance procedures. It would have been too expensive for each studio to do it over and over again every time it hired someone, nor could the Producers' Association do it for its members—an actor or actress who did not receive clearance would have a juicy conspiracy-not-to-hire suit. Caught between the fear of right-wing stigmatization and boycott (if they did not clear their employees) and the fear of expensive lawsuits (if they performed the job themselves), the studios were only too pleased to turn to "crusaders" like Gang to perform the odious task. In point of fact, their gratitude to, and trust of, Martin Gang became so great that a suspected employee's refusal to employ the attorney (e.g., Bess Taffel) automatically connoted that the screen artist was "guilty" as charged and unrepentant, hence to be discharged by the studio. In an era of fear and trembling, men like Gang became experts in the ways and means of expediting and certifying the collapse of the weak and the frightened.

A person who believed that he or she was unemployable would retain Gang, not as a lawyer, but as a conduit or "skid-greaser" to employability. Gang would investigate the circumstances which had led to the black- or graylisting and report back to his client. Once convinced of his client's willingness to do penance, Gang would set his clearance procedure in motion. If the client had been named before HUAC, William Wheeler would be called in to Gang's office to hear the formal recantation and arrange for a session before the Committee in Washington.[39] If the client's name appeared on some organization's list of "Reds," a letter or affidavit was composed (under Gang's direction) answering all the "charges" and promising answers to any subsequent accusations. A screenwriter who retreated in indignation from Gang's methods wrote:

> Mr. Gang told me that I must prepare myself for questioning, and I must do so with great thoroughness. I must make a full list of all my activities, all my associations, all my writings, all my articles, speeches, meetings, lectures, contributions, subscriptions, to any and all movements no matter how slightly radical or innocent I might think them to be. . . .[40]

This done, Gang would see to it that informal, but effective, word of the client's reemployability went out to the studios, via the good offices of Roy Brewer or some other renowned reactionary of the Motion Picture Alliance such as actor Ward Bond. Gang used Brewer for two reasons: 1) a central clearer was needed to avoid the expense and time of repetitious clearance performances; 2) most of the problems were caused by the Motion Picture Alliance, and "Brewer was the one voice of sanity there" and, in addition, "a decent, honest man."[41] Depositions taken years later from some of the most powerful executives and producers in the motion picture industry—Spyros Skouras, Y. Frank Freeman, Dore Schary—attested, indirectly, to Gang's success.

Compared to the American Legion, however, Brewer and Gang were mom-and-pop grocery stores. With over seventeen thousand posts and nearly 3 million members nationwide, the Legion became the supermarket of the clearance industry through the threat of boycotting films to which suspected "subversives" had contributed and publishing articles which attacked films and individuals by name, and the industry as a whole. Eric Johnston and a committee of prominent executives from the Producers' Association (Nicholas Schenck, Spyros Skouras, Barney Balaban, Nate Spingold) sought a meeting with the Legion's national commander, Donald Wilson, to "arrange" a procedure whereby Hollywood artists could clear themselves of any taint of radicalism and the Hollywood studios could elude wholesale condemnation. The meeting occurred in Washington, D.C., on March 31, 1952. The film representatives asked Wilson to provide them with the

15. John Wexley in the mid-1940s, as he embarked on the screen-play for *Cornered*.

16. Screenwriter John Paxton, producer Adrian Scott, and director Edward Dmytryk look over the script of *Crossfire*, the first anti-anti-Semitic feature film from the Hollywood studios (RKO, 1947). (Courtesy, *Hollywood Reporter*.)

THE MAKERS: JOHN PAXTON, ADRIAN SCOTT, EDWARD DMYTRYK

17. Ring and Frances Chaney Lardner, newly married and honeymooning at the HUAC hearings, October 1947.

18. Ben Margolis, attorney for the "unfriendly Nineteen" and the "Hollywood Ten."

I'M NO COMMUNIST

19. Tough-guy Humphrey Bogart admits to the movie fan magazine world that he had been "duped" by the Reds, 1948. (Courtesy, *Photoplay*.)

20. Screenwriter Gordon Kahn, a member of the Hollywood Nineteen and a "premature" graylistee, just prior to exile in Mexico, 1948.

21. Sam and Sadie Ornitz, with their granddaughter Laurel, just after his release from the federal prison in Springfield, Missouri, 1951.

22. Screenwriter Michael Wilson posed with his family—daughters Rebecca and Rosanna and wife Zelma—prior to his adamant refusal to "cooperate" with HUAC and his subsequent blacklisting, 1951. (Zelma Wilson is Sylvia Gussen Jarrico's sister.)

23. Paul, Sylvia, and Bill Jarrico making a rare "political" appearance during the height of the blacklist, Los Angeles, Christmas, 1955.

24. Joan, Michael, and Adrian Scott during his tenure as a black market television writer, 1959.

25. Ben and Norma Barzman, *en famille*, midway through their exile in France, 1962.

26. One of the few Hollywood Communists who retained his belief in communism, Lester Cole, talking with Soviet film director Roman Karmen at the Documentary Film Festival, Leipzig, German Democratic Republic, 1973.

27. Albert Maltz, many years after the shouting and persecution stopped, still believed what he wrote thirty-five years earlier, in 1940: "Beneath all else is this: a man must hold to his purpose. This—nothing less—is the underground stream of his life."

28. Screenwriter-director Abraham Polonsky relaxes in his post-blacklist years. "A free man always elects himself to the life he is going to lead. . . ."

names of all screen artists or workers connected in any way with communism which his organization had compiled. They also requested that the Legion create or oversee a clearance-by-letter procedure by which the named (under studio pressure) could clean their pasts. Of the 300 names given the producers by Wilson, it turned out that only two had been subpoenaed by HUAC. The other 298 became instant candidates for the unemployment line. *Variety* reported that "all the major studios are checking the loyalties of their employees against a list and dossiers furnished . . . by the American Legion. . . . [The studios are asking] that the answers be objective and couched in terms that can be made public, if necessary."[42]

Thus it transpired that the American Legion, just like the clearance agencies of shadier repute, having offered unasked its good offices as exposers and prosecutors of "Communists," was now requested to act in the role of judge for those accused who wished to plead *nolo contendere*. Approximately one hundred of the people listed by the Legion chose to write the clearance letter. In it they had to answer satisfactorily the following questions:

1. Is this charge accurate?
2. Why did you join the listed organizations?
3. Who invited you to join them?
4. Whom did you invite to join?
5. Did you resign? When?[43]

Thus, once again, the name of the game was names. Having watched the Communists and ex-Communists agonize over this question of conscience, the liberals were now invited to join in. Nor could there be any doubt that the vast majority of people now led into the arena were liberals, most of them anti-Communist, to be sure—but men and women nevertheless who had worked hard for such causes as Roosevelt and the New Deal, the Anti-Nazi League, the Hollywood Writers' Mobilization, or HICCASP. (To escape the graylist, a liberal would have had to have insistently espoused an anti-Communist line—as, for example, Philip Dunne and Melvyn Douglas did.) The majority recoiled from groveling before the ancient adversary and turning over fresh victims to it, and those who capitulated often wrote letters which were tortured mixtures of defiance and defensiveness.

Once the tears had dried on the page, the letter was sent to one of several anointed clearing agents—Brewer, George Sokolsky, Vincent Hartnett (who began his career with ABC and then moved over to Aware, Inc.), or James F. O'Neil, publisher of *Firing Line*. If the correspondent had "properly" admitted to, and explained, the charges, and if he had provided names, and if his tone were convincingly sincere and contrite, then he could usually return to work (i.e., have his name removed from the graylist). If questions still remained, as they often did, then another letter would be required. Johnny Green, equally renowned as a liberal and as the musical director at MGM, had to write three such letters to save his position.

When first approached by MGM's "clearance vice president," Louis K. Sidney, Green refused to write the letter, calling it (and the request) "an affront" both to his character and his intelligence. Nicholas Schenck, the head of Loew's, was summoned, and he and Green finally reached an agreement: Green said he would write a letter in which he would explain his political activities, but that he would not apologize for any of them. Green's letter was rejected by Sidney and Floyd Hendrickson, head of the studio legal department; they felt that the wording would alienate the "judges." Green rejected their advice until it was pointed out to him that his job was on the line. The second, revised, letter was also deemed unacceptable. Finally, with the studio brass breathing down his neck, Green composed a one-page letter in which he stated a series of patriotic ideals by which he felt every American should be guided. This letter cleared him. Johnny Green's situation, however, was quite unique. MGM's top executives, Dore Schary, L. K. Sidney, and Nicholas Schenck, had all been longtime friends—he was considered a company man.[44]

There was a gray area on the graylist for people who, though they could in no sense be linked to communism, could be construed as having defended Communists, by supporting either the Ten (e.g., Howard Koch) or the Screen Writers Guild (e.g., Mary McCall and Sheridan Gibney). The atmosphere of political suspicion and financial insecurity of the 1948–52 period offered the studios an opportunity, in the cases of McCall and Gibney, to rid themselves of two labor union veterans, each of whom had led the Guild in a move to oppose the Producers' Association's cooperation with the anti-Communist crusade. Both writers believe that the sudden, inexplicable downswings which their careers took immediately after their respective tenures as SWG president ended (Gibney's in 1948; McCall's in 1952), which lasted for over a decade, stemmed directly from their militant trade unionism. Gibney, who earned over $200,000 during the years 1945–47, worked a total of two weeks in 1948. In 1949 he became an independent producer, but failed to make any films; in 1950 he sold a story to Columbia. McCall, who had twenty-two screen credits between 1937 and 1950, and two in 1952, had only two more in the ensuing decade. In addition, her husband and two sons, all of whom were in the military, suddenly lost their security clearances.

Gibney, of course, had been compromised by Jack Warner's nonsensical blathering before HUAC. The decisive factor in the decline of Gibney's screenwriting career was not, however, his "exposure" by Warner; if it had been, Gibney's retention of Martin Gang would have sufficed to clear him. Rather, Gibney was unlucky enough to be Guild president during the SWG's initiation of a legal action challenging the blacklist, and thus to become identified with it. In early 1948 the Screen Writers Guild appropriated $5,000 to engage the prestigious Washington law firm of Arnold, Fortas, and Porter to file an anti-blacklist suit against the producers. The case, *Screen Writers Guild, Inc.* v. *Motion Picture Association of America et al.*, was intended to protect currently employed screenwriters, not as a plea for the SWG members of the Hollywood Ten.

For her part, McCall had incurred studio wrath when, as Guild president in 1951, she had led the SWG's legal battle to prevent Howard Hughes from removing Paul Jarrico's name from an RKO film he had written prior to his HUAC appearance, *The Las Vegas Story*. The SWG took Hughes to court, claiming that he had breached the credit allocation section of the collective bargaining agreement between the Guild and the producers. Hughes won.

As the Gibney and McCall episodes make clear, the studios were periodically capable of confounding public black- and graylists with management's own private shitlists. On the other hand, there were producers who periodically tried to persuade especially valuable studio properties to cooperate with HUAC or the American Legion. With the exception of RKO, probably every major studio, at one time or another, extended itself or its resources to protect an endangered screen artist whose films consistently made money. Marguerite Roberts, for example, wrote a number of successful films for MGM in the forties. After she had taken the Fifth before HUAC, in September 1951, she was approached over twenty times by her employers in their efforts to convince her to clear herself. The studio even offered to pay for her lawyer if she would reappear before the Committee, name a few names (to salve her "tender" conscience, it was suggested that she name those already named), and, in general, revise her behavior toward HUAC. Roberts steadfastly refused, had her contract bought up, lost a major screen credit (*Ivanhoe*), and was blacklisted until well into the sixties.

One of the most churlish of the moguls, Harry Cohn, achieved something of a reputation as the studio boss most willing to obey only minimally the anti-Communist crusade law. Many times he urged Larry Parks, Lillian Hellman, and Guy Endore to clear themselves—if necessary, to go insincerely through the formalities—so that he could continue to employ them. In the case of actress Judy Holliday, for whom Cohn had a special personal regard, tinged with something short of frenzy at the idea that Columbia Pictures might lose a superstar (and a bundle of money on her two recently released films), he hired the distinguished lawyer Simon H. Rifkind to advise her. He also paid one Kenneth Bierly, ex-FBI, ex-American Business Consultants, a substantial sum of money "to clear up the confusion about Judy Holliday."[45] Holliday, who chose not to exhibit either the recalcitrance or the dignity of Roberts, Hellman, or Endore, was indeed cleared to continue with her very successful film career.

Cohn also assisted, in obscure ways, the removal of Carl Foreman's name from the blacklist. Although Cohn had refused to back Foreman's Fifth Amendment position in 1951, fired him, and threatened to withhold Foreman's share of Columbia Pictures' purchase price ($25 million) for the producing company Foreman had helped found with Stanley Kramer, Cohn agreed, in the summer of 1956, to an employment contract with the screenwriter. There was one catch—the agreement would not take effect until Foreman appeared before HUAC and gained clearance without using the Fifth Amendment. Foreman would not discuss the matter with us, but Paul Jacobs described the "clearance" meeting in the pages of *The Reporter*, two years after the event:

On August 8, Foreman and his attorney met in Washington with Chairman Walter and Richard Arens, committee director. . . . Arens maintains that he didn't even know the meeting with Foreman was scheduled until a few minutes before it took place. In fact, he said he didn't even know who Carl Foreman was. . . . All went well at the cozy meeting until Arens, evidently not well briefed on the "arrangements," asked Foreman about other Party members. . . . [Walter] upheld Foreman's refusal to give names.[46]

Walter issued no clearance; Columbia signed Foreman; and the HUAC chairman refrained from attacking Columbia.

In 1958, the Columbia release *The Key* carried a single screenplay credit: Carl Foreman.

Many of the blacklisted people with whom we talked are positive that Buchman and Foreman made their passages through the treacherous waters of HUAC assisted by large sums of money. No one with whom we talked, however, could offer any tangible evidence for his or her belief. John Cogley, who probably saw more evidence than any other single person, told HUAC in 1956: "I found no evidence that clearances were sold or that one could buy a clearance."[47]

Whatever name one accords the years 1948–53—"the time of the toad," "scoundrel time," or "the plague years"—they were finally a period of individual crisis, in its literal meaning of confronting decision. Hollywood—so accustomed to forming and molding public opinion—was suddenly besieged by organizations and forces claiming (believably) to incarnate that very opinion (now angry); organizations and forces oblivious to, or scornful of, Hollywood's self-admiration. Inside the walls the time for heroism and dramatics passed swiftly, followed by far longer years of imprisonment within the decisions of an hour or a day. The decisions to resist rendered large numbers of people—artists who, many of them, for all their sincere political activism, were accustomed to wealth, celebrity, and professional accomplishment—overnight pariahs, exiles within their own city. The decision to surrender rendered other artists moral cripples in their own, as well as many of their colleagues', eyes. It was a time of personal testing. The weak found themselves willing to betray almost (but not quite) everything—beliefs, friends, integrity, pasts—in order to save their vocations. The self-declared "strong" underwent the temptations of St. Anthony, yet chose devastation—perhaps without fully comprehending its endless arid vistas. The political culture which had once nourished weak and strong alike was eradicated, never to return. But the political voice of the strong was not altogether silenced; instead it adapted itself as best it could to the conditions of exile.

12
Exile and Return:
the Aftermath, 1953 to Present

> Living through the blacklist and exile was like having gone to
> war—it was a rich and rewarding experience, but I would not
> want to go through it again.
>
> —Ben Barzman

The Emigrés

"I was no longer, at [the time of the blacklist, remembered Guy
Endore] a member of the Communist Party, but I was still, so to
speak, a member, because now we were all blacklisted together. The
endless meetings [over] these things for so many years . . . I can't
begin to tell you what kind of a nightmare it was, and I always had
the feeling that it was useless to fight this thing legally."[1] But he and
other black- and graylisted screen artists *did* fight these excommuni-
cations legally, as well as politically, professionally, and artistically—
with little success. The political atmosphere had to change before the
blacklist could begin to end.

The situation of writers, who could change their names or employ
"fronts," was somewhat better than that of actors, directors, and
producers, who could not change their faces. Nevertheless, the persecution left its mark on everyone. "Every time I sat down at the typewriter, bitter and aggrieved feelings intruded upon my screen work,"
said Carl Foreman. "I wanted to write angry letters rather than a
script." Some of the Ten could not even compose letters. Sadie Ornitz
remembered that when her husband, Sam, returned home from prison
in mid-1951, "he was badly shaken by the treatment of prisoners. He
wanted to write about it. He thought he could finish the book in three
to six months, but the words would not come. He never wrote it."

Adrian Scott's writing was "blocked" by "a mass of jagged tension," which hung on for months after his release.

The blacklist and the hostile political atmosphere not only impaired the confidence and creativity of left-wing screen artists, it also deprived them of the social relationships within the radical subculture which had nurtured them in the period before 1947. Nevertheless, it was economic necessity, not lack of solidarity, which caused the dispersal of the impenitent writers, directors, and actors to points quite distant from Hollywood. Many artists came to realize that their chance of employment in the arts increased in direct proportion to the miles they put between themselves and their former home. A small handful, the *very* fortunate, had saved sufficient money or been awarded a tidy enough sum in contract settlements to retire on a standard of living approximating the one they had known. Two such were Marguerite Roberts and her husband, novelist John Sanford, who moved to Santa Barbara, a hundred miles from Los Angeles, but "a world away from Hollywood." The great majority of the blacklisted, however, were obliged to hustle, and a significant percentage (particularly the well-known) to emigrate. If not for the passport hurdles erected by the Department of State, many more screen artists undoubtedly would have left this country, or left earlier than they did.

The pilgrimage out was, in a quirkish sort of way, international fascism's revenge on Hollywood. The immigration of the thirties became the emigration of the fifties, as the great tide of political refugees now moved away from the film capital. Bertolt Brecht and Thomas Mann, who had long since returned to the Germany they had once fled, were subsequently joined in Europe by a slew of their comrades of the Popular Front: Stewart, Scott, Carl Foreman, and Joseph Losey went to England; Wilson, Jarrico, Ben Barzman, and Jules Dassin, to France. Mexico received the single largest contingent of expatriates: Maltz, Butler, Bright, and Kahn, who each remained there for many years; Trumbo, who left after about a year to return to Hollywood; and Lardner and Ian McLellan Hunter, both of whom found the pickings there slim and headed for New York after a short stay. There they became part of the largest exile colony, including Abraham Polonsky, Walter Bernstein, Millard Lampell, Henry Meyers, Edward Eliscu, Jay Gorney, and Mortimer Offner.

Wherever they migrated, however, the blacklisted artists could not leave behind the problems Hollywood caused for them. Their politics and their notoriety marked them in the most banal of ways. They found, for example, that they had become classed by insurance underwriters as "practitioners of a hazardous vocation." Endore's agent told him, "blacklisted people . . . are rated like steeplejacks and gangsters; they must pay an additional fifty percent premium [on their life insurance] because their chances of living out a normal life are that much lower than average."[2] Wherever they lived, the blacklisted experienced emotional pressures as dispiriting to them as their political and professional isolation. It was to be, as Sylvia Jarrico noted, "a horrible period. I couldn't eat or sleep properly. The pressure was so intense that if I had not been morally strengthened by my political past, the current situation would have been crushing, unbearable." No longer living in the same city, their political and social community fragmented, these shared burdens and pressures bound together the blacklisted as they made their separate ways.

A few of the exiles found life in a new culture endurable—so much so, indeed, that some did not return to Hollywood even when the blacklist began to break in the early 1960s. Hugo Butler did the best screenwriting of his life in Mexico. He wrote two (uncredited) scripts for Luis Buñuel (*The Adventures of Robinson Crusoe* and *The Young One*) and two semi-documentary films (*Torero* and *Los Pequeños Gigantes*) on Mexican subjects.* *Torero* won the Robert Flaherty award at the Venice Film Festival. The British Screenwriters Guild nominated Ben Barzman and Millard Lampell for an award for their script for *Blind Date* (released in this country as *Chance Meeting*) in 1959. And Albert Maltz wrote two novels, one play, and five film scripts during his eleven-year sojourn in Mexico City. After seven lean years writing for television in Hollywood, Adrian Scott managed, in London, to recapture the income, standard of living, and freedom from pursuit he had enjoyed prior to October 1947 in Hollywood, while Michael Wilson pseudonymously co-authored two Hollywood blockbusters, *The Bridge on the River Kwai* and *Lawrence of Arabia.* Jarrico, Sidney Buchman, and Donald Ogden Stewart chose to expatriate permanently; the Barzmans lived in Paris and Nice for twenty-seven years. By and large, however, foreign exile was not to the liking of most who underwent it and they returned home as soon as it became professionally possible.

The Barzmans had not fled Hollywood to avoid a subpoena or to find work. He was under contract to MGM in early 1949 when a

---

* These scripts were written in English for an independent production company formed by George Pepper, the former executive secretary of the Hollywood Democratic Committee. American investors provided the majority of the funds.

transatlantic telephone call changed his and his family's lives. Edward Dmytryk was calling from London to tell Barzman that the script—*Christ in Concrete*—which the screenwriter had written, free of charge, was going to be produced by the J. Arthur Rank Studio. Dmytryk urged Barzman to leave for England to assist in the rewrite and production of the script. Excited by the prospect, Barzman convinced the studio to release him from his contract, and he took his family to London, fully intending to return once the film was completed. Subsequent reports from the United States made it clear to Barzman that if he returned to Hollywood he would be unemployable there. It was to be fourteen years before the family reappeared on American soil.

They lived in Paris between 1949 and 1954. During that time, Norma had her passport lifted and was told that it would only be returned "when you are on an American ship bound for America with the passport stamped 'valid for one way trip only.'" (It was not returned until 1958.) Ben, who had been born in Canada, was denaturalized in 1954. When his citizenship was reinstated in 1963, he was presented with a bill for back taxes he owed for his nine years as a non-American.

They then spent six months in Nice and, in August 1954, decided that it was time to settle down. (They had three children.) Norma returned to Paris and purchased a house in Auteuil. They lived in Paris until 1958, after that alternating between winters in London (working for Joseph Losey) and summers in Spain (working for Samuel Bronston). They returned to Los Angeles in 1976.

Living abroad was a very dialectic experience for me [recalled Ben Barzman (who now lives in Los Angeles)]. We were afforded a variety of experiences and exposed to trends in film making which would not have been available to us in America (Italian neorealism, French New Wave). The film producers who sought us out had a political viewpoint similar to our own and we worked, for the most part, with congenial material. In addition, we attended numerous left-wing film congresses where cinematic problems were discussed in a political context.

As blacklisted American screenwriters we were welcomed by the artistic and intellectual community of Europe—not just the left-wing section of it. We came to know Picasso, Sean O'Casey, Joliot-Curie, and others. But the stimulation which came from being exposed to extraordinary figures peaked after about nine or ten years. When it did, in 1958, however, it still was not professionally possible for us to return to the United States.

During the entire experience I felt cheated and victimized; I experienced resentment, humiliation, and rage. The feelings of exclusion, alienation, and uprootedness never really left me. As a writer, I felt circumscribed—a writer needs to be steeped in the mainstream of the culture he is writing about. I did not feel I was a part of the French community.

We were, however, very close with the other blacklisted Americans. We helped each other—were very protective toward one another—because we shared a common vulnerability and a common threat: the American Embassy. Foreign service people exerted tremendous pressure on the French government to get rid of us, and "cultural attachés" hovered around the cutting rooms and film studios. As long as we stayed out of politics, however, the French authorities gave us no trouble. In fact, when the Americans denaturalized me, the French government gave me a *titre de voyage* so I could travel to other European countries for film assignments.

Politics, of course, was off limits for all the exiles, most of whom had been warned by their host governments (or knew enough) to stay quiescent. Maltz experienced something rather worse than this: his political enemies remained quite active. Shortly after arriving in Cuernavaca, he wrote Biberman about the "inauguration of a campaign here directed against those North American politicals who are at the moment in Mexico." The Mexican right-wing clerical newspaper, *Excelsior* (a "mouthpiece for the American Embassy"), had begun to publish a series of diatribes on "Reds in Cuernavaca," aimed at bringing an end to asylum for North Americans in Mexico. The outlook for the exiles was further dimmed by the fate of Gus Hall, Ohio state chairman and national board member of the CPUSA, a rumored victim of the informal extradition process between the FBI and the Mexican police. Hall's "deportation" (following his flight from a Smith Act conviction) had the entire left-wing American expatriate community nervously awaiting the early morning knock on the door.[8] (The local police had, without warning, rousted Hall from his hotel room at gunpoint, handcuffed him, driven him to the airport, and unceremoniously shoved him aboard an FBI-chartered plane. The plane landed in Laredo, Texas, the next morning, October 10, 1951, where Hall was "apprehended.")

Within a year, the Mexican expatriates were once again subjected to Red-baiting—north-of-the-border-style. In August 1952, Richard English, screenwriter and sometime hack journalist, who had authored

Dmytryk's recantation in *The Saturday Evening Post*, penned a slanderous, highly erroneous "account" of the behavior of the blacklisted writers south of the border.[4] Though the accusations were fallacious old bromides—"the American Commies have been feeding anti-U.S. propaganda for use behind the Iron Curtain out of Mexico via Havana"—the antagonisms which the article was expressly designed to create, and English's revelation that "the Mexican FBI keeps up a complete file on [the exiles], down to the last peso on their current bar bills," further aggravated the writers' chronic anxieties.

The blacklisted who wanted to travel were dogged by another severe political problem—passports. Throughout the fifties the United States Government made it difficult for Communists or suspected Communists to receive or keep passports. Secretary of State Dean Acheson announced, in May 1952, that passports were being withheld from alleged Communists, from anyone whose "conduct abroad is likely to be contrary to the best interest of the United States," or from anyone who appeared to be "going abroad to engage in activities which will advance the Communist movement."[5] It was, recalled Albert Maltz, a form of house arrest, which did not end until 1958.

Carl Foreman lived three years in London, incapable of traveling elsewhere because the State Department had annulled his passport after he had arrived in England. Adrian Scott feared that each trip back to the States would entrap him there because his passport would be withheld when he presented it at American customs. "Without fail, every time we came through Immigration," said Joan Scott, "we were given the works. We would present our passport, and no sooner would the official look at the number than he would reach for a red book and check our names against a list. Then we would be separated from a planeload of people and conducted to a special area of the airport where we were left to cool our heels for an hour or more. All the while uniformed officials came and went and conferred among themselves in whispers. When they spoke to us it was in the most surly fashion imaginable." The experiences of Foreman and Scott were not isolated examples, and the blacklistees soon learned the contingent nature of civil liberties and rights in America.

The Blacklisted on the Black Market

Their regular sources of income severed, and legal fees mounting, the "unfriendly" witnesses had to scramble for money. No sooner had Trumbo, Maltz, Cole, and Lawson returned home from the 1947 hearings than they were at work writing scripts under assumed names, at rates well below their usual standards. After 1951 the situation changed completely—the majors ceased trafficking in the black market altogether, and there were few independents willing to risk opprobrium for the benefit of cut-rate talent. There was almost no film work available until the mid-fifties, and even then assignments hardly flowed. The black market was a buyers' paradise; some of the finest screenwriting talent in the world became available at bargain rates to small, independent producers who turned out grade "C" films on shoe-string budgets.

Those few who managed to survive through black market work did so writing for television. And even there, the black market did not really open until 1953. Once it did, however, blacklisted writers found that underground television work, because of the networks' constantly increasing demand for new story material and the producers' desire to use the same writers in ongoing series, paid more than underground film work. Also, it was easier to "hide" in the networks than in the movie studios. Not only did Abraham Polonsky make more money turning out "You Are There" episodes than he ever did at movie writing, but he—and his blacklisted co-authors, Walter Bernstein and Arnold Manoff—derived a certain satisfaction from their work for the CBS series (even though their names never appeared on the screen). The three of them developed a supportive *esprit de corps* in the course of selecting historical subjects who were exemplars of defiant individualism, civil disobedience, philosophical radicalism, and personal integrity. They relished the opportunity to mirror their own self-images in the twenty-four-minute scripts they wrote about Joan of Arc, Socrates, Galileo, the first Salem witchcraft trial, etc.

For most writers, however, the pickings were slimmer, and grew more so as the blacklist grew longer. Many of the men and women were obliged to jockey for a limited number of limited opportunities. Nor was talent the only touchstone of the selection process. Luck, connections, reputation, and the ability to write speedily under pressure counted for more than brilliance. Those who could hustle in this fashion earned enough to survive, but they had to work long, long hours for slight personal fulfillment. By comparison with the hazards, insecurities, and fears of the black market, the writers' buildings must have seemed like havens of the Muse.

The greatest worry of the black market seller was that his identity might somehow become known to the blacklisters. Some producers obviously knew the real identity of their writers. For example, the

King Brothers were aware that Dalton Trumbo ("Robert Rich") was scripting "The Brave One," and Hannah Weinstein had enlisted Ring Lardner and Ian McLellan Hunter to write the popular TV series "The Adventures of Robin Hood." Most assignments, however, required that aliases obtain behind as well as on the screen—i.e., that a writer's identity be hidden from the producer as well as from the viewer. Few film makers or television staff producers were brave enough to risk the loss of their jobs should the identity of their writer become known. To avoid a second cashiering, the blacklisted simply avoided the whole problem by hiding their identities behind a front. Pen names were bad enough—"cashing a check made out to an imaginary person is not a simple matter when your own name cannot appear as endorser. You have to open a bank account under your alias"[6]—but the problems encountered with fronts were worse. *Noms de plume* were manipulable words; fronts were often refractory people. Al Levitt was the "back room" behind two fronts; neither of them worked out. During the first experience Levitt wrote scripts which another man submitted to producers (as in the film *The Front*). They then split the salary checks fifty-fifty. As time went on, however, success went to the front's head and he began to resent Levitt and demand more money. "All you do is sit here at a typewriter," he carped, "I have to go to those damned meetings and sweat out questions [about the script] that I can't answer."

After a time, Levitt tried again to establish a functioning front operation. This time the personalities meshed harmoniously enough, but after a few months the new front caved in, not from fear of discovery, but because, said Levitt, "his psyche could not take putting his name on my work."

"Take a pseudonym," he told me, "and we will write together and attend story conferences together." I feared that someone would blow the whistle on me and that he would suffer as a result. The first time we walked into a studio together I felt like I was on enemy territory. Some of the people there knew who I was—they shot me peculiar looks when they heard my "name"—but no one acknowledged me. The second time I was not so lucky. A secretary looked up and said, "Aren't you Al Levitt?" My partner panicked and ran from the room. I told the secretary I was no longer using that name, canceled the appointment, and followed my co-author to the car. There, the guy who had been pushing me to enter studios and had been joking about my paranoia admitted that he had "lost his head" under the pressure.

In short, it was not easy to be an anonymous writer or a front. One wife who fronted for her husband recounted how producers and executives were always inquiring innocently, "How [and who] is your husband?" She not only had to invent a phony identity for her blacklisted spouse, she had to invent one "that wouldn't intrigue people enough either to pursue the subject or arrange a social get-together. I told my business associates that he was a troubleshooter for White Front stores." (Her husband was indignant when he found this out.) Even so, one especially satisfied producer insisted on meeting the husband of this "wonderful young writer." "Happily" outside circumstance intervened (the cocktail party was canceled) to spare the couple the expense of hiring a male stand-in, as they had prepared to do. (In fact, the couple had a whole repertoire of "contingency plans" about how to appear "uncoupled" should they accidentally bump into a producer of one of their scripts.)

The mushrooming of phony names, and the secrecy surrounding all black market transactions, occasionally produced humorous episodes. In his *Wit and Wisdom of Hollywood*, Max Wilk reports an anecdote concerning blacklisted screenwriter Walter Bernstein. Under the pseudonym "Bob Rogers," Bernstein wrote a script for one producer. Some time later, as "Dick Jones," he was assigned to rewrite a script handed to him by another producer. It was the "Rogers" script.[7] Where Bernstein used two *noms de plume*, Robert Lees wrote under three. For a time it was said that there were more aliases than fleas on the "Lassie" show.

For the most part, though, the black market regulars found the experience anything but funny. As Lawson told Victor Navasky, "[that kind of authorship] corrupted everything and everybody it touched. You took jobs you didn't want, and you didn't even have an opportunity to talk over story points or changes that were made in your work."[8] For men such as Lawson, who had fought for two decades in the Screen Writers Guild to win a fair credit system and who were accustomed to seeing their names on the screen, this kind of anonymity and usurpation of artistic authority cut to the heart. "It hurt like hell not getting credits and accolades for the films I wrote," said Carl Foreman, whose black market scripts included co-authorship of the Academy Award-winning *The Bridge on the River Kwai*.

Considerations of political or social content in a script now, of course, became unheard-of luxuries for men and women blacklisted because of their political views. Ninety-nine per cent of the material that one encountered on the black market did not, in any case, "lend itself" to making "statements." As craftsmen of great professional pride, the blacklisted writers put their best efforts into the schlock they were given, but after the small taste of honey of war and postwar films—*Thirty Seconds Over Tokyo, Sahara, Crossfire, The Boy with Green Hair, Home of the Brave*, etc.—the black market fare was sour mash. Al Levitt's front said to him one day, only partly in jest, "I can see why you got blacklisted—so your name wouldn't have to appear on this shit."

The Politics of Exile and the Exiles' Politics

Opportunities for political activism virtually ceased to exist in the "new era." For one thing the impenitent radicals were by now political pariahs. (Guy Endore wrote, "You feel like the lepers of the Middle Ages, you ought to tinkle a bell and cry out the old warning, 'Unclean!' 'Unclean!' "[9]) Ian Hunter recalled that he and his colleagues "could not even support the political candidates of our choice for fear of smearing the latter with a 'Red' brush." Indeed, as late as 1969, liberal Steve Allen would warn the campaign managers of Los Angeles mayoral candidate Thomas Bradley of the "capital" Bradley's "reactionary opponents will certainly make" over a fund-raising dinner to be hosted by Dalton Trumbo. Allen stated: "It would in no way affect my own admiration for Mr. Bradley that Mr. Trumbo might be one of his supporters but—to go over the ground again—*if* (a) Mr. Trumbo is today of the Communist persuasion (something he has every legal right to be), and *if* (b) this fact is publicized by Mr. Bradley's rightist political opposition, then (c) the March 14th affair will almost certainly be used in such a way as to cost Mr. Bradley a perhaps significant number of votes in this not-always-politically-enlightened city."[10]

For another thing, the movement lived on only as a wraith in the minds of the dispersed left-wingers. The once thriving ICCASP and its Hollywood chapter were by now shadows of their old selves, although the national organization (called, after 1948, the National Council of Arts, Sciences, and Professions) managed an impressive swan song, worthy of inclusion in the annals of the old Popular Front. At the height of the Cold War and anti-Communist crusade, in March 1949, the NCASP sponsored a Cultural and Scientific Conference for World Peace at the Waldorf-Astoria. Harassed by police and government agents, picketed by right-wing groups, and with many of its invited international delegates unable to attend because the State Department revoked or refused visas, the Conference nonetheless managed to attract eighteen thousand people to its closing peace rally at Madison Square Garden, at which John Howard Lawson and Lillian Hellman spoke.[11] That, however, marked the end of NCASP as a generator of newsworthy propaganda. The organization itself finally gave up the ghost in 1955.

The Southern California chapter, with its nucleus of screenwriters still active, also endured through the early fifties. It published a few radical pamphlets—"A Survey of Discrimination in the Health Field in Los Angeles," "The Truth About Korea," and "Can We Live with the Atom?"—before passing into oblivion.

The Hollywood branches of the CPUSA disintegrated at about the same time as the Arts, Sciences, and Professions. HUAC had, of course, mortally wounded the Party's screen artist sections, but it took Khrushchev's revelations about Stalin's crimes and the Soviet invasion of Hungary to apply the *coup de grâce*. Paul Jarrico, who presided over the liquidation of the Party in Hollywood, said that by 1956 there were not even enough people left "to sit down as a group and figure out what we had done wrong." As individuals, however, Communists and ex-Communists passed through what seems to have been a Gethsemane of doubt and self-questioning as they realized (in Jarrico's words) "that all the terrible things that our enemies had been saying about us were true, and that we had been defending indefensible things." Jeff Lawson remembered "my father and his friends going over and over the Khrushchev speech, trying to explain it to themselves. I felt sorry for them; what a tragedy to have to come to that. It put them in a terrible bind." The shock "dislocated" Albert Maltz for six months.

For conscientious Communists like Jarrico, Lawson, Maltz, and others, the great time of suffering was not 1947–48 or the ensuing blacklist, but the shock and dismay of seeing the fabric of their political faith as so many veils of illusion. "The fight with HUAC seemed like a good, healthy political battle," said Jarrico. "We were losing, sure, but we had ammunition and the will to go on fighting." But in 1956 they found the enemy within. "The Party had set itself up as the judge and possessor of truth. It was like discovering the Messiah had feet of clay." This was the dismal end of communism among the screen artists. Only a few surmounted the crisis of the mid-fifties and remained in the CP.

Even though the organizations began to disappear, some political activity continued. Hollywood radicals participated in anti-HUAC, anti-atomic bomb, anti-Korean War, and pro-Rosenberg demonstrations.

The latter generated an especial fervor among some of the blacklisted; Lardner, Wexley, Biberman, Wilson, and others took the risk of expressing public solidarity, in one way or another, with the husband and wife convicted of conspiracy to commit espionage. Wilson, in fact, was one of several dozen people to show up on the steps of the Federal Building in downtown Los Angeles to participate in a night-long vigil on the eve of the Rosenbergs' execution on June 19, 1953. Toward morning, Wilson recalls, an ex-Party comrade turned informer, Roy Huggins, drove up in a Cadillac convertible with the top down, and screamed out, "They're going to fry you Commie bastards, too!" and drove off.

In such a climate, and bereft of institutional forums and support, the Hollywood radicals focused on challenges closer to home—for example, forming the political consciousness of their children. The offspring of the blacklisted do not remember much organized politicking on their parents' part in the fifties or sixties, but many of them do recall an ongoing dinner table education. Rebecca Wilson speaks for many of her counterparts when she describes the earnestness of her parents' evening political discussions with the children. "They wanted us to have their values, to be pro-working class, pro-black, pro-Chicano, pro- all oppressed peoples." The "curriculum" emphasized principles, values, and perspectives, not political activism or sectarian indoctrination.

Beyond this, the Hollywood left-winger was reduced to acts of individual political witness, often enough made to the one-man audience dogging his trail like an unwelcome succubus, the FBI agent. Government surveillance became a constant for those on the blacklist. The "unfriendly" witnesses knew their phones were tapped; they knew their neighbors and friends were being questioned; they knew they could count on regular visits from polite, crew-cut agents in gray suits and fedoras attempting to discover what the blacklistees were doing, where they were working, whom they were seeing. "We lived with the constant sense of feeling hunted," said Sylvia Jarrico (who was fired from her editorial position on the *Hollywood Quarterly* for refusing to sign the University of California loyalty oath).

So everyone got used to "living with the agents." Jeff Lawson regularly steeled himself for the sight of "the man sitting in a car across the street from my house." Donald Ogden Stewart's son, Ames, could literally not walk out the front door without an agent calling to him, "Hey, Ames, d'ya want to talk to us today?" The ringing doorbell became an alarm signal. Kate Lardner, Ring's daughter, remembers that

Hugo Butler was visiting one day when the doorbell sounded. She went to answer it, and Butler pushed her aside, saying that children should never answer the door. (Butler probably did not want to answer it himself—for fear of being handed another subpoena.) More than any other external exigency, even the need to make a living, the constant FBI and governmental attention and the fears generated by government funding of "relocation camps" for "political subversives"† suppressed thoughts of reviving the old political movement.

Though the blacklisted Hollywood radicals dared not act collectively on behalf of the kinds of public causes which would once have mobilized them, they did enroll in a new "cause"—that of their own professional reinstatement. Along the way they often took the opportunities offered them by circumstances to duel with old enemies and speak out for traditional friends, but the modes of their new politics had indubitably narrowed.

They fought on two fronts: against the blacklist, and against the conspiracy and fears which tried to deny them free expression.

The Legal Fight Against the Blacklist

By 1952 it was fairly clear that judges were as infected by the anti-Communist frenzy of the times as were politicians, and that legal action held only the slimmest hope of success. And yet the blacklisted persevered because "the principle of the fight mattered," said Paul Jarrico. He launched the first important legal counteroffensive of the new generation of blacklistees. As a result of his public announcement that he preferred going to jail "like my courageous friends in the Hollywood Ten to crawling in the mud [of informing] like Larry Parks," Jarrico was literally locked out of the studio (RKO) where he was

---

† Section 103 (a) of the McCarran Internal Security Act, passed over President Truman's veto in September 1950, read: "Whenever there shall be in existence [an "Internal Security Emergency"], the President, acting through the Attorney General, is hereby authorized to apprehend and by order detain, pursuant to the provisions of this title, each person as to whom there is reasonable ground to believe that such person probably will engage in, or probably will conspire with others to engage in, acts of sabotage. . . ."

James V. Bennett, director of the Federal Bureau of Prisons, announced in September 1952 that $775,000 had already been expended for the "activation and rehabilitation" of six relocation camps, which were capable of holding well over sixty thousand Communists. (John Wexley, *The Judgment of Julius and Ethel Rosenberg*, New York: Cameron & Kahn, 1955, p. 148.)

under contract. The screenplay on which he had been working was given to other writers. Howard Hughes refused to abide by the ruling of the Screen Writers Guild that Jarrico be given a co-credit for *The Las Vegas Story*, and filed a declaratory judgment suit against Jarrico, charging breach of the morals clause. Jarrico counterclaimed with a $350,000 damage suit against RKO, while the Guild filed its own suit to compel the studio to live up to the credit arbitration agreement.

On November 26, 1952, Superior Court judge Orlando Rhodes ruled that Jarrico's refusal to answer HUAC's questions constituted a violation of the morals clause. He stated that taking the Fifth Amendment to avoid testifying had come to be associated in the public mind with Communist Party membership or sympathy, either of which rendered the invoker an "object of public disgrace, obloquy, ill will and ridicule."[12] Though Jarrico appealed his case all the way to the Supreme Court of the United States, the verdict stood. As such, it represented far more than a personal loss for Paul Jarrico, for in effect the American court system partly sabotaged the legal principle of mutuality of contract and undercut the civil protection afforded by the Fifth Amendment by accepting studio management's contention that reliance on the Bill of Rights amounted, *prima facie*, to a violation of the morals clause of a contract.

The Guild's action, meanwhile, not only failed of its own weight when a flaw was discovered in the union's contract with studio management,‡ but essentially brought all further Guild anti-blacklist activity to a complete halt. The producers agreed to renegotiate their collective bargaining agreement with the Guild only if the SWG agreed to drop the anti-trust suit filed in 1948, as well as to acquiesce in the studios' refusal to give screen credits to alleged Communists and "unfriendly" witnesses. In 1953 the Guild voted by an overwhelming 9–1 margin in favor of whitewashing the blacklist.[18] One year later the Guild voted to deny membership in the union to known Communists. In this, as in many other instances, the obsessions, fears, and diversions engendered by anti-communism worked dramatically against the interests and progress of organized artists in the entertainment industry.

Daunted but stubborn, and with no other recourse save abandoning the battle altogether, the blacklisted persevered with their litigations. In March 1953, twenty-three "unfriendly" witnesses—fourteen

---

‡ The credit arbitration clause was worded in such a way that it left the writer alone to pursue judicial redress if the Guild and the recalcitrant studio could not come to an agreement—i.e., the Guild had no legal standing to sue a motion picture studio for breach of this clause.

writers, six actors, and three other film workers—announced their intent to file a $51 million damage suit in Los Angeles Superior Court, charging the studios with conspiracy to blacklist. *Wilson* v. *Loew's*, filed in July, fared no better than any other attempts by blacklisted film personnel to secure redress of their grievances through the courts. Superior Court judge Ellsworth Meyer sustained the demurrers of the defendants and dismissed the complaint. The California District Court of Appeals upheld the lower court in June 1956, the California Supreme Court refused to hear the case, and the United States Supreme Court upheld the lower court in March 1958. As before, the plaintiffs were informed at every judicial level that, appearances to the contrary notwithstanding, loss of employment as a result of refusal to testify before HUAC did not qualify as an infringement on their right of association or opinion, nor did it deprive them unfairly of their "economic welfare." As late as 1960 another group of blacklisted screen artists tried the tack offered by Washington attorney David Shapiro—to take on the Producers' Association with weapons provided by the Sherman Antitrust Act. The case, *Nedrick Young et al.* v. *Motion Picture Association of America, Inc.*, was launched at a large gathering at Carnegie Hall in September 1961. It dragged on for five years, and was finally settled for $100,000.

Thus, for the blacklisted, the legal route was not a road to victory and vindication, but part of the ongoing struggle with the forces of repression. As Robert L. Richards, a blacklisted screenwriter who spent money, energy, and years suing the studios, wrote to Ben Margolis in 1962, "It concerns not merely the issue of job reinstatement for a comparative handful of Hollywood people, but can result in a decisive blow at the whole process of trial-by-committee and political firings that has intimidated and silenced untold numbers of people in this country for the past fifteen years."[14]

The Struggle to Be Heard

The significant (and ironical) personal victory which a handful of left-wing screenwriters wrought for themselves out of the defeat and destruction of their professional careers was that for the first time they succeeded in commingling their artistic with their political impulses. Involuntarily freed from the obligation to maintain reputations as commercially viable script writers, hence to turn out shootable screenplays on subjects which barely interested them, a number of writers now had the time, inclination, and material out of which to produce political and creative work. "We suffered from a terrible sense of isolation," said Michael Wilson, "and political writing was an attempt to break out and reestablish contact with society, to be heard." That their efforts at communication here, as elsewhere, were destined to go unheeded and unsupported did not mean that they failed. The small corpus of literary and film work turned out by a group of the most talented blacklisted writers remains unique in the annals of screen history and significant to the political formation of later generations of left-wingers.

In the course of its short life, the *Hollywood Review*, published by the film members of the Southern California chapter of the Arts, Sciences, and Professions, produced a quality of radical criticism heretofore unknown (and unexpected) from the film industry Left. Sustained by the energies of Helen Levitt and Sylvia Jarrico, it far surpassed the work that film radicals—or for that matter, anyone else —had done in the regular CP organs (*New Masses, Daily Worker, People's World*) of the thirties and forties. Though the *Review* reached very few people—Al Levitt guessed five hundred ("we had the feeling we were shouting into an empty barrel")—the work of turning out the paper absorbed the attention of an important contingent of the blacklisted and gave them hope and satisfaction. In all, nine issues of the periodical appeared at irregular intervals between January 1953 and June 1956. It was not intended by the editors to be a general political journal, but a critical review focusing on American films— more specifically on the increasing violence, sadism, hatred, bigotry, and glorification of brutality perpetrated on audiences by the entertainment industry. Each issue contained one major article which attempted to link trends in motion pictures with the developments of the Cold War, or to critique film depiction of minorities, women, and the foreign-born.

Two decades before Molly Haskell's *From Reverence to Rape*, Sylvia Jarrico's "Evil Heroines of 1953" offered a radical feminist analysis and commentary on the calculated and unjust treatment of women in American movies.[15] Noting that while the majority of women's roles continued to spotlight characters cut from the homespun cloth of romance, domesticity, and subservience to men, there had emerged a newer, postwar stereotype which Jarrico called "women of will." She is "a killer . . . , a long-range calculator and absolutely ruthless . . . a force of evil." This "spine-tingling change," a Cold War production, was not a mere wrinkle of fashion or a chance occurrence, but represented a deliberate counterattack by a male-dominated industry (and society) on a new and potentially powerful social force, the millions of women trained or made confident and conscious by the war mobilization.

> The complacent theme that submission is the natural state of women has given way to the aggressive theme that submission is the *necessary* state of women. . . . Hollywood's sinister heroines constitute a sharpened attack on the opportunities and capacities of real women to take effective action in behalf of themselves, their families, their communities, and their nation.

In two cogent essays Michael Wilson sought to expose Hollywood's enlistment in the Cold War. A new kind of war film had appeared, wrote Wilson, which glorified "concepts required of the Korean War: blind obedience, the killer instinct, sacrificial death." The latent purpose of these films was to "inculcate a martial spirit that would not fade away with any eventual cessation of hostilities in Korea."[16] Furthermore, a new kind of hero had emerged in adventure films: "[he is] dead-pan, he walks alone, like a stalking cat, seeking a personal solution to a social problem; he prefers violence to debate." He is a ruthless, contemptuous, inhuman killer, and the films in which he appears, wrote Wilson, "are not escapist, but propaganda films, expressing the doctrines of Manifest Destiny, the American Century, and white supremacy in gaudy technicolor."[17]

In these, as in other articles focusing on blacks, workers, TV, the Cold War "thaw" of 1956, and the blacklist, writers like Sylvia Jarrico, Wilson, Al Levitt, Lawson, and Scott continued in the *Hollywood Review* the fight that they had undertaken from their first years in Hollywood. Eventually, however, the paper's funds dried up, and no new sources of income arose to replace those contributed by the Arts, Sciences, and Professions, which folded in 1955. Also, Jarrico and Wilson decamped for Paris and brighter job prospects. With their departure the *Hollywood Review* went out of existence.

Its life span exactly coincided with that of the *California Quarterly*, a monument to blacklisted screenwriter Philip Stevenson's determination to maintain a forum for radical writers and poets. He and his co-editors (Lawrence P. Spingarn, Thomas McGrath, Wilma Shore, Sonora Babb, and Dolph Sharp) published stories and poems by Aimé Césaire, B. Traven, Pablo Neruda, Louis Aragon, Ray Bradbury, Nelson Algren, and a host of other, younger writers. One issue (Summer 1953) was devoted to *Salt of the Earth*, a film made by blacklistees. (See page 417.) In the first issue (Autumn 1951), which appeared on the morrow of Stevenson's uncooperative appearance before HUAC, the editors noted that they had founded the *Quarterly* "on the conviction that more good writing will come out of the nineteen-fifties than is likely to achieve publication. . . . Contemporary writing is threatened equally by censorship and obscurantism."

Those screenwriters who turned to novel writing in the early and mid-fifties discovered the harsh truth of those quoted words.

Albert Maltz had moved to Mexico "partly to avoid getting recommitted to political activity. I wanted to concentrate now on being a writer." And yet the urge to "be political" did not subside. He wrote to Biberman that "I continue to swing like a God damn pendulum" between the urge to return home and join the political fight, and the urge to stay in Mexico and write. Writing, after all, could itself be "a weapon that reaches very wide."[18] One of the books that Maltz wrote in exile—*A Long Day in a Short Life*—was probably his finest novel in the marriage it effected between the political and the aesthetic. Juxtaposing the day in prison of Floyd Varney, Caucasian, with that of a fellow inmate, Huey Wilson, black man, Maltz's subtle story manages to touch on numerous socio-political themes, from an unjust system of criminal justice to racism to class conflict to black pride and consciousness, without appearing didactic or discursive. Nevertheless, seventeen American publishers, including Little, Brown, which had published Maltz's three previous novels, rejected the new manuscript. By contrast, sixteen overseas houses, including publishers in England, Denmark, Norway, Sweden, Holland, Italy, and Argentina, accepted it. The book sold well in England and the German Democratic Republic, and enjoyed a moderate success in most of the other countries in which it appeared.

Ring Lardner, Jr., Philip Stevenson, and John Wexley fared somewhat better than Maltz—that is, they were able to find American firms which would publish their books. Lardner's satirical novel about the Cold War and the dangers of uncritically embracing an ideology, *The Ecstasy of Owen Muir*, however, was rejected by all the major houses to which it was sent. It was published, finally, by Angus Cameron, a blacklistee from the publishing industry.* Ignored by critics, boycot-

---

* Cameron had been chief editor at Little, Brown. At the same time, he had been active with the Boston People's Educational Center (a socialist school), and an open supporter of Henry Wallace's campaign for the presidency. Singled out by *Counterattack*, he was forced to resign his position

ted by most bookstores, the book enjoyed a favorable response in England.

Philip Stevenson used a pseudonym, Lars Lawrence, to avoid Lardner's difficulties. G. P. Putnam's Sons purchased the first volume of his ambitious tetralogy about working-class life in New Mexico, *The Seed*. In the opus Stevenson drew on his memory of events he had witnessed in the thirties to sketch an anthropological mural of the culture and events (a miners' strike and its violent aftermath) which engulfed a proletarian Mexican-American community in the Southwest. *The Seed*, though it came closer than any other American novel to presenting a realistic, sympathetic literary portrayal of working-class life, was poorly publicized; only a few hundred copies were sold.

John Wexley, for his part, produced a magisterial, in-depth dissection of the Rosenberg case. Considering the virulent and hostile atmosphere surrounding defenders of the executed "spies," and the primitive state of investigative journalism, *The Judgment of Julius and Ethel Rosenberg* (recently updated and reissued) was a monumental accomplishment. In it, Wexley carefully and thoroughly destroyed the government's case.

The most important single achievement of the blacklisted, however, was not a literary but a cinematic enterprise. As early as 1948, Herbert Biberman had organized a company called Film Associates, Inc., with the intention of making movies which would combine high standards of technical excellence with progressive story content. Biberman and his friends had high hopes for their undertaking; they had a property and plans to shoot it in Mexico. They had even secured the collaboration of the Actors' Lab Theater, a group of left-wing actors from the old Group Theatre of the thirties. But the demands of the Ten's legal defense, jail, the blasts of the Tenney Committee against the Actors' Lab, which caused it to fold, and the return of HUAC brought an end to Film Associates, Inc.[19]

"It wasn't until 1951, when we were good and dead professionally,

---

in 1951. With Albert E. Kahn, author of a critical commentary on postwar America, *High Treason: The Plot Against the People* (1950), Cameron formed a publishing company in 1953. It was, recalled Abraham Polonsky, "the only place a blacklisted screenwriter could get published." Cameron and Kahn (and later Cameron Associates, Inc.) brought out Polonsky's *A Season of Fear*, Alvah Bessie's *The Un-Americans*, and John Wexley's *The Judgment of Julius and Ethel Rosenberg*.

that we could get involved in movies that packed a real social and political wallop," said Paul Jarrico, alluding to *Salt of the Earth*, the film produced in 1953–54 by a company founded entirely by blacklisted artists. So great was the founders' commitment to Independent Productions Corporation that Biberman, Scott, and Jarrico vowed to take no other work until the company was established. They outlined an ambitious program: a film on Paul Robeson to be written by John Howard Lawson and Carlton Moss; a film on the trial of a black woman (Helen Johnson) to be written by Dalton Trumbo; a short feature on the life of Frederick Douglass to be called *The House on Cedar Hill*, written by Al Levitt and Moss; a documentary of trade unions; and *Salt of the Earth*.

Reality overtook the bold prospectus—only *Salt* got made. It was a unique film in the degree it succeeded in drawing together the political ideas and film-making talents of the screen artists involved. *Salt of the Earth* relates the story of a strike of Mexican-American mine workers and the rise to feminist and union consciousness of their wives. From the outset the production faced the same forces of political and cultural oppression which had cost its makers their jobs in Hollywood and closed the doors of American publishing houses to their literary efforts.[20] In May 1952 Roy Brewer not only refused Independent Productions Corporation an IATSE film crew with which to produce *Salt*, but promised to do everything in his power to prevent the making of the movie. Throughout 1953, while production was in progress, the Jarricos, Biberman, Wilson, and others connected with it were bitterly attacked from the floor of Congress, in the pages of the *Hollywood Reporter*, from the offices of the IATSE and RKO studios. Local vigilante groups arose in the New Mexico towns where *Salt* was being filmed, and one night a pitched gun battle took place at the ranch where the film crew was living.

Despite all of these obstacles, not to mention Brewer's strenuous efforts to interfere with post-production work, *Salt* was finished and copies printed for distribution. It premiered in a few theaters in New York in March 1954, and enjoyed good reviews and excellent box office. Yet no distributor, major or minor, would pick up the film. Ben Margolis said that in four decades of legal experience he had never seen a more complete boycott or more egregious violation of the anti-trust laws. He termed it "a complete breakdown of law and order. And the frustration of it was we couldn't hope to win satisfaction in court." The producers of *Salt* nonetheless mounted a juridical battle to win enforcement of the anti-trust laws against the conspiracy to blacklist their film; the litigation dragged on for ten years before Independent Productions lost.

Salt of the Earth has always enjoyed a fairly active underground and international life. It was well received in Europe, winning the International Grand Prix for best film shown in France (1955) and the Karlovy Vary award at the Czechoslovakian Film Festival of the same year. Although it has not to this day received commercial distribution, and therefore has not made back the money it cost, it continues to be shown on college campuses, in museums and art houses, and in union halls; it has become, in fact, one of the leading "cult films" of the American Left. At the outset, its producers had hoped that *Salt* would return a large enough profit to finance the company's other film projects; by the end, however, simply getting the film made at all constituted a major achievement for the men and women involved. "It refurbished our sense of political usefulness," said Sylvia Jarrico, the assistant producer; "the film was useful not just to ourselves but to that marvelous bunch of workers in New Mexico" (many of whom appeared in *Salt*). Al Levitt thought that the sheer fact of the film's appearance infused hope in the hearts of blacklisted artists everywhere.

The End of the Blacklist

Though Dalton Trumbo is usually credited with unraveling the blacklist and blazing the trail back to the major studios, his experience with *The Brave One* was only part of the occasion, and certainly not the cause.[21] The blacklisted, in the early sixties, were favored by the political winds which once blew so ill for them. "Peaceful coexistence" with the Soviet Union and the election and inauguration of John F. Kennedy signaled a liberalized political climate in the United States. Only under these circumstances could the absurdities attendant to ghosts and *noms de plume* walking off with Academy Awards have signaled the beginning of the end of the motion picture blacklist.

Like everyone else, Trumbo did business on the black market in order to support himself and his family; he was, in fact, compulsive about this financial goal, writing to Biberman, when the latter invited him to join Independent Productions:

> I am, from today [August 1951] on and for some time in the future, not interested in pamphlets, speeches, or progressive motion pictures. I have got to earn money—a considerable sum of it—very quickly. I cannot and will not hypothecate two or three

months, or even a month, for any project that doesn't contain the possibility of an immediate and substantial sum.[22]

In fact, Trumbo wrote a very long script for IPC on the trial of a black woman. Biberman and Jarrico criticized it and some testy letters were exchanged over the project.

Instead, Trumbo, on his return from Mexico in 1953, established himself as a kind of central clearinghouse for black market work. He and Michael Wilson accepted every assignment which came their way, trying to secure for their colleagues the scripts they did not have time to do themselves. In 1956 one of Trumbo's pseudonyms, "Robert Rich," unexpectedly won an Academy Award (Best Motion Picture Story) for *The Brave One*, and it slowly dawned on the writer that here might be a means of turning his economic way of life into a political assault on the blacklist. He began deliberately to augment and manipulate the industry's considerable interest in "Robert Rich," making it appear as if there were a thriving black market all over Hollywood responsible for virtually every important film of the last five years.

Trumbo bided his time as he calculated the effects of the systematic campaign of gossip, innuendo, and whispers he was orchestrating. He revealed the identity of "Robert Rich" only after fellow blacklistee Nedrick Young had announced that the "Nathan E. Douglas" who had written the script for *The Defiant Ones* was none other than Nedrick Young, the blacklisted screenwriter. Since the film was favored to win a screenwriting Oscar for "Douglas" and his co-author Harold J. Smith, the Academy was forced to rescind its rule disqualifying Fifth Amendment witnesses from Academy Award consideration. Three days later, on January 16, 1959, Trumbo told the world that he was indeed the "Robert Rich" who had scripted *The Brave One*.

One year later Otto Preminger took the decisive step and announced that Trumbo had written *Exodus* and that the writer's name would appear on the screen. Preminger's courage bolstered that of Kirk Douglas, who agreed to give Trumbo screen credit for *Spartacus*. The year was 1960, and it proved to be an important watershed. Thereafter, in a slow-moving column, the "lepers" began to return from their valley.

A few did, that is; but not all—and not even a large minority. In all perhaps 10 per cent of the blacklisted artists managed to recover active professional lives in the film industry. It was not mainly continued political prejudice which kept most of the radicals out of the business after the blacklist died, but the competitive nature of the game itself. A decade or more without a screen credit made it difficult, usually impossible, for the older generation to get jobs—particularly in a market of significantly declining production rates. Fashions had changed, talent had perhaps withered for want of exercise, new and younger faces popped up where older, more familiar associates had once sat. Undoubtedly many of the "other 90 per cent" took a stab or two at recovering their former careers and fortunes, but the hurdles were too high and could not be cleared.

As the long night of the blacklist slowly lifted, there appeared something of a tendency, particularly noticeable among those like Trumbo who had appeared to triumph over long odds, if not precisely to forgive and forget, then at least to try to reconcile antagonists with embracing, anodyne formulas. "It will do no good to search for villains or heroes because there were none," Trumbo told the Writers Guild of America West when he gratefully accepted its Laurel Award in 1970. "There were only victims." "Only victims" did not appeal to many of Trumbo's colleagues among the Ten and the Left in general. Maltz, for one, angrily reacted: "To say that those who aided and applauded these committees, and did their bidding, were also 'victims' along with those who opposed them and thereby suffered public humiliation, slander, job blacklist and blasted careers, is factual nonsense and lacking in moral judgment."[23]

Indeed it would appear that Trumbo, in his uncharacteristic effort to be magnanimous and polite, also showed himself to be uncharacteristically apolitical. As a lifelong radical he should not have overlooked the crucial dimension of moral choice which his phrase "only victims" seems to discount. The fact is neither side—informer or blacklisted—qualified as "victim," if the term is understood as meaning helpless. Dmytryk, Kazan, Parks, and Collins were no more "swept up" in a flood tide they did not understand than were Lawson, Lardner, or Polonsky. Nearly every conscious, politically thoughtful person in Hollywood—i.e., virtually all the liberals and radicals—knew perfectly well who the opposition was, what it stood for, and what resisting or capitulating to it would imply. The blacklisted were therefore not victims, as Maltz seemed to suggest, any more than the turncoats were. Neither side stood still before the superior force which swept over Hollywood; the blacklisted were those who chose to fight, while the informers submitted in order to save their professional and personal lives. Those who fought were resoundingly and endlessly defeated in nearly every facet of their struggle, but the defeated are not necessarily the victimized.

As for "heroes," perhaps Trumbo is closer to the truth; perhaps he is not. It depends, one would suppose, largely on who is doing the defining, and when. The blacklisted have certainly always enjoyed heroic status among elements of the Left; and in recent (post-1975) years their image or mystique has permeated through to the mainstream of the "new" Hollywood. Without making a judgment on a question which by definition does not lend itself to "final" statements, the historian would simply note that if heroism is to mean a display of ample measures of courage, intelligence, transcendence, fidelity, and solidarity in the face of an organized assault on basic democratic rights, at moments when such traits entail suffering, loss, and insecurity, then a large number of the blacklisted were heroes. If, on the other hand, the word is intended to denote Plutarchian or Homeric traits of purity, strength, selflessness, omniscience, then, to a man and a woman, the blacklisted fell short.

Conclusion: the Effects of the Blacklist

Any human tragedy or testing, however regrettable and evil, offers the opportunity for transcendence and growth as well as collapse and destruction. A few of the blacklisted disintegrated completely under the enormous pressure of losing career, income, status, friends, perhaps family. The deaths of at least a half-dozen people—including actors John Garfield, J. Edward Bromberg, and Canada Lee—can be traced directly to their ensnarement in the anti-Communist dragnet of the early fifties. Dozens of other blacklistees lost husbands and wives, mental and physical health as a result of their misfortune.

Undoubtedly many of the blacklisted who survived intact would agree with Michael Wilson's judgment that "many of us grew during that period rather than withered. It tested our mettle; we came out the better for it. We attained a more abiding and profound humanism, a greater compassion, and a philosophical perspective on our own lots, which could certainly have been much worse. Compared to political refugees in other lands we had it relatively easy."

Some of the children of the blacklist developed close ties with one another, establishing something almost like a kinship. In New York City, where Tim Hunter (son of Ian) grew up, there was a small group of "outcast" families. Merely friends and acquaintances before the events of 1951–53, they became welded together in sustaining, nourishing ways thereafter. "I grew up with a real sense of loyalty and community, a sense of an extended family. I knew that if anything happened to my parents, there were other 'parents' who would care for me." Michael Butler (son of Hugo) described similar feelings about his youth in Mexico City: "The bond which held together the American political expatriates was probably shared by few groups anywhere. We cut through a lot of bullshit in our need to stick together."

Such testimonies could be multiplied almost indefinitely. For the most part the exiled withstood the challenge and rose to the occasion. Yet they and their dependents would all agree that it would have been better to have reaped such personal and spiritual benefits under different circumstances—circumstances of their own choosing.

Far less strengthening or positive was the blacklist's impact on the film industry. As a place to work Hollywood became much less interesting and original. Never daring in the first place, the studios withdrew before the lengthening shadows of HUAC and McCarthy into the dictated confines of patriotic conformity and circumscribed creativity. Controversial or "social" subjects, at best only a minor portion of previous production schedules, were no longer even countenanced as story material at the majors. (John Paxton was not even permitted to write in a black cab driver in a film about suicide he was writing for Darryl Zanuck.) Indeed, it was only in contrast with Hollywood's output in the fifties that many artists, including those very same radicals who hotly criticized the limitations of the earlier eras, began to conclude that movies of the thirties and forties were so "daring" or so good. Hollywood films of the fifties did not lack *any* political or social content, however; they contained a conservative, vindictive, triumphal content which betrayed the new forces and attitudes at work in the industry. The studios took giant steps backward in their depictions of women, war, crime, and government on film, while the near complete exclusion of the poor, workers, blacks, and minorities (with the exception of American Indians, who existed simply as screaming bodies to be picked off by blue-suited cavalry or trigger-happy cowboys) provided mute witness to the studios' enlistment as auxiliaries in the greater struggle unleashed by HUAC.

Such conclusions were not merely those of the *Hollywood Review* staffers. Nearly everyone noticed sooner or later the ice age which had descended on Hollywood. Leonard Spigelgass, a successful screenwriter and a moderate liberal, testified in a deposition that the Waldorf resolution:

> had the effect upon this industry of stifling the creation of original stories which might "probe the dark corners and dark places of our society." There came as a result a distinct fear on the part of many people . . . a fear of writing and creating those materials which they normally would [have chosen to work on] before this resolution was written. I can go on with a long list of classic American folklore which we no longer use and which I no longer use because I feel it will not sell and, if I may say as a postscript, it is because there is fear prevalent among the second level of the producers predicated and based entirely and only upon [the Waldorf Statement].[24]

Arthur Miller discovered that a clearance procedure for scripts existed which almost seemed to duplicate that for employees. Miller had offered a screenplay about waterfront labor racketeering to Harry Cohn. Cohn felt obliged to submit the material to Roy Brewer, who called it "fallacious" and turned it over to the FBI for its "expert" consideration. No AFL union countenanced racketeering, averred Brewer, and, more to the point, "no writer loyal to the United States would have conceived such a script, whose effect would only be to create turmoil on the New York docks across which flowed the supplies for our armies in Korea." Miller's script met a predictable fate at the hands of Brewer, Cohn, and the FBI: "it was decided that all I had to do was change the script so that instead of union racketeers terrorizing the workers, it would be the Communists."[25] (The film which Columbia eventually made about longshore labor, On the Waterfront (1954), was written and directed by informers—Budd Schulberg and Elia Kazan—and glorified the hero's decision to testify against his former friends and union comrades.)

Nor, according to David Niven, did the Hollywood society which remained after the departure of the blacklisted reflect the inner glow of the newly purified:

> Hollywood was deeply wounded . . . and for years friendships, careers, marriages, and reputations lay in tatters as the arguments waxed and waned about who had behaved well, who had behaved badly, and who had saved their skins at the expense of others.[26]

The blacklist was a scourge. Everything, including America, withered from contact with it.

Epilogue

It was early in the winter of 1974. The Hollywood Left had not known organized existence for two decades. Many of its most energetic animators were dead: Ornitz, Kahn, Scott, Biberman, Young, Butler. Quiescence reigned among the survivors. During the anti-war movement of the sixties, a few of them had appeared at some demonstrations, but, by and large, age, ill health, the grind of earning a living, or weariness indisposed most of the former blacklisted to political activity. Now when the telephone or doorbell rang, it was a much better bet that the inquirer was a journalist or writer requesting an interview than a government agent asking questions.

Alone in these crepuscular shadows, Sadie Ornitz received her copy of the Encyclopedia Judaica, an Israeli publication, containing biographical sketches of prominent Jewish people. When she looked up the entry for her husband, she discovered that the authors had chosen to ignore completely Sam's political work in the anti-fascist fronts, his union efforts, the struggles of the Ten, and instead to produce a venomous indictment of Ornitz for an alleged anti-Semitic tone and content in his novels:

> Ornitz, a professed atheist, saw no virtues in Jewish immigrant life and wished to end Jewish isolation by a policy of outright assimilation. He defied Jewish opinion with his violently hostile portrayals of Jewish types, notably the money-chasing "allrightniks" detested by contemporary leftists and anti-Semites.[27]

While it was true that Ornitz, like many Jewish writers of the interwar era, wrote critically and humorously of Jewish immigrant life (notably in his popular *Haunch Paunch and Jowl,* 1923), the Encyclopedia entry was extraordinarily unjust and inaccurate in its judgment of Ornitz, a man who had greatly valued and delighted in his Jewish heritage.

Sadie Ornitz, a woman who cherished her husband's memory and shared his political mettle, telephoned Albert Maltz. Maltz came immediately, read the piece, and then composed a letter which he sent out to everyone still alive in the old Hollywood Left. He asked his former comrades:

For [Sadie Ornitz's] sake, but more importantly, to rescue the good name of an honorable man for future generations, this untrue and dreadful characterization of Ornitz must be changed when the next edition of this *Encyclopedia* is printed. Will you write a letter . . . stating that you know this biography is untrue and asking that it be changed in the next edition?

"To rescue the good name of an honorable man" proved a cause which drew indignant letters (to the Encyclopedia editors) from the familiar names which have appeared in the pages of this book: Maltz, Cole, Bessie, Lardner, Jarrico, Lees, Jean Butler, Sklar, Rosenwein, Edward Biberman, and many more. Once again, as they had done for the Screen Writers Guild, the Anti-Nazi League, the Popular Front, the Hollywood Democratic Committee, the Hollywood Ten, and the struggle against the blacklist, the Old Guard answered the call to battle. Despite mistakes, regrets, and defeats, amid the passing of years, the waning of energies, and the weakening of social and personal ties, in new times and a very different world, their spirit of community and struggle endured.

Afterword

This book, in part a product of the dissatisfaction engendered in us by the historical shortcomings and extreme anti-communism of previous efforts, has, in turn, occasionally rendered us dissatisfied and impatient with those people we thought would be our best sources of information: former members of the Hollywood branches of the CPUSA. Ironically, the majority of them—who should be most interested in setting the record straight—remain mute and unresponsive to the issues most frequently distorted by their anti-Communist foes: the role of the Communist Party in progressive political and social activity of the thirties and forties and the question of their relationship to it. A graphic demonstration of the difficulty which former Hollywood Communists still have with public acknowledgment occurred at a Blacklist Retrospective in May 1977 in Los Angeles. *Salt of the Earth,* the proudest cinematic event in the Left's experience, had just been screened. On the theater stage sat five people who had been instrumental in the making of the film, answering questions from the audience. A man asked: "What was the relation between the basic themes of the film—labor, ethnic, and female consciousness—and the Communist Party line?" The moment of truth. The audience held its breath. The panel members were silent. We, knowing they all had been Party members and knowing further that the race question, the woman question, and the trade union question had been the topics of many endless discussions in the Hollywood branches of the Party, sat expectantly in our chairs. Finally, Michael Wilson, who wrote the script, once again angrily dodged the question: "We were *all* political—the film came out of our political beliefs."

In short, the struggle over the right to remain silent on these interrogatories has come to figure as the Hollywood Left's Battle of the Marne in the war against political repression in America. The veterans of this conflict are enthusiastically willing to discuss most questions save the central ones of "Are you now or have you ever been?", "Who else is or was?", and "What did the experience connote?" This reticence is historically understandable, perhaps even justified, but it makes the historians' job all the more difficult, even distasteful, when he has to become pushy in an interview or make use of the testimony of informers and turncoats.

Such is the aura about discussing the Party that even we, as historians, have noticed again and again a reserve on our parts both toward asking for particulars from our sources and divulging them in print. Through examining our impatience and reticence as well as that of our sources, and by discussing this whole delicate question with a small handful of particularly candid, trusting Party members of the 1936–56 period, we have derived a set of reasons which, we believe, explains why a Party member might justifiably refuse to speak. First, and most obviously, having suffered unfairly and profoundly for refusing, under degrading circumstances, to answer that question, the Communists and fellow travelers are now loath to be candid. Indeed some have developed a kind of First Amendment fetishism—"it's my right not to speak." This reaction is especially understandable in view of the fact that nearly all the latter-day authors of books and articles on this subject have been anti-Communist in tone if not in practice. If you have gone to prison or lost your job for saying nothing to Robert Stripling or Frank Tavenner, why speak openly to Robert Vaughn or Stefan Kanfer? (Silence in the face of hostile interpretations or perceived misuse of confidences has now swung from left to right to keep pace with the nature of the histories now being written. Informers Richard Collins and Leo Townsend told us that they were no longer giving interviews because they felt that their remarks were twisted and used out of context. Right-winger John Lee Mahin noted that he, and Roy Brewer and Morrie Ryskind, were tired of dueling with interviewers whose politics were so obviously hostile to their own.)

Secondly, the way in which the question is usually asked implies a reductionist understanding of the problem—"Oh, you were, were you? Well then, that explains everything"—which betrays the complexity, subtleties, and intangibilities of historical evidence. Membership in the Communist Party meant many things to the screen people and there were nearly as many kinds of Communists as there were individual Communists. Specifically there were key differences according to degree of commitment, psychological disposition, length of stay in the Party, reasons for joining and leaving, in which era one joined the Party, where one joined, one's activities within the Party, etc. In sum, simply knowing that a man or woman was a "Communist," and knowing nothing else about him or her, is to know rather less than one imagines. Until recently only the Communists themselves seemed to understand this.

Thirdly, many of the men and women who might justifiably be posed this question are still professionally active in show business and are therefore concerned about what further travails may devolve upon them for late-in-the-day indiscretions. In an industry as competitive as film or television, where there might be forty reasons why one person does not get the job he or she hopes for, why add a possible forty-first? It may well be temporarily fashionable to have been a blacklistee; and someone of the current invulnerability of Lillian Hellman may win applause by publicly rebuking, on national television no less, the Academy of Motion Picture Arts and Sciences for its supineness before the forces of reaction in the forties and fifties. Nevertheless, open admission of past or present membership in the CPUSA can be a high-risk venture in America in any era.

The fourth and final reason for reticence issues from the preservative, protective instincts of the political Left anywhere. This is a multifaceted sensitivity: protection of the ongoing movement itself; protection of the history of the movement from the Philistines and adversaries who would willfully distort or destroy it; protection of the individual's personal memories of youthful purpose and fulfillment from the armchair criticisms of even "friendly" historians. Having been periodically savaged by the forces of government and the Right since the days of Daniel Shays, the Left has evolved an automatic instinct to safeguard its very existence that occasionally functions like a retreating general husbanding his troops even at the expense of abandoning fortresses and positions to the enemy. This is a defensible strategy sometimes, but there comes a limit to what one may give up without effectively doing the enemy's work for him. Thus left-wingers in America, particularly Communists, have occasionally assumed stands of extreme incommunicability and exclusivity, and even outright dishonesty or intentional self-blindness, in their felt need to protect themselves, their movement, and their memories. The danger becomes, then, a twofold one: leftists may either distort the truth altogether—as when they abandon all critical self-scrutiny and engage in the worst sort of apologetics[1]—or take the truth to their graves for fear of its being misunderstood by outsiders and newcomers.

Linda Rageh, the daughter of a Communist labor organizer, eloquently summed up for another interviewer the Left's tangled sensitivities on the question of its past:

It is terrible to realize that the real complexity of the labor and
left struggle cannot be communicated—partly because people . . .
are unwilling to re-experience the bitter emotions of the past by
examining them [and] partly because the left itself is still so precious that everyone who fought for it wants to protect it from
the ignorance of those who might not understand.[2]

The hesitancy and concern are comprehensible, even well taken, but
when they dictate long-term policy, then the Left risks intentional or
unintentional betrayal of its fundamental task of education as well as
its traditional faith in historical truth on whose side it sees itself doing
combat. For the peril exists that the Left, out of a self-preservative instinct taken to extremes, will remain suspect *terra incognita* for precisely the new generations who want and need to know the whole
truth. The truth is, of course, a complex, manifold thing, and left-
wingers must not countenance their own or anyone else's caricature or
distortion of it, but they must also, finally, not shy away from telling
all that that they know and trusting that the truth of what they know
is ultimately stronger than the insensitivities, ignorance, and malign intentions of outsiders, newcomers, and adversaries.

Appendix 1

Original Occupations of Early Screenwriters

One small group of early screenwriters did not have far to travel. A few of the ex-scenarists (e.g., Anita Loos, Jules Furthman, and Sonya Levien) managed to hang on to their nests while the tree shook under them; most of the old-timers, however, were forlornly shuffling out the studio gates by the time the new breed of writers arrived. (Had they lived long enough, the scenarists might have enjoyed a moment of rueful satisfaction when, a quarter century later, many successful screenwriters were unable to make the transition to television.)

Most of the newcomers had made important marks and reputations in other forms of writing before coming to Hollywood. Out of the world of newspaper journalism emerged Ben Hecht, a crime reporter for the Chicago *Daily News;* Gene Fowler, an editor of the New York *Daily Telegraph;* and numerous others, including John Bright, Ring Lardner, Jr., Dudley Nichols, Nunnally Johnson, Alvah Bessie, Charles MacArthur, and Joseph Mankiewicz. A literary notch or two above them was the *New Yorker* school of screenwriters: Herman Mankiewicz, Robert Benchley, Charles Brackett, Dorothy Parker, Donald Ogden Stewart, and John O'Hara. Later on in the decade, *The Saturday Evening Post* would contribute its brand of less sophisticated and less literary tale-weavers whose scripts (*Beau Geste, Western Union, Union Pacific*, etc.) nonetheless seemed better suited for an era eager for narrative, adventure, wild landscapes, and traditional values. This group included, among others, Borden Chase, Ernest Haycox, Robert Carson, and Norman Reilly Raine.

The New York stage sent large delegations from two different groups. The left-wing theater (e.g., the New Playwrights, the Theatre Union, the Group Theatre) gave Hollywood some of its future "Reds": John Howard Lawson, Albert Maltz, Francis Edwards Faragoh, Philip Stevenson, and two men who escaped prosecution at the hands of Congress in the late forties/early fifties, Clifford Odets and

Michael Blankfort. The legitimate stage exported Lester Cole, Samson Raphaelson, John Wexley, Edwin Justus Mayer, and Morrie Ryskind, and, on consignment only, George Kaufman, Moss Hart, Marc Connelly, S. N. Behrman, Sidney Kingsley, Sidney Howard, John Van Druten, and Lillian Hellman.

Vaudeville, burlesque, and radio produced a small but gifted and highly successful group of screenwriters: Ken Englund, Hal Kanter, Harry Tugend, Ed Hartmann, Irving Brecher, Leonardo Bercovici. These men, and others like them, had garnered valuable experience writing to order for a demanding group of stand-up comics—Phil Baker, Fred Allen, Bert Lahr, etc.—and for the various radio theaters.

Ironically, the inhabitants of literature's most prestigious territory— the novel—had the least success with the new craft of screenwriting. The journalists were flexible and unpretentious troubleshooters—their skills were in considerably greater demand in Hollywood, and they proved more adaptable to screenwriting than their more erudite and literary peers. The playwrights knew how to write dialogue. But the novelists, for all their celebrity, could not adjust easily to the new trade. Scott Fitzgerald, William Faulkner, Dashiell Hammett, Damon Runyon, Mary Roberts Rinehart, Aldous Huxley, Sinclair Lewis, and, somewhat later, Raymond Chandler and James Cain never really established themselves firmly in Hollywood.

A few soon-to-be successful screenwriters had little or no professional reputation when they arrived at Los Angeles' Union Station. Humble and famous alike, however, soon found that screenwriting was an arcane trade demanding a compound of skills and dispositions quite unrelated to the mainline practice of writing. Thus students of the theater—aspiring, middle-rank, or failed playwrights like Norman Krasna, Sheridan Gibney, Sidney Buchman, Jo Swerling, Preston Sturges, and Robert Riskin—were not at a disadvantage in Hollywood as compared to their admired colleagues, Kaufman, Hart, et al. On the contrary, as time would show, their youth and hunger provided them with a flexibility and toughness that stood them in better stead with producers than the refined skills and brittle dispositions of many of the literary elders.

Flexibility and toughness were engendered by other experiences as well. Dalton Trumbo, Samuel Ornitz, and John Huston had made their livings as a bakery goods packer, social worker, and knockabout, and all wrote on the side. A fair number of hopefuls emerged from a variety of professional experiences: lawyers, Emmet Lavery, Howard Koch; teachers, Waldo Salt, Karl Tunberg; actors, George Seaton,

Robert Lees, Horace McCoy; short story writers, Irwin Shaw; magazine free-lance, Mary McCall; advertising, John Lee Mahin; and finally college "lit" majors: Philip Dunne, Paul Jarrico, Harold Buchman, Carl Foreman, Richard Collins, Bess Taffel, Michael Wilson, and Budd Schulberg.

Appendix 2

Screen Writers Guild Officers and Board Members

1933–45

PRESIDENTS
Ralph J. Block
Charles Brackett
Lester Cole*
Sheridan Gibney
Emmet Lavery
John Howard Lawson*
Mary McCall, Jr.
Dudley Nichols
Ernest Pascal

EXECUTIVE OFFICERS
Hugo Butler*
Philip Dunne
Howard Estabrook
Francis Faragoh*
Frances Goodrich
James M. Hilton
Boris Ingster
Talbot Jennings
Michael Kanin
Ring Lardner, Jr.*
Seton I. Miller
Edward E. Paramore, Jr.
Frank Partos
Maurice Rapf*
Wells Root

Robert Rossen*
Dore Schary
Dwight Taylor

EXECUTIVE BOARD
Melville Baker
Claude Binyon
Harold Buchman*
Jerome Chodorov*
Richard Collins*†
Marc Connelly
Delmer Daves
Walter DeLeon
Helen Deutsch
Julius Epstein
Joseph Fields
Oliver Garrett
Jay Gorney*
Albert Hackett
Dashiell Hammett*
Lillian Hellman*
F. Hugh Herbert
David Hertz
Paul Jarrico*
Gordon Kahn*
Howard Koch*
Harry Kurnitz

---

* Named as, or self-confessed, member of the Communist Party.
† HUAC informer.

John Larkin
Leonard Lee
Gladys Lehman
William Ludwig
Richard Maibaum
Benjamin Markson
Brian Marlow
Edwin Justus Mayer
Jane Murfin
Henry Myers
John F. Natteford
George Oppenheimer
Samuel Ornitz*
Nat Perrin
Gertrude Purcell*†
Samson Raphaelson
Betty Reinhardt
Fred Rinaldo*

Robert Riskin
Allen Rivkin
Marguerite Roberts*
Stanley Roberts*†
Stanley Rubin
Waldo Salt*
Raymond Schrock
Budd Schulberg*†
Adrian Scott*
Allan Scott
Sol Shor*†
Donald Ogden Stewart*
Jo Swerling
Leo Townsend*†
Dalton Trumbo*
Harry Tugend
Anthony Veiller
John Wexley*

* Named as, or self-confessed, member of the Communist Party.
† HUAC informer.

Appendix 3

Key Political Activists in Hollywood

LIBERALS   RADICALS

1930s

James Cagney	Ben Barzman
Eddie Cantor	Leonardo Bercovici
Bette Davis	Herbert Biberman
Melvyn Douglas	John Bright
Philip Dunne	J. Edward Bromberg
Florence Eldridge	Harold Buchman
Julius Epstein	Sidney Buchman
Philip Epstein	Hugo and Jean Butler
John Ford	Charles Chaplin
John Garfield	Lester Cole
Ira Gershwin	Richard Collins
Johnny Green	Edward Dmytryk
Oscar Hammerstein II	Arnaud d'Usseau
Paul Henreid	Guy Endore
Katharine Hepburn	Francis Faragoh
Miriam Hopkins	Dashiell Hammett
Ernst Lubitsch	Lillian Hellman
Fredric March	Paul and Sylvia Jarrico
Lewis Milestone	Gordon Kahn
Paul Muni	Howard Koch
Dudley Nichols	Ring Lardner, Jr.
Allen Rivkin	John Howard Lawson
Edward G. Robinson	Robert Lees
Dore Schary	Melvin Levy
Walter Wanger	Samuel Ornitz
Orson Welles	Dorothy Parker
Nathanael West	Maurice Rapf
William Wyler	Robert Rossen
	Waldo Salt

LIBERALS   RADICALS

John Sanford
Budd Schulberg
Gale Sondergaard
Lionel Stander
Donald Ogden Stewart
Robert Tasker
Dalton Trumbo
John Wexley
Michael Wilson

1940s

John Huston   Alvah Bessie
Danny Kaye   Henry Blankfort
Gene Kelly   Carl Foreman
                                          Edward Huebsch
                                          Millard Lampell
                                          Ben Maddow
                                          Albert Maltz
                                          Arnold Manoff
                                          Larry Parks
                                          Abraham Polonsky
                                          Adrian Scott
                                          Philip Stevenson
                                          Nedrick Young

Appendix 4

For reasons which research has not made clear, the list of names which appeared in the *Hollywood Reporter* did not coincide with the schedule of witnesses prepared by HUAC for October.

<table>
<tr><td>Hollywood Reporter
September 22, 1947</td><td>Appeared in Washington
October 1947</td></tr>
<tr><td>PRODUCERS:</td><td>PRODUCERS:</td></tr>
<tr><td>Eric Johnston</td><td>Jack Warner</td></tr>
<tr><td>Louis B. Mayer</td><td>Louis B. Mayer</td></tr>
<tr><td>Jack Warner</td><td>James K. McGuinness</td></tr>
<tr><td>Samuel Goldwyn</td><td>Walt Disney</td></tr>
<tr><td>Walt Disney</td><td>Dore Schary</td></tr>
<tr><td>Dore Schary</td><td>Adrian Scott†</td></tr>
<tr><td>James K. McGuinness</td><td>Eric Johnston</td></tr>
<tr><td>Adrian Scott</td><td></td></tr>
<tr><td>ACTORS:</td><td>ACTORS:</td></tr>
<tr><td>Gary Cooper</td><td>Adolphe Menjou</td></tr>
<tr><td>Charles Chaplin</td><td>Robert Taylor</td></tr>
<tr><td>Adolphe Menjou</td><td>Robert Montgomery</td></tr>
<tr><td>Robert Montgomery</td><td>George Murphy</td></tr>
<tr><td>George Murphy</td><td>Gary Cooper</td></tr>
<tr><td>Larry Parks</td><td>Larry Parks*†</td></tr>
<tr><td>Robert Taylor</td><td>Ronald Reagan</td></tr>
<tr><td>Ronald Reagan</td><td></td></tr>
<tr><td>WRITERS:</td><td>WRITERS:</td></tr>
<tr><td>Rupert Hughes</td><td>Ayn Rand</td></tr>
<tr><td>Clifford Odets</td><td>John Charles Moffitt</td></tr>
<tr><td>Donald Ogden Stewart</td><td>Rupert Hughes</td></tr>
</table>

* Not called to testify.
† "Unfriendly" witness.

Hollywood Reporter September 22, 1947	*Appeared in Washington* October 1947
WRITERS: Alvah Bessie Bertolt Brecht Lester Cole Howard Koch Ring Lardner, Jr. John Howard Lawson Albert Maltz John Charles Moffitt Howard Rushmore Morrie Ryskind Waldo Salt Dalton Trumbo	WRITERS: Howard Rushmore Morrie Ryskind Fred Niblo, Jr. Richard Macaulay John Howard Lawson† Dalton Trumbo† Albert Maltz† Alvah Bessie† Samuel Ornitz† Emmet Lavery Ring Lardner, Jr.† Lester Cole† Bertolt Brecht† Richard Collins*† Gordon Kahn*† Howard Koch*† Waldo Salt*†
DIRECTORS: Leo McCarey Lewis Milestone Sam Wood Herbert Biberman Edward Dmytryk	DIRECTORS: Sam Wood Leo McCarey Herbert Biberman† Edward Dmytryk† Lewis Milestone*† Irving Pichel*† Robert Rossen*†
OTHERS: Cedric Gibbons Roy Brewer Sam Moore Lela Rogers William Pomerance Joseph E. Davies	OTHERS: Oliver Carlson Lela Rogers Roy Brewer

---

* Not called to testify.
† "Unfriendly" witness.

Appendix 5

Memo to Studio Heads William Dozier and
Charles Kormer Suggesting *Crossfire* as
a Project for the Studio—RKO

from Adrian Scott

THE BRICK FOXHOLE
or
THE PEACE TIME HITLER'S CHILDREN
or
LET'S MAKE THREE STARS
or
A POWELL PICTURE FOR $250,000
or
HOW CAN YOU LOSE?

Dear Charlie and Bill:

The variety of titles alone suggests what fecund material this is. As a
few executives will attest (and as I myself admit) on the question of
titles my I.Q. is about as low as an I.Q. can be. But this is irrelevant.

This is the prospectus you suggested I write on THE BRICK FOX-
HOLE.

I believe FOXHOLE can be made for $250,000. This way: Dmy-
tryk, Paxton and I, at our present rate of picture making, turn out two
pictures a year. Say this picture is done for the 1947 schedule. Consider this as an additional picture; a *third* picture from all of us. This
means that we are charged our normal rates on two pictures and on
this a certain fixed fee—say $5,000 apiece, or nothing if we can keep
Leon's blood pressure from engulfing us all.

This picture will be shot in 21–25 days, reducing production expense to a minimum. Dmytryk has agreed that this can be done if the schedule is well planned and if the sets are clearly visualized before the picture starts. (The precedent is THE INFORMER which John Ford shot in 18 days.) This is a highly practical plan of operation. Dmytryk knows how to shoot fast and he will be helped by a tight script without one superfluous scene, a script written and timed for length.

On the question of the cast: The plan is to use our boys, Mitchum, Tierney, Bill Williams, etc., and where the group we have is not satisfactory, to look among the returned veterans for new and interesting personalities. As we discussed—the opportunity for making stars is not at all remote. The characters in this book are all dynamite. We should come through with at least one star if the boys are carefully selected. (Precedent: DESTINATION TOKYO. Out of this Warners got Robert Hutton, William Prince and Dane Clark.)

Dick Powell is very interested in this project. Powell's dough is pretty high for us if we expect to bring it in for $250,000. But maybe it can be done. If the production cannot afford the $50,000, perhaps the studio will be willing to arrange some percentage deal with him.

The girls in the cast are fairly simple. There are two. Neither of the parts is large but one is dynamite. The girl, Ginny, has the earmarks of a star-making role. The other one, Mary, is simply cast with some newcomer.

The story changes (which I've incorporated in the enclosed synopsis) are simple and in no wise distort the meaning of Brooks' book. Here they are:

1st) The war is over. The soldiers are on terminal leave or are awaiting discharge.

2nd) The incident which propels Jeff's misery. In the book it is the chance overhearing of scuttlebutt in the barracks— regarding his wife's unfaithfulness. In the book this is the straw that makes a lonely, unhappy fellow even more lonely and unhappy. The coincidence of this is invalid. The change would go something like this: Mary and Jeff have had a fight. It doesn't matter about what. Some difference regarding their future, where they will live, how they will live, what his job will be when he gets out. It is not important that a major issue should involve them. Something slight will intensify the misery and loneliness of an already miserable guy. In the midst of this, a letter comes from a friend which relates that Mary was out with an old beau of hers. Subsequently the episode turns out to be innocent but it serves the purpose of starting Jeff's story.

3rd) This is a story of personal fascism as opposed to organized fascism. The story, in a very minor sense to be sure, indicates how it is possible for us to have a gestapo, if this country should go fascist. A character like Monty would qualify brilliantly for the leadership of the Belsen concentration camp. Fascism hates weakness in people; minorities. Monty hates fairies, negroes, jews and foreigners. In the book Monty murders a fairy. He could have murdered a negro, a foreigner or a jew. It would have been the same thing. In the picture he does murder a jew. This analysis, incidentally, is absolutely correct in the opinion of the author. The picture would deal exclusively with Monty's anti-semitism.

4th) Ginny's being a whore. We could suggest this as many pictures have suggested whores by indirection. She would be a B girl, working in a barroom. She is *kind* to Jeff, warms up to him, is maternal to him. She manages to fill a gap in his loneliness. She would like a man like Jeff for her own. But the circumstances of the war (that is over) have caused a distortion in her, i.e. made her a whore, that will prevent her now from ever achieving a normal life. She is a pathetic child of a woman, and yet is capable of great anger and passion as shown in the scene when she is cross-examined by Keeley and Jeff's wife.

5th) The policeman, Finlay. A very good cop, incidentally. He would be a Roman Catholic and an Irishman. He understands anti-semitism because he's Irish and a Catholic. He understands it more clearly than other people because his grandfather, who immigrated to this country from Ireland, was murdered in a riot against the Irish people. This actually happened in New York City and Philadelphia in the last century. He would be our spokesman.

6th) The final and concluding sequences are due for an overhaul. The fight between Monty and Keeley in the museum is tough to swallow. Monty's death is a must, of course. And it may be that he will be killed by Keeley. For the present we are looking for a series of taut suspense sequences during which the soldiers led by Keeley try to trap Monty and then finally succeed.

I believe we could enlist the help of Justice Frank Murphy in this picture. Perhaps he would agree to speak a foreword to the picture as representative of his committee. It would do an incalculable amount of good.

Dmytryk, Paxton and I want to make this picture for two reasons. First, we are ambitious. We want to make fine pictures. This will make a fine picture.

Secondly, and more important, is this: Anti-semitism is not declining as a result of Hitler's defeat. The recent negro race riots even in a high school (an unheard of event in this country) is symptomatic of the whole cancer. Anti-semitism and anti-negroism will grow unless heroic measures can be undertaken to stop them. This picture is one such measure.

This will never in our hands be a depressing pamphlet. It will have all the rugged excitement and speed of MURDER, MY SWEET and a white hot issue to boot.

The enclosed synopsis merely indicates how the picture can be done. I have not included any of the magnificent scenes that Brooks has written, many of which can be inserted intact.

Appendix 6

The Waldorf Statement

Members of the Association of Motion Picture Producers deplore the action of the ten Hollywood men who have been cited for contempt. We do not desire to prejudge their legal rights, but their actions have been a disservice to their employers and have impaired their usefulness to the industry.

We will forthwith discharge or suspend without compensation those in our employ and we will not re-employ any of the ten until such time as he is acquitted or has purged himself of contempt and declares under oath that he is not a Communist.

On the broader issues of alleged subversive and disloyal elements in Hollywood, our members are likewise prepared to take positive action.

We will not knowingly employ a Communist or a member of any party or group which advocates the overthrow of the Government of the United States by force or by illegal or unconstitutional methods. In pursuing this policy, we are not going to be swayed by hysteria or intimidation from any source. We are frank to recognize that such a policy involves dangers and risks. There is the danger of hurting innocent people. There is the risk of creating an atmosphere of fear. Creative work at its best cannot be carried on in an atmosphere of fear. We will guard against this danger, this risk, this fear. To this end we will invite the Hollywood talent guilds to work with us to eliminate any subversives, to protect the innocent, and to safeguard free speech and a free screen wherever threatened.

Appendix 7

Roster of "Important" Informers

Name	Profession	Credits	Names
Leopold Atlas	writer	5	37
George Bassman	composer	15	3
George Beck	writer	5	18
Martin Berkeley	writer	15	155
Lee J. Cobb	actor	22	20
Richard Collins	writer	8	23
Danny Dare	producer	7	7
Edward Dmytryk	director	24	26
Sterling Hayden	actor	7	7
Roy Huggins	writer	9	19
Elia Kazan	director	7	11
Roland Kibbee	writer	6	18
David Lang	writer	13	75
Marc Lawrence	actor	68	14
Isobel Lennart	writer	13	21
Melvin Levy	writer	7	9
Paul Marion	actor	23	29
Clifford Odets	writer	6	6
Larry Parks	actor	26	12
Gertrude Purcell	writer	18	1
David Raksin	composer	18	11
Meta Reis	story department	0	20
Stanley Roberts	writer	29	29
Robert Rossen	director	19	54
Bernard Schoenfeld	writer	4	21
Budd Schulberg	writer	5	15

Name	Profession	Credits	Names
Sol Shor	writer	27	47
Leo Townsend	writer	10	37
Pauline Townsend	writer	0	83
Frank Tuttle	director	12	36
Elizabeth Wilson, née Betty Anderson	writer	0	45

Notes

Introduction

1. New York *Times*, January 12, 1920, Part II, p. 28. "Following the Secretary of the Interior's address, the motion picture representatives went into session to arrange the campaign. . . ."
2. Letter from Nat Segaloff, November 7, 1976, Section 2, p. 24.

Chapter 1

1. Mae D. Huettig, *Economic Control of the Motion Picture Industry*, Philadelphia: University of Pennsylvania Press, 1944, pp. 52, 59–62; F. D. Klingender and Stuart Legg, *Money Behind the Screen*, London: Lawrence & Wishart, 1937, p. 63.
2. Tom Dardis, *Some Time in the Sun*, New York: Charles Scribner's Sons, 1976, p. 192.
3. Letter to Sam Ornitz, September 11, 1930, Samuel Ornitz Collection, The Wisconsin Center for Theater Research, 48 AN, Box 1.
4. *Variety*, February 29, 1940, pp. 1 and 5.
5. United States, National Recovery Administration, *Report Regarding Investigation Directed to Be Made by the President in His Executive Order of Fair Competition for the Motion Picture Industry*, prepared by Sol A. Rosenblatt, July 7, 1934, Washington, D.C.: U. S. Government Printing Office, 1934, p. 24.
6. "Conversation Piece," *The Screen Guilds' Magazine*, 2, March 1935, p. 5.
7. William Fadiman, *Hollywood Now*, New York: Liveright, 1972, p. 106.
8. Max Wilk, *The Wit and Wisdom of Hollywood*, New York: Warner Paperback Library, 1973, p. 170.
9. "Elegy for Wonderland," *Esquire*, March 1959, pp. 56–60, reprinted in Arthur F. McClure, *The Movies: An American Idiom*, Rutherford, N.J.: Fairleigh Dickinson University Press, 1971, p. 359.
10. "Writing for the Movies," *Focus on Film*, Winter 1970, p. 52.
11. Transcript of discussion at the American Film Institute, October 19, 1971, T-77, p. 14.
12. *Behind the Screen*, New York: Delacorte Press, 1965, p. 383.

13. Andrew Laskos, "Screenwriter as Star: Shaking the Shackles," Los Angeles *Times Calendar*, August 29, 1976, p. 44, quoting Wells Root.
14. Dardis, 157.
15. James R. Silke, *Here's Looking at You, Kid*, Boston: Little, Brown & Co., 1976, p. 67, quoting Jim Webb.
16. Anita Loos, *Kiss Hollywood Good-by*, New York: The Viking Press, 1974, p. 119.
17. Quoted in Wayne Warga, "What Happened to Ruth Davis?" Los Angeles *Times Calendar*, February 27, 1977, p. 84.
18. *Bring on the Empty Horses*, New York: G. P. Putnam's Sons, 1975, p. 83.
19. Quoted in Tom Flinn, "William Dieterle: The Plutarch of Hollywood," *The Velvet Light Trap*, No. 15, Fall 1975, p. 28.
20. Letter from Charles Katz to Martin Popper, July 6, 1951, Robert Kenny/Robert Morris Collection, The Wisconsin Center for Theater Research, 29 AN, Box 6.
21. Deposition of Lester Cole, *Cole* v. *Loew's, Inc.*, September 10, 1948, p. 55.
22. Quoted in Frank MacShane, *The Life of Raymond Chandler*, New York: E. P. Dutton & Co., Inc., 1976, p. 110.

Chapter 2

1. Dave Davis and Neal Goldberg, "Organizing the Screen Writers Guild—An Interview with John Howard Lawson," *Cineaste*, 8, no. 2, p. 8.
2. Donald Ogden Stewart, American Film Institute Oral History Project, December 1971, p. 94.
3. Bob Thomas, *Thalberg: Life and Legend*, Garden City, N.Y.: Doubleday & Company, 1969, p. 268.
4. Samuel Marx, *Mayer and Thalberg: The Make-Believe Saints*, New York: Random House, 1975, p. 207.
5. *My First Hundred Years in Hollywood*, New York: Random House, 1964, p. 224.
6. Mae D. Huettig, *Economic Control of the Motion Picture Industry*, Philadelphia: University of Pennsylvania Press, 1944, pp.100–2.
7. *Variety*, October 16, 1933, p. 3.
8. Ibid., December 16, 1934, pp. 1 and 2; December 24, 1934, p. 1; January 29, 1935, p. 1.
9. Garth Jowett, *Film: The Democratic Process*, Boston: Little, Brown & Co., 1976, p. 473; United States, National Recovery Administration, Division of Review, *Evidence Study No. 25 of the Motion Picture Industry*, prepared by Daniel Bertrand, November 1935, p. 16. See also James Rorty, "Dream Factory," *Forum*, September 1935, pp. 162–65;

Anthony Dawson, "Motion Picture Economics," *Hollywood Quarterly*, 3 (1948), pp. 217–40.

10. Donald Ogden Stewart, in a speech to the League of American Writers' Congress, 1939, reprinted in Stewart, ed., *Fighting Words*, New York: Harcourt, Brace & Co., 1940, p. 136.

11. Leo C. Rosten, *Hollywood: The Movie Colony, the Movie Makers*, New York: Harcourt, Brace & Co., 1941, p. 318.

12. The letter, dated December 1, 1933, is in the Samuel Ornitz Collection, The Wisconsin Center for Theater Research, 48 AN, Box 1.

13. *Variety*, August 9, 1934, p. 5.

14. Quoted in Fred Lawrence Guiles, *Hanging on in Paradise*, New York: McGraw-Hill Book Co., 1975, p. 37.

15. Quoted in William Froug, *The Screenwriter Looks at the Screenwriter*, New York: The Macmillan Co., 1972, p. 244.

16. These goals were typed out on four pages of onionskin paper. They are in the possession of Lester Cole. Page three is missing.

17. "The Handshake," *The Screen Writers' Magazine*, July 1934, p. 1.

18. John Howard Lawson, "Notes from an Exile," *The Screen Writers' Magazine*, July 1934, p. 22.

19. Christopher Dudley Wheaton, *A History of the Screen Writers Guild (1920–1942): The Writers' Quest for a Freely Negotiated Basic Agreement*, University of Southern California: unpublished Ph.D. thesis, 1974, pp. 81–83.

20. *Variety*, September 20, 1933, p. 1.

21. Ibid., September 23 and 25.

22. Ibid., September 6, 1933, p. 1.

23. Frances Marion, *Off with Their Heads!*, New York: The Macmillan Co., 1972, p. 240.

24. Guiles, p. 254; *Film Comment*, May–June, 1976, pp. 53–54.

25. *Variety*, August 26, 1939, p. 1.

26. Ibid., August 19, 1939, pp. 1 and 8.

27. Ibid., November 8, 1933, pp. 1 and 13.

28. Ibid., September 23, November 13, and November 27, 1933.

29. Ibid., March 1, 1934, p. 1; March 10, pp. 1 and 3.

30. Ibid., April 6, 1934, p. 16.

31. Ibid., March 18, 1935, p. 1.

32. "The Wagner Act—Reality or Prophecy?" *Screen Guilds' Magazine*, August 1935, p. 15.

33. *Variety*, July 17, 1935, p. 1.

34. Ibid., March 30, 1936, p. 4.

35. Ibid., March 28, 1935, p. 4.

36. Ibid., March 30, 1936, p. 4.

37. Ibid., April 3, 1936, pp. 1 and 12.

38. Ibid., April 27, 1936, pp. 1 and 11.

39. Ibid., April 30, 1936, p. 6.
40. Ibid., April 30, 1936, p. 4.
41. Los Angeles *Examiner*, April 27, 1936.
42. William P. Mangold, "Hollywood Fights Its Writers," *The New Republic*, May 27, 1936, p. 70.
43. *Variety*, August 24, 1939, p. 12.
44. Ibid., August 4, 1937, pp. 1 and 13.
45. Mangold, p. 71.
46. *Variety*, August 18, 1939, pp. 1 and 6.
47. Wheaton, p. 122.
48. *Variety*, May 2, 1936.
49. Ibid., April 27, 29, and 30, 1936.
50. Ibid., May 1, 1936, p. 1.
51. Ibid., August 23, 1939, pp. 1 and 9.
52. Ibid., August 24, 1939, pp. 1 and 10.
53. Ibid., May 4, 1936, p. 2.
54. Ibid., May 12, 1936, pp. 1 and 4.
55. Testimonies of Horace McCoy and Robert Presnell before the NLRB, quoted in *Variety*, August 25 and 26, 1939.
56. Dalton Trumbo, *Additional Dialogue: The Letters of Dalton Trumbo, 1942–1962*, ed. Helen Manfull, New York: M. Evans and Co., 1970, p. 569.
57. Ibid.
58. *Variety*, May 9, 1936, p. 6 (paid advertisement).
59. Ibid., March 17, 1937, pp. 1, 18 and 19.
60. *Hollywood Reporter*, May 6, 1936.
61. *Variety*, June 29, 1938, p. 1.
62. Ibid., January 28, 1939, pp. 1 and 4.
63. Ibid., August 5, 1939, pp. 1 and 4.

Chapter 3

1. Karl Marx and Friedrich Engels, *Manifesto of the Communist Party*, Peking: Foreign Languages Press, 1972, pp. 43–44.
2. *NO! In Thunder*, Boston: Beacon Press, 1960, p. 162.
3. Jon Wiener, "The Communist Party Today and Yesterday: An Interview with Dorothy Healey," *Radical America*, 11 (May–June 1977), p. 26.
4. Max Gordon, "The Communist Party of the Nineteen-Thirties and the New Left," *Socialist Revolution*, 27 (January–March 1976), p. 18.
5. "Theses of the Sixth Comintern Congress on the International Situation and the Tasks of the Communist International," in Helmut Gruber, *Soviet Russia Masters the Comintern*, Garden City, N.Y.: Anchor Books, 1974, p. 221.

6. "Pinks Plan to Stalinize Studios," *Variety*, September 16, 1933, pp. 1 and 3.

7. "The Writers' Congress," *The Nation*, May 15, 1935, p. 571.

8. Joseph North, ed., *New Masses: An Anthology of the Rebel Thirties*, New York: International Publishers, 1969, p. 349.

9. *The Best Times: An Informal Memoir*, New York: The New American Library, 1966, p. 215.

10. John Howard Lawson, "Biographical Notes," *Zeitschrift für Anglistik und Amerikanistik*, 4 (1956), p. 74.

11. Ibid.

12. Dave Davis and Neal Goldberg, "Organizing the Screen Writers Guild—An Interview with John Howard Lawson," *Cineaste*, 8, p. 6.

13. November 15, 1932, Samuel Ornitz Collection, The Wisconsin Center for Theater Research, 48 AN, Box 1.

14. " 'Inner Conflict' and Proletarian Art: A Reply to Michael Gold," *New Masses*, April 17, 1934.

15. *Film: The Creative Process*, New York: Hill & Wang, 1964, pp. 123–24.

16. "Biographical Notes," p. 74.

17. Quoted in Gerald Rabkin, *Drama and Commitment: Politics in the American Theater of the Thirties*, Bloomington: Indiana University Press, 1964, p. 161.

18. United States 82nd Congress, 1st session, July 6, 1951, Committee on Un-American Activities, *Communist Infiltration of the Hollywood Motion Picture Industry*, Washington, D.C.: U. S. Government Printing Office, 1951, Vol. 2, p. 1,837.

19. Ring Lardner, Jr., *The Lardners: My Family Remembered*, New York: Harper & Row, 1976, p. 256.

20. 1951 HUAC hearings, Vol. 1, p. 600.

21. Louis B. Fleming, "Mavericks Marching in Red Ranks," February 27, 1978, p. 1.

22. 1951 HUAC hearings, Vol. 2, p. 1,861.

23. Ibid., Vol. 1, p. 600.

24. United States 84th Congress, 1st session, June–July 1955 and April 1956, Committee on Un-American Activities, *Investigation of Communist Activities in the Los Angeles Area*, Washington, D.C.: U. S. Government Printing Office, 1955 and 1956, Vol. 6, p. 5,791.

25. Lardner, pp. 255–56.

26. Christopher Caudwell, *Illusion and Reality*, London: Macmillan and Co., 1937, pp. 318 and 325.

27. *Intellectuals and the War*, New York: Workers Library Publishers, 1940, pp. 18, 56, 58.

28. Herbert Biberman, "Frank Capra's Characters," *New Masses*, July 8, 1941, p. 27.

29. Paul Trivers, "Hollywood Writers Move Up," *New Masses*, September 14, 1943, pp. 20–21; Robert Rossen, "New Characters for the Screen," *New Masses*, January 18, 1944, pp. 18–19.

30. Dalton Trumbo, "Hollywood Pays," *Forum and Century*, February 1933, p. 119.

31. "Editorial Statement," *Hollywood Quarterly*, 1 (1945), p. 1.

32. "The Negro in Hollywood," *Political Affairs*, June 1950, pp. 65, 67, 70.

33. "On Our Cultural Work," *Party Voice*, January 1957, p. 5.

34. Guy Endore, *Reflections of Guy Endore*, UCLA Oral History Project, 1964, pp. 132 and 140.

35. Henry Ephron, *We Thought We Could Do Anything: The Life of Screenwriters Phoebe and Henry Ephron*, New York: W. W. Norton & Co., 1977, pp. 31–32.

36. Peggy Lamson, *Roger Baldwin: Founder of the American Civil Liberties Union*, Boston: Houghton Mifflin Co., 1976, p. 195.

Chapter 4

1. Interview by Max Wilk for American Film Institute's Oral History Project, December 1971, p. 88.

2. Louis Nizer, *New Courts of Industry: Self-Regulation Under the Motion Picture Code*, New York: The Longacre Press, 1935, pp. xvi–xvii.

3. We are indebted to David Talbot and Barbara Zheutlin for allowing us to use this quotation from their interview with John Bright, October 1975.

4. "My Name Isn't Costello," *Screen Guilds' Magazine*, February 1937, p. 7.

5. Diana Serra Cary, *The Hollywood Posse*, Boston: Houghton Mifflin Co., 1975, p. 127.

6. Jack L. Warner, *My First Hundred Years in Hollywood*, New York: Random House, 1964, p. 215.

7. *The Best Times: An Informal Memoir*, New York: The New American Library, 1966, p. 47.

8. "Biographical Notes," *Zeitschrift für Anglistik und Amerikanistik*, 4 (1956), p. 73.

9. Ibid.

10. Michael Paul Rogin and John L. Shove, *Political Change in California*, Westport, Conn.: Greenwood Publishing Co., 1970, p. 127.

11. Upton Sinclair, *The Autobiography of Upton Sinclair*, New York: Harcourt, Brace and World, 1962, p. 260.

12. Bob Thomas, *Thalberg: Life and Legend*, Garden City, N.Y.: Doubleday & Company, 1969, p. 269.

13. Samuel Marx, *Mayer and Thalberg: The Make-Believe Saints*, New York: Random House, 1975, p. 236.

14. *Variety*, October 27, 1934, p. 2.
15. Thomas, p. 269.
16. Kyle Crichton, *Total Recoil*, Garden City, N.Y.: Doubleday & Company, 1960, pp. 246–47.
17. *Variety*, October 23, 1934, p. 4.
18. Carey McWilliams, *Southern California Country*, ed. Erskine Caldwell, New York: Duell, Sloan & Pearce, 1946, p. 298.
19. *Variety*, March 9, 14, 21, and April 26, 1934.
20. New York *Times*, June 10, 1928, reprinted in Richard Koszarski, ed., *Hollywood Directors, 1914–1940*, London: Oxford University Press, 1976, p. 199.
21. Erika and Klaus Mann, *Escape to Life*, Boston: Houghton Mifflin Co., 1939, p. 265.
22. Salka Viertel, *The Kindness of Strangers*, New York: Holt, Rinehart & Winston, 1969, pp. 211–15; Charles Chaplin, *My Autobiography*, New York: Simon & Schuster, 1964, p. 434; Marta Feuchtwanger's contribution to the UCLA Oral History Project.
23. Mann, p. 266.
24. Klaus Völker, *Brecht: A Biography*, New York: The Seabury Press, 1978, p. 286.
25. S. N. Behrman, *Tribulations and Laughter*, London: Hamish Hamilton, 1972, p. 231.
26. United States Congress, House of Representatives, Committee on Un-American Activities, 80th Congress, 1st session, October 1947, *Hearings Regarding the Communist Infiltration of the Motion Picture Industry*, Washington, D.C.: U. S. Government Printing Office, 1947, p. 145.
27. *The Nation*, May 29, 1935, p. 623. McWilliams underscored his warning in a much longer pamphlet, *It Can Happen Here: Active Anti-Semitism in Los Angeles*, Los Angeles: American League Against War and Fascism and Jewish Anti-Nazi League of Southern California, 1935.
28. While present-day biographers of Long—most notably T. Harry Williams (New York: Knopf, 1969)—argue that "dictator" and "fascist" are European terms which do not really apply to Long or his methods, the style of his campaigns and leadership seemed demagogic and tyrannical to many of his contemporaries, and thus potentially fascist in their import. For example, see Raymond Gram Swing, *Forerunners of American Fascism*, New York: Julian Messner, 1935.
29. Arthur M. Schlesinger, Jr., *The Politics of Upheaval*, Boston: Houghton Mifflin Co., 1960, p. 518.
30. Both the liberal historian William Leuchtenberg (*Franklin D. Roosevelt and the New Deal, 1932–1940*, New York: Harper Torchbooks, 1963, p. 276) and the left-wing James Weinstein ("Response to Max Gordon," *Socialist Revolution*, 27, January-March 1976, p. 55)

qualified—with "in retrospect"—their assertions that there was no domestic fascist menace in the United States during the thirties.

31. *The Best Times: An Informal Memoir*, New York: The New American Library, 1966, p. 140.

32. Donald Ogden Stewart, *By a Stroke of Luck*, New York: Paddington Press, 1975, p. 210.

33. Ibid., p. 213.

34. Ibid., p. 216.

35. Ibid., p. 218.

36. Ibid., p. 217.

37. Ibid., p. 221.

38. Ibid., p. 222.

39. Ella Winter, *And Not to Yield: An Autobiography*, New York: Harcourt, Brace & World, 1963, p. 222.

40. Donald Ogden Stewart, Oral History Project, American Film Institute, December 1971, pp. 20–21.

41. Prince Hubertus zu Loewenstein, *Towards the Further Shore: An Autobiography*, London: Victor Gollancz, 1968, p. 171.

42. Loewenstein, p. 171.

43. Viertel, p. 181.

44. Hy Kraft, *On My Way to the Theatre*, New York: The Macmillan Co., 1971, pp. 145–46.

45. *Variety*, October 20, 1936, p. 5.

46. *Hollywood Reporter*, August 24, 1938, pp. 1 and 2.

47. Stewart, *By a Stroke . . .* , p. 231.

48. *Hollywood Now*, October 7, 1938, p. 2.

49. *Hollywood Reporter*, November 26, 1938, p. 2.

50. Allen Guttmann, *The Wound in the Heart: America and the Spanish Civil War*, New York: The Free Press of Glencoe, 1962, p. 4.

51. Harold Clurman, *The Fervent Years*, New York: Hill & Wang, 1957, p. 189.

52. Dorothy Parker, "Incredible, Fantastic . . . and True," *New Masses*, November 23, 1937.

53. Leuchtenberg, pp. 238–72 *passim*.

54. "California Speaks," *TAC*, October 1939, pp. 11 and 31.

55. "Declaration of Policy of the Motion Picture Democratic Committee, Passed as a Resolution at Its General Membership Meeting on February 12, 1939," Melvyn Douglas Collection, The Wisconsin Center for Theater Research, 100 AN, Box 1.

56. Dalton Trumbo, *Harry Bridges: A Discussion of the Latest Effort to Deport Civil Liberties and the Rights of American Labor*, Hollywood: League of American Writers, 1941, p. 27.

57. Speech delivered in Hollywood to the Arts, Sciences and Professions Council, May 25, 1949, reprinted in Albert Maltz, *The Citizen Writer*, New York: International Publishers, 1950, p. 37.

58. See Jerold S. Auerbach, *Labor and Liberty: The La Follette Committee and the New Deal*, Indianapolis: The Bobbs-Merrill Co., 1966.
59. Letter to Screen Directors Guild, November 24, 1952, Herbert Biberman/Gale Sondergaard Collection, The Wisconsin Center for Theater Research, 58 AN, Box 1. The "spectacle" which so infuriated Biberman—a brutal strikebreaking effort organized by the growers and abetted by the police and sheriff departments—is described in Carey McWilliams, *Factories in the Field*, Santa Barbara: Peregrine Publishers, 1971, pp. 255-56.
60. "Organization Report," July 1939, Melvyn Douglas Collection, The Wisconsin Center for Theater Research, 100 AN, Box 1.
61. "Oh, I Thought You Said the Name Was Costello," *Screen Guilds' Magazine*, March 4, 1937, p. 18.
62. Winter, p. 233.
63. "Hollywood Gets Wise!" *TAC*, June 1939, p. 16.

Chapter 5

1. Draft of a letter to *Time* magazine, June 1940, Melvyn Douglas Collection, The Wisconsin Center for Theater Research, 100 AN, Box 1.
2. Quoted in Frank A. Warren III, *Liberals and Communism*, Bloomington: Indiana University Press, 1966, p. 104.
3. Joseph E. Davies, *Mission to Moscow*, New York: Simon & Schuster, 1941, pp. 453-56.
4. Winston S. Churchill, *The Gathering Storm*, Boston: Houghton Mifflin Co., 1948, p. 394.
5. Peggy Lamson, *Roger Baldwin: Founder of the American Civil Liberties Union*, Boston: Houghton Mifflin Co., 1976, p. 201.
6. Al Richmond, *A Long View from the Left*, New York: Delta, 1975, p. 283; George Charney, *A Long Journey*, Chicago: Quadrangle, 1968, p. 123; Benjamin Gitlow, *The Whole of Their Lives*, New York: Charles Scribner's Sons, 1948, p. 304; see also John Gates, *The Story of an American Communist*, New York: Thomas Nelson & Sons, 1958, pp. 74-77.
7. Peggy Dennis, *The Autobiography of an American Communist*, Berkeley: Creative Arts Book Co., 1977, p. 136.
8. Guy Endore, *Reflections on Guy Endore*, UCLA: Oral History Project, 1964, p. 144.
9. Leo C. Rosten, *Hollywood: The Movie Colony, the Movie Makers*, New York: Harcourt, Brace & Co., 1941, p. 141.
10. Allen Guttmann, *The Wound in the Heart: America and the Spanish Civil War*, New York: The Free Press of Glencoe, 1962, p. 66.
11. Quoted in Dennis, p. 135.
12. *The Secret Diary of Harold L. Ickes*, Vol. 3, *The Lowering Clouds, 1939-1941*, New York: Simon & Schuster, 1954, p. 73.

13. Melvyn Douglas Collection, 100 AN, Box 1.
14. Ibid.
15. Ibid.
16. The report of this meeting is in the Douglas Collection.
17. Melvyn Douglas Collection, 100 AN, Box 1, March 3, 1940.
18. Ibid., June 8, 1940.
19. Ibid., February 4, 1940.
20. Sally Reid, "Is Melvyn Douglas a Communist?" *Photoplay*, September 1940, p. 88.
21. *Hollywood Citizen News*, August 16, 19, 20, 21, 1939.
22. For a discussion of the origins and fabricators of the doctrine of "Red fascism" see Les K. Adler and Thomas G. Paterson, "Red Fascism: The Merger of Nazi Germany and Soviet Russia in the American Image of Totalitarianism, 1930's–1950's," *American Historical Review*, 75 (April 1970), pp. 1,046–64.
23. For a systematic critique of this equation see Arno J. Mayer, *Dynamics of Counter-Revolution in Europe, 1870–1956*, New York: Harper Torchbooks, 1971, pp. 9–34.

Chapter 6

1. "COMMAND, Don't Beg!" *Black & White*, February 1940, p. 4.
2. *Additional Dialogue: Letters of Dalton Trumbo, 1942–1962*, ed. Helen Manfull, New York: M. Evans and Co., 1970, p. 29.
3. *The Fervent Years*, New York: Hill & Wang, 1957, p. 273.
4. *Labor Radical*, Boston: Beacon Press, 1970, p. 399.
5. See Jane Mathews, *The Federal Theatre, 1935–1939*, Princeton: Princeton University Press, 1967. For an account of Red-baiting in other WPA projects see Jerre Mangione, *The Dream and the Deal: The Federal Writers Project, 1935–1943*, Boston: Little, Brown & Co., 1972, p. 290; and Milton Meltzer, *Violins and Shovels: The WPA Arts Projects*, New York: Delacorte Press, 1976, pp. 138–39.
6. Deposition of Sheridan Gibney, *Screen Writers Guild, Inc.* v. *Motion Picture Association of America, Inc.*, U. S. District Court, Southern District, New York, civil action no. 46-165, December 27 and 28, 1950, p. 75.
7. Ibid., p. 76.
8. August Raymond Ogden, *The Dies Committee*, Washington, D.C.: The Catholic University of America Press, 1945, p. 211; Walter Goodman, *The Committee*, Baltimore: Penguin Books, Inc., 1969, p. 101.
9. *Hollywood Citizen News*, August 6, 1939, pp. 1 and 3.
10. Ogden, pp. 212–13; Alanna Nash, "Cancelled," *Take One*, July-August 1977, p. 31.
11. August 16, 1940.

12. See Edward L. Barrett, Jr., *The Tenney Committee*, Ithaca: Cornell University Press, 1951.

13. *Variety*, July 28, 1941.

14. Ibid., July 2, 1941.

15. Richard Schickel, *The Disney Version*, New York: Avon Books, 1969, pp. 209–16.

16. *Variety*, February 16 and 18, 1942.

17. Jack B. Tenney, *California Legislator*, UCLA Oral History Project, 1969, Vol. 3, p. 1,129.

18. *Variety*, January 14, 1941, pp. 1 and 5.

19. Academy of Motion Picture Arts and Sciences, *Press Clipping File on the Senate Subcommittee War Film Hearings*, Vol. 1, August 1–October 15, 1941, ed. Donald Gledhill, Hollywood: Academy Press, 1941.

20. Quoted in Harold J. Salemson, "Swastika over Hollywood," *The Clipper*, October 1941, p. 9.

21. September 10, 1941, reprinted in *Press Clipping File*, Second Day, p. 14.

22. *Variety*, May 26, 1943; June 1, 1943; November 8, 1943.

23. Zechariah Chafee, Jr., *Free Speech in the United States*, Cambridge, Mass.: Harvard University Press, 1946, p. 463.

24. Ibid., pp. 442–43.

25. Richard P. Traina, *American Diplomacy and the Spanish Civil War*, Bloomington: Indiana University Press, 1968, p. 192.

26. League of American Writers Collection, Bancroft Library, University of California, 72/242, part 7.

27. Dalton Trumbo, *Harry Bridges: A Discussion of the Latest Effort to Deport Civil Liberties and the Rights of American Labor*, Hollywood: League of American Writers, 1941.

28. *Soviet Diplomacy and the Spanish Civil War*, Berkeley: University of California Press, 1957, pp. 46 and 88.

29. Speech to a meeting of the Hollywood Peace Forum, reprinted in the *Sunday Worker*, February 11, 1940, p. 6.

30. *"We Hold These Truths . . .": Statements on anti-Semitism by 54 leading American writers, statesmen, educators, clergymen and trade-unionists*, New York: League of American Writers, 1939.

31. George Sklar and Albert Maltz, *Peace on Earth: An Anti-War Play*, New York: Samuel French, 1936, pp. 115–16.

32. V. J. Jerome, *Intellectuals and the War*, New York: Workers Library, 1940, p. 14.

33. *Should American Writers Support Our Participation in the War?*, transcript of speeches in the League of American Writers Collection, part 15.

34. August 26, 1939, p. 1.

35. *Statement to American Writers and Artists* [1940], League of American Writers Collection, part 7.

36. Ralph B. Levering, *American Opinion and the Russian Alliance, 1939–1945*, Chapel Hill: University of North Carolina Press, 1976, p. 34.

37. Minutes of the Executive Board meetings of the Hollywood Branch of the League of American Writers, January 28, 1940, League of American Writers Collection, part 15.

38. Minutes of the National Executive Board meetings, League of American Writers Collection, part 2.

39. Minutes of the National Executive Board, June 19 and 27, 1940.

40. Minutes of the Hollywood Executive Board, March 27, 1941.

41. Clifton Brock, *Americans for Democratic Action*, Washington, D.C.: Public Affairs Press, 1962, p. 45.

42. *Bulletin of the League of American Writers*, July 21, 1941, League of American Writers Collection, part 1.

43. *Bulletin*, January 3, 1942.

44. Mark Lincoln Chadwin, *The Hawks of World War II*, Chapel Hill: University of North Carolina Press, 1968, pp. 243, 245.

45. David Dubinsky and A. H. Raskin, *David Dubinsky: A Life with Labor*, New York: Simon & Schuster, 1977, p. 292.

46. Levering, pp. 43 and 55.

47. American Society for Russian Relief, Inc., *USA-USSR: A Story of Friendship and Aid, 1941–1946*, New York [1947].

48. United States Congress, Senate, *Investigation of the National Defense Program, Hearings Before a Special Committee Investigating the National Defense Program*, 78th Congress, 1st session, part 17, February 16, 1943, "Army Commissions and Military Activities of Motion Picture Personnel," Washington, D.C.: U. S. Government Printing Office, 1943; *Variety*, September 9, 1942, pp. 1 and 4; *Variety*, September 18, 1944, p. 10; for a detailed analysis of the strains between the American occupation forces in Germany and film executives over the distribution of Hollywood films there see Thomas H. Guback, *The International Film Industry*, Bloomington: Indiana University Press, 1969.

49. Stewart, *By a Stroke of Luck*, New York: Paddington Press, 1975, p. 262.

50. Ring Lardner, Jr., *The Lardners: My Family Remembered*, Harper & Row, 1976, p. 290.

51. John Keats, *You Might As Well Live: The Life and Times of Dorothy Parker*, New York: Simon & Schuster, 1970, pp. 233–35.

52. Paul Trivers, "Hollywood Writers Move Up," *New Masses*, September 14, 1943, pp. 20–21; Robert Rossen, "New Characters for the Screen," *New Masses*, January 18, 1944, pp. 18–19.

53. United States Congress, House of Representatives, Committee on Un-American Activities, 80th Congress, 1st session, October 1947, *Hear-*

ings Regarding the Communist Infiltration of the Motion Picture Industry, Washington, D.C.: U. S. Government Printing Office, 1947, p. 138.

54. "Communism and the Movies: A Study of Film Content," in John Cogley, *Report on Blacklisting*, Vol. 1, *The Movies*, The Fund for the Republic, 1956, pp. 211–12.

55. *Labor Radical*, Boston: Beacon Press, 1970, p. 177.

56. *Variety*, December 10, 1941, and January 14, 1942.

57. This admonition was delivered by screenwriter Anthony Veiller, OCD representative to the HWM, March 28, 1942, Melvyn Douglas Collection, The Wisconsin Center for Theater Research, 100 AN, Box 2.

58. The scripts are collected in Arch Oboler and Stephen Longstreet, eds., *Free World Theatre: Nineteen New Radio Plays*, New York: Random House, 1944.

59. Quoted (with ellipses) in John Morton Blum, *V Was for Victory: Politics and American Culture During World War II*, New York: Harcourt Brace Jovanovich, 1976, p. 25.

60. *Writers' Congress: The Proceedings of the Conference Held in October 1943 Under the Sponsorship of the Hollywood Writers' Mobilization and the University of California*, Berkeley: University of California Press, 1944, p. 4.

61. Ibid., p. 56.

62. League of American Writers Collection, Part 7.

63. Ralph Block to Carey McWilliams, March 10, 1942, Carey McWilliams Papers, Hoover Institution on War, Revolution and Peace.

64. Speech by Polonsky at a Blacklist Retrospective held at the Los Feliz Theater, Los Angeles, May 1, 1977.

65. May 23, 1945, p. 34; July 11, p. 32; October 10, p. 31.

66. Blum, p. 183.

67. We are indebted to Pauline Finn for access to a bound copy of the scripts for "Reunion, U.S.A."

68. Guy Endore wrote two powerful pamphlets for the Committee, both of which enjoyed wide circulation: *The Sleepy Lagoon Case* (1943) and *The Sleepy Lagoon Mystery* (1944). All the Committee's materials, including newspaper clippings, letters from the imprisoned boys, etc. are in the Special Collections department of the UCLA Graduate Research Library, Archive number 107.

69. Remi Nadeau, *Los Angeles: From Mission to Modern City*, New York: Longmans, Green and Co., 1960, pp. 242–44; Carey McWilliams, "What We Did About Racial Minorities," in Goodman, pp. 96–97.

70. The script and selected animation panels were printed in *Hollywood Quarterly*, 1 (July 1946), pp. 72.

71. Melvyn Douglas Collection, The Wisconsin Center for Theater Research, 100 AN, Boxes 3 and 4.

72. "Moving the West-Coast Japanese," *Harper's*, September 1942, p. 369.
73. February 28, 1942, p. 8.
74. Quoted in Art Preis, *Labor's Giant Step*, New York: Pioneer Publishers, 1964, p. 141.

Chapter 7

1. "The Documentary and Hollywood," *Hollywood Quarterly*, 1 (January 1946), p. 166.
2. *Hollywood Reporter*, June 5, 1947, p. 1.
3. James Green, "Fighting on Two Fronts: Working Class Militancy in the 1940's," *Radical America*, July-August 1975, pp. 20–21.
4. Alonzo L. Hamby, *The Imperial Years: The United States Since 1939*, New York: Weybright and Talley, 1976, pp. 92–93.
5. United States Congress, House of Representatives, 78th Congress, 2nd session, *House Reports, Miscellaneous*, Vol. 2, January 10–December 19, 1944, "Report No. 1311—The C.I.O. Political Action Committee," March 29, 1944, Washington, D.C.: U. S. Government Printing Office, 1944, pp. 1–2.
6. *Variety*, February 7, 1944, p. 5.
7. Ibid.
8. *Weekly Variety*, September 12, 1945, p. 34.
9. *PM*, July 2, 1944.
10. *Variety*, March 15, 1944, p. 3.
11. *Hollywood on Trial*, a film written by Arnie Reisman, directed by David Helpern, Jr., and produced by James C. Gutman, 1976.
12. Quoted in John Cogley, *Report on Blacklisting*, Vol. 1, *The Movies*, The Fund for the Republic, 1956, p. 11.
13. *Variety*, April 19, 1944.
14. Arthur F. McClure, *The Truman Administration and the Problems of Postwar Labor, 1945–1948*, Rutherford, N.J.: Fairleigh Dickinson University Press, 1969, pp. 45 and 181.
15. Len De Caux, *Labor Radical*, Boston: Beacon Press, 1970, p. 446; Art Preis, *Labor's Giant Step*, New York: Pioneer Publishers, 1964, p. 257; Ludwig Teller, *A Labor Policy for America: A National Labor Code*, New York: Baker, Voorhis, & Co., 1945, pp. 309–10.
16. Cabell Phillips, *The Truman Presidency*, New York: The Macmillan Co., 1966, p. 112.
17. New York *Times*, November 6, 1945, p. 1.
18. I. F. Stone, *The Truman Era*, New York: Monthly Review Press, 1953, pp. 80–82; Lawrence S. Wittner, *Cold War America: From Hiroshima to Watergate*, New York: Praeger Publishers, 1974, p. 88.
19. Night letter from George Pepper to President Truman, September 25, 1945, Hollywood Democratic Committee Collection, The Wisconsin Center for Theater Research, 31 AN, Box 9.

20. Patricia Killoran, "The Truth About Hollywood's Film Strike."
21. This three-page form letter, written on official IATSE stationery and signed by Brewer (this particular specimen was addressed to Gregory Peck) is in the Hollywood Democratic Committee Collection, 31 AN, Box 9.
22. *Variety*, March 26, 1945.
23. Minutes of the SWG Executive Board, September 17, 1945. (All references to SWG minutes are taken from copies in the possession of former Guild president Sheridan Gibney.)
24. SWG minutes, October 5, 1945.
25. *The Screen Writer*, May 1946, pp. 40–41; *The Screen Writer*, July 1946, p. 40.
26. SWG minutes, October 8, 1945.
27. Hollywood Democratic Committee Collection, 31 AN, Box 9.
28. "The Real Facts Behind the Motion Picture Lockout," a speech delivered at the Olympic Auditorium, October 13, 1945, Hollywood Ten Collection, Southern California Library for Social Studies and Research.
29. SWG minutes, October 15, 1945.
30. United States Congress, House of Representatives, 80th Congress, 2nd session, Special Sub-Committee of the Committee on Education and Labor, *Jurisdictional Disputes in the Motion Picture Industry*, Vol. 3, February-March 1948, Washington, D.C.: U. S. Government Printing Office, 1948, pp. 2,106, 2,107, and 2,117.
31. SWG minutes, September 20, 1946.
32. February 1947, p. 46.
33. *Jurisdictional Disputes*, pp. 1,570–1,571.
34. McClure, p. 163.
35. David Dubinsky and A. H. Raskin, *David Dubinsky: A Life with Labor*, New York: Simon & Schuster, 1977, p. 276; Len De Caux, *Labor Radical*, Boston: Beacon Press, 1970, p. 440.
36. Quoted in Clifton Brock, *Americans for Democratic Action*, Washington, D.C.: Public Affairs Press, 1962, p. 52.
37. Lawson's remark was from a speech he delivered to the Executive Board of the Hollywood Democratic Committee, August 18, 1944, Hollywood Democratic Committee Collection, 31 AN, Box 1; Trumbo's from a speech he made to a Writers for Roosevelt meeting, September 6, 1944, reprinted in *New Masses*, September 26, 1944, p. 29.
38. "History of the Hollywood Democratic Committee," (written by George Pepper), Hollywood Democratic Committee Collection, 31 AN, Box 1, p. 37.
39. The letter or article, "On the Dissolution of the Communist Party of the United States," is reprinted in Robert V. Daniels, ed., *A Documentary History of Communism*, Vol. 2, New York: Vintage Books, 1960, pp. 139–42.

40. Peggy Dennis, *The Autobiography of an American Communist*, Berkeley: Creative Arts Book Co., 1977, p. 174.

41. Ring Lardner, Jr., *The Lardners: My Family Remembered*, New York: Harper & Row, 1976, p. 317.

42. Reprinted in Henry Hart, ed., *American Writers' Congress*, New York: International Publishers, 1935, p. 69.

43. "Background to Error," *New Masses*, February 12, 1946, pp. 23–25.

44. In the issues of February 12, 23, March 2, and 16; reprinted in *Mike Gold: A Literary Anthology*, ed. Michael Folsom, New York: International Publishers, 1972, pp. 283–91.

45. "Moving Forward," *New Masses*, April 9, 1946, pp. 8–10, 21–22.

46. *Essays on Literature, Philosophy, and Music*, New York: International Publishers, 1950, pp. 25, 31, and 42.

47. "On Our Cultural Work," *Party Voice*, January 1957, p. 5.

48. *Letters on Literature and Politics, 1912–1972*, selected and edited by Elena Wilson, New York: Farrar, Straus & Giroux, 1977, p. 255.

49. Ibid., p. 286.

50. *Eurocommunism and the State*, London: Lawrence and Wishart, 1977, p. 117.

51. March 14, 1947, Philip Stevenson Collection, The Wisconsin Center for Theater Research, 69 AN, Box 2.

52. Herbert Biberman, "Freedom of Choice: The First Freedom," undated manuscript in the Herbert Biberman/Gale Sondergaard Collection, The Wisconsin Center for Theater Research, 58 AN, Box 15.

53. Speech delivered at an HWM forum, March 12, 1947, Dalton Trumbo Collection, The Wisconsin Center for Theater Research, 24 AN, Box 75.

54. "Areas of Silence," *Hollywood Quarterly*, 3 (Fall 1947), p. 51.

55. Irving Bernstein, *Hollywood at the Crossroads: An Economic Study of the Motion Picture Industry*, Hollywood: Hollywood AFL Film Council, 1957, pp. 17 and 18.

56. Ibid., pp. 23, 24, 31–32.

57. Clive Hirschhorn, *Gene Kelly*, Chicago: Henry Regnery Co., 1974, p. 158.

58. *Variety*, April 21, 1938, pp. 1 and 5; "120,000 American Ambassadors," *Foreign Affairs*, October 1939, pp. 45–59.

59. Margaret Thorp, *America at the Movies*, New Haven: Yale University Press, 1939, pp. 280–81.

60. September 9, 1943, pp. 1 and 5.

61. United States Department of State, *Memorandum on the Postwar International Information Program of the United States*, prepared by Arthur W. Macmahon, Washington, D.C.: U. S. Government Printing Office, 1945, p. xviii.

62. *Variety*, January 14, 1944, p. 4.

63. Department of State *Memorandum*, p. 76.

64. Ibid., p. 80.

65. "Mr. Eric Johnston's Tour," *The Screen Writer*, July 1947, pp. 12–13.

66. For a history of the manner in which the FBI established its informer network and dossier file see Frank Donner, "How J. Edgar Hoover Created His Intelligence Powers," *The Civil Liberties Review*, 3 (February-March 1977), pp. 34–51; Athan G. Theoharis, "The F.B.I.'s Stretching of Presidential Directives, 1936–1953," *Political Science Quarterly*, 91 (Winter 1976–77), pp. 652–72. For an account of how the Bureau reacted when it was exposed see Richard Harris, "Reflections: Crime in the F.B.I.," *The New Yorker*, August 8, 1977, pp. 30–42.

67. Ring Lardner, Jr., "First Steps in Arithmetic," *The Screen Writer*, August 1947, p. 17.

68. "Witch-Hunting in Hollywood," *The Screen Writer*, June 1947, p. 17.

69. *The Screen Writer*, September 1946, p. 3.

70. "Snowball in the Spring," *The Screen Writer*, June 1947, p. 3.

71. *The Screen Writer*, September 1946, pp. 45–51.

Chapter 8

1. Boston: Little, Brown & Co., 1944, p. 431.

2. United States Congress, House of Representatives, Committee on Un-American Activities, 84th Congress, 1st session, *Investigation of Communist Activities in the Los Angeles Area*, Vol. 2, June 30, 1955, p. 1,760.

3. *Hollywood Reporter*, May 19, 1947, p. 16.

4. New York *Times*, March 28, 1947, p. 15.

5. New York: E. P. Dutton & Co., 1948, pp. 11 and 31.

6. *Hollywood Reporter*, April 21, 1947, p. 1.

7. *Variety*, May 5, 1947, pp. 1 and 8; May 29, 1947, p. 7.

8. *Variety*, May 16, 1947, p. 3.

9. Deposition of Lester Cole, September 10 and 11, 1948, *Cole* v. *Loew's, Inc.*, in the District Court of the United States, Southern District of California, Central Division, No. 8005-Y, pp. 137–38.

10. United States Congress, House of Representatives, Committee on Un-American Activities, 80th Congress, 1st session, October 1947, *Hearings Regarding the Communist Infiltration of the Motion Picture Industry*, Washington, D.C.: U. S. Government Printing Office, 1947, pp. 312–13.

11. Deposition of E. J. Mannix, March 31, 1948, *Cole* v. *Loew's*.

12. *Hollywood Reporter*, July 23, 1947, p. 1.

13. Cole deposition, pp. 140–41.

14. *Hollywood Reporter*, September 30, 1947, pp. 1 and 4.

15. Ring Lardner, Jr., *The Lardners: My Family Remembered*, New York: Harper & Row, 1976, p. 320.

16. Albert Maltz, *The Citizen Writer*, New York: International Publishers, 1950, p. 28.

17. Ibid., p. 40.

18. See Telford Taylor, *Grand Inquest*, New York: Ballantine Books, 1961, pp. 218–19, 242–43. In 1955 the Supreme Court upheld the use of the Fifth; see *Quinn* v. *U.S.*, 349 U.S. 155, *Emspak* v. *U.S.*, 349 U.S. 190, and *Bart* v. *U.S.*, 349 U.S. 219, all decided in May 1955.

19. See Leonard Levy, *Origins of the Fifth Amendment*, New York: Oxford University Press, 1968.

20. Letter dated April 2, 1973, courtesy of Albert Maltz.

21. Alvah Bessie, *Inquisition in Eden*, New York: The Macmillan Co., 1965, p. 189.

22. Walter Goodman, *The Committee*, Baltimore: Penguin Books, 1969, p. 302.

23. Robert Kenny/Robert Morris Collection, The Wisconsin Center for Theater Research, 29 AN, Box 6.

24. October 15, 1947, p. 11.

25. *Hollywood Reporter*, October 16, 1947, pp. 8 and 9.

26. From Howard Koch's "Introduction to the Printed Record," *Thought Control in the U.S.A.: The Collected Proceedings of the Conference on the Subject of Thought Control in the United States*, called by the Hollywood Arts, Sciences and Professions Council, P.C.A., July 9–13, 1947, Los Angeles, 1947, p. 2.

27. Letter to Edward L. Barrett, Jr., July 1949, quoted in *The Tenney Committee*, Ithaca, New York: Cornell University Press, 1951, p. 364.

28. A copy of this broadsheet is in the Hollywood Democratic Committee Collection, The Wisconsin Center for Theater Research, 31 AN, Box 1.

29. New York *Times*, October 26, 1947, p. 53.

30. A full list of contributors—a who's who of leading men and women—is in the Hollywood Democratic Committee Collection, 31 AN, Box 4.

31. A copy of the letter, without a date, is in the possession of Philip Dunne.

32. *The Screen Writer*, 3, June 1947, p. 4.

33. Circular from Lavery to SWG members, October 20, 1947, Alvah Bessie Collection, The Wisconsin Center for Theater Research, 59 AN, Box 1.

34. 1947 HUAC hearings, pp. 10–16.

35. Letter from Gordon Kahn to Charles Katz, January 31, 1948, Kenny/Morris Collection, 29 AN, Box 12.

36. 1947 HUAC hearings, p. 138.

37. "Congress and Hollywood," October 23, 1947, p. 24.

38. October 27, 1947, p. 17.

39. Quoted in letter from Kahn to Katz.
40. 1947 HUAC hearings, pp. 291, 293–94.
41. The letter, dated October 28, 1947, is in the Samuel Ornitz Collection, The Wisconsin Center for Theater Research, 48 AN, Box 1.
42. 1947 HUAC hearings, pp. 306–8, 323.
43. 1947 HUAC hearings, p. 404.
44. 1947 HUAC hearings, p. 364.
45. Reprinted in Robert Vaughn, *Only Victims: A Study of Show Business Blacklisting*, New York: G. P. Putnam's Sons, 1972, p. 324.
46. Cole deposition, pp. 163–64.
47. November 2, 1947, part IV, pp. 6 and 8; part I, pp. 1 and 16.
48. November 5, 1947, p. 18.
49. New York *Times*, November 3, 1947, p. 19.
50. N. D. Daniels, "Hollywood After the Hearings," *New Masses*, 65 (November 25, 1947), pp. 4–5.
51. Humphrey Bogart, "I'm No Communist," *Photoplay*, March 1948, p. 53.
52. Quoted in Dalton Trumbo, "Honor Bright and All That Jazz" (first printed in 1956), reprinted in *The Time of the Toad*, New York: Perennial Library, 1972, p. 140.
53. Quoted in Clive Hirschhorn, *Gene Kelly*, Chicago: Henry Regnery Co., 1974, p. 159.
54. Trumbo, "Honor Bright," p. 140.
55. Conference on Thought Control, p. 87.
56. An edited version of Lavery's testimony is included in Eric Bentley, ed., *Thirty Years of Treason*, New York: The Viking Press, 1971, p. 173.
57. Kenny/Morris Collection, 29 AN, Box 6.
58. Ibid.
59. Bessie Collection, 59 AN, Box 1.
60. *Hollywood Reporter*, November 20, 1947, p. 4.

Chapter 9

1. Speech delivered at "A Salute to John Howard Lawson," November 12, 1955, courtesy Alfred Levitt.
2. United States Congress, House of Representatives, 80th Congress, 1st session, October 1947, Committee on Un-American Activities, *Hearings Regarding the Communist Infiltration of the Motion Picture Industry*, Washington, D.C.: U. S. Government Printing Office, 1947, p. 10.
3. *Motion Picture Herald*, February 22, 1936, pp. 15 and 16.
4. *Variety*, February 24, 1937, p. 1.
5. United States 82nd Congress, 1st session, July 6, 1951, Committee on Un-American Activities, *Communist Infiltration of the Hollywood*

Motion Picture Industry, Washington, D.C.: U. S. Government Printing Office, 1951, Vol. 1, p. 198.

6. *The Pat Hobby Stories*, New York: Charles Scribner's Sons, paperback, 1962, p. 117.

7. October 10, 1936, p. 1.

8. Dave Davis and Neal Goldberg, "Organizing the Screen Writers Guild —An Interview with John Howard Lawson," *Cineaste*, 8, No. 2, p. 10.

9. Lawson, "More Than Make Believe," *TAC*, August 1938, p. 5.

10. July 1938, p. 47.

11. Hicks, "How Red was the Red Decade?" *Harper's*, 207 (July 1953), p. 57.

12. Winchell Taylor, "Secret Movie Censors," *The Nation*, 197 (July 9, 1938), pp. 38–39.

13. Ibid., p. 39.

14. Davis and Goldberg, p. 10.

15. Lawson, "More Than Make Believe," p. 5. For a more complete study of the *Blockade* controversy, see Larry S. Ceplair, "The Politics of Compromise in Hollywood: A Case Study," *Cineaste*, 8, No. 4, pp. 2–7.

16. "Confessions of a Nazi Spy," *TAC*, April 1939, p. 19.

17. *Variety*, July 21, 1939, p. 4.

18. Quoted in Gordon Sager, "Hollywood Carries on for Neville," *TAC*, October 1939, p. 14.

19. *Variety*, May 22, 1940, pp. 1 and 4.

20. Wolfe Kaufman, "War, Propaganda and Hollywood," *The Clipper*, August 1, 1940, p. 27.

21. 1947 HUAC hearings, pp. 71 and 74.

22. 1947 HUAC hearings, p. 39.

23. 1951 HUAC hearings, Vol. 1, pp. 235–36.

24. Richard Moody, *Lillian Hellman, Playwright*, New York: Pegasus, 1972, pp. 139–40.

25. Letter from Koch to the Los Angeles *Times Calendar*, June 5, 1977, p. 2.

26. *Writers' Congress: The Proceedings of the Conference Held in October 1943 Under the Sponsorship of the Hollywood Writers' Mobilization and the University of California*, Berkeley: University of California Press, 1944, p. 34.

27. " 'Wilson' and the Box Office," September 5, 1944, pp. 27–28.

28. 1951 HUAC hearings, pp. 416–17; Richard English, "What Makes a Hollywood Communist?" *The Saturday Evening Post*, May 19, 1951, p. 148; Edward Dmytryk, *It's a Hell of a Life but Not a Bad Living*, New York: Times Books, 1978, p. 70.

29. Dmytryk, p. 71.

30. *Hollywood Reporter*, October 3, 1947, p. 9.

31. Scott, "You Can't Do That," speech given at a Conference on the Subject of Thought Control in the United States, reprinted in *Thought Control in the United States of America: The Collected Proceedings of the Conference on the Subject of Thought Control in the United States, Called by the Hollywood Arts, Sciences & Professions Council, Progressive Citizens of America, July 9–13, 1947,* Los Angeles: 1947, p. 325.

32. Ibid., pp. 325–28.

33. Ibid., p. 330.

34. Russell Campbell, "Interview with Leo Seltzer: 'A Total and Realistic Experience,'" *Jump Cut,* pp. 14, 26.

35. *Film in the Battle of Ideas,* New York: Masses & Mainstream, 1953, p. 91.

36. Tony Safford, "Interview with Samuel Brody: 'The Camera As a Weapon in the Class Struggle,'" *Jump Cut,* pp. 14, 30.

37. *Variety,* November 16, 1936, p. 11.

38. Speech given at the Fourth Congress of the League of American Writers, June 1941, reprinted in *Mike Gold: A Literary Anthology,* Michael Folsom, ed., New York: International Publishers, 1972, pp. 246–47.

39. Excerpt from Lawson's appeal brief to the United States Supreme Court, *Variety,* August 12, 1949, p. 6.

40. 1951 HUAC hearings, Vol. 1, p. 294.

41. Polonsky, American Film Institute Seminar, November 13, 1974, p. 44.

Chapter 10

1. *People's World,* November 7, 1947, p. 3.

2. November 20, 1947, pp. 1 and 15.

3. Deposition of Lester Cole, *Cole* v. *Loew's, Inc.,* United States District Court, Southern District of California, No. 8005-Y, September 10 and 11, 1948, p. 178.

4. Los Angeles *Times,* February 13, 1952, p. 5.

5. The letter, dated November 16, 1947, is in the Robert Kenny/Robert Morris Collection, The Wisconsin Center for Theater Research, 29 AN, Box 12.

6. The letter, written on MGM stationery, and dated November 28, 1947, is in the Kenny/Morris Collection, 29 AN, Box 12.

7. Deposition of N. Peter Rathvon, *Cole* v. *Loew's, Inc.,* March 26, 1948, pp. 48, 71–77, 120.

8. Handwritten notes of Robert Kenny, intended for use in the cross-examination of Eric Johnston, Kenny/Morris Collection, 29 AN, Box 1.

9. Deposition of Dore Schary, *Independent Productions Corporation* v. *Loew's, Inc., et al.,* United States District Court, Southern District of New York, March 13, 1964, p. 29.

10. Deposition of Louis B. Mayer, *Cole* v. *Loew's, Inc.*, March 10, 1948, p. 56.

11. Schary deposition, p. 40.

12. Ibid., p. 36.

13. Rathvon deposition, pp. 92–93.

14. The letters, dated November 26, 1947, are in the Kenny/Morris Collection, 29 AN, Box 6.

15. *Part of Our Time*, New York: Simon & Schuster, 1955, pp. 182, 183, 300.

16. *The Committee*, Baltimore: Penguin Books, 1969, pp. 213 and 214.

17. Kanfer, *A Journal of the Plague Years*, New York: Atheneum, 1973, p. 84.

18. "The Blacklist and the Cold War," New York *Times*, October 3, 1976, section 2, p. 16.

19. *Talking Pictures*, New York: Penguin Books, 1975, p. 346.

20. Ibid., p. 256.

21. "Edward Dmytryk Is a Self-Made Man As Well As a Serious-Minded Director," *Films in Review*, February 1962, p. 86.

22. New York: E. P. Dutton & Co., 1968.

23. New York: Frederick Ungar Publishing Co., 1974.

24. Henry Ephron, *We Thought We Could Do Anything: The Life of Screenwriters Phoebe and Henry Ephron*, New York: W. W. Norton & Co., 1977, p. 86.

25. Quoted in Kanfer, p. 88.

26. Letters from Herman Selvin, Loeb & Loeb, to Charles Katz, November 10 and 12, 1948, Kenny/Morris Collection, 29 AN, Box 6.

27. *Weekly Variety*, November 12, 1947, p. 18.

28. November 8, 1947, Melvyn Douglas Collection, The Wisconsin Center for Theater Research, 100 AN, Box 3.

29. November 28, 1947, Melvyn Douglas Collection, 100 AN, Box 3.

30. Quoted in Alvah Bessie, *Inquisition in Eden*, New York: The Macmillan Co., 1965, p. 224.

31. Rathvon deposition, p. 127.

32. Deposition of Leonard Spigelgass, *Screen Writers Guild, Inc.* v. *Motion Picture Association of America, Inc.*, Southern District of New York, 46-165, June 14, 1950, p. 71.

33. Ibid.

34. *Hollywood Reporter*, December 2, 1947, p. 1.

35. Spigelgass deposition, pp. 73–74; *Hollywood Reporter*, December 3, 1947.

36. *Hollywood Reporter*, December 22, 1947, p. 21.

37. Ibid., December 15, 1947, p. 1.

38. Ibid., January 14, 1948, p. 1.

39. *Hollywood Reporter*, January 6, 1948, pp. 1 and 2.

40. Lillian Ross, "Onward and Upward with the Arts," *The New Yorker*, February 21, 1948, p. 48.
41. Ibid., p. 46.
42. March 29, 1948, pp. 1 and 10.
43. United States Congress, House of Representatives, Committee on Un-American Activities, 80th Congress, 1st session, October 1947, *Hearings Regarding the Communist Infiltration of the Motion Picture Industry*, Washington, D.C.: U. S. Government Printing Office, 1947, pp. 28–29.
44. August 11, 1948, p. 5.
45. November 26, 1947, p. 15.
46. Quoted in John Cogley, *Report on Blacklisting*, Vol. 1, *The Movies*, The Fund for the Republic, 1956, p. 77.
47. United States Congressional Record: Proceedings and Debates of the 80th Congress, First Session, Vol. 93, part 9, November 18, 1947, to December 19, 1947, Washington, D.C.: U. S. Government Printing Office, 1947, p. 10,771.
48. Ibid., pp. 10,777–78.
49. Ibid., p. 10,776.
50. Ibid., p. 10,773.
51. Ibid., p. 10,782.
52. Ibid., pp. 10,778 and 10,793.
53. The outlines, opening and closing statements, and printed briefs are in the Kenny/Morris Collection, 29 AN, Boxes 7 and 13.
54. The letter, dated March 7, 1948, is in the Kenny/Morris Collection, 29 AN, Box 6.
55. 167 F2d 250, March 18, 1948.
56. Kenny/Morris Collection, 29 AN, Box 14.
57. The circular, dated August 20, 1948, is in the Kenny/Morris Collection, 29 AN, Box 14.
58. 176 F2d 52.
59. 176 F2d 53.
60. Quoted in "Fellow Citizens: Our Husbands Are in Prison!", Hollywood: The Committee to Free the Hollywood Ten, [1950].
61. *Variety*, August 2, 1950, pp. 1 and 3.
62. Typescript of statement, dated December 20, 1948, is in the Kenny/Morris Collection, 29 AN, Box 6.
63. Quoted in David Caute, *The Great Fear: The Anti-Communist Purge Under Truman and Eisenhower*, New York: Simon & Schuster, 1978, p. 143.
64. 185 F2d 652 and 653, November 22, 1950.
65. 216 F2d 851, November 4, 1954.
66. Los Angeles *Times*, April 29, 1952, p. 4.
67. Mayer deposition, pp. 37–38.

68. Deposition of E. J. Mannix, *Cole* v. *Loew's, Inc.*, March 31, 1948, pp. 41–42.

69. Rathvon deposition, pp. 87–90.

70. Deposition of George A. Hickey, *Cole* v. *Loew's, Inc.*, November 19, 1948, pp. 23–30.

71. The report is in the Kenny/Morris Collection, 29 AN, Box 15.

72. Ibid., Box 12.

73. Ibid., Box 13.

74. August 5, 1948, Albert Maltz Collection, The Wisconsin Center for Theater Research, 17 AN, Box 15.

75. Letter from Trumbo to Phil Berg, March 8, 1948, reprinted in *Additional Dialogue: Letters of Dalton Trumbo, 1942–1962*, ed. Helen Manfull, New York: M. Evans and Co., 1970, p. 88.

76. Letter to Ben Margolis, December 4, 1960, Herbert Biberman/Gale Sondergaard Collection, The Wisconsin Center for Theater Research, 58 AN, Box 102; letter to Screen Writers Guild, May 16, 1949, Albert Maltz Collection, 17 AN, Box 15.

77. Handwritten petition for parole, September 8, 1950, Kenny/Morris Collection, 29 AN, Box 5.

78. Letter to Kenny, April 25, 1951, Kenny/Morris Collection, 29 AN, Box 15.

79. Letter to Margolis, July 25, 1950, Biberman/Sondergaard Collection, 58 AN, Box 1; letter to Kenny, July 20, 1950, Kenny/Morris Collection, 29 AN, Box 5.

80. July 19, 1950, Kenny/Morris Collection, 29 AN, Box 5.

81. April 25, 1951, Ibid., Box 15.

82. Ibid., Boxes 5 and 6.

83. Richard English, "What Makes a Hollywood Communist?", *The Saturday Evening Post*, May 19, 1951, p. 147.

84. Ibid., p. 147.

85. Edward Dmytryk, *It's a Hell of a Life but Not a Bad Living*, New York: Times Books, 1978, p. 72.

86. English, pp. 149–50.

87. Excerpt from Dmytryk's second appearance before HUAC, April 25, 1951, reprinted in Eric Bentley, ed., *Thirty Years of Treason*, New York: The Viking Press, 1971, p. 398.

88. New York *Times*, September 11, 1950, p. 18.

89. Bentley, p. 404.

90. Letter from Roy Brewer, Ronald Reagan, and others to the *Hollywood Reporter*, June 6, 1951.

91. *The 1950–51 Motion Picture Almanac*, New York: Quigley Publications, 1950, p. 636.

92. Dmytryk, p. 147.

93. "Return to the Free World," *New Masses*, June 1951, p. 13.

Chapter 11

1. United States Congress, House of Representatives, 83rd Congress, 2nd session, February 6, 1954, *Annual Report of the Committee on Un-American Activities for the Year 1953*, Washington, D.C.: U. S. Government Printing Office, 1954, p. 23.

2. George W. Kirchwey, *A Survey of the Workings of the Criminal-Syndicalism Law of California*, Los Angeles: California Committee of the ACLU, 1926, pp. 9–10.

3. *The Witness and I*, New York: Columbia University Press, 1974, pp. 30–31.

4. *Safeguarding Civil Liberties*, UCLA: Oral History Project, 1974, p. 120.

5. Stephen H. Fritchman, *Heretic: A Partisan Autobiography*, Boston: Beacon Press, 1977, pp. 122–23.

6. Interview with Max Wilk for the American Film Institute's Oral History Project, December 1971, pp. 22–23.

7. *Losey on Losey*, ed. Tom Milne, Garden City, N.Y.: Doubleday & Company, 1968, p. 90.

8. Richard Moody, *Lillian Hellman, Playwright*, New York: Pegasus, 1972, pp. 232–33.

9. *Variety*, December 22, 1950, pp. 1 and 6.

10. Ibid., February 12, 1951, p. 5.

11. United States Congress, House of Representatives, 82nd Congress, 2nd session, February 17, 1952, Committee on Un-American Activities, *Annual Report of the Committee on Un-American Activities for the Year 1951*, Washington, D.C.: U. S. Government Printing Office, 1952, p. 7.

12. United States Congress, House of Representatives, 82nd Congress, 1st session, July 6, 1951, Committee on Un-American Activities, *Communist Infiltration of the Hollywood Motion Picture Industry*, Washington, D.C.: U. S. Government Printing Office, 1951, Vol. 2, p. 1,509.

13. March 12, 1951, p. 6.

14. March 5, 1951, p. 11.

15. *Variety*, October 13 and 18, 1950; Thomas F. Brady, "Hollywood Divided by Loyalty Pledge Issue," New York *Times*, October 22, 1950.

16. Ibid., June 3 and July 19, 1951.

17. Ibid., March 21, 1951, p. 9; Sondergaard's letter, dated March 13, appeared in *Variety*, March 16, p. 5.

18. Ibid., October 10, 1950.

19. *Growing Up in Hollywood*, New York: Harcourt Brace Jovanovich, 1976, pp. 203–4. (His emphasis.) See also Kenneth L. Geist, *Pictures Will Talk: The Life and Films of Joseph L. Mankiewicz*, New York: Charles Scribner's Sons, 1978, pp. 173–206.

20. *Variety*, October 23, 1950.

21. Ibid., October 27, 1950.
22. Ibid., March 21, 1951.
23. April 9, 1952, p. 3.
24. May 3, 1951, Biberman/Sondergaard Collection, The Wisconsin Center for Theater Research, 58 AN, Box 1.
25. 1951 HUAC hearings, Vol. 1, p. 107.
26. Los Angeles *Examiner*, April 13, 1951, p. 5.
27. For her reflections on her appearance and demeanor see William Overend, "When Comedy Stopped for Lucy," Los Angeles *Times*, November 24, 1976, part IV, pp. 1 and 15.
28. April 12, 1951, Biberman/Sondergaard Collection, 58 AN, Box 1.
29. Victor S. Navasky, "To Name or Not to Name," New York *Times Magazine*, March 25, 1973, p. 111.
30. Quoted in Stefan Kanfer, *A Journal of the Plague Years*, New York: Atheneum, 1971, p. 173.
31. *Wanderer*, New York: Alfred A. Knopf, 1963, pp. 390–91.
32. *Variety*, January 28 and February 6, 1952; *Weekly Variety*, January 30, 1952, pp. 2 and 18.
33. Lawrence S. Wittner, *Cold War America: From Hiroshima to Watergate*, New York: Praeger Publishers, 1974, pp. 91–92.
34. Pollock's affidavit for *Young et al.* v. *Motion Picture Producers Association, Inc.*, April 11, 1961, pp. 4–9.
35. United States Congress, House of Representatives, 84th Congress, 2nd session, July 1956, Committee on Un-American Activities, *Investigation of So-Called "Blacklisting" in Entertainment Industry—Report of the Fund for the Republic, Inc.*, Washington, D.C.: U. S. Government Printing Office, 1956, Vol. 5, pp. 5,230 and 5,237.
36. John Cogley, *Report on Blacklisting*, Vol. 1, *The Movies*, Fund for the Republic, 1956, pp. 83–84.
37. Robert Kenny/Robert Morris Collection, The Wisconsin Center for Theater Research, 29 AN, Box 17.
38. Deposition of Martin Gang, *Independent Productions Corp.* v. *Loew's, Inc. et al.*, May 4, 1964, pp. 45 and 88.
39. Ibid., p. 72.
40. Cogley, p. 90.
41. Gang deposition, pp. 64–68.
42. May 21, 1952.
43. "X" [a group of Hollywood writers], "Hollywood Meets Frankenstein," *The Nation*, June 28, 1952, p. 630.
44. We are indebted to Greg Bernstein for allowing us to use portions of the interview he conducted with Johnny Green.
45. Cogley, pp. 115–16.
46. "Good Guys, Bad Guys, and Congressman Walter," May 15, 1958, pp. 30–31.
47. 1956 HUAC hearings, Vol. 5, p. 5,223.

Chapter 12

1. *Reflections on Guy Endore*, UCLA Oral History Project, 1964, p. 153.
2. "Life on the Blacklist," *The Nation*, December 20, 1952, p. 568.
3. These events and their impact are described in great detail in a letter from Maltz to Biberman, October 29, 1951, the Biberman/Sondergaard Collection, The Wisconsin Center for Theater Research, 58 AN, Box 1.
4. "Mexico Clamps Down on Stalin," *The Saturday Evening Post*, August 30, 1952, pp. 16–17, 41, and 44.
5. Thomas I. Emerson and David Haber, *Political and Civil Rights in the United States*, Buffalo, N.Y.: Dennis & Co., 1958, pp. 504–5, quoted in David Caute, *The Great Fear*, New York: Simon & Schuster, 1978, p. 245.
6. Ring Lardner, Jr., "My Life on the Blacklist," *The Saturday Evening Post*, October 14, 1961, p. 42.
7. New York: Warner Paperback Library, 1973, p. 292.
8. "To Name or Not to Name," New York *Times Magazine*, March 25, 1973, p. 119.
9. Endore, "Life on the Blacklist," p. 568.
10. Reprinted, along with Trumbo's responses and related correspondence, in Dalton Trumbo, "The Happy Jack Fish Hatchery Papers," *Esquire*, January 1970, pp. 73–77, 166–74.
11. The New York *Times* carried complete reports in its editions of March 24–28, 1949.
12. Los Angeles *Times*, November 27, 1952, part 1, p. 2.
13. *Variety*, February 5, 1953; Robert Ardrey, "Hollywood: The Toll of the Frenzied Forties," *The Reporter*, March 21, 1957, p. 31.
14. August 7, 1962, Biberman/Sondergaard Collection, The Wisconsin Center for Theater Research, 58 AN, Box 102.
15. *Hollywood Review*, June–July 1953.
16. "Conditioning the American Mind: War Films Show Vicious Over-All Policy," January 1953.
17. "Hollywood's Hero: Arrogant Adventurers Dominate Screen—Goodbye Mr. Deeds," April–May 1954.
18. March 2, 1952, Biberman/Sondergaard Collection, 58 AN, Box 1.
19. Delia Nora Salvi, *The History of the Actors' Laboratory, Inc., 1941–1950*, U.C.L.A.: unpublished Ph.D. thesis, 1969, pp. 185–86.
20. The full story of the making of *Salt of the Earth* and the miners portrayed in the film is excellently told by Deborah Silverton Rosenfelt in her commentary on Michael Wilson's script (*Salt of the Earth*, Old Westbury, N.Y.: The Feminist Press, 1978); and in Herbert Biberman, *Salt of the Earth*, Boston: Beacon Press, 1965.
21. The best account of the professional experience of the blacklistees is in

Howard Suber, *The Anti-Communist Blacklist in the Hollywood Motion Picture Industry*, U.C.L.A.: unpublished Ph.D. thesis, 1968; for details on Trumbo's black market career see Bruce Cook, *Dalton Trumbo*, New York: Charles Scribner's Sons, 1977.

22. *Additional Dialogue: Letters of Dalton Trumbo, 1942–1962*, Helen Manfull, ed., New York: M. Evans and Co., 1970, p. 228.
23. Maltz's most recent restatement of this theme occurred in a letter to the Los Angeles *Times Book Review*, April 3, 1977, p. 2.
24. *Screen Writers Guild, Inc.* v. *Motion Picture Association of America, Inc.*, June 14, 1950, p. 89.
25. Arthur Miller, "The Year It Came Apart," *New York*, December 30, 1974–January 6, 1975, p. 42.
26. *Bring on the Empty Horses*, New York: G. P. Putnam's Sons, 1975, p. 95.
27. Jerusalem: The Macmillan Co., 1971, Vol. 12, pp. 1,472–73.

Afterword

1. Joseph North, former editor of the *Daily Worker*, penned a particularly egregious example of Communist "apologetics": *No Men Are Strangers*, New York: International Publishers, 1958.
2. Quoted by Deborah Rosenfelt in *Salt of the Earth*, Old Westbury, N.Y.: The Feminist Press, 1978, p. 99.

Bibliography

Interviews

Murray Abowitz
Ben and Norma Barzman
Edward Biberman
Sonja Dahl Biberman
Michael Blankfort
Ellenore Bogigian
Jean Butler
Michael Butler
Lester Cole
Sid Davison
Melvyn Douglas
Philip Dunne
Ted Ellsworth
Ken Englund
Pauline Lauber Finn
Carl Foreman
Sheridan Gibney
Dorothy Healey
Edward Huebsch
Ian McLellan Hunter
Tim Hunter
Leo Hurwitz
Paul Jarrico
Sylvia Jarrico
Barbara Kahn
James Kahn
Charles Katz
Pearl Kibre
Stanley Kramer
Kate Lardner
Ring Lardner, Jr.
Emmet Lavery

Jeff Lawson
Alfred Levitt
William Littlejohn
Martin Ludwig
Mary McCall, Jr.
Carey McWilliams
John Lee Mahin
Albert Maltz
Ben Margolis
Milton Merlin
Joy Micon
Sam Moore
Karen Morley
Sadie Ornitz
Seniel Ostrow
John Paxton
Paul Perlin
Abraham Polonsky
William Pomerance
Allen Rivkin
Marguerite Roberts
Samuel Rosenwein
John Sanford
Joan Scott
George Sklar
Ray Spencer
Bess Taffel
Leo Townsend
Chris Trumbo
Karl Tunberg
Gore Vidal
Haskell Wexler

John Wexley   Bert Witt
Rebecca Wilson   Jeane Wood
Michael Wilson   William Wyler

Archives

American Film Institute, Beverly Hills, California
Bancroft Library, University of California, Berkeley
Hoover Institution on War, Revolution and Peace, Stanford
Margaret Herrick Library of the Academy of Motion Picture Arts and
    Sciences, Beverly Hills, California
Motion Picture Association of America, Inc., New York
Southern California Library for Social Studies and Research, Los Angeles
UCLA Special Collections Library
UCLA Theater Arts Library
University of Southern California Theater Arts Library
University of Wyoming Special Collections Library
Walter P. Reuther Library of Labor and Urban Affairs, Wayne State Uni-
    versity, Detroit
The Wisconsin Center for Theater Research, Madison
Writers Guild of America West

Books and Articles:

Aaron, Daniel. *Writers on the Left.* New York: Harcourt, Brace and
    World, 1961.
Aaron, Daniel, and Bendiner, Robert, eds. *The Strenuous Decade: A Social
    and Intellectual Record of the Nineteen-Thirties.* Garden City, N.Y.:
    Anchor Books, 1970.
Academy of Motion Picture Arts and Sciences. *Press Clipping File on the
    Senate Sub-Committee War Film Hearings,* Vol. I, August 1–October
    15, 1941, ed. Donald Gledhill. Hollywood: Academy Press, 1941.
Academy of Motion Picture Arts and Sciences and Writers Guild of
    America West. *Who Wrote the Movie and What Else Did He
    Write?* Los Angeles, 1970.
Academy of Sciences of the U.S.S.R. and Soviet War Veterans' Commit-
    tee. *International Solidarity with the Spanish Republic, 1936–1939.*
    Moscow: Progressive Publishers, 1975.
Adler, Les K., and Paterson, Thomas G. "Red Fascism: The Merger of
    Nazi Germany and Soviet Russia in the American Image of Totali-
    tarianism, 1930's–1950's," *American Historical Review,* 75 (April
    1970), 1,046–64.
Alexandre, Laurie Ann. *The John Reed Clubs.* California State University,
    Northridge: unpublished master's thesis, 1977.

Almond, Gabriel A. *The Appeals of Communism*. Princeton: Princeton University Press, 1954.

American Society for Russian Relief, Inc. *USA-USSR: A Story of Friendship and Aid, 1941–1946*. New York, [1947].

Arakie, Margaret. *The Broken Sword of Justice: America, Israel and the Palestine Tragedy*. London: Quartet Books, 1973.

Ardrey, Robert. "Hollywood: The Toll of the Frenzied Forties," *The Reporter*, March 21, 1957, 29–33.

Arthur, Thomas H. *The Political Career of an Actor: Melvyn Douglas and the New Deal*. Indiana University: unpublished Ph.D. thesis, 1973.

Audience Research, Inc. *Congressional Investigation of Communism in Hollywood: What the Public Thinks*. Princeton, December 17, 1947.

Auerbach, Jerold S. *Labor and Liberty: The La Follette Committee and The New Deal*. Indianapolis: The Bobbs-Merrill Co., 1966.

Balio, Tino. *United Artists: The Company Built by the Stars*. Madison: The University of Wisconsin Press, 1976.

Barrett, Edward L., Jr. *The Tenney Committee*. Ithaca: Cornell University Press, 1951.

Baxter, John. *The Hollywood Exiles*. New York: Taplinger Publishing Co., 1976.

——. *Hollywood in the Thirties*. New York: Paperback Library, 1970.

Behrman, S. W. *Tribulations and Laughter*. London: Hamish Hamilton, 1972.

Belfrage, Cedric. *The American Inquisition, 1945–1960*. Indianapolis: The Bobbs-Merrill Co., 1973.

Belknap, Michael R. *The Smith Act: A Study in Political Justice*. University of Wisconsin: unpublished Ph.D. thesis, 1973.

Beloff, Max. *The Foreign Policy of the Soviet Union*. 2 vols. New York: Oxford University Press, 1947 and 1949.

Bendiner, Robert. *Just Around the Corner: A Highly Selective History of the Thirties*. New York: Harper & Row, 1967.

Benson, Frederick R. *Writers in Arms: The Literary Impact of the Spanish Civil War*. New York: New York University Press, 1967.

Bentley, Eric, ed. *Thirty Years of Treason*. New York: The Viking Press, 1971.

Bergman, Andrew. *We're in the Money*. New York: New York University Press, 1971.

Bernstein, Irving. *Hollywood at the Crossroads: An Economic Study of the Motion Picture Industry*. Hollywood: Hollywood AFL Film Council, December 1957.

Bessie, Alvah. *Inquisition in Eden*. New York: The Macmillan Co., 1965.

——. *The Soviet People at War*. New York: The American Council on Soviet Relations, [1942].

Biberman, Herbert. *Salt of the Earth*. Boston: Beacon Press, 1965.

Bilderback, William W. *The American Communist Party and World War II*. University of Washington: unpublished Ph.D. thesis, 1973.

Biskind, Peter. "The Way They Were," *Jump Cut*, May–June 1974, 24–28.

Blotner, Joseph. "Faulkner in Hollywood," in *Man and the Movies*, ed. W. R. Robinson. Baton Rouge: Louisiana State University Press, 1967. Pp. 261–303.

Bluem, A. William, and Squire, Jason S., eds. *The Movie Business: American Film Industry Practice*. New York: Hastings House, publishers, 1972.

Blum, John Morton. *V Was for Victory: Politics and American Culture During World War II*. New York: Harcourt Brace Jovanovich, 1976.

Boyer, Richard O., and Morais, Herbert M. *Labor's Untold Story*. New York: Cameron Associates, 1955.

Braudy, Leo. *The World in a Frame: What We See in Films*. Garden City, N.Y.: Anchor Press, 1976.

Brock, Clifton. *Americans for Democratic Action*. Washington, D.C.: Public Affairs Press, 1962.

Brownlow, Kevin. *The Parade's Gone By . . .* New York: Ballantine Books, 1968.

Burke, Kenneth. "The Writers' Congress," *The Nation*, May 15, 1935, 571.

Burke, Robert E. *Olson's New Deal for California*. Berkeley: University of California Press, 1953.

Carew Hunt, R. N. "Willi Munzenberg," in *International Communism*, ed. David Footman, St. Antony's Papers, No. 9. Carbondale: Southern Illinois University Press, 1960. Pp. 72–87.

Carr, Edward Hallett. *The Soviet Impact on the Western World*. New York: The Macmillan Co., 1954.

Carr, Robert K. *The Constitution and Congressional Investigating Committees*. New York: Carrie Chapman Catt Memorial Fund, 1954.

———. *The House Committee on Un-American Activities, 1945–1950*. Ithaca: Cornell University Press, 1952.

Carter, Dan T. *Scottsboro: A Tragedy of the American South*. Baton Rouge: Louisiana State University Press, 1969.

Cary, Diana Serra. *The Hollywood Posse*. Boston: Houghton Mifflin Co., 1975.

Cattell, David T. *Communism and the Spanish Civil War*. Berkeley: University of California Press, 1955.

———. *Soviet Diplomacy and the Spanish Civil War*. Berkeley: University of California Press, 1957.

Caudwell, Christopher. *Illusion and Reality*. London: Macmillan and Co., 1937.

Caughey, John W., ed. *Their Majesties the Mob*. Chicago: University of Chicago Press, 1960.

Caughey, John and Laree. *Los Angeles: Biography of a City.* Berkeley: University of California Press, 1976.

Caute, David. *The Fellow-Travelers: A Postscript to the Enlightenment.* London: Weidenfeld & Nicolson, 1973.

——. *The Great Fear: The Anti-Communist Purge Under Truman and Eisenhower.* New York: Simon & Schuster, 1978.

Chadwin, Mark L. *The Hawks of World War II.* Chapel Hill: University of North Carolina Press, 1968.

Chafee, Zechariah, Jr. *Free Speech in the United States.* Cambridge, Mass.: Harvard University Press, 1946.

Chaplin, Charles. *My Autobiography.* New York: Simon & Schuster, 1964.

Chaplin, John R. "Hollywood Goes Closed Shop," *The Nation,* February 19, 1936, 225–26.

Charney, George. *A Long Journey.* Chicago: Quadrangle Books, 1968.

Chase, Donald, ed. *Filmmaking: The Collaborative Art.* Boston: Little, Brown and Co., 1975.

Childs, David. "The British Communist Party and the War, 1939–41: Old Slogans Revived," *Journal of Contemporary History,* 12 (April 1977), 237–53.

Churchill, Winston S. *The Gathering Storm.* Boston: Houghton Mifflin Co., 1948.

Ciment, Michel. *Kazan on Kazan.* New York: The Viking Press, 1974.

Claudín, Fernando. *The Communist Movement: From Comintern to Cominform.* Vol. 2. Trans. Francis MacDonough. New York: Monthly Review Press, 1976.

Cleland, Robert G. *California in Our Time (1900–1940).* New York: Alfred A. Knopf, 1974.

Clubb, Edmund O. *The Witness and I.* New York: Columbia University Press, 1974.

Clurman, Harold. *The Fervent Years.* New York: Hill & Wang, 1957.

Coffee, Lenore. *Storyline: Recollections of a Hollywood Screenwriter.* London: Cassell & Co., 1973.

Cogley, John. *A Canterbury Tale.* New York: The Seabury Press, 1976.

——. *Report on Blacklisting.* 2 vols. The Fund for the Republic, 1956.

——. "Return Engagement," *Commonweal,* June 7, 1957, 251–54.

Cole, Wayne S. *America First: The Battle Against Intervention, 1940–1941.* Madison: The University of Wisconsin Press, 1953.

——. *Senator Gerald P. Nye and American Foreign Relations.* Minneapolis: The University of Minnesota Press, 1962.

Connelly, Marc. *Voices Offstage: A Book of Memoirs.* New York: Holt, Rinehart & Winston, 1968.

Cook, Bruce. "The Black Years of Dalton Trumbo," *American Film,* October 1975, 30–36.

——. *Dalton Trumbo.* New York: Charles Scribner's Sons, 1977.

Cooke, Alistair. *A Generation on Trial: U.S.A. v. Alger Hiss.* New York: Alfred A. Knopf, 1950.

Corliss, Richard, ed. *The Hollywood Screenwriters.* New York: Avon, 1972.

———. *Talking Pictures.* New York: Penguin Books, 1975.

Cowley, Malcolm. *Exile's Return.* New York: The Viking Press, 1956.

Crichton, Kyle. *Total Recoil.* Garden City, N.Y.: Doubleday & Company, 1960.

Cripps, Thomas. *Slow Fade to Black: The Negro in American Film, 1900–1942.* New York: Oxford University Press, 1977.

Crossman, Richard, ed. *The God That Failed.* New York: Bantam Books, 1949.

Crowther, Bosley. "The Birth of a Nation," in *Black Films and Film-Makers,* ed. Lindsay Patterson. New York: Dodd, Mead & Co., 1975. Pp. 75–83.

Curtiss, Thomas Quinn. *Von Stroheim.* New York: Farrar, Straus & Giroux, 1971.

Daniels, Robert V., ed. *A Documentary History of Communism.* 2 vols. New York: Vintage Books, 1960.

Daniels, Roger. *Concentration Camps USA: Japanese Americans and World War II.* New York: Holt, Rinehart & Winston, 1972.

Dardis, Tom. *Some Time in the Sun.* New York: Charles Scribner's Sons, 1976.

Davies, Joseph E. *Mission to Moscow.* New York: Simon & Schuster, 1941.

Davis, Dave, and Goldberg, Neal. "Organizing the Screen Writers Guild —an Interview with John Howard Lawson," *Cinéaste* (8), 4–11, 58.

Davis, John. "Notes on Warner Brothers' Foreign Policy, 1918–1948," *Velvet Light Trap,* 4 (Spring 1972), 23–33.

De Caux, Len. *Labor Radical.* Boston: Beacon Press, 1970.

Delmer, Sefton. *Black Boomerang.* New York: The Viking Press, 1962.

De Mille, Agnes. *Dance to the Piper.* Boston: Little, Brown & Co., 1951.

De Mille, William C. *Hollywood Saga.* New York: E. P. Dutton & Co., 1939.

Deming, Barbara. *Running Away from Myself.* New York: Grossman Publishers, 1969.

Dennis, Peggy. *The Autobiography of an American Communist.* Berkeley: Creative Arts Book Co., 1977.

DeVol, Kenneth S., ed. *Mass Media and the Supreme Court.* New York: Hastings House Publishers, 1971.

Diamond, Sigmund. "Veritas at Harvard," *New York Review of Books,* April 28, 1977, 13–17; May 26, 1977, 42–45; July 14, 1977, 38–41.

Divine, Robert A. *The Illusion of Neutrality.* Chicago: The University of Chicago Press, 1962.

———. *Roosevelt and World War II.* Baltimore: The Johns Hopkins Press, 1969.

Dmytryk, Edward. *It's a Hell of a Life but Not a Bad Living*. New York: Times Books, 1978.

Doenecke, Justus D. "Non-Interventionism of the Left: The Keep America out of the War Congress," *Journal of Contemporary History*, 12 (April 1977), 221–36.

Donner, Frank. "How J. Edgar Hoover Created His Intelligence Powers," *The Civil Liberties Review*, 3 (February–March 1977), 34–51.

——. *The Un-Americans*. New York: Ballantine Books, 1961.

Dos Passos, John. *The Best Times: An Informal Memoir*. New York: The New American Library, 1966.

Dowdy, Andrew. *"Movies Are Better Than Ever."* New York: William Morrow & Co., 1973.

Draper, Theodore. *American Communism and Soviet Russia*. New York: The Viking Press, 1960.

Dubinsky, David, and Raskin, A. H. *David Dubinsky: A Life in Labor*. New York: Simon & Schuster, 1977.

Dubofsky, Melvyn, and Van Tine, Warren. *John L. Lewis: A Biography*. New York: Quadrangle/The New York Times Book Co., 1977.

Dunne, Father George H. *Hollywood Labor Dispute*. Los Angeles: Conference Publishing Co., n.d.

Editors of *Look*. *Movie Lot to Beachhead*. Garden City, N.Y.: Doubleday, Doran & Company, 1945.

Ehret, Richard C. *A Descriptive Analysis of the Hearings Held by the House Committee on Un-American Activities in 1947 and 1951 on the Communist Infiltration of the Motion Picture Industry, and Their Relationship to the Hollywood Labor Movement*. UCLA: unpublished master's thesis, 1969.

Eisler, Hanns. *Composing for the Films*. New York: Oxford University Press, 1947.

Ekirch, Arthur A., Jr. *The Decline of American Liberalism*. New York: Longmans, Green & Co., 1955.

Endore, Guy. *Let's Skip the Next War*. Hollywood Peace Forum, 1940.

——. "Life on the Blacklist," *The Nation*, December 20, 1952, 568.

——. *Reflections on Guy Endore*. UCLA: Oral History Project, 1964.

English, Richard. "Mexico Clamps Down on Stalin," *The Saturday Evening Post*, August 30, 1952, 16–17, 41, 44.

——. "What Makes a Hollywood Communist?", *The Saturday Evening Post*, May 19, 1951, 30–31, 147–50.

Ephron, Henry. *We Thought We Could Do Anything: The Life of Screenwriters Phoebe and Henry Ephron*. New York: W. W. Norton & Co., 1977.

Esslin, Martin. *Brecht: The Man and His Work*. Rev. ed. Garden City, N.Y.: Anchor Books, 1971.

Executive Staff of the Screen Actors Guild. *Memorandum re 1945 Strike*. [Hollywood, 1945.]

Fadiman, William. *Hollywood Now.* New York: Liveright, 1972.

Farber, Stephen. *The Movie Rating Game.* Washington, D.C.: Public Affairs Press, 1972.

Fast, Howard. *The Naked God.* New York: Frederick A. Praeger, 1957.

Feis, Herbert. *Churchill, Roosevelt, Stalin.* Princeton: Princeton University Press, 1957.

"Fellow Citizens: Our Husbands Are in Prison!" Hollywood: Committee to Free the Hollywood Ten, [1950].

Felton, James. "Panic in Hollywood," *'48*, April 1948, 134–42.

Fiedler, Leslie A. *No! in Thunder.* Boston: Beacon Press, 1960.

"Film and Photo League: Radical Cinema in the 30's," *Jump Cut* (14), 23–33.

Fordin, Hugh. *Getting to Know Him: A Biography of Oscar Hammerstein II.* New York: Random House, 1977.

———. *The World of Entertainment.* Garden City, N.Y.: Doubleday & Company, 1975.

The Fourteenth Chronicle: Letters and Diaries of John Dos Passos. Edited and with a biographical narrative by Townsend Ludington. Boston: Gambit, 1973.

Franklin D. Roosevelt and Foreign Affairs. Vol. III, September 1935–January 1937. Ed. Edgar B. Nixon. Cambridge, Mass.: The Belknap Press, 1969.

Freeland, Richard M. *The Truman Doctrine and the Origins of McCarthyism.* New York: Shocken Books, 1974.

French, Philip. *The Movie Moguls.* Chicago: Henry Regnery Co., 1969.

Fried, Richard M. *Men Against McCarthy.* New York: Columbia University Press, 1976.

Frischauer, Willi. *Behind the Scenes of Otto Preminger.* New York: William Morrow & Co., 1974.

Fritchman, Stephen H. *Heretic: A Partisan Autobiography.* Boston: Beacon Press, 1977.

Froug, William. *The Screenwriter Looks at the Screenwriter.* New York: The Macmillan Co., 1972.

Furnas, J. C. *Stormy Weather: Crosslights on the Nineteen Thirties, An Informal Social History of the United States, 1929–1941.* New York: G. P. Putnam's Sons, 1977.

Gaer, Joseph. *The First Round: The Story of the CIO Political Action Committee.* New York: Duell, Sloan & Pearce, 1944.

Gassner, John, and Nichols, Dudley, eds. *Best Film Plays of 1943–1944.* New York: Crown Publishers, 1945.

———. *Twenty Best Film Plays.* New York: Crown Publishers, 1943.

Geist, Kenneth L. *Pictures Will Talk: The Life and Films of Joseph L. Mankiewicz.* New York: Charles Scribner's Sons, 1978.

Gerber, Albert B. *Bashful Billionaire: The Story of Howard Hughes.* New York: Lyle Stuart, 1967.

Gilbert, James B. *Writers and Partisans: A History of Literary Radicalism in America.* New York: John Wiley & Sons, 1968.

Girdner, Audrie, and Loftis, Anne. *The Great Betrayal: The Evacuation of the Japanese-Americans During World War II.* New York: The Macmillan Co., 1969.

Gitlow, Benjamin. *The Whole of Their Lives.* New York: Charles Scribner's Sons, 1948.

Glazer, Nathan. *The Social Basis of American Communism.* New York: Harcourt, Brace and World, 1961.

Goldman, Eric F. *Rendezvous with Destiny.* New York: Vintage Books, 1956.

Goldstein, Malcolm. *The Political Stage: American Drama and Theater in the Great Depression.* New York: Oxford University Press, 1974.

Goldstein, Robert Justin. "The FBI's Forty-Year Plot," *The Nation,* July 1, 1978, 10–15.

Goodhart, Philip. *Fifty Ships That Saved the World: The Foundation of the Anglo-American Alliance.* Garden City, N.Y.: Doubleday & Company, 1965.

Goodman, Jack, ed. *While You Were Gone: A Report on Wartime Life in the United States.* New York: Simon & Schuster, 1946.

Goodman, Walter. *The Committee.* Baltimore: Penguin Books, 1969.

Gordon, David. "Mayer, Thalberg and MGM," *Sight and Sound,* 45 (Summer 1976), 186–87.

Gordon, Max. "The Communist Party of the Nineteen-Thirties and the New Left," *Socialist Revolution,* #27 (January–March 1976), 11–48.

Gornick, Vivian. *The Romance of American Communism.* New York: Basic Books, 1977.

Gottlieb, Robert, and Wolt, Irene. *Thinking Big: The Story of the Los Angeles Times, Its Publishers and Their Influence on Southern California.* New York: G. P. Putnam's Sons, 1977.

Graham, Hugh Davis, ed. *Huey Long.* Englewood Cliffs N.J.: Prentice-Hall, 1970.

Graham, Sheilah. *The Garden of Allah.* New York: Crown Publishers, 1970.

Griffith, Robert. *The Politics of Fear: Joseph R. McCarthy and the Senate.* Lexington: The University Press of Kentucky, 1970.

Griffith, Robert, and Theoharis, Athan, eds. *The Specter: Original Essays on the Cold War and the Origins of McCarthyism.* New York: New Viewpoints, 1974.

Gross, Babette. *Willi Munzenberg: A Political Biography.* Trans. Marian Jackson. [East Lansing]: Michigan State University Press, 1974.

Gruber, Helmut. *Soviet Russia Masters the Comintern*. Garden City, N.Y.: Anchor Books, 1974.

Guback, Thomas H. *The International Film Industry*. Bloomington: Indiana University Press, 1969.

Guiles, Fred Lawrence. *Hanging On in Paradise*. New York: McGraw-Hill Book Co., 1975.

Guttmann, Allen. *The Wound in the Heart: America and the Spanish Civil War*. New York: The Free Press of Glencoe, 1962.

"Hal B. Wallis" (interview). *Dialogue on Film*, 4 (March 1975).

Hamby, Alonzo L. *Beyond the New Deal: Harry S. Truman and American Liberalism*. New York: Columbia University Press, 1973.

——. *The Imperial Years: The United States Since 1939*. New York: Weybright & Talley, 1976.

Hampton, Benjamin B. *History of the American Film Industry: From Its Beginnings to 1931*. New York: Dover Publications, 1970.

Harper, Alan D. *The Politics of Loyalty: The White House and the Communist Issue, 1946–1952*. Westport, Conn.: Greenwood Publishing Co., 1969.

Harrington, Michael. *Fragments of the Century*. New York: Saturday Review Press/E. P. Dutton & Co., 1973.

Harris, Leon. *Upton Sinclair: American Rebel*. New York: Thomas Y. Crowell Co., 1975.

Haver, Ron. "RKO Years," *American Film*, 3 (December 1977–January 1978), 28–34.

Hayden, Sterling. *Wanderer*. New York: Alfred A. Knopf, 1963.

Hecht, Ben. *Charlie*. New York: Harper & Brothers, 1957.

——. *A Child of the Century*. New York: Simon & Schuster, 1954.

——. "If Hollywood Is Dead or Dying as a Moviemaker, Perhaps the Following Are Some of the Reasons," *Playboy*, November 1960, 56–57, 130–39.

Hellman, Lillian. *Scoundrel Time*. Boston: Little, Brown & Co., 1976.

Henderson, Robert M. *D. W. Griffith: His Life and Work*. New York: Oxford University Press, 1972.

Herman, Lewis. *A Practical Manual of Screen Playwriting*. New York: World Publishing Co., 1963.

Hicks, Granville. "How Red Was the Red Decade?", *Harper's*, July 1953, 53–61.

Higham, Charles. *The Art of the American Film, 1900–1971*. Garden City, N.Y.: Doubleday & Company, 1973.

——. *Cecil B. DeMille*. New York: Charles Scribner's Sons, 1973.

——. *Hollywood at Sunset*. New York: Saturday Review Press, 1972.

——. *Warner Brothers*. New York: Charles Scribner's Sons, 1975.

Higham, Charles, and Greenberg, Joel. *Hollywood in the Forties*. New York: A. S. Barnes & Co., 1968.

Himelstein, Morgan Y. *Drama Was a Weapon*. New Brunswick: Rutgers University Press, 1963.

Hirschhorn, Clive. *Gene Kelly*. Chicago: Henry Regnery Co., 1974.

Hofstadter, Richard. *The American Political Tradition*. New York: Vintage Books, 1974.

Holmes, John Clellon. "15¢ Before 6:00 PM: The Wonderful World of the Thirties," *Harper's*, December 1965, 51–55.

Houseman, John. *Run-Through*. New York: Simon & Schuster, 1972.

Howe, Irving, and Coser, Lewis. *The American Communist Party: A Critical History (1919–1957)*. Boston: Beacon Press, 1957.

"How Should the Movies Aid National Defense?", *Town Meeting*, #6, March 3, 1941, Columbia University Press.

Huettig, Mae D. *Economic Control of the Motion Picture Industry*. Philadelphia: University of Pennsylvania Press, 1944.

Hunnings, Neville March. *Film Censors and the Law*. London: George Allen & Unwin, 1967.

Hyde, Douglas. *I Believed*. New York: G. P. Putnam's Sons, 1950.

Hynes, Samuel. *The Auden Generation: Literature and Politics in England in the 1930s*. New York: The Viking Press, 1977.

Ickes, Harold. *The Secret Diary of Harold L. Ickes*. Vol. 3, *The Lowering Clouds, 1939–1941*. New York: Simon & Schuster, 1954.

Inglis, Ruth A. *Freedom of the Movies*. Chicago: University of Chicago Press, 1947.

Israel, Lee. "Judy Holliday," *MS.*, December 1976, 72–74, 90–96.

Ivens, Joris. *The Camera and I*. New York: International Publishers, 1969.

Jacobs, Lewis. *The Rise of the American Film*. New York: Teachers College Press, 1968.

Jacobs, Paul. "Good Guys, Bad Guys, and Congressman Walter," *The Reporter*, May 15, 1958, 29–31.

Jennings, C. Robert. "The Hollywood 10, Plus Twenty," Los Angeles *Times, West Magazine*, September 3, 1967, 10–17.

Jerome, V. J. *Intellectuals and the War*. New York: Workers Library Publishers, 1940.

——. "The Negro in Hollywood Films," *Political Affairs*, 29 (June 1950), 58–92.

Jobes, Gertrude. *Motion Picture Empire*. Hamden, Conn.: Archon Books, 1966.

Johnston, Eric. "Messengers from a Free Country," *The Saturday Review of Literature*, March 4, 1950, 9–12.

——. *We're All in It*. New York: E. P. Dutton & Co., 1948.

Johnston, Verle B. *Legions of Babel: The International Brigades in the Spanish Civil War*. University Park: The Pennsylvania State University Press, 1967.

Josephson, Matthew. *Sidney Hillman: Statesman of American Labor*. Garden City, N.Y.: Doubleday & Company, 1952.

Jowett, Garth. *Film: The Democratic Art*. Boston: Little, Brown & Co., 1976.

Kael, Pauline. *I Lost It at the Movies*. Boston: Little, Brown & Co., 1954.

——. "Raising Kane," in *The Citizen Kane Book*. Boston: Little, Brown & Co., 1971. Pp. 3–84.

——. "Trash, Art, and the Movies," in *Going Steady*. New York: Bantam Books, 1971. Pp. 103–58.

Kahn, Gordon. *Hollywood on Trial*. New York: Arno Press and the New York *Times*, 1972.

Kanfer, Stefan. *A Journal of the Plague Years*. New York: Atheneum, 1973.

Karsh, Bernard, and Garman, Phillips L. "The Impact of the Political Left," in *Labor and the New Deal*, eds. Milton Derber and Edwin Young. Madison: The University of Wisconsin Press, 1957. Pp. 79–119.

Kazin, Alfred. *Starting Out in the Thirties*. Boston: Atlantic Monthly Press/Little, Brown & Co., 1962.

Keats, John. *You Might As Well Live: The Life and Times of Dorothy Parker*. New York: Simon & Schuster, 1970.

Kempton, Murray. *Part of Our Time*. New York: Simon & Schuster, 1955.

Kennan, George F. *Russia and the West Under Lenin and Stalin*. Boston: Little, Brown & Co., 1960.

——. *Soviet Foreign Policy, 1917–1941*. Princeton: D. Van Nostrand Co., 1960.

Kennedy, Joseph P. *The Story of the Films*. Chicago: A. W. Shaw Co., 1927.

Kenny, Robert W. *My First Forty Years in California Politics, 1922–1962*. UCLA: Oral History Project, 1964.

Klein, Michael and Jill. "Native Land: An Interview with Leo Hurwitz," *Cinéaste* (6), 2–7.

Klingender, F. D., and Legg, Stuart. *Money Behind the Screen*. London: Lawrence & Wishart, 1937.

Knightley, Phillip. *The First Casualty*. New York: Harcourt Brace Jovanovich, 1975.

Kopkind, Andrew. "Hollywood Politics: Hearts, Minds and Money," *Ramparts*, August–September 1975, 45–48.

Koszarski, Richard, ed. *Hollywood Directors, 1914–1940*. New York: Oxford University Press, 1976.

Kracauer, Siegfried. "National Types as Hollywood Presents Them," in *The Cinema, 1950*, ed. Roger Manvell. Harmondsworth: Penguin Books, 1950. Pp. 140–69.

Kraft, Hy. *On My Way to the Theatre*. New York: The Macmillan Co., 1971.

Kulik, Karol. *Alexander Korda: The Man Who Could Work Miracles.* New Rochelle, N.Y.: Arlington House, Publishers, 1975.

Lamont, Corliss, ed. *The Trial of Elizabeth Gurley Flynn by the American Civil Liberties Union.* New York: The Horizon Press, 1968.

Lamson, Peggy. *Roger Baldwin: Founder of the American Civil Liberties Union.* Boston: Houghton Mifflin Co., 1976.

Landsberg, Melvin. *Dos Passos' Path to U.S.A.: A Political Biography, 1912–1936.* Boulder: The Colorado Associated University Press, 1972.

Langer, William L., and Gleason, S. Everett. *The Undeclared War, 1940–1941.* New York: Harper & Bros., 1953.

Lardner, Ring, Jr. *The Lardners: My Family Remembered.* New York: Harper & Row, 1976.

———. "My Life on the Blacklist," *The Saturday Evening Post,* October 14, 1961, 38–44.

Larrowe, Charles P. *Harry Bridges: The Rise and Fall of Radical Labor in the United States.* New York: Lawrence Hill & Co., 1972.

Lasch, Christopher. "The Cultural Cold War: A Short History of the Congress for Cultural Freedom," in *Towards a New Past: Dissenting Essays in American History,* ed. Barton J. Bernstein. New York: Vintage Books, 1969. Pp. 322–59.

Lash, Joseph P. *Roosevelt and Churchill, 1939–1941.* New York: W. W. Norton & Co., 1976.

Latham, Aaron. *Crazy Sundays.* New York: The Viking Press, 1970.

Latham, Earl. *The Communist Controversy in Washington.* Cambridge, Mass.: Harvard University Press, 1966.

Lavery, Emmet G. *Notes and Footnotes.* UCLA: Oral History Project, 1962.

Lawrence, Jerome. *Actor: The Life and Times of Paul Muni.* New York: G. P. Putnam's Sons, 1974.

Lawson, John Howard. "Biographical Notes," *Zeitschrift für Anglistik und Amerikanistik,* 4 (1956), 73–76.

———. *Film: The Creative Process.* 2nd ed. New York: Hill & Wang, 1967.

———. *Film in the Battle of Ideas.* New York: Masses & Mainstream, 1953.

———. *Theory and Technique of Playwriting and Screenwriting.* New York: G. P. Putnam's Sons, 1949.

Lawson, R. Alan. *The Failure of Independent Liberalism, 1930–1941.* New York: G. P. Putnam's Sons, 1971.

Lazitch, Branko. *Biographical Dictionary of the Comintern.* Stanford: The Hoover Institution Press, 1973.

Leab, Daniel J. *From Sambo to Superspade.* Boston: Houghton Mifflin Co., 1975.

Lemisch, Jesse. *On Active Service in War and Peace: Politics and Ideology in the American Historical Profession.* Toronto: New Hogtown Press, 1975.

LeRoy, Mervyn. *Take One*. New York: Hawthorn Books, 1974.

Leuchtenberg, William E. *Franklin D. Roosevelt and the New Deal, 1932–1940*. New York: Harper Torchbooks, 1963.

Levenstein, Aaron (in collaboration with William Agar). *Freedom's Advocate*. New York: The Viking Press, 1965.

Levering, Ralph B. *American Opinion and the Russian Alliance, 1939–1945*. Chapel Hill: The University of North Carolina Press, 1976.

Levin, Murray B. *Political Hysteria in America*. New York: Basic Books, 1971.

Levy, Leonard W. *Origins of the Fifth Amendment*. New York: Oxford University Press, 1968.

"Liberal Anti-Communism Revisited: A Symposium," *Commentary*, 3 (September 1967), 31–79.

Lingeman, Richard R. *Don't You Know There's a War On?: The American Home Front, 1941–1945*. New York: G. P. Putnam's Sons, 1970.

Logan, Somerset. "The Battle of Hollywood," *The New Republic*, August 7, 1929, 308–10.

Loos, Anita. *Kiss Hollywood Good-by*. New York: The Viking Press, 1974.

Losey on Losey. Ed. Tom Milne. Garden City, N.Y.: Doubleday & Company, 1968.

Lovell, Hugh, and Carter, Tasile. *Collective Bargaining in the Motion Picture Industry*. Berkeley: University of California Institute of Industrial Relations, 1955.

Loewenstein, Prince Hubertus zu. *Towards the Further Shore: An Autobiography*. London: Victor Gollancz, 1968.

——. *The Tragedy of a Nation: Germany, 1918–1934*. New York, 1934.

Lundberg, Ferdinand. *Imperial Hearst*. New York: Equinox Cooperative Press, 1936.

Lynd, Alice and Staughton. *Rank and File: Personal Histories by Working-Class Organizers*. Boston: Beacon Press, 1973.

McAleer, John. *Rex Stout: A Biography*. Boston: Little, Brown & Co., 1977.

McAuliffe, Mary Sperling. *Crisis on the Left: Cold War Politics and American Liberals, 1947–1954*. Amherst: The University of Massachusetts Press, 1978.

MacCann, Richard Dyer. *The People's Films*. New York: Hastings House Publishers, 1973.

McCarthy, Todd, and Flynn, Charles. *Kings of the Bs: Working Within the Hollywood System*. New York: E. P. Dutton & Co., 1975.

McClure, Arthur F. *The Movies: An American Idiom*. Rutherford, N.J.: Fairleigh Dickinson University Press, 1971.

——. *The Truman Administration and the Problems of Postwar Labor,*

1945–1948. Rutherford, N.J.: Fairleigh Dickinson University Press, 1969.

MacDougall, Curtis D. *Gideon's Army*. 3 vols. New York: Marzani & Munsell, 1965.

MacGowan, Kenneth. *Behind the Screen*. New York: Delacorte Press, 1965.

———. "When the Talkies Came to Hollywood," *The Quarterly of Film, Radio and Television*, 10 (1955–56), 288–301.

MacShane, Frank. *The Life of Raymond Chandler*. New York: E. P. Dutton & Co., 1976.

McWilliams, Carey. *Factories in the Field*. Santa Barbara: Peregrine Publishers, 1971.

———. "Hollywood Plays with Fascism," *The Nation*, May 29, 1935, 623–24.

———. *It Can Happen Here: Active Anti-Semitism in Los Angeles*. Los Angeles: American League Against War and Fascism/Jewish Anti-Nazi League of Southern California, 1935.

———. *Japanese Evacuation: Interim Report*. New York: Institute of Pacific Relations, 1942.

———. "Moving the West-Coast Japanese," *Harper's*, September 1942, 359–69.

———. *Prejudice. The Japanese American: A Symbol of Racial Intolerance*. Boston: Little, Brown & Co., 1944.

———. *Southern California Country*. Ed. Erskine Caldwell. New York: Duell, Sloan & Pearce, 1946.

———. *What About Our Japanese-Americans?* New York: Institute of Pacific Relations, 1944.

———. *Witch Hunt: The Revival of Heresy*. Boston: Little, Brown & Co., 1950.

Maltz, Albert. *The Citizen Writer*. New York: International Publishers, 1950.

Mamatey, Victor S. *Soviet Russian Imperialism*. Princeton: D. Van Nostrand Co., 1964.

Mangione, Jerre. *The Dream and the Deal: The Federal Writers' Project, 1935–1943*. Boston: Little, Brown & Co., 1972.

Mangold, William P. "Hollywood Fights Its Writers," *The New Republic*, May 27, 1936, 70–71.

Mann, Erika and Klaus. *Escape to Life*. Boston: Houghton Mifflin Co., 1939.

Marion, Frances. *Off with Their Heads!* New York: The Macmillan Co., 1972.

Markowitz, Norman D. *The Rise and Fall of the People's Century: Henry A. Wallace and American Liberalism, 1941–1948*. New York: The Free Press, 1973.

Martin, Charles H. *The Angelo Herndon Case and Southern Justice.* Baton Rouge: Louisiana State University Press, 1976.

Martin, Jay. *Nathanael West: The Art of His Life.* New York: Farrar, Straus & Giroux, 1970.

Martin, Olga J. *Hollywood's Movie Commandments.* New York: The H. W. Wilson Co., 1937.

Marx, Samuel. *Mayer and Thalberg: The Make-Believe Saints.* New York: Random House, 1975.

Mathews, Jane D. *The Federal Theatre, 1935–1939.* Princeton: Princeton University Press, 1967.

Mayer, Edwin Justus. *A Preface to Life.* New York: Boni and Liveright Publishers, 1923.

Mayersberg, Paul. *Hollywood: The Haunted House.* New York: Stein & Day, 1968.

Meister, Dick, and Loftis, Anne. *A Long Time Coming: The Struggle to Unionize America's Farm Workers.* New York: Macmillan Publishing Co., 1977.

Meltzer, Milton. *Violins & Shovels: The WPA Arts Projects.* New York: Delacorte Press, 1976.

Mike Gold: A Literary Anthology. Ed. Michael Folsom. New York: International Publishers, 1972.

Miller, Arthur. "The Year It Came Apart," *New York*, December 30, 1974–January 6, 1975, 30–44.

Miller, John C. *Crisis in Freedom: The Alien and Sedition Acts.* Boston: Atlantic Monthly Press/Little, Brown & Co., 1952.

Mr. Dooley Remembers: The Informal Memoirs of Finley Peter Dunne. Ed. with an introduction and commentary by Philip Dunne. Boston: Atlantic Monthly Press/Little, Brown & Co., 1963.

Mitchell, Broadus. *Depression Decade.* New York: Holt, Rinehart & Winston, 1962.

Mitford, Jessica. *A Fine Old Conflict.* New York: Alfred A. Knopf, 1977.

Monroe, Eason. *Safeguarding Civil Liberties.* UCLA: Oral History Project, 1974.

Moody, Richard. *Lillian Hellman, Playwright.* New York: Pegasus, 1972.

Moreau, Genevieve. *The Restless Journey of James Agee.* New York: William Morrow & Co., 1977.

Moremen, Merrill Raymond. *The Independent Progressive Party in California, 1948.* Stanford University: M.A. unpublished thesis, 1950.

Munk, Michael. "*The Guardian:* From Old to New Left," *Radical America*, 2 (March–April 1968), 19–28.

Murray, Robert K. *Red Scare: A Study in National Hysteria, 1919–1920.* Minneapolis: University of Minnesota Press, 1955.

Nadeau, Remi. *Los Angeles: From Mission to Modern City.* New York: Longmans, Green & Co., 1960.

Nash, Alanna. "Cancelled," *Take One*, 5 (July–August 1977), 23–41.

Nash, George H. *The Conservative Intellectual Movement in America, Since 1945.* New York: Basic Books, 1976.

National Council of American-Soviet Friendship. *Partners for Peace: A selection of the leading addresses delivered at the American-Soviet Friendship rally in Madison Square Garden* [November 16, 1944], *The Red Army Day Celebration* [February 22, 1945] *and International Women's Day Broadcast* [March 7, 1945], *1944–1945.* New York, [1945].

——. *U.S.A. U.S.S.R.: A selection of the leading addresses delivered at the Madison Square Garden meeting and at the opening luncheon session of the Congress of American-Soviet Friendship held in New York City: November 6–18, 1943.* New York, [1943].

Navasky, Victor S. "To Name or Not to Name," New York *Times Magazine,* March 25, 1973, 34–35, 110–12, 118–21.

Nettl, J. P. *The Soviet Achievement.* New York: Harcourt, Brace & World, 1967.

Niven, David. *Bring on the Empty Horses.* New York: G. P. Putnam's Sons, 1975.

Nizer, Louis. *New Courts of Industry: Self-Regulation Under the Motion Picture Code.* New York: The Longacre Press, 1935.

Nolan, William F. *Dashiell Hammett: A Casebook.* Santa Barbara: McNally & Loftin, 1969.

——. *John Huston: King Rebel.* Los Angeles: Sherbourne Press Inc., 1965.

Nollau, Gunther. *International Communism and World Revolution.* New York: Frederick A. Praeger, 1961.

North, Joseph. *No Men Are Strangers.* New York: International Publishers, 1958.

——, ed. *New Masses: An Anthology of the Rebel Thirties.* New York: International Publishers, 1969.

Oboler, Arch, and Longstreet, Stephen, eds. *Free World Theatre: Nineteen New Radio Plays.* New York: Random House, 1944.

Ogden, August Raymond. *The Dies Committee.* Washington, D.C.: The Catholic University of America Press, 1945.

On the Eve of Prison: Two Addresses by Gale Sondergaard and Albert Maltz. Hollywood: Arts, Sciences, and Professions Council, 1950.

Oppenheimer, George. *The View from the Sixties.* New York: David McKay Co., 1966.

Packer, Herbert L. *Ex-Communist Witnesses.* Stanford: Stanford University Press, 1962.

Parrish, Michael E. "Cold War Justice: The Supreme Court and the Rosenbergs," *American Historical Review,* 82 (October 1977), 805–42.

Parrish, Robert. *Growing Up in Hollywood.* New York: Harcourt Brace Jovanovich, 1976.

Patterson, Frances Taylor. "The Author and Hollywood," *The North American Review*, 244 (Autumn 1937), 77–89.

Pechter, William. "Interview with Abraham Polonsky," *Film Quarterly*, 15 (Spring 1962), 50–54.

Perry, Louis B. and Richard S. *A History of the Los Angeles Labor Movement, 1911–1941*. Berkeley: University of California Press, 1963.

Phillips, Cabell. *The 1940s: Decade of Triumph and Trouble*. New York: Macmillan Publishing Co., 1975.

——. *The Truman Presidency*. New York: The Macmillan Co., 1966.

Phillips, Leona Rasmussen. *D. W. Griffith: Titan of the Film Art*. New York: Gordon Press, 1976.

Phillips, William. "What Happened in the Fifties," *Partisan Review*, 43 (1976), 337–40.

Poe, Elizabeth. "Credits and Oscars," *The Nation*, March 30, 1957, 267–69.

Polonsky, Abraham. "How the Blacklist Worked in Hollywood," *Film Culture*, 50–51 (Fall-Winter 1970), 41–48.

——. American Film Institute Seminar, November 13, 1974.

Powdermaker, Hortense. *Hollywood: The Dream Factory*. Boston: Little, Brown & Co., 1950.

Preis, Art. *Labor's Giant Step*. New York: Pioneer Publishers, 1964.

Preston, William, Jr. *Aliens and Dissenters*. Cambridge: Harvard University Press, 1963.

——. "The 1940s: The Way We Really Were," *The Civil Liberties Review*, 2 (Winter 1975), 4–38.

Prickett, James Robert. *Communists and the Communist Issue in the American Labor Movement, 1920–1950*. UCLA: unpublished Ph.D. thesis, 1975.

Priestley, J. B. *Midnight on the Desert*. New York: Harper & Brothers Publishers, 1937.

Rabkin, Gerald. *Drama and Commitment: Politics in the American Theatre of the Thirties*. Bloomington: Indiana University Press, 1964.

Randall, Richard S. *Censorship of the Movies*. Madison: University of Wisconsin Press, 1968.

Rauch, Basil. *Roosevelt from Munich to Pearl Harbor*. New York: Barnes & Noble, 1950.

Raymond Chandler Speaking. Eds. Dorothy Gardner and Katherine Sorley Walker. Boston: Houghton Mifflin Co., 1962.

Reagan, Ronald (and Richard G. Hubler). *Where's the Rest of Me?* New York: Duell, Sloan & Pearce, 1965.

Reeves, Thomas C. *Freedom and the Foundation: The Fund for the Republic in the Era of McCarthyism*. New York: Alfred A. Knopf, 1969.

Reisz, Karel. "Hollywood's Anti-Red Boomerang," *Sight and Sound*, 22 (January–March 1953), 132–37, 148.

Rhode, Eric. *A History of the Cinema: From Its Origins to 1970.* New York: Hill & Wang, 1976.

Riasanovsky, Nicholas V. *A History of Russia.* 3rd ed. New York: Oxford University Press, 1977.

Richmond, Al. *A Long View from the Left.* New York: Delta, 1975.

Rivkin, Allen, and Kerr, Laura. *Hello Hollywood.* Garden City, N.Y.: Doubleday & Company, 1962.

Robeson, Paul. *Here I Stand.* London: Dennis Dobson, 1958.

Robinson, David. *Hollywood in the Twenties.* New York: A. S. Barnes & Co., 1968.

Robinson, Edward G. (with Leonard Spigelgass). *All My Yesterdays: An Autobiography.* New York: Hawthorn Books, 1973.

Rogin, Michael Paul, and Shove, John L. *Political Change in California.* Westport, Conn.: Greenwood Publishing Co., 1970.

Rosefelt, Reid. "Celluloid Sedition?: The Strange Case of the Hollywood Ten," *Velvet Light Trap,* 11 (Winter 1974), 2–5.

Rosenstone, Robert A. *Crusade on the Left: The Lincoln Battalion in the Spanish Civil War.* New York: Pegasus, 1969.

Ross, Lillian. "Onward and Upward with the Arts," *The New Yorker,* February 21, 1948, 32–48.

——. *Picture.* New York: Avon Books, 1969.

Ross, Murray. "The C.I.O. Loses Hollywood," *The Nation,* October 7, 1939, 374–77.

——. *Stars and Strikes: Unionization of Hollywood.* New York: Columbia University Press, 1941.

Rosten, Leo C. *Hollywood: The Movie Colony, the Movie Makers.* New York: Harcourt, Brace & Co., 1941.

Rovere, Richard H. *The American Establishment and Other Reports, Opinions, and Speculations.* New York: Harcourt, Brace & World, 1962.

——. *Arrivals and Departures: A Journalist's Memoirs.* New York: Macmillan Publishing Co., 1976.

A Salute to John Howard Lawson. Eds. Paul and Sylvia Jarrico, Sonja Dahl Biberman, Helen Blair. Los Angeles, November 12, 1955.

Salvi, Delia Nora. *The History of the Actors' Laboratory, Inc., 1941–1950.* UCLA: unpublished Ph.D. thesis, 1969.

Sands, Pierre Norman. *A Historical Study of the Academy of Motion Picture Arts and Sciences (1927–1947).* New York: Arno Press, 1973.

Saposs, David J. *Communism in American Unions.* New York: McGraw-Hill Book Co., 1959.

Schapiro, Leonard. *The Communist Party of the Soviet Union.* New York: Vintage Books, 1964.

Schapsmeier, Edward L. and Frederick H. *Prophet in Politics: Henry A. Wallace and the War Years, 1940–1965.* Ames: The Iowa State University Press, 1970.

Schickel, Richard. *The Disney Version.* New York: Avon Books, 1969.

Schlesinger, Arthur M., Jr. *The Coming of the New Deal.* Boston: Houghton Mifflin Co., 1959.

——. *The Politics of Upheaval.* Boston: Houghton Mifflin Co., 1960.

——. *The Vital Center.* Boston: Houghton Mifflin Co., 1949.

Schorer, Mark. *Sinclair Lewis: An American Life.* New York: McGraw-Hill Book Co., 1961.

Schumach, Murray. *The Face on the Cutting Room Floor.* New York: William Morrow & Company, 1964.

Shannon, David A. *The Decline of American Communism.* New York: Harcourt, Brace & Co., 1959.

——. *The Socialist Party of America.* New York: The Macmillan Co., 1955.

Sheean, Vincent. *Not Peace But a Sword.* New York: Doubleday, Doran & Company, 1939.

Sherman, Eric. *Directing the Film: Film Directors on Their Art.* Boston: Little, Brown & Co., 1976.

Silke, James R. *Here's Looking at You, Kid.* Boston: Little, Brown & Co., 1976.

Sinclair, Upton. *The Autobiography of Upton Sinclair.* New York: Harcourt, Brace & World, 1962.

Sklar, Robert. *Movie-Made America.* New York: Random House, 1975.

Snyder, Robert L. *Pare Lorentz and the Documentary Film.* Norman: University of Oklahoma Press, 1968.

Soderbergh, Peter A. "The Grand Illusion: Hollywood and World War II, 1930–1945," *The University of Dayton Review,* 5 (Winter 1968–1969), 13–21.

Sorrell, Herbert K. *You Don't Choose Your Friends.* UCLA Oral History Project, 1963.

Sperber, Murray A. *And I Remember Spain.* New York: Collier Books, 1974.

Spigelgass, Leonard. American Film Institute Seminar, October 19, 1971.

Starobin, Joseph R. *American Communism in Crisis, 1943–1957.* Cambridge: Harvard University Press, 1972.

Stein, Walter J. *California and the Dust Bowl Migration.* Westport, Conn.: Greenwood Press, 1973.

Stern, Daniel. *Final Cut.* New York: The Viking Press, 1975.

Stewart, Donald Ogden. *By a Stroke of Luck.* New York: Paddington Press, 1975.

——. (Interview with Max Wilk.) American Film Institute, Louis B. Mayer Oral History Project, December 1971.

——. "Writing for the Movies" (with Allen Eyles and John Gillett), *Focus on Film,* 5 (Winter 1970), 49–57.

——, ed. *Fighting Words.* New York: Harcourt, Brace & Co., 1940.

Stone, I. F. *The Truman Era*. New York: The Monthly Review Press, 1953.

Sturak, John Thomas. *The Life and Writings of Horace McCoy, 1897–1955*. UCLA: unpublished Ph.D. thesis, 1966.

Suber, Howard. *The Anti-Communist Blacklist in the Hollywood Motion Picture Industry*. UCLA: unpublished Ph.D. thesis, 1968.

Swindell, Larry. *Body and Soul: The Story of John Garfield*. New York: William Morrow & Co., 1975.

Taylor, Telford. *Grand Inquest*. New York: Ballantine Books, 1961.

Taylor, Winchell. "Secret Movie Censors," *The Nation*, July 9, 1938, 38–40.

Tebbel, John. *The Life and Good Times of William Randolph Hearst*. New York: E. P. Dutton & Co., 1952.

Teichmann, Howard. *George S. Kaufman: An Intimate Portrait*. New York: Dell Publishing Co., 1973.

Tenney, Jack B. *California Legislator*. 4 vols. UCLA Oral History Project, 1969.

Theoharis, Athan G. "The F.B.I.'s Stretching of Presidential Directives, 1936–1953," *Political Science Quarterly*, 91 (Winter 1976–1977), 652–72.

——. *Seeds of Repression*. Chicago: Quadrangle Books, 1971.

Thomas, Bob. *King Cohn*. New York: G. P. Putnam's Sons, 1967.

——. *Thalberg: Life and Legend*. Garden City, N.Y.: Doubleday & Company, 1969.

Thompson, Morton. "Hollywood Is a Union Town," *The Nation*, April 2, 1938, 381–83.

Thorp, Margaret F. *America at the Movies*. New Haven: Yale University Press, 1939.

Traina, Richard P. *American Diplomacy and the Spanish Civil War*. Bloomington: Indiana University Press, 1968.

Trilling, Diana. *Claremont Essays*. New York: Harcourt, Brace & World, 1964.

——. "Liberal Anti-Communism Revisited," in *We Must March My Darlings*. New York: Harcourt Brace Jovanovich, 1977. Pp. 41–66.

Trumbo, Dalton. *Additional Dialogue: Letters of Dalton Trumbo, 1942–1962*. Ed. Helen Manfull. New York: M. Evans & Co., 1970.

——. "Blacklist-Black Market," *The Nation*, May 4, 1957, 383–87.

——. "The Fall of Hollywood," *The North American Review*, August 1933, 140–47.

——. *Harry Bridges: A Discussion of the Latest Effort to Deport Civil Liberties and the Rights of American Labor*. Hollywood: League of American Writers, 1941.

——. "Hollywood Pays," *Forum and Century*, February 1933, 113–19.

——. *The Real Facts Behind the Motion Picture Lockout*. (Speech delivered at the Olympic Auditorium, Los Angeles, October 13, 1945; Hollywood Ten Collection, Southern California Library for Social Studies and Research.)

——. *The Time of the Toad: A Study of Inquisition in America and Two Related Pamphlets.* New York: Perennial Library, 1972.

The Truth About Hollywood. Hollywood: Council of Hollywood Guilds and Unions, 1944.

Tucker, Robert C. *The Soviet Political Mind.* New York: Frederick A. Praeger, Publisher, 1963.

Tuska, Jon, et al., eds. *Close Up: The Contract Director.* Metuchen, N.J.: The Scarecrow Press, 1976.

Ulam, Adam B. *The Rivals: America and Russia Since World War II.* New York: The Viking Press, 1971.

United States Congress, Congressional Record: Proceedings and Debates of the 80th Congress, 1st session, Vol. 93, part 9, November 18–December 19, 1947. Washington, D.C.: U. S. Government Printing Office, 1947.

United States House of Representatives, House Reports, Miscellaneous, 78th Congress, 2nd session, Vol. 2, January 10–December 19, 1944, Report no. 1311: "The C.I.O. Political Action Committee," Washington, D.C.: U. S. Government Printing Office, 1944.

United States 80th Congress, 2nd session, February–March 1948, Special Sub-Committee of the Committee on Education and Labor. *Jurisdictional Disputes in the Motion-Picture Industry.* Vol. 3. Washington, D.C.: U. S. Government Printing Office, 1948.

United States 82nd Congress, 2nd session, February 17, 1952, Committee on Un-American Activities. *Annual Report of Committee on Un-American Activities for the Year 1951.* Washington, D.C.: U. S. Government Printing Office, 1952.

United States 83rd Congress, 2nd session, February 6, 1954, Committee on Un-American Activities. *Annual Report of the Committee on Un-American Activities for the Year 1953.* Washington, D.C.: U. S. Government Printing Office, 1954.

United States 82nd Congress, 1st session, July 6, 1951, Committee on Un-American Activities. *Communist Infiltration of the Hollywood Motion Picture Industry.* 4 vols. Washington, D.C.: U. S. Government Printing Office, 1951.

United States 83rd Congress, 1st session, 1953, Committee on Un-American Activities. *Communist Infiltration of the Hollywood Motion Picture Industry.* 3 vols. Washington, D.C.: U. S. Government Printing Office, 1953.

United States 80th Congress, 1st session, October 1947, Committee on Un-American Activities. *Hearings Regarding the Communist Infiltration of the Motion Picture Industry.* Washington, D.C.: U. S. Government Printing Office, 1947.

United States 84th Congress, 1st session, June–July 1955 and April 1956,

Committee on Un-American Activities. *Investigation of Communist Activities in the Los Angeles Area.* Vols. 2, 4–6. Washington, D.C.: U. S. Government Printing Office, 1955 and 1956.

United States 84th Congress, 2nd session, July 1956, Committee on Un-American Activities. *Investigation of So-Called "Blacklisting" in Entertainment Industry—Report of the Fund for the Republic, Inc.* Washington, D.C.: U. S. Government Printing Office, 1956.

United States Senate, 78th Congress, 1st session, February 16, 1943, A Special Committee Investigating the National Defense Program. *Army Commissions and Military Activities of Motion Picture Personnel.* Washington, D.C.: U. S. Government Printing Office, 1943.

United States Temporary National Economic Committee, 76th Congress, 3rd session, 1941. *Investigation of Concentration of Economic Power: Monograph no. 43, The Motion Picture Industry—A Pattern of Control.* Washington, D.C.: U. S. Government Printing Office, 1941.

United States Department of State. *Memorandum on the Postwar International Information Program of the United States.* Washington, D.C.: U. S. Government Printing Office, 1945.

United States Judiciary, *Federal Reporter,* several volumes.

United States, *Federal Supplement,* several volumes.

United States, *United States Reports,* several volumes.

United States National Labor Relations Board. *In the Matter of Metro-Goldwyn-Mayer Studios, and Motion Picture Producers Association, et al., and Screen Writers Guild, Inc.: Decision and Direction of Election, June 4, 1938.*

United States National Recovery Administration, Division of Review. *Evidence Study No. 25 of the Motion Picture Industry.* November 1935.

United States, *The Motion Picture Industry Study.* February 1936.

United States, *Report Regarding Investigation Directed to Be Made by the President in His Executive Order of November 27, 1933, Approving the Code of Fair Competition for the Motion Picture Industry.* Washington, D.C.: U. S. Government Printing Office, 1934.

Vaughn, Robert. *Only Victims: A Study of Show Business Blacklisting.* New York: G. P. Putnam's Sons, 1972.

Vidal, Gore. "Art, Sex and Isherwood," *The New York Review of Books,* December 9, 1976, 10–18.

——, "Who Makes the Movies?", *The New York Review of Books,* November 25, 1976, 35–39.

Vidor, King. *A Tree Is a Tree.* New York: Harcourt, Brace & Co., 1952.

Viertel, Salka. *The Kindness of Strangers.* New York: Holt, Rinehart & Winston, 1969.

Volker, Klaus. *Brecht: A Biography.* New York: The Seabury Press, 1978.

Walton, Richard J. *Henry Wallace, Harry Truman, and the Cold War.* New York: The Viking Press, 1976.

Wanger, Walter F. "The Motion Picture in the Fight for Freedom," *Free World*, November 1943, 443–47.

——. "120,000 American Ambassadors," *Foreign Affairs*, October 1939, 45–59.

——. "OWI and Motion Pictures," *Public Opinion Quarterly*, 7 (Spring 1943), 100–10.

War Activities Committee, Motion Picture Industry. *Movies at War*. New York, [1945].

Warner, Jack L. *My First Hundred Years in Hollywood*. New York: Random House, 1964.

Warners Revisited. *Velvet Light Trap*, Fall 1975.

Warren, Frank A. III. *Liberals and Communism*. Bloomington: Indiana University Press, 1966.

Warshow, Robert. *The Immediate Experience*. Garden City, N.Y.: Doubleday & Company, 1962.

Wasserman, Harry. "Ideological Gunfight at the RKO Corral," *Velvet Light Trap*, 11 (Winter 1974), 7–11.

Watkins, George S., ed. *The Motion Picture Industry*. *The Annals of the American Academy of Political and Social Science*, 254 (November 1947).

Weaver, John D. *El Pueblo Grande: A Non-Fiction Book About Los Angeles*. Los Angeles: Ward Ritchie Press, 1973.

Weinstein, James. *Ambiguous Legacy: The Left in American Politics*. New York: New Viewpoints, 1975.

——. "Response to Max Gordon," *Socialist Revolution*, no. 27 (January–March 1976), 48–59.

Wenden, D. J. *The Birth of the Movies*. New York: E. P. Dutton & Co., 1975.

Wesley, David. *Hate Groups and the Un-American Activities Committee*. 2nd ed. (revised). New York: Emergency Civil Liberties Committee, 1962.

West, Blake. "Notes on Refusal to Testify Before the House Committee on Un-American Activities," *Tulane Law Review*, 24 (December 1949), 237–40.

Westerfield, H. Bradford. *Foreign Policy and Party Politics, Pearl Harbor to Korea*. New Haven: Yale University Press, 1955.

Wetter, Gustav A. *Dialectical Materialism: A Historical and Systematic Survey of Philosophy in the Soviet Union*. Peter Heath, trans. New York: Frederick A. Praeger, Publishers, 1958.

Wexley, John. *The Judgment of Julius and Ethel Rosenberg*. New York: Cameron & Kahn, 1955.

Wheaton, Christopher Dudley. *A History of the Screen Writers Guild (1920–1942): The Writers' Quest for a Freely Negotiated Basic Agreement*. University of Southern California: unpublished Ph.D. thesis, 1974.

Wiener, Jon. "The Communist Party Today and Yesterday: An Interview with Dorothy Healey," *Radical America*, 11 (May–June 1977), 25–45.

Wilk, Max. *The Wit and Wisdom of Hollywood*. New York: Warner Paperback Library, 1973.

Willen, Paul. "Who 'Collaborated' with Russia?", in *Causes and Consequences of World War II*, Robert A. Divine, ed. Chicago: Quadrangle Books, 1969. Pp. 202–24.

Williams, Jay. *Stage Left*. New York: Charles Scribner's Sons, 1974.

Wilson, Edmund. *Letters on Literature and Politics, 1912–1972*. Selected and edited by Elena Wilson. New York: Farrar, Straus & Giroux, 1977.

Winter, Ella. *And Not to Yield: An Autobiography*. New York: Harcourt, Brace & World, 1963.

Wittner, Lawrence S. *Cold War America: From Hiroshima to Watergate*. New York: Praeger Publishers, 1974.

Wood, Alan. *Mr. Rank*. London: Hodder & Stoughton, 1952.

Wood, Michael. *America in the Movies*. New York: Basic Books, 1975.

———. "Hollywood's Last Picture Show," *Harper's*, January 1976, 79–82.

Wood, Tom. *The Bright Side of Billy Wilder, Primarily*. Garden City, N.Y.: Doubleday & Company, 1970.

Wright, Richard. *American Hunger*. New York: Harper & Row, 1977.

Writers at Work: The Paris Review Interviews, Third Series. New York: The Viking Press, 1967.

Writers' Congress: The Proceedings of the Conference Held in October 1943 Under the Sponsorship of the Hollywood Writers' Mobilization and the University of California. Berkeley: University of California Press, 1944.

Writers Take Sides: Letters About the War in Spain from 418 American Authors. New York: League of American Writers, 1938.

Wyman, David S. *Paper Walls: America and the Refugee Crisis, 1938–1941*. Amherst: University of Massachusetts Press, 1968.

Yarnell, Allen, *Democrats and Progressives*. Berkeley: University of California Press, 1974.

X [a group of Hollywood writers]. "Hollywood Meets Frankenstein," *The Nation*, June 28, 1952, 628–31.

Zhdanov, Andrei A. *Essays on Literature, Philosophy, and Music*. New York: International Publishers, 1950.

Zheutlin, Barbara, and Talbot, David. "Albert Maltz: Portrait of a Hollywood Dissident," *Cinéaste* (8, #3), 2–15, 59.

Zukor, Adolph. *The Public Is Never Wrong*. New York: G. P. Putnam's Sons, 1953.

Newspapers and Periodicals

The Actor (1940)

Anti-Nazi News (November 1936–January 1939; also entitled *News of the World* and *Hollywood Now*)

Black & White (1939–40)

The California Quarterly

The Clipper (Hollywood chapter, League of American Writers, August 1940–November 1941)

The Coast (1938–42)

Equality (1939–40)

Film Comment

Film Culture

Free World (1941–46)

Hollywood Citizen News

Hollywood Quarterly

Hollywood Reporter

Hollywood Review (Southern California Chapter of the Arts, Sciences, and Professions)

I Carbs

Los Angeles *Examiner*

Los Angeles *Times*

Masses & Mainstream

New Masses

New Theater

New York *Times*

People's World

Photoplay

Radical America

Screen Actor (1940–47)

The Screen Guild Magazine (1936–38)

The Screen Guilds' Magazine (1934–36)

The Screen Player (1934)

The Screen Writer (1941–48)

TAC (1938–39)

Variety

Weekly Variety

Novels and Plays

Bessie, Alvah. *The Un-Americans*. New York: Cameron Associates, Inc., 1957.

Blankfort, Michael. *The Brave and the Blind*. Indianapolis: The Bobbs-Merrill Co., 1940.

———. *I Met a Man*. Indianapolis: The Bobbs-Merrill Co., 1937.

———. *A Time to Live*. New York: Harcourt, Brace & Co., 1943.

Fitzgerald, F. Scott. *The Last Tycoon*. New York: Charles Scribner's Sons, 1941.

———. *The Pat Hobby Stories*. New York: Charles Scribner's Sons, 1962.

Lardner, Ring, Jr. *The Ecstasy of Owen Muir*. New York: New American Library, 1972.

Lawrence, Lars [Philip Stevenson]. *The Seed: A Trilogy. Morning Noon and Night*. Berlin: Seven Seas Publishers, 1958. *Out of the Dust*. New York: G. P. Putnam's Sons, 1956. *Old Father Antic*. New York: International Publishers, 1961. *The Hoax*. London: John Calder, 1961.

Maltz, Albert. *Afternoon in the Jungle*. New York: Liveright, 1971.

———. *Black Pit*. New York: G. P. Putnam's Sons, n.d.

———. *The Cross and the Arrow*. Boston: Little, Brown & Co., 1944.

———. *The Journey of Simon McKeever*. Boston: Little, Brown & Co., 1949.

———. *A Long Day in a Short Life*. London: May Fair Books, 1957.

———. *The Morrison Case*. Unpublished, 1952.

———. *Private Hicks*. Unpublished, 1935.

———. *The Underground Stream*. Boston: Little, Brown & Co., 1940.

———. *The Way Things Are and Other Stories*. New York: International Publishers, 1938.

Miller, Arthur. *The Crucible*. New York: Bantam Books, 1959.

Ornitz, Samuel B. *Haunch Paunch and Jowl*. New York: Boni and Liveright, 1923.

Peters, Paul, and Sklar, George. *Stevedore*. New York: Covici-Friede, 1934.

Polonsky, Abraham. *The Enemy Sea*. Boston: Little, Brown & Co., 1943.
——. *A Season of Fear*. New York: Cameron Associates, 1956.
——. *The World Above*. Boston: Little, Brown & Co., 1951.
Rouverol, Jean [Jean Butler]. *Juarez: A Son of the People*. New York: Crowell-Collier Press, 1973.
Schulberg, Budd. *The Disenchanted*. London: The Bodley Head, 1951.
Sklar, George, and Maltz, Albert. *Merry Go Round*. Unpublished, 1932.
——. *Peace on Earth*. New York: Samuel French, 1936.
Trilling, Lionel. *The Middle of the Journey*. New York: The Viking Press, 1947.
Trumbo, Dalton. *Johnny Got His Gun*. New York: Bantam Books, 1970.

About the Authors

LARRY CEPLAIR was educated at U.C.L.A. and the University of Wisconsin, and received his Ph.D. in European social history in 1973. He has taught history in New York and Los Angeles. He is co-author, with Steven Englund, of a biographical study of the young Trotsky, and has written studies on French labor, political film making, and labor organizing in Hollywood.

STEVEN ENGLUND, 34, is a son of the screenwriter Ken Englund, who was president of the Screen Writers Guild and the Writers Guild of America in the late fifties. Mr. Englund is a former Marshall Scholar and has been a correspondent for *Time* magazine's Behavior section. His articles have appeared in the London *Times Literary Supplement*, the New York *Times Magazine*, *The New York Review of Books*, *Le Nouvel Observateur*, the *Columbia Journalism Review*, the Los Angeles *Times*, *Sports Illustrated*, and other publications. Co-author with Edward Ford of *For the Love of Children* (Anchor Press/Doubleday, 1977) and *Permanent Love* (Winston Press, 1979), he has taught French history at the University of California, Los Angeles, and is currently writing a book (to be published by Doubleday in 1981) in Waupaca, Wisconsin, about a murder which became a celebrated feminist case.

Index